Early Modern Women

DATE DUE

DEC 1 4 2001		
MAR 3 '03		

Early Modern Women Poets

(1520–1700)

An Anthology

EDITED BY
JANE STEVENSON and PETER DAVIDSON

WITH CONTRIBUTIONS FROM
Meg Bateman, Kate Chedgzoy, and Julie Saunders

OXFORD
UNIVERSITY PRESS

OXFORD
UNIVERSITY PRESS

Great Clarendon Street, Oxford OX2 6DP
Oxford University Press is a department of the University of Oxford.
It furthers the University's objective of excellence in research, scholarship,
and education by publishing worldwide in
Oxford New York

Athens Auckland Bangkok Bogotá Buenos Aires Calcutta
Cape Town Chennai Dar es Salaam Delhi Florence Hong Kong Istanbul
Karachi Kuala Lumpur Madrid Melbourne Mexico City Mumbai
Nairobi Paris São Paulo Shanghai Singapore Taipei Tokyo Toronto Warsaw
and associated companies in Berlin Ibadan

Oxford is a registered trade mark of Oxford University Press
in the UK and certain other countries

Published in the United States
by Oxford University Press Inc., New York

British Library Cataloguing in Publication Data
Data Available

Library of Congress Cataloging in Publication Data
Data available
ISBN-0-19-818426-3
ISBN-0-19-924257-7 *(pbk.)*

Typeset by Kolam Information Services Pvt Ltd, Pondicherry, India
Printed in Great Britain
on acid-free paper by
Biddles Ltd.,
Guildford and King's Lynn

IN MEMORY OF

JEREMY FRANK MAULE

11 August 1952–25 November 1998

*

This life is worke-day even att the Best
butt christian death, an holly day of Rest.

ACKNOWLEDGEMENTS

WE would like to acknowledge the research grants offered by the University of Warwick RDSO and Humanities Research Centre in support of travel and research assistance for this project.

We are grateful for help received from the Bodleian Library, particularly the staff of Duke Humfrey's Library; Cambridge University Library, particularly Brian Jenkins and the other staff of the Rare Books Room, and Jayne Ringrose and Godfrey Waller of the Manuscripts Room; the British Library; Oliver Pickering and the Brotherton Library; Susanna Robson of the Special Collections in the National Art Library; Hannah Repath of Bray; the Wiltshire County Record Office at Trowbridge; Angela Broome in the Royal Institute of Cornwall, and to the curators in the Department of Textiles at the Victoria and Albert Museum. Although we have not reproduced texts from their collections, we are also grateful to the Royal Library, Brussels; the Royal Library, The Hague; and the Bibliotheca Apostolica, Vatican City.

We must also thank the following institutions for permitting us to use texts and readings from manuscripts and books in their care: the Bodleian Library, Corpus Christi College, and Magdalene College in Oxford; the British Library, the Library of Friends' House, the National Maritime Museum, Greenwich , the National Art Library, the Victoria and Albert Museum, and the Public Record Office in London; the University Library and the Pepys Library, Magdalen College, in Cambridge; the Brotherton Library, Leeds; the Northamptonshire Record Office, Northampton; the Nottinghamshire Archives, Nottingham; The Marquis of Salisbury, Hatfield House; Edinburgh University Library, The Scottish Record Office, and the National Library of Scotland in Edinburgh, Aberdeen University Library; the National Library of Wales in Aberystwyth; the Archives Départmentale du Nord in Lille; the Royal Library, Stockholm; the Pierpont Morgan Library, New York; the Henry E. Huntington Library, San Marino, California; the Folger Shakespeare Library in Washington DC; the Beinecke Rare Books and Manuscripts Library, Yale University, particularly, as always, the Osborn Collection and Stephen Parks; the Clarke Library in Los Angeles; Cornell University Library; the Houghton Library, Harvard University. For permission to reproduce texts we are grateful to Oxford University Press; the Scottish Gaelic Texts Society; and the Bord na Gaelge in Dublin; also to the editors of those scholarly journals who are thanked individually in the footnotes.

Apart from our contributing editors, Kate Chegdzoy (entirely responsible for the Welsh texts and translations), Meg Bateman (who helped us to select Gaelic texts, and made most of the translations), Marie-Louise Coolahan (who researched Irish texts), and Julie Sanders (who oversaw the inclusions from the Countess of Pembroke, Mary Wroth, and the Tixall poets, and read an early stage of the biographies, to their infinite betterment), the following individuals have been generous with help, suggestions, and references: Susan Bassnett, Peter Beal, Andrew Biswell, Bernard Capp, Louise Carpenter, Sarah Dunnigan, Margaret Ezell, Joyce Froome, David Hall, Frances Harris, Daniel Höhr, Arnold Hunt, James Knowles, Roger Lonsdale, Donald and Sheona Low, Lynne Magnusson, Mairín ní Dhonnchadha, David Norbrook, Colm Ó Baoill, Breandán Ó Buachalla, Liam O Murchú, Oliver Pickering, Sasha Roberts, Sarah Ross (whom we would particularly like to thank for the transcription of the poem by Julea Palmer which we include), Sabina Sharkey, Alison Shell, Nigel Smith, Gillian Spraggs, Winifred Stevenson, Janet Todd, Betty Travitsky, Sue Wiseman, Louise Yeoman. We would like to give special mention to the generosity of Elizabeth Clarke, Vicki Burke, and Marie-Louise Coolahan, both *in propriis personis*, and as officers of the Nottingham Trent University Perdita Project Database for Early Modern Women's Manuscript Miscellanies, for the way that they have shared findings with us. Marie-Louise most kindly took a last-minute hand with Irish-language texts, and introduced us to Liam O Murchú, for which (and to whom) we are especially grateful. We are happy to acknowledge the support and encouragement received from participants in the Trinity/Trent Colloquium for the study of early modern women and manuscripts. The very existence of such a forum, deliberately set up to cut across the lamentable divisiveness and lack of scholarly generosity which characterize the contemporary academy in Britain, must be acknowledged with gratitude.

We would also like to record our gratitude to the scholars who have worked on the prosopography of early modern women writers, whose findings we have gratefully used; notably Meg Bateman, Maureen Bell, Margaret Ezell, Germaine Greer, Elaine Hobby, Dorothy Latz, Colm Ó Baoill, George Parfitt, Melinda Sansone, Simon Shepherd, and Janet Todd.

Siobhàn Keenan, Jonathan Key, and Ian McLellan have at various stages been able and multi-competent research assistants: Jonathan Key is particularly to be thanked for memorable steadiness under fire in the latest stages of the work.

We have also been the recipients of the most generous help and advice from Germaine Greer—particularly with respect to the poetry of Eleanor Wyatt and Anne Wharton—she has been our 'Arctick star' as the project has come to completion, as well as one of our keenest and most helpful critics.

As the dedication records, this book was fostered by Jeremy Maule, who contributed much to it, and, to our profound regret, did not live to see it finished.

J. S.
P. D.

CONTENTS

CONTENTS

xii CONTENTS

xiv   CONTENTS

xvi

CONTENTS

xxii CONTENTS

CONTENTS xxiii

INTRODUCTION

THIS anthology is the result of a lengthy and careful search of manuscript, printed, and epigraphic sources of many kinds. While the reader
will, we hope, find in it a good selection of the work of established early
modern poets, from Isabella Whitney to Aphra Behn, they will also find
many poems published here for the first time. One of the main principles we have applied in selecting texts for inclusion has been that of
representing the sheer energy and diversity of women's cultural activity
in the British islands and in the communities of exiles from those
islands. It would appear, however, that this diversity has only been
recently recognized.

> English women's writing, until the past few decades, was racially homogeneous
> and regionally compact, with little ethnic, religious, or even class diversity.

This astonishing remark was made by Elaine Showalter as recently as
1991.[1] If even a writer as committed to the professional study of
women's writing as the author of *A Literature of Their Own* can make
a mistake on this scale, then we are justified in our main principle of
inclusion, which is to demonstrate the range and variety of women's
verse in early modern England. Thus, it is a central part of our project
to bring the ethnically and linguistically distinct Celtic provinces as well
as the writings of exiles for their beliefs to the attention of our readers.
Even if we were to consider only writing from English-speaking areas,
we might see what by the standards of modern America is ethnic
homogeneity,[2] but we also see women vigorously expressing every con-
ceivable shade of religious opinion from baroque Catholicism to the
most eschatologically visionary varieties of Nonconformity; and every
possible political stance from Royalism to millenarian anarchy. There is
as much diversity on issues of gender: the women of the early modern

---

[1] Elaine Showalter, *Sister's Choice: Tradition and Change in American Women's Writing*
(Oxford: Clarendon Press, 1991), 2–3. Similarly, Margaret Ferguson has called Lewalski to
task for generalizing on the basis of élite women's literary production in a review essay,
'Moderation and its Discontents: Recent Work on on Renaissance Women', *Feminist
Studies* 20:2 (1994), 358–61.

[2] There was a small black population in early modern England (for example, a black
Spaniard introduced the modern steel needle into England in Queen Mary Tudor's reign),
but no writing is known to survive from this group. The Jews were proscribed from
England for most of this period until Cromwell allowed them to return. Probably the most
noticeable sub-groups were French Protestant refugees (Huguenots), and Dutch Protestant refugees from the Spanish Netherlands. Both communities produced literary women,
such as Esther Inglis, or Langlois, a professional calligrapher working mostly in Edinburgh, and Catherine Tishem, or Thysmans, of Norwich, mother of the internationally
famous Latin poet, Jan Gruter, who read Latin, Greek, French, Italian, and English, and
taught Latin and Greek to her son.

British islands express opinions which range from vehement defence of patriarchal authority to mystical individualism. In terms of class, early modern women poets run the gamut from, on the one hand, the pedlar Jane Hawkins's prophecies, and Honor Strangman's and Jennyfer Benny's obscene libel, to, on the other hand, the highly coded and controlled exchange of verses and emblems, compliments and warnings between Queen Elizabeth I and her cousin Mary Stuart. We have poems from working-class women, middle-class women, citizens (i.e. members of the mercantile élite), country gentlefolk, nuns, and courtiers. We have also included poems by women who used Latin and Greek, which languages were less of a male monopoly than they are sometimes thought to be, and women who were native speakers of Scottish Gaelic, Welsh, Lowland Scots, Irish, and French. These 'other voices' help to remind us that, despite centuries of metropolitan attrition, this has always been a multicultural archipelago.

I

While we have tried to give some representation of the whole canon of prolific poets such as Katherine Philips, Aphra Behn, and Hester Pulter, we have also consistently found room for writing which illustrates the way in which verse was used in the relatively oral culture of early modern England for purposes which are not primarily literary, such as libels, slanders, news, instruction, and charms. All these types of verse are used by working women alongside the hitherto more visible manifestations of popular culture, such as execution narratives or political ballads: all these kinds of verse, of course, are often the inexpert productions of occasional poets, but they are of vital interest as the surviving representatives of a vast, vanished repertory of everyday verse composition, verse writing, and verse circulation.[3] We have also included very minor occasional verse from women who are primarily interesting for historical reasons, such as Elizabeth Queen of Bohemia, and, where we know that both a mother and daughter wrote verse, we have made a point of including verse from both generations. While the Sidneys have long been famous as a literary family, they are not unique in this respect: a brief verse survives from Lady Falkland's mother, Lady Tanfield; Lady Eleanor Davies the prophetess was the mother of Lucy, Countess of Huntingdon. In a different social context, Jane Sowle, Quaker and professional printer, was the mother of Elizabeth Bradford, also a printer, who was one of the earliest women to write verse in

---

[3] As Barry Reay has pointed out in *Popular Culture in Seventeenth-Century England* (London: Routledge, 1988), 15, cheap chapbooks and printed ballads formed the childhood reading of the élite, and continued to be read for relaxation by all levels of society: 'low culture' was a continuous part of the lives of even the highly educated.

America. We have also taken a particular interest in poems which reflect directly on the experience of being a woman, or a woman writer, and in poems from one woman to another.

The poets represented in this anthology are arranged chronologically, insofar as this is possible. Chronological order has the advantage of contextualizing the individual writers, in that it becomes possible to set each author in the context of her contemporaries (to whom she may in some cases be seen reacting), and also to chart women's responses to political and social issues and events. Chronological ordering makes a historical approach to the texts possible, while in no sense militating against any other possible stance. However, while it is of direct help to the reader, it presents serious problems to the editors. The social phenomenon of writing poetry for scribal publication (or, indeed, publication in print) is not a simple one even when it is happening amongst conventionally educated men; an additional layer of social considerations complicates the survival of work by women. Consequently, many of our authors are completely obscure: sometimes a contextless name is attached to a poem, sometimes, even, an imprecise circumlocution such as 'Lady B.' or 'A Young Lady'. Where the authors' dates of birth are known; we order them simply in chronological precedence. This is not without its difficulties, but our lack of information about many of these writers makes it impossible to adopt any more sophisticated approach. The relationship between floruit (period of active composition) and chronological age is often far from certain, complicating the question of whether two writers of the same age belong in literary terms to the same generation.[4]

At one extreme, we have Anna Alcox, whom we know to have been 6 when she wrote down her versions of two popular religious ballads, and the poem of the 10-year-old future Countess of Panmure. At the other extreme, we have a number of widows composing epitaphs for themselves or their husbands, in some cases after many years of marriage. There is one example, which chronology excludes (the verse dates from 1728) of a self-epitaph written in extreme old age reflecting on a life which would appear to have spanned much of the seventeenth century, and part of the eighteenth.[5] This, however, does not mean that we can to any extent graft our contemporary experience onto the early modern world, and deduce that all widows or women writing their own epitaphs, are, by modern standards, elderly.

[4] An example of the way in which the life of even an élite woman may be inadequately or partially recorded is that of Lady Elizabeth Tyrwhit, for whom we do not even have dates of birth and death, though she was a person of some importance.

[5] Edinburgh, Scottish Record Office, GD56/158. The self-epitaph is that of Mary Scott, who died at Dunkeld, 26 Feb. 1728. 'Twice did I see old prelacy pull'd down | and twice the cloak was tumbled by the Gown | ane end of Stewart's race I saw; nay More | I saw my Countrey sold for English ore | Such desolation in my time has been | I have an end of all perfection seen.'

Both very old and very young poets might seem to be special cases, but they point towards a specific problem about the chronology of writing and women's lives, illustrated by the poetic career of Bathsua Makin, who published a book of poetry at 16 under her maiden name of Rainolds, fell silent in her young adulthood, and circulated additional verse perhaps thirty years later. Under various circumstances, young girls such as Anna Alcox, Bathsua Rainolds, or the Seymour sisters wrote poetry: extreme precocity was admired in the early modern period, and work by very young women commanded an audience. But there is also some evidence that women might take to verse quite late in life, quite often as an aspect either of contemplative religious exercises, or of augmenting the position of her family (since poetry for familial monuments may often be seen as a gesture of extending and preserving the collective status of the family line). It may also, of course, be that in the case of so accomplished a poet as Katherine, Lady Dyer, known only from two poems (both family epitaphs), work from late life is preserved because it is, literally, on stone, while work on paper may be deliberately destroyed by its writer, or fall victim to the indifference of posterity. Consider, for example, the sad case of Elizabeth Holles, mother of the antiquary (and therefore, obsessive keeper of paper) Gervase Holles, born in 1578.[6]

[she had] the best and choysest education, wch render'd hir, who had judgment beyond most of her sex, aequally accomplisht with the best of them ... And to prove that a great fancy may sometimes accompany great virtues, shee compiled in verse the passages of hir whole life.

Unfortunately, 'my uncle Holles (after hir death) borrowed [it] from my father with importunity, and lost [it] as negligently.'

Elizabeth Cary's biography suggests one possible paradigm for women's literary activity. Observing that between 1609 and 1625, she gave birth to eleven children, her daughter noted that 'she being continually after as long as she lived with [her husband] either with child or giving suck', she wrote no poetry in the years of her marriage.[7] But, while we might suggest that the pattern offered by Elizabeth Cary or Bathsua Makin may not have been uncommon—literary aspirations realized in two phases, virginity and widowhood—it is far from universal. Hester Pulter, to take another example, mother of no less than fifteen children, notes that she wrote much of her poetry during the long periods of lying-in which social custom demanded of those who

---

[6] Gervase Holles, *Memorials of the Holles Family*, ed. A. C. Wood, Camden Society 3rd ser. 55 (1937), 219. Elizabeth Holles's mother, incidentally, was also an educated woman, who had been taught by the wife of John Stanhope, Archbishop of York.

[7] 'The Lady Falkland: A Life', in Elizabeth Cary, *The Tragedy of Mariam, The Fair Queen of Jewry*, ed. Barry Weller and Margaret W. Ferguson (Berkeley, Los Angeles, and London: University of California Press, 1994), 194.

had just given birth. This simply strengthens the point that it is almost impossible to extrapolate general rules from the way in which any one woman managed the relationship between her life and her writing. On the whole, it is probable that it is Hester Pulter who is the exception, and that Damaris, Lady Masham speaks for many in saying "Tis in Vain that you bid me Preserve my Poetry; Household Affairs are the Opium of the Soul', since other writers support her, including Mary Oxlie:

> From an untroubled mind should Verses flow;
> My discontents makes mine too muddy show;
> And hoarse encumbrances of houshold care
> Where these remaine, the Muses ne're repaire.

In dealing with anonymous poetry, or poetry attributed to a named woman about whom nothing is known, we have had to make a number of working assumptions. A *terminus ante quem* is provided by the manuscript, or printed source: this may be gained from the colophon, from the date of the paper, or from palaeographic evidence. Contextual information, style, or other considerations may help to refine the actual date of composition. Let us say, then, that a particular poem is datable to c.1620. Where would we put it in our list? In summary, we have not presumed to impose one generalization where a conjectural dating governs the place of any one writer in the sequence: we have had generally to assume a floruit of late twenties to mid-thirties for most kinds of literary activity. We have made an exception, however, in the cases of the few wholly undated and uncontexted epitaphs, where, in the absence of other information, we have assumed a 'late floruit' of around 40. While far from perfect, this scheme does at least address the problem of the relationship between poetic composition and women's lives, and attempts to honour the difference between the lives of men and women in our period. Happily, the cases where conjectures of this sort have had to be applied are comparatively few.

A consistent problem in the making of this collection has been that of identifying infiltrators. It is of course the case that many men have written poems in a female persona: the classical poet Ovid provided them, in his *Heroides*, with impeccable precedent for so doing. Among these, the poet and musician Thomas Campion (1567–1620) is a particularly interesting example, in that, while the words which he puts in the mouth of female speakers may sometimes be frank in their delight in physical pleasures, they are very far from stereotyping women as lustful or gluttonous.[8] It is also the case that even when we have a poem

---

[8] For a general discussion see Gail Reitenbach, 'Maydes are simple, some men say: Thomas Campion's Female Persona Poems', in *The Renaissance Englishwoman in Print*, ed. Anne M. Haselkorn and Betty S. Travistsky (Amherst: University of Massachussetts Press, 1990), 80–95.

attributed to a named and historically attested woman, it may not be her
own work: this is particularly problematic in the case of Elizabeth I, who
deliberately created herself as a quasi-symbolic being, a focus for
national feeling to whom 'appropriate' utterances could be ascribed
within the complex system of her propaganda.[9] This phenomenon is
not unique to her. The ascription of a series of erotic sonnets to her
cousin Mary, Queen of Scots by her religious enemies in Scotland is
motivated chiefly by political considerations, by their attempt to prove
her to be an adultress and accessory in the murder of her husband. In
this case, it seems highly unlikely that their contrafactions (almost
certainly based on fragments of pre-existing, French-language texts)
would have passed as the work of any native speaker of French. It is
to be noted that up until this point, these sonnets have barely been
examined for textual, contextual, or palaeographic evidence.[10] In equally
complex if less grave circumstances, although there is a good case for
one of the poems attributed to Anne Vavasour (*c*.1560–after 1622: the
mistress of the Earl of Oxford, then of Sir Henry Lee) being actually her
own work, the echo-poem in her voice which begins ' "O heavens",
quoth she, "who was the first that bed in me this fevere" ' is more
probably the work of Oxford himself, or another member of their
circle.[11] Other highly visible women, such as Frances Howard, Lady
Somerset,[12] also attract pseudepigraphic verse.

The case for including anonymous poetry in a woman's voice has to
be carefully thought through in each case; and the case we would make
for including what we do is the following. In the sixteenth and seventeenth centuries, there is a vast amount of poetry *about* women. Some of
it attacks them, some defends them. This poetry, and other publicly
available analyses of women's psychology and behaviour, such as con-
duct-books, attributes to them a set of consistently stereotyped features.
Poetry in which a woman speaker condemns herself out of her own

---

[9] While there is a good case for those poems attributed to Elizabeth that we have
included, other poems, such as 'When I was fair and young', which attributes to her a
regret at not yielding to importunate suitors, and is headed 'Verses made by the queine
when she was supposed to be in love with mountsyre [the duke of Anjou]' in Rawl. Poet.
85, fo. 11ʳ, are almost certainly fictional.

[10] The manuscript is in Cambridge University Library, MS Oo VII 47: their context
(which has itself been barely examined until now) is that of a dossier of various evidences
against Mary collected in Scotland and sent to England to be used as evidence against her.
It is an index of the strange a-historical attitude widely held towards such early-modern
figures as Mary Stuart that no examination has hitherto been made of these sonnets in the
context of Mary's authenticable autograph verse. On all grounds, paleographic, ortho-
graphic, and metrical, they would appear to disqualify themselves conclusively from being
her work, or indeed the production of any native speaker of French, and have therefore
been excluded from this anthology.

[11] Steven W. May, *The Elizabethan Courtier Poets: The Poems and their Context* (New
York: Columbia University Press, 1991), 282–3.

[12] Oxford, Bodleian Library MS Ashmole 38, p. 50.

mouth as 'bad' according to this model—such as 'Lady ffretchevell's song of the wives'[13]—can be reasonably assumed to be written by a man: the more the poem focuses on the hapless, cuckolded, and intimidated men that the speaker has subdued, the more certain this is. Similarly, a poem spoken by a young virgin who has just discovered the delights of heterosexual intercourse expresses a long-established male fantasy,[14] and is most unlikely to be by a woman. A few woman poets of the period, notably Aphra Behn, write about the pleasures of sex, but their stance is not voyeuristic in this way. By the same token, a poem in a woman's voice which expresses her joy in chastity, silence, and obedience, or dwells narcissistically on her own physical beauty, is also highly suspect. But, on the other hand, anonymous verse which strikes out in a different direction from either of these stereotypic and male-centred positions has at least a chance of being what it claims to be.

Context is also a relevant consideration. If a poem appears in a miscellany with a number of other poems by women, or in one which women had a recognizable hand in compiling (such as the Devonshire and Tixall manuscripts) its chances of being what it says it is are naturally increased. An isolated, anonymous poem in a female voice in a collection made by a man may be what it seems (an example might be the two poems apparently by a woman, perhaps the same woman, in the sixteenth-century commonplace book of Humfrey Newton),[15] but in general, the chances are against it. The 'woman's poems' in Bodley, Rawl. Poet. 85,[16] assembled by John Finet and other Cambridge men in the late 1580s form a useful case in point. The manuscript includes a group of poems from the Earl of Oxford and his circle, one of which is the echo-poem mentioned above, while another is 'Thoughe I seeme strange' which has a far better case to be Anne Vavasour's work. But its presence in Finet's manuscript is explicable by the Oxford connection. The other (anonymous) 'women's poem' in the same manuscript, 'Howe can the feeble forte but yeeld at last', is not contextualized as part of a group; and its content puts it under immediate suspicion: its tone is

---

[13] Oxford, Bodleian Library, MS Douce 357, fo. 96ᵛ, 'Lady ffretchevell's song of the wives, to the tune of Four able Phisitians are lately come down': the wives' only interest in life is cuckolding their husbands. It should also be noted that Lady Fretchevel is the subject of another lampoon (in Oxford, Bodleian Library MS Firth C.15, fo. 212) suggesting that she is a rampantly oversexed hermaphrodite attracted to both men and women.

[14] e.g. London, British Library MS Harl. 7392, fo. 74ᵛ, a manuscript compiled in the 16th cent. by Humphrey Coningsby, who matriculated at Christ Church, Oxford, in 1581 and became MP for St Albans.

[15] R. H. Robbins, 'Poems of Humfrey Newton, Esq., 1466–1536', *Publications of the Modern Language Association of America* 65 (1950), 249–81.

[16] L. A. D Cummings, 'John Finet's Miscellany' (1960), Washington University doctoral thesis: Bodleian Library Oxford, Diss. films 273, L. G. Black, 'Studies in some Related Manuscript Poetic Miscellanies' (1971), Bodleian Library D.Phil. d 5094. John Finet the compiler began collecting poems at court and continued at Cambridge between 1584 and 1590. Later he became Master of Ceremonies to James I.

strongly suggestive of (male) university poetry, since it moves gradually into sly jesting on women's sexuality, and the familiar male fantasy that 'no means yes'.[17] The assumption that this is a male-authored poem is perhaps confirmed by the presence in the manuscript of an overtly obscene poem 'Naye, phewe, nay pish', which is also about a woman who raises an initial clamour but moves towards a position of complacent yielding: this is, on the whole, what early-modern university wits expected women to be like.

A wholly different class of attributed poetry which must be treated with equal caution is the ballad. For example, *The wofull lamentacon of mrs. Anne Saunders, which she wrote with her own hand, being prisoner in newgate, Iustly condemned to death* (1573), despite its title, is almost certainly the work of some anonymous ballad-maker.[18] Two poems by Anne Askew which were printed by John Bayle as part of her prison writings are accepted by most critics as her own work, but a ballad in her voice, 'I am a woman poore and blinde' is unlikely to be anything but Protestant propaganda verse. The hugely popular ballad by Ann Morcott which we include was printed anonymously as a broadsheet, but since it is attributed to this otherwise unknown woman in the more literary context of Thomas d'Urfey's *Pills to Purge Melancholy* (published in 1719), there is no reason to discount the attribution. In summary, our policy with work which is dubious in any of these ways in the claims which it makes for female authorship, is to treat it with extreme caution, but, having taken due consideration of context, provenance and *genre*, not to treat anonymity or the possibility of a poem *in persona* as an insuperable obstacle to inclusion.

Anonymity leads onto the whole question of naming, which is far more problematic for women than it is for men. We have already spoken about women who choose not to identify themselves by name at all, but even when women are identifiable, the problems of naming are far from at an end. Some well-known early modern women writers are commonly referred to by their maiden names (such as Catherine Trotter), others (such as Aphra Behn) by the name of a first or subsequent husband. Some, in their own lifetime, adopted a variety of strategies, for example Elizabeth Rowe, who began her public career as 'Philomela', published a second volume as Elizabeth Singer, and was known thereafter as Mrs Rowe. We have attempted (perhaps mistakenly) to impose order on this chaos. The primary name given for each woman whose poetry is included is her married name—in the case of those married several times, the name of her first husband, on the principle that this is the name by which most women were known during their adult lives. This inevitably

---

[17] The poem is preserved in three Oxford manuscripts (see Crum H1340), in one of which it is attributed to a 'Mistress M.R.': it is also attributed to Sir Philip Sidney.

[18] Hyder E. Rollins, *Old English Ballads* (Cambridge, Mass.: Harvard University Press), 340.

creates some oddities, especially among the much-married. Queen Catherine Parr, for example, is not immediately obvious as Lady Borough, nor Martha Moulsworth instantly recognizable as Martha Prynne, while the hapless Lady Jane Grey must appear as Lady Jane Dudley, in acknowledgement of her extremely brief marriage. Besides those of our contributors who are royal and/or polyandrous, the other set of women who are inadequately served by the application of this principle are the Scots, who according to Scottish custom, did not inevitably change their name on marriage, but usually used their maiden name throughout their lives,[19] and the handful of Americans, who customarily used both names (e.g. Sarah Whipple Goodhue; who thus becomes Sarah Goodhue, née Whipple). But, since a considerable number of the women we include are not well known, with the result that no forms of their names are familiar, we have elected to treat them consistently. The exception we have allowed is women writing in Celtic languages, who are normally (not always) identified by patronymics: to impose surnames on them would be to imitate the behaviour of their English overlords. In order to solve the occasional difficulties which arise from this attempt at consistency, therefore, the author-index gives *all* known names for each woman. This has the additional merit of occasionally shedding light on women's relatedness to one another through the female line. Maiden names (where known) and names of second and subsequent husbands (where appropriate, and known) are given, as are titles. Women who entered religion and changed their *first* names are treated on a principle analogous to our treatment of the married. Since the name in religion is the name of the woman in her adult life, it is the central one. The formulation 'Dame Constantia (Anne) Cary' represents a woman born with the name Anne Cary, known in her chosen vocation of nun as Dame Constantia.

II

It has been generally assumed until relatively recently that early modern women's writing, like their lives, belongs in the realm of social history: the history of the private, the personal, and the quotidian, unless the woman in question was actually a queen. It has also been assumed, though not by all scholars of the subject, that women wrote primarily about their personal emotions, their religion, perhaps, their husbands and children. They did, of course, but it is a great mistake to imagine that none of them looked beyond their own domestic circle—they wrote about much else besides. Moreover, since Patrick Collinson, in his Cambridge inaugural lecture, pleaded for social history 'with the politics

---

[19] There are further complexities here, in that Scottish women of the upper classes would generally break this rule to take their husband's title, or his surname together with the territorial designation accompanying a Scottish titular barony.

put back',[20] historians have become increasingly conscious that the public and the private can not be effectively divided in the early modern period. For one thing, almost nothing *was* private in the twentieth-century sense of the word. As David Cressy has summarized the question,[21]

all life was public in early modern England, or at least had public, social or communal dimensions. That is not to say that there was no inwardness, no interiority, no possibility of retreat from public affairs; of course there was. But against the demands of family, community and society, the early modern world allowed no separate private sphere (in the modern sense), no place where public activity did not intrude. Even within the recesses of domestic routine, every action, every opinion, was susceptible to external interest, monitoring, or control. Walls had ears, and everybody's business was a matter of credit, reputation or common fame.

Thus, as a number of historians have demonstrated, the private was considered relevant to the public world, and was not truly private in the modern sense of the word. But it is equally true to turn this proposition over, and assert that public affairs were relevant to the private worlds of individual women.

One thing which this anthology illustrates is that a substantial number of the early modern women who wrote verse did so from a standpoint of engagement with political or religious events. For example, in 1589, Anne Dowriche moves from an appalled evocation of the massacre of French Protestants on St Bartholomew's eve in Paris in 1572 to a consideration of the limits of obedience to an unjust king. In the 1640s, Anne Bradstreet's 'Dialogue between Old England and New' is a long and serious poem which attempts to locate contemporary politics in the context of English history, going back as far as the Saxon conquest. At about the same time, Hester Pulter, Royalist gentlewoman, wrote with equal engagement both about the fortunes of the Royalists in war and about the loss of a much-loved daughter to smallpox. After the Restoration, Lucy Hutchinson, just as committed, but on the Parliamentarian side, wrote a series of superb poems, bitter not merely with the tears of her personal widowhood, but with the ashes of passionately resented political defeat. Such notable public events as the Plague, the Great Fire of London, the 'Popish Plot', and the 'Glorious Revolution' of 1688, are all directly reflected in the verse of contemporary women: not merely courtiers such as Anne Killigrew and the Countess of Winchilsea who were directly involved on a personal level, but working-class sectaries such as Anne Wentworth. Later, in 1693, the flippant Alicia D'Anvers,

[20] Patrick Collinson, *De Republica Anglorum: Or, History with the Politics Put Back* (Cambridge, 1990).

[21] David Cressy, 'Response: Private Lives, Public Performance, and Rites of Passage', in *Attending to Women in Early Modern England*, ed. Betty S. Travitsky and Adele F. Seeff (Newark: University of Delaware Press/Associated University Presses, 1994), 187–97, at 187.

reflecting the mood of a nation emotionally exhausted by fifty years of conflict, presents, even as she mocks, the series of crises which made the England she knew in the prologue to *The Oxford-Act*. At the very end of the century, the anonymous Scottish author of *The Golden Island* writes 152 lines in defence of a venture which she perceives as a crucial step in freeing her nation from the threatened economic hegemony of England.

Another principal subject is of course religion; a term which covers a variety of types of writing. 'Religious verse' may mean more or less private exercises in religious meditation, or didactic or polemic verse aimed at convincing others. Religious allegiance is a crucial aspect of early modern history; as Catholic monarchs were succeeded by Protestants and *vice versa*, with corresponding shifts in policy. Religious issues also add to the tension between the Celtic speakers of Ireland and parts of the Scottish Highlands and the political centre in London. Religion is also one of the subjects on which a woman was entitled not merely to have an opinion, but to express it, at least within limits and in the Quaker community, for example, polemic and controversy were seen to be as much women's concern as they were men's. So, women's writing on religion covers a wide range of spheres of activity: Lady Scourie's quiet, beautifully achieved paraphrase of the Song of Songs is, as it were, balanced by the public assertions of Mary Adams's *Warning to the Inhabitants of England*.

Another subject, besides love, religion, and politics, which was frequently addressed by early modern women poets is work. We may tend to assume that all adult women in early modern England were married, since marriage was so evidently the social ideal and the declared purpose of women's lives, but the reality is different. Only 32 per cent of women were married at any one time— this has something to do with the fact that 40 per cent of the population was under 21 but, even if one excludes children from the statistics, about half the adult female population was unmarried in the late sixteenth century.[22] Faced with social crisis, manufacturing towns such as Manchester and Norwich reacted by outlawing independent single women: if women could not marry, they were to be forced into service, that is, subordination within someone else's household.[23] The fact that this legislation is repeated indicates that it was not successful, and women were seeking to live independently, 'at their own hands', thus, in competition with men. It is perhaps not surprising that employment and independence is a theme in women's verse, represented here by Isabella Whitney, Elizabeth With,

[22] These statistics are derived from Tim Stretton, *Women Waging Law in Elizabethan England* (Cambridge: Cambridge University Press, 1998), 103, and Paul Griffiths, 'Masterless Young People in Norwich, 1560–1645', in *The Experience of Authority in Early Modern England*, ed. Paul Griffiths *et al.* (London, Macmillan, 1996), 146–86, at 152–3.

[23] Griffiths, 'Masterless Young People', 152, 168.

Hannah Wolley, Elizabeth Tipper, and the author of the anonymous sampler verse which we include.

Another important theme, especially towards the end of this period, is women's writing itself. Many of the poets who write in the last decades of the seventeenth century are highly conscious of a tradition of women's writing, and take up positions in reference to writers of the previous generation: as they present it, their writing is sanctioned by that of Aphra Behn or Katherine Philips, sometimes by both. The more professional women writers of the end of the century are also consciously mutually supportive: Catherine Trotter, Delarivier Manley, Mary Pix, and Sarah Field, all write in support of one another's publications. They are strongly aware of creating a public arena for one another: Mary Pix, for example, describes Sarah Field's poetry as 'A Sacred Sanction to the writing Fair'.[24] Another feature of this generation is an overt, polemical feminism, centred mostly on the crippling effects of social convention, and also on women's lack of access to education. Mary Astell and Lady Mary Chudleigh, for example, write in this vein, as does Sarah Field.

Delarivier Manley, Mary Pix, and several other writers of the same generation were writing to support themselves. Ever since Virginia Woolf invited women to strew roses on the grave of Aphra Behn, on the grounds that she had earned her living by her pen, historians of women's writing have been particularly interested in the idea of the professional woman writer. But apart from the last generation we include, that is, writers born after 1670, the concept is a problematic one in the period covered by this anthology. Very few early modern women were professional poets, outside the Gaelic culture of highland Scotland. In the sixteenth century, and the first half of the seventeenth, the rewards of authorship, for men as well as women, were indirect. People who needed to think in terms of earning money from their writing did not expect to do so by publishing as such: it was the patronage system, rather than actual payment for on books sold, that gave verse writing an economic dimension. For example, Aemilia Lanyer certainly needed to make money, and published *Salve, Rex Iudaeorum*, but the return for this investment was more probably the favour of the great ladies to whom it is dedicated, (especially Margaret Clifford, Countess of Cumberland), than anything earned by sales of the book itself.[25] The same is probably true of her contemporary, the Latin poet Elizabeth Jane Weston. The connection between verse and patronage was automatic as late as 1660, since Ann Lee pointedly refutes it in the case of her own restoration ode:

---

[24] *Poems on Several Occasions, together with a Pastoral*, by Mrs S.F., London, Printed and to be sold by J. Nutt, [1706].

[25] Barbara K. Lewalski, 'Of God and Good Women: the Poems of Aemilia Lanyer', in *Silent but for the Word*, ed. Margaret P. Hannay (Kent, Oh.: Kent State University Press, 1985), 203–24.

My lynes goe not a fishing for great friends
For end they'le have, but they will have no ends.

In the second half of the seventeenth century, however, there was profit
to be made by prose. After the Restoration, the theatre was the obvious
choice for women who needed to make money, since it offered a direct
form of reward (the profits of the third night went to the author), but by
the 1680s, for reasons both technological and social, prose fiction
became a profitable enterprise, and so professional writers such as Aphra
Behn and Delarivier Manley, who had begun their careers as playwrights, began writing fiction.

Therefore, economic motives for women's verse writing were not
paramount throughout the period covered by this anthology. The
reasons for making verse public were various: apart from a desire to
attract patronage, we also find evidence of a personal desire for fame,
most clearly seen in the Duchess of Newcastle, various shades of belief
in the importance of the subject which the poet is writing about, and the
extreme case of writers convinced of the extreme urgency of their
subject in that they are mouthpieces of the Holy Spirit, which is the
motive which impels a number of early modern writers, from Eleanor
Davies to Anna Trapnel, into verse.

There has been a great deal of scholarly attention paid recently to the
ways in which poetry was circulated in the early modern period. Substantial numbers of women did not publish through the medium of
print, not because they feared the press, but because they preferred to
reach a more carefully targeted and restricted audience with manuscript
copies. (It is worth noting that such an established male poet as bishop
Henry King (1592–1669) published almost exclusively by the circulation
of manuscript.[26]) This is true even up to the end of the seventeenth
century, though by then the practise of scribal publication was becoming somewhat old-fashioned: Delarivier Manley's play, *The Lost Lover*,
performed and printed in 1696, features an 'Affected Poetess' called
Orinda, who sweeps on stage with the following words:[27]

Lard, *Marina*, I finish't a Copy of Verses last night, which I have sent to half a
score of my Friends for their approbation, I bestow'd the last upon admirable
Sir Amorous Courtal, but I'le send you one of them...

Orinda, despite Manley's admiration for the original Orinda (Katherine
Philips), is a comic character. To Manley, a notable member of the new
class of commercial women writers, this way of circulating text is simply

---

[26] See Margaret J. Ezell, *The Patriarch's Wife: Literary Evidence and the History of the
Family* (Chapel Hill and London: University of North Carolina Press, 1987), 65, for
examples.
[27] *The Lost Lover, or, The Jealous Husband; a Comedy*, as it is Acted at the Theatre
Royal by His Majesty's Servants, written by Mrs. Manley, London, printed for R.
Bentley, in Covent-Garden, 1696, act II, sc. 1, p. 13.

affected: this attitude is a testimony to the rapid cultural change in England after the Restoration, since in fact, the circulation of manuscript seems to have served the original Katherine Philips very well, and to have won her both fame and approbation.[28]

III

The survival of women's work is an even more hit-or-miss matter than that of men. Very little of what survives, therefore, falls uncomplicatedly into the category of the genuinely private. Women who really did not want their writings to be read after their death burned them, or selected carefully what they wished posterity to know about them.[29] Some verse survives in miscellany manuscripts put together by women themselves: in some cases (the manuscript of Katherine Austin is a case in point) with the intention of leaving the book to their children.[30] Quite a lot more survives in miscellany manuscripts put together by men, such as the 'verses by my mother in her own hand', kept by Anthony Hammond, and the friendship poem of Francellina Stapleton, preserved by her neighbour John Newdigate. But the majority of the women's poems that survive do so in print, even in the sixteenth century. Probably the earliest book of verses to be published by Englishwomen under their own names, and during their lifetime, is in Latin: a book of distichs mourning the Queen of Navarre published in Paris by three daughters of the Duke of Somerset in 1550.[31] The next book of verse to be printed under the name of an Englishwoman is that of Isabella Whitney, in 1567. While the first is the work of three young aristocrats, the second was written by an impoverished, middle-class waiting-gentlewoman—from the beginning, women's writing was not homogeneous in terms of class, language, subject-matter, or intention.

As printing got cheaper, the sheer variety of women whose work was printed is startling. This again is a point where modern expectations sharply fail to match early modern realities: print does not inevitably imply either that very many copies were produced, or that they were

---

[28] Peter Beal, *In Praise of Scribes* (Oxford: Clarendon Press, 1998), 147–91.

[29] In widely differing degrees, the Countess of Pembroke (through superb scribal copies), the Tixall poets (in circulated manuscript), and the Duchess of Newcastle (in print, and by presentation of her books to selected libraries—Oxford, Cambridge, and Leiden in the Netherlands) are examples of writers consciously selecting and organizing their own oeuvre and reputation.

[30] Note also Dame Sarah Cowper, a copious writer, many of whose works survive in the Hertfordshire Record Office. Her History of the World, written in 1686 is dedicated thus: 'To my Daughter Judith Cowper I leave this Book, Desiring her to leave it [to] some sone of our ffamily to be kept in memory of Sarah Cowper' (Hertfordshire Record Office, D/ EP F 41, fo. 1ʳ).

[31] See Brenda M. Hosington, 'England's First Female-Authored Encomium: The Seymour Sisters' Hecatodistichon (1550), to Marguerite de Navarre. Text, Translation, Notes, and Commentary', *Studies in Philology* 93 (1996), 117–63.

widely distributed. Indeed, a print run of twenty or so copies, for pamphlets such as those of Anne Wentworth or Elizabeth With, would, despite the fact that book-history has not yet devoted much attention to the phenomenon, appear to be perfectly possible. The religious community whose pamphlets have the highest rate of survival is the Quakers: this is partly because of the Quaker tradition itself, which allowed women to preach and speak in public, and partly because the Quakers decided in 1672 to preserve two copies of all writings produced by their movement since its inception, and were very successful in doing so: the result is a treasure-house of ephemeral pamphlets, many of which are by women.[32] The other group of pamphlets to survive in quantity are those produced in the years of the Civil War: this is entirely due to the decision of a London bookseller, George Thomason, to try and preserve a copy of all tracts and cheap publications available in London in those years. This inclusive collection similarly reveals that many women, even working and poorly educated ones, took to print on matters which concerned them.[33] Later in the century, this type of evidence disappears, not necessarily because women stopped publishing tracts, but simply because there was no successor to George Thomason. It is highly probable that in fact, urban, working-class radicals of both sexes continued to circulate printed tracts among themselves. Such evidence as we have, mostly anecdotal, suggests that it was both easy and cheap, at least in London, to find a printer and get a few copies of a short pamphlet printed.

The orally composed poetry of the Celtic countries is even more vulnerable to breaks in the line of transmission than verse printed in pamphlets, since for many decades, or even centuries, the surviving poems and songs depended for their survival exclusively on the memories of members of the families who upheld the bardic tradition; people who were themselves gravely at risk, due to the hostility of their English overlords to the language, culture, and customs of the Celtic-speaking peoples.

IV

In a predominantly Celtic milieu, print culture is a subsection, of unknown dimensions, of culture in general. While we would argue that

---

[32] Women Quakers wrote 220 of the 3,853 Quaker tracts published before 1700. Eighty-two of the 650 authors of these tracts were women. See Hugh Barbour, 'Quaker Prophetesses and Mothers in Israel', in *Seeking the Light: Essays in Quaker History in Honor of Edwin B. Bronner*, ed. J. William Frost and John M. Moore (Wallingford and Haverford, Pa.: Pendle Hill Publications and Friends Historical Association, 1986), 46.

[33] Thomason collected 23,000 items in 2,000 volumes. Their survival hung by a thread until 1762: the collection was 'ignored and neglected by the British establishment for almost a century', and was finally bought for a pittance. David Stokes, 'Disposing of George Thomason's Intractable Legacy, 1664–1762'. *The Library* 6th ser. 14 (1992), 337–56.

the remains of a lively working-class oral culture can be discerned in early modern England; the early modern Gaeltacht (a useful shorthand phrase for speakers of Irish and the closely-related Scottish Gaelic, the separate case of Wales will be considered below) maintained both a low *and* a high culture entirely in the oral domain. Ireland had maintained a class of professional poets and guardians of culture, the *filid*, since before the birth of Christ, who passed knowledge from one generation to the next via a highly efficient system of oral teaching and verse composition. Since poetry was thus a profession, akin to, and of equal status with, law, it is hardly surprising to find that it excluded women. 'Low' culture, meanwhile, was more directly analogous to poetic activity elsewhere in the British Isles: mnemonic verse, elegy, romance, entertainment, satire.

The period covered by this anthology is precisely that of the passing of the old order in Gaelic society. The Elizabethan and Cromwellian conquests of Ireland, and the Cromwellian subjugation of the Highlands, were attended by a deliberate attempt to destroy the guardians of Gaelic culture as natural leaders of resistance. In sixteenth-century Ireland, poets, scholars, and men of learning were hanged or otherwise murdered as deliberate policy, while those who survived were persecuted as 'carroughes, bards, rhymers and common idle men and women' (the phrase of John Perrot, Lord President of Munster, in 1571). In Scotland, the sixth of the 'Statutes of Iona', a series of measures aimed at de-Gaelicizing the Highlands enacted in 1609, lays down that

It is inactit that everie gentilman or yeaman [yeoman] within the said Ilandis... sall put at the leist thair eldest sone, or haveing no childrene maill thair eldest dochter, to the scuillis on the Lawland [in the Lowlands],... quihill [so that] they may be found able sufficientlie to speik, reid, and wryte Inglische.

The sophisticated, intricate poetry of the bardic order was profoundly vulnerable in this new political climate, particularly given the length and intensity of the training of a *fili*, and the flight, death, or proscription of the noble families who had patronized them, which destroyed their economic basis. The chief effect of this on poetry is the breakdown of the 'classic' Gaelic literary language: the Gaelic poetry which we include from the sixteenth century is mostly 'art' poetry, intertextual with a poetic tradition going back a thousand years, syllabic in structure, and requiring a trained ear to be appreciated;[34] while from the seventeenth century, we have 'folk' poetry, composed in common, demotic metres, responding in less sophisticated ways to the immediate pressure of events or emotions. This 'new poetry' has a regular stress.[35]

---

[34] For an overview of professional Irish poetry, see Osborn Bergin, *Irish Bardic Verse* (Dublin: Institute for Advanced Studies, 1970).

[35] *Gàir nan Clàrsach (The Harps' Cry): An Anthology of Seventeenth Century Gaelic Poetry*, ed. Colm Ó Baoill, tr. Meg Bateman (Edinburgh: Birlinn, 1994), 2.

The destruction of the class of professional poets may have in itself opened up some opportunities for women. *Banfilid* (female poets) were not unknown in Ireland, either in literature, legislation, or life. As with more familiar educational systems, it is probable that few women could have had access to bardic schools: the rough conditions of the trainee poet's life make it probable that only the daughter of a poet could be thus educated. But the bardic order, by the late Middle Ages, had come to exclude women as a policy.[36] According to the professional poets, women's proper relation to bardic activity is as patrons: they are frequently mentioned in this capacity.[37] A small amount of Irish women's poetry is beginning to come to light: a woman calling herself Caitlín Dubh (Dark Kathleen) has left a collection of five poems from the early seventeenth century, mostly addressed to connections of the earl of Thomond. Unfortunately, editorial work has not proceeded to a point where a sample could be included here,[38] though her work is extremely interesting, and vehemently engaged with the politics of her time: her poem on the death of Donough O'Brien ends, in a way traditional in Irish poetry, with the personification of Ireland as a woman: 'behold Ireland henceforth: she exchanged the ancestry of beauty, she seized blackness over the appearance of white purity. She is blind, she has lost her hearing, her leg has been broken, her footsteps have been stopped, the end of the man to whom she gave her suffrage.'[39] We are, however, able to include a long poem from another Irishwoman of the same generation, Fionnghuala, inghean Bhriain Uí Domhnaill.[40]

There is one verse-form, however, which was very strongly associated with Irish women: the 'keen' (from *caointe*: song).[41] English observers were greatly struck by the 'howls' at Irish funerals, and regarded them as proof of Irish barbarity.[42] A faint echo of this is sometimes also seen among English-language speakers in Ireland. In Rathcoole, for example, a community grew up which was English by speech but Irish by social formation: 'they have a sort of jargon speech peculiar to themselves.' John Dunton records the lament of a mother over her son Robin's grave:

[36] Katherine Simms, 'Women in Gaelic Society during the Age of Transition', in *Women in Early Modern Ireland*, ed. Margaret MacCurtain and Mary O'Dowd (Edinburgh: Edinburgh University Press, 1991), 32–42

[37] Bernadette Cunningham, 'Women and Gaelic Literature, 1500–1800', ibid. 147–59, at 149–51.

[38] In Maynooth, MS M 107 fos. 193^r–211^r, headed 'Caitilín dub cct.' (cecinit: 'sang/composed these'), mentioned by Breandán Ó Buachalla, *Aisling Ghéar: Na Stiobhartaigh agus an tAos Léinn 1603–1788*, (Dublin: An Clóchomhar, 1996), 667 n. 86: our thanks to Marie-Louise Coolahan for alerting us to this. Professor Liam O Murchú, University of Cork, is preparing an edition.

[39] Translation Marie-Louise Coolahan.

[40] Our thanks to Professor O Murchú for giving us this text and translation.

[41] Ann Partridge, 'Wild men and Wailing Women', *Éigse* 18 (1980), 27–33.

[42] Anne Lawrence, 'The Cradle to the Grave: English Observation of Irish Social Custom in the Seventeenth Century', *The Seventeenth Century*, 3.1 (1988), 63–84, at 79.

'Ribeen a Roon, Ribbeen mourneen, thoo ware good for loand stroand and mounteen, for rig a tool and roast a whiteen, reddy tha taakle gather tha baarnacks drink a grote at nauny hapennys.'[43] This pathetic doggerel is clearly assonantal, as is Celtic poetry, rhetorically structured, and dependent on Irish: as such, it is a rare record of a tradition at the point of extinction, expiring in English with memories of Irish words and Irish verse-forms. In those parts of the country where Irish language culture flourished, it would seem that there were many keens uttered, but none recorded. Another poet from the linguistic borders is Bríd Iñían Iarla Chille Dara (*c*.1590–after 1607) who would appear to have been capable of composing a poem in Irish while in her teens, but a few years later, claimed, in a letter to the authorities written in English, that she was incapable of understanding a conversation in Irish (in order to be able to claim ignorance of the 'treasonable' activities of her husband, who had fled abroad).

The situation in Gaelic Scotland seems to have been very different. It produced a series of distinguished woman poets whose work came to be perceived as classic. Màiri nighean Alasdair Ruaidh (*c*.1615–1705) seems to have been a professional: she was official panegyrist to the MacLeods, and her work is seen as an honoured example of the professional bardic art.[44] Sileas na Ceaphaich (*c*.1660–*c*.1729), composing towards the end of the seventeenth century, has left a very substantial oeuvre on a variety of subjects, some personal, some public. A particular genre of panegyric song called *luinneag* was strongly associated with women composers,[45] Women's poems even survive from the fifteenth and sixteenth century. They include *Griogal Cridhe*, in which the speaker, a Campbell, laments the execution of her husband Gregor MacGregor of Glenstrae in 1570.[46] If the proportion of Scottish Gaelic verse in this collection may seem high, it should be remembered that it is representative of the remarkably large canon of surviving poetry composed by women from before the year 1700. It would not be wholly inaccurate to conjecture that Scottish Gaelic society would seem to have been the culture, out of the three kingdoms and the four nations, where women could function as poets in the most unproblematic way.

It is surprising that the same cannot be said for Lowland, Scots-speaking Scotland, where, although women enjoyed a degree of legal autonomy in advance of that allowed by most early modern legal codes,

[43] Edward McLysaght, *Irish Life in the Seventeenth Century* (Cork: Irish University Press and Cork University Press, 3rd edn. 1969), 354.

[44] John MacInnes, 'The Panegyric Code in Gaelic Poetry and its Historical Background', *Transactions of the Gaelic Society of Inverness* 50 (1976–8), 435–98, at 446–9. Her work is edited by J. Carmichael Watson.

[45] John MacInnes, 'The Choral Tradition in Scottish Gaelic Songs', *Transactions of the Gaelic Society of Inverness* 46 (1969–70), 44–65.

[46] William Gillies, 'Some Aspects of Campbell History', *Transactions of the Gaelic Society of Inverness* 50 (1976–78), 256–95, at 264.

there seems to be comparatively little surviving writing by women, and almost no evidence of women being educated to a high standard. (At the time of writing, Anna Hume seems very much an exception.) This may be a 'false reading': academic study of the culture of Reformation Scotland has, until comparatively recently, assumed that theocratic hostility to the arts precluded most cultural production, but the work of scholars such as Louise Yeoman and Sarah Dunnigan now suggests that there is more seventeenth-century manuscript poetry than has hitherto been assumed. This whole subject is changing by the year, as more exploration of the sixteenth and seventeenth century sources is undertaken.

This being said, the brief account of women poets in Scotland given here is inevitably going to look more disjointed than the accounts of other cultures given above, a matter of a survey of individuals for whom a cultural context cannot yet be perceived clearly. One such is the author of an accomplished poem in the Bannatyne manuscript (1568) who seems to have have been close enough to court poetic circles to have elicited a reply from Alexander Scott, but even her identity can only be conjectured and no other work certainly from the same hand survives. The verbal culture of Mary's court followed the Queen's own linguistic background in Latin and French and, despite the Queen's own composition of a quantity of assured and sophisticated verse in French, there seems to be no evidence that any other women at court were moved to follow her example: the sonnet possibly by Mary Beaton, one of her intimates and ladies in waiting, dates from the early rule of her son, James VI.[47]

Again, while there is a substantial canon of court poetry associated with the Scottish court of James VI so far, only one woman has been clearly identified existing on the fringes of the 'Castalians', and it is clear, despite the polish of her surviving sonnet, that Christian Lindsay was held not in particularly high regard by her contemporaries. A very interesting and accomplished sonnet-sequence called 'A Ladyis Lamentation', travelling with the poems of Alexander Montgomerie, may be the work of a woman in court circles, though she cannot be identified.[48] It is also to be wished that more was known about Elizabeth Coburne (née Douglas) who has the most shadowy of poetic existences, despite the urbanity of her surviving work, two complimentary poems addressed to the poet William Fowler, who, at some later time, wrote a funerary verse on her death. With both of these women, there is a strong presumption that they wrote much more than survives, but the rest of their canon is yet to be found.

[47] Edinburgh, National Library of Scotland MS 2065, fo. 6^r.
[48] In *The Poems of Alexander Montgomerie*, nos. xxxiii–xxxviii, ed. James Cranstoun, Scottish Texts Society, 3 vols. (Edinburgh and London: William Blackwood & Sons, 1887), i.105–8.

Outwith the court, most of the poets writing in Scots are isolated in context as in time: Mary Oxlie, Anna Hume, Lady Culross, Lady Scourie, and the 'Lady of Honour' (who wrote on the disastrous colonial enterprise which ended Scottish autonomy for nearly three centuries) remain, for the moment, figures moving in different generations, different circles, different parts of Scotland.

The question of orally transmitted verse in lowland Scotland is also partially obscured by lack of surviving evidence, but the trial of Isobel Gowdie would at least suggest that a repertory of charm-verses existed on the edges of the popular tradition. Whether these can be seen as exclusively a possession of women's culture is a question to which it is impossible to return a simple answer. The same might be said of the problematic territory of the Scots narrative ballad. While there is no doubt that these ballads were current in early modern Scotland (indeed ballads and dance tunes lived for centuries in Scottish memory) and it is equally certain that the first collectors in the later eighteenth century collected their sets of ballads from women, it is again difficult to draw any kind of division between male and female oral traditions in the early modern period. The set of proverbial or prudential verses known as 'The Lady Lothian's Lilt' exist on the edge of this category of circulating verses, although in this case there is a consistent attribution of the text to a single originator, and the last verse leaves in no doubt that that originator was a woman. In summary, at the time of writing, the distribution of verse by women in lowland Scotland would seem to be a matter of isolated centres of activity and of activity by individuals, displaying none of the patterns of family tradition or local or sectarian encouragement which can be discerned elsewhere in the British Islands.

Writing by Welsh women is similarly sporadic in the early modern period, although for slightly different reasons, encroaching Anglicisation and absence of aristocratic patronage amongst them (those of the Welsh aristocracy who might have functioned as patrons on the scale of the Irish-speaking Earls in Ireland had mostly begun to drift to England by the period covered by this anthology). There are only between thirty and forty poems by women surviving for the sixteenth and seventeenth centuries, although there were most probably others which have not survived. The relation of Welsh and English complicates matters to a greater degree than in the other Celtic countries, in that many Welsh people in the period began to use English for purposes of business and public affairs, thus providing an alternative language for expression of public concerns. This was not a wholesale rejection of the indigenous language; since bardic poetry continued to be patronized by superficially Anglicized gentry. This bilinguality was radically different from Ireland or highland Scotland where most Gaelic speakers were either monoglot or had Latin or a Continental language as second language, and where the only language in common with élite English speakers seems to have beeen Latin. Thus a set of oppositions governed language-use in early modern Wales, whereby English cames to be perceived as forward and outward-looking, while Welsh was perceived as retrospective and directed inward towards the family and the cultural tradition of the past. Both men and women use the different languages in different contexts. Again, as in Ireland, women were excluded from the bardic tradition, which was an exclusively male phenomenon, whereas poetry in more popular metres was at the centre of culture and community. For all these reasons, and for the specific reason that Welsh composition was often oral, as opposed to written English (so much so that it seems that in bilingual Pembrokeshire in 1600 English was the only written language) the survival of women's verse, like Scottish Gaelic verse, is often dependent on intermediaries, initially on inheritors to remember the composition, and, later antiquarians to give it its first written form. (Women's writing in prose—letters, prayers, and quotidian material—is usually in English.) This is not to deny the existence of contemporary manuscripts containing poems by women, but it is noteworthy that most Welsh verse from this period, by women and men, has remained in manuscript until comparatively recently. In the early modern period, material printed in Welsh tended to be material translated from English, and very little original composition in the language saw print. This is certainly the case with women's poetry, as evidenced by the fact that all the Welsh verse in this collection is derived either from contemporary manuscript or from subsequent antiquarian collections.

To complete this necessarily very brief survey, it is important to consider for a moment the work of those women who were members of the invisible nation of the British Islands, those who were driven into either literal or internal exile on account of their proscribed Catholicism. Popular Catholic writing is manifested in ballads, with the attendant problem of the unknowability of the gender of the inheritor of the ballad tradition. (The ballad redactions of the child Anna Alcox are a fair representation of this popular tradition.) In some of the parts of England where there were substantial numbers of recusant Catholics (in Lancashire and in parts of Staffordshire and Herefordshire), obviously Catholic material survives in charms and blessings, such as those which emerged at the trial of the Lancashire 'witches' of the Device family. At gentry level, the sort of cultural formation which went with being a recusant made Catholic families unusually cohesive and aware of each other, very much given not only to intermarriage, but also to the exchange of visits, letters and verses. It is hard to assess the degree to which Catholic women's culture differs from that of their Protestant contemporaries: it is certainly true that those who remained in England held strongly to the traditional festivals of the year, indeed to an idea that they were the upholders of a kind of authentic Englishness, and thus a retrospective element, a looking back to the last century, may be discerned in some Catholic culture. On the other hand, those who went into exile in northern France or the Low Countries were very much involved with the new, baroque culture of the counter-reformation, and, given that many Catholic children were illegally educated in the religious houses and colleges abroad then returned to their families, this culture was also disseminated through recusant England. The work of the Catholic poets in this collection is essentially not unlike like that of their gentry contemporaries at first glance (obviously the writing of the exiled nuns is, of its nature, very different from any other sort of religious writing in the book), but the assumptions about law, legitimacy, and religion which underlie it offer a sharp perception of that strange aspect of early modern English life which consigned a substantial number of the traditional élite to the status of outlaws within their own countries.

V

In conclusion, it remains to give some account of the editorial policies and principles which have guided this collection and edition. The statement which began this introduction is, with remarkably few exceptions, literally true. Almost every text in the book has been examined afresh in its primary state by one of the editors, or one of the contributing editors. All sources are precisely given in the notes on the text. There are, of course, a few exceptions: where a recent edition, with a textual policy as cautious as our own exists, it has seemed pointless duplication of labour to do anything but use it: the poems of the Countess of Pembroke are a case in point. Similarly, texts of poems in Gaelic are usually taken from the earliest scholarly record, which will be detailed in full in the notes on the text but it must be remembered that the earliest written record may come years or centuries after the poem's composition. The same is broadly true for the few women's poems in Irish which we have been able to gather. Poems from inscribed sources, whether they are from samplers or monuments, have been given in upper and lower case where the originals generally have upper-case letters in two different sizes.

Where there has been a choice of copy text (and the number of poems which survive in more than one text is surprisingly few) our principle has been to try and identify the text nearest to what the author chose to *circulate* in her lifetime. Thus, for a poet such as Katherine Philips, who circulated verse in manuscript, fair-copy manuscripts made from her own papers are the obvious choice, rather than the posthumous printed editions. For women who chose to publish in print in their own lifetimes, such as Jane Barker, we have preferred printed text even to fair-copy manuscript, though we have collated such manuscripts wherever possible.

Orthography and punctuation are a major issue for an edition such as this. According to Oxford house-style, we have normalized u/v and i/j, and expanded abbreviations, but we have not altered spellings other-wise. This is not a trivial matter. For example, a poem which we considered although we did not include it, 'O happy dames', attributed in Tottel's *Miscellany* to Henry Howard, Earl of Surrey, but arguably by Mary Shelton,[49] looks almost modern in Tottel's printed text, but virtually Middle English in the orthography of the Devonshire manu-script. We include two poems by Elizabeth Taylor, one from a miscel-lany manuscript, one from a printed text: the manuscript poem looks semi-literate, while the confidence and elegance of her writing is far more clearly to be seen in print. But keeping something of the appear-ance of source-texts is important, because it locates them in time, keeps them in relation to their original context. Whenever confronted with the minimalist punctuation and capitalization of early modern texts from manuscript, the reader should perhaps remember that authorial manu-scripts of the eighteenth and nineteenth centuries—the examples of George Eliot and Walter Scott spring to mind—were routinely sent to the printer unpunctuated in the expectation that punctuation would be supplied in the printing-house.

Even so, punctuation has been one of the most difficult editorial questions which have had to be answered as this book has neared completion. Stated briefly, the problem is this: in an anthology as wide-ranging in time and in genre as this one, texts in vastly different states of finish of presentation have to coexist. Where we have a printed source or a manuscript source designed for circulation, punctuation and accidentals have been followed exactly (with the usual reservation that unequivocal printer's or scribe's errors have been emended), but when we come to texts from informal manuscript sources, the problem often is that they have no punctuation of any sort, and thus look strangely unfinished or provisional. Our solution has been arrived at after much thought, and that is that those texts which are completely unpunctuated have here been supplied with sparse, indeed skeletal punctuation and a clear note that this has been done will be found in the notes on the poem in question. It is not an ideal solution, but it answers temporarily the problem of poems which simply look unfinished to a modern eye. We might emphasize that we have not interfered with accidentals in poems which had, in the source-text, a funtional system of punctuation of any

---

[49] Jonathan Goldberg, *Desiring Women Writing: English Renaissance Examples* (Stanford: Stanford University Press, 1997), 144–63.

sort. A case in point is Katherine Philips, where the highly individual authorial punctuation serves not only as a guide to the way in which she imagined her work being read aloud, but also serves to identify scribal copies made directly from authorial originals. Apart from this, all texts are given as found in copy-text, subject only to the usual Oxford University Press normalizations, detailed above.

The study of early modern women's poetry is an academic industry of twenty years' growth, which has seen an extraordinary amount of activity. This anthology is a work of consolidation. In making it, we have had to explore areas which have received little attention, but we have also made grateful use of a great deal of excellent work. Our book is in itself part of a process: we hope, at least, to provide readers with reliable and authentic texts of a wider range of women's verse from the early modern period than has been hitherto available, but are aware that, particularly in the case of Scottish poets, scholarly work proceeding in harmony with our own may, in the next few years, produce new texts and connections. This will always be the case, but for the present, we hope that we have been faithful in producing, for the time being, a just representation of what we know of the women poets who wrote in a diversity of modes and languages in the years between 1520 and 1700.

'ALIA'

THERE are two poems in a female voice in the miscellany of Humfrey Newton, both redacted by him, but signalled as womens' compositions: this one is headed *alia*: 'another [female]'. It appears to be a poem of leave-taking from an erstwhile girlfriend, alternatively it may have been written by a man in a female persona. The reference to the monetary cost of her favours supports the latter interpretation, but the geniality of the poem speaks in favour of the former.

I   *'Farewell, that was my lef so dere'*

Farewell, that was my lef so dere,
Fro her that loved you so well.
Ye were my lef from yere to yere:
Wheder I were your I connot tell.
To you I have byn trew and lell   5
At all tymes unto this day;
And now I say farewell, farewelle,
I tak my lef for ever and ay.

Your lof, forsoth, ye have not lost:
If ye loved me, I loved you, iwys   10
Bot that I put you to gret cost;
Therfor I have you clipt and kist
Bot now, my luf, I most nedes sesse
And tak me to hym that me has tan.
Therfore tak ye another wher ye list: 15
I gif you good lef, sertayn

Gif ye me licence to do the same.
This tokyn truly I you betak
In remenbrance of my name.
Send me a tokyn for my sake.   20
Wheder it be send erly or late,
I shall it kepe for old qwayntance
And now to Crist I you betake
To save and kepe in wert and sance.

1 *lef*: life   5 *lell*: loyal   8 *lef*: leave   10 *iwys*: certainly   11 *Bot*: except   12 *clipt*: embraced   13 *sesse*: cease   14 *tan*: taken   16 *good lef*: permission   18 *you betak*: entrust to you   22 *qwayntance*: acquaintance   24 *wert and sance*: wit and sense

ANONYMOUS

(*c*.1520)

THIS poem has the form of a carol, which in the Middle Ages, means a dance-tune, with a refrain; and is completely anonymous. It is therefore not certainly of female authorship. However, few English carols are in a female voice, and those that are, are mostly extremely misogynistic. This expression of sad fidelity runs counter to the carols' general assumption of women's fickleness and lust, which speaks in its favour. The text has alternative feminine pronouns written inter-linearly—'sche', 'hyre', etc., recasting it for a male speaking voice.

2   *'Wolde God that hyt were so'*

Wolde God that hyt were so
As I cowde wysshe bytuyxt us two

The man that I loved al ther best
In al thys contre, est other west,
To me he ys a strange gest.   5
What wonder est thow I be wo?

When me were levest that he shold duelle
He wold noȝht sey onys far welle
He wold noȝht sey onys farewell
When tyme was come that he wold go.   10

In places ofte when I hym mete
I dar noȝht speke but forth I go
With herte and eyes I hym grete
So trywe of love I know no mo

As he ys myn hert love   15
My dyrward dyre, iblessed he be,
I swere by God that ys above
Non hath my love but only he.

I am Icomfortyd in every syde
The colures wexeth both fres and newe   20
When he ys come and wyl abyde
I wott ful wel that he ys trywe.

I love hym trywely and no mo
Wolde God that he hyt knywe:
And ever I hope hyt schal be so   25
Then schal I chaunge for no new.

---

4 *est other west*: east or west   7 *me were levest*: I most wanted; *duelle*: stay   8 *onys*: once   15 *hert love*: the love of my heart   16 *dyrward dyre*: precious darling

ANONYMOUS
(c.1520)

T HE 'Welles MS' is an early sixteenth-century poetical miscellany, containing no poems of known authorship, written in several different hands. Quite a number of poems in it are written from a woman's point of view, and are arguably of female authorship. The three selected here are very different, though all are verse letters. The first has a somewhat carol-like form, though it does not have a refrain. In the manuscript, it forms part of a composite, thirteen-stanza poem which appears to have been compiled from three or more separate lyrics: the stanza which comes third forms the beginning of a completely different song in Aberystwyth, National Library of Wales MS Porkington 10, and in some manuscript fragments discovered in the Chapter Library of Canterbury. The speaking voice in the first part is male. Apart from these two witnesses to stanza three, there are no other manuscripts so it is not possible to prove conclusively that stanzas 10–13, which are certainly in a female voice, and strike off in a different direction from the previous stanzas, had currency as a separate poem.

3   *'Evyn as mery as I make myght'*

Evyn as mery as I make myght
ytt ys nott as I wolde,
for to on I have my troweth i-plyght
and a-noder hathe my harte yn holde.

He that hathe my trowthe i-plyght,   5
he dwellyd with me a whyle;
but he that hathe my hart yn holde,
I wylle hym never be-gyle.

I must take as I have bake,
thereof I have my fyll;   10
butt I must drynke as I have brewe
wheder ytt be good or yll.

All my harte I have here wrytton,
to send yow yn a byll;
ytt shalbe to your vnderstandyng   15
I have nott all my wyll.

3 *troweth i-plyght*: I am promised to one   6 *dwellyd*: stayed   8 *be-gyle*: deceive   9 *take as I have bake*: proverbial, current at least from mid-sixteenth century: I must keep the bargain I have made   14 *byll*: letter

ANONYMOUS
(*c*.1520)

THE playful doggerel 'from one young woman to another' is included as an early witness to relations between women. It was evidently written as a New Year's gift, as were other poems in this collection (see no. 149) and offers, again, a picture of early sixteenth-century womanhood which stands at an acute angle to cliché. The poem mines a vein of grotesque humour often found in medieval comic writing. The ending now appears both lame and extraordinary: 'Beshetyn' is probably the past tense of the verb 'beshut', but at the very least this is a pun: given the cloacal nature of much contemporary humorous writing, we must see this as more comic, and less violent, than it appears to a modern sensibility.

4   *A lettre sende by on yonge woman to a-noder,*
      whiche aforetyme were felowes to-geder

My loving frende, amorous Bune,
I cum ambelyng to you by the same tokyn
that you and I have be to-geder,
and settyn by the fire in colde wether,
and wyth vs noo moo but our Gullett,   5
with all the knakes in hur buggett;
hur trumpett and hur merye songe
now for to here, I thinke itt longe.
Come amble me to hur, I you praye,
and to Agnes Irpe as bright as daye.   10
I wolde you were here to lokke our gates,
butt alas itt ys to fare to the jakes.
Fare-well faire Agnes Blakamoure,
I wolde I hadde you here in stoore,
for you wolde come with al your harte;   15
farewell! farewell! my ladye darke.
Commande me to Wyllum, I you desyre,
and praye hym to wyshe vs some of his fyre,
for we have none butt a coole or a stykke,
and so we dryve a-waye the weke.   20
and commande me also to the roughe Hollye
that turnethe itt ofte into Godes bodye,
and to all your oder felowes besyde
as well as I hadde ther names discryed.
and praye John cossall to be goode and kynde,   25
for the nexte yere he wylbe blynde;
and bydde Humffrey doo hym no shrowd turne,
for then Sir John muste hym worune.
and commande me to Thomson, that talle man
whiche shulde have a lather to pisse in a can;   30

and also to Nicholas with the blake berde,
on whome to loke itt makes me a-ferde
My vnclez and my aunte be merye and glade
and, thankes be to God, I am nott sadde,
and Christoffer, your frende, ys off goode cheere   35
and many tymes he wissheth hym ther.
Faire tokens I wolde have sende
butt I lakked money for to spende.
And thys, fare-you-well! the goode Newe Yere,
I pray you be merye and off good cheere,   40
and, for the love of swete Seynt Denyes,
att thys my letter thinke noo vnkyndnes,
for to make you all merye I doo ryme
and nowe to leave I thinke itt tyme.
Att nyne off the clokke thys was wrytten;   45
I wolde you were all beshetyn.

finis

2 *ambelyng*: strolling   5 *noo moo*: no more   6 *knakes*: toys, trifles, jokes; *buggett*: bag   8 *here*: hear   12 *jakes*: lavatory   19 *coole*: coal   20 *dryve a-waye*: pass   22 i.e. he swears a lot   27 *shrowd*: sharp, unkind   28 *worune*: warn   30 *lather*: ladder (suggesting that 'tall' is a sarcasm and he was actually short—so short he needed to climb a ladder to piss successfully into a chamber-pot)   37 *tokens*: presents (New Year was the season for exchanging gifts)   41 *Seynt Denyes*: St Denis, or Dionysius, first bishop of Paris: French kings were buried in his church. Devotion to St Denis came to England with the Normans   45 *nyne*: i.e extremely late, since people normally rose at dawn   46 *beshetyn*: safely shut in for the night (from *beshut*: enclose, surround): probably with a joking double-entendre, 'that you dirty yourselves'

ANONYMOUS

(*c*.1520)

THE longest of the poems included here from the 'Welles MS' is a response in rhyme-royal, through which we can see the shadowy form of a stereotyped early Tudor 'lover's complaint', which is here received by a serious-minded and earnest young woman, who experiences considerable difficulty in mapping the 'cruel lady' of Tudor love lyric onto her own sense of self. She observes, acutely, that despite her lover's catastrophic vocabulary it is hard to believe that he is in any real sense suffering. By contrast, her own dignified statement of commitment is plainly expressed, and carries conviction.

5   *'Right best beloved and most in assurance'*

Right best beloved and most in assurance
of my trew harte, I me recommende
hartely unto yow with-owten vareance;

and have receyved the whiche ye to me did send,
wherby I perceyve your loving harte and minde;   5
desiring yow in the same soo to continewe,
and then for your grett paynes comfforte may insuye.

Thanking me for my kindnes in times paste,
your desire is I shuld kepe in mynde
the purpose I was in when ye spake with me laste.   10
Truly, unconstant you shall me never fynde,
but ever to be trewe, feithfull and kinde,
and to yow beire my trew harte withouten vareance,
desiring you to make me noo dyssemblance.

Also, wher you saye that my bewtye soo sore   15
shuld you inflame with persing violence,
that with extreme love of me you shuld be caught in snare:
I mervell thereof gretly without douttance
that itt shuld have suche might or puisance,
for I knowe right well I was never so bewtiouse   20
that I shuld you constren to be soo amerous.

Also wher you saye that absens shuld be
the grettest payne that can be devised
unto on that is in grette extremitee
and with paynfful love soore tormented: 25
itt is of a truthe, itt can nott be denyed
butt that absens causeth ofte penciffenes;
butt I suppose you be in noo such distresse.

Also itt is truth that throughe povertye
many on dare nott put hym-selffe in prease;   30
butt I take you for none of them, trulye,
butt that you durst, if that itt did yow please,
your-selffe put forthe your harte for to ease.
for how shuld I your sorowez redresse
but iff that ye to me doo them pleynly expresse?   35

Also wher you desire me that I shuld nott shrinke,
butt that I shuld continewe in the same mynde
that you lafte me in, soo that then you might thinke
that there were some truthe in womans kinde:
surely in the same mynde ye shall me styll fynde,   40
soo that you shall nott nede me forto mistruste,
though peraventure you have fonde some unjuste.

Itt is a trewe proverbe and off olde antiquite,
'dispraise nott all, though on have offended'.
Butt they be worthye prasse that stydfast and trowe be,   45
and they disprease, that oderwayez have intended:

yett say well, 'By the worst the best may be amended',
for my love ye sett uppon a perffitt gronde.
noo dissayte in me truly shal be founde

Butt I wylbe trewe, though I should continewe   50
all my hole lyffe in payne and hevynesse.
I will never change you for any other newe.
Yow be my joye, my comfforte and gladnes,
whome I shall serve with all dilligence.
Exyle me never from your harte soo dere,   55
whiche unto my harte have sett you most nere.

Fynally, this scedule forto conclude,
my purpose is certen according to the same,
myndyng for your sake all fantasyez to exclude
off love fayned, and the contrarye to attaine: 60
and by lyke usage off us shall springe the fame
unto the presence off Venus, that goddes eternall,
whoo off hur goodnes grante joye to trewe lovers all.

finis

13 *beire*: bear, maintain   14 *dyssemblance*: equivocation   18 *douttance*: doubt   19
puisance: power   21 *constren*: constrain, compel   27 *penciffenes*: thoughtful melancholy   30 *in prease*: forward   41 *forto*: to   42 *peraventure*: perhaps   44 *on*:
one   46 *disprease*: (of) dispraise   49 *dissayte*: deceit   57 *scedule*: document   62
Venus: medieval love-lyric often apostrophizes the Roman goddess of love, despite the
undoubted Christian commitment of its writers

LADY MARGARET HOWARD, née STEWART, later DOUGLAS, LADY LENNOX
(1515–1578)

LADY MARGARET was the daughter of Margaret Tudor, Queen of Scotland,
by her second husband, Archibald, sixth earl of Angus, and was thus the half-
sister of King James V of Scotland, and the niece of Henry VIII. She was
brought up in England, at the royal court. Although there were some doubts as
to the legitimacy of Margaret Tudor's second marriage, she was unquestionably
a Tudor, with a claim to be considered in the royal succession, which she passed
on to her daughter and grandsons. By the act passed after the execution of Anne
Boleyn, declaring both Mary and Elizabeth illegitimate, Margaret was necessarily advanced to the position of the lady of highest rank in England. Since she
had been born in England (at Harbottle Castle, Northumberland), and was very
much a protégée of her uncle Henry VIII, her claim to the succession was held
to outrival that of her half-brother James V of Scotland, and her marriage was
thus a matter of state. But as a young woman, she fell passionately in love with
Thomas Howard, and married him in secret. Clandestine marriage with a
woman so close to the throne was construed as treason. The relationship was

discovered by Henry VIII in June, 1536, and the pair were separated. Howard was incarcerated in the tower, and Margaret was removed to Syon House. The 'Devonshire Manuscript', which contains a variety of poems from the circle of Anne Boleyn and her associates, includes poems exchanged between them. In October, 1537, she was released from Syon and her husband died of an ague in the Tower. Margaret was rehabilitated at court by 1539, in which year she was appointed First Lady to Anne of Cleves. When Catherine Howard replaced Anne of Cleves as Queen, she kept this position. Unluckily, she was again detected in a clandestine affair, this time with the new Queen's brother Sir Charles Howard, and was once more imprisoned at Syon. She was released in 1541 (to make room for her quondam mistress) and went to Kenninghall with her old friend the Duchess of Richmond. She married the Earl of Lennox in 1544, and moved with him to Temple Newsam in Yorkshire. A year later, their first son, Henry Stuart, Lord Darnley (who was to marry Mary Queen of Scots), was born, the first of eight children, all of whom predeceased her. The Devonshire Manuscript passed into her hands at the time of her second marriage, having probably first belonged to the Duchess of Richmond. From her, it passed to Charles Lennox, her second son, who put it in the library at Chatsworth House, where he and his wife (Elizabeth Cavendish) lived after their marriage in 1574. King Henry's affection for her was sharply diminished after her marriage to Lennox, since she began to manifest Catholic leanings, and his last will excluded her from the succession.

Lady Margaret was a masterful and politically active woman. According to the Calendar of State Papers (Spanish), XI, 293-7, she was Mary Tudor's choice for the succession rather than Elizabeth, perhaps because of their religious sympathy, which no doubt increased her sense of her own consequence. Elizabeth was understandably suspicious of her. Her plan to marry Darnley to Mary Stuart was revealed to Elizabeth by untrustworthy servants, and Lady Margaret was incarcerated in the royal palace at Sheen: when the marriage finally took place, she was sent to the Tower. She was still there in 1567, when Mildred Cecil, Lady Burleigh, was sent to break the dreadful news that her son had been shockingly murdered at Kirk o'Field near Edinburgh: Cecil comments, 'The Queens Majesty sent yesterday my lady Howard and my wife to Lady Lennox in the Tower to open this matter unto her; who could not by any means be kept from such passion of mind as the horribleness of the fact did require.' She made herself so ill with grief that a doctor had to be sent for. The last of her many periods of imprisonment was after the marriage of her younger son Charles Lennox to Elizabeth Cavendish, daughter of Elizabeth Shrewsbury ('Bess of Hardwick'), which produced the ill-fated Arbella Stuart; yet another politically motivated, clandestine marriage.

The identification of the authors of individual poems in the Devonshire manuscript is a palaeographic and evidential minefield. But the attribution of the poems ascribed to her here is strengthened considerably by the obviously Scottish origin of its writer, since no other Scot is known to have been part of this circle: note the rhyme 'constancy/dy', the spelling 'pairpose', Scots plural forms (with their implied sounded final syllable) such as 'herys' and 'dooris' and the verb 'welld'. Indeed, it might now be asserted that the Scots orthography of a group of poems in the Devonshire manuscript make Lady Douglas the *most* identifiable author in that collection.

6   *'Now that ye be assemblld heer'*

Now that ye be assemblld heer
　　All ye my ffreynds at my request
Specyally you my ffather dere
　　That off my blud ar the nerest
　　Thys vnto you ys my request   5
That ye woll pacyently hyre
　　By thys my last words exprest
My testement yntyer

And thynk nat to ynterrupte me
　　Ffor syche wyse provyded have y   10
That thogh ye welld yt woll nat be
　　This touer ye se ys strong and hye
　　And the dooris fast barred have y
That no whight my pairpose [me] let shold
　　For to be quen of all Ytaly   15
Nat on day lenger leve I wold

Therffor suet father, I you pray
　　Ber thys my deth with pacyence
And tourment nat your herys gray
　　But frely pardoun myn ofence   20
　　Sythe yt prosedeth off lovers ffervence
And off my harts constancy
　　Let me nat ffrom the sweet presence
Of hym that I have caseyt to dy.

(1537)

4 her mother lived till 1541, but she had separated from Margaret's father in 1519. Margaret was brought up by her father and at Henry's court; 8 *yntyer*: complete   10 *Ffor syche wyse*: against such an eventuality   12 *touer*: tower   14 *whight*: wight, person; *let shold*: should prevent   16 *Nat on*: not one   17 *suet*: sweet   20 *herys gray*: grey hairs   22 *ffervence*: fervency   23 *Let*: keep

7   *'the sueden chance ded mak me mues'*

the sueden chance ded mak me mues
off hym that so lat was my ffrend
soe strangly now he do me ues
that Y well spy hes uavaryng mynd
Wharffor y mak a promes nou   5
to brek my ffansy and nat to bou
What cowld he say mor than he ded

or what aperrance more could he show
Allways to put me out off dred

3 *strangly*: stranly MS; *ues*: use   4 *uavaryng*: wavering

CIRCLE OF ANNE BOLEYN
(1530s)

THE circumstances outlined in this poem suit Lady Margaret, though
we hesitate to attribute the poem to her, since there are no Scots markers in it.

8   *'I ame not she by proweff of syt'*

I ame not she by proweff of syt
  Kan make a joke off al my woo,
Nor yn suche thynges I do delyt
  But as they be so must they show.
My wowers meshape hath hapt so ryt,   5
  Thus off my ffrynd to make my ffo,
That thoo I wold yt laked nyt
  To cloke my greffe wer yt doth grow.

(1536?)

1 *proweff*: proof   5 *meshape*: mishap; *ryt*: right   7 *nyt*: night   8 *greffe*: grief

KATHERINE, LADY BOROUGH, née PARR, later
NEVILLE, TUDOR, SEYMOUR
(1512–1548)

KATHERINE PARR is of course principally famous for becoming the sixth and
last wife of Henry VIII. She was brought up at court, where her widowed
mother was a member of Catherine of Aragon's inner circle, entrusted with
running the palace school, attended by Princess Mary, the daughters of Henry
VIII's sister Mary, and the children of the ladies-in-waiting, including her own
Katherine. Katherine Parr and Princess Mary thus became intimate friends.
Under the tuition of the Spanish humanist Juan Luis Vives, the pair learned
Latin and French, logic, rhetoric, some mathematics, music, and theology. She
was a lifetime 'insider' at the Tudor court. Less predictably, this background
caused her to set a very high value on friendship with other women: the alumnae
of the palace school were friends for life.

Katherine's first marriage (in 1526), was to an elderly widower, Edward, Lord Borough of Gainsborough in Lincolnshire. Its most important future consequence was that Katherine attracted the devoted admiration and loyalty of a neighbour's daughter, Anne Askew (see nos. 12–13). After Lord Borough's death, she went back to court, but as Anne Boleyn's star rose, and life at court disintegrated for the friends of Katherine and Mary, she decided to marry the middle-aged Lord Latimer, of Snape Hall, Richmondshire. After the fall of Anne Boleyn and the marriage of Henry with Jane Seymour, Katherine made her first appearance at court for three years: she and the Duchess of Suffolk (another alumna of the palace school) united in a concerted effort to persuade Henry to relent towards Princess Mary—efforts which were, after some tense moments, successful. She then returned home to Yorkshire, where the family promptly became embroiled in the popular uprising known as the Pilgrimage of Grace; a protest against the dissolution of the monasteries. Lord Latimer joined the rebels, apparently in the hope of moderating their intentions. When Henry brought the rebellion under control, Latimer found himself in danger of his life. Katherine sought a private interview with Henry, and contrived to talk him over to mercy. She is also known to have succeeded in obtaining her uncle Sir George Throgmorton's release from the Tower, and in the process, assisted in the fall of Henry's chief minister, Thomas Cromwell, beheaded in 1540.

Henry's fifth wife, Katherine Howard, lost her head in 1542. Lord Latimer died in the same year, and Katherine returned once more to court. Here, for probably the first time in her life, she fell in love, with the physically magnificent, if politically inept, Sir Thomas Seymour. However, when Henry himself proposed to her, she kept her feelings to herself, and took on her third elderly husband, marrying the King in 1543. The fact that Sir Thomas was thereupon sent on one foreign mission after another suggests that she had studied the inglorious career of Katherine Howard with advantage. Henry was at this point in need of a nurse rather than a mistress, hugely fat, often ill, and liable to disastrous mood-swings. Katherine bent her considerable talents to winning the King's children. By August, she had succeeded in collecting all of them under one roof, and in gaining the love even of the suspicious Elizabeth. Henry's trust in his last wife is indicated by the fact that she was made Regent during his absence in France. The only point in her career as Queen when her unobtrusively efficient grasp on the reins was shaken was due to her old friend, Anne Askew. For the first time in her life, Katherine found she had personal enemies, anxious to bring her down. But Anne stood firm, through hours of cross-examination and torture on the rack. Katherine, meanwhile, contrived to make her peace with the King. Anne Askew died at the stake, but she died alone. Henry followed her six months later, leaving Katherine's position unassailable.

Thomas Seymour, the new king's uncle, became Lord Admiral, and renewed his courtship of Katherine. Edward VI, after initial obtuseness, was talked into approving his stepmother's marriage. Elizabeth went to live with the new couple at Chelsea, an experiment which was abandoned after some indiscreet romps made the ménage the subject of public gossip. Katherine then fell pregnant, to the delight of herself and her friends. Her daughter was born in August 1548. All seemed well at first, but Katherine began to show symptoms of puerperal fever, and died on 5 September, rapidly followed by her child. Lady Jane Grey was her chief mourner. The verses here are from a French translation of her *Lamentacion*: Katherine studied French, and it is possible that she made this as a translation exercise: she encouraged her stepdaughters to undertake comparable tasks.

9   from *'Considerant ma vie misérable'*

Christ a son pere obeisant estoit
Iusque a la mort a luy se submettoit
Mais las I'estoys en toute iniquite
Opiniastre encontre verite.
Christ fut bening et d'un cueur gracieux   5
Mais i'estois fiere et d'un port glorieux
Christ desprisoit le monde en chacun lieu
Mais i'e l'aymois et en fai sois mon Dieu
Christ vint icy pour ses freres servir
Mais i'appetois de me les asservir   10
Christ deprisoit tout gloire mondaine
Mais ie preuois peine d'en estre plene
Christ aymoit mieux pauvrete et simplesse
Mais l'aymois miex biens honneir et richesse
Christ estoit doux, aux pauvres pitoyable   15
Mais i'estois rude et bien peu confortable
Christ prioit Dieu pour tous ses ennemis
Mais ie hayois les miens et leurs amis
Christ s'efforcoit de pecheurs convertir
Mais ie n'alloys de rien les divertir.   20

(after 1547)

9   From *'In contemplation of my wretched life'*

Christ was obedient unto his father
even to the death of the cross,
and I disobedient, and most stubborn
even to the confusion of trueth.
Christ was meke and humble in heart,   5
I moste proud and vainglorious.
Christ dispised the worlde with all the vanities thereof,
and I made it my god because of the vanities.
Christ came to serve his brethren,
I coveted to rule over them.   10
Christ dispised wordly honor
and I muche delited to attain the same,
Christ loved the base and simple thinges of the world
and I estemed the moste fayre and pleasunt thinges.
<Christ loved povertie, and I welth.> [not translated]   15
Christ was ientle, and mercyfull to the poore,
and I harde hearted and unientle.
Christ prayed for his enemies,
and I hated mine [French adds: and their friends].

Christ rejoysed in the convercion of synners,   20
and I was not greved to se theyr revercion to synne.

ALIS FERCH GRUFFYD AB IEUAN AP
LLEYWELYN FYCHAN
(fl. *c*.1540–1570)

GRUFFYD AB IEUAN AP LLYWELYN FYCHAN was a nobleman and poet from Llewenni Fechan near St Asaph, in north-east Wales. Surviving verses are associated with two of his daughters, Alis and Catrin (see below, no. 27). Nothing is known of their biographies.

10 *Englynion o waith Alis ach Ryffydd ap Iefan*
   pan ofynodd ei thad pa fath wr a fyne hi

   hardd fedrus campus pes caid—a dewr
        I daro o bai raid
   mab o oedran cadarn blaid
   A gwr o gorph goreu a gaid

   fy nhad a ddywede ym hyn—mae gorau   5
        Yw garu dyn gwrthun
   Ar galon sydd yn gofyn
   Gwas glan hardd ysgafn i hun

10 *Verses written by Alis daughter of Gryffydd son*
   of Iefan when her father asked her what sort of
   husband she would like

   Beautiful, accomplished, splendid—if he can be had—and brave
        to strike were there need
   a youth in age, wall-strong,
   and a man of the finest body to be had

   My father told me this—that best   5
        for me is to love a repulsive man
   yet the heart asks for
   a lad pure, lovely, and light of its own

11 *pan ofynne ei thad yn wr gweddw beth a*
   ddoede hi am iddo amcanu priodi llances o lodes

Llances o lodes lwydwen—feinael
   A fynne gael amgen
   hi a rodded yn ireddwen
   chwithe nhad aethoch yn hen

Yn gleiriach bellach heb allu—duw n borth   5
   ond or barth ir gwelu
   Gwanwr ai ben un gwnnu
   Ni thale dim ich ael ddu

Rhai a heurai o hiroed, or blaen
   fyned draen im troed   10
   Dylys yw ngorph llei delwy
   Dygwyl y ffair digloff wy

11 *When her father a widower asked what she*
   would say to his intention of marrying
   a young girl

A fair young fine-browed lass
   would demand a better
   Fresh and pure she would be given
   you my father have got old

Decrepit you can hardly without God's help   5
   get from hearth to bed
   a weak man his head going white
   wouldn't satisfy your black-browed one

[*father's reply*] Some asserted long life before now
   put a thorn in my foot   10
   my body is sure where I should be
   on fairs and feastdays, nothing holds me back.

ANNE KYME, née ASKEW
(1521–1546)

ANNE ASKEW's claim to fame is as a Protestant martyr, hailed as a true servant of God by both John Bale and John Foxe. She wrote *The first examinacyon* in 1545, an account of her first imprisonment and interrogation, and *the lattre examinacyon* in 1546, just before she was burned as a heretic at Smithfield. Her writing was edited and published by John Bale. She was the well-educated and very religious second daughter of Sir William Askew of Stallingborough, near Grimsby, and a childhood friend of Katherine Parr. Her older sister was betrothed to Thomas Kyme of Kelsey, but died before the marriage took place, whereupon her father insisted that she act as substitute. She and Kyme had two children, but the marriage was not a happy one, and ended when he turned her out of the house. She went to London, where she was received by Protestant sympathizers, in 1545. In the same year, she was charged with heresy, interrogated, and tortured, in the hopes that she would implicate important people: this attempt seems to have been aimed at Katherine Parr's circle (she was specifically asked if 'my lady of Suffolk, my lady of Sussex, my lady of Hertford, Lady Deny and lady FitzWilliam'—all strong Protestants—were involved). It was in any case a failure. She was released, and charged with heresy again in 1546, and subjected to the full rigours of torture, notably the rack. She refused to recant, and was burned on 16 July 1546, so crippled that she had to be carried to the stake in a chair: bags of gunpowder were hung round her to shorten her sufferings.

The two poems given here, appended to the first and second examinations respectively, are probably her work: a ballad in her voice also survives ('I am a woman poor and blind'), which is an exploitation of her status as Protestant heroine by some unknown hand.

12   *The voyce of Anne Askewe out of the*
54. Psalme of David, called, Deus in nomine tuo.

> For thy names sake, be my refuge,
>   And in thy truthe, my quarell judge.
> Before the (lorde) let me be hearde,
>   And with faver my tale regarde
> Loo, faythlesse men, agaynst me ryse,   5
>   And for thy sake, my deathe practyse.
> My lyfe they seke, with mayne and myght
>   Whych have not the, afore their syght
> Yet helpest thu me, in thys dystresse,
>   Savynge my sowle, from cruelnesse.   10
> I wote thu wylt revenge my wronge,
>   And vysyte them, ere it be longe.
> I wyll therfor, my whole hart bende,
>   Thy gracyouse name (lorde) to commende.
> From evyll thu hast, delyvered me,   15
>   Declarynge what, myne enmyes be.
>   Prayse to God.

>   (1546)

11 *wote*: know

13   *The Balade whych Anne Askewe made and sange whan she was in Newgate.*

Lyke as the armed knyght
Appoynted to the fielde
With thys world wyll I fyght
And fayth shall be my shielde.
    faythe is that weapon stronge   5
Whych wyll not fayle at nede
My foes therfor amonge
Therwith wyll I procede.
    As it is had in strengthe
And force of Christes waye   10
It wyll prevayle at lengthe
Though all the devyls saye naye.
    faythe in the fathers olde
Obtayned ryghtwysnesse
Which make me verye bolde.   15
To feare no worldes dystresse.
    I now rejoyce in hart
And hope byd me do so
For Christ wyll take my part
And ease me of my wo.   20
    Thu sayst lorde, who so knocke
To them wylt thu attende
Undo therfor the locke
And thy stronge power sende.
    More enmyes now I have.   25
Than heeres upon my heed
Lete them not me deprave
But fyght thy in my steed.
    On the my care I cast
For all their cruell spyght   30
I sett not by their hast
For thu art my delyght.
    I am not she that lyst
My anker to lete fall
For euerye drysling myst   35
My shyppe substancyall.
    Not oft use I to wryght
In prose nor yet in ryme
Yet wyll I shewe one syght
That I sawe in my tyme.   40
    I sawe a ryall trone
Where Justyce shuld have sytt
But in her stede was one

Of modye cruell wytt.
Absorpt was ryghwysnesse   45
As of the ragyng floude
Sathan in his excesse.
Sucte up the gyltelesse bloude.
Than thought I, Jesus lorde
Whan thu shald judge us all   50
Harde is it to recorde
On these men what wyll fall.
Yet lorde I the desyre
For that they do to me
Lete not them tast the hyre   55
Of their inyquyte.

(1547)

14 *ryghtwysnesse*: righteousness   26 *heeres... heed*: hairs...head   34 *anker*:
anchor   35 *dryslyng myst*: drizzling mist   41 *trone*: throne   55 *hyre*: reward

LADY ELIZABETH TYRWHIT
(fl. *c*.1548–1582)

ELIZABETH TYRWHIT was the daughter of Sir Goddard Oxenbridge, Knight
Banneret, by his second wife, Anne the daughter of Sir Thomas Fyne of
Claversham. She married Sir Robert Tyrwhit of Leighton Buzzard, Master of
the Horse to Queen Katherine Parr. Lady Tyrwhit was the god-daughter
of Queen Katherine Parr, and was with her at her death: it was she who bitterly
accused Sir Thomas Seymour of hastening her end by refusing her proper
medical care after the birth of her child (Haynes, *Burleigh Papers* i, 107–9).
Like all of Queen Katherine's inner circle, she was staunchly Protestant. Her
husband was the man appointed to enquire into an embarrassing incident of the
future Queen Elizabeth's youth; a flirtation with Katherine Parr's husband, Sir
Thomas Seymour, in 1649. Lady Tyrwhit was appointed by the Privy Council
to supervise Princess Elizabeth after the removal of her beloved Mrs Katherine
Ashley, to Elizabeth's fury: 'she wept all that night and lowered all the next day.'
More to the point, she never forgave either of them, and after Elizabeth became
Queen, they discreetly retired to their estate at Leighton Bromswold in Huntingdonshire. Lady Tyrwhit's tomb survives, much worn, in the church of
Leighton Bromswold. Though there are full-size effigies of herself and her
husband, Sir Robert Tyrwhit, no inscriptions are now visible. Their only
child, Katherine, married Sir Henry d'Arcy and died in 1567.

Lady Tyrwhit's devotion to the more extreme forms of Protestantism is
suggested by a remark in a letter of Sir Robert Tyrwhit's to Protector Somerset
in 1548: 'my wyffe is not sayne in Divynnity, but is half a Scripture woman' (i.e.
a Calvinist). (Ellis, *Letters* ii. 129–40) Lady Tyrwhit was the author of prose
*Morning and evening praiers, with divers psalmes, hymnes and meditations, made and
set forth by the Lady Elizabeth Tyrwhit*, London, H. Middleton for C. Barker,

1574. This was published as a tiny 32° book, presumably to make it easy to carry about. The single copy which survives is in effect a jewel: it was set into a gold and enamel case with a carrying-ring and a chain, to be hooked onto a lady's belt as part of a châtelaine (the mistress of the house's collection of keys, etc., kept on the belt for a combination of security and easy access). It is now in the British Museum (see further Hugh Tait: 'The girdle-prayerbook or "Tablett"', *Jewellery Studies* 2 (1985)). She contributed to the *Monument of Matrones* (1582), edited by Thomas Bentley, to which Lady Frances Abergavenny also contributed. The 'Second Lampe of Virginitie' is a valuable source for women's religious writing in the Renaissance. The editor describes this section as giving the reader a 'tast' of those queens, noble ladies, and godly gentlewomen who from their tender and maidenly years have sacrificed their time, substance, and physical well-being to scriptural studies, and the compiling and translating of religious books.

14   *The Hymne of the daie of* judgment

Sweet Iesus of thy mercie, our pitifull praiers heare:
   That we may be on thy right hand, when thou shalt appeare.
For thou shalt come with heavenlie power, and sit on the throne:
   None shall judge the quicke and dead, but thou Christ alone.
O Christ cast us not awaie, in that daie of ire: 5
   When thou shalt send before thee, a hot consuming fire.
To purge all creatures, defild with Adams sinne:
   Then a new heaven and earth, O Lord thou wilt beginne.
Then the elect shall be blessed, upon thy holie hill:
   But the wicked shall be damned, that have withstood thy will.   10
The sheepe shall be safe, and defended in the fold:
   The goates shall wander, in hunger, storme and cold.
Thy Saints shall behold thee, in thy throne of light:
   The reprobates shall ever, have fearefull things in sight.
Wailing in wretchednese, with everlasting paine: 15
   Yet Lord be mercifull, our lives are but vaine.
Our flesh shall fade, death hath digd our grave:
   Yet of thy mercie Lord, thy sinfull creature save.
And blesse us in the time of grace, before the daie of ire:
   When the corrupt elements, shall be purgd with fire.   20

    We laud thee Father for thy grace,
      [We praise thee Sonne which made us free:
    We thanke the holie Spirit for our solace
      Which is one God and persons three.]

                    (before 1582)

2 *right hand*: cf. Psalm 16: 11   4 *quicke*: Acts 10: 42   6 *fire*: Revelations 13: 13   8 *new heaven*: Revelations 21: 1   9 *holie hill*: Psalms 99: 9   11–12 Matthew 25: 32   13 *throne*: Revelations 4: 2

15 *An Hymne of the state of all Adams* posteritie.

I am the fruit of Adams hands, through sin lockt in satans bands,
Destined to deth, the child of ire, a flaming brand of infernall fire:
Borne I was naked and bare, and spend my time in sorowe and care,
And shall returne unto the dust, and be deprived of carnall lust.
Yet thou father didst Jesus send, to pardon them that did offend: 5
We laud him in the work of might, that we be blessed in his
   sight.

MILDRED CECIL, née COOKE, LADY BURLEIGH
(1526–1589)

MILDRED was the oldest daughter of Sir Anthony Cooke of Gidea Hall in
Essex. His family consisted of five daughters and four sons, of whom four
daughters became famous as scholars. The details of their curriculum are
unknown, but they were certainly taught the Classical languages, Italian, probably French, and Latin and Greek verse composition. The youngest daughter
(Margaret) appears to have died in her late teens, but the surviving four
impressed their contemporaries as outstandingly learned. Mildred, Lady Burleigh, second wife of William Cecil, was almost certainly the eldest. She married
Cecil on 21 December 1545, and much of the family's story thereafter can be
explained by this connection. At the time of his second marriage, however, he
was only 25. Henry VIII was still on the throne, and Cecil's political importance
was negligible, while Mildred was merely the daughter of an old University
friend. Cecil emerges into political visibility only in the reign of the boy-king
Edward VI, as a servant of the king's uncle, the Lord Protector, Duke of
Somerset. His rise thereafter, which involved his deftly detaching himself
from his first patron's ruin, is a testimony to his own political acumen, and
also to the capacity of late-sixteenth-century England to utilize the talents of
new men.

   Her literary life was concerned mostly with translation from Greek. Giles
Lawrence, of Christ Church, Oxford, was her Greek tutor in her youth; and
claimed that she 'egalled if not overmatched' contemporary Grecians. Mildred's
manuscript translation of a sermon by St Basil survives as BL MS Royal
17.B.xviii. She is also said to have translated 'a peece' of the fourth-century
bishop of Constantinople, St John Chrysostom, though she refused to publish
her work once she heard that someone else had also done a translation: this
information comes from the anonymous *Life of Burghley* written c.1600, and
may be an erroneous reference to the translation from St Basil already
mentioned. She took pleasure in reading the works of the fourth-century
Greek Fathers of the Church—of particular interest to Anglican theologians,
then and later, since they represented an ancient strand of Christian thought
which was disassociated from the Roman Church. An anonymous translation of
John Chrysostom's commentary on the Epistle to the Ephesians was dedicated

to Anne Cecil, Mildred's daughter, in 1581, suggesting a continued interest in Greek patristic writing in the Cecil household in the third generation (and also that Mildred passed on to her daughter the kind of education she had had herself: there is clear evidence that Anne Cecil read Latin).

Conyers Read in his life of Burghley comments on Mildred's influence in general, 'without doubt she brought into Cecil's life a strong puritan influence and her intercession with her husband was often sought by those of that persuasion . . . we shall find her participating actively in Cecil's intellectual and in his official life.' Mildred Cecil has left almost no personal writing, and those of her letters that survive are essentially political documents. One, written in Latin, is to her cousin Sir William Fitzwilliam, Lord Deputy of Ireland, advising him to stick to his post for the time being, and indicates something of her canny sense of political realities. She was seen as important enough to correspond with by international humanists such as George Buchanan, Franciscus Junius, and Charles Utenhove, and also by leading politicians (Scots and English) from the earliest days of Cecil's appointment as Elizabeth's principal adviser. The word 'housewife' attached to Mildred Cecil, though true after a fashion, carries wholly inappropriate implications. In effect, in addition to her other responsibilities, Mildred ran what was recognized as the best private school in England. The anonymous biography states that, 'most of the principal gentlemen of England preferred their sons and heirs to [Cecil's] service', which has abundant contemporary corroboration. Mildred Cecil died on 4 April, 1589, and was buried in Westminster Abbey with her daughter Anne, under a very long Latin inscription from her husband, recording his devoted affection for her.

16 Ὡς πρώτιστα ἔναιον ἐπὶ χθόνι πολυβοτείρῃ

'Ὡς πρώτιστα ἔναιον ἐπὶ χθόνι πολυβοτείρῃ
νήπιοι ἄνδρες ὕλας κόσμος ἄκοσμος ελω
ὡς φρόνιμοι ἐγενοντ''ἄνδρες πολυδένδρεος ὕλη
Ὑ λων τοις κήποις ἀνθέμεοισι πόρεν.
Νυν δ ἐφύτευσε καλὸν σοφος ὡς ἐκ νηρίτου ὕλης   5
Ὕλη ἐφαρμοσσων ὄν ποτε κ ηπον ὁρας

1 ʼἐπὶ χθόνι πολυβοτείρῃ/ on the fruitful earth: direct quotation from Hesiod, *Works and Days*, 510   2 κόσμος/universe: untranslatable wordplay: κʼοσμος means both 'order' and 'the created world'. κόσμος/ακοσμος; 'world that is disorderly/no world' is a phrase used in a poem in the *Greek Anthology*, vii. 561; ʼὕλας/woods: ʼὕλη is both 'a wood', and a word used philosophically to signify 'primal chaos'   5 ἐκ νηρίτου ὕλης/from the immense forest: from Hesiod, *Words and Days*, 511

16 *As when at first primitive men were dwelling on the fruitful earth*

As when at first primitive men were dwelling in the fruitful earth,
A universe that was not yet orderly established the woods:
As men grew wise, the tree-filled forest
Was transformed into flowery gardens of the woodlands.

Now, the Wise Man (Sylva) has cultivated beauty, just as, from the
    immense forest,   5
a wood is created where now you see a garden.

LADY MARY CHEKE, née HILL, later
MACWILLIAM
(c.1527–1616)

LADY MARY was the daughter of Richard Hill, sergeant of the wine cellar to
Henry VIII. She married John Cheke in about 1547. Her second husband was a
royal pensioner, Henry MacWilliam, with whom she received a lease from the
crown in 1565 or 1566, indicating that she was widowed and remarried before
that time. Lady Mary was an important confidential servant of the Queen. She
was numbered among the extraordinary ladies of the Privy Chamber at Elizabeth's coronation, though only as an ordinary one at her funeral. But she was
clearly one of Elizabeth's most intimate attendants through the reign, partly for
reasons of sheer continuity. Her name appears regularly in New Year gift rolls,
always as Lady Cheke, and in 1562, Cecil appointed her one of four ladies, all
wives of knights, to accompany Elizabeth to a proposed meeting with Mary,
Queen of Scots (which never, of course, took place). The one poem attributed to
her was probably written in the late 1590s and circulated quite widely in
manuscript miscellanies. Nine copies survive: six are anonymous, while two
record her authorship.

17   Erat quaedam mulier *[a reply to John*
    Harington's poem, Erat quidem homo*]*

    That no man yet could in the bible find
    A certaine woman, argues men are blinde
    Blinde as the Preacher, who had little learninge
    The Certaine cause of this soe ill discerning.
    A Certaine woman of the multitude   5
    Sayd, blest be the pappes that gave our Saviour foode
    A Certaine woman too, a milstone threw
    And from the wall, Abimilech she slew.
    There likewise was, as holy writ doth say
    A Certaine woman named Lydia   10
    Nay more (though it by men be ou'swai'de)
    The text records, there was a certaine maide.
    Which proves directly certaine women then.
    And certaine too, more certaine far than men.
    Your Preacher then may well stand much perplext   15
    To see how grossely, he bely'd the text.
    And blush his sermon was no better suted

Then by a woman thus to be confuted.
Yit for his comfort, one true note he made
When (there is now, no certaine man) he said.   20

(1590s)

6 *pappes* Luke 11: 27   7 *milstone* Judges 9: 53   10 *Lydia* Acts 16: 14, 40   11 *ou'swai'de*:
overswayed, argued against   12 perhaps Luke 24: 22

ANNE BACON, née COOKE
(1528?–1610)

ANNE BACON was the second of the five highly educated daughters of Sir
Anthony Cooke. She married the physically gross, but intelligent and formidable
Nicholas Bacon, Lord Keeper of the Great Seal of England to Queen Elizabeth,
early in the 1550s, as his second wife. They had three children, Anthony and
Francis, and a daughter, who died in childhood. Anthony became a not wholly
successful politician, but Francis became one of the most prodigious intellects of
the age. Anne was widowed in 1576, and thereafter took full advantage of her
status as *femme sole*. As widow, she resided at Gorehambury, in receipt of one-
third of Sir Nicholas's patrimony, a position which gave her a great deal of
power over her sons, who were perpetually short of money.

Her first appearance in the public record is as one of Mary Tudor's gentlewomen during her brother's lifetime: on Mary's accession, in 1553, she became a
member of the Queen's privy chamber. She published a book of sermons translated
from the Italian of Bernadino Ochino in 1550, when she was 22, and early in the
reign of Elizabeth, she also published an English translation of an extremely
important book, John Jewell's *An Apology for the Church of England*.

A large number of letters survive from Anne Bacon, to her brother-in-law,
William Cecil, Lord Burleigh, and to her sons, particularly Anthony, many of
them preserved among the Tenison MSS in Lambeth Palace Library. They
present a mixture of religious exhortation, maternal anxiety, and worldly good
sense: she clearly believed that neither of her sons was remotely capable of
organizing his own affairs, and was perpetually anxious lest they default from
the austerest principles of Calvinism. Moreover, she was short-tempered, and
got worse as she aged: a hapless servant reporting back to Nicholas in 1594 noted
plaintively, 'I will give none offence to make her angry, but nobody can please
her long together.' She was inclined, on the evidence of this correspondence, to
fly off the handle, and then relent: when she believed that Anthony had been
consorting with Catholics, another intermediary reported that 'she let not to say
that you are a traitor to God and your country; you have undone her; you seek
her death...' one can almost hear her. It is hardly surprising to find that the
sentiment 'you have little enough, if not too little, regarded your kind and no
simple mother's wholesome advice from time to time' is a regular theme of her
correspondence with her sons. What is more interesting is to find that she uses
Latin and Greek as a first and second level of concealment in her letters to her
sons: 'Be not too bold with κυρίῳ θησαυραρίῳ [The Lord Treasurer: Bur-
leigh]. Lose not his φιλίαν [friendship]. You know what I mean...be not
overcredulous or too open. *Sub omni lapide latet anguis* [a viper lurks under

every stone]. Similarly, in another letter to Anthony, a direct and negative judgement of Archbishop Whitgift is written in Greek. She was notably secretive: many letters insist that her correspondence is not to be shown to anyone. On the whole, Latin seems to be used to convey personal tenets: Greek, when her opinion might be seen as subversive.

All of the Cooke sisters except the youngest (who died in the year of her marriage, probably in childbirth) wrote poetry. A dedicatory poem in a presentation manuscript of the *Giardino cosmografico coltivato* by Bartholo Sylva of Turin, made for Lord Leicester by the circle of Protestant activists who included the Cooke sisters and the preacher Edward Dering (Cambridge, CUL Ii.5.37), appears to be Anne's work: the signature is erased, leaving only the initials A...B..., with the right number of spaces for Anna Baconia. Schleiner has suggested that the erasure is highly comprehensible (all other names are given in full), since Anne's husband, Sir Nicholas Bacon, was responsible for prosecuting Edward Dering in the Star Chamber the year after the manuscript's completion, and permanently depriving him of his licence to preach. The poem is short but complex: it builds a comparison between Sylva's manuscript and the Garden of Eden (the thorns, for example, evoke Genesis 3: 18).

18   *A—B—in D.B. Sylva*

Se titulo prodit liber hic, quantasque recondat
    Ipse suo fidens nomine monstrat, opes.
Promittit mundum, promittit sidera, sed quem
    Ad se non rapient nomina tanta virum?
Nec coelum tenebris, nec mundus sentibus horret.   5
    Scilicet artificem sentit uterque manum.
SYLVA prius, sed nunc est hortus amoenior, ut tu
    Quisquis es, in mediis ex patiere rosis.

                                    (1572)

18   *A—B—on the learned Bartholo Sylva*

By this title, the book declares itself, and the amount of riches that
        it conceals,
    itself trusting in its own name, it shows forth.
It promises the world, it promises the stars: what man
    do such names not attact to it?
Heaven does not abhor darkness, nor the world thorns,   5
    For thus each perceives the hand of the maker.
There was first a WOOD, but now, a still lovelier garden, so that
        you,
    whoever you are, may attain the roses at its centre.

FRANCES NEVILL (née MANNERS), LADY ABERGAVENNY
(after 1527–1576)

Lady Frances Abergavenny was the daughter of Thomas Manners, Earl of Rutland and Eleanor, the daughter of Sir William Paston. She married Henry Nevill (b. 1527), 33rd Baron Bergavenny, or Abergavenny, before 31 January 1556. Her verses in the *Monument of Matrones* are preserved in the context of advice to her daughter, thus allying her writing with the genre of 'mother's advice'. Lady Abergavenny's daughter, Mary, the recipient of her work in the *Monument of Matrones*, was their only child, born in 1554. She married Sir Thomas Fane of Bodsill, Kent. There is no indication that Lady Abergavenny herself intended to publish her work, which Thomas Bentley describes as actively solicited by him from the various ladies involved in his collection.

19   *A necessarie praier in Meeter against vices*

O Lord my God, make thou my hart repentant for to be,
  The spirit of contrition, do thou ingraffe in me.
Unto mine eies let there be given aboundant teares of weeping,
  And let my hands be occupied with often almes giving.
O thou my king quench out of me all foul fleshlie desire,   5
  And with the love of thee alone set thou my hart on fire.
O my redeemer drive awaie the spirit of pride from me,
  And graunt to me that great treasure of meeke humilitie.
Take from me O my Saviour, the furious rage of ire,
  The shield of patience give to me, the which I do desire.   10
O Creator roote out of me all spitefulnesse of mind,
  And graunt in stead thereof againe meekenes that I may find.
O bountifull father give me a faith that shall endure,
  With hope agreeing therunto, and charitie most sure.
O thou my guide keepe from my lips all lieng vanitie,   15
  And from my mind drive far awaie all vaine unconstancie.
All wavering take thou from my hart, and from my mouth scoffing,
  With all proud lookes and gluttonie, backbiting and slandering.
Covetousnes wipe cleare awaie, with curiositie,
  The fond desire of vaine-glorie, with all hypocrisie.   20
Let me never the poore despise, nor yet the weake oppresse.
  And let me not blaspheme, for then I die remediless.
O thou which didst me forme and make, take all rashnesse from
    mee,
  And leaue me not such a mind as, will not with peace agree.
Take from me ydlenesse and sloth, and heavie lumpishnesse,   25
  Take from me disobedience, and eke all, stubbornnesse.
O my God, for thy deere sonnes sake, I humblie beseech thee,

To graunt me the works of mercie, with aboundance of pittie,
That I may thee both love and feare, and eke pitie the poore,
   Make me good men alwaies to love, and wicked to abhor.   30
Make me so little to esteeme those things that wordlie bee,
   With hart and voice that I may crave in heaven to be with
      thee.

Amen

(before 1582)

EMMA FOXE
(d. 1570)

THIS poem was collected from a monumental brass in Aldeburgh, Suffolk, suggesting that Emma Foxe was a woman of substance. The use of tomb-verses to warn and exhort the living—either passing readers, or as here, the subject's immediate family—is not uncommon in the sixteenth and seventeenth centuries. Emma Foxe's poem is almost a 'mother's advice', though placed on a public monument rather than in a private book. A number of other women left verses for use on their monuments: we include one by Katherine Killigrew (no. 36), but there are others, such as the verses of Elizabeth Peirce (d. 1671) in Bath Abbey.

20 'To you that lyfe possess grete troubles do befall'

To you that lyfe possess grete troubles do befall,
When we that slepe by Dethe do feel no harm at all.
An honeste lyfe dothe bringe a joyfull deathe at last,
And lyfe agayne begins when dethe is once past.
My louinge ffoxe ffarewell, God guyde thee with his grace,   5
Prepare thyselfe to come and I will geve the place.
   My children all adewe, and be ryghte sure of this,
   You shal be brought to Duste as emma ffoxe your Mother is.

(1570)

ELIZABETH I
(1533–1603)

BRIEFLY, Elizabeth I was the daughter of Henry VIII and Anne Boleyn. Her mother was executed before she was 2, and she herself was bastardized by her father: something which we should perhaps remember, since it helps to explain her lifelong insecurity about other claimants to the throne. Her position

throughout the reign of her half-sister Mary Tudor was a very stressful one: she
was effectively under house arrest, though she clearly had sufficient access to
news to learn from some of Mary's mistakes. She came to power on Mary's
death in November, 1558, and ruled without marrying for more than forty years
without ever clarifying her intentions for the succession. Her position as female
sovereign was neither unparalleled nor unprecedented (the English had had a
chance to get used to a female ruler under Mary), but no other reigning Queen
of the sixteenth century anywhere in Europe exploited her position so effectively. Her reign was a complex one. It was necessary to create some degree of
religious unity: the Anglican settlement which was achieved predictably out-
raged both Catholics and the more extreme Protestants, and religious issues
rumbled on throughout the reign. Her foreign affairs problems were dominated
by Spain, France, and Scotland, and for decades, she used the prospect of her
marriage as an important tool of her diplomatic relations with all three
states. Her diplomacy and also her handling of domestic problems were both
dominated by her lack of money: she was extremely reluctant to go to war,
which was hugely expensive, and she was often accused of miserliness (particularly by those who had to fight on her behalf), but she was almost powerless
to increase her revenues except by pleading with Parliament for subsidies: this
was partly because pre-industrial England was not very wealthy, and partly due
to the Queen's sense of the weakness of her position which made her reluctant
to push her luck. Her preferred method of dealing with difficulties was to
vacillate as long as possible until either a consensus emerged, or the problem
evaporated. Crises of the reign included a Catholic rising in 1570, which aimed
to put Mary, Queen of Scots on the throne (and beyond measure increased
general English paranoia about Catholics), and the Spanish Armada's attack on
England in 1588, a complete victory which was due to a combination of good
seamanship on the English side, and absolutely extraordinary luck with the
weather.

Elizabeth is known to have versified at various points in her life. As the self-
created centre of a powerful national mythology (discussed by Roy Strong and
others), she was also the object of a considerable quantity of verse *in persona*.
The case for each separate poem therefore has to be carefully considered. It is
unlikely that any poems bewailing prolonged virginity are authentic, however
often they may be attributed in manuscript. However, the case for 'The dread of
future foes' is a good one, particularly because of its excellent provenance,
recorded by the Queen's godson, Sir John Harington, and preserved in *Nugae
Antiquae:*

Good Madam. Herewith I commit a precious jewel, not for your ear, but your eye; and
doubt not but you will rejoyce to wear it even in your heart: It is of her Highness own
enditing, and doth witness, how much her wisdom and great learning do outweigh even
the perils of state, and how little all worldly dangers do work any change in her mynde. My
Lady Wilougby did covertly get it on her Majesty's tablet, and had much hazard in so
doing; for the Queen did find out the thief, and chid for spreading evil bruit of her writing
such toyes, when other matters did so occupy her employment at this time; and was fearful
of being thought too lightly of for so doinge. But marvel not, good Madam, her Highness
doth frame herself to all occasions, to all times, and all things, both in business and
pastime, as may witness this her sonnet.

The text in MS Egerton 2642 has a suggested date of composition of 1569–70:
thus the poem was written in the context of the arrival of Mary, Queen of Scots
in England in 1568, and the subsequent Northern rebellion of 1569/70: this is

also suggested in Puttenham's *Arte of English Poesie* (1589), 247. The context described by Harington tends to suggest that the poem was written as an act of private meditation, in Elizabeth's personal notebook (her 'tablet'): though she was perhaps sufficiently pleased by it to leave it lying about where a maid of honour could find it: since she was a woman of profoundly devious, ambivalent and indirect mind, even she may not have known whether she wished it to be circulated or not. The brief Latin and English cry of frustration we also print here has a good case for authenticity because it was *not* circulated, but preserved in one of his own books by her chancellor (the English is her own version of the Latin).

Other poems which have an excellent case for authenticity are the answer-poems to Paul Melissus and Sir Walter Raleigh. Paul Melissus Schede was born in Franconia in 1539, and lived principally in Heidelberg, where he came under the patronage of the Elector Palatine. He became famous as a poet in Greek and Latin, and as a musician, and received a variety of honours: he was named Poet Laureate by the emperor Maximilian II in 1564, and given the title of Count Palatine in Italy in 1579. He also spent time in Paris, where he became friendly with members of the Pléiade, and had close friends among English diplomats. He remained a firm Protestant, but was on good terms with many individual Catholics, and so was frequently employed on missions to unite the Protestant princes of Germany in a league against the Catholic powers of Europe. He had a variety of contacts with Elizabeth. In a letter he wrote to her in August 1585, he claims to have admired her for thirty years. One of the poems in his *Mele sive Odae* (published 1580), implies that Elizabeth had actually read his work and expressed an interest in him, while another takes courtly flattery to the length of speaking of himself as a slave, with Elizabeth as his mistress: it is this poem to which a reply survives. Its authorship can never be certain, but writing of a reply to a poem of flattery is common among cultivated Renaissance princes, and Elizabeth was known on other occasions to respond to a potential challenge to her eloquence. It is certainly far more sophisticated than the other Latin verse printed here, but the short verse is an improvisation, and this poem a very polished performance. The importance of Melissus is a relevant factor. He was very widely admired; and his courtship of her therefore genuinely flattering. He was also a diplomatic agent of the German Protestant Princes, with whom Elizabeth was seeking to unite in a league against Catholic Europe. These are both cogent reasons for offering a gracious rejoinder. Another support for its authenticity is the textual position of the poem. He prints the 'Responsum Reginae' after his own initial poem in *Mele sive Odae*, but when he reprints his own poem in *Schediasmata* (1586), he leaves out the 'Responsum', which may suggest that it was not his own work.

The Armada Song cannot be proved to be by Elizabeth, but it is within the range of possibility: the interesting thing about it is that it is a canticle: the reference is to the Crossing of the Red Sea, and the two songs of praise uttered by Moses and Miriam. The reference to the fiery pillar and cloud is also a clear allusion to Exodus. Elizabeth is either another Miriam (on grounds of gender) or functionally another Moses: the reference within the poem itself is more obviously to the Canticle of Moses. Early modern women frequently look for some authority for their work: among the possibilities offered by the Old Testament, the prophetess Deborah is the most frequently evoked (see nos. 183, 251: Elizabeth is compared to Deborah on a number of occasions), but Miriam's jubilant song of praise as the Israelites watched the destruction of their

Egyptian pursuers, overwhelmed by water, is another occasion when a woman's public utterance is clearly sanctioned by context. Another work which we believe to be probably genuine is a long poem in French. It is in her most scribbly and private hand, with many scorings-out: the first page is missing, and it is clearly an early draft, probably preserved by accident or as a curiosity (Hatfield House, Cecil Papers 147, nos. 150–4, fos. 207–14).

21   *GENUS INFŒLIX VITÆ*

> Multum vigilavi, laboravi, presto multis fui,
> Stultitiam multorum perpessa sum,
> Arrogantiam pertuli, Difficultates exorbui,
> Vixi ad aliorum arbitrium, non ad meum.
>
> A haples kynde of lyfe is this I weare,   5
> Moch watche I dure, and weary toilings daier;
> I serve the route, and all their follies beare;
> I suffer pryde, and suppe full hard assaise;
> To others will, my life is all addrest,
> And no ware so, as might content me best.   10

This above was written in a booke by the Queenes majestie.

(*c*.1570)

22 'The dread of future foes exyle my present Joy'

The dread of future foes exyle my present Joy
And wit mee warns to shunne soche snares as thretten myne annoy
ffor fallshood now doth flow and subjects fayth doth ebbe
which shold not be yf reason rewld or Wysdome wove the webbe.
But clowds of Joyes untried, doth cloke aspiring minds   5
Which turne to rage of late report, by chaunged course of minds
The topps of hope suppose, the roote of Rue shalbee.
and fruteles of their graffed guile as shortlie yow shall see
The dazeled eyes with pride, with great ambition blynde
shalbe unsealld by worthie wights, whose foresight falshood fyndes   10
The daughter of Debate, that discord ay doth sow
Shall reape no gaine where former rule, still peace hath taught to
    know
No fforain banisht wight, shall ankor in this Port
Our Realm brooks no seditious sects, Let them elswhere resort
My Rustie sword through rest, shall first his edge imploy   15
To poll the topps that seekes such chaunge or gapes for further Joy.

ffinis
Elizabetha
Regina

2 *as thiretten miue annoy*: as might cause me harm   8 *graffed guile*: grafted (i.e. insidiously introduced)   11 *daughter of Debate*: Mary Queen of Scots

23   *Reginae Responsum*

    Grata Camena tua est, gratissima dona, Melisse:
        Gratior est animi dulcis imago tui.
    At quae tanta movet te causa, quis impetus urget,
        Ex homine ingenuo servus ut esse velis?
    Haud nostrum est arctis vates includere septis,   5
        Aut vel tantillum deminuisse caput.
    Tu potius liber fieres, laxante patrona
        Vincula, si famula conditione fores.
    Sed vatum es princeps; ego vati subdita, dum me
        Materiam celsi carminis ipse legis,   10
    Quem regum pudeat tantum coluisse poetam,
        Nos ex semideis qui facit esse deos?

                        (before 1580)

23   *The Queen's Answer*

Your song is welcome, Melissus, a most welcome gift
Yet more welcome is the sweet image of your soul
But how great a cause moves you, what impulse urges
That, though free-born, you want to be a slave?
It is hardly our custom to keep poets in narrow confines   5
Or to restrict their rights even in the smallest degree.
Rather, you would be made free, your mistress
Would loose your chains, if you had been in a servile state.
But you are prince of poets; I am the poet's subject, when
You make me the matter of your lofty verse   10
What king would be ashamed to cherish such a poet
Who turns us from heroes into gods?

24 *A songe made by her Majestie and songe before*
her at her cominge from white hall to Powles
through Fleete streete in Anno domini 1588.

    songe in December after the scatteringe of the Spanishe
    Navy

    Lok and bowe downe thyne eare o Lorde
    from thy bryght spheare behould and see
    Thy hand maide and thy handy worke
    Amongest thy pristes offeringe to thee

zeale for incense Reachinge the skyes   5
my selfe and septer sacryifise

My sowle assende this holy place
Ascribe him strengthe and singe his prayse
For he Refraynethe peryures spyrite
And hathe done wonders in my Daies   10
he made the wynds and waters rise
To scatter all myne enemyes

This Josephes Lorde and Israells god
the fyry piller and dayes clowde
That saved his saincts from wicked men   15
And drenchet the honor of the prowde
And hathe preservud in tender love
The spirit of his Turtle Dove.

finis

(1588)

3 *hand maide*: reminiscence of the *Magnificat*, Luke 2: 28   7 *assende*: Psalm 24: 3   9
peryures: perjurers'   10 *wonders*: Exodus 15: 11   11 *wynds and waters*: Exodus 16: 10
[this whole poem evokes the Canticle of Moses, Exodus 15: 1–18, and the Magnificat,
Luke 2: 46–55]   14 *fyry piller*: Exodus 13:21   16 *drenchet*: drenched, drowned

ANNE LOK (née VAUGHAN, later DERING, PROWSE)
(*c*.1535–after 1590)

ANNE LOK, or Locke, was the elder daughter of Stephen Vaughan, a member
of the Merchant Adventurer's company in the time of Henry VIII. From 1538,
he was governor of the Merchant Adventurers' factory at Antwerp. During his
sojourn in Antwerp, he converted to Protestantism, married (his wife's name is
unknown, but she was described as 'witty and housewifely'), and had three
children, Anne, Jane, and Stephen. This wife died in 1545, and he remarried on
his return to London, choosing the widow of a London mercer, of uncomprom-
isingly Protestant outlook, and in 1549, he died. Anne married Henry Lok,
probably around 1552, a mercer with interests in Antwerp who also happened to
be her father's neighbour in Cheapside. Nothing is known of the circumstances
in which she acquired her unusually extensive education. The Loks were
cultivated and rather literary in their tastes. Henry Lok could write Latin, in
the italic hand which was then becoming fashionable. They were also extremely
Protestant. It was as a result of their religious enthusiasm that Anne Lok made
probably the most important friendship of her life, with John Knox, who first
met Anne Lok in London in the winter of 1552/3, and lived with the young
couple for a time before leaving England. They entered into a passionate
spiritual friendship, of great importance to both, which is witnessed by thirteen
surviving letters from Knox to Anne Lok. Once settled in Geneva, Knox bent
his iron will to persuading his friend to leave her husband and family and join

him in exile. Six months later, Anne Lok arrived in Geneva accompanied by two small children, Henry and Anne, and a maid, but without her husband. She buried Anne within four days of their arrival; probably a grim witness to the difficulties of the journey.

One witness to how she spent her time in Geneva is her translation of John Calvin's sermons on the song of Hezekiah, which she dedicated to her fellow religious exile, Catherine Bertie, dowager duchess of Suffolk, together with *A meditation of a penitent sinner*, a metrical paraphrase of the fifty-first psalm, which she published in 1560. Queen Mary died in 1558, and the Marian exiles began flooding homewards, including Anne Lok, who was back in her husband's house in Cheapside by June 1559. Nothing further is heard of her until 1571, when her husband died: she was presumably a leading light among the London 'godly', but published nothing, and had no public profile. Henry Lok bequeathed her all his worldly goods and appointed her sole executrix of his will, a testimony that that no breath of scandal can ever have touched her association with Knox.

She very promptly married again: not another businessman, but one of the most outstanding extreme Protestant preachers of the day, Edward Dering, five years her junior. Given the centrist religious instincts of Elizabeth, Dering was virtually certain to spend his life in trouble. He had already insulted the Queen to her face, at a sermon preached before her in February 1570, and for the rest of his short career, his zeal was matched only by his lack of tact. In May, 1571, the Cooke sisters involved the Derings in the creation of a beautiful presentation manuscript of the *Sylvae* of the Italian Protestant Bartolo Silva for the Earl of Leicester (the principal supporter of extreme Protestantism among those closest to the Queen), with dedicatory poems from all four sisters, Anne, and Edward Dering himself. However much good this may have done, it could not counteract Dering's continued rashness. He lectured on the Epistle to the Hebrews at St Paul's in 1573, which had two effects: he was thought by some to be the most notable preacher of his day, but he was also brought before the Star Chamber in May of that year, and silenced at the Queen's personal command in December, despite the best efforts of Katherine Killigrew. Dering, meanwhile had other troubles. He was tubercular, and by the summer of 1575, he had begun to spit blood. He died in 1576. Anne's last marriage was a much calmer affair: she married an Exeter draper, Richard Prowse, three times Mayor of Exeter, sometime before 1583, and spent the last decade or so of her life in Devon. In 1590, she sent another work of her own to the press, a translation from Jean Taffin's French text, *Of the markes of the children of God and of their comfort in afflictions*, which she dedicated to Ann, countess of Warwick: 'Everie one in his calling is bound to doo somewhat to the furtherance of the holie building, but because great things by reason of my sex I may not doo, and that which I may I ought to doo, I have according to my duetie brought my poore basket of stones to the strengthning of the walles of that Jerusalem whereof (by grace) wee are all both citizens and members.' Anne Lok's son, another Henry Lok, inherited literary tendencies from both parents. He published a versified version of Ecclesiastes, two hundred religious sonnets, and a large number of sonnets addressed to a variety of powerful people, seeking a patronage which he never, in the event, obtained. His mother's verse is of a different order: it is clearly intended to 'doo somewhat to the furtherance of the holie building'. Like other Protestant women writers, she can be clear that her work is not transgressive, since it is God's work she is about.

25   *Anna Dering in Bartholomeum Sylvam*
     Medicum Tauriniensium.

Ut iuvat umbriferum levibus nemus omnes susuris
Luminaque in viridi cuncta calore tenet
Sic exculta tuis tua mens iuvat artibus omnes
O SYLVA, omnigenis sylva repleta bonis.

(1572)

1 *omnes*: omne' MS

25   *Anna Dering on Bartolomeo Silva,*
     Doctor of Turin.

Just as the shady grove delights all with its whispering breezes,
and comprehends all shades in the colour green,
Thus your sophisticated mind delights everyone with your arts,
O SILVA, a 'wood' brimming over with all kinds of excellence.

26   *The necessitie and benefit of* AFFLICTION

Great trouble and vexation,
  the righteous shall sustaine:
By Gods determination,
  whil'st here they doe remaine.
Which grievous is and irkesome both   5
  for flesh and bloud to beare:
Because by nature we are loth
  to want our pleasure here.
And eke because our enemy
  that auncient deadly foe,   10
Sathan, with cruell tyrannie,
  the worker of our woe
Doth still provoke the wicked sort,
  in sinne which doe delight:
To please themselves, and make great sport   15
  to vexe us with despight.
Yet doe the righteous by the crosse,
  moe blessed things obtaine
Then any way can be the losse,
  the dolor, or the paine.   20
The losse is that which in few daies,
  would passe, fade and decay
Even of it selfe: the gaine alwaies

no man can take away.
All earthly estimation   25
   the crosse may cleane deface:
But heavenly consolation,
   the soule does then imbrace.
Afflictions wordly pleasures will
   abandon out of minde: 30
Then is the Soule more earnest still,
   the joyes of heaven to finde.
The wordly riches, goods and wealth,
   by troubles may depart:
The inward joyes and saving health,   35
   may wholly rule the heart
In trouble friends doe start aside,
   as cloudes doe with the winde:
But Gods assistance doth abide,
   to cheare the troubled minde.   40
If we should feele these losses all
   at once, by sudden change:
We may not be dismaid withall,
   though it seeme very strange.
Job lost his friends, he lost his wealth,   45
   and comfort of his wife:
He lost his children and his health,
   yea all, but wretched life.
When all was gone, the Lord above
   did still with him remaine: 50
With mercy, kindnesse and with love
   assuaging all his paine.
Teaching him by experience,
   that all things fickle be:
(Which subject are to human sence)   55
   and yeeld all misery.
But godlinesse within the heart,
   remaineth ever sure:
In wealth and woe, it is her part,
   true comfort to procure.   60
Afflictions turn'th these worldly joyes
   to greater paine and woe
Because the love was linc'kt with toyes,
   Religion is not so.
For when mans heart doth most delight   65
   in pleasure, wealth and pride:
Religion then will take her flight,
   she may not there abide.
Whereby our soules in wofull plight,
   continually remaine: 70

Yet have not we the grace or might
   from such lusts to refraine.
In which estate most willingly
   (though tending right to hell)
We count our chiefe felicity,   75
   and love therein to dwell.
Therefore the Lord which is above,
   regarding us below:
With mercy, pitty, grace, and love,
   that alwaies from him flow;   80
Doth mix with griefe these earthly things
   wherein we doe delight
Which to our soules all sorrow brings,
   or else removes them quite.
Then doth the holy word of God,   85
   most comfortable seeme:
Which we (before we felt the rod)
   meere folly did esteeme.
The world which earst most pleasant was
   now loathsome seemes to be: 90
It doth appeare (as in a glasse)
   all fraught with miserie.
Then feare wel hell, then flie we sinne,
   then seeke we heaven the more:
To use good meanes we then begin,   95
   which we despisde before.
Then can we pray, then can we call,
   to God for strength and grace
Which things before might not at all,
   with us have any place   100
Then heare we with attentiveness,
   then read we with all care:
Then pray we with great ferventnesse,
   no travaile then we spare.
Then shall we see, feele and confesse,   105
   the state wherein we dwelt:
To be nothing but wretchednesse,
   though worldly joyes be felt
Because the soule by godlinesse,
   more comfort doth receive   110
In one day, than by wordlinesse,
   which they full soone shall leave.
Then we with *David* shall confesse,
   that God from heaven above
(By humbling us) doth well expresse   115
   his mercy and his love.
For ere we felt the scourging rod,

we errde and went astray:
But now we keepe the law of God,
    and waite therein alway   120
Then for Religion love the Crosse,
    though it doe bring some paine:
The joy is great, small is the losse,
    but infinite the gaine.

FINIS

(1615)

45 *Job*: Job chs. 1–2   77 *which*: whith copytext   113 *David*: e.g. Psalm 69, 94: 12

CATRIN FERCH GRUFFYDD AB IEUAN AP LLYWELYN FYCHAN, or CATRIN FERCH GRUFFYDD AP HYWEL O LANDDEINIOLEN
(fl. 1555)

GRUFFYD AB IEUAN AP LLYWELYN FYCHAN was a nobleman and poet
from Llewenni Fechan near St Asaph, in north-east Wales. Surviving verses are
associated with two of his daughters, Alis (see above, no. 10) and Catrin. There
is some confusion in the manuscripts between Catrin the daughter of this
Gruffyd and the daughter of another bard, Gruffydd ap Hywel o Landdeiniolen,
of Anglesey: for example, two poems, 'Gweddïo ac wylo i'm gwely' and 'Iesu
Duw Iesu dewisaf ei garu' are attributed in two manuscripts to both Catrin ferch
Gruffydd ab Ieuan, and Catrin ferch Gruffydd ap Hywel. Sixteen poems
apparently written by sixteenth-century Welsh women are attributed to one or
more of Alis, the two Catrins, and an even more shadowy Gwen, allegedly sister
to Alis and Catrin. Nothing is known of the lives of any of these women.

27   *Owdwl foliant i Grist*

    1 Gweddïo ag wylo i'm gwely—y nos
         yn eissie cael cysgy
      ar Dduw tad a'r ganhiady
      gael mynd atto i'r fro fry

    2 Gael fry y gallu a golles—ar gam   5
         cael gymyn a chyffes
      a marw yn llyn mawr yw'r lles
      drwy Dduw nid yn Iddewes

    3 O bum Iddewes ddiles feddylie—o'r gwaetha
         yn gweithio y Sulie   10
      a gwyro deg o'r geirie
      o'r nod a erchis Duw ne'

4 Duw ne' yw'r gore mewn gwarant—cadarn
  yn cadw 'i holl blant
  gwir Dduw a gâr faddeuânt   15
  i'm meddwl a chwbwl o'm chwant

5 Chwant i'r golud symud a'm siomi—yn llwyr
  a rhoi'r lles i golli
  a chyn dywad tylodi
  rhyfalch mi a wn oeddwn i   20

6 Myfi ar Dduw tri bob tro—o'm gofal
  a gyfyd fy nwylo
  teilwng fo imi weddïo
  un mab Mair fo ai cair i'm co

7 Cof am hwnn a ddylwn ai addoli—â'r galon   25
  a gwilied 'i sorri
  rhag dyfod heb gymodi
  rhaid im Duw gwynn d'ofyn do

8 Erlyn a gofyn yn gyfion—a wrendy
  ferwyndod fy nghalon   30
  f'arglwydd oll er d'archollion
  a'th friw a gefaist i'th fron

9 Briw'r fron a'r galon heb goelio—gynt
  ag ynte heb ddigio
  er dolur traed a dwylo   35
  trugaredd drwy 'i fowredd fo

10 Er 'i 'sgwrsio a'i guro a'r—geirie dig
   a mab Duw yn diodde'
   Duw gwirion aeth â'r gore
   Duw a wnaeth daiar a ne'   40

11 Estyn gie yr breichie a'u brychu—ar lled
   a'r lladron o bob tu
   gwisgo'r goron a gwasgu
   ar ei dâl o'r Iddew du

12 A thridie godde' ei giddio—yn ddiddig   45
   a'i ddeuddeg yn wylo
   ag o'r bedd heb rybuddio
   Fo a gododd pann fynnodd fo

13 yr Iddewon creulon yn crio—o ddig
   wedi i Dduw 'u twyllo   50
   gwedi iddo godi a'u gado
   Un Mab Mair ddiwair oedd o

14 Fynghyffes fy hanes a henwa'—i ddyn
　　ag i Dduw yn gynta'
　　mynych waith i damuna' 55
　　o'm pechod ddyfod yn dda

15 Caru 'r da yn fwyaf oedd feie—moddion
　　nid meddwl am ange
　　a siarad peth sy' ore
　　nid da imi ond Duw ne' 60

16 Cybyddu a thyrru ni theriais—er Duw
　　nag er dim a glowais
　　a'r bechie mawr a bechais
　　sy'n gruge dan furie f'ais

17 Fy hynod bechod bechie—dideilwng 65
　　i d'olwg 'u madde
　　yr un Duw a fu'n diodde
　　ar y groes nid oes ond e

18 Duw nef yw'r gore o'r gyfraith—o'n poen
　　i'n prynnu ar unwaith 70
　　Duw yn gwbwl Duw yw'n gobaith
　　Duw sy'n ne' bie bob iaith

19 Fyngweddïer bore sy'barod—ar allel
　　ewyllys y Drindod
　　byw mewn buched ddibechod 75
　　yr hwnn i mynnwn y mod

20 Darfu'r nod a'r amod ar yma—byth
　　fo ballodd y mowrdda
　　cael myned a ddamuna
　　at Dduw gwir Dduw ag awr dda. 80

Catrin ferch Gruffydd ap Howel o lan Ddyniolen yn Môn ai
cant

27　　　　　*A praise poem to Christ*

1 I pray and weep in my bed at night
　　(craving sleep)
　　to God the Father to give me his permission
　　to go to him in the region above

2 above I shall (I lost strength by falsehood) 5
　　have communion and confession
　　and there is much benefit in dying like this,
　　in God not as a Jewess

3 Oh! I have been a sinner, thinking vain thoughts and worse
   working on the Sabbath   10
   and twisting ten of the commandments
   of the purpose that thou, God in heaven, command

4 God in heaven is best (in strong authority)
   at keeping all of his children
   the true God loves forgiveness,   15
   for my thoughts and all of my desires

5 Remove my desire for wealth and disappoint me totally
   and give me the benefit of losing
   that before poverty set in
   I know that I was too proud   20

6 Every time and in every tribulation, I to the three-in-one
   raise my arms [i.e. in prayer]
   It is right for me to pray
   [to] the son of Mary who is on my mind.

7 I should remember Him and worship him from the heart   25
   and take care not to displease him
   lest I come without being reconciled
   I must, dear Lord, seek thee

8 I pursue and request sincerely he who listens
   to the pain of my heart   30
   because, my perfect Lord, of thy wounds
   and the bruises thou suffered to thy breast

9 Long ago, I believed not in the pain to the breast and heart
   and he was not angry
   because of the wounds to hands and feet,   35
   mercy is to be had through his majesty

10 Despite scourging and beating him, and angry words
   and the suffering of God's son
   Dear God took the best
   God who made heaven and earth   40

11 The sinews of his arms were stretched apart and maimed
   and the thieves were either side of him
   He wore the crown on his head and it was pressed
   on his forehead, by the black Jew

12 For three days, he, contented, suffered to be hid   45
   and his twelve [disciples] wept
   and from the tomb, without warning,
   he resurrected when he willed it so

13 The cruel Jews cried with anger
   after God had deceived them   50
   after he resurrected and left them.
   He was the son of pure Mary.

14 My confession and my history I state to man
    and to God first
  many a time I wish   55
  that I could be cleansed from my sins

15 The fault of my devotion was that I loved good best
    not remembering death
  and talking (the thing that is best)
  is not good for us, unless [we talk] of God in heaven   60

16 I did not tarry to covet or heap [wealth], in despite of God
    or because of any thing that I heard of
  and the large sins that I sinned
  are swellings under the walls of my breast

17 My remarkable burdens of sin are unworthy   65
    in your sight to be forgiven
  The one God that suffered
  on the cross, there is only him.

18 God in heaven is the best of the law—from our pain
    he redeems us at once   70
  God, perfect God, is our hope;
  God who is in heaven is the author of all tongues

19 My morning prayers are ready—by the power
    of the will of the Trinity,
  [I wish] to live the sinless life,   75
  is what I would insist on

20 Aims and conditions have expired, and here now
    the great goodness has ceased
  I desire to go,
  to God, true God, at a good hour.   80

ANNE DUDLEY, née SEYMOUR, later UNTON, with MARGARET and JANE SEYMOUR
(after 1535–1587/8, after 1535–?? 1541–1551)

THE Seymour sisters seem to have resembled their near-contemporaries, the four daughters of Anthony Cooke in being conscious of themselves as a group. They wrote a joint poem for the tomb of Marguerite de Valois, authoress and Queen of Navarre, who was buried in Paris in 1551, turn and turn about: the youngest of the three, Jane, was a precocious 10-year-old at the time: it is probably reasonable to imagine that her older sisters gave her some help. The writing of a *tombeau* (a series of funerary poems) was a common way of honouring a person of literary distinction in sixteenth-century France.

The sisters were the daughters of Edward Seymour, Duke of Somerset, and Lord Protector, who ended his life disgraced and executed. They were the children of a family in the very process of rising from minor gentry to aristocracy. Their aunt, Jane Seymour (1509–37), was the third wife of Henry VIII. Their uncle, Thomas Seymour, was the last husband of Henry's sixth wife, Catherine Parr; and appears also to have made advances to the young Princess Elizabeth. They were three of the ten children whom Seymour had by his second wife, Anne Stanhope. Somerset's estates were settled on his issue by his second wife rather than the children of his first marriage by an act of Parliament passed in 1540 (because there were serious doubts raised about the first wife's fidelity, and thus the legitimacy of her offspring), which will have given them a stronger financial position after their father's fall than they could otherwise have expected. Jane, the youngest (1541–61), was directly involved with her father's political life: he was accused of plotting to marry her to the sickly young prince, Edward VI, whose early death brought Mary Tudor and then Elizabeth I to the throne. This seems very far from unlikely: there was a potential bar had they been Catholics, in that Jane and Edward were first cousins (he was the son of Jane Seymour), but the Seymour family had come out firmly as Protestants. The education of the Seymour girls has to be seen in this highly political context. The girls with a direct claim on the throne such as Mary Tudor, Elizabeth, Lady Jane, and Lady Katherine Grey, were all highly educated. Seymour was in effect identifying his children as potential future princesses by lavishing the resources on them that he did: his sister's brief but glorious career had perhaps suggested to him that a family's advancement could be furthered by its daughters as well as its sons.

Anne married twice, as her funeral sermon indicates (her first husband was Lord Lisle, son of the Duke of Northumberland, making her the sister-in-law of Lady Jane Grey, her second a Berkshire knight, Sir Edward Unton), while Margaret and Jane died unmarried, probably because of their father's disgrace: after his fall in 1551, the five unmarried sisters were dumped on their aunt Elizabeth, then a relatively poor widow, who was hardly in a position to advance their fortunes: they may or may not have returned to their mother's care after she was released from the Tower in 1553, but in any case, Lady Seymour kept a very low profile after her husband's fall. Anne made her second marriage in 1555, rusticated at Faringdon, had seven children in ten years, and in 1566, 'fell into lunacy', though according to her son's later testimony, 'she enjoyed lucid intervals'. Nothing more is heard of Margaret, who perhaps died. Jane became a Maid of Honour, first to Mary, then to Elizabeth, and was the prime mover in the disastrous marriage between her brother, Edward Seymour, and Lady Jane Grey's younger sister Katherine, though she died (in 1561) just before the scandal broke.

The ambitiousness of the Seymours as a family is probably witnessed by the sisters' distichs: as 'learned maids', there was a social propriety which they could invoke in writing on the death of another notably learned lady; but to produce something so very long, under the auspices of a man with such strong connections to the French court, can only be seen as a bid to raise their status. It is also interesting that they are informed (presumably by Denisot) of Marguerite's actual behaviour on her deathbed: she is known to have pronounced the name of Jesus three times as she died, which is directly reflected in distich 89 (Margaret's).

28   *From the* Hecatodistichon

I. *Anne*

Haec sacra Reginae cineres tegit urna Navarrae,
 Urna tegens tenui grande cadaver humo.

II. *Margaret*

Regina hic, qua non alia est, vel nomine maior
 Vel pietate prior, MARGARIS alma jacet.

III. *Jane*

Margaris alma jacet, sed corpore: mente non olim   5
 Dum vixit iacuit, nec modo functa jacet.

IV. *Anne*

Divini vates versus non busta parate
 Queis sita Margaridos molliter ossa cubent.

V. *Margaret*

Carminibus quicunque valent, cantuque Poetae,
 Margaridem cantu, carminibus que sonent.   10

VI. *Jane*

Quae super egressa est sexus, mentem, modumque,
 Regina (heu) periit, si periisse potest.

VII. *Anne*

Corpus humum, sed mens coelum, quod anabat utrumque
 Iam tenet: antiquis gaudet utrunque locis.

VIII. *Margaret*

Idem Reginae cineres, atque ossa Navarrae   15
 Non idem claudit Spemque, Fidemque lapis.

IX. *Jane*

Quicquid ab aeterno potuit mortalibus usquam
 Esse boni, aut sancti Margaris obtinuit.

X. *Anne*

Illa bono et sancto toties operata, bonoque
 Et sancto fruitur, perfruiturque Deo.   20

XI. *Margaret*

Reginae, in terris quicquid Sol lumine lustrat,
 Quicquid et Oceanus proluit, est tumulus.

XII. *Jane*

Non haec Reginam claudit brevis urna Navarrae:
 Claudere Reginam tam brevis urna nequit.

28   *From the* Hecatodistichon

I. Anne

This sacred urn holds the ashes of the Queen of Navarre
Holding an urn, I hold a corpse of great substance.

II. Margaret

A Queen this, whom no other equals, either greater in name
or beforehand in piety: sweet MARGARET lies here.

III. Jane

Sweet MARGARET rests here, but in body: while she lived
she used not to rest in mind, nor does she lie dead.

IV. Anne

Poet, do not prepare pyres of divine verse
but, a thousandfold, the site where the bones of MARGARET rest.

V. Margaret

All who are capable of verse and the songs of a poet
utter MARGARET in a song, with verses.

VI. Jane

She who has gone is above her sex in mind and quality
A queen (alas) has died, insofar as she was able to die.

VII. Anne

The body now inhabits the earth, but the mind heaven
which each used to love; each rejoices in its ancient home.

VIII. Margaret

The same encloses the ashes and bones of the Queen of Navarre
The same stone does not enclose her hope and faith.

IX. Jane

Whatever from eternity can ever be good in mortals,
or holy, MARGARET possessed.

X. Anne

She, as many times as she performed good and holy works
enjoys good and holy deeds, and is rewarded by GOD.

XI. Margaret

Whatever the Sun bathes with its light on land,
Whatever, also, the Ocean moistens, is the tomb of the Queen.

XII. Jane

This little urn does not enclose the Queen of Navarre
so small an urn cannot hold a Queen.

LADY JANE DUDLEY (née GREY)
(1537–1554)

THE unfortunate Lady Jane Grey, the 'nine day's queen', was a victim of Tudor politics: her father-in-law, John Dudley, Duke of Northumberland, attempted to put her on the throne of England (she was the granddaughter of Henry VIII's sister Mary), and in consequence, she was beheaded at the age of 16. Like other Tudor royal ladies, she received an extensive humanist education. Her tutor, Dr Harding, began teaching her Latin, Greek, and modern languages at 7. As she grew up, she became a convinced Protestant, and also an enthusiastic scholar. A frank conversation with the educationalist Roger Ascham when she was 14 suggests an element of compensation for, or withdrawal from, her mistreatment by her parents:

> when I am in presence either of father or mother, whether I speak, keep silence, sit, stand, or go...I must do it, as it were in such weight, measure and number, even so perfectly as God made the world, or else I am so sharply taunted, so cruelly threatened, yea, presently sometimes, with pinches, nips, and bobs, and other ways which I will not name for the honour I bear them, so without measure misordered, that I think myself in hell till time come that I must go to Master Aylmer, who teacheth me so gently, so pleasantly, with such fair allurements to learning, that I think all the time nothing whilst I am with him. And when I am called from him, I fall on weeping because whatsoever I do else but learning is full of grief, trouble, fear, and wholly misliking unto me.

As this passage indicates, Lady Jane was an unlucky and victimized girl long before she was disastrously catapulted into high politics. But she was also sharp-tongued, observant, and self-respecting. As Carole Levin has pointed out, there was little of the passive victim in her makeup. When she found herself in the Tower, facing execution, she began her last letter to her father with the words, 'Father, although it hath pleased God to hasten my death by you, by whom my life should rather have been lengthened...' which suggests that she was not above returning hurt for hurt.

That she was a good Latinist is beyond question. Three Latin letters on religious topics to Henry Bullinger, a Calvinist, survive: they were written after her marriage since they are signed 'Jane Duddeley'. Her long final letter to her sister Katherine was in Latin. Most of her writing (whether in in English or Latin) was done in the Tower, under sentence of death, and it is therefore unsurprising that it is concerned mostly with Protestant theology: her relationship with God was her most urgent practical problem. Two verse graffiti in Latin from the Tower suggest that if her life had been a happier and longer one, she might have written poetry.

29 'Certaine verses written by the said ladie Jane with a pinne'

Non aliena putes homini quae obtingere possunt,
Sors hodierna mihi, cras erat illa tibi.

JANE DUDLEY

Deo iuvante, nil nocet livor malus:
Et non iuvante, nil iuvat labor gravis
                    Post tenebras spero lucem.

1 *Non aliena putes homini/Do not think anything alien to mankind*: cf. Terence, *Heavton Timorvmenos*: Homo sum: nil a me alienum puto (I am a man: I count nothing human foreign to me)

29   'Certaine verses written by the said ladie Jane with a pinne'

Do not think anything alien to mankind which may befall one:
This is my fate today, tomorrow it may be yours.

                                                    Jane Dudley

With God's help, wicked malice can do one no harm;
If He helps not, then the hardest work is in vain
                    After darkness, I hope for light.

ELIZABETH HOBY (née COOKE, later LADY RUSSELL)
(1540–1609)

LADY ELIZABETH HOBY was the third of the learned daughters of Sir Anthony Cooke. Her two marriages might seem less brilliant than those of her sisters Anne Bacon and Mildred Cecil, but both her husbands were important people. When Sir Thomas Hoby (the translator of Castiglione's *Courtier*) died as ambassador to France in 1566, Elizabeth I sent her a personal letter of condolence, which includes the pledge, 'we would have you rest yourself in quietnes, with a firm opinion of our especiall favour towards you'. In 1592 she was honoured by a visit from the Queen to her estates at Bisham (the entertainment she put on on this occasion included an extremely unusual prioritizing of poetic composition over needlework as proper feminine activity: 'How doe you burne time, and drowne beauty, in pricking of clouts, when you should be penning of sonnets?')
    Like her sisters, Lady Hoby was a competent writer in both Latin and Greek. Though almost all of her poetry that survives consists of epitaphs, she was undoubtedly the finest poet among them. She also translated *A Way of Reconciliation...touching the True Nature and Substance of the Body and Blood of Christ from Latin to English* (published 1605), dedicated to her daughter Anne Herbert, with a short Latin poem. For her religious interests, see the biographical notes on her sister Katherine Killigrew.
    There is a fair number of surviving letters from Elizabeth, mostly in the Cecil papers: Elizabeth (perhaps due to the complications of two marriages, with children from both) was the most litigious of the Cooke sisters. Her letters are written very much as from the head of the family, and move easily in the field of English common law, about which she was clearly well informed enough to be able to cite precedents. A steady stream of letters preserved in the Cecil papers at

Hatfield kept Burghley and later, Robert Cecil alive to the interests of the Russells. Most of these letters indicate a strong desire to maintain the Russell status: both daughters were at court, as Elizabeth often was herself, and this was a considerable expense and worry. In the letters to Robert, whom she addressed with the freedom of an aunt, Elizabeth comes over as autocratic, intemperate, and expressive. For instance, following a quarrel with a protegée called Anne Lovelace, she comments, 'neither list I while I breathe to be thus bearded by a girl's tearing out of my teeth what I meant to be her preferment in my parish if she had kept my favour.' She was clearly a Puritan without being a prude, since Sir John Harington notes that he read her his scatological essay, *The Metamorphosis of Ajax*.

Among the property which Lady Russell inherited from her second husband was the use of a castle belonging to the Queen, in the capacity of castellan: she brought a court case to the Star Chamber to confirm her right to hold it, in May 1606. The judges took one look at her case and decided it was invalid, and moved to adjourn immediately for lunch—but Lady Russell was not a woman who could be treated so cavalierly: 'the Ladye, interruptinge them, desyred to be hearde, & after many denyalls by the Courte, vyolentelye & with greate audacitie beganne a large discourse, & would not by any meanes be stayed nor interrupted, but wente one for the space of halfe an howre or more.' She lost, as she was bound to, since the office of castellan was a military one, but she was at least successful in making herself heard.

The Hoby tombs at Bisham are an interesting expression of their originator's attitudes to herself and her family: the layout of her tomb stresses her own centrality, while the only daughter to marry into the peerage kneels in the next most prominent position, facing her, in her countess's robes, and her sons meekly bring up the rear. One of these, Thomas Postumus Hoby, with whom she was pregnant when she struggled back from France with her husband's corpse, married the heiress Margaret Dakins, who as Margaret Hoby, wrote a now-famous diary. She organized elaborate funerals for both her husbands, and planned her own funeral with scrupulous observance of the heraldic rules. In a letter to Sir William Dethick, Garter King of Arms, she inquired 'what number of mourners were due to her calling; what number of waiting women, pages, and gentlemen ushers; of chief mourners, lords, and gentlemen; the manner of her hearse, of the heralds, and church, &c'.

30 *ELIZABETH HOBAEA conjux, ad THOMAM HOBAEUM, Equitem Maritum*

O dulcis conjux, animae pars maxima nostrae,
    Cujus erat vitae, vita medulla meae.
Cur ita conjunctos divellunt invida fata?
    Cur ego sum viduo sola relicta thoro?
Anglia fælices, fælices *Gallia* vidit,   5
    Per mare, per terras noster abivit amor,
Par fortunatum fuimus dum viximus una,
    Corpus erat duplex, spiritus unus erat.
Sed nihil in terris durat charissime conjux,
    Tu mihi, tu testis flebilis esse potes.   10
Dum patriae servis, dum publica commoda tractas,

Occidis, ignota triste cadaver humo.
Et miseri nati flammis febrilibus ardent.
Quid facerem tantis, heu mihi mersa malis!
Infælix conjux, infælix mater oberro, 15
Te vir adempte fleo, vos mea membra traho.
Sic uterum gestans, redeo terraque Marique
In patriam luctu perdita, mortis amans.
Chare mihi conjux, et praestantissime *Thoma*,
Cujus erat rectum, et nobilie quicquid erat. 20
Elizabetha, tibi quondam gratissima sponsa,
Haec lacrymis refert verba referta piis.
Non potui prohibere mori, sed mortua membra,
Quo potero, faciam semper honore coli.
Te Deus, aut similem Thomae mihi redde maritum, 25
Aut reddant Thomae me mea fata viro.

(*c.*1566)

30 *ELIZABETH HOBY, wife, to THOMAS
HOBY, Knight, her husband.*

Beloved husband, greatest part of our soul,
whose life was once the marrow of my life,
Why have envious fates divided those who were joined?
why am I left alone in a widow's bed?
England saw us happy, France saw us happy, 5
our loves has passed over seas and lands,
While we lived as one, we were equally blessed,
there was one body, and but a single soul
But, darling husband, nothing endures in this world,
you can be a tearful witness of this for me. 10
While you were serving your country, and dealt with public affairs,
You died, a sad corpse, in alien ground.
And the pitiful children burned in feverish flames.
What could I do, alas, immersed in such misery?
Unhappy wife, unhappy mother, I wander about 15
I weep for you, man taken from me, I weep for my own limbs.
I leave these anguished lands, I bring back home this stolen body of
my husband,
and the strengthless limbs of his children.
Carrying the burden of my womb, I return, by sea and land,
to my native place, lost in grief, loving death. 20
My dearest husband, and my most excellent *Thomas*,
in whom everything that was was right, and noble,
Elizabeth, once your most happy wife,
brings back these words which she recalls with holy tears.
I cannot withstand death, but those dead limbs, 25
as far as I can, I will always hold in honour.
O God, either return to me a husband the image of Thomas,
or let my fate return me to Thomas my husband.

31 *ELIZABETHAE HOBEAE, Matris, in obitum*
       duarum filiarum ELIZABETHAE,
              et ANNAE, Epicedium

ELIZABETHA jacet (eheu mea viscera) fato
   Vix dum maturo, virgo tenella jaces.
Chara mihi quondam vixisti filia matri,
   Chara Deo posthac filia vive patri.
Mors tua crudelis, multo crudelius illud,   5
   Quod cecidit tecum junior ANNA soror
ANNA patris matrisque decus, post fata sororis,
   Post matris luctus, aurea virgo jaces!
Una parens, pater unus erat, mors una duabus,
   Et lapis hic unus corpora bina tegit.   10
Sic volui mater tumulo sociarier uno,
   Uno quas utero laeta gemensque tuli.

       Istae duae generosae, optimaeque spei
       sorores, eodem anno viz. 1570
       Eodemque Mense, viz. Februario,
       paucorum dierum spatio
       interjecto, in Domino
       obdormiverunt.

                                                    (1570)

2 *Vix...matura viro*: reminiscence of *Aeneid* VII. 53, 'iam matura viro'

31 *An epicedium by ELIZABETH HOBY,*
their mother, on the death of her two daughters
          ELIZABETH and ANNE

ELIZABETH lies here (alas for my heart), thus fated:
   You lie here, scarcely mature, a tender virgin
When you lived, you were a daughter dear to her mother
   Now, live dear to God and your [dead] father.
Your death was cruel, but there was one still crueller:
   the one which cut down your younger sister ANNA with you.
ANNA, you were the glory of your father and mother; after your
         sister's end
   and after your mother's grief, here you lie, golden virgin!
There was one mother, one father, one death, for the pair
   And this one stone hides both their bodies.
Thus I, their mother, wanted to unite them in a single tomb,
   weeping, whom I once carried in the same happy womb

       These two noble and most hopeful sisters
       in the same Year, i.e. 1570
       In the same Month, i.e. February
       only a few days apart,
       slept in the Lord.

ISABELLA WHITNEY
(*c*.1540–after 1580)

ISABELLA was probably the sister of Geoffrey Whitney, author of *A Choice of Emblemes* (1586), and may have been born in Cheshire at Coole Pilate near Nantwich, where the Whitneys were an old gentry family. She was, however, 'bred' at London and she tells us that her parents had lived at Smithfield, outside the City walls. She is described as 'a yonge Gentilwoman' in the title of her first publication, but it is evident that her immediate family had fallen through the floor of gentry status. Although Isabella was a woman of some education (she knew, for example, the classical myths), two of her sisters were serving as 'waiting gentlewomen', and she had had such a job herself some time previously to the publication of her first book, *The Copy of a Letter* (?1567). She was, she says, 'very weake in purse'. In 1672 she lost her post as a servant and fell dangerously ill, but found comfort in Sir Hugh Plat's *Flowers of Philosophy* (1572) a collection of neo-Stoic adages, which she decided to versify in her second book, *A Sweet Nosegay, or Pleasant Poesy*. The opening section of one-hundred-and-ten 'philosophical flowers' is followed by a series of 'Familiar Epistles' in which she imagines herself living in the country and writing to her friends and relatives. The recipients of her letters include Geoffrey, a second brother, Brooke, two younger sisters in service, and a married sister, Anne Baron. The family was scattered, presumably because they were all scratching a living as best they might, and met infrequently. Impecunious and single, writing for Isabella Whitney was an aspect of her attempts to earn a living, but also a resource in the personal sense; it filled time in which she would otherwise have been lonely and at a loose end.

Her 'Copy of a Letter' is an English reflection of a Latin genre which originates with Ovid's *Heroides*: epistolary poems of complaint written in the first person, and attributed to mythic heroines notable for their unhappy love. As a genre, *heroides* were extremely popular with Renaissance poets all over Europe, and there are numerous English examples. It was an obvious form for a jilted woman to adopt: the fact that the poem is called a 'Copy of a Letter' (Ovid's original *heroides* are presented as letters) directly indicates that it is intended to be read as *heroides*—and may also indicate that Whitney, in conforming herself to existing generic expectations, may not have been expecting to be read absolutely literally. The extensive Classical reference in the letter is another indication that she wants her poem to be read as Ovidian rather than as purely autobiographical.

Her 'Wyll and Testament' is a shopper's guide to Elizabethan London; a perambulation of the city with its intensely active economic life; one of the few English poems offering a cityscape to set beside those which envision the countryside or a country house (such as those of Aemilia Lanyer and Anne Kemp, nos. 59 and 193). It is possible that in addition to the two books published under her name, the epitaph for William Gruffith in *The Gorgeous Gallery of Gallant Inventions* is also by Isabella Whitney. This was registered for publication by Richard Jones on 20 Dec. 1577, and apparently published as a broadside before being added as a filler to *The Gorgeous Gallery*. One reason for upholding this suggestion is that a W.G. contributed to *The Copy of a letter*, remarking that 'six yeares long ... I bod for thee', which tempts us to identify the 'unconstant lover' with William Gruffith. The epitaph is written in reply to, or objection to, an earlier epitaph on Gruffith which the writer feels fails to do him justice: this is by I.H., possibly Jasper Heywood. Another pointer in the same direction is that the relatively rare by-form 'preace' for 'press' is used both in the first line of this poem, and in the 'Wyll and Testament'.

32   *I.W. To her unconstant Lover*

As close as you your weding kept
    yet now the trueth I here:
Which you (yer now) might me have told
    what nede you nay to swere?

You know I alwayes wisht you wel   5
    so wyll I during lyfe:
But sith you shal a Husband be
    God sent you a good wyfe.

And this (where so you shal become)
    full boldly may you boast: 10
That once you had as true a Love,
    as dwelt in any Coast.

Whose constantnesse had never quaild
    if you had not begonne:
And yet it is not so far past,   15
    but might agayne be wonne.

If you so would: yea and not change
    so long as lyfe should last:
But yf that needes you marry must?
    then farewell hope is past.   20

And if you cannot be content
    to lead a single lyfe?
(Although the same right quiet be)
    then take me to your wife.

So shall the promises be kept,   25
    that you so firmly made:
Now chuse whether ye wyll be true,
    or be of SINONS trade.

Whose trade if that you long shal use,
    it shal your kindred stayne: 30
Example take by many a one
    whose falshood now is playne.

As by ENEAS first of all,
    who dyd poore DIDO leave,

Causing the Quene by his untrueth   35
  with Sword her hart to cleave,

Also I finde that THESEUS did,
  his faithfull love forsake:
Stealyng away within the night,
  before she dyd awake.   40

JASON that came of noble race,
  two Ladies did begile:
I muse how he durst shew his face,
  to them that knew his wile.

For when he by MEDEAS arte,   45
  had got the Fleece of Gold
And also had of her that time,
  al kynd of things he wolde.

He toke his Ship and fled away
  regarding not the vowes;   50
That he dyd make so faithfully,
  unto his loving Spowes,

How durst he trust the surging Seas
  knowing himselfe forsworne?
Why dyd he scape safe to the land,   55
  before the ship was torne?

I think King Aeolus stayd the winds
  and Neptune rulde the Sea:
Then might he boldly passe the waves
  no perils could him slea.   60

But if his falsehed had to them,
  bin manifest befor:
They wold have rent the ship as soone
  as he had gon from shore.

Now may you heare how falsenes is   65
  made manyfest in time:
Although they that commit the same,
  think it a veniall crime.

For they, for their unfaithfulnes,
  did get perpetuall Fame: 70
Fame? wherefore dyd I terme it so?
  I should have cald it shame.

Let Theseus be, let Jason passe,
  let Paris also scape:
That brought destruction unto Troy   75
  all through the Grecian Rape,

And unto me a Troylus be,
   if not you may compare:
With any of these parsons that
   above expressed are. 80

But if I can not please your minde,
   for wants that rest in me:
Wed whom you list, I am content,
   your refuse for to be.

It shall suffise me simple soule, 85
   of thee to be forsaken:
And it may chance although not yet
   you wish you had me taken.

But rather then you shold have cause
   to wish this through your wyfe: 90
I wysh to her, ere you her have,
   no more but losse of lyfe.

For she that shal so happy be,
   of thee to be elect:
I wish her vertues to be such, 95
   she nede not be suspect.

I rather wish her HELENS face,
   then one of HELENS trade:
With chastnes of PENELOPE
   the which did never fade. 100

A LUCRES for her constancy,
   and Thisbie for her trueth:
If such thou have, then PETO be
   not PARIS, that were rueth.

Perchance, ye will think this thing rare 105
   in on woman to fynd:
Save Helens beauty, al the rest
   the Gods have me assignd.

These words I do not spek thinking
   from thy new Love to turne thee: 110
Thou knowst by prof what I deserve
   I nede not to informe thee.

But let that passe: would God I had
   Cassandraes gift me lent:
Then either thy yll chaunce or mine 115
   my foresight might prevent.

But all in vayne for this I seeke,
   wishes may not attaine it

Therfore may hap to me what shall,
and I cannot refraine it.   120

Wherfore I pray God be my guide
and also thee defend:
No worser then I wish my selfe,
untill thy lyfe shal end.

Which life I pray God, may agayne,   125
King Nestors lyfe renew:
And after that your soule may rest
amongst the heavenly crew.

Therto I wish King Xerxis wealth,
or els King Cressus Gould: 130
With as much rest and quietnesse
as man may have on Mould.

And when you shall this letter have
let it be kept in store?
For she that sent the same, hath sworn   135
as yet to send no more.

And now farewel, for why at large
my mind is here exprest?
The which you may perceive, if that
you do peruse the rest?   140

28 *SINON*: Greek double agent, betrayed Troy   33–6 *ENEAS*: Vergil, *Aeneid*, bk 4
passim   37–40 *THESEUS*: abandoned Ariadne on Naxos   41–52 *JASON*: abandoned
his wife Medea, a sorceress, who had assisted him to acquire the Golden Fleece, in order to
marry Creusa   57 *Aeolus*: Greek god of the winds   58 *Neptune*: Greek god of the
sea   74 *Paris*: abducted Helen, causing the Trojan War   77 *Troylus*: proverbially faithful
partner of the false Cressida (cf. Chaucer, *Troilus and Criseyde*)   97 *HELEN*: of Troy,
legendary beauty but unfaithful wife   99 *Penelope*: faithful wife of Odysseus   101
LUCRES: Lucretia, Roman heroine who committed suicide to save her honour   102 *Thisbe*:
lover of Pyramus, who killed herself thinking he was dead.   103 *PETO?*   103 *rueth*: a
pity   114 *Cassandra*: Prophetess, daughter of Priam of Troy   126 *Nestor*: Greek hero
who reached extreme age   129 *Xerxis*: Xerxes, famously wealthy king of Persia   130
Cressus: Croesus, King of Lydia, also famously wealthy

33   *The Aucthour (though loth to leave the Citie) upon*
      her Friendes procurement, is con-strained to departe:
      wherfore (she fayneth as she would die) and maketh
      her WYLL and Testament, as foloweth: With large
      Legacies of such Goods and riches which she moste
      aboundantly hath left behind her; and therof maketh
      LON-don sole executor to se her Legacies performed.

A communication which the Auctor had
to London, before she made her Wyll.

The time is come I must departe,
    from thee ah famous Citie:
I never yet to rue my smart,
    did finde that thou hadst pitie.
Wherefore small cause ther is, that I   5
    should greeve from thee to go:
But many Women foolyshly,
    lyke me, and other moe,
Do such a fyxed fancy set,
    on those which least desarve,   10
That long it is ere wit we get,
    away from them to swarve,
But tyme with pittie oft wyl tel
    to those that wil her try:
Whether it best be more to mell,   15
    or utterly defye.
And now hath time me put in mind,
    of thy great cruelnes:
That never once a help wold finde,
    to ease me in distres.   20
Thou never yet, woldst credit geve
    to boord me for a yeare:
Nor with Apparell me releve
    except thou payed weare.
No, no, thou never didst me good,   25
    nor ever wilt I know;
Yet am I in no angry moode,
    but wyll, or ere I goe
In perfect love and charytie,
    my Testament here write: 30
And leave to thee such Treasurye,
    as I in it recyte.
Now stand a side and geve me leave
    to write my latest wyll:

And see that none you do deceave,   35
  of that I leave them tyl.

    The maner of her
  Wyll, and what she left to London:
  and to all those in it: at her departing.

I whole in body, and in minde,   40
  but very weake in Purse:
Doo make, and write my Testament
  for feare it wyll be wurse.
And fyrst I wholy doo commend,
  my Soule and Body eke: 45
To God the Father and the Son,
  as long as I can speake.
And after speach: my Soule to hym,
  and Body to the Grave
Tyll time that all shall rise agayne,   50
  their Judgement for to have.
And then I hope they both shal meete,
  to dwell for aye in joye:
Whereas a trust to see my Friends
  releast, from all annoy.   55
Thus have you heard touching my soule,
  and body what I meane:
I trust you all wyll witnes beare,
  I have a stedfast brayne.
And now let mee dispose such things,   60
  as I shal leave behinde;
That those which shall receave the same,
  may know my wylling minde.
I firste of all to London leave
  because I there was bred: 65
Brave buildings rare, of Churches store,
  and Pauls to the head.
Betweene the same: fayre streats there bee,
  and people goodly store:
Because their keeping craveth cost,   70
  I yet wil leave him more.
First for their foode, I Butchers leave,
  that every day shall kyll:
By Thames you shal have Brewers store,
  and Bakers at your wyll.   75
And such as orders doo observe,
  and eat fish thrice a weeke:
I leave two Streets, full fraught therwith,
  they neede not farre to seeke.
Watlyng Streete, and Canwyck streete,   80

I full of Wollen leave:
And Linnen store in Friday streete,
   if they mee not deceave.
And those which are of callyng such,
   that costlier they require: 85
I mercers leave, with silke so rich,
   as any would desyre.
In Cheape of them, they store shal finde
   and likewise in that streete:
I Goldsmithes leave, with Juels such,   90
   as are for Ladies meete.
And Plate to furnysh Cubbards with,
   full brave there shall you finde:
With Purle of Silver and of Golde,
   to satisfye your minde.   95
With Hoods, Bungraces, Hats or Caps,
   such store are in that streete:
As if on ton side you should misse
   the tother serves you forte.
For Nets of every kind of sort,   100
   I leave within the pawne:
French Ruffes, high Purles, Gorgets and Sleeves
   of any kind of Lawne.
For Purse or knives, for Combe or Glasse,
   or any needeful knacke   105
I by the Stoks have left a Boy,
   wil aske you what you lack.
I Hose doo leave in Birchin Lane,
   of any kynd of syse:
For Women stitchte, for men both Trunks   110
   and those of Gascoyne gise.
Bootes, Shoes or Pantables good store,
   Saint Martins hath for you:
In Cornwall, there I leave you Beds,
   and all that longs thereto.   115
For Women shall you Taylors have,
   by Bow, the chiefest dwel:
In every Lane you some shall finde,
   can doo indifferent well.
And for the men, few Streetes or Lanes,   120
   but Bodymakers bee:
And such as make the sweeping Cloakes,
   with Gardes beneth the knee.
Artyllery at Temple Bar,
   and Dagges at Tower hyll: 125
Swords and Bucklers of the best,
   are nye the Fleete untyll.

Now when thy Folke are fed and clad
  with such as I have namde:
For daynty mouthes, and stomacks weake,   130
  some Junckets must be framde:
Wherfore I Poticaries leave,
  with Banquets in their Shop:
Phisicians also for the sicke,
  diseases for to stop.   135
Some Roysters styll, must bide in thee,
  and such as cut it out:
That with the guiltless quarel wyl,
  to let their blood about.
For them I cunning Surgions leave,   140
  some Playsters to apply,
That Ruffians may not styll be hangde,
  nor quiet persons dye.
For Salt, Otemeale, Candles, Sope,
  or what you els doo want: 145
In many places, Shops are full,
  I left you nothing scant.
Yf they that keepe what I you leave,
  aske Mony: when they sell it:
At Mint, there is such store, it is   150
  unpossible to tell it.
At Stiliarde store of Wines there bee,
  your dulled mindes to glad:
And handsome men, that must not wed
  except they leave their trade.   155
They oft shall seeke for proper Gyrles,
  and some perhaps shall fynde:
(that neede compels, or lucre lures)
  to satisfye their mind
And neare the same, I houses leave,   160
  for people to repayre:
To bathe themselves, so to prevent
  infection of the ayre.
On Saturdayes I wish that those,
  which all the weeke doo drug: 165
Shall thyther trudge, to trim them up
  on Sondayes to looke smug.
Yf any other thing be lackt
  in thee, I wysh them looke:
For there it is: I little brought   170
  but nothyng from thee tooke.
Now for the people in thee left,
  I have done as I may:
And that the poore, when I am gone,

have cause for me to pray.   175
I wyll to prisons portions leave,
    what though but very small:
Yet that they may remember me,
    occasion be it shall:
And fyrst the Counter they shal have,   180
    least they should go to wrack:
Some Coggers, and some honest men,
    that Sergantes draw a back.
And such as friends wyl not them bayle,
    whose coyne is very thin: 185
For them I leave a certayne hole,
    and little ease within.
The Newgate once a Monthe shal have
    a sessions for his share:
Least being heapt, Infection might   190
    procure a further care.
And at those sessions some shal skape
    with burning nere the Thumb:
And afterwards to beg their fees,
    tyll they have got the some.   195
And such whose deedes deserveth death,
    and twelve have found the same:
They shall be drawne by Holborne hill,
    to come to further shame:
Well, yet to such I leave a Nag   200
    shal soone their sorrowes cease:
For he shal either breake their necks
    or gallop from the preace.
The Fleete, not in their circuit is,
    yet if I geve him nought: 205
It might procure his curse, ere I
    unto the ground be brought.
Wherfore I leave some Papist olde
    to underprop his roofe:
And to the poore within the same,   210
    a Boxe for their behoofe.
What makes you standers by to smile,
    and laugh so in your sleeve:
I thinke it is, because that I
    to Ludgate nothing geve.   215
I am not now in case to lye,
    here is no place of jest:
I dyd reserve, that for my selfe,
    yf I my health possest.
And ever came in credit so   220
    a debtor for to bee.

When dayes of paiment did approch,
    I thither ment to flee.
To shroude my selfe amongst the rest,
    that chuse to dye in debt: 225
Rather than any Creditor,
    should money from them get.
Yet cause I feele my selfe so weake
    that none mee credit dare:
I heere revoke: and doo it leave,   230
    some *Banckrupts* to his share.
To all the Bookebinders by Paulles
    because I lyke their Arte:
They ery weeke shal mony have
    when they from Bookes departe.   235
Amongst them all, my Printer must,
    have somwhat to his share:
I wyll my friends these Bookes to bye
    of him, with other ware.
For Maydens poore, I Widdoers ritch,   240
    do leave, that oft shall dote:
And by that meanes shall mary them,
    to set the Girles aflote.
And wealthy Widdowes wil I leave,
    to help yong Gentylmen: 245
Which when you have, in any case
    be courteous to them them:
And see their Plate and Jewells eake
    may not be mard with rust.
Nor let their Bags too long be full,   250
    for feare that they doo burst.
To ery Gate under the walles,
    that compas thee about:
I Fruit wives leave to entertayne
    such as come in and out.   255
To Smithfeelde I must something leave
    my parents there did dwell:
So carelesse for to be of it,
    none wolde accompt it well.
Wherfore it thrice a weeke shall have,   260
    of Horse and neat good store,
And in his Spitle, blynd and lame,
    to dwell for evermore.
And Bedlam must not be forgot,
    for that was oft my walke: 265
I people there too many leave,
    that out of tune doo talke.
At Bridewel there shal Bedelles be,

and Matrones that shal styll
See Chalke well chopt, and spinning plyde,   270
　　and turning of the Mill.
For such as cannot quiet bee,
　　but strive for House or Land:
At Th'innes of Court, I Lawyers leave
　　to take their cause in hand.   275
And also leave I at ech Inne
　　of Court, or Chauncelrye:
Of Gentylmen, a youthfull roote,
　　full of Activytie:
For whom I store of Bookes have left,   280
　　at each Bookebinders stall:
And part of all that London hath
　　to furnish them withall.
And when they are with study cloyd:
　　to recreate theyr minde: 285
Of Tennis Courts, of dauncing Scooles,
　　and fence they store shal finde.
And every Sonday at the least,
　　I leave to make them sport.
In divers places Players, that   290
　　of wonders shall reporte.
Now London have I (for thy sake)
　　within thee, and without:
As come into my memory,
　　dispearsed round about   295
Such needfull thinges, as they should have
　　heere left now unto thee:
When I am gon, with conscience
　　let them dispearsed bee.
And though I nothing named have,   300
　　to bury mee withall:
Consider that above the ground,
　　annoyance bee I shall.
And let me have a shrowding Sheete
　　to cover mee from shame: 305
And in oblivyon bury mee
　　and never more mee name
Ringins nor other Ceremonies,
　　use you not for cost:
Nor at my buriall, make no feast,   310
　　your mony were but lost.
Rejoyce in God that I am gon,
　　out of this vale so vile,
And that of ech thing, left such store,
　　as may your wants exile.   315

I make thee sole executor, because
  I lov'de thee best.
And thee I put in trust, to geve
  the goodes unto the rest.
Because thou shalt a helper neede,   320
  In this so great a chardge,
I wysh good Fortune, be thy guide, least
  thou shouldst run at lardge.
The happy dayes and quiet times,
  they both her Servants bee.   325
Which well wyll serve to fetch and bring,
  such things as neede to thee.
Wherfore (good London) not refuse,
  for helper her to take:
Thus being weake, and wery both   330
  an end heere wyll I make.
To all that aske what end I made,
  and how I went away:
Thou answer maist: like those which heere,
  no longer tary may.   335
And unto all that wysh me well,
  or rue that I am gon:
Doo me comend, and bid them cease
  my absence for to mone.
And tell them further, if they wolde,   340
  my presence styll have had:
They should have sought to mend my luck;
  which ever was too bad.
So fare thou well a thousand times,
  God sheelde thee from thy foe: 345
And styll make thee victorious,
  of those that seeke thy woe.
And (though I am perswade) that I
  shall never more thee see:
Yet to the last, I shal not cease   350
  to wish much good to thee.
This xx of October I,
  in ANNO DOMINI:
A Thousand: v hundred seventy three
  as Alminacks descry.   355
Did write this Wyll with mine own hand
  And it to London gave:
In witnes of the standers by,
  whose names yf you will have.
Paper, Pen, and Standish were: 360
  at that same present by:
With Time, who promised to reveale,

as fast as she could hye
The same: least of my nearer kyn,
for any thing should vary: 365
So finally I make an end
no longer can I tary.

FINIS. by Is. W.

(20 October 1573)

6 *to go*: go copytext   15 *mell*: compromise with   67 *Pauls*: St Paul's is the metropolitan
church of London   77–8 *orders . . . weeke*: in 1563, to strengthen the fisheries, an act was
passed increasing from two to three the number of fast-days on which eating meat was
forbidden   80 *Watlyng . . . Canwyck*: two streets known for their cloth-dealers (the latter
was originally inhabited by candle-makers) 88 *Cheape*: Cheapside   92 *Plate*: silver dishes
94 *Purle*: thread of gold or silver wire, used in embroidery and borders 96 *Bungraces*:
shades worn on the front of women's bonnets as protection from the sun   99 *forte*: for
it   101 *pawne*: arcade of the Royal Exchange, selling fabrics   102 *high Purles*: kind of
ruff; *Gorgets*: wimples covering neck and bosom   111 *Gascoyne*: baggy breeches   112
Pantables: slippers   113 *Saint Martins*: probably St Martin-le-Grand, a market for cheap
clothes and boots   117 *Bow*: Church of St Mary le Bow   121 *Bodymakers*:
tailors   123 *Gardes*: ornamental borders   125 *Dagges*: large pistols   127 *nye . . . untyll*:
near to the Fleet; *Fleete*: prison for those condemned by the Star Chamber or Chancery   131 *Junckets*: sweet delicacies   132 *Poticaries*: apothecaries, i.e. chemists   133
Banquets: an after-dinner meal of fruits, sweetmeats, and wine   142 *styll*: already
dead   150 *Mint*: the mint in the Tower 152 *Stiliarde*: Stillyard, a hall for Hanse
merchants who were known for trading strong Rhine wines   154 *handsome men*: apprentices; *must not wed*: apprentices had to remain unmarried during their seven year
terms which usually began at the age of fourteen   156 *Gyrles*: prostitutes   165 *drug*:
drudge   167 *smug*: neat   180 *Counter*: two debtors' prisons, on Poultry and
Bread streets   182 *Coggers*: cheats, gamesters   186 *hole*: subterranean level of the
Counter for prisoners without money   187 *little ease*: name of a notorious cramped
cell that prevented the prisoner from standing or sitting   188 *Newgate*: criminal
gaol   194 *beg . . . fees*: convicts could become licensed beggars to pay their fines   200
Nag: the gallows at Tyburn   203 *preace*: press   215 *Ludgate*: prison for debtors and
bankrupts   216 *case*: a position to   232 *Paulles*: St Paul's Churchyard, famous for its
book-sellers   236: *my Printer*: Richard Jones   256: *Smithfeelde*: north-west of London,
the site of Bartholomew Fair   261 *neat*: cattle   262 *Spitle*: St Bartholomew Hospital   264 *Bedlam*: Hospital of St Mary of Bethlehem, a lunatic asylum   268 *Bridewel*:
women's penitentiary   287 *fence*: fencing grounds   363 *hye*: dispatch

KATHERINE DOWE
(fl. before 1588)

BARTHOLOMEW DOWE, in his *Dairie Booke for Good Huswives*, 1588, attributes this short verse to his dairywoman mother Katherine. Didactic verse of
various kinds, perhaps most famously Thomas Tusser's *A Hundreth Points of
Good Husbandry* (editions from 1557), is a strong feature of Elizabethan verse-
making, but didactic verse attributable to women is relatively uncommon. The
self-image in this verse is a strong one, of active, vigorous, and self-respecting
professionalism. He records of her, with justifiable pride, that she kept seven
score cows (140) at 'a Grange belonging to an Abbie of white Monkes, called

Sibeton Abbie, five miles from Dunwiche, and foure miles from Framlingham Castle' (Suffolk). She was the head dairywoman with seven maids under her, one for every twenty cows. As Dowe makes clear, caring for and milking this many animals, to say nothing of processing the milk (which had to be kept, scalded, and turned into butter and cheese), implied getting up at 4 a.m., year in, year out, with the dairy always kept cold as possible. Mrs Dowe's robust practicality is a note seldom struck in women's poetry, but probably important to the lives of many actual women.

34   *'Arise earelie'*

> Arise earelie
> Serve God devoutly.
> Then to thy work busilie.
> To thy meate joyfully.
> To thy bed merilie   5
> And though thou fare poorely,
> And thy lodging homelie.
> Yet thank God highly.
>
> Ka. Dowe

3 *busilie*: vigorously   7 *homelie*: poor, simple

KATHERINE KILLIGREW (née COOKE) (1542?–1583)

KATHERINE, fourth daughter of Sir Anthony Cooke, married in 1558. Her husband was Sir Henry Killigrew, a distinguished Cornish soldier and diplomat of pronouncedly Puritan views, a protegé of Robert Dudley, Lord Leicester (who was the principal patron of Elizabethan Puritans). He served the Queen with distinction in the Palatinate, the Low Countries, and later in his career, in Scotland, where he was entrusted with a variety of highly confidential missions.

While she was not as publicly distinguished as her oldest sister, Katherine was personally friendly with a number of internationally known Protestant humanists, notably George Buchanan, who presented a manuscript of his poems to her (now Paris, BN nouv. acq. lat. 106, written *c*.1575), and wrote one poem to, and two about her. Her principal appearances in the historical record associate her strongly with the Elizabethan Puritan movement: in particular, she was intimately friendly with the charismatic and talented preacher Edward Dering, who became her spiritual adviser in the 1570s: some of his half of the correspondence survives, in his *Certaine Godly and Comfortable Letters* (1597). Other associates of the same kind include Andrew Melville and William Charke, both of whom wrote verses on her monument, which is recorded in Stowe's *Survay of London* (1633). The Killigrews owned an estate at Helmdon, which was probably

Katherine's principal residence, but she also spent part of her time in London, in their house in St Paul's churchyard.

Her marriage was notably successful. Sir Henry, while physically unimpressive (Leicester speaks of him as 'little Hal Killigrew'), shared her literary leanings: he himself wrote verse in French (e.g. PRO SP 70/22, fo. 400, 70/23, fo. 792). He also clearly appreciated strong-minded women: Louise de Coligny, wife of William the Silent, speaks of him as a friend, and his second wife, the Frenchwoman Jaél de Peigne, was, like his first, literary. A variety of letters and documents from both partners testify to their concern for one another's well-being during the frequent separations caused by Sir Henry's profession, including the poem from Lady Killigrew to her sister Mildred given here. A letter from Sir Henry to his brother-in-law Cecil, for instance, written in 1573, testifies to his desire to be reunited with the wife and children he had not seen for nine months (BL MS Cotton Caligula C. IV, fo. 104). Katherine's health gave intermittent cause for concern, and a number of Sir Henry's letters refer to his anxiety at having to leave her. Katherine was the mother of four daughters, Anne, Elizabeth, Mary, and Dorothy, and died in childbirth with the last of them in August 1583. All four daughters lived to grow up and marry (some more than once).

The first poem is the only occasional verse to survive from one Cooke sister to another, but it was probably one of many. The poem is simple, but the stance quite complex, since author and subject are sisters, from a notably cohesive and loyal family, but are also in a hierarchical relationship: not only is Lady Burleigh the oldest (no small matter in the sixteenth century), but Sir Henry's career, and therefore the Killigrews' welfare, is dependent on Cecil's patronage. Lady Killigrew assumes, almost certainly correctly, that her sister is able to influence whether Sir Henry will be called on for further duties. She is probably wholly serious in signalling that she will be considerably distressed if she and her husband are not promptly reunited, but the message is conveyed in a light and courtly fashion which underlines her position as her sister's client: the insistence on positive-comparative-superlative which dominates the poem reduces its assertiveness, both by its playfulness, and because it evokes and recalls the formal grammatical study which she and her sister once shared. The second, short poem is a personal credo, of some interest, since it was written to be inscribed in a public place, and its author was a leading light of the Elizabethan Puritan movement. The appropriate attitude of the living to the dead was a minefield for early Protestant theologians because of the entrenched, and psychologically satisfying, Catholic tradition of interaction between the dead and the living, and of prayer for the dead: Lady Killigrew's formulation of her immediate expectations here would have delighted John Calvin.

35 *'Si mihi quem cupio cures Mildreda remitti'*

> Si mihi quem cupio cures Mildreda remitti,
> Tu bona, tu melior, tu mihi sola soror:
> Sin male cessando retines, vel trans mare mittis,
> Tu mala, tu peior, tu mihi nulla soror.
> Is si Cornubiam, tibi pax sit et omnia laeta,   5
> Sin mare, Ciciliae nuncio bella. Vale.

(1570s)

35   *'Mildred, if you take the trouble to send me*
     what I want'

> Mildred, if you take the trouble to send me what I want,
> You are a good – you are the best – you are my only sister.
> If you cruelly keep him back by delaying, or send him overseas,
> You are a bad – you are the worst – you are no sister to me.
> If it is to be Cornwall, peace and all joy to you:
> If it's the sea, I declare war on (Mrs) Cecil. Farewell.

36   *in mortem suam haec Carmina dum vixerat*
     scripsit D. Katharina Killigreia

> Dormio nunc Domino, Domini virtute resurgam,
>   Et σωτῆρα meum carne videbo mea.
> Mortua ne dicar, fruitur pars altera, Christo
>   Et surgam capiti, tempore, tota, meo.

(in or before 1583)

36   *The lady Katherine Killigrew wrote this poem*
     about her own death

> I sleep now with the Lord, by the Lord's strength will I rise up,
>   And I will see my Saviour in my flesh.
> I shall not say I am dead, my other part flourishes,
>   And I will rise whole, in time, with Christ as my head.

MARY STUART, QUEEN OF SCOTS
(1542–1587)

THE daughter of James V, who died a week after her birth, Mary, Queen of Scots was sent to France as the bride-to-be of the Dauphin François at the age of 5. Her mother, meanwhile, ruled Scotland on her behalf as Queen Dowager. Her marriage to François was ended by his very early death, whereupon she returned to Scotland as ruling Queen in 1561. Her personal reign was brief and disastrous: it was dominated by ecclesiastical politics, as the Catholic Queen struggled with a strong Calvinist Church, and also by Mary's own obsession with being named the heir of Elizabeth. She married Henry Stuart, Lord Darnley, son of the Earl of Lennox and Margaret Douglas, in July 1565. Their affection for each other lasted only a matter of months, and their only child, the future James VI, was born less than a year later, in June 1566. In February, 1567, the house where Darnley was staying was blown up, and he himself found strangled in the garden: it was widely rumoured that his murderer was the Earl of Bothwell, who, with extraordinary imprudence, she married three months after Darnley's death, in a Protestant service. The Scottish lords raised an army against her, she was forced to abdicate, and imprisoned in a castle on Loch Leven in June of the same year, while Bothwell escaped to Scandinavia. She escaped from Loch Leven in 1568, raised a force against her illegitimate half-brother, who was acting as Regent for the infant James, and was defeated. She retreated over the Solway into England, and threw herself on the mercy of Elizabeth, a complete failure of political judgement. Elizabeth put her under a house-arrest which gradually solidified into an imprisonment which lasted for nineteen years. After unequivocal evidence of her complicity in plots against the life of the English Queen, Elizabeth was, with extreme reluctance, persuaded to sign the warrant for her execution. The legality of this action against the anointed monarch of a neighbouring state was uncertain then, and has been much debated since. It gave rise to the only point in Mary's life when she can be seen acting with real intelligence, her own orchestration of her execution as a martyrdom for the Catholic faith, and a bid for canonization.

As a girl in France, the future Queen Mary had an education appropriate to her rank: she learned Latin, which she could write as well as read, and Italian, as well as such feminine skills as embroidery. She acquired Scots, and may have spoken some English, though throughout her life, she seems to have thought most easily in French, the language in which she wrote almost all her poems. She very much admired the new poetry of the 'Pléiade', and most of her own verse is couched in the idioms of her favourite Ronsard, to whom she wrote a poem. Two short Latin distichs attest to her competence in that language. Two longer Latin poems are attributed to her: one, 'Adamas loquitur', is the work of George Buchanan, the other, 'Domine deus speravi in te', is a pious forgery unlikely to have been composed earlier than the eighteenth century.

37   *'En mon triste et doux chant'*

En mon triste et doux chant
D'un ton fort lamentable,
Je jette un deuil trenchant,
De perte incomparable,
Et en souspirs cuysans   5
Passe mes meilleurs ans.

Fut-il un tel malheur
De dure destinée,
Ny si triste douleur
De dame fortunée,   10
Qui mon cœur et mon oeil
Vois en bière et cercueil?

Qui, en mon doux printemps
Et fleur de ma jeunesse,
Toutes les peines sens   15

D'une extrême tristesse,
Et en rien d'ay plaisir,
Qu'en regret et desir?

Ce qui m'estoit plaisant
Ores m'est peine dure;   20
Le jour le plus luisant
M'est nuit noire et obscure,
Et n'est rien si exquis,
Qui de moy soit requis.

J'ay au cœur et à l'oeil   25
Un portrâict et image
Qui figure mon deuil
Et mon pasle visage,
De violettes taint,
Qui est l'amoureux tainct.   30

Pour mon mal estranger
Je ne m'arreste en place;
Mais j'ay eu beau changer,
Si ma douleur n'efface;
Car mon pis et mon mieux   35
Sont les plus déserts lieux.

Si en quelque séjour,
Soit en bois ou en prée,
Soit sur l'aube du jour,
Ou soit sur la vesprée,   40
Sans cesse mon cœur sent
Le regret d'un absent.

Si parfois vers ces lieux
Viens à dresser ma veue,
Le doux traict de ses yeux   45
Je vois en une nue;
Soudain je voy en l'eau
Comme dans un tombeau.

Si je suis en repos,
Sommeillant sur ma couche,   50
J'oy qu'il me tient propos,
Je le sens qu'il me touche:
En labeur, en recoy
Tousjours est près de moy.

Je me vois autre objet,   55
Pour beau qui se présente,
A qui que soit subject,
Oncques mon cœur consente,

Exempt de perfection,
A ceste affection.   60

Metz, chanson, icy fin
A si triste complainte,
Dont sera le refrain:
Amour vraye et non faincte
Pour la séparation   65
N'aura diminution.

(1560)

20 *Ores* [arch.]: now   29 *taint* [arch.]: smothered   31 *estranger* [arch]: to set at a distance

37   *'In my sweet and sad song'*

In my sweet and sad song,
Of most lamenting tone,
I look deeply
At my incomparable loss,
And in bitter sighs   5
I pass my best years.

Is there an equal sorrow
Of hard destiny
Or as sad a grief
Of the Lady Fortune,   10
As that which, my heart and eye,
I see in coffin and bier?

Who, in my sweet spring
And flower of my youth,
Feel all the pains   15
Of the greatest sorrow
And take pleasure alone
In regret and longing.

He who was my delight
Now is my hard pain   20
The brightest day
Is dark night to me;
There is no fine thing
Which I desire now.

In my heart and eyes   25
I have a portrait and image
Which represents my mourning
And pale cheeks
Of smothered roses
Which were once the complexion of love.   30

Trying to flee my pain
I do not rest in one place,

But I need to change
Thus to relieve my sorrow,
As my best and worst   35
Are my most desert places.

If my wanderings
Should be in wood or field,
Should be at daybreak
Or at twilight,   40
Ceaselssly my heart feels
Sorrow for the one who is absent.

If sometimes towards such places
I should direct my gaze,
The sweet glance of his eyes   45
I see in the clouds
I look into the water
As if into a tomb.

If I am resting
Sleeping on my couch,   50
I hear him speaking to me,
I feel him touch me,
In work, in entertainment at court,
He is always with me.

I see no other thing   55
As beautiful if he is not in it,
To no other matter
Will my heart ever agree,
Cut off from wholeness
By this grief.   60

End this song here
End this sad lamentation,
Whose refrain shall be:
True love, not feigned,
Is not diminished   65
By separation.

38 *Carmina Italica et Gallica scripta per Regina Scotiae ad Angliae Reginam*

Il pensier che mi nuoce insieme e giova
   Amaro e dolce al mio cor cangia spesso
   E fra tema e speranza lo tien'si oppresso
   Che la quiette pace unque non trova.

Però, se questa carta à voi rinuova   5
   Il bel disio di vedervi in me impresso
   Cio fa il grand' affanno ch'in sestesso
   Ha, non puotendo homai da se far prova

Ho vedeto talhor vicino al porto
  Rispinger have in mar contrario vento 10
  E nel maggior' seren' turbarse il Cielo

Cosi sorella chara temo e pavento
  Non gia per noi, ma quante volte à torto
  Rompe fortuna un ben'ordito vello?

Ung seul penser qui me proffute el nuit
  Amer et doulx change en mon cueur sans cesse
  Entre le doubte et l'espoir il m'oppresse
  Tant que la paix et le repos me fuit

Donc, chere soeur, si ceste carte suit 5
  L'affection de nous veoir qui me presse;
  C'est que ie viz en peine et en tristesse
  Si promptement l'effect ne s'en ensuit

Jay veu la nef relascher par contraincte
  En haulte mer, proche d'entrer au port, 10
  Et le serain se convertir en trouble

Ainsi ie suis en soucy et en craincte
  Non pas de vous, mais quantes fois à tort
  Fortune rompt voille et cordage double?

38 *Verses in Italian and French, written by the
    Queen of Scots to the Queen of England*

A single thought which benefits and harms me
Bitter and sweet alternate endlessly in my heart.
Between hope and fear this thought weighs down on me
So much that peace and rest flee from me

So, dear sister, if this paper reiterates 5
My pressing desire to see you;
It is because I see in pain and sorrow
The immediate outcome if this request should fail.

I have seen the ship blown by contrary winds
On the high seas, near to the harbour mouth 10
And the calm turning to troubled water

Likewise [sister] I live in fear and terror
Not on account of you, but because there are times
When Fortune can destroy sail and rigging at once.

39   *'Celuy vraiment na poinct de courtoisie'*

> Celuy vraiment na poinct de courtoisie
> Qui en bon lieu ne montre son scavoir
> Estant requis descripre en poesie:
> Il vauldroit mieux du tout n'en poinct avoir
>
> *
>
> Les Dieux, les Cieux, La Mort, and la haine et l'enuie   5
> Sont sourds, irès, cruels, animès contre moy
> Prier, Soufrir, Pleurer, à chascun estre amye
> Sont les remedes qu'entent d'ennuitz ie voy

                                                    (1582)

39   *'He is, in truth, lacking in civility'*

> He is, in truth, lacking in civility
> Who fails, at the time when it is required, to show his knowledge
> Being required to write in verse:
> He wishes above all to have nothing to do with it.
>
> *
>
> The Gods, the Heavens, Death, hatred and envy   5
> Are deaf, angry, cruel, stirred up against me;
> To pray, to suffer, to weep, to be a friend to all
> Are the cures for the many vexations which I see

ANONYMOUS
(before 1568)

THIS poem is preserved in the Bannatyne Manuscript, written in 1568, which is a principal witness to the élite literary culture of Lowland Scotland in the mid-sixteenth century. There was apparently a fashion for 'heart' poems in Scottish literary circles in the 1550s, since a number of examples survive. There is an answer to this poem by the poet Alexander Scott in the same manuscript, (fos. 235[b]–236[a]), notably respectful in tone, in a way which suggests a reply to a patroness rather than a lover.

40   *'Haif hairt in hairt ʒe hairt of hairtis haill'*

> Haif hairt in hairt ʒe hairt of hairtis haill
> Trewly sweit hairt ʒour hairt my hairt sall haif
> Expell deir hairt my havy hairtis baill

Praying ȝow hairt quhik hes my hairt in graif
Sen ȝe sweit Hairt my hairt may sla and saif   5
Lat not deir hairt my leill hairt be forloir
Excelland hairt of every hairtis gloir.

Glaid is my Hairt with ȝow suiet Hairt to rest
And serve ȝow hairt with hairtis observance
Sen ȝe ar hairt with bayth our hairtis possest   10
My Hairt is in ȝour hairtis governance
Do with my hairt ȝour hairtis sweit plesance
ffor is my hairt thrall ȝour hairt untill
I have no hairt contrair ȝor hairtis will

Sen ȝe haif hairt my faythfull hairt in cure   15
Uphald the hairt quhilk is ȝour hairtis awin
Gif my hairt be ȝour hairtis serviture
How may ȝe thoill ȝour trew hairt be ourthrawin
Quhairfoir sweit hairt not suffer so be knawin
But ȝe be hairt my hairtis rejosing   20
As ȝe ar hairt of hairtis conforting.

---

1 *haill*: whole   2 *haif*: have   3 *baill*: bale, injury   4 *quhik*: which; *in graif*: in your power   7 *gloir*: glory   8 *suiet*: sweet   13 *thrall*: enslaved   16 *awin*: own   18 *thoill*: endure

NIGHEAN DHONNCHADH,
THE DAUGHTER OF DUNCAN CAMPBELL
OF GLENLYON
(fl. 1570)

THE circumstances of this poem, which is attributed to Campbell of Glenlyon's daughter, are that it was composed after Gregor MacGregor of Glenstrae was captured, tried, and beheaded by Glenlyon at Taymouth Castle in 1570. Gregor MacGregor had eloped with Glenlyon's daughter, against the wishes of her father, who had intended to marry her to the Baron of Dull. Glenlyon's anger was exacerbated by the fact that the MacGregor had refused to take the Campbell name in return for protection. Glenlyon's daughter was forced to witness her husband's execution at the hands of her father. In this poem, which oral tradition attributes to her, she expresses her love for her husband, and her repudiation of her own clan. Since any possibility of happiness or security in the Highlands depended on membership of a clan, her position as a young widowed mother who had forsworn her father's protection was a calamitous one, and her evident foreboding that her child will not live to grow up was entirely rational.

41 *'Moch madainn air latha Lùnasd''*

Moch madainn air latha Lùnasd'
  Bha mi sùgradh mar ri m'ghràdh,
Ach mun tàinig meadhon latha
  Bha mo chridhe air a'chràdh.

Ochain, ochain, ochain uiridh   5
  Is goirt mo chridhe, a laoigh,
Ochain, ochain, ochain uiridh
  Cha chluinn t' athair ar caoidh.

Mallachd aig maithibh is aig càirdean
  Rinn mo chràdh air an-dòigh,   10
Thàinig gun fhios air mo ghràdh-sa
  Is a thug fo smachd e le foill.

Nam biodh dà fhear dheug d'a chinneadh
  Is mo Ghriogair air an ceann,
Cha bhiodh mo shùil a'sileadh dheur,   15
  No mo leanabh féin gun dàimh.

Chuir iad a cheann air ploc daraich,
  Is dhòirt iad fhuil mu làr:
Nam biodh agam-sa an sin cupan
  Dh'òlainn dìth mo shàth.   20

Is truagh nach robh m'athair an galar,
  Agus Cailean Liath am plàigh,
Ged bhiodh nighean an Ruadhanaich
  Suathadh bas is làmh.

Chuirinn Cailean Liath fo ghlasaibh,   25
  Is Donnchadh Dubh an làimh,
'S gach Caimbeulach th' ann am Bealach
  Gu giùlan nan glas-làmh.

Ràinig mise réidhlean Bhealach,
  Is cha d'fhuair mi ann tàmh: 30
Cha d'fhàg mi ròin de m'fhalt gun tarraing
  No craiceann air mo làimh.

Is truagh nach robh mi an riochd na h-uiseig,
  Spionnadh Ghriogair ann mo làimh:
Is i a' chlach a b'àirde anns a' chaisteal   35
  A' chlach a b'fhaisge do'n bhlàr.

Is ged tha mi gun ùbhlan agam
  Is ùbhlan uile aig càch,
Is ann tha m' ubhal cùbhraidh grinn
  Is cùl a chinn ri làr.   40

Ged tha mnathan chàich aig baile
'Nan laighe is 'nan cadal sàmh,
Is ann bhios mise aig bruaich do lice
A' bualadh mo dhà làimh.

Is mór a b'annsa bhith aig Griogair   45
Air feadh colle is fraoich,
Na bhith aig Baran crìon na Dalach
An taigh cloiche is aoil.

Is mór a b'annsa bhith aig Griogair
Cur a' chruigh do'n ghleann,   50
Na bhith aig Baran crìon na Dalach
Ag òl air fìon is air leann.

Is mòr a b'annsa bhith aigh Griogair
Fo bhrata ruibeach ròin,
Na bhith aig Baran crìon na Dalach   55
A' giùlan sìoda is sròil.

Ged a bhiodh ann cur is cathadh
Is latha nan seachd sion,
Gheigheadh Griogair dhòmh-sa cragan
'S an caidlimid fo dhìon.   60

Ba hu, ba hu, àsrain bhig,
Chan 'eil thu fhathast ach tlàth:
Is eagal leam nach tig an latha
Gun dìol thu t'athair gu bràth.

(1570)

1 *Lùnasd/Lammas* (1 August), probably an error introduced in oral transmission, for Tùrnais (Palm Sunday), since MacGregor was beheaded in April   9 *Mallachd/a curse*: this is a curse on her father (19–20): a trope of Scottish/Irish mourning songs, used, for example, in Ailean Dubh O'Connell's 'Lament for Art O'Leary', and in 'the Dowie Dens of Yarrow': see *Éigse* 18 (1980) 29–33   22 *Cailean Liath/Grey Colin*: Colin Campbell of Glenorchy, married to a Ruthven   27 *Bealach/Taymouth*: MacGregor was executed at Taymouth Castle   47 *Baran...na Dalach/Baron of Dull*: whom her father had wanted her to marry

41   *'Early on Lammas morning'*

Early on Lammas morning
I was sporting with my love,
but before noon came upon us
my heart had been crushed.

Alas, alas, alas and alack,   5
sore is my heart, my child,
alas, alas, alas and alack
your father won't hear our cries.

A curse on nobles and relations
who brought me to this grief,   10
who came on my love unawares
and took him by deceit.

Had there been twelve of his kindred,
and my Gregor at their head,
my eye would not be weeping   15
nor my child without a friend.

They put his head on an oaken block
and spilled his blood on the ground,
if I had had a cup there
I'd have drunk my fill down.   20

A pity my father was not diseased
and Grey Colin stricken with plague,
even though Ruthven's daughter
would wring her hands dismayed.

I'd put Grey Colin under lock and key   25
and Black Duncan in heavy irons,
and every Campbell in Taymouth
I'd set to wearing chains.

I reached the lawn of Taymouth
but for me that was no balm,   30
I left no hair of my head unpulled
nor skin upon my palms.

If only I had the flight of the lark
with Gregor's strength in my arm,
the highest stone in the castle   35
would be the closest to the ground.

Though now I'm left without apples
and the others have them all,
my apple is fair and fragrant,
with the back of his head on the mould.   40

Though others' wives are safe at home
lying sound asleep,
I am at the edge of your grave
beating my hands in grief.

I'd far rather be with Gregor   45
roaming moor and copse
than be with the niggardly Baron of Dull
in a house of lime and stone.

I'd far rather be with Gregor
driving the cattle to the glen   50
than be with the niggardly Baron of Dull
drinking beer and wine.

I'd far rather be with Gregor
under a rough hairy skin

than be with the niggardly Baron of Dull 55
dressed in satin and silk.

Even on a day of driving snow
when the seven elements reel,
Gregory would find me a little hollow
where we would snugly sleep. 60

Ba hu, ba hu, little waif
you still are only young
but the day when you revenge your father
I fear will never come.

ELLIN THORNE
(c.1576)

NOTHING is known of Ellin Thorne except her name and the fact that she was clearly a person of some education. The miscellaneous manuscript which preserves this elegant poem attributed to her is one with strongly Catholic connections: it contains an exhortation to Cranmer, 'Points of Religion propperly to be Known by Priests', and a translation of the rule of St Benedict into English verse. Such of the songs and ballads as are datable seem to cluster around 1576. Ownership marks suggest that it belonged to Henry Savile of Banke (1568–1617), and to Sir John Anstis (1669–1744/5), Garter King of Arms, who may have given it to the British Library. The possibility that Henry Savile had a hand in compiling the book as well as owning it is suggested by the links with Yorkshire which it reveals: three ballads have explicit, and five implicit, connections with that county. A number of placenames is scribbled on fo. 148^v: the nine which can be identified are of places in the West Riding of Yorkshire (they include Thorn).

42 *Ellin thorne songe*

Would god that deth with cruell darte
and fatall sesters thre
before had perste my virgins harte
or I did fancye the

Cupido then his force had bent 5
and golden bowe in vaine
my womans harte hade not ben rent
with this most rewfull paine

His denting darte no soner flew
from sounding silver stringe 10
but pinchinge paines eke dolores newe
within my brest did springe

O lukeless happ unhapy luke
some lyones me feede
some Savage tiger gave me suke   15
un thankfulness me brede

Els I not once had fended the
whoss shynning comely graice
constraines me nowe to rune I se
a captives Rufull rayce   20

O spile me not but spedely
thie mercy here extende
and I wyll serve the faithfully
unto my latter ende.

2 *fatall sesters*: the Fates   13 *luke*: luck   14 *lyones me feede*: lioness fed me   15 *gave me*
suke: gave me suck   16 *me brede*: bred me   17 *fended the*: offended thee   21 *spile*:
destroy

MARIE COLLYN, née HARVEY
(1555/6–after 1600)

MARIE HARVEY was the child of a prosperous yeoman family, baptized in May
1567. She was the younger sister of Gabriel Harvey of Saffron Walden. On 31
March 1600 she married a yeoman, Philipp Collyn, in Waldon. Nothing more is
heard of her until she brings a suit against her brother in 1608 which arose from
her father's will: this stipulated that Gabriel Harvey should pay her £60 within
four years of his death. The will provided that if this sum was not paid, Harvey
would forfeit the greater part of the inheritance to come to him after their
mother's death (which did not occur until 1613): his chronic cash-flow problems
meant that he never had the ready money to pay her. Marie waited fifteen years
to complain of his delinquency, suggesting a deliberate attempt to enrich herself
at her brother's expense. The suit was eventually settled amicably, and she
dropped out of history.

As a teenager, Marie Harvey, who was barely of gentlewoman status, seems to
have dropped unselfconsciously into verse for the sake of emphasis. Such of her
writing as survives is preserved by her brother, Gabriel Harvey, who seems to
have made a dossier recording the encounters around Christmas, 1574 between
his sister Marie and Philip Howard, Earl of Surrey, both of whom were about 17
(perhaps in case of future slanders against Marie's sexual reputation). Harvey's
account notes a series of meetings, the first accidental, the following engineered
by Howard, and a series of gifts from him to her. Marie was determined not to
surrender her virtue, but was far from indifferent to such gifts as a gold ring. At
one point, Marie was induced to write her dangerous admirer a letter, which
took her some time. Letters are then fired to and fro, carried by Howard's
confidential servant, referred to as P. In her letters, dropping into simple rhyme
seems to be a way of saying, 'please believe I mean what I say'. Later in this one-
sided affair, when Howard had talked her into a meeting which she then thought

better of, she left him a thirty-six-line poem by way of diplomatic apology, the poem given here. The tone of transparent simplicity is misleading, since Marie Harvey is telling a pack of lies: according to her brother, 'ye maide purposely tooke a iorny a seven miles of, in ye morning before six a clocke, dreading ye wurst if mie lord should chaunce to cum.' The poem is an excuse, an apology, and an attempt at temporizing. The week before this was sent, Howard had actually tried to rape her, and a few days later, Harvey himself intervened tactfully but firmly to put a stop to the whole affair. Marie's verse, in this narrative, is used by her to deflect or disarm Howard's lust, anger, or rapacity. Her stratagems for keeping this relationship in her control rather than Howard's are fascinating, but language is the only one which is of present concern. Verse may be a poor weapon against an aristocratic 17-year-old male bent on sexual gratification, but it was a weapon of sorts. I would also suggest that she is using verse to indicate that she has a point of view, she is a speaking subject, not just a female object—perhaps even making a Pamela-like bid through her very facility with words to be recognized as a woman of sufficient social status not to be used and discarded even by a Howard. Marie Harvey was not a lady, she was not even a gentlewoman, strictly speaking, but the literacy of these letters imply that she was not a wench, and hint that she should not be treated as one.

43 *'The thursday before new yeares day (being on the satterdy) the Maide, by councell of on, she trustid well, excussid herself on this wise to Milord.'*

Milord I thanke you hartely
For your late liberalitie.
I would I were hable to requite
Your Lordships bowntie with the like.
Marry, mie hart is not so franke,   5
But mie habilitie is as scante
Therefore, in steade of a leifer gift
I bequeath you this paper for a shift.
You se I am disposid to rime,
Though it be cleen out of time.   10
I hope your Lordship will have me excusid
As longe as you feel not yourself abusid.
To be short Milord, thus it is I wis,
I could not be at home according to prommis.
I would not, perhaps it may to you seem,   15
I pray you, Milord, do not so misdeem.
Truly I was sent for, to spend this good time
A fewe miles of with a kinsman of mine.
Whether mi father in hast wuld so faine have me goe,
That I could not, nor durst not for mielife, say noe.   20

    So that I was faint
      At his commaundiment:

To take a jornye
   That I litle ment.
I pray you Milord   25
   Have me excusid,
Though by mie frends
   I be thus rulid.
The truth is, I am not mine owne Maide,
My frends to disobey I am afraide.   30

An other time as good
   To speake your minde;
In the meane time if you seeke
   You can not but finde.
Your honors to commaund   35
In anie honest demaund.

                             M.

                   (Christmas, 1573)

6 *habilitie*: ability   7 *leifer*: more acceptable   11 *Lordship*: L. MS   21 *faint*: fain

ANNE FIELD, née VAVASOUR, later
RICHARDSON
(*c*.1560–after 1622)

ANNE VAVASOUR was the daughter of Henry Vavasour of Copmanthorpe in Yorkshire. She came to court as a Gentlewoman of the Bedchamber in 1580, when the Earl of Oxford was estranged from his wife Anne Cecil, the daughter of Lord Burghley. The context of the surviving poem appears to be this affair. In 1581, she gave birth to a son in the Maiden's Chamber: Oxford attempted to flee the country, and both the guilty parties were temporarily put in the Tower. Her son was acknowledged by Oxford as his own, since he was allowed to assume Oxford's own surname of Vere: as Sir Edward Vere, he had a respectable and meritorious career as a professional soldier. At some point after this public debacle, Anne Vavasour moved in with a much older admirer, Sir Henry Lee, the Queen's Champion, at Woodstock. Lee's wife died in 1590, and she was visibly *maîtresse en titre* at Woodstock later that same year. She remained at Woodstock until Lee's death, and is said in her epitaph to have been buried in his grave.

By 1590, Anne Vavasour was married to one John Field. Since she undoubtedly lived with Sir Henry Lee, and Field was the recipient of an annuity from Sir Henry, this was evidently a marriage intended to do no more than give her child a name should she conceive one: they had one son, Thomas Vavasour, or Freeman, who was appointed Yeoman of the Armour in 1607/8. Her position in her later years was quite a socially secure one: in September 1608, Anne of Denmark did her and Lee the courtesy of paying a visit to a little lodge which he had a short distance from Ditchley. John Chamberlain describes the incident: 'the Queen, before her going out of this County, dined with Sir Henry Lee at his

Little Rest, and gave great countenance, and had long and large discourse with Mrs Vavasour; and, within a day or two after, sent a very fair jewell valued above £100, which favour hath put such new life into the old man, to see his sweet-heart so graced, that he says he will have one fling more at the Court before he die.' Lee died in 1611, which created a considerable problem. Since his property was largely entailed, he was forced to leave the bulk of it to his heir-at-law, a great-nephew, Henry Lee Rainsford, but he provided for Anne with care: a jointure, the total yearly value of which was £700, an annuity for their son, and bonds to protect her interests left with her brother, Sir Thomas Vavasour, and another family friend. The heir attempted to repudiate these extensive claims on his estate, but was overruled by the court: she came less well out of a second suit, in which the heir attempted to recover jewels, gold, hangings, silver, and other valuables which she had removed from the property before the heir took possession. Her final brush with the law came in 1618, and is again recorded by John Chamberlain: 'Mrs Vavasour, old Sir Henry Lee's woman, is like to be called in question for having two husbands now alive.' Field, it may be presumed, had disappeared from her life, if indeed he was ever part of it: she took a chance, and married one John Richardson of Durham at some time before 1621, in which year they co-signed a lease. The resultant bigamy case, brought against her by Lee's heir, came before the High Commission, and was determined on 1 February 1621. Anne was condemned to a fine of £2,000, but in the following year, the prerogative of the crown (perhaps in this case, influenced by Queen Anne's patronage of her) was invoked to exempt her.

The poem reflects an emotionally and practically complex situation. Her love for Oxford was necessarily clandestine, since he was married: her 'hande' may refer to a betrothal, while the possession of her 'glove' probably refers to some individual appointing himself her champion in the courtly love sense: the obvious candidate for this role is Sir Henry Lee, whose attraction to her predates the disastrous affair with Oxford, on the incontrovertible evidence of his tilting armour, one suit of which was decorated with the initials AV accompanied by true-love knots.

44   *'Thoughe I seeme straunge sweete freende be thou not so'*

Thoughe I seeme straunge sweete freende be thou not so
  Do not annoy thy selfe with sullen will
Myne harte hathe voude allthoughe my tongue saye noe
  To be thyne owne in freendly liking styll
Thou seeste me live amongest the Lynxes eyes   5
  That pryes innto each privy thoughte of mynde
Thou knowest ryghte well what sorrows may aryse
  Ife once they chaunce my setled lookes to fynde
Contente thy selfe that once I made an othe
  To sheylde my selfe in shrowde of honest shame   10
And when thou lyste make tryall of my trouthe
  So that thou save the honoure of my name

And let me seme althoughe I be not coye
To cloak my sadd conceyts with smylinge cheere
Let not my jestures showe wherein to joye   15
Nor by my lookes let not my loue appeere.
We seely dames that falles suspecte, do feare
And live within the moughte of envyes lake
Muste in oure heartes a secrete meaning beare
Far from the reste whiche outwardlye we make   20
Go where I lyke, I lyste not vaunte my love
where I desyre there moste I fayne debate
One hathe my hande an other hathe my glove,
But he my harte whome I seeme most to hate
Then farewell freende I will continue straunge   25
Thou shalt not heere by worde or writinge oughte
Let it suffice my vowe shall never chaunge
As for the rest I leave yt to thy thoughte.

5 *Lynxes*: proverbially sharp-sighted   16 *love*: lovee MS   18 *moughte*: mouth

CATHERIN LLWYD, née OWEN
(d. 1602)

CATHERIN OWEN was married to the poet Dafydd Lllwyd of Henblas, Anglesey, whose 'Elegy for Catherin Owen who died 11 June in the year of Christ 1602' gives the date of her death. Nothing else is known of her except that she evidently had a son called Siôn (John). Like contemporary Scottish women, Welsh women evidently kept their fathers' names on marriage. Both this poem and her husband's elegy are preserved in a seventeenth-century Welsh poetic miscellany.

45 *At Siôn Lloyd: cynghorion y fam i'w hetifedd*

Fy mab Siôn o Fôn, 'rwy i—di weniaith
    yn d'annerch miawn difri'
ag o'm gwir fodd yn rhoddi
at hyn fy mendith i ti.

Bendithied, rhwydded, aml i rhoddo—Duw   5
    yt ras da er ffrwytho;
arnad, Siôn, i danfono
mal y gwlith i fendith Fo.

Clywais fod hynod hoen walch—hoff eurddysg
    ith fforddiaw yn ddi falch;   10

y masdr Williams, dra haelwalch,
yw'r glain gwiw a'r galon gwalch.

Y paun nid adwaen, noedig—ydyw,
    odiaeth ŵr ddysgedig;
o'th flysia'r iaith felysig,   15
nad, er fy mwyn, ddwyn ei ddig.

Taled tad y rhad, lle mae'r hyder—byth
    'i boen a'i flinder,
i Mastr Williams bob amser,
organ parch a'r genau pêr.   20

Dewis gyfeillion diwair—dysgedig,
    dysg wady rhai drygair:
nag ynnill Siôn, oganair,
er mwyn mab y Forwyn Fair.

Coylia, meddylia ddilin—daioni,   25
    fal dyna dy ffortun;
a gwylia dy dri gelyn,
a châr Dduw a chowyr ddyn.

Dy dri gelyn hyn a henwais—ydynt
    odiaeth ar bob malais: 30
y byd a'r cnawd, trallawd trais,
lew rhuedig, llwyr wadais.

Gweddïaf, galwaf ar geli—ŵr hael,
    ar i hwn dy groisi:
gwyddost pwy sy'n rhoi'i gweddi   35
dinam, dy fam ydwyf fi.

Bydd draw yn ddistaw ddiystryn—chwerwedd,
    broch eiriau a'i hynnyn;
er gwrando garw gair undyn
edrych beth a ddoythych, ddyn.   40

Er yt gael gafael drwy gofiaw—mwynedd
    fy mendith i'th lwyddaw,
Siôn dal hyn sy' yn d'eiliaw
er Duw, lwydd bawb ar dy law.

Dy famaeth helaeth pei holen'—f'enaid   45
    yw'r fwynnaidd Rhydychen;
tyn Siôn draw, â'th ddwy bawen,
burion happ i bronnau hen.

                    Catherin Owen dy fam a'i gwnaeth

46 *Rhydychen/Oxford*: Jesus College, Oxford, was strongly associated with Welsh students.

45 *To Siôn Lloyd: the mother's advice to her heir*

My son Siôn of Anglesey, I am without flattery
    addressing you in all seriousness
and by my own goodwill I give
in addition to this my blessing to you.

God bless you, speed you, frequently give you   5
    good grace in order to flourish
on you, Siôn, to bestow
as the dew his blessing.

I heard that a remarkable man of noble vigour, dear golden learning
    guides you in humility;   10
Master Williams, very generous and noble,
is this fine jewel with the noble heart.

This peacock that I know not, noteworthy is he
    and an excellently erudite man;
if you crave sweet language,   15
do not, for my sake, incur his anger

May the father of blessings where there is faith forever pay
    for his pain and his trouble
Master Williams always,
organ of respect with pure lips.   20

Choose loyal, learned companions,
    learn to disown those who speak ill:
and do not incur, Siôn, defamation
for the sake of the Virgin Mary's son.

Believe, think on following goodness,   25
    as it is your destiny;
and beware your three enemies
and love God and true men.

Your three enemies that I named, they
    excel at all malice: 30
The world and the flesh, tribulation and violence,
the roaring lion, I renounced absolutely.

I shall pray, I shall call on God — generous man
    for him to bless you:
do you know who offers her prayer   35
without defect ? I am your mother

Be quiet there, bitterness,
    angry words, do not incite.
Though hearing the rough words of another,
watch what you yourself say, man.   40

Though you hold fast by remembrance to the gentleness
    of my blessing to speed you,
Siôn, hold to this that gives you succour
for God's sake, that those at your side prosper.

Your abundant nursemaid if they ask, dear soul, 45
  is gentle Oxford;
Grasp there Siôn, with your two paws,
the good fortune of her old breasts.

            Catherin Owen your mother made this

CHRISTIAN LINDSAY
(fl. 1580/86)

CHRISTIAN LINDSAY was part of a circle of court poets active in Scotland in the mid-1580s, known as 'the Castalian Band'. She may have been married to John of Dunrod, sheriff of Lanark, and she was more certainly a member of the Crawford family, and a cousin of the Bishop of Ross.

Robert Hudson was a musician and poet, with the title of 'court violar'. Her surviving poem is a plea to Alexander Montgomerie that he and his fellow poets at court not forget him. She appears, with the implication that she is a writer, in a poem by James VI, complaining that Montgomerie has given her grounds for the accusation that 'poets lie':

> Not yett woulde ye not call to memorie
> What grounde ye gave to Christian Lindsay by it
> For now she sayes, which makes us all full sorie
> Your craft to lie; with leave, now have I tried.

Another sonnet of Montgomerie's from 1580/86, again addressing the court violar Robert Hudson, says:

> Ye can pen out tua cuple and ye pleis
> Yourself and I, old Scot and Robert Semple
> Quhen we are deid, that all our dayis bot daffis
> Let Christian Lyndesay wryte our epitaphis.

This last suggests that Edinburgh court poets regarded her as part of their circle, but did not take her verse very seriously.

46   *Christen Lyndesay to Ro. Hudsone*

Oft haive I hard, bot ofter fund it treu,
  That courteours kyndnes lasts but for a vhyle.
Fra once ȝour turnes be sped, vhy then adeu,
  ȝour promeist freindship passis in exyle.
Bot, Robene, faith, ȝe did me not beguyll;   5
  I hopit ay of ȝou as of the lave:
If thou had with, thou wald haif mony a wyle,
  To mak thy self be knaune for a knaive.
Montgomrie, that such hope did once conceave
  Of thy guid-will, nou finds all is forgotten.   10

Thoght not bot kyndnes he did at the craiv,
He finds thy friendship as it rypis is rotten.
The smeikie smeithis cairs not his passit travel,
Bot leivis him lingring, déing of the gravell.

11 *craiv*: crave   12 *rypis*: ripens   13 *smeikie smeithis*: smoky smiths; *travel*: work
14 *déing*: dying; *gravel*: urinary disease

MARGARET CLIFFORD, COUNTESS OF CUMBERLAND, née RUSSELL
(1560–1616)

MARGARET CLIFFORD was the daughter of the Earl of Bedford, who had George Clifford, Earl of Cumberland, as his ward: Bedford took the opportunity to bring his ward's fortune into the family by betrothing him to his daughter. Clifford's mother was Lady Eleanor Brandon, younger daughter of Charles Brandon, Duke of Suffolk, and Mary Tudor, daughter of Henry VII: he was thus the first cousin of the ill-fated Lady Jane Grey. They married in 1577, and the marriage collapsed in 1591, whereupon she took her daughter, Anne Clifford, and they went to live with her sister Anne, Countess of Warwick. Both were cultivated patronesses supporting such writers as Edmund Spenser and Samuel Daniel (whom she hired as her daughter Anne's tutor), and notably, Aemilia Lanyer (nos. 58–9): it was Margaret Clifford's brother's estate at Cookham which Lanyer celebrated in her long poem. She was a notably cultivated and well-educated woman, with wide interests which included alchemy and architecture. This epitaph (which is on one of her business partners) is the only verse of hers known to survive; though alchemical manuscripts preserved in the Cumbrian County Archives at Kendal (studied by Penny Bayer in a forthcoming Warwick University Ph.D.) suggest something of her intellectual circle and interests.

47 *Epitaph for Richard Cavendish, engraved on his monument in Hornsey church*

Candish deriv'd from Noble Parentage
Adorn'd with Vertuous and heroicke partes
Most learned bountifull Devout and Sage
Grac'd with the graces Muses and the Artes
Deer to his Prince in English Court admird   5
Beloved of great and Honourable Peeres
Of all estemed embraced and desired
Till Death Cut of his well employed yeeres.
Within this earth his earth entombed lies
Whose heavenly part Surmounted has the skies.   10

(1601)

1 *Candish*: Richard Cavendish (d. 1600) was a life-long student at Oxford, Cambridge, and abroad; he translated Euclid into English. The monument is in St Mary's Church, Hornsey, Middlesex.

MARY HERBERT (née SIDNEY), COUNTESS OF PEMBROKE
(1561–1621)

MARY HERBERT was the daughter of Mary Dudley and Henry Sidney, and the sister of Sir Philip. Her grandfather, William Sidney, was entrusted with the care of the infant Edward VI, and Henry Sidney, in consequence, was one of the hand-picked group of young nobles brought up and educated with their future king. Her mother was daughter to the ambitious and high-flying John Dudley, Duke of Northumberland (executed 1553), and sister of Elizabeth's favourite, the Earl of Leicester. Her parents' lives were bound up with the court; her cousins and aunts served Mary, and later Elizabeth. When Mary was born, at Tickenhall near Bewdley, on the Welsh border, she was her parents' fourth child. Her brother Philip was seven years her senior. In 1562, the Queen fell ill with smallpox, and her life was despaired of. It was Lady Sidney who was entrusted with the desperately responsible task of nursing her. Elizabeth made an excellent recovery, Lady Sidney caught the disease herself, and was terribly disfigured. She never fully recovered, though she bore three more children, and though she continued to appear at court (veiled or masked) she and Sir Henry often lived apart. This separation was expedited by Sir Henry's appointment as Lord Governor of Ireland and Lord President of the Council of the Marches of Wales. Mary Sidney therefore spent a more retired childhood than might have been predicted: sometimes in Dublin, probably more often in Wales, usually at Ludlow Castle, or in the main family home, Penshurst Place, subject of Ben Jonson's country-house poem of 1611.

Mary was taught fashionable accomplishments, the lute, the virginals, embroidery. She and her sisters had at various times a governess, Anne Mantell, a 'skolemaster', Mr Thornton, and an Italian teacher, Mistress Maria. She certainly learned French and Italian, since she was later to translate from these languages, and probably Latin and Greek. Her brother Robert (b. 1563) had books bought for him; no equivalent items are listed in the accounts specifically for the girls, but they may have used their brother's and their father's books. In 1575, Mary was presented at court, and in 1577, she married Henry Herbert, Earl of Pembroke, staunchly Protestant, more at home in Welsh than in English, and about thirty years her senior, and entered on a life of even greater splendour than she had been born to.

The close relationship between Mary Herbert and her brother Sir Philip Sidney was built up after her marriage, since he had effectively left home when she was 6. He paid extended visits to her home at Wilton in the year of her marriage, and often spent time with her thereafter. His *Arcadia* resulted from these visits, as his dedication states: 'you desired me to doe it, and your desire to my heart is an absolute commandment.' Her first child was born in 1580, and was followed by three others. In 1585, Sir Philip Sidney was killed at Zutphen, amid massive international publicity. Mary's translations of the Psalms began as a project to revise and complete the metrical version of the Psalms that her brother had left unfinished. After her husband's death in 1601 she was granted a royal manor in Bedfordshire by James I and built Houghton House, where she resided until her death from smallpox in 1621. The Countess was the most celebrated literary patron in late-Elizabethan England. Among the poets who enjoyed her patronage were Nicolas Breton, Thomas Moffet, and Samuel Daniel. According to John Aubrey, she built a laboratory at Wilton reserved for her own use and that of her chemist, the brash but brilliant Adrian Gilbert. Aubrey offers a drastically different version of the Countess from the pious psalmist, but his version of her character and life must be treated with extreme caution.

The Countess's translations of the Psalms were not literal translations, but original poems in innovative verse forms. They were also texts of Protestant theology and scholarship: among the authorities she consulted were Clement Marot's French translation of the Psalms, commentaries by Théodore de Bèze and Jean Calvin, and the Geneva Bible. They remained unpublished until 1823, but were known and admired by Ben Jonson, George Herbert, and John Donne. Her other translations included Robert Garnier's closet tragedy, *Marc Antoine*, and Philippe du Plessis-Mornay's *Discourse of Life and Death*, which were published together in 1592, and Petrarch's *Triumph of Death*, which remained in manuscript. Her elegy to her brother, 'To the Angell Spirit of Sir P. Sidney', was published with Samuel Daniel's works in 1623. 'Thenot and Piers' was presumably written for a projected visit of the Queen's to Wilton in the late 1590s which never took place. This is probably the earliest piece of Renaissance English writing for dramatic performance written by a woman. It aims to please and flatter Elizabeth, and does so with considerable adroitness. The Queen (well into her sixties, and committed to a fiction of youthfulness) is associated with perpetual Spring. Similarly, though Elizabeth obstinately refused to name a successor, more and more courtiers and politicians in the 1590s were discreetly opening negotiations with James VI of Scotland: Mary Herbert offers the consoling fiction, 'to us none else but only shee'. The structure of the work is theological; it draws on the tradition of describing God in negatives, since no positives can be superlative enough.

48   *Miserere Mei Deus.*

Psalm 51

O lord, whose grace no limitts comprehend;
sweet lord, whose mercies stand from measure free;
To mee that grace, to mee that mercie send,
And wipe o lord my sinnes from sinnfull mee
O clense, o wash my fowle iniquitie: 5
 clense still my spotts, still wash awaie my staynings,
 till staines and spotts in me leave no remaynings.

For I, alas, acknowledging doe know
my filthie fault, my faultie filthiness
to my soules eye unceasantlie doth show   10

which done to thee, to thee I doe confesse,
Just, judge, true wittnes; that for righteousnes
    thie doome maie passe against my guilt awarded,
    thy evidence for truth maie be regarded.

My mother, loe! when I began to be,   15
conceaving me, with me did sinne conceave:
and as with living heate she cherisht me,
corruption did like cherishing receave.
but loe, thie love to purest good doth cleave,
    and inward truth: which hardlie els discerned,   20
    my trewand soule in thy hid schoole hath learned.

Then as thie self to leapers hast assign'd,
with Hisop, lord, thy Hisop, purge me soe:
and that shall clense the leaprie of my mind.
make over me thie mercies streames to flow,   25
Soe shall my whitnes scorn the whitest snow.
    to eare and hart send soundes and thoughts of gladdnes,
    that brused bones maie daunce awaie their saddnes.

Thie ill-pleas'd eye from my misdeedes avert:
Cancell the registers my sinnes containe: 30
create in me a pure, cleane, spottless hart:
inspire a sprite where love of right maie raigne.
ah! cast me not from thee: take not againe
    thie breathing grace: againe thie comfort send me,
    and let the guard of thy free sprite attend me.   35

Soe I to them a guiding hand wilbe,
whose faultie feete have wandred from thie way:
and turn'd from sinne will make retorne to thee,
whom, turn'd from thee sinne erst had ledd astraie.
O God, God of my health, O doe away   40
    my bloody crime: soe shall my tongue be raised
    to praise thy truth, enough can not be praised.

Unlock my lipps, shut up with sinnfull shame:
then shall my mouth ô lord, thy honour sing;
for bleeding fuell for thy alters flame,   45
to gaine thy grace what bootes it me to bring?
burnt-offrings are to thee no pleasaunt thing.
    the sacrifice that god will holde respected,
    is the heart-broken soule, the sprite dejected.

Lastly, O lord, how soe I stand or fall,   50
leave not thy loved Sion to embrace:
but with thie favour build up Salems wall,
and still in peace, maintaine that peacefull place.

then shalt thou turne a well-accepting face
  to sacred fires with offred guiftes perfumed: 55
  till ev'n whole calves on alters be consumed.

21 *trewand*: truant   22 *leapers*: lepers   23 *Hisop*: hyssop (a herb)   46 *bootes it*: what
does it avail me?

49   *Deus Judicium*

Psalm 72

Teach the kings sonne, who king hym self shalbe,
  thy judgmentes lord, thy justice make him learn:
To rule thy Realme as justice shall decree,
    And poore mens right in judgment to discern.
      then fearelesse peace,   5
      with rich encrease
        the mountaynes proud shall fill:
      and justice shall
      make plenty fall
        on ev'ry humble hill.   10

Make him the weake support, th'opprest relyve,
  supply the poore, the quarrell-pickers quaile:
soe agelesse ages shall thee reverence give,
    till eies of heav'n, the sunn and moone, shall faile
      and thou againe   15
      shalt blessings rayne,
        which down shall mildly flow,
      as showres thrown
      on meades new mown
        whereby they freshly grow.   20

During his rule the just shall ay be greene,
  and peacefull plenty joine with plenteous peace:
while of sad night the many-formed queene
    decreas'd shall grow, and grown again, decrease.
      from sea to sea   25
      he shall survey
        all kingdoms as his own:
      and from the trace
      of Physons race,
        as farr as land is known.   30

The desert-dwellers at his beck shall bend:
  his foes them suppliant at his feete shall fling:
the kinges of Tharsis homage guifts shall send;
    so Seba, Saba, ev'ry Iland king.
      nay all, ev'n all   35

shall prostrate fall,
    that crownes and Scepters weare:
and all that stand
at their command,
    that crownes and Scepters beare.   40

For he shall here the poore when they complaine;
  and lend them help, who helplesse are opprest:
his mercy shall the needy sort sustaine;
  his force shall free their lyves that lyve distrest.
    from hidden sleight   45
    from open might
      hee shall their soules redeeme:
    his tender eyes
    shall highly prise,
      and deare their bloud esteeme.   50

So shall he long, so shall he happy live;
  health shall abound, and wealth shall never want:
they gold to hym, Arabia gold, shall give,
  which scantness dere, and dereness maketh scant,
    they still shall pray   55
    that still he may
      so live, and flourish so:
    with out his praise
    no nights, no daies,
      shall pasport have to go.   60

Looke how the woods, where enterlaced trees
  spread frendly armes each other to embrace,
joyne at the head, though distant at the knees,
  waving with wind, and lording on the place:
    so woods of corne   65
    by mountaynes borne
      shall on their showlders wave:
    and men shall passe
    the numbrous grasse,
      such store each town shall have.   70

Looke how the Sunne, soe shall his name remayne;
  as that in light, so this in glory one:
all glories that, at this all lights shall stayne:
  nor that shall faile, nor this be overthrowne.
    the dwellers all   75
    of earthly ball
      in hym shall hold them blest:
    as one that is
    of perfect blisse
      a patterne to the rest.   80

O God who art, from whom all beeings be;
  eternall Lord, whom Jacobs stock adore,
and wondrous works are done by only thee,
  blessed be thou, most blessed evermore.
    and lett thy name,   85
    thy glorious fame,
      no end of blessing know:
    lett all this Round
    thy honour sound,
      so lord, ô be it so.   90

50   *De Profundis.*

Psalm 130

From depth of grief
  where droun'd I ly,
lord for relief
  to thee I cry:
my ernest, vehment, cryeng, prayeng,   5
graunt quick, attentive, heering, waighing.

O Lord, if thou
  offences mark,
who shall not bow
  to beare the cark?   10
but with thy justice mercy dwelleth,
and makes thy worshipp more, excelleth.

Yea makes my soule
  on thee, ô lord
dependeth whole,   15
  and on thy word,
though sore with blott of sinne defaced,
yet surest hope hath firmly placed.

Who longest watch
  who soonest rise,   20
can nothing match
  the early eyes;
the greedy eies my soule errecteth,
while gods true promise it expecteth.

Then Israel   25
  on god attend:
attend him wel,
  who still thy frend,
in kindnes hath thee deere esteemed,
and often, often, erst redeemed.   30

Now, as before;
    unchanged he
will thee restore
    thy state will free;
all wickedness from Jacob driving   35
forgetting follies, faultes forgiving.

51 *A Dialogue betweene two shepheards,* Thenot
and Piers, *in praise of* ASTREA, *made by the*
excellent Lady, the lady Mary Countess of
Pembrook *at the Queenes Maiesties being at her*
house at Anno 15

Then. I sing divine ASTREAS praise,
    O Muses! help my wittes to raise,
        And heave my Verses higher.
Piers Thou needst the truth, but plainely tell,
    Which much I doubt thou canst not well,   5
        Thou art so oft a lier.

Then. If in my song no more I show,
    Than Heav'n, and Earth, and Sea do know,
        Then truely I have spoken.
Piers Sufficeth not no more to name,   10
    But being no lesse, the like, the same,
        Else lawes of truth be broken.

Then. Then say, she is so good, so faire,
    With all the earth she may compare,
        Not Momus selfe denying.   15
Piers Compare may thinke where likenesse holds,
    Nought like to her the earth enfoldes,
        I lookt to finde you lying.

Then. ASTREA sees with Wisedomes sight,
    Astrea workes by Vertues might,   20
        And joyntly both do stay in her.
Piers Nay take from them, her hand, her minde,
    The one is lame, the other blinde,
        Shall still your lying staine her?

Then. Soone as ASTREA shewes her face,   25
    Strait every ill avoides the place,
        And every good aboundeth.
Piers Nay long before her face doth showe,
    The last doth come, the first doth goe,
        How lowde this lie resoundeth!   30

Then. ASTREA is our chiefest joy,
Our chiefest guard against annoy,
Our chiefest wealth, our treasure.
Piers Where chiefest are, there others bee,
To us none else but only shee; 35
When wilt thow speake in measure?

Then. ASTREA may be justly sayd,
A field in flowry Roabe arrayd,
In Season freshly springing.
Piers That Spring indures but shortest time, 40
This never leaves *Astreas* clime,
Thou liest, instead of singing.

Then. As heavenly light that guides the day
Right so doth shine each lovely Ray,
That from *Astraea* flyeth. 45
Piers Nay, darkness oft that light enclowdes,
Astreas beames no darknes shrowdes;
How lowdly *Thenot* lyeth!

Then. ASTREA rightly terme I may
A manly Palme, a Maiden Bay, 50
Her verdure never dying.
Piers Palm oft is crooked, Bay is lowe,
She still upright, still high doth growe
Good *Thenot* leave thy lying.

Then. Then Piers, of friendship tell me why, 55
My meaning true, my words should ly,
And strive in vaine to raise her?
Piers Words from conceit do only rise,
Above conceit her honour flies;
But silence, nought can praise her. 60

(late 1590s)

15 *Momus*: Greek god of ridicule, therefore a fault-finder   50 *Palme*: associated both with
royalty and virginity *Bay*: evergreen; the reward of poetry

ANONYMOUS
(*c.*1500/1525)

COMPOSED in the first quarter of the sixteenth century, this is a keen, or
mourning song, the earliest Gaelic woman's poem in the vernacular (as distinct
from poems in learned metres, some of which survive from the fifteenth
century). It is held, on internal evidence, to have been composed by a woman
whose husband was killed on their wedding day. In some versions, the husband

is named as Eòghan: there was unfortunately no chief of Mackintosh called
Eòghan between 1500 and 1525, so somewhere in oral transmission, the name of
Eòghan's clan has been lost and Mackintosh substituted, though this does not in
itself militate against the thesis that the poem is correctly attributed to a woman.
The fact that the clan-name does not appear in the verse itself means that it was
easy for it to get lost in transmission. The keen is sung to the pipe tune, *Cumha
Mhic an Tòisich*, 'MacIntosh's Lament', but it is not known whether this was the
original tune.

52   *Bealach a' Ghàraidh*

    Ochain a Laoigh, leag iad thu,
Ochain a Laoigh, leag iad thu,
Ochain a Laoigh, leag iad thu,
    'M bealach a' ghàraidh

'S truagh nach robh mis' an sin,   5
'S truagh nach robh mis' an sin,
'S truagh nach robh mis' an sin,
    Is ceathr' air gach làimh dhomh.

An leann thog iad gu d' bhanais,
An leann thog iad gu d' bhanais,   10
An leann thog iad gu d' bhanais,
    Air d' fharaire bhà e.

Bha mi 'm bhrèidich's am ghruagaich,
Am bhrèidich 's am ghruagaich,
Am bhrèidich 's am ghruagaich,   15
    'S am bhantraich san aon uair ud.

Gun chron air an t-saoghal ort,
Gun chron air an t-saoghal ort,
Gun chron air an t-saoghal ort,
    Ach nach d'fheud thu saoghal bhuan fhàistinn.   20

    Ochain a Laoigh, leag iad thu, &c.

52   *The Breach in the Wall*

    Alas, my love, they knocked you down,
Alas, my love, they knocked you down,
Alas, my love, they knocked you down,
    In the breach in the wall.

It is a shame I was not there,   5
It is a shame I was not there,
It is a shame I was not there,
    With four men at either hand.

The ale they brought to your wedding,
The ale they brought to your wedding,
The ale they brought to your wedding,   10
   Was drunk at your wake.

I was a bride and a maiden,
A bride and a maiden,
A bride and a maiden   15
   And a widow all at once.

You had no fault to speak of,
You had no fault to speak of,
You had no fault to speak of,
   But that you did not betoken a long life.   20

     Alas, my love, they knocked you down, &c.

ANNE WRIGGLESWORTH
(fl. 1584)

MRS WRIGGLESWORTH got into a good deal of trouble with this verse, which
was the object of a libel case brought against her. She was a working-class
woman in Hertfordshire, and she is only unusual among the many early modern
women scolds, ballad-makers, and libellers we know of in that the text of her
ballad is preserved. It is problematic, however, in that she denied writing it. Her
claim that 'she hard it as she came to the market to Oxford abowte Christmes
last of one Robert Nevell who did synge it by the way' fits neither the implied
female *persona* of the rhyme, nor Anne Wrigglesworth's repeating the rhyme
over a number of months 'and for good will she told the same to Goodwife
Willyams and her doughter, and to Goodwife Cadman and her daughter, becaus
she thought it was made to their discreditt.' She was dismissed with a caution.
In any case, the important point here is her use of the rhyme, rather than
questions of authorship of an *urtext* which is a notoriously elusive concept at this
oral level of the use of verse.

53   *'Yf I had as faire a face as John Williams'*

Yf I had as faire a face as John Williams
   his daughter Elzabeth hasse,
Then wold I were a taudrie lace as Goodman
   Bolts daughter Marie dosse;

And if I had as mutch money in my pursse   5
   as Cadmans daughter Margaret hasse,
Then wold I have a basterd lesse
   Then Butlers mayde Helen hasse.

1 *Williams*: Willms MS   3 *were*: wear

ELIZABETH, LADY TANFIELD, née SYMONDES
(?1565–1628)

ELIZABETH SYMONDES was the daughter of Giles Symondes of Claye, Norfolk and wife of Sir Laurence Tanfield, a lawyer, who became Lord Chief Baron of the Exchequer. Her mother was Catherine Lee, sister of Sir Henry Lee, the lover of Anne Vavasour (no. 44). As allegations of fraud and corruption proliferated against him, common rumour openly suggested that Lady Tanfield was equally ready to take bribes to influence her husband's legal judgements. Her husband's tenants at Great Tew, Oxfordshire, complained of her that 'she saith that the inhabitants of Tu are more worthy to be ground to powder than to have any favour shewed to us, and that she will play the devil amongst us'. Sir Laurence's defence of his enclosing activities is weakened by the numerous complaints against him elsewhere (HMC, *Third report*, 31). She and her husband left such a legacy of hatred behind them that there is a local legend in Burford, Oxfordshire (where Sir Laurence is buried), that if the level of the river sinks beneath a certain point, the Tanfields will return from hell. As late as the eighteenth century, when a drought sent the river down towards this level, the locals turned out to pour in water to prevent this from happening. The couple's sole child and heiress, also Elizabeth, was a poet and playwright, and is represented in this volume. It is therefore interesting that a portrait of a lady in masque costume now in the Tate Gallery (T03031) is thought to be Lady Tanfield. As her daughter's biography will show, the relationship between them was not good, but the portrait may suggest that they had an interest in drama in common.

54   *Tomb of Sir Lawrence Tanfield obiit 30 Ap. 1625 erected by Lady Tanfield 1628.*

Here shadow lie
Whil'st life is sadd,
Still hopes to die
To him she hadd

In bliss is hee,   5
Whom I lov'd best
Thrise happie shee
With him to rest.

So shall I be
With him I loved   10
And hee with mee
And both us blessed

Love made me Poet
And this I writt,
My harte did doe yt   15
And not my witt.

ANON: possibly MARIE LAUDER, née MAITLAND
(born after 1528, fl. before 1586)

MARIE MAITLAND was the daughter of Richard Maitland, Lord Lethington (1496–1586), who was Keeper of the Great Seal of Scotland until 1567, despite having gone blind. Her mother was Mary, daughter of Sir Thomas Cranston of Crosbie, and she was one of four daughters and three sons. The statesman William Maitland of Lethington, the eldest son of Sir Richard (b. *c.*1528) was her brother. Marie Maitland married Alexander Lauder of Hatton, and her son George Lauder was the author of a number of poems very highly regarded by the early nineteenth-century Scottish antiquarian David Laing.

In a manuscript written either by or for Marie Maitland, there survives this overtly lesbian poem from a woman in love with another woman, expressing a wish that one of them change sex so they can marry. The addressee is unknown: there is not enough evidence for the life of Marie Maitland to allow us to identify any of her personal friends. The bulk of the MS is written in two styles, 'a small but clear form of the old Scottish hand', and a large Italic lettering. As Arthur F. Marotti has pointed out (*Manuscript Print and the Renaissance English Lyric*. (Ithaca, NY & London: Cornell University Press, 1995), 25–6), women almost always wrote italic: it is therefore possible that the italic hand is that of Marie Maitland. Perhaps the likeliest hypothesis is that this poem is by Marie Maitland herself. A poem to her, 'To your self' (in the same manuscript, fo. 126) makes considerable claims for her as a poet: stanza 1 compares her to Sappho, stanza 2 to Olimpia Morata, fifteenth-century Latin poet and polymath. Conceivably, other anonymous poetry in this manuscript may be the work of the same poet: I would suggest the possibility that no. lxxi, fo. 116, 'gif faithfulnes 3e find' is hers, on stylistic grounds.

55   *'As phœbus in his spheris hicht'*

     As phœbus in his spheris hicht
     precellis the kaip Crepusculein
     And phœbe all the starris licht
     your splendour so madame I wein
     Dois onlie pas all feminine   5
     In sapience superlative
     Indewit with vertewis sa devine
     as leirned pallas redivive.

     And as be hid vertew unknawin
     The adamant drawis yron thairtill   10
     your courtes nature so hes drawin
     My hairt youris to continew still
     Sa greit Joy dois my spreit fulfill
     contempling your perfectioun
     Ye weild me holie at your will   15
     and raviss my affectioun.

Your perles Vertew dois provoike
and loving kyndnes so dois move
My Mynd to freindschip reciproc
That treuth sall try sa far above   20
The auntient heroicis love
as salbe thocht prodigious
ad plaine experience sall prove
Mair holie and religious.

In amitie perithous   25
to theseus wes not so traist
Nor Till Achilles patroclus
nor pilades to trew orest
Nor yit achates luif so lest
to gud Ænee nor sic freindschip   30
Dauid to Ionathan profest
nor Titus trew to kynd Iosip.

Nor yit Penelope I wiss
so luiffed ulisses in hir dayis
Nor Ruth the kynd moabitiss   35
Nohemie as the scripture sayis
nor portia quhais worthie prayiss
In romaine historeis we reid
Qha did devoir the fyrie brayis
To follow brutus to the deid   40

Wald michtie Jove grant me the hap
With yow to have your brutus pairt
and metamorphosing our schap
my sex intill his vaill convert
No brutus then could caus ws smart   45
as we doe now unhappie wemen
Then sould we bayth with Joyfull hairt
honour and bliss the band of hymen

Yea certainlie we sould efface
Pollux and castoris memorie   50
and gif that thay deservit place
amang the starris for loyaltie
Then our mair perfyte amitie
mair worthie recompence sould merit
In hevin eternall deitie   55
amang the goddis till Inherit.

And as we ar thocht till our wo
nature and fortoun doe coniure
and hymen also be our fo
Yit luif of vertew dois procuire   60

freindschip and amitie sa suire
with sa greit fervencie and force
Sa constantlie quhilk sall Induire
That not but deid sall ws divorce.

And thoucht adversitie ws vex   65
Yit be our freindschip salbe sein
Thair is mair constancie in our sex
Than ever amang men hes bein
no troubill / torment / greif / or tein
nor erthlie thing sall ws dissever   70
Sic constancie sall ws mantein
In perfyte amitie for ever.

2 *kaip Crepusculein*: cape of twilight   3 *phœbe*: the moon   6 *onlie*: is the only one
to   8 *pallas*: Minerva, goddess of wisdom; *redivive*: brought back to life   10 *yron
thairtill*: iron to it   15 *holie*: wholly   25 *perithous/Theseus* mutually devoted
friends   27 *Achilles/patroclus*: friends and lovers from Homer's *Iliad*   29 *achates*:
Achates, faithful friend of Aeneas (Virgil, *Aeneid*)   31 *David*: loved Jonathan with a
love 'surpassing the love of women', 1 Samuel 18: 1   32 *Titus*: Roman emperor, said to
have taken Josippus as a lover.   33 *Penelope*: faithful wife of Ulysses (Homer,
Odyssey)   35 *Ruth*: was passionately devoted to her mother-in-law Naomi (Ruth 1:
16)   37 *portia*: wife of Brutus, deprived of other means to commit suicide on his
death, did so by swallowing live coals (brayis)   40 *to the deid*: unto death   43 *schap*:
shape   44 *vaill*: will   50 *Pollux*: and Castor, devoted brothers, the sons of Leda, turned
into stars as the Twins

'E.D.' [ELIZABETH ?COBURNE, née
DOUGLAS]
(fl. 1587)

A NUMBER of women poets flourished at the Scottish court of King James.
These verses by E.D. were written to accompany 'The Triumphs of the most
famous Poet, Mr Frances Petrarke, translated out of italian into inglish [i.e.
lowland Scots] by Mr Wm Foular, P. of Hallicke', dedicated to Lady Jean
Fleming and Lady Thirlstane, 12 Dec. 1587. She may have been the Elizabeth
Douglas whom Fowler records as a patroness in a published, single-sheet
funerary poem (unfortunately undated). Another possible candidate is Elizabeth
Douglas, Countess of Errol, to whom Fowler dedicated a sonnet, the youngest
daughter of William Douglas, Earl of Morton, who married Francis Hay, ninth
Earl of Errol. E.D.'s poems are preserved in autograph: an elegant italic, laid out
as a presentation page.

   Fowler, her subject, was of burgess background, and rose to favour by means
of verse writing. He was younger than the other court poets of James VI, nearer
the king's own age. He was for many years court official and a royal secretary,
and was over a long period an intelligencer for Walsingham. He became
secretary to Queen Anne. He later ousted the court poet Montgomerie from
place, as Montgomerie had ousted his predecessor Polwarth. 'Fowler as a poet

was copious and determined, well-lettered and wide-ranging, his work bearing witness to the new interest in Italian poetry' (H. M. Shire, *Song, Dance and Poetry of the Court of Scotland under King James VI* (Cambridge: Cambridge University Press, 1969, 81). His translation of the *Trionfi*, which is iambic pentameter, incorporates glosses into the text in medieval style. Interestingly, another sonnet addressed to Fowler, possibly by Lady Mary Beton, which was presumably written a little earlier, urges him to abandon lyric in favour of the imitation of Petrarch (Edinburgh, National Library of Scotland 2065, fo. 6ʳ). He was the uncle of the better-known William Drummond of Hawthornden, a friend of Ben Jonson's, also celebrated in a dedicatory poem by a woman friend, Mary Oxlie.

This poem is a testimony to the fashionable poetry of the 1580s, and a reminder that much of what we think of as quintessentially Elizabethan poetry —Sidney, Marlowe, Shakespeare—was not actually published before 1590. The idea that seven cities contended for the title of Homer's birthplace is a trope originating in the Greek Anthology.

56   *E.D. in prayse of Mr W fouler her freind*

The glorious greks dois prayse their *Homers* quill
and citeis sevin dois stryve whair he was borne
The *latines* dois of *Virgill* vaunt at will
And Sulmo thinks her ovid dois adorne
The *Spanioll* laughs (save *Lucan*) all to scorne   5
and *France* for *Ronsard* standis and settis him out
The better sorte for *Bartas* blawis the horne
and England thinks her *Surrey* first but doubt
To prayse thair owen these countreis gois about
Italians lyke *Petrarchas* noble grace   10
Who weill deservis first place amangs that rout
But *Fouler* thou fare dois thame all deface
    No *vanting* Grece no *Romaine* now will stryve
    They all do yeilde sen Fouler dois arryve.

(1587)

This poem may be intended to invoke Martial, *Epigrams*. 1. 61, a poem on the birthplaces of celebrated authors   1–2 *Homer*: died forgotten and obscure; seven cities later claimed to be his birthplace   3 *Virgill*: author of the *Aeneid*   4 *Sulmo*: birthplace of Ovid, author of *Metamorphoses* and other poems   5 *Lucan*: a Latin poet of Spain, author of the *Pharsalia*   6 *Ronsard*: Pierre de Ronsard (1524–85), much admired French lyric poet   7 *Bartas*: Guillaume Salluste, Sieur du Bartas (1544–90), greatly admired in England (notably by Anne Bradstreet) following the English translation of his *Weekes* by Joshua Sylvester; *blawis the horne*: signals appreciation   8 *Surrey*: Henry Howard, Earl of Surrey (1517–47). Many of his poems were printed in *Tottel's Miscellany* in 1557: like Fowler, he studied Italian models, especially Petrarch; *but doubt*: without doubt   10 *Petrarchas*: Francesco Petrarca (1304–74) one of the first important Italian poets to write in the vernacular, crowned Poet Laureate in Rome in 1341, immensely influential as a love-poet   11 *rout*: group

57   *E.D. in commendation of the Author and*
his choise

When *Alexander* entred phrygian land
Achilles tombe he weeping did behauld
O happie Wight who suche a trumpet fand
& happye thou who hes his vertewes tauld
Thou happye Laura thou by fame enrold   5
And happ to the o Petrarch dois befall
Thy glorye shee, her prayse thou dois unfold,
How may thy fame o *Fouler* then be small
Who sings Dame Lauras prayse but fein3et all
This verteous Dame to whome thy worke thou gevis   10
to her of right those triumphs sing thou shall
No *Laura* heir but ladye *Jeane* it is
    O ladye live! thy Fouler the extolls
    Whose golden pen thy name in fame enrolls.

(1587)

Title *choise*: Petrarch's *Canzoniere*, translated by Fowler as *The Triumphs of Love*   1–2
Alexander: the Great—he paid a famous visit to the tomb of Achilles   3 *trumpet*:
Homer   5 *Laura*: Petrarch's mistress, to whom he addressed the *Canzionere*   9 fein3et:
invented   12 *heir*: here; *Jeane*: Lady Jean Fleming, dedicatee of Fowler's translation

AEMILIA LANYER (née BASSANI)
(1569–1645)

AEMILIA was the daughter of Baptista Bassani, described as 'a native of Venice'
in his will, and Margaret Bassani or Johnson, described in the same document as
his 'reputed wieff' (PRO 11/58, fo. 154). Aemilia was the couple's second child:
an elder sister, Angela, was married to Joseph Hollande, gentleman, by 1576.
Aemilia was christened on 17 January 1569. Her father was 'one of the Musi-
tions of our Sovereigne Ladye the Quenes majestie' and a man of some property:
at the time of his death, he owned three houses in Spitalfields, and was in a
position to leave his younger daughter a dowry of £100, besides the rents and
use of the three houses after the death of their mother Margaret. Baptista
Bassani's will was witnessed on 3 January 1576, so he presumably died in that
month, when Aemilia was 7. Most of what is known about her life at this stage is
derived from the casebooks kept by the astrologer Simon Foreman, whom she
consulted in 1597. He notes that she recalled that 'her mother did outlive her
father—and the wealth of her father failed before he died & he began to be
miserable in his estate' (Oxford, Bodleian Library Ashmole 226, fo. 95ᵛ).

    Despite this unpromising start, either Bassani or Margaret Johnson was able
to invoke some patronage for their young daughter, since her poem 'To the
Ladie Susan, Countesse Dowager of Kent', speaks of her as 'the Mistris of my
youth'. She also told Foreman that she had been brought up in Kent. Thus, it

seems as though she was educated in the Countess's household, which may explain how she acquired an education. When she was 18, her mother died. At or around this time, Aemilia became the mistress of the Lord Chamberlain, Henry Cary, Lord Hunsdon, some forty-five years her senior. On her own testimony (to Simon Foreman), he was generous to her: she was 'maintained in great pomp', had forty pounds a year of her own, and was wealthy in money and jewels. She was hastily married to Alfonso Lanyer, one of the Queen's musicians, in 1592 when it was found that she had become pregnant. Her son, born early in 1593, was named Henry, presumably as an unequivocal signal that Henry Cary, not Alfonso Lanyer, was his father. This marriage of convenience was not a success at first: by her way of it, 'her husband hath delte hardly with her and spent and consumed her goods and she is nowe . . . in debt'. Her several visits to Foreman indicate that she was not in good health during her early married life. She reported that she suffered repeated miscarriages, and bore a daughter, Odillya, in 1598, who lived for less than a year. However, the window on her affairs opened by the Foreman consultations suggests mutual loyalty between Aemilia and her husband, despite their differences. The couple hoped to rise in the world: in 1597, Lanyer went to sea with the Earl of Essex, hoping to be knighted (a hope which was not fulfilled). By September that year, Aemilia's indebtedness led Foreman to hope that she might be willing to prostitute herself to him: 'she is nowe very needy and in debte & it seams for Lucrese sake wilbe a good fellowe for necessity doth compell.' In fact, though she allowed him a certain amount of fumbling, he never actually achieved his aim, and the consultations ceased.

The Lanyers' income stabilized somewhat in 1604, when Alphonso received a patent from King James granting him the income from weighing hay and grain. Before 1609, Aemilia spent some time at Cookham with Margaret, Countess of Cumberland, and her daughter, Anne Clifford. These visits were the inspiration for her *Description of Cooke-ham*, and also perhaps the starting-point of *Salve, Deus*, as she suggests in lines 1–6 of the former poem. Alphonso died in 1613, and the patent became the subject of litigation between his widow and his own relatives. In 1617, Aemilia founded a school at St Giles in the Field, which she kept until 1619: this venture came to an end after a series of suits and countersuits beween her and her landlord over rent and building repairs. Little is known of her later life. She probably joined the household of her son Henry, who also became a court musician (a flautist): he died in 1633, at the age of 40, and the fact that thereafter Aemilia's continued legal battles with the Lanyers over the patent are carried on in the name of herself and her grandchildren (Mary and Henry) suggests that she may have had a role in helping their mother Joyce (née Mansfield) to care for them. She was buried on 3 April 1645 at St James, Clerkenwell, where she is listed as a 'pensioner', a term which suggests that she had received some steady support from a patron, perhaps from the King.

58 *from* Salve Deus Rex Judaeorum (*ll. 745–840*)

Now *Pontius Pilate* is to judge the Cause
Of faultlesse *Jesus*, who before him stands;
Who neither hath offended Prince, nor Lawes,
Although he now be brought in woefull bands:
O noble Governour, make thou yet a pause,   5
Doe not in innocent blood imbrue thy hands;

But heare the words of thy most worthy wife,
Who sends to thee, to beg her Saviours life.

Let barb'rous crueltie farre depart from thee,
And in true Justice take afflictions part;
Open thine eies, that thou the truth mai'st see,
Doe not the thing that goes against thy heart,
Condemne not him that must thy Saviour be;
But view his holy Life, his good desert.
    Let not us Women glory in Mens fall,
    Who had power given to over-rule us all.

Till now your indiscretion sets us free,
And makes our former fault much lesse appeare;
Our Mother *Eve*, who tasted of the Tree,
Giving to *Adam* what shee held most deare,
Was simply good, and had no powre to see,
The after-comming harme did not appeare:
    The subtile Serpent that our Sex betraide,
    Before our fall so sure a plot had laide.

That undiscerning Ignorance perceav'd
No guile, or craft that was by him intended;
For had she knowne, of what we were bereav'd,
To his request she had not condiscended.
But she (poore soule) by cunning was deceav'd,
No hurt therein her harmelesse Heart intended:
    For she alleadg'd Gods word, which he denies,
    That they should die, but even as Gods, be wise.

But surely *Adam* can not be excusde,
Her fault though great, yet hee was most too blame;
What Weakenesse offerd, Strength might have refusde,
Being Lord of all, the greater was his shame:
Although the Serpents craft had her abusde,
Gods holy word ought all his actions frame,
    For he was Lord and King of all the earth,
    Before poore *Eve* had either life or breath.

Who being fram'd by Gods eternall hand,
The perfect'st man that ever breath'd on earth;
And from Gods mouth receiv'd that strait command,
The breach whereof he knew was present death:
Yea having powre to rule both Sea and Land,
Yet with one Apple wonne to loose that breath
    Which God had breathed in his beauteous face,
    Bringing us all in danger and disgrace.

And then to lay the fault on Patience backe,
That we (poore women) must endure it all;

We know right well he did discretion lacke,
Beeing not perswaded thereunto at all;
If *Eve* did erre, it was for knowledge sake,
The fruit beeing faire perswaded him to fall:
    No subtill Serpents falshood did betray him,   55
    If he would eate it, who had powre to stay him?

Not *Eve*, whose fault was onely too much love,
Which made her give this present to her Deare,
That what shee tasted, he likewise might prove,
Whereby his knowledge might become more cleare;   60
He never sought her weakenesse to reprove,
With those sharp words, which he of God did heare:
    Yet Men will boast of Knowledge, which he tooke,
    From *Eves* faire hand, as from a learned Booke.

If any Evill did in her remaine,   65
Beeing made of him, he was the ground of all;
If one of many Worlds could lay a staine
Upon our Sexe, and worke so great a fall
To wretched Man, by Satans subtill traine;
What will so fowle a fault amongst you all?   70
    Her weakenesse did the Serpents words obay;
    But you in malice Gods deare Sonne betray.

Whom, if unjustly you condemne to die,
Her sinne was small, to what you doe commit;
All mortall sinnes that doe for vengeance crie,   75
Are not to be compared unto it:
If many worlds would altogether trie,
By all their sinnes the wrath of God to get;
    This sinne of yours, surmounts them all as farre
    As doth the Sunne, another little starre.   80

Then let us have our Libertie againe,
And challendge to your selves no Sov'raigntie;
You came not in the world without our paine,
Make that a barre against your crueltie;
Your fault beeing greater, why should you disdaine   85
Our beeing your equals, free from tyranny?
    If one weake woman simply did offend,
    This sinne of yours, hath no excuse, nor end.

To which (poore soules) we never gave consent,
Witnesse thy wife (O *Pilate*) speakes for all;   90
Who did but dreame, and yet a message sent,
That thou should'st have nothing to doe at all
With that just man; which, if thy heart relent,
Why wilt thou be a reprobate with *Saul*?

To seeke the death of him that is so good,   95
For thy soules health to shed his dearest blood.

1–8 Based on Matthew 27: 19. Pilate's wife had a dream in which she saw him sentence the innocent Christ to death, and sent an urgent message to the court advising Pilate to release him; later tradition made her a Christian   66 Genesis 2: 21–3

59   *The Description of Cooke-ham*

Farewell (sweet Cooke-ham) where I first obtain'd
Grace from that Grace where perfit Grace remain'd;
And where the Muses gave their full consent,
I should have powre the virtuous to content:
Where princely Palace will'd me to indite,   5
The sacred Storie of the Soules delight.
Farewell (sweet Place) where Virtue then did rest,
And all delights did harbour in her breast:
Never shall my sad eies againe behold
Those pleasures which my thoughts did then unfold: 10
Yet you (great Lady) Mistris of that Place,
From whose desires did spring this worke of Grace;
Vouchsafe to thinke upon those pleasures past,
As fleeting worldly Joyes that could not last:
Or, as dimme shadowes of celestiall pleasures,   15
Which are desir'd above all earthly treasures.
Oh how (me thought) against you thither came,
Each part did seeme some new delight to frame!
The House receiv'd all ornaments to grace it,
And would indure no foulenesse to deface it.   20
The Walkes put on their summer Liveries,
And all things else did hold like similies:
The Trees with leaves, with fruits, with flowers clad,
Embrac'd each other, seeming to be glad,
Turning themselves to beauteous Canopies,   25
To shade the bright Sunne from your brighter eies:
The cristall Streames with silver spangles graced,
While by the glorious Sunne they were embraced:
The little Birds in chirping notes did sing,
To entertaine both You and that sweet Spring.   30
And *Philomela* with her sundry leyes,
Both You and that delightfull Place did praise.
Oh how me thought each plant, each floure, each tree
Set forth their beauties then to welcome thee:
The very Hills right humbly did descend,   35
When you to tread upon them did intend.
And as you set your feete, they still did rise,
Glad that they could receive so rich a prise.

The gentle Windes did take delight to bee
Among those woods that were to grac'd by thee.   40
And in sad murmure utterd pleasing sound.
That Pleasure in that place might more abound:
The swelling Bankes deliver'd all their pride,
When such a Phœnix once they had espide.
Each Arbor, Banke, each Seate, each stately Tree,   45
Thought themselves honor'd in supporting thee,
The pretty Birds would oft come to attend thee,
Yet flie away for feare they should offend thee:
The little creatures in the Burrough by
Would come abroad to sport them in your eye;   50
Yet fearefull of the Bowe in your faire Hand,
Would runne away when you did make a stand.
Now let me come unto that stately Tree,
Wherein such goodly Prospects you did see;
That Oake that did in height his fellows passe,   55
As much as lofty trees, low growing grasse:
Much like a comely Cedar streight and tall,
Whose beauteous stature farre exceeded all:
How often did you visite this faire tree,
Which seeming joyfull in receiving thee,   60
Would like a Palme tree spread his armes abroad,
Desirous that you there should make abode:
Whose faire greene leaves much like a comely vaile,
Defended Phebus when he would assaile:
Whose pleasing boughes did yeeld a coole fresh ayre,   65
Joying his happinesse when you were there.
Where beeing seated, you might plainely see,
Hills, vales, and woods, as if on bended knee
They had appeard, your honour to salute,
Or to preferre some strange unlook'd for sute: 70
All interlac'd with brookes and christall springs,
A Prospect fit to please the eyes of Kings:
And thirteene shires appear'd all in your sight,
Europe could not affoard much more delight.
What was there then but gave you all content,   75
While you the time in meditation spent,
Of their Creators powre, which there you saw,
In all his Creatures held a perfit Law;
And in their beauties did you plaine descrie,
His beauty, wisdome, grace, love, majestie.   80
In these sweet woods how often did you walke,
With Christ and his Apostles there to talke;
Placing his holy writ in some faire tree,
To meditate what you therein did see:
With *Moyses* you did mount his holy Hill,   85

To know his pleasure, and performe his Will.
With lovely *David* you did often sing,
His holy Hymnes to Heavens Eternall King.
And in sweet musicke did your soule delight,
To sound his prayses, morning, noone, and night.   90
With blessed *Joseph* you did often feed
Your pined brethren, when they stood in need.
And that sweet Lady sprung from *Cliffords* race,
Of noble *Bedfords* blood, faire streame of Grace;
To honourable *Dorset* now espows'd,   95
In whose faire breast true virtue then was hous'd:
Oh what delight did my weake spirits find
In those pure parts of her well framed mind:
And yet it grieves me that I cannot be
Neere unto her, whose virtues did agree   100
With those faire ornaments of outward beauty,
Which did enforce from all both love and dutie.
Unconstant Fortune, thou art most to blame,
Who casts us downe into so lowe a frame:
Where our great friends we cannot dayly see,   105
So great a diffrence is there in degree.
Many are placed in those Orbes of state,
Parters in honour, so ordain'd by Fate;
Neerer in show, yet farther off in love,
In which, the lowest alwayes are above.   110
But whither am I carried in conceit?
My Wit too weake to conster of the great.
Why not? although we are but borne of earth,
We may behold the Heavens, despising death;
And loving heaven that is so farre above,   115
May in the end vouchsafe us entire live.
Therefore sweet Memorie doe thou retaine
Those pleasures past, which will not turne againe:
Remember beauteous *Dorsets* former sports,
So farre from beeing toucht by ill reports;   120
Wherein my selfe did alwaies beare a part,
While reverend Love presented my true heart:
Those recreations let me beare in mind,
Which her sweet youth and noble thoughts did finde:
Whereof depriv'd, I evermore must grieve,   125
Hating blind Fortune, carelesse to relieve.
And you sweet Cooke-ham, whom these Ladies leave,
I now must tell the griefe you did conceave
At their departure; when they went away,
How every thing retaind a sad dismay: 130
Nay long before, when once an inkling came,
Me thought each thing did unto sorrow frame:

The trees that were so glorious in our view,
Forsooke both flowres and fruit, when once they knew
Of your depart, their very leaves did wither,   135
Changing their colours as they grewe together.
But when they saw this had no powre to stay you,
They often wept, though speechlesse, could not pray you;
Letting their teares in your faire bosoms fall,
As if they said, Why will ye leave us all?   140
This being vaine, they cast their leaves away,
Hoping that pitie would have made you stay:
Their frozen tops like Ages hoarie heaires,
Showes their disasters, languishing in feares:
A swarthy riveld ryne all over spread,   145
Their dying bodies half alive, half dead.
But your occasions call'd you so away,
That nothing there had power to make you stay:
Yet did I see a noble gratefull minde,
Requiting each according to their kind,   150
Forgetting not to turne and take your leave
Of these sad creatures, powrelesse to receive
Your favour when with griefe you did depart,
Placing their former pleasures in your heart;
Giving great charge to noble Memory,   155
There to preserve their love continually:
But specially the love of that faire tree,
That first and last you did vouchsafe to see:
In which it pleas'd you oft to take the ayre,
With noble *Dorset*, then a virgin faire: 160
Where many a learned Booke was read and skand
To this faire tree, taking me by the hand,
You did repeat the pleasures which had past,
Seeming to grieve they could no longer last.
And with a chaste, yet loving kisse tooke leave,   165
Of which sweet kisse I did it soone bereave:
Scorning a sencelesse creature should possesse
So rare a favour, so great happinesse.
No other kisse it could receive from me,
For feare to give backe what it took of thee: 170
So I ingratefull Creature did deceive it,
Of that which you vouchsaft in love to leave it.
And though it oft had giv'n me much content,
Yet this great wrong I never could repent:
But of the happiest made it most forlorne,   175
To shew that nothing's free from Fortunes scorne,
While all the rest with this more beauteous tree,
Made their sad consort Sorrowes harmony.
The floures that on the banks and walkes did grow,

Crept in the ground, the Grasse did weepe for woe.   180
The Windes and Waters seem'd to chide together,
Because you went away they know not whither:
And those sweet Brookes that ranne so faire and cleare,
With griefe and trouble wrinckled did appeare.
Those pretty Birds that wonted were to sing,   185
Now neither sing, nor chirp, nor use their wing;
But with their tender feet on some bare spray,
Warble forth sorrow, and their owne dismay.
Faire *Philomela* leaves her mournefull Ditty,
Drownd in dead sleepe, yet can procure no pittie: 190
Each arbour, banke, each seate, each stately tree,
Lookes bare and desolate now for want of thee;
Turning greene tresses into frostie gray,
While in cold griefe they wither all away.
The Sunne grew weake, his beames no comfort gave,   195
While all greene things did make the earth their grave:
Each brier, each bramble, when you went away,
Caught fast your clothes, thinking to make you stay:
Delightfull Eccho wonted to reply
To our last words, did now for sorrow die: 200
The house cast off each garment that might grace it,
Putting on Dust and Cobwebs to deface it.
All desolation then there did appeare,
When you were going whom they held so deare.
This last farewell to *Cooke-ham* here I give,   205
When I am dead thy name in this may live,
Wherein I have perform'd her noble hest,
Whose virtues lodge in my unworthy breast,
And ever shall, so long as life remaines,
   Tying my heart to her by those rich chaines.   210

(c.1609–10)

The earliest example of the Stuart country-house poem, anticipating the two chief strands of
the genre: the praise of hospitality and the, often symbolically interpreted, description of the
estate. Title *Cooke-ham*: in Berkshire near Maidenhead. The royal manor was leased to the
Countess of Cumberland's brother, William Russell of Thorhaugh, in 1603; the Countess
resided periodically there until *c*.1605   6 *sacred Storie*: Christ's passion as related in the
Salve Deus   31 *Philomela*: nightingale; *leyes*: songs 32 *delightfull Place*: *locus amoenus* of
classical tradition   51 *Bowe*: the Countess is imagined as Diana, the goddess of hunting and
chastity   55–61 *Oake... Palme*: these are the trees which associate with the (female)
personification of holy Wisdom in Ecclesiasticus 24: 17–19, thus paying an audacious and
elegant compliment to the Countess   83 *holy writ*: compare Lady Anne Clifford, who
pinned up texts and sayings all round her room for general edification   85 Exodus 24: 13–8,
25–32, 33   91–2 *Joseph... need*: Joseph fed his brothers when famine struck, although they
had sold him into service in Egypt (Genesis 42–5)   93–5 Lady Anne Clifford, daughter of
Lady Margaret (Russell) Clifford, married Richard Sackville, Lord Buckhurst, third earl of
Dorset, on 25 February 1609   112 *conster*: construe   119 *Dorsets former sports*: masques
and dancing; Lady Anne performed at court in *The Masque of Beauty* (1609) and *The Masque
of Queens* (1610)   145 *riveld ryne*: wrinkled bark   210 *her*: the Countess of Cumberland

ANNE DOWRICHE, née EDGCUMBE
(fl. 1589–1596)

ANNE DOWRICHE came from a prominent West Country family, the Edge-cumbes of Mount Edgecumbe, Cornwall. Her father's will was proved in 1560, at which point she was described as 'under age', so she was perhaps born *c.* 1550. Her sister Margaret Denny, née Edgecumbe was a maid of honour to Elizabeth I. Her mother, who was probably the sister of Sir Richard Rogers, was once accused of wrecking in Mount's Bay and trafficking in stolen goods. More respectably, her father, Sir Richard Edgcumbe, and her brother Piers both became MPs. In 1580, she married Hugh Dowriche, a Devon gentleman, graduate of Oxford, and rector first of Honiton (1587) then of Lapford in Devon, and bore him four children, as well as writing commendatory verses for *The Jaylors' conversion*, a religious pamphlet by him published in 1599. In 1589 Anne published *The French History*, a long historical poem on the massacre of Protestants in and around Paris on St Bartholomew's Eve (24 August) 1572, which ought to be read in the context of the defeat of the Spanish Armada in the summer of 1588. Her major source was François Hotman's *True and Plain Report of the Furious Outrapes of France* (1573), which was also used by Marlowe for his *Massacre at Paris* (*c.*1592). The narrator is an Englishman who in the opening scene encounters a Huguenot exile while walking in the woods, and persuades him to recount his country's sufferings, which the Frenchman does 'in verse'. The concluding section of her volume consists of 'The Judgement of the Lord against this bloody and perjured King of France, Charles the 9th [1574]', which anticipates the assassination of the Duc de Guise in 1598. George Boase's *Bibliotheca Cornubiensis* (i. 118) also credits her with *A Frenchman's Songe, made upon ye death [of] ye French King, who was murdered in his own Court, by a traiterous Fryer of St Jacobs order, 1st Aug. 1589*, licensed to Edward Allde, in 1589 (perhaps a translation), of which no copy is known to survive. England responded with horror to the massacre of Protestants in and around Paris on St Bartholomew's Eve, 1572: her work expresses widely held senti-ments. Her second book also relates to the iniquities of the French: the assassination of Henri III, the last of the Valois, by a young friar called Jacques Clément. Anne's niece, also Anne Dowriche, with whom she has sometimes been confused, married first Richard Trefusis of Trefusis, then Ambrose Man-nington, the MP for Launceston in 1629, and died in 1638.

60   *The Admiralls being slaine, they likewise*
        murdred most cruellie not onelie all such frends,
        Phisitians, Preachers, and all other that were found
        hidden in the Admirals lodging, but also as manie
        as were suspected to be of that religion within the
        towne or anie where els, were lamentablie put to
        the sword, as here folowing we may plainlie see

These furies frying thus, yet thus were not content
But in the house, from place to place, like greedie houndes they went.
To search the chambers all and corners of receipt;
That from the wolfe the sheep might save his throate by no deceipt.
And such as sleeping were found naked in their bed,   5
Or gone to hide or save themselves they first cut of their head
And after fiercelie pierst with wounds both great and deepe;
Which being done, like cruell currs they throw them on a heap.
Among which wofull troope two Noble youths there were
And Pages of most worthie birth which likewise died there.   10
With these, among the rest a man of noble fame,
The Countie *Rouchfoucault* was forst at last to tast the same.
Whom for his pleasant wit the King did seeme to love;
Yet in this furie nothing might the King to mercie move.
But now in hast must be to death untimelie sent,   15
To yeeld again unto the Lord the life that he had lent.
So him at first *De Nance* commanded was to kill;
But he most stoutlie did[a] refuse this guiltlesse blood to spill.
[b]Shall I, said he, consent to doo this fearfull thing
To shed this blood, because I am commanded by the King?   20
No, God forbid, I know I have a soule to save;
So bloodie spot, to save my life, my name shall never have.
I know there is a day, a day that[c] Saints desire;
When of our deeds the king above a reckoning will require.
Obaie the King,[d] that's true, in things that honest be: 25
When I obey in wicked hests, wo worth the time to me.
For Ioab did not well[e] King David to obay,
When wickedlie the King him bad Uriah for to slay.
Those Elders did offend which shewde themselves too prone,
Those wicked letters to obey poore[f] Naboth for to stone.   30
And cursed[g] Doeg which obaide a wicked will,
Shall cursed stand for that he did the Lords annointed kill.
A murder to be done the King doth now request,
My God commands the contrary: now which to chuse wer best?
The King doth threaten death, and God doth threaten hell,   35
If for the King I should forsake my God, should I doo well?

What others see ô King, I cannot well divine,
To kill the uncondemned man, it is no charge of mine.
To slaie my deadlie foe except there were some cause
I would not yeeld; much less my frend against our sacred laws.   40
What envie doth report, ô King I cannot saie;
But this my frend a faithfull man to me hath been alwaie.
ʰTherefore I praie your Grace your rigor to asswage,
Or bid some other whom you list to execute your rage.
In matters that be good if that you list to use   45
My service, you shall see that I no peril will refuse.
Therefore I praie your Grace this answere for to take,
Which unto *Saule*ⁱ his Soldiers once were not afraid to make.
De Nance to kill his frend no wight shall ever see,
Though for refusall he were sure beheaded for to be.   50
Take heed (ô noble King) what sprite you follow now
Let no man force you doo the thing that God doth disallow
While good king *David* was by whoredome brought asleep,
He did the thing, which being wakt did force his hart to weep
While *Saule* in mallice was against good David bent,   55
He ranne to that which afterward with teares he did lament.
And whilest that *Iezabel* great mischiefe did intend
Against poore *Naboth*, she at last came to a fearfull ende.
Looke well therefore (ô king) before you leape too farre,
Least in the end this testie scab do breed a lasting scarre.   60
Well I can saie no more, but God preserve your Grace,
And graunt your soule when breath is gone with him a resting place.'

                                                          (1589)

[*Dowriche's own marginal notes*]
   ᵃ Mounsier de Nance Captaine of the Guard, refuseth to kill the Countie Rouchfoucault.   ᵇ His speeches used both privatlie to his frends, and also to the King, upon
the refusal.   ᶜ Rev. 6.10.   ᵈ Rom. 13.1, 1 Pet. 2.13, Tit. 3.1.   ᵉ 2 Sam.
11.16.   ᶠ 1 Kings 21.11.   ᵍ 1Sam. 22.18.   ʰ His speeches to the
king.   ⁱ Sam. 22.17.

12 *Rouchfoucault*: François de la Rochefoucauld, Prince de Marsillac   57 *Iezabel*: Jezebel
plotted to have Naboth executed (1 Kings 21); this incident prompted Elijah to predict
that dogs would eat Jezebel's corpse (1 Kings 21: 23); in Jehu's coup she was thrown out of
the window by her own attendants and trampled to death

61   *Verses written by a Gentlewoman upon the Jaylors Conversion*

            The man is blest which can indure,
              Whose hart doth never slide,
            When for his sinne, with fierie scourge,
              His patience shal be tride.

No daunting feare can once attainte,   5
   The conscience that is cleare:
The wicked waile that have no faith,
   When dangers doe appeare.
The rod that doth correct our life,
   And sinfull waies reprove,   10
Is said, to be a certaine signe
   Of Gods eternall love.
No tempting tryall from the Lord,
   No griefe or dire annoye,
Can sever once the faithfull hart,   15
   From Christ, his onely joye.
Though sinfull flesh doe oft rebell,
   And fancie file our fall,
Yet happie man, that can returne,
   When God beginnes to call.   20
Though God permit his chosen flocke,
   Sometimes to walke astraie:
Yet sets he both the times and meanes,
   To wayne them from their waie.
How long did Paule, with cruell hart,   25
   The Church of Christ molest?
Till called home to see the truth,
   His blindnesse did detest.
How cruell was this Jaylors hart,
   To vex the poore elect?   30
Till trembling earth by mightie power,
   His madnesse did detect.
The God, that makes the haughtie hils,
   And Libans Cedars shake
When he shall take his cause in hand,   35
   Will make the prowdest quake.
To comfort his, that be in neede,
   The Lord is alwaies prest,
And all that haps to his elect,
   Is alwaies for the best.   40
Which in this picture here is seene,
   By that, which shall insew,
Lord graunt us grace, when he doth call,
   To frame our lives anew.

                  A.D.
                (1596)

ANNE DORMER, LADY HUNGERFORD
(d. 1603)

LADY HUNGERFORD was not only a leading recusant herself, but the sister of a still more famously Catholic lady, Jane Dormer, Duchess of Feria, one of Mary Tudor's favourite ladies-in-waiting. Her grandmother, Jane Nudigate, Lady Dormer, was also a notably steadfast Catholic. Anne and Jane were the children of William Dormer and Mary Sidney, sister of Sir Henry Sidney, thus, first cousins of the Countess of Pembroke. Lady Dormer took herself off to Flanders on the accession of Elizabeth with her granddaughter Jane Dormer, and settled in Louvain where she lived for twelve years till 1571, acting as a refuge and harbour for banished priests and English Catholic gentlemen. Her other granddaughter, Anne, Lady Hungerford, went out to Louvain the year her grandmother died (separating from her husband to do so), and took over the household, living on the Continent for thirty-two years. She was a friend of Margaret of Austria, Duchess of Parma, and died in 1603, probably in old age.

The text printed by John Bucke is a meditation on the rosary, a specifically Catholic devotional practice, execrated by Protestants: the beads are held in the hand, and allowed to slip through the fingers one at a time, accompanied by a repetition of the short prayer, 'Ave Maria'. After every ten Aves, a 'Pater Noster' (the Lord's Prayer) is said. Lady Hungerford expanded the set meditations on the Joyful Mysteries of the Virgin, with additional meditations on themes suggested by each clause of the prayer. As it is presented in its original form, the centre of the page is taken up by a large picture of a rosary, with the stanzas of the 'Meditacion' arranged around it anticlockwise, beginning at the twelve o'clock position. Each stanza is also accompanied by a small picture, the whole forming a richly polysemic devotional focus. (The page is reproduced, at about half the original size, in Patricia Crawford's *Women and Religion in England, 1500–1720* (London and New York: Routledge, 1993) 81.)

62   *The Lady Hungerford's Meditacions*
upon the Beades

IN NOMINE PATRIS
If my disciple thou wilt be
  take up thy crosse and follow me:
The crosse that was most odious
  is by my death made glorious.   5

AVE MARIA

With humble mynde I take my way,
   unto the blessed virgin pure:
Upon my knees Ave to saye,
   that she may helpe my sinnes to cure.   10

GRATIA PLENA

O Marie meeke haile full of grace
   whom when Elizabeth did veu
She sayde ther was with her in place
   the mother of her lord Jesu   15

DOMINUS TECUM

O lady deare our lorde with thee
   whom shipheards first in manger finde
A starr from th'east did guyd kinges three
   to visit him with devout mynde.   20

BENEDICTA TU IN MULIERIBUS

Among women thou blessed be,
   who skapte the swordes that thinfantes slew
Whiles Herod sought most cruelly,
   with all to kill thy sonne Jesu.   25

ET BENEDICTUS FRUCTUS VENTRIS TUI

The fruit of thy wombe blessed be,
   whom wrongfully to death they drew:
What greater crosse coulde come to thee,
   than this thou bare with Christ Jesu.   30

SANCTA MARIA ORA PRO NOBIS

O holy mother praye for me,
   whose sinnes deserve eternall payn
That after death my soule maye be,
   where my sweete Jesu now doth raygn.   35

Marie bare Christ at yeres fifteen,
   he lived in earthe thre and thirtie:
Fyfteen yeres after was she seen
   assumpt to heaven at threskore three.

1,6,11, etc. The rosary prayer: 'Hail Mary, full of grace, the Lord is with thee. Blessed art thou among women, and blessed is the fruit of thy womb, Jesus. Holy Mary, pray for us'   36–9: Epiphanius of Cyprus (fourth century) stated that Mary gave birth to Christ at 15, a figure which was generally accepted thereafter, but subsequent calculations of the age at death of the Virgin put it anywhere between 60 and 72.

JANE SEAGER
(fl. 1589)

THE only evidence for Jane Seager's existence is the vellum MS which she presented to Queen Elizabeth, which contains a suite of ten poems on the Sybilline prophecies of the coming of Christ with a final poem to the Queen. By its nature, it gives little away about the author, except that she was very well educated, and extremely skilful. The little book is an object d'art, a pleasure to look at and to touch, elegantly bound by her in red velvet and gold braid, with an inset illuminated picture (*verre eglomisé*), which is apparently also her work. The text itself is equally aesthetic. It is written in a very calligraphic italic with a facing transcription for each poem into the shorthand system invented by Timothy Bright a couple of decades earlier. There is nothing in her book to indicate why she was so concerned to interest the Queen in Bright's 'characterie'. Jane Seager was almost certainly the daughter of Sir William Segar, scribe, limner, calligrapher, and Garter King at Arms in the later part of Elizabeth's reign, since the script in this book is identical with that of Sir William: either he taught her his hand, or he wrote it for her, and it is hard to see why he should have done either unless she was his child.

63   *To Queen Elizabeth*

Lo thus in breife (most sacred Majestye)
I have sett downe whence all theis Sibells weare
What they foretold, or saw, we see, and heare,
And profett reape by all their prophesy
Would God I weare a Sibell to divine   5
In worthy vearse your lasting happynes:
Then only I should be Characteres
Of that, which worlds with wonder might defyne
But what need I to wish, when you are such,
Of whose perfections none can write to-mutch.   10

2 *Sibells*: The Sibyls were pre-Christian prophetesses held to have predicted the future birth of Christ. This book consists of versions of the prophecies associated with each of the Sibyls in turn   7 *Characteres*: characteress; (female) delineator

64   *Lybica*

Behold, behold, the day shall come when as
A Joyfull Prince shyning upon his seed
His churche with graces shall illuminat:
And cleare the darcknes which through synne was bred
He shall unlock the uncleane lipps of them   5
That guilty are, and being true and just,

He shall his people love, but for his foes
They shall not come, nor stand before his sight:
He shall indue with blessings from above
The Queene his Churche, the more for our behove.   10

(1589)

Title *Lybica*: the Libyan Sibyl. The prophecies of the Sibyls circulated initially in Greek: the Latin tradition begins with the fourth-century Roman writer Lactantius, who lists ten Sibyls. Seager's poems are put in the mouths of these ten.

ELIZABETH COLVILLE, née MELVILLE, LADY CULROSS
(?1570s–after 1630)

THE date of her birth is unknown, but she was the daughter of Sir James Melville Laird of Halhill (a courtier, diplomat, and memoir-writer) and Christina Boswell. Her uncle, also James Melville, was a Presbyterian minister, professor of Oriental languages at St Andrews, and the author of a famous diary written in racy, idiomatic Scots. By 1598 Elizabeth was married to John Colville of Wester-Cumbrae, who later inherited, although he did not assume, the title Lord of Culross. Their first son, Alexander, was an eminent Scottish Episcopalian and biblical scholar; for a time he held the chair of Hebrew and theology at the University of Sedan. Another son, Samuel Colvil, also wrote verse: he was the author of 'the Whig's Supplication or Scotch Hudibras'. Elizabeth Melville was, like her husband, deeply and sincerely Presbyterian.

Her verses were in circulation by the year of her marriage, since Alexander Hume, Rector of Logie, dedicated his *Hymns or Sacred Songs* (1599) to her, praising her for her pious verses and religious temperament. Her dream-poem, 'A Morning Vision' was published by James Melville in *A Spiritual Propine*, in 1598, and *Ane Godlie Dreame*, in ottava rima, was first published in 1603, at a time when the Presbyterians were attempting to persuade James to repeal his laws forbidding Presbyterian 'prophesyings', and reprinted seven times up to 1727. She lived into old age, since she was at a prophesying in Lanarkshire in 1630, where she attracted the approving notice of the leader John Livingstone. Her 'Sonnet sent to Blackness' is addressed to John Welsch, son-in-law of John Knox, who was imprisoned in Blackness Castle in 1605 for refusing to give information about the Presbyterian Assembly at Aberdeen, and condemned to death for treason, a sentence which was commuted to banishment and executed in October, 1606. It is preserved in an almost entirely Anglicized orthography: William K. Tweedie, *Select Biographies edited for the Wodrow Society, chiefly from manuscripts in the library of the Faculty of Advocates* (Edinburgh: Wodrow Society, 1845), contains some of her letters and may shed some light on her own practice). She may also be the author of 'Away vaine world bewitcher of my heart', a lyric of wordly renunciation in Edinburgh University Library De 3. 70, fos. 81^{r-v}. The fact that the poem appears in the 1603 and 1606 editions of *Ane Godlie Dreame*, considerably Anglicized, might seem to strengthen the case for Melville, though Rod Lyall has suggested that it is actually by Montgomerie.

65 *from Ane Godlie Dreame, compylit in Scottish Meter be M.M. Gentelvvoman in Culross, at the requeist of her freindes*

I luikit up unto that Castell fair,
Glistring lyke gold, and schyning silver bricht:
The staitlie toures did mount above the air,
Thay blindit mee, they cuist sa greit ane licht.
My heart was glad to sie that joyfull sicht,   5
My voyage than I thocht was not in vaine,
I him besocht to guyde me thair aricht,
With manie bowes never to tyre againe.

Thocht thou be neir, the way is wonderous hard,
Said hee againe, thair foir thou mon be stout,   10
Fainte not for feir, for cowards are debard,
That hes na heart to go thair voyage out.
Pluck up thy heart and grip me fast about,
Out throw yon trance together wee man go:
The yet is law, remember for to lout,   15
Gif this war past, wee have not manie mo.

I held him fast, as hee did gif command,
And throw that trance together than wee went:
Quhairin the middis grit pricks of Iron did stand,
Quhairwith my feit was all betorne and rent.   20
Tak courage now said hee, and be content,
To suffer this: the pleasour cums at last:
I answerit nocht, bot ran incontinent
Out over them all, and so the paine wes past.

Quhen this was done my heart did dance for joy,   25
I was sa neir, I thoucht my voyage endit:
I ran befoir, and socht not his convoy,
Nor speirit the way, becaus I thocht I kend it:
On staitlie steps maist stoutlie I ascendit,
Without his help I thocht to enter thair: 30
Hee followit fast and was richt sair offendit,
And haistelie did draw me down the stair,

Quht haist said hee, quhy ran thou so befoir?
Without my help, thinks thou to clim sa hie?
Cum down again, thou ȝit mon suffer moir,   35
Gof thow desyres that dwelling place to sie:
This staitlie stair it is not maid for thee;
Hald thow that course, thow sall be thrust aback:
Allace said I, lang wandring weiriet mee,
Quhilk maid mee rin the neirest way to tak.   40

Than hee began to comfort mee againe,
And said my freind thow man not enter thair:
Lift up thy heart, thou ʒit mon suffer paine,
The last assault perforce it mon be sair.
This godlie way althocht it seime sa fair,   45
It is too hie thou cannot clim to stay:
Bot luik belaw beneath that staitlie stair,
And thou sall sie ane uther kynde of way.

I luikit doun and saw ane pit most black
Most full of smoke and flaming fyre most fell: 50
That uglie sicht maid mee to flie aback,
I feirit to heir so manie shout and ʒell.
I him besocht that hee the treuth walt tell,
Is this said I, the Papists purging place?
Quhair they affirme that sillie saulles do dwell,   55
To purge thair sin, befoir they rest in peace?

The braine of man maist warlie did invent
That Purging place, he answerit me againe:
For gredines together thay consent
To say that saulles in torment mon remaine,   60
Till gold and gudes relief them of thair paine,
O spytfull spreits that did the same begin:
O blindit beists your thochts are all in vaine,
My blude alone did saif thy saull from sin.

(1603)

4 *cuist*: cast   14 *trance*: transom   15 *yet*: gate; *lout*: bow   16 *Gif this war*: once this
is   28 *speirit*: asked; *kend*: knew   54 *purging place*: Purgatory   59 *gredines*: greediness

66   *A Sonnet sent to Blackness*
      to Mr John Welsch, by the Lady Culross

My dear Brother, with courage bear the crosse
Joy shall be joyned with all thy sorrou here
High is thy hope disdain this earthly drosse!
Once shall you see the wished day appear

Now it is dark thy sky cannot be clear,   5
After the clouds it shall be calm anone,
Wait on his will whoes blood hath bo't the[e] dear
Extoll his name tho outward joyes be gone.

Look to the Lord thou art not left alone,
Since he is thine quhat pleasure canst thou take   10
He is at hand, and hears thy heavy groan
End out thy faught, and suffer for his sake

A sight most bright thy soul shall shortly see
When shew of Glore thy rich reward shall be:

10 *quhat*: what   12 *End out thy faught*: fight to the end

LADY ANNE SOUTHWELL (née HARRIS)
(1571–1636)

ANNE was the daughter of Elizabeth Pomeroy and Thomas Harris, the second
of their four children. Her father was a member of parliament. She married
Thomas Southwell, squire of Spixworth in Norfolk, on 24 June 1594. Some
time thereafter, the young couple went to Ireland to participate in the plantation
of Munster, and lived at Poulnalong Castle, about seven miles from Kinsale.
The Southwells worked hard to be accepted by the upper echelons of the
colonial establishment: her miscellany includes a letter to Viscount Falkland,
the Lord Deputy of Ireland, and poems addressed to George Touchet, the first
Earl of Castlehaven, and Cicely, or Cassandra, MacWilliams, Lady Ridgeway. In
the copy of a letter bound into the miscellany Southwell reproves Lady Ridgeway for her aversion to verse and proceeds to mount a cogent defence of poetry
on the grounds of inspiration and didactic value. Sir Thomas Southwell died in
1626, and shortly after, Lady Anne married Captain Henry Sibthorpe, and
moved with him to Clerkenwell. In 1631, they rented a house in Acton, West
of London, where she formed friendships with Roger Cox, the assistant curate at
St Mary's Church, Daniel Fealty, a preacher, and Robert Johnson, the court
lutenist and composer. She died on 2 October 1636, and is probably buried in St
Mary's Church, Acton. No children are mentioned.

Her commonplace book, Folger V b 198, is a bound folio volume, the water-
marks of which date to before 1600. It is fairly characteristic of the genre: it
contains a variety of compositions, prose and poetry, by Lady Southwell herself,
the writings of others collected by her, including poems by Sir Walter Raleigh
and Henry King, inventories of her belongings, her accounts for the rent of the
Acton house, a paraphrase of Seneca's 'booke of Providence' (fo. 8), an abstract
of Suetonius (fo. 30ᵛ), notes from Augustine's *City of God* (fos. 66ᵛ–67), a mini-
bestiary (fo. 68–68ᵛ), and apophthegms (fo. 69–69ᵛ). Her epitaph, transcribed in
the miscellany, is the main source for her life (fos. 73, 74). There is also a list of
books belonging to Lady Southwell and her second husband, which includes
translations of Pliny, Suetonius, Sallust, Eusebius, and Calvin, among others.
Most of the original poetry is on the Decalogue; expanded versions of poems on
two of the commandments also appear in a presentation copy for the King (BL
Landsdowne MS 740).

67   *To the kinges most excellent Majestye*

Darest thou my muse present thy Battlike winge,
before the eyes of Brittanes mighty kinge?
Hee that all other states exceedes as farre

as doth the sunne a litle glimmering starre
To whose blest birth the Cherubins did tender   5
all the endowments for a princely splendor
You lines, excuse my boldness in this matter
and tell the truth; my hart's too big to flatter.
Yf in the search of this world I could find
one to exceed the vertues of thy minde   10
the height of my ambition would aspire
to offer up these sparckles to that fire.
since all fall shorte of thy soules qualitye
more short then of thy states abilitye:
Tis thy attractive goodnes gives mee scope   15
to come (dread soveraigne) on the [arm]es of hope
and offer up this tribute to thy meritt
this sacrifice to thy devinest spiritt.
I know in God there doth noe ill abide
nor in his true Epitome, noe pride   20
Thou art the nursing father of all pietye
the mightye champion for the Deitye.
This of the high Jehovah I doe singe
to whome doth this belonge, but to the kinge
Great God of heaven, thankes for thy gracious favours   25
Great King on earth, accept the poor endeavours

of your mat^{yes} most humble
and faythfull subiect

Anne Southwell

21 *nursing father*: this was a phrase favoured by James I

68   *'All maried men desire to have good wifes'*

All maried men desire to have good wifes:
but few give good example by thir lives
They are owr head they wodd have us thir heles.
this makes the good wife kick the good man reles.
When god brought Eve to Adam for a bride   5
the text says she was taene from out mans side
A simbole of that side, whose sacred bloud.
flowed for his spowse, the Churches savinge good.
This is a misterie, perhaps too deepe
for blockish Adam that was falen a sleepe.   10

3 *heles*: heels   5 Genesis 2: 21

69   *An Elegie written by the Lady A.S. to the*
      Countesse of London Derrye supposyenge hir to
           be dead by hir longe silence

Since thou fayre soule, art warblinge to a spheare
from whose resultances these quicknd were
Since thou hast layd that downy Couch aside
of Lillyes, Violetts, and roseall pride
And lockt in marble chests, that Tapestrye   5
that did adorne the worlds Epitome,
soe safe, that Doubt it selfe can never thinke,
fortune or fate hath power, to make a chinke,
Since, thou for state, hath raisd thy state, soe farr,
To a large heaven, from a vaute circular,   10
because, the thringinge virtues, in thy breste
could not have roome enough, in such a chest,
what need hast thou these blotted lines should tell,
soules must againe take rise, from whence they fell,
From paradice, and that this earths Darke wombe   15
is but a wardrobe till the day of Dome?
To keepe those wormes, that on hir bosome bredd,
till tyme, and death, bee both extermined,
Yet in thy passage, fayre soule, let me know
what things thou saw'st in riseinge from below?   20
Whether that Cynthia regent of the flood
With in hir orbe admitt of mortall brood?
Whether the 12 Signes serve the Sun for state?
Or elce confine him to the Zodiaque?
And force him retrograde to bee the nurse   25
(whoe circularly glides his oblique course)
Of ALMA MATER, or unfreeze the womb
of madam Tellus? which elce proves a tombe,
whether the starrs be Knobbs uppon the spheres?
Or shredds compos'd of Phoebus goulden hayres?   30
Or whether th'Ayre be as a cloudy sive?
the starrs be holes through which the good soules drive?
whether that Saturne that the six out topps
sit ever eatinge of the bratts of Opps?
Whose Jealousye is like a sea of Gall   35
vnto his owne proves periodicall?
But as a glideinge star whoe falls to earth
Or lovers thoughts, soe soules ascend theyr birth,
which makes mee thinke, that thyne had noe one notion,
of those true elements, by whose true motion,   40
All things have life, and death, but if thyne eyne,
should fix a while upon the Christalline,

Thy hungrye eye, that never could before,
see, but by fayth, and faythfully adore,
should stay, to mark the threefould Hierarchye,   45
differinge in state, not in foelicitye
How they in order, 'bout Jehova move,
In severall offices, but with one love,
And from his hand, doe hand in hand come downe,
till the last hand, doe heads of mortalls crowne.   50
Fayne would I know from some that have beene there?
what state or shape coelestiall bodyes beare?
For man, to heaven, hath throwne a waxen ball,
In which hee thinks h'hath gott, true formes of all,
And, from the forge howse, of his fantasie,   55
hee creates new, and spins out destinye.
And thus theise prowd wormes, wrapped in lothsome rags,
shutt heavens Idea upp, in letherne baggs.
Now since in heaven are many Ladyes more,
that blinde devotion busyley implore,   60
Good Lady, freind, or rather lovely Dame,
if yow, be gone from out this clayie frame,
tell what yow know, whether th'saynts adoration?
will stoope, to thinke on dusty procreation,
And if they will not, they are fooles (perdye)   65
that pray to them, and robb the Trinitye,
The Angells joy in our good conversation,
Yet see us not, but by reverberation,
And if they could, thow saints as cleere eies have,
if downe yow looke to earth, then to the grave,   70
Tis but a Landskipp, more, to look to Hell
in viewinge it, what strange thinges may yow tell!
From out that sulphrous, and bitumnous lake,
where Pluto doth his Tilt, and Tournay make,
where the Elizium, and theyr purgatorye   75
stande, like two suburbs, by a promontarye,
poets, and popleings, are aequippollent,
both makers are, of Gods, of like descent,
poets make blind Gods, whoe with willowes beates them,
popelings makes Hoasts of Gods, and ever eates them.   80
But let them both, poets, and popelings, passe
whoe deales too much with eyther, is an Asse
Charon conduct them, as they have devised.
the Fall of Angels, must not bee disguised,
As 'tis not tirrany, but louinge pittye   85
that Kings, build prisons, in a populous cittye
Soe, the next way, to fright us back to good,
is to discusse the paynes, of Stigian flood.
In Eve's distained nature, wee are base,

And whipps perswade us more, then love, or grace,   90
Soe, that if heaven, should take a way this rodd,
God would hate us, and wee should not love God,
For as affliction, in a full fedd state,
like vinegar, in sawces, doe awake
dull Appetites, and makes men feed the better,   95
soe when a Lythargye, or longnes doth fetter,
the onely way, to rouse againe our witts,
is, when the surgions cheifest toole is whips.
Brasse hath a couseninge face and lookes like gould
but where the touchstone comes it cannot hold.   100
That Sonne of ours, doth best deserve our rent,
that doth with patience beare, our chastisement,
each Titmouse, can salute the lusty springe,
and weare it out, with joyllye reuellinge,
but your pure white, and vestall clothed swan,   105
sings at hir death, and never sings but than,
O noble minded bird, I envy thee,
for thou hast stolne, this high borne note from mee.
But as the prophett, at his Masters feete
when hee ascended, up the Welkin fleete   110
Watcht, for his cloake, soe every bird, and beast,
When princely Adam, tumbled from the nest,
catcht, from his knoweinge soule, some qualitie,
and humbly kept it, to reedifye,
theyr quondam Kinge, and now, man goes to schoole,   115
to every pismire, that proclaymes him foole,
But stay my wanderinge thoughts, alas where made I?
In speaking to a dead, a senceless Lady.
Yow Incke, and paper, be hir passeinge bell,
The Sexton to hir knell, be Anne Southwell.   120

(1627)

Title *the Countesse of London Derrye*: Cicely (d. 1627) (she apparently also used the name
Cassandra), sometime maid of honour to Queen Elizabeth, sister and co-heir of Henry
MacWilliam. She married Sir Thomas Ridgway (d. 1632), a Devonshire gentleman, who
went on the Azores expedition under Essex, served in Ireland and was knighted, and
employed in the colonization of Ulster; created Earl of Londonderry August 1622   21
Cynthia: moon controlling the tides   28 *Tellus*: goddess of the earth   77 *aequippollent*:
equally powerful   80 Protestants thought that the Mass implied a cannibalistic feast;
they conceived of Holy Communion as a commemorative ritual   109 *the prophett*:
Elijah   116 *pismire*: ant   119 compare Isabella Witney's *Wyll and Testament*, 364–5

70   *An Epitaph, uppon Cassandra Mac*
Willms wife to Sr Thomas Ridgway Earle of
London Derry by ye Lady A.S.

Now let my pen bee choakt with gall.
since I have writt propheticall
I wondred, that the world did looke,
of late, like an vnbayted hooke
Or as a well, whose springe was dead   5
I knew not, that her soule was fledd
Till that the mourneinge of hir Earle
did vindicate, this deare lost pearle.
You, starr gasears that view the skyes?
saw yow of late a new star rise?   10
Or can yow by your Art discover
hir seate neere the coelestiall mover?
She is gone that way, if I could find her,
and hath not left, hir match behind hir,
I'le prayse noe more, hir blest condicion,   15
but follow hir, with expedition.

(1627)

9 *gasears*: gazers   12 *coelestiall mover*: God, the 'unmoved mover' (a concept which
derives from Aristotle)

ESTHER KELLO (née INGLIS/LANGLOIS)
(1571–1624)

ESTHER INGLIS, 'l'unique et souveraine Dame de la plume', as she was termed
in 1612, was the daughter of Hugenot refugees who came initially to London,
but settled in Scotland. If she was born in France, then her date of birth can be
established by the 1571 register of aliens, which notes that in the parish of
Blackfriars in London in that year were Nicholas Inglishe, Frenchman, schoolmaster, and householder, Mary his wife, David his son, and 'Yester' his
daughter, and that they '[came] into this realm about two years past for religion'
(R. E. G. and E. F. Kirk, *Returns of Aliens Dwelling in the City and Suburbs of
London, Henry VII–James I*, Publications of the Hugenot Society of London, ii.
15). A book which she wrote in 1624 gives her age as 53; which would make her
born in 1571, but it is possible that deliberately or otherwise, she knocked two
years off her age. Her father was schoolmaster in Edinburgh from 1574, and was
responsible for 'forming of his pupils hands to a perfyte schap of lettir'. Her
mother was Marie Presot, also a calligrapher, who is known to have written two
small books for the library of James VI (*Miscellany of the Scottish History Society*,
Scottish History Society (1893), i. li): a sheet of her work survives in the
Newberry Library, Chicago. Her brother called himself 'David, *cognomento*

Anglus, *natione* Gallus, et *educatione* Scotus', which was also, perhaps, how
Esther saw her own nationality. Esther grew up to be the most famous of
early modern woman calligraphers, patronized by Elizabeth I and James I.
Surviving specimens of her work range in date from 1586 to 1624. She married
a Calvinist pastor, Bartholomew Kello (who was also noted for his writing), in
1596. She and Kello lived in Edinburgh for a number of years before accompanying James VI to London. He was collated to the rectory of Willingdale
Spain, near Chelmsford in 1607, and in 1615, they returned to Edinburgh. They
had one son, Samuel, who graduated from Edinburgh University and became
minister of Spixall in Suffolk.

71   *Priere a Dieu*

Seigneur a ton hôneur
    et par ta grace aussi
J'ai parfait ce LIVRET
    ainsi Seigneur ainsi
Pour ne fair oncques rien   5
    au monde qui ne duise
Ton Sainct Esprit toujours
    en ce sentier humain
Assuere, ouvre, redresse,
    illumine, conduise,   10
Mon cœur, mon œuil, mon pied,
    mon esprit et ma main.
        Ainsi soit il

71   *Prayer to God*

Lord to your honour
and by your grace
I have perfected this little book
Thus, Lord, thus
(So that I may never do anything   5
In the world which does not draw
Your Holy Spirit always
Into this journey through human life)
Steady, open, direct
illumine, lead,   10
My heart, my eye, my foot,
my spirit and my hand
        Amen. So may it be.

MARTHA PRYNNE (née DORSETT, later THROUGOOD, MOULSWORTH) (1577–after 1632)

SINCE virtually all that we know of Martha Prynne is derived entirely from the poetic autobiography we have here, there is little point in rehearsing such details as we have of her life. She was clearly well educated: she was taught Latin, though she found no use for this in later life, and her sometimes unorthodox reading (for example, the Byzantine historian Nicephorus, whom she must have accessed in Latin) suggests that she, one of her husbands, or most probably, her father had an extensive library. Her poem suggests a life of reading and thinking about religious issues, and is in the tradition of spiritual autobiography. Her third husband, Bevil Molesworth, of Hoddesdon, Hertfordshire, esq., was a partner in the Great Farm of Customs. He was entitled to bear the coat of arms of the Mortimers, the family of the medieval Earls of March. His will (P.C.C. 11/159, fo. 32) was proved by Martha on 9 March 1631/2. It was made in the first year of the reign of Charles I and Molesworth describes himself as already 'weake in body with age'. In the preamble he expresses orthodox Protestant hopes about the resurrection of his body from the 'Purgatory of the earth' and he asks to be interred under the font of Broxbourne church, where his only son, Bevil Molesworth, is buried. Clearly wealthy, he left money for an annual lectureship at the same church. He had two married daughters and one grandson, Bevil Hill: Martha's poem suggests that these daughters were her stepchildren.

72   *The Memorandum of Martha Moulsworth Widdowe*

	The tenth day of the winter month November	
	A day which I must duely still remember	
	did open first theis eis, and shewed this light	
Nouember 10th 1632	Now on thatt day uppon thatt daie I write	
	This season fitly willinglie combines	5
	the birth day of my selfe, and of theis lynes	
my muse is a tell	The tyme the clocke, the yearly stroke is one	
clocke, and echoeth	thatt clocke by ffiftie five retourns hath gonn	
everie stroke w^th	How ffew, how many warnings itt will give	
a coupled ryme	he only knowes on whome we are, and live.	10
so many tymes		
vix 55	In carnall state of sin originall	
Acts 17 28 and [?]	I did nott stay one whole day naturall	
	The seale of grace in Sacramentall water	
	so soone had I, so soone become the daughter	
	of earthly parents, and of heavenlie ffather	15
	some christen late for state, the wiser rather.	
Luke 10:14	My Name was Martha, Martha took much payne	
	our Saviour christ her guesse to entertayne	
	God gyve me grace my Inward house to dight	

Revel: 3.20

that he with me may supp, and stay all night.   20

Luke 24.29

My ffather was a Man of spottles ffame
of gentle Birth, and Dorsett was his name
He had, and left lands of his owne possession
he was of Levies tribe by his profession
his Mother oxford knowenge well his worth   25
arayd in scarlett Robe did send him fforth.
By him I was brought upp in godlie pietie
In modest chearefullnes, and sad sobrietie
Nor onlie so, Beyond my sex and kind
he did with learning Lattin decke [my] mind   30
And whie nott so? the muses ffemalls are
and therfore of Us ffemales take some care
Two Universities we have of men
o thatt we had but one of women then

O then thatt would in witt, and tongs
  surpasse   35
All art of men thatt is, or ever was
But I of Lattin have no cause to boast

Lattin is not the most
marketable mariadge
mettall

ffor want of use, I longe agoe itt lost

Had I no other portion to my dowre
I might have stood a virgin to this houre   40
Butt though the virgin Muses I love well
I have longe since Bid virgin life ffarewell
Thrice this Right hand did holly wedlocke
  plight
And thrice this Left with pledged ringe was
  dight
three husbands me, and I have them enjoyde   45
Nor I by them, nor they by me annoyde
all lovely, lovinge all, some more, some
  lesse
though gonn their love, and memorie I
  blesse.

1 Husband, Mr Nicolas
Prynne, Aprill 18
1598

Untill my one and twentieth yeare of Age

I did nott bind my selfe in Mariadge   50
My springe was late, some thinke thatt sooner
  love
butt backward springs doe oft the kindest
  prove
My first knott held five yeares, and eight
  months more
then was a yeare sett on my mourninge score

2nd Mr Tho: Througood

My second bond tenn years nine months did
  last   55

ffebruary 3 1604

three years eight Months I kept a widowes
  ffast
The third I tooke a lovely man, and kind

3rd Mr Bevill
Moulswoorth
June 15, 1619

such comlines in age we seldome ffind

ffrom Mortimers he drewe his pedigre
their Arms he bore, not bought with Heraulds fee   60
third wife I was to him, as he to me
third husband was, in nomber we agree
eleven years, and eight months his autume lasted
a second spring to soone awaie it hasted
was never man so Buxome to his wife   65
with him I led an easie darlings life.
I had my will in house, in purse in Store
what would a woman old or yong have more?
Two years Almost outwearinge since he died
And yett, and yett my tears ffor him nott dried   70
I by the ffirst, and last some Issue had
butt roote, and ffruite is dead, which makes me sad

My husbands all on holly dayes did die
Such day, such waie, they to the Saints did hye
This life is worke-day even att the Best   75
butt christian death, an holly day of Rest
the ffirst, the ffirst of Martirs did befall
Saint Stevens ffeast to him was ffuneral
the morrowe after christ our fflesh did take
this husband did his mortall fflesh forsake   80
the second on a double sainted day
To Jude, and Symon tooke his happy way
This Symon as an auncient Story Sayth

Niceph: Histo:
Jude ver: 3

did ffirst in England plant the Christian ffayth
Most sure itt is that Jude in holy writt   85
doth warne us to Mayntayne, and ffight ffor itt
In which all those that live, and die, may well
hope with the Saints eternally to dwell
The last on Saint Mathias day did wend
unto his home, and pilgrimages ende   90
this feast comes in that season which doth bringe
vppon dead Winters cold, a lyvelie Springe
His Bodie winteringe in the lodge of death
Shall ffeele A springe, with budd of life, and Breath

corrin: 15.42
phillip: 3.21

And Rise in incorruption, glorie, power   95
Like to the bodie of our Saviour

Matt: 22.18

In vayne itt were, prophane itt were ffor me
I shall call husband in the Resurrection
ffor then shall all in glorious perfection
Like to th'immortall heavenlie Angells live   100

verse 30

Who wedlocks bonds doe neither take nor give
But in the Meane tyme this must be my care
of knittinge here a fourth knott to beware
A threefold cord though hardlie yett is broken

Ecclesiast 4.2

Another Auncient storie doth betoken   105
thatt seldome comes A Better; whie should I

then putt my Widowehodd in jeopardy?
the Virgins life is gold, as Clarks us tell
the Widows silvar, I love silvar well.

(November the 10th 1632)

18 *guesse*: guest   60 *bore*: bought deleted MS   78 *St Stevens*: 26 December   82 *Symon*: 28 October   83 The reference is to Nicephorus Xanthopolus (Callistos), *Ecclesiastica Historia* 2. 40: there were two Latin editions of this Greek text in the sixteenth century (Basel, 1561, and Paris, 1562), and one in 1630   85 *Jude*: the Epistle of Jude, the last letter in the New Testament   89 *St Mathias*: 14 May

LUCY RUSSELL (née HARINGTON), COUNTESS OF BEDFORD (1581–1627)

LUCY HARINGTON was the daughter of John Harington of Exton and Anne Kelway. She, her brother John, and her sister Frances were well educated: she learned Italian, French, and Spanish, though probably not Latin. She was distantly related to the Countess of Pembroke through her grandmother, Lucy Sidney, and also to John Harington of Kelston, the poet. In 1594, at the age of 13, she was married to Edward Russell, third Earl of Bedford, bringing him the estate of Minster Lovell and a dowry of £3,000. Despite this, Bedford was continually in debt, even before his association with Essex's rebellion earned him a fine of £20,000 (later reduced to £10,000). She and her husband fared better in the next reign. Immediately after the death of Queen Elizabeth, the Countess and her mother went post-haste to Edinburgh to pay their respects to James I and Queen Anne. The investment was a lucky one. The Countess was appointed to the Queen's bedchamber, and became, and remained, a recognized favourite among Queen Anne's ladies, while Lord and Lady Harington were entrusted with the care and education of Princess Elizabeth (a charge which, like most dealings with the Stuarts, proved cripplingly expensive, however honourable). Lord and Lady Harington accompanied the princess to the Palatinate after her marriage to the Elector in 1613, and Lady Harington remained her chief attendant. Lord Harington's death in 1613 and her brother John's death the following year left her the heir to two-thirds of the Harington estate: unfortunately far from straightening out her financial problems, this compounded them, since the care of the Princess Elizabeth had left the estate encumbered by nearly £40,000 debt.

Between 1608 and 1617, Lucy, Countess of Bedford lived either at Twickenham, where she was hostess to a variety of literary guests (including John Donne, Ben Jonson, Samuel Daniel, John Dowland, and George Chapman), or at court. After 1617, her chief residence was Moor Park, where she laid out a splendid garden. In 1619, she contracted smallpox, and lost much of her beauty, though she remained an important figure at court until the accession of Charles I in 1625. She had no children who survived infancy. She died in the same month as her husband, May 1627, but had herself buried with the Haringtons at Exton, an indication of the extent to which she remained identified with her family of birth. One of her principal concerns in later life was the

promotion of the cause of the exiled Elizabeth of Bohemia, to whom she was
bound by close ties of loyalty and personal affection. She actually visited
Elizabeth at the Hague in 1621, at considerable personal risk.

The Countess of Bedford is a figure of great importance in the culture of the
Stuart court. It was she who recommended Samuel Daniel to the Queen to
create the Christmas masque of 1604, and she took a prominent role in many
masques thereafter. Perhaps her greatest coup was with Ben Jonson/Inigo Jones'
Masque of Blackness on 6 January 1605, in which she partnered the Queen. For
the following decade, she was at the centre of all such dramatic performances to
centre on the Queen and her ladies. She is also important as a patroness: a
considerable number, and wide variety of works were dedicated to her in both
poetry and prose. She promoted Samuel Daniel and Ben Jonson, but her name is
most closely associated with John Donne (whose poem 'Twick'nam Garden' is
named for her estate). She supported his ever-unsuccessful quest for public
office, stood godmother to his second daughter, and gave him financial support.
It is Donne who is our chief witness to the Countess's own poetry: he exchanged
poems with her on at least two occasions, mentioned in his letters, and also
records seeing some other verse which was either improper or satiric: 'I . . . make
a petition for verse, it is for those your Ladyship did me the honour to see in
Twicknam garden, except you repent your making; and having mended your
judgment by thinking worse, that is, better, because juster, of their subject.
They must needs be an excellent exercise of your wit, which speak so well of so
ill: I humbly beg them of your Ladyship, with two such promises, as to any
other of your compositions were threatenings; that I will not show them, and
that I will not believe them; and nothing should be so used that comes from your
brain or breast.' The emphatic promise that the verse will be kept within a
narrow and discreet circle explains why these *leviora* do not survive: they also
suggest that the Countess may have exercised tight control over the circulation
of all her writings. There is no indication that she made any effort to save or
collect her own poems: she was perhaps, in her own eyes, primarily the subject
of poetry and the patroness of poets, seeing her own writing as essentially
ephemeral. Her only surviving poem is from a poetic exchange with Donne in
1609, on the death of Cecilia Bulstrode, a response to, and correction of, his own
poem.

There is not the slightest indication that Lucy, Countess of Bedford, suffered
from lack of a sense of self-worth. For most of her adult life, she was virtually
femme sole: with father and brother dead, and her husband disgraced and in debt,
she was free to do much as she pleased. She was recognized as one of the most
important women in the court after the Queen herself, she enjoyed her position
as Maecenas, collector, patron, performer. Lord Falkland likened her to Hypatia, the Alexandrian mathematician and Neoplatonic philosopher. Her indifference to the survival of her own writing has little, if anything, to do with self-
censorship. Her one poem reveals some interesting things about her. It is
sufficiently confident and skilful to suggest that it was one of many, and it also
confirms the Calvinist leanings suggested by the many dedications to her of
works by prominent English Calvinists and Puritans (and if this seems to sit
strangely with the conspicuous consumption and display of her work on the
masque, we should remember that James I was also a Calvinist).

73   *'Death be not proud, thy hand gave not this blow'*

Death be not proud, thy hand gave not this blow,
Sinne was her captive, whence thy power doth flow;
The executioner of wrath thou art,
But to destroy the just is not thy part.
Thy comming, terrour, anguish, griefe denounce;   5
Her happy state, courage, ease, joy pronounce.
From out the Christall palace of her breast,
The clearer soule was call'd to endlesse rest,
(Not by the thundering voyce, wherewith God threats,
But, as with crowned Saints in heaven he treats,)   10
And, waited on by Angels, home was brought,
To joy that it through many dangers sought;
The key of mercy gentle did unlocke
The doores 'twixt heaven and it, when life did knock.
Nor boast, the fairest frame was made thy prey,   15
Because to mortall eyes it did decay;
A better witnesse than thou art, assures,
That though disolv'd, it yet a space endures;
No dramme thereof shall want or losse sustaine,
When her best soule inhabits it again.   20
Goe then to people curst before they were,
Their spoyles in Triumph of thy conquest weare.
Glory not thou thy selfe in these hot teares
Which our face, not for hers, but our harme weares,
The mourning livery given by Grace, not thee,   25
Which wils our soules in these streams washt should be,
And on our hearts, her memories best tombe,
In this her Epitaph doth write thy doome.
Blinde were those eyes, saw not how bright did shine
Through fleshes misty vaile the beames divine.   30
Deafe were the eares, not charm'd with that sweet sound
Which did i'th spirit-instructed voice abound.
Of flint the conscience, did not yeeld and melt,
At what in her last Act it saw, heard, felt.
Weep not, nor grudge then, to have lost her sight,   35
Taught thus, our after stay's but a short night:
But by all soules not by corruption choaked
Let in high rais'd notes that power be invoked.
Calme the rough seas, by which she sayles to rest,
From sorrowes here, to a kingdome ever blest;   40
And teach this hymne of her with joy, and sing,
The grave no conquest gets, Death has no sting.

                                            (1609)

21 This line refers to the Calvinist doctrine of predestination to salvation or damnation   42 1 Corinthians 15: 55

ELIZABETH JANE LEON (née WESTON, 'WESTONIA') (1582–1612)

WHAT is known of Elizabeth Weston's life is drawn from her poems, particularly a long autobiographical poem written on the occasion of her mother's death, printed in Prague, 1606, and included here. Elizabeth Weston's mother was named Joanna. She knew Latin well, according to her daughter, which may militate against Susan Bassnett's suggestion that she was the Joan Cooper who married Edward Kelley. Joan Cooper may or may not have been the mother of John Francis Weston, born in 1580, and Elizabeth Jane, born in 1582. In any case, when Elizabeth Jane was 6 months old, their father died. The children were looked after for some time by their grandparents, but the grandmothers both died, and the children's fates were then reconsidered. Meanwhile, if Joan Cooper is Joanna Kelley, she remarried swiftly, since she was Edward Kelley's wife by 1583 (the children may, however, have continued to be fostered by their grandparents for some time). She was brought up a Catholic: in the poem on her mother, she recalls being signed with the cross by her. A further level of ambiguity in the whole situation is introduced by Vaclav Kaplicky's biography of Kelley (in Czech), which states that Kelley married Elizabeth's mother, already a Lady Weston, in Prague at some point between 1589 and 1591, with two imperial ministers as witnesses, suggesting that Joanna Weston arrived there independently of Kelley, perhaps as a religious exile. It may be that Kelley married Joan Cooper in 1583, but that she did not long survive the marriage, and he remarried another Joan, or Jane (Joanna, in Latin), the mother of the Weston siblings, after 1589.

Edward Kelley was a con-man, magician, and alchemist closely associated with John Dee. His early history is completely unknown. Dee records his saying in 1583: 'I cannot abide my wife; I love her not, nay, I abhor her, and there in the house I am misliked, because I favour her no better.' Another reference to Kelley's wife in the Dee papers is a prayer for her to be granted children, in 1587. It appears that her marriage with Kelley was infertile, and the problems between them related (at least in part) to his longing for children. The Cooper/Kelley marriage was possibly annulled, in 1588, since Dee's diary records that on 12 October in that year, Joan Cooper left Kelley at Trebon to return to England. Kelley passed as Catholic in Bohemia, and it would have been relatively easy to disallow a Protestant marriage. At some unknown point in their early lives, Elizabeth's mother Joanna (whoever she was) brought her own children into Kelley's household, perhaps most probably at the ages of 7 and 9 respectively. Unlike some step-parental relationships, this one was a great success, and apparently assuaged Kelley's longing for fatherhood. After some Continental wanderings, Kelley moved back to Prague in 1589, and impressed Rudolf II so greatly that he received a knighthood. He also claimed he was an Irish nobleman, descended from the ancient Irish lords of Huí Máine, in Connacht. But in 1591, Kelley's relations with the emperor soured. His household was arrested and tortured, while Joanna was put under house-arrest, he was imprisoned, and in 1597, died in custody.

Kelley was conscientious about educating his stepchildren: John Francis was sent to study at the Catholic University of Ingolstadt. In 1591, Lady Kelley and Elizabeth moved to Jilove, and she went to school there: her headmaster was Jan Sarsan Vodnansky. She went on to study Latin and other languages with John Hammond, who had earlier been employed by Dee as tutor to his children: and she also mentions in a poem that both she and her mother studied with the musician Philippe de Monte.

The background to Kelley's arrest is that he was telling his various patrons that he knew how to transmute base metals into gold. Not only did Rudolf believe him, so did Elizabeth I, Edward Dyer, who was sent to Prague at least twice to try and retrieve him, and Lord Burghley. One of Kelley's more revealing purchases in the days when Rudolf was showering him with money was a gold-mine in Jilove, near where his wife and step-daughter lived. This must have given him the wherewithal to produce the odd teaspoonful of gold, after a careful deployment of special effects, but once his patrons began pressing him to produce gold by the pound, or preferably the ton, he was in serious trouble. He either had to admit fraud, or fulfil his promises: he seems to have resisted doing either until eventually he died of ill-treatment. Elizabeth Weston, who was 15 at the time of his death, believed in him absolutely. She saw him as an unjustly mistreated man, and campaigned vigorously for the restitution of his property to herself and her mother.

Kelley's death left her (and her mother) on their own financial resources, especially since John Francis died soon after his stepfather. Astonishingly, she responded to this by becoming a writer. Her literary activity seems to have been conducted with complete professionalism. A very large proportion of her total oeuvre consists of poems in praise of various grandees, mostly in Prague: this is exactly what one would expect from a writer in the public arena, dependent on patronage. In 1603, she married Johannes Leo of Eisenach, a lawyer, and an agent of Christian van Anhalt. He was also interested in alchemy. Weston continued to write, while the pair had seven children (four sons and three daughters) before her early death. Three daughters survived her.

Prague in the late sixteenth and early seventeenth centuries was a magnet for the European intelligentsia, especially those with alchemical interests. Weston's male friends and associates included Paul Melissus (a man with many friends, also associated with Elizabeth I and Johanna Pallantia, as well as with Sir Philip Sidney), and Oswald Croll, whose *Basilica Chymica* (Prague, 1609) includes poems from Paul Melissus and from Weston. Rudolf II's Prague provided an environment relatively friendly to women writers and scholars. Highly-educated women contemporaries included Elizabeth Albertina à Kameneck, daughter of one of Rudolf's counsellors, Mikuláš Albert z Kaménka, and the Danish Sophie Brahe, sister of Tycho, who made her home there. The daughter of the distinguished politician and nobleman Wacker von Wackenfels, Helena Maria, was educated following her example, but died of smallpox aged 10.

In spite of having made her life in Bohemia, Weston remained highly conscious of herself as an Englishwoman. One of the poetic stances she adopted in her work was to identify herself with Ovid, who was exiled in Pontus, where he wrote his *Tristia*. This also comes out strongly in her poem to James I. She was a very self-conscious literary artist. She was dissatisfied with the first edition of *Parthenicon*: a poem in her own hand in the copy in the British Library expresses her feelings that the book did not adequately express her achievement.

74 *De Inundatione Pragae ex continuis pluviis orta, anno 96*

Evocat iratos Caeli inclementia ventos;
  Imbreque continuo nubila mista madent.
Molda tumet multum vehemens pluvialibus undis
  Prorumpens ripis impetuosa suis.
Largaque per latos diffundit flumine campos,   5
  Et rapidus siccos protulit amnis agros.
Spumosus, verrit per praeceps omnia gurges:
  Et misere insanis cuncta feruntur aquis.
Hinc seges, hinc fructus distracti fluctibus undant:
  Inde vir, inde thorus, foeminaque inde natat.   10
Cerne, trabes, pinus, et tecta natantia, cerne;
  Volvuntur rapidis prodigiosa vadis.
Septa procelloso late stant gurgite mersa:
  Sic alto pereunt omnia mersa mari!
Cymba forum sulcat, piscis delubra Deorum   15
  Contemerat; refugis fluctibus ara madet.
Adstant adtonitae, sed veste liquente catervae,
  Insuetisque dolent cuncta perire malis.
Talis erat facies furibundum cernere Moldam
  Et similes undae Deucalionis erant.   20
Tu qui monstra freti rabidosve domare furores
  Jhova potes, nutu tot mala merge tuo.

                                        (1596)

20 *Deucalionis*: the classical flood which overwhelmed the earth: parallel to the more familiar Hebrew story. The just Deucalion was saved when all else perished

74 *On the flooding of Prague, which arose from continuous rain in the year 1596*

The severity of Heaven calls out the angry winds
  The massed clouds are perpetually sodden with rain
The furious Moldau is greatly swollen with storm-waters
  Impetuous, it is breaking its own banks,
And in its abundance it overflows in a flood across the wide plains   5
  So the swift river overwhelms the dry fields.
Foaming, the headlong flood sweeps over all
  And tragically, everything is borne off by the maddened water.
Here grain, here jumbled fruit bobs on the waves,
  There a man, a bed, a woman swims: 10
See, beams, pinewood, roofs, floating,
  Strange things are whirled round in the rapid eddies.

Far and wide, house walls stand submerged in the stormy gulf,
  Thus all things perish, drowned in deep water!
A dinghy rows over the town square, fish make free with the shrines of the
  Gods,   15
  Altars are soaked by the surging waves.
A crowd stands about, stunned, with dripping clothes,
  They are grieving that everything has perished in an unforseen calamity.
Thus it was to see the face of the furious Moldau
  —it was like Deucalion's flood.   20
You who quell monsters and the raging furies of the sea,
  Powerful Jehovah, drown all these evils with your nod.

75   *In obitum nobilis et generosae foeminae,*
      dominae Ioannae post mortem magnifici et
      generosi domini Edovardi Kellei de Imany,
      equitis aurati sacraeque Caesarae Maiestatis
      consiliarii, derelicta viduae, matris suae
      honorandissimae charissimaeque
      lachrymaebunda effudit filia

       Mortis inexpletae quae vis, et quanta potestas
         Hac nisi sit tactus, dicere nemo potest.
       Hanc saevire quidem per corpora sola putaram,
         Nec jaculis animum posse ferire suis:
       Sed res ipsa docet longe contraria: laesam   5
         Vulnere, et expertam me facit ista loqui.
       Major in internam mortis truculentia mentem,
         Corporis inque, artus assolet esse minor.
       Hoc ubi prostratum telo trajecit acuto,
         Ictibus haud poterit pluribus esse locus.   10
       Nescio quot stimulis mens est obnoxia: quotque
         Pectoris in sensus praevalet illa modis?
       Nam tibi quot charos extinguit sanguine junctos,
         Et quot amicorum morte perire facit.
       Tot tibi, sive tuo, quasi praesens, vulnera cordi   15
         Infligit, toties te cruciando necat.
       Non adimit vitam, verum in mala plura reservat;
         Dum ferit, in plagas vult superesse novas.
       Quas ita ferre grave est, ut tela novissima quivis
         Talibus exemptus sustinuisse velit.   20
       Ipsa ego quae tulerim mortis sub pectore morsus,
         Durius est ipsa morte referre mihi.
       Me ferit infantem; menses cum nata fuissem
         Vix senos, miserae vulnera dura dedit.

Quae non illa quidem, sed ploret adultior aetas   25
    Ipsum (proh superi) mi rapiendo patrem.
Quod vix incepi teneris sentiscere in annis
    Vulnus, quum stimulis institit illa novis.
Atque aviam summa feritate necavit utramque,
    Neptis ego quarum cura suprema fui.   30
Inde miserta mei celso sunt Numina caelo,
    Qui vice sit patris dant vitricumque mihi.
Quo contenta fui, qui ceu pater alter amavit,
    Cui fuit ut fratris, sic quoque cura mei.
Sed rapit impatiens mihi mors et Livor eundem,   35
    Sic mea spes tumido pressa furore jacet.
Frater erat reliquus de tot, materque, propinquis,
    Sperabam his hostem parcere velle tribus.
Sed neque, mors istis satiata doloribus, instat
    Non intermissis me cruciare malis.   40
Protinus et fratrem medio sub flore juventae.
    Sternit, et haec nobis gaudia falce metit.
Hic etiam lachrymis et iniqua sorte squalentem
    Lumine conspexit lucidiore Deus.
In thalamos jungit, levet ut mea damna, maritum   45
    Fratre magis charum, sitque iterata Trias.
Faenora conjugii post tempora justa sequuntur
    Et genitrix avia est facta, vir ipse parens,
Filiolam primo partu, puerumque secundo
    Dat Deus, ut levius damna priora feram.   50
Sed mors quae paucis invita pepercerat annis,
    Rursus in invisum suscipit arma caput.
Spemque patris parvum divellit ab ubere natum
    Vulneribus renovans signa vetusta novis.
Haec reparare Diis quoque visum damna, puellus   55
    Qui maesti referat spem patris, alter adest.
Atropos hic odiis iterum succensa novatis,
    Eheu barbarico plena furore fremit.
Quoque magis favit Numen caeleste misellae,
    Hoc minus illa mihi desinit esse minax.   60
Nec mora grande malum parat, et furibunda dolore
    Qui superat reliquum, saucia corda quatit.
Nam, mea te genitrix, vitali lumine privat,
    Vt misera ingenti sim spoliata bono.
Mater enim quid sit, quae sit jactura parentum   65
    Quam pupillorum lachryma crebra docet?
His ego juncta meae lugubria fata parentis,
    Heu procul a patris dissita sede, gemo.
Non plus maternis me vocibus illa monebit,
    Nec mihi cui dicam, consule mater, erit.   70

Non ea plus soboli benedicens prona mihique
   Signa dabit fronti, pectoribusque crucis.
Ah morior quoties hanc interiisse recordor,
   Vsque adeo innato pectus ab igne dolet.
Siccine mors geminas tibi fas vibrare sagittas?   75
   Sic paenis Titii me cruciare cupis?
Siccine cum superis audes contendere bello?
   Et versare dolos, et dare verba mihi?
Desine, saevitum nimis est, tua spicula conde,
   Sint saltem posthaec mitia fata mihi.   80
Sed rumpare licet Deus est qui damna levabit,
   Hic qui discutiat nubila mentis, erit.
Hic virtute sua reliquos servabit amicos,
   Comprimet et vires, mors inimica, tuas.
Sit soboles mihi salva, precor, vivatque maritus,   85
   Caetera quae tulerit sors, animosa feram.
Et licet ipsa sequar matrem, cum venerit hora,
   Vitae causa mihi, mors, melioris erit.
Tu vero aeternum genitrix veneranda Valeto
   Hasque meas lachrymas ultima dona cape.   90

Elisabetha Ioanna Leonis
ex familiaVestoniorum Angla

(1606)

76 *Titii*: Tityus was one of the great sinners of Greek myth, a titan who was tormented in
the underworld by a vulture which fed on his liver

75 *On the Death of the Noble and Gentle Woman, Lady Joanna Kelley after the death of the Magnificent and Gentle Sir Edward Kelley of Imania, Knight, Counsellor of his Sacred Majesty Caesar, having been left widow: a daughter sheds grieving tears for her most honourable and beloved mother*

Whatever force insatiable death has, how much power,
   No one could say until his touch was on her.
He, as I believe, expends his savagery on bodies alone,
   Nor is he able to strike the soul with his darts:
But the thing itself teaches something far opposite: 5
   I am injured by this wound, and it has made me unable to speak of it.
The savagery of death is greater in the inward mind,
   In the limbs of the body, it is generally less.
Where he attacks the fallen with a sharp dart,
   There can scarcely be a place for many blows.   10
I do not know how many of his stings the mind can oppose: how often
   It may prevail over the senses of the breast?

For in your life, he destroyed as many beloved relatives by blood
    as he caused friends to perish in death.
So many for you, as if wounds which he just now inflicted on your heart,   15
    How often he killed, to torment you
He did not snatch away life, for it reserved in truth, many worse ills,
    When he made them, he wished to conquer new torments.
Thus, it was hard to bear those things, as the most recent dart,
    With which he wished to maintain the one set aside in these things.   20
I myself, when I suffered the bite of death in my breast,
    Found it harder than to assign that death to myself.
It came upon me as an infant; When I had lived scarcely six months since
    my birth,
    It dealt hard wounds to the helpless
Which, though I did not at the time, I later bewailed, at a more adult age   25
    O Gods! it snatched away my father himself from me.
I had scarcely begun to understand the loss, because of my tender years,
    When he followed it up with new darts
And killed both grandmothers with great cruelty,
    I, the granddaughter, was their last care.   30
Thence the gods of high heaven had pity on me,
    Since they gave a substitute father, as a stepfather for me.
With whom I was happy, who I loved as a second father,
    Who cared for me just as he cared for my brother.
But impatient death snatched him from me, and its malice   35
    Thus my hope lay, pressed down by swelling anger.
I had one brother left, and a mother, of so many relations:
    I used to hope that the enemy would consent to spare us three.
But Death was is never satisfied with so many griefs,
    It pursued me, to torment me with incessant evils.   40
First of all, it laid low my brother, in the middle of his flowering youth,
    And mowed down this joy of ours with its scythe.
God looked on this mourning also, with tears
    And put this unjust fate in a more brilliant light.
He linked me in marriage, that I might rise above my misfortunes,   45
    With a husband dearer than my brother, that we might again be a trio.
I was rewarded, after an appropriate period of marriage had intervened,
    And my mother was made a grandmother, my husband a father,
I had a little girl as my first baby, and a boy
    Was given by God as my second, that I might carry more lightly the first loss   50
But unwilling death, who had spared for a few years,
    Again took weapons into its dreadful head.
It tore a tiny baby, its father's hope from the breast,
    Renewing its old scar with new wounds.
When the gods saw this loss, they replaced it, another little boy,   55
    Who recalled the hope of his sad father, came along.
Atropos, incensed again with rage at this new one,
    Alas, growled, full of barbaric fury.
Also God in heaven more favoured the miserable one,
    That menace turned away from me.   60
But without much delay, it prepared an evil, and my wounded heart,
    Which overcame the remainder, shook with furious grief.

For you, my mother, were deprived of light and life,
   So that I, the miserable, might be deprived of so great a good.
For what might a mother be, if there should be a loss of parents   65
   Whom the frequent tears of the eyes might teach?
My grim fate is linked with that of my parents,
   Alas, I groan, in a seat far from my father's.
No more will she warn me with maternal admonition,
   Nor may I say that my mother will be my counsellor.   70
Nor will she again bless her child as she lies,
   Making the sign of the cross on my forehead and breast.
Ah, how often do I die, as I remember her death,
   To the point where my breast mourns, consumed with its own fire.
Death, is it your habit thus to hurl twin arrows?   75
   Do you thus desire to torment me with the pains of Tityus?
Do you thus dare to wage war with the gods
   And exchange tricks, and give words to me?
Cease, it is too great among rages, lay aside your darts,
   They may be, at any rate, afterwards, a mitigation of my fate.   80
But it is permitted to God to destroy this: he who which will lift the curse,
   This will be, which dispels clouds from the mind.
This will save the friends who remain by its virtue,
   And enemy death, it will overcome your strength.
Thus, I pray, save my children, may my husband live,   85
   The rest which fortune brings, I will bear with courage.
And when it is allowed, I will follow that mother, when the hour comes,
   The origin of life for me, death will be better.
An eternal farewell to you, most honoured mother,
   Take the last gift, of these my tears.   90

76   *In 2. Ovidii Trist.*

Sors tua, Naso tuae praecium artis, plurima mecum
   De proprio voluit participare malo:
Cujus in haec tandem creverunt agmina vires,
   Effundi solitas ut superent lacrymas.
Duco reluctantes extrema per omnia Musas: 5
   Nec mihi, qua pergo quave recedo, via est.
Perpetuìm igitur luctus iniere Calendae,
   Exiit auspiciis ultima meta meis!
Torqueor, et miseri quaerens solamina casus,
   Tristibus inficior, Naso, misella tuis.   10
Ultima enim primi repetens documenta libelli,
   Eventus video fati utriusque paros.
Dum mea me in similem rapuerunt tempora sortem:
   Quamvis dissimiles causa det ipsa modos,
Qui te Sarmaticas mensis projecit in oras,   15
   Prima idem fati visus origo mei.
Missus in exilium freta per diversa luisti
   Supplicio culpam tu graviore tuam:

Exsul ego heîc dudum peregrinae supplico terrae,
   Que mala dat quovis horridiora freto.   20
Te piger hospitio profugum rigor excipit Ursae,
   Qua jacet extremo terra subacta gelu:
Arcophylax nostro non multum a vertice distat:
   Longaque Phoebum atris nubibus addit hyems:
Una tibi Nerei movet inclementia bilem,   25
   Quam tamen amplexu vel Thetis una levat.
In me perpetuos armat fera turba furores.
   Ah dolor! in me aditus impetus omnis habet!
Scribenti, cartam feriunt tibi gurgitis undae:
   Et mea, sed lacrymis, scripta rigata madent.   30
Propria tu defles incommoda: me omnia solam,
   Quae vix ingenuae sunt toleranda, gravant.
Tu patriam, incolumes patriae sed linquis amicos
   Mi pater et patrii hoc interiere lares.
Sauromatae infestant crebris tibi cuncta rapinis: 35
   Et mihi, quae non dat, gens furibunda rapit!
Noxia fecisti tu lumina: et artis honorem
   Laesisti: poenas carmen, et error habet:
Pro pietate mihi crudelis reddita merces:
   Culpa etenim tanti nulla probata mali.   40
Jamque tui tecum poterat querimonia luctus
   Fortia Magnanimi frangere corda viri.
Quem non et tenerae moveant lamenta puellae,
   Damnaque barbaricis vix superanda Getis?
Ergo tuo liceat mea fata dolere dolore!   45
   Ah melior quanto sors tua forte mea est!

Title 2 *Ovidii Trist*: the *Tristia* ('sorrows') are elegiac poems by Ovid written in AD 8–12, the early years of the poet's exile to Tomis (mod. Constanta), a precarious outpost of civilization on the Black Sea. The second *Tristia* (Book 1, ii) describes a storm on Ovid's voyage to Tomis in December AD 8   1 *Naso*: Ovid's full name was Caius Ovidius Naso   7 *Calendae*: the first day of each month, therefore, the passing months   11 *Ultima...primi...libelli*: *Tristia*, 1, xi; this epilogue stresses the physical dangers of Ovid's journey, which present a metaphor for the poet's condition   15 *Sarmaticas*: Ovid used 'Sarmatia's land' for the region in which Tomis was situated (1. ii. 82)   25 *Nerei*: Nereus, a sea-god. *Tristia* 1 was written in the course of the sea voyage (1. xi. 1–8)   35 *Sauromatae*: Sarmatians, a nomad people related to the Scythians; their incursions into the lower Danube basin are a pre-occupation of Ovid's in the *Tristia*   44 *Getis*: Getae, a Thracian tribe occupying the banks of the lower Danube; they later acquired the name of Daci (Dacians)

76   *On the second Tristia of Ovid*

Your lot, O Ovid, the price of your art,
   Wishes to participate in many ways with my own misfortunes
Which, at length, have grown to this powerful multitude
   So that they overcome the tears I am accustomed to weep.

I lead resistent Muses through all remote regions, 5
    Nor for me is there a way by which I can go forward or return,
Therefore, the Calends usher in perpetual grief
    The last turning-point of my fortunes is gone past.
I am tortured, and seeming consolation for my unhappy lot,
    I, the unhappy, O Ovid, do not admit your griefs. 10
Going back to the last piece in your first book,
    I can see that the events of our respective fates are equal.
Since my own times have snatched me up with a similar mishap—
    Though dissimilar causes brought about this result.
The month which precipitated you onto the Sarmantian shore, 15
    The same one seemed the first origin of my fate.
Sent into exile, over many seas,
    You atoned for your misdeed with a more terrible punishment:
Just as I, an exile in a foreign land, beseech from here,
    A land which gives misfortunes more savage than the sea. 20
The lazy chill of the Bear received you as a refugee, with hospitality,
    Which lies at the end of the earth, conquered by ice:
Arctophylax stands not far over my head:
    And long winter muffles the Sun with black clouds.
One savagery of Nereus excites your indignation, 25
    Which, however, Thetis resolves with a single embrace.
A fierce crowd arms itself against me with perpetual rages,
    Oh, the grief! An attack always finds access to me!
As you write, the waves of the sea strike your page:
    But my damp writing is moistened with tears. 30
You weep for your own trials: I, alone, am oppressed by all things,
    Which, for a gentlewoman, are scarcely to be borne.
You left your fatherland, your friends, but you left them safe.
    Here, the spirits of my father and my fatherland are both destroyed
All the Sauromatae attacked you with frequent raids: 35
    And for me, what it does not give, an enraged people snatches!
You have made your talents harmful: and stained the honour of art:
    The poem, and your sin, have their punishments.
On account of my piety, a cruel reward is returned:
    Even though no crime is proved answering to such evils. 40
If your griefstricken complaint were able to move
    The strong heart of a Great-souled man;
Who would not also be moved by the laments of a tender girl,
    And losses scarcely surmountable by the barbarian Getae?
Therefore, may I grieve for my fate, through your grief 45
    Ah, how much better your luck was than mine!

77   *Ad Lectorem*

Omnia praesenti; Lector, quaecunque libello
    Nomine sub nostra publica fata vides
Non me diffiteor scripsisse, sed altera causa est,
    Cur commissa typis haec minus esse velim

Nimirum quod sint congesta sine ordine cuncta,   5
   Iunctaque 'Parthenicis quae nova nupta dedi
Itaque' typographicis scateant hinc indeque mendis
   (Quas vereor tribuat ne mihi livor iners?)
Pro libituque meas opplet sine iure pagellas
   Nescio cui fidens, alter amicitiae.   10
Doctarum series hinc est superaddita Vatum
   In qua cum gratis sunt male grata simul
Hinc omissa scias mea plurima, multo videbis
   Hinc modulis passim mixta aliena meis
Hunccine Westoniae diei vis, quaso, libellum   15
   Tu, qui Westoniae vix sinis esse locum?
At melius proprios integro Codice laudes
   Condere, quo digne concelebrere, fuit.
uam tu foemineis iunxisse poemata opellis,
   Grandia sic parvis et minuisse modis.   20
il moror ista tamen Lector mihi inde sinistri
   Si capit, et dextra singula mente legit.
empus erit sine te (faveat modo Parca) pagella
Impleat ut numeris Westonis ipsa suas.

77   *To the Reader*

Everything you see, Reader, in the little book before you
is published under my name.
I do not conceal that I have written; there is another reason
Why I did not want to see these things committed to type:
Everything is incredibly jumbled together, with no order   5
And linked to the *Parthenicon*, which I gave when newly married
here, there and everywhere, they are full of printers' errors
(and I fear idle malice will attribute them to me)
An un-friend, trusting I know not who, at his own whim
has filled my pages, without justification.   10
In this book, there is superadded a series of learned Poets
Which, while free,are also superfluous:
You must realise many of my poems have been left out
You will find others' poems randomly mixed up with mine
Do you want, I ask, a book of the days of Westonia   15
You, who have scarcely alloted any space *to* Westonia?
It would have been better to earn proper praises for an intact book
Which we could both worthily have rejoiced in.
Since you have linked these poems with a woman's minor works
Great things are diminished by contact with lesser.   20
However, I will not delay the Reader, if he takes the negative
away from me, and reads the positive, with an open mind.
A time will come when without you (if Fate permits)
the page will be filled up with Westonia's own poems.

ELIZABETH CARY (née TANFIELD), COUNTESS OF FALKLAND
(c.1585–1639)

ACCORDING to a herald's notebook preserved as BL Harley 1754 (fo. 71), Elizabeth was the daughter of Laurence Tanfield of Burford and Elizabeth Symonds of Clay in Norfolk. Her mother's mother was Catherine Lee, sister of Sir Henry Lee, the lover of Anne Vavasour. Elizabeth Cary was her parents' sole heir, which made her, regardless of personal temperament, inclination, and the fact that she was short and stout, a marital prize. She married Henry Cary, Viscount Falkland, Lord Deputy of Ireland. Having been brought up as a Protestant, Elizabeth Cary converted to Catholicism from personal conviction. Several of her daughters subsequently became nuns, and one, Dame Lucy Magdalen Cary, wrote a biography of her mother (Lille, Archives du Nord 20H9: see forthcoming edition by Heather Wolfe). She was very well educated, as Dame Lucy testifies: 'Afterwards, by herself, without a teacher, and while still a child, she learned French, Spanish and Italian (which she always understood quite perfectly). She learned Latin in the same manner (without being taught) and understood it perfectly when she was young, translating the Epistles of Seneca from Latin to English. After having long discontinued it, she was much more imperfect in it, so when a little time before her death she translated some of Blosius out of Latin, she was fain to help herself somewhat with the Spanish translation.' She was a bookworm from a child. Her mother disapproved of her reading so much, so she persuaded the servants to supply her with candles. By the time of her marriage in 1602, her candle-debt stood at some £200.

Her marriage with Sir Henry Cary was very much a family arrangement: her husband was actually fighting in the Netherlands for the first year of the marriage, and was much abroad until 1606. Elizabeth Cary remained at home for the first year of her married life, but in 1603, her mother-in-law insisted she join the Cary household. Lady Katherine was even stricter than her own mother, and forbade her to read at all. As a result, she took to writing, 'for her private recreation, on several subjects and occasions, all in verse'. After Sir Henry's return in 1606 from a spell as a prisoner of war in Spain, he began a successful career at court, which culminated with his appointment as Lord Deputy of Ireland in 1622. Sir Henry's life as a courtier of course required his young wife's participation. Since her daughter Dame Lucy records that 'dressing was all her life a torture to her' (she used to walk about her dressing-room reading while her gentlewomen pinned garments on her more or less at random), it is probable that she took little pleasure in this way of life. She also gave birth to eleven children between 1608 and 1624, and experienced prolonged bouts of depression. She accompanied her husband to Ireland, where she took the opportunity to learn Gaelic. Her teacher may have been Richard Bellings (secretary to the Supreme Council of the Catholic Confederation in the Irish civil war): she was the recipient of his dedication in *A Sixth Booke to the Countesse of Pembrokes Arcadia* (Dublin, 1624).

The view of the duty of married women expressed in *Mariam* is unusually extreme: we must remember that the woman who wrote it was gradually moving towards a position where she was to act in direct and complete defiance of her husband's wishes. She had leanings towards Catholicism from perhaps 1605, but at the time when she wrote *Mariam*, she conformed, outwardly at least, to her husband's strict Protestantism. We may perhaps think that she is aiming to convince herself with the argument she presents here. The marriage broke down in 1625, due, among other things, to Cary's persecution of Irish Catholics, and he sent her home to England. Her conversion to Catholicism was made public in 1626 when the King was informed. Sir Henry virtually disowned her at the news: she was confined to her rooms for six weeks; and in the longer term, when she failed to renounce her conversion, he stopped her allowance, took away her children, and refused to pay for her maintenance. Her mother was equally opposed: 'I perceive by your last letters ... that I shall never have hope to have any comfort from you ... My desire was ... to have you live with your husband, and to live in that religion wherein you were bred.' After appeals from both parties, the Privy Council ruled that Sir Henry must pay her maintenance and the debts which she had by then accrued. The couple remained completely estranged until 1631, when Queen Henrietta Maria arranged for a partial reconciliation. In 1633, Elizabeth helped to nurse her husband on his deathbed. She died in 1639, in impoverished circumstances.

The family was split down the middle by religion. Elizabeth Cary was able to bring her daughters and some of her sons over to Catholicism, but not her oldest son, Lucius. Due to her financial troubles, Lucius acted as the guardian of his younger siblings on his father's death, but Elizabeth concentrated her mind on regaining care of them and encouraging them to convert. Magdalena was the first to join her in her religion, then between them, they converted the others. Elizabeth Cary contrived to send her younger sons abroad for a Catholic education, at the English Benedictines in Paris, despite fierce opposition from the Cary family: in this, she was covertly aided by Queen Henrietta Maria, who paid for the boys' education. At least four of her daughters entered English religious houses in the Low Countries: Anne (Dame Clementina), Lucy (Dame Magdalena), Augustina, and Maria, while one of her sons also became a Benedictine. Her life by one of her daughters (Dame Lucy) is the principal source for her biography. It is clear from her narrative that the daughter in question found her mother an embarassment in her own teenage years: but that later, after she had chosen to become a nun, they became very close.

In the 1620s and 1630s, Elizabeth Cary's principal literary interests reflected the centrality of Catholicism in her life. She worked on a translation of Cardinal Perron's *Replique a la response du serenisme roy de la Grande Bretagne* (Perron was an internationally important figure, with a considerable influence on the religious life of England), which was printed with a dedication to her patroness, Queen Henrietta Maria: most of the copies were seized and burnt. She also composed verse lives of St Mary Magdalen, St Agnes, and St Elizabeth of Portugal, and also many verses to the Virgin and other saints: these appear to have been lost, though it is not wholly impossible that they may turn up in convent records, having been kept by her daughters. She was buried as a Catholic in the Queen's chapel.

78   *Chorus*

Tis not enough for one that is a wife
To keepe her spotles from an act of ill;
But from suspition she should free her life,
And bare herself of power as well as will.

Tis not so glorious for her to be free,   5
As by her proper self restrained to be.

When she hath spatious grounde to walke upon,
Why on the ridge should she desire to goe?
It is no glory to forbear alone,
Those things that may her honour overthrowe   10
    But tis thanke-worthy, if she will not take
    All lawful liberties for honours sake.

That wife her hand against her fame doth reare,
That more than to her Lord alone will give
A private word to any second eare,   15
And though she may with reputation live.
    And though most chast, she doth her glory blot,
    And wounds her honour, though she killes it not.

When to their Husbands they themselves doe bind,
Doe they not wholy give themselves away?   20
Or give they but their body not their mind,
Reserving that though best, for others pray?
    No sure, their thoughts can no more be their owne,
    And therefore should to none but one be knowne.

Then she usurpes upon anothers right   25
That seeks to be by publike language grac't:
And though her thoughts reflect with purest light,
Her mind if not peculiar is not chast.
    For in a wife it is no worse to find
    A common body, then a common mind.   30

And every mind though free from thought of ill,
That out of glory seeks a worth to show:
When any's ears but one therewith they fill,
Doth in a sort her pureness overthrow.
    Now *Mariam* had, (but that to this she bent)   35
    Been free from fear, as well as innocent.

6 *proper*: own   28 *peculiar*: reserved to one person   30 *common*: with overtones of prostitution

79   *To the Queens most Excellent Majestie*

'Tis not your faire out-side (though famous GREECE
    Whose beauties ruin'd kingdomes never sawe
A face that could like yours affections drawe)
    Fittes you for the protection of this peice

It is your heart (your pious zealous heart)   5
    That by attractive force, brings great PERROONE
To leave his SEYNE, his LOYRE, and his GARROONE;
    And to your handmaide THAMES his guiftes impart:
But staie: you have a brother, his kinge borne,
    (Whose worth drawes men from the remotest partes,   10
To offer up themselves to his desartes.)
    To whom he hath his due allegiance sworne
      Yet for your sake he proves ubiquitarie
      And comes to England, though in France he tarrie.

(1630?)

1 the addressee is Queen Henrietta Maria   2 *beauties*: reference is primarily to Helen of Troy, but perhaps also to the famous courtesan Thais, who persuaded Alexander to burn Persepolis   6 *PERROONE*: Cardinal Perron   7 *SEYNE* etc.: French rivers, Seine, Loire, Garonne   9 *brother*: Louis XIII

LADY MARY WROTH (née SIDNEY)
(1587–c.1652)

LADY MARY WROTH was the eldest daughter of Sir Robert Sidney, first Earl of Leicester, and Barbara Gamage. She was the product of a notably literary family: her father, her aunt Mary Sidney, and her uncle Sir Philip were all known as poets. She was brought up at Penshurst and in The Netherlands, when her father succeeded his brother as Governor of Flushing (Vlissingen). She married Sir Robert Wroth, the heir of a family of wealthy and socially ambitious landowners without courtly connections, in 1604. Though they appear to have had little in common—his interests were business, local affairs, hunting and fishing, hers were courtly and literary—they remained on friendly terms. In 1614 he died and, having entertained King James too lavishly, left his widow in debt for the rest of her life. Her only legitimate child, James, was not born till after ten years of marriage, a month before his father's death, pehaps because they spent little time together. She had two more children in her widowhood, a son, William, and a daughter, Catherine, the result of an affair in the 1620s with her cousin William Herbert, third Earl of Pembroke, whom she had known from childhood.

    Her career as a courtier began in 1602, when she was 15, in the last years of Elizabeth's reign. Even as a married woman, she continued to be part of Queen Anne's entourage, living at court while her husband stayed in Essex. Revealingly, she continued to use the Sidney coat of arms, suggesting that she thought of herself as a Sidney rather than as Wroth's wife. While at court, she participated in a number of masques. Most importantly, she danced in the first masque written for Queen Anne, Jonson's *The Masque of Blackness*, where she played the nymph Baryte. The thoughts on blackness in the sonnet 'like to the Indians' included here may be connected with this experience.

    Lady Wroth lost favour with Queen Anne, and retired to Penshurst during 1612–20, where she composed a sprawling prose romance, with intermingled

songs and poems, which offers satirical descriptions of court intrigues in the quest
for royal favour. It was published in 1621 as *The Countess of Montgomeries Urania*,
named for her cousin/lover's sister-in-law (as the *Arcadia* had been dedicated to
its author's sister, the Countess of Pembroke), but sonnets connected with the
romance were being read in manuscript by Wroth's friends at least as far back as
1613, and the Folger manuscript contains several poems that were not printed in
1621. It is the first full-length work of prose fiction published by an English-
speaking woman, and appeared as an impressive folio volume. While the engraved
title-page designed by Simon van der Passe might suggest that it was published by
her desire, the fact that the text is incomplete, with the last line finishing in mid-
sentence, and that there is no preliminary material such as a formal dedication to
the Countess of Montgomery, suggests that it was pirated. Certainly, Wroth
insisted to the Duke of Buckingham that the books of *Urania* 'were sold against
my mind I never purposing to have them published'. A sequel was written but
never published (the MS, itself unfinished, is in the Newberry Library, Chicago).
Appended to the *Urania* is an elaborate sonnet sequence called *Pamphilia to
Amphilanthus* from which the poems anthologized here are taken: similarly, it is
the first collection of Petrarchan love poetry to be published by a woman—rather
belatedly, in terms of the history of the English Petrarchan sonnet, since the form
was at its most fashionable thirty years earlier. Wroth received many tributes from
contemporary writers for her work, including Ben Jonson, George Chapman, and
Joshua Sylvester. The first of these claimed that since reading her sonnets he has
become 'A better lover and much better poet'. There are hints in *Urania* and the
sonnets linking Wroth to Pamphilia ('all-loving') and Amphilanthus ('lover of
two') to William Herbert, her faithless lover. The 'Crown of Sonnets' is based on
the Italian poetic form, the *corona*, in which the last line of each sonnet serves as the
first line of the succeeding one. Selections from her poetry given here follow
the printed text: an edition based on the Folger manuscript, by Josephine Roberts,
was published in 1983. Mary Wroth also wrote a long pastoral entertainment,
Love's Victory, recently edited by Michael Brennan, and published privately by
the Roxburgh Club in 1988.

The last selection from Lady Mary Wroth is wholly different. Sir Edward
Denny objected fiercely to *Urania*, which he perceived to be making covert
allusion to embarrassments within his own family. When he did not manage to
persuade her to withdraw it, he wrote a sort of pasquinade against her, attacking
her personally, but also as a woman writer, a copy of which is preserved among
the manuscripts of Sir Henry Jukes Lloyd Bruce. Far from being overwhelmed
by the attack, she rose to it very precisely with a reply, given here, which uses
the same set of rhyme-words as Denny's libel, and cleverly turns it back on him.
Little is known of Wroth's later life, except that she resided at Woodford, where
she appears on the tax rolls and bills for the sale of land.

80   *A crowne of Sonetts dedicated to Love*

1.

In this strang labourinth how shall I turne?
    wayes are on all sids while the way I miss:
    if to the right hand, ther, in love I burne;
    lett mee goe forward, therin danger is;

If to the left, suspition hinders bliss,   5
     lett me turne back, shame cries I ought returne
     nor fainte though crosses with my fortunes kiss;
     stand still is harder, allthough sure to mourne;

Thus lett mee take the right, or left hand way;
     goe forward, or stand still, or back retire;   10
     I must thes doubts indure with out alay
     or help, butt traveile find for my best hire;

yett that which most my troubled sence doth more
is to leave all, and take the thread of love.

11 *alay*: allay, mitigation   12 *traveile*: could mean both labour and travel

2.

Is to leave all, and take the thread of love
     which line straite leads unto the soules content
     wher choyce delights with pleasures wings doe move,
     and idle phant'sie never roome had lent,

When chaste thoughts guide us then owr minds ar bent   5
     to take that good which ills from us remove,
     light of true love, brings fruite which none repent
     butt constant lovers seeke, and wish to prove;

Love is the shining starr of blessings light;
     the fervent fire of zeale, the roote of peace,   10
     that lasting lampe fed with the oyle of right;
     Image of fayth, and wombe for joyes increase.

Love is true vertu, and his ends delight,
his flames ar joyes, his bands true lovers might.

       .   .   .   .

13.

Free from all fogs butt shining faire, and cleere
     wise in all good, and innosent in ill
     wher holly friendship is esteemed deere
     with truth in love, and justice in our will,

In love thes titles only have theyr fill   5
     of hapy lyfe maintainer, and the meere
     defence of right, the punnisher of skill,
     and fraude; from whence directnes doth apeere,

To thee then lord commander of all harts,
     ruller of owr affections kinde, and just   10
     great king of Love, my soule from fained smarts
     or thought of change I offer to your trust

This crowne, my self, and all that I have moe
except my hart which you beestow'd beefore;

14.

Except my hart which you beestow'd before,
    and for a signe of conquest gave away
    as worthles to bee kept in your choyse store
    yett one more spotles with you doth nott stay.

The tribute which my hart doth truly pay   5
    faith untouch'd is, pure thought discharge the score
    of debts for mee, wher constancy bears sway,
    and rules as Lord, unharm'd by envyes sore,

Yett other mischiefs faile nott to attend,
    as enimies to you, my foes must bee;   10
    curst jealousie doth all her forces bend
    to my undoing; thus my harmes I see.

Soe though in Love I fervently doe burne,
In this strange labourinth how shall I turne?

81   Sonnet XIX

Come, darkest night, becoming sorrow best;
    Light, leave thy light, fit for a lightsome soul;
    Darkness doth truly suit with me oppressed,
    Whom absence' power doth from mirth control:
The very trees with hanging heads condole   5
    Sweet summer's parting, and of leaves distressed
    In dying colours make a griefful roll,
    So much, alas, to sorrow are they pressed.
Thus of dead leaves her farewell carpet's made:
    Their fall, their branches, all their mournings prove,   10
    With leafless, naked bodies, whose hues vade
    From hopefull green, to wither in their love:
If trees and leaves for absence mourners be,
No marvel that I grieve, who like want see.

                                        (1621)

11 *vade*: possibly for 'fade', or from Latin *vadere*: to go

82   Sonnet XXII

Like to the Indians, scorchèd with the sun,
    The sun which they do as their god adore,

So am I used by love: for evermore
I worship him: less favours have I won;
Better are they who thus to blackness run,   5
    And so can only whiteness' want deplore,
    Than I who pale and white am with grief's store,
Nor can have hope, but to see hopes undone.
Besides, their sacrifice received 's in sight
    Of their chose saint, mine hid as worthless rite.   10
    Grant me to see where I my offerings give;
Then let me wear the mark of Cupid's might
    In heart, as they in skin of Phoebus' light;
    Not ceasing offering to live while I live.

                                        (1621)

83   *Sonnet XXXVIII*

What pleasure can a banish'd creature have
    In all the pastimes that invented are
    By wit or learning? Absence making warre
Against all peace that may a biding crave.

Can wee delight but in a welcome grave,   5
    Where we may bury paines? and so be farre
    From loathed company, who alwaies jarre
Vpon the string of mirth that pastime gave.

The knowing part of joy is deem'd the heart,
    If that be gone what joy can joy impart   10
    When senslesse is the feeler of our mirth?

No; I am banish'd and no good shall finde,
    But all my fortunes must with mischiefe binde,
    Who but for misery did gaine a birth.

                                        (1621)

84   *Song*

    Dearest if I by my deserving,
    May maintaine in your thoughts my love,
        Let me it still enjoy,
        Nor faith destroy:
    But pitty Love where it doth move.   5

    Let no other new Love invite you,
    To leave me who so long have servd:
        Nor let your power decline

But purely shine
On me, who have all truth preserv'd.   10

Or had you once found my heart straying,
Then would not I accuse your change,
    But being constant still
    It needs must kill
One, whose soule knowes not how to range.   15

Yet may you Loves sweet smiles recover,
Since all love is not yet quite lost,
    But tempt not Love too long
    Lest so great wrong
Make him think he is too much crost.   20

85   *Sonnet II*

Love like a Jugler comes to play his prize,
    And all mindes draw his wonders to admire,
    To see how cunningly he (wanting eyes)
    Can yet deceive the best sight of desire.

The wanton Childe, how can he faine his fire   5
    So prettily, as none sees his disguise,
    How finely doe his trickes; while we fooles hire
    The badge, and office of his tyrannies.

For in the ende such Jugling he doth make,
    As he our hearts instead of eyes doth take;   10
    For men can onely by their flights abuse

The sight with nimble, and delightfull skill,
    But if he play, his gaine is our lost will,
    Yet Child-like we cannot his sports refuse.

(1621)

86   *Railing Rimes returned upon the Author by*
        Mistress Mary Wrothe

Hirmophrodite in sense in Art a monster
    as by your railing rimes the world may Conster
Your spitefull words against a harmless booke
    shews that an ass much like the Sire doth looke
Men truly noble fear no touch of Blood   5
    Nor question make of others much more good
Can such comparisons seeme the want of witt
    When oysters have enflamd your blood with it

But it appeares your guiltiness gapt wide
    And filld with Dirty doubt your brains swolne tide   10
Both frind and foe in deed you use alike
    And your madd witt in sherry aequall strike
These slaunderous flying flames raisd from the pott
    You know are false and raging makes you hott
How easily now do you receave your owne   15
    Turnd on your self from whence the squibb was throwne
When these few lines not thousands writt at least
    Mainly thus prove your self the drunken beast
This is far less to you then you have doune
    A Thrid but of your owne all wordes worse spunn   20
By which you lively see in your own glasse
    How hard it is for you to ly and pass
Thus you have made your self a lying wonder
    Fooles and their pastimes should not part asunder
Take this then now lett railing Rimes alone   25
    For wise and worthier men have written none.

2 *Conster*: construe, guess

ISOBEL BEAUMONT with JOHN COLEMAN, a
servant
(1589–after 1607)

At the age of 18, an upper-class young woman, Isobel Beaumont, joined forces with a disgruntled servant, John Coleman, to write a lampoon on the head of the household, her older brother, Henry Beaumont: this pasquinade is addressed, in mock commiseration, to his wife. She and Coleman may have been lovers: he later claimed that they were married. Such verses could potentially cause a great deal of trouble. Whereas some types of public mockery, such as 'rough music' or skimmingtons were essentially normative, in that they were used to express disapproval of men who could not control their wives or women who refused to be controlled, pasquinades were perceived as disruptive to hierarchy and patriarchal order. This one, in which a young woman flouts the authority of her brother, mocks his sexuality, and combines with a servant to encourage her sister-in-law to take up adultery, is a classic example of the kind of thing the authorities liked least. Copies of this verse passed around, and also circulated orally, and were perceived at the time as materially damaging to the status and authority of Henry Beaumont.

87 *'Poor Bess Turpin, I pytty thy case as farr as I can'*

    Poor Bess Turpin, I pytty thy case as farr as I can
    For maraying of no boddy in stead of a man

For when he was at the biggest of his growing and best of himself
He was but the moyetie of a man and a lecherous elf.

Aske but the whoores in London and they will telle all   5
For whose sakes he lyes fast bounde in the scriveners stall
But this you will confesse and so will your mother
That if you make no body cuckold you may lye with another.

4 *moyetie*: half; *elf*: a kind of fairy, the overtones are of small size, spitefulness, perhaps
dangerousness   6 *scriveners stall*: place where writing was done

HESTER WYAT
(*c*.1600)

HESTER WYAT was probably one of the descendants of the famous mid-Tudor
poet Sir Thomas Wyatt: a number of Wyatt women wrote poetry, notably
Eleanor Wyatt. Nothing is known of her life.

88 *A poem made by a friend of mine in answere
to One who Ask't why she wrotte.*

What makes me write, my dearest Freind, you aske,
For our sexe always thought too great a taske.
I grant you this yet 'tis no ill spent time
And my thoughts natur'ly fall into Rime
Rude and unpolish't from my pen they flow,   5
So Artless I my native tongue scarce know.
Learning the Wit and judgement must improve,
Refine the verse each tender passion move,
While me no muse assists nor God of Love;
Like those whose hearts with suden greife oprest,   10
No kind freind near on whose Lov'd constant Breast
Leening their drooping Heads they may complain,
To Groves which no return can make again
They sigh ther woes to ease their killing pain.
So whilst in solitude the days I pass   15
Paper I make my Freind and minds true Glass,
To that myselfe unbosome free from fear
Of a false womans tongue or lissening Eare,
Blessing their fate who your deare sight enjoye,
Pleasures their hours their happy hours imploy.   20
This to us Rurall Nimphs is now deny'd,
A Life which is you know my humble share,
Free from Ambition, nor yet clog'd with Care,

Nor need I tell you Freind this dismall truth
How vice and folly has possest our Youth,   25
So empty is our Sex, yet so vain grow'n,
And more debauch't the other ne're were known.
Out of such company whats to be brought?
Scandal or nonsense not one solid thought.
With Joy I from these noysy Crouds retire   30
And from my thoughts of my owne Heart inquire,
Shou'd we not to our selves this great debt pay?
The little time that fleeting Life does stay
Wear worthless if unthinkyd thrown away.
Then I my secret thoughts colect and write   35
Cause this improves me most does most delight
And whilst with innocence my time I spend,
That soonest leads to the proposed end,
No guilty blush my cheeks dye to impart.
These Lines my Freind, chast as the Authors Heart,   40
Happy if they can answere your desire
Tho they in flames bright as your Eyes Expire.

34 *Wear*: were; *unthinkyd*: unthinkingly

A MAID OF HONOUR
(fl. 1603)

IN *The Crown Garland of Golden Roses*, a collection of songs mostly on the
subject of English monarchs, first published in 1612. Claude Simpson in *The
British Broadside Ballad*, 576–8, notes that 'Phillida flouts me', the ballad which
gives the tune its name dates to *c*.1600, and is thus compatible with the Queen's
death in 1603. Unfortunately, 'Gone is Elizabeth' can *not* be sung to this tune
without inordinate repetition, suggesting that this little poem, whatever its
provenance, was not written to fit it.

89   *A short and sweet Sonnet made by one of
the Maids of Honour, upon the death of
Queen Elizabeth, which she sewed upon a
Sampler, in Red Silke.*

to a new *Tune*, or to 'Philida *flouts me*'.

Gone is *Elizabeth*,
      whom we have lov'd so dear
She our kinde Mistresse was
      full foure and fortie yeares.

England she govern'd well,   5
    not to be blamed:
Flanders she succour'd still,
    and Ireland tamed.
France she befriended,
    Spain she hath foiled.   10
Papists rejected,
    and the Pope spoiled.
To Princes powerfull,
    to the World vertuous
To her Foes merciful   15
    to Subjects gracious,
Her Soul is in Heaven
    The World keepes her Glory:
Subjects her good deeds,
    and so ends my Story.   20

A GENTLEWOMAN
(fl. 1603)

ALL that is known about the author of this poem is provided by a note in the manuscript: 'A gentlewoman y^t married a yonge Gent who after forsooke whereuppon she tooke hir needle in wch she was excele[n]t and wo^{r}ked upo[n] hir Sampler thus'.

90   *A Gentlewoman yt married a yonge Gent*
        who after forsooke whereuppon she tooke hir
        needle in which she was excelent and worked
           upon hir Sampler thus

Come give me needle stitchcloth silke and haire,
That I may sitt and sigh and sow and singe,
For perfect collours to discribe the aire
A subtile persinge changinge constant thinge.

No false stitch will I make my hart is true,   5
Plaine stitche my sampler is for to complaine
Now men have tongues of hony, harts of rue,
True tongues and harts are one, Men makes them twain.

Giue me black silk that sable suites my hart
And yet som white though white words do deceive   10
No greene at all for youth and I must part,

Purple and blew, fast love and faith to weave.
Mayden no more sleepeless ile go to bedd
Take all away, the work works in my hedd.

(before 1603)

7 *rue*: extremely bitter herb associated with regret

ANONYMOUS
(before 1624)

THE earliest redaction of this well-known poem is recorded by John Aubrey. In a
passage on funeral customs, he notes that in Yorkshire, 'till about 1624 at the
Funerall a woman came (like a *Praefica*) and sang this following song . . .' This is to
say, while the actual authorship of this composition is as unrecoverable as that of
most ballads, it formed part of women's traditional lore and culture in early modern
Yorkshire. Aubrey himself collected it from a Mr Mawlese, who told him that in his
father's youth some sixty years previously (from 1628, the date of writing, i.e. the
1560s) the song was sung at country funerals. Later versions of the 'Lyke Wake
Dirge' have been collected, suggesting that it continued in oral circulation for
centuries: it is unlikely to have found its way out of Aubrey's *Remaines* back into
circulation. It represents a folk redaction of the Catholic concept of purgatory and
'salvation by works', obstinately surviving a hundred years after the Reformation.

91   *'The Lyke Wake Dirge'*

This ean night this ean night;
   every night and awle:
Fire and Fleet and Candle-light
   and Christ receive thy Sawle.

When thou from hence doest pass away   5
   every night and awle
To Whinny-moor thou comest at last
   and Christ receive thy silly poor Sawle.

If ever thou gave either hosen or shun
   every night and awle   10
Sit thee down and putt them on
   and Christ receive thy Sawle.

But if hosen nor shoon thou never gave nean
   every night etc,
The Whinnes shall prick thee to the bare beane   15
   and Christ etc.

From Whinny-moor that thou mayst pass
   every night etc:

To Brig o' Dread thou comest at last
    and Christ etc: 20

From Brig of Dread that thou mayst pass,
    every night etc:
To Purgatory fire thou com'st at last
    and Christ etc:

If ever thou gave either Milke or drinke,   25
    every night etc:
The fire shall never make thee shrink
    and Christ etc:

But if milk nor drink thou never gave nean,
    every night and awle: 30
The Fire shall burn thee to the bare bane
    and Christ receive thy Sawle.

3 *Fleet*: water (flood)   7 *Whinny-moor*: in Yorkshire   9 *hosen or shun*: stockings or shoes   15 *Whinnes*: gorse; *beane*: bone

ELEN GWDMAN
(fl. 1609)

NOTHING is known of this woman, but the title of the poem associates her with Talyllyn in Anglesey.

92   *Cwynfan merch ifanc am ei chariad:*
y ferch oedd Elen Gwdman o Dalyllyn a'r mab
oedd Edward Wyn o Fodewryd, y Mesur Rogero

Pob merch ifanc sy'n y byd
Mewn glân feddylfryd calon;
Gogelwch, gwyliwch fod yn drwch
I fab, o byddwch ffyddlon.

Myfi a ŵyr oddi wrth y clwy'   5
Ac i chwi 'rwy'n conffesu;
Pâr y dristwch sydd i'm bron
O achos ffyddlon garu.

Gŵr bonheddig gweddaidd, glân,
Ifiengaidd, oedran lysti,   10
A fai'n tramwy'r fan lle bawn,
Yn fynych cawn ei gwmni.

Ei gamp a'i barabl yn fy ngŵydd
A'i sadrwydd oedd yn peri,
Ei olwg troead fal yr ôd,   15
I'm tyb oedd ei fod i'm hoffi.

Gwybu Giwpyd ar fyr dro,
Fy mod i'n lecio ei foddion,
Ac a saethodd ergyd trwm,
Do, saeth o blwm i'm calon.   20

Yna'r aethom yn gla' ein dau
Heb neb yn addef'i feddwl;
Ni wydde'r un ond ei glwy'i hun
Er bod pob un mewn trwbwl.

O wan hyder, nid oedd o   25
Yn presuwmio gofyn
Dim trugaredd ar fy llaw,
Ond diodde' draw fal'r oenyn.

A minne oedd yn ŵyl neu'n fud,
Heb feiddio doedyd wrtho;   30
na rhoi amna'd mewn un lle
O'm clwy, lle galle dybio.

Y fi yn tybied nad oedd o
Ond cownterffetio ffansi;
Ac ynte'n meddwl nad oedd wiw   35
Geisio i'm briw mo'r eli.

Ni fuom felly'n cyfri'r sêr
Ac eisiau specer rhyngom;
Pan ddaeth ffortun, fe wyr Crist,
I mi a thrist newyddion.   40

Clywed ddarfod i'w ffrins o
Yn gaeth ei rwymo ag arall;
'Roedd yn rhaid iddo diodde'n frau
Y naill ai'r iau neu'r fwyall.

Ymgyfarfod ar ôl hyn   45
A dechrau yn syn ymholi;
Ar y Dynged bwrw'r bai,
Ni wydde'nd rhai mo'n c'ledi.

Gan ei fod o'n canu'n iach,
Bellach mi gonffesa';   50
O hyn allan, er ei fwyn,
Dros f'oes yn forwyn triga'.

Ffrins a chenedl, ffôl a ffel,
'Rwy'n rhoddi ffarwel i chwi;

Mi af i Rufain, drwy nerth Duw,   55
Dros f'oes i fyw mewn nyn'ri.

Canu a dawnsio, progres, parlio,
Yr ydw'i'n bario'ch cwmni;
Prudd-dota, ymprydio a gweddïo,
Mae gen i groeso i'r rheini.   60

Merch a'i canodd sydd â'i bryd
Ar roddi'r byd i fyny;
Ac o fawl i'r Iesu gwyn
Ni cheisia' ond hyn mo'r canu.

92   *A young woman's complaint about her*
sweetheart; the girl was Elen Gwdman from
Talyllyn and the lad was Edward Wyn from
Bodewryd, to the tune 'Rogero'

Every young woman in the world,
In pure mind and heart;
Be wary, watch that you be wicked
To a lad, O be faithful.

I know from my own wound   5
And I confess to you:
The spear of sadness is in my breast
Because of loving faithfully.

A fine, noble graceful man,
In the lusty age of youth,   10
As he passed by the place where I lived,
I often enjoyed his company.

His virtues and his speech in my presence
His appearing sudden like the snow
And his sobriety were causes   15
To make me think he liked me.

Cupid knew in a short time
That I liked his ways,
And he struck a heavy blow,
Yes, an arrow of lead to my heart.   20

Then we both became sick
But neither confessed his thoughts;
Each knew only his own wound
Even though both were in pain.

Being of frail confidence, he did not   25
Presume to ask
Mercy at my hand,
But suffered there like a little lamb.

And I too was shy or dumb,
Not daring to tell him   30
Nor giving any sign anywhere
Of my wound, that he might suspect.

I imagined that he was just
Feigning a fancy
And he thought it was not fit   35
To try to salve my bruise.

Thus we were not counting the stars
And lacking a go-between;
When fortune brought, Christ knows,
To me sad news.   40

I heard that his friends had
Bound him tightly to another
He had to suffer swiftly
Either the yoke or the axe.

Meeting each other after this   45
And starting to enquire in amazement;
Blame fell on Destiny
That our friends knew not our troubles.

Since he is saying goodbye,
I will further confess: 50
From now on, for his sake,
I will live a maid all my life.

Friends and kinfolk, foolish and wise,
I say farewell to you;
I'll go to Rome, with God's strength,   55
To live all my life in a nunnery.

Singing and dancing, processions, gossip
I renounce your company;
Gravity, fasting, and prayer,
For these I have a welcome.   60

A girl sang this, who has set her heart
On giving up the world;
And in praise to pure Jesus
I will not seek to sing anything but this.

ELEANOR DAVIES (née TOUCHET, later DOUGLAS) (LADY ELEANOR AUDLEY) (1590–1652)

ELEANOR DAVIES was daughter of George Touchet, 11th Baron Audley, created earl of Castlehaven in 1616, and Lucy, daughter of Sir James Mervin of Fonthill Giffard. When she was between 10 and 15 years old, she and her mother joined her father in Ireland, which Lady Audley hated. She was well educated, and had some Latin; she probably composed the Latin text of her tract *Prophetia*—there is no *a priori* reason to assume that she did not, since she includes Latin passages in other tracts and wrote Latin words in the margin in her own hand.

She married Sir John Davies, who had been appointed King's Solicitor in Ireland in 1603, and Attorney in 1606, in 1609. Her daughter Lucy was born in 1613. One son, Richard, died in infancy. Another, Jack, was apparently dumb, and a source of anxiety, but was drowned as a child. She and Davies returned to England in 1619. Lucy was married in 1623, to Ferdinando, son and heir of Henry Hastings, fifth Earl of Huntingdon. Her brother Mervin, Lord Audley and second Earl of Castlehaven, meanwhile married the Countess of Huntingdon's sister Anne, widow of Lord Chandos. Lady Eleanor's life took an unexpected turn in 1625, when she received a message from the Prophet Daniel. Her husband, Sir John, took a dim view of this, and burned the book she had written: for her part, she told him he would die in three years and started wearing mourning. Relations became strained, and he did indeed die at the end of 1626.

Only three months after his death, she married Sir Archibald Douglas, in March 1627. She became much given to prophesying death. In 1631, her brother was tried and executed for a range of sexual crimes which included sodomy and prostituting his wife to his servants. In the same year, her second husband was stricken with some sort of seizure, after which he was at least intermittently insane. In 1633, she moved to Holland for six months, where it was much easier for her to print (since the Low Countries had no censorship laws), and from whence she issued a spate of pamphlets. On her return, her books were seized, and she was called before the Court of High Commission. The burning of her prophecies was ordered by Archbishop Laud, and bitterly resented by her, and she was imprisoned in the Gatehouse at Westminster, from whence she was released in 1635. In 1636, she was living in Lichfield, where the cathedral was being renovated in keeping with Laud's High Anglicanism. Her protestation against this culminated when she sat herself on the bishop's throne, declared herself primate and metropolitan, and poured hot tar and wheat paste on the new altar hangings. The brief poem included here was written during this episode. That December, she was brought to London and committed to Bedlam without a hearing.

As England moved into Civil War, she became more and more certain of her mission. From *c*.1641–3, her writing centres on criticism of Britain and its rulers. From 1644, she became more concerned with the Last Judgement. In early 1647 she was once again imprisoned in the Gatehouse at Westminster. *The Gatehouse Salutation*, printed in February 1646, recalls her earlier experience of imprisonment at the Gatehouse (1633–5) and, in the context of her expectations of the Second Coming, reflects upon the courts of law sitting at Westminster. Although the tract rhymes, it was printed as continuous prose except for the last two lines. The verses are identified with the 'new song' of Revelation 5: 9, and it is directed that they are to be sung 'To the Tune of Magnificat': this suggests a self-identification with Mary, not as Virgin, or even as Mother of God, but as 'The Handmaid of the Lord': in the Magnificat, Mary speaks with the authority of a prophet.

93 *When hee was come to the other side of the contrye, of the Gergesenes, there mett him two: possessed with Devils Coming Out of the Tombes. 8 Math: Mark.*

Travelors poore Tombes thes. avoide and flee.
Wide Mouthes untam'd. No chaine that Beare can tye.
Insasiable worme, Tounge Brideled Bee.
Spirits uncleane which restles rage and Crye.
Devils administer. adjure. yee see.   5
Epicure swine feeding. Chok'd Thousands Twaine.
Named Legion. in his righte. Minde againe.

Soe howese of god poluted smell and veiw.
A fayre of Fatherless; weepe Thames and Trent
Theifes theire correction howese fitter for you.   10
Heere Marrage. Lawe. Bonds. all assunder rent.
A Mercement for. Empted uncleanness Strive

Men Mercieless. Lett this Whipp. smale suffice.
Fetters beware. A Touche. to you bee wise.
Braune to digest in Choler. not refuse   15
Friendly Musterd. a little. to peruse.

You Ducking Lowe. rooteing. yee that Beraye
Your rayement white, Fryers, [ ]
    awaye no staye.

(Litchfeild January. 1636)

Title *Gergesenes*: Gergesa, on the southern shore of the Sea of Galilee   3 *Insasiable worme*: one of the torments of hell in Mark 9: 44   6 *Epicure*: the philosophy of Epicurus (341–270 BC) was (wrongly) associated with mindless hedonism, in phrases such as 'the fattest swine of Epicurus' sty'. In Matt. 8: 28–32, Jesus casts devils out of two dangerous lunatics living in the tombs, and makes them go into a herd of pigs. In the version in Mark 5: 2–13, the devils say that their name is Legion (meaning a division of the Roman army), 'for we are many', and there were two thousand swine   10 *correction howese*: reformatory   12 *A Mercement*: amercement, fine as penalty for an offence; *Empted*: discharged, emptied   14 *Touche*: probably punning on her own name, Touchet   15 *Braune*: a dish of pressed, preserved pork, which was eaten with mustard, here in the sense of spiritual food? *Choler*: anger   17 *Beraye*: betray

94   *THE GATEHOUSE SALUTATION*

From the Lady *ELEANOR*.

Revelat. cap. 4

Serving for Westminsters Cathedral, their old Service.
And Courts of Westminster, those Elders sitting, &c.

February, 1646
Revel. cap. 4.
Post hæc vidi, & ecce ostium apertum in Cælo, &c.
New PSALM or SONG;
The CONTENTS

The Holy Ghost first knocks, so high extold, shews the end come,
by New writ witnessed and Old; in whose Kalender the time set
out, a week expired of Centuries thereabout; When as Twenty four
from *Normand* Race sprung, cast their Crowns down, Times hour-
glasse (as 'twere) run.   5

So opend the aforesaid gate or door, what winged Beasts be those
four; what restlesse eyes those day and night; the first ruff a Lyon
like: The other smooth as a Calfs skin soft: the fourth an Eagle
flying aloft: Midst them one visag'd as a MAN, which knot unloose
he who can: what eyes these before and behind, *Holy, Holy, &c.* all   10
of one minde; *Which was, which is to come,* say, *Glory to Father,
Spirit,
Son.* Inthroned, powther'd within whose Robe, in right hand whose
the Starry Globe, the likenesse of the Judgment Day, as Resurrec-
tion robes display.   15
                              Benedicite omnia opera.
                              The four Beasts, *&c.*
Bethlems Manger sometime the Throne, as its describ'd, where she
did grone; a Feather-bed cald otherwise, some Dormix curtains
wrought with eyes; their work both sides alike doth shew, full of   20
holes, besides all eaten so; A Rug and Blankets thereon laid, a woful
prisoner, the aforesaid, whose companions tedious hours, no better
Church than prisoners towers: As Elders white arrayed so shine,
Four and twenty first crownd of time: Seasons four, also with Feast
days, crowns resign; aloud him praise, all proclaiming Eternity,   25
away with tyrant Time they cry.

All Blessing, Power, Honor, say, to him dedicate a third day;
worship no Throne but his alone, besides whom King nor Priests
is none: Like as with twain that covered their face, other twain with
flying apace, their feet covered also with train, Time past, present,   30
and futures reign.

So Tabernacles three let us make, one for Moses, Christs, and
Elias sake; as for those that adore the Beast, no Sabbath have, day
or nights rest.

Lo Moonday she cœlestial virgin bride, as *Behold, I make all*   35
things new, Gates wide, new Earth, &c. Jerusalems peaceable rest,
Spouse of the Sun, our splendant new Moon's feast, Monethly, the
golden Tree of life like renders its fruit, no more pain, prison,
strife: As spar'd a million of *Belial* Sons, better then touch one of

those sacred ones: O kisse this precious Altar Coal, purges division,   40
makes ye whole.

Away with former fashions old and past: New Lights appear,
new Song record at last; he that is otherwise at his peril, as he that
righteous is, be he so still.

       So Gates and Prison Doors be no more shut,   45
       The King of Glory comes, your souls lift up.

Farewell.

To the Tune of Magnificat.

FINIS

Post hæc vidi, etc.: Rev. 4: 1, 'after this I looked and behold, a door was opened in heaven'   1 *Holy Ghost...knocks*: Rev. 3: 20   3 *week...of Centuries*: 700 years; *Twenty four*: she means that the royal line of England will come to an end after twenty-three successors to William the Conqueror have reigned (discounting regencies and failed bids for power, Charles I was the twenty-fourth)   6 *winged Beasts*: the 'four beasts full of eyes' (considered to be symbols of the four Evangelists) in Rev. 4: 6–7   13 *powther'd*: powdered; *right hand...Globe*: cf. Rev. 5: 1   16: *Benedicite*: blessed are all His works   18 *Bethlems manger*: she was committed to Bethlehem hospital (Bedlam), but associates her wretched state with the Nativity   19 *Dormix*: dornick (originally imported from Tornrijk in Belgium), a fabric, usually woollen, used for hangings and furnishing. Presumably 'wrought with eyes' is bitterly ironic, meaning moth-eaten and full of holes: fabrics were sometimes adorned with all-over embroidery, but this was very expensive   29 *twain*: seraphim, described thus in Iaaiah 6: 2   32 *Tabernacles three*: Mark 9: 5, 'let us make three tabernacles, one for thee, and one for Moses, and one for Elias'   35 *Moonday*: Monday; *virgin bride*: Rev. 21: 2. the New Jerusalem, the bride, descends from the heavens and all the earth's splendour is gathered into her   37 *Monethly...fruit*: Rev. 22: 2   39 *Belial Sons*: repeated usage in Old Testament for the incorrigibly wicked, e.g. Judges 19: 22   40 *Coal*: Isaiah 6: 6   45 *Gates*: Ps. 24: 7   48 *Magnificat*: Mary's song of thanks to God for choosing her to bear his son (Luke 1: 46)

BRÍD INÍAN IARLA CHILLE DARA
(BRIGID O'DONNELL, née FITZGERALD)
(*c*.1590–after 1607)

THIS poem is the reply to a poem written possibly by the bard Eochaidh Ó hEoghusa on behalf of Cúchonnacht Og Maguire. In this poem, Maguire claims to speak as a ghost, slain by the angelic vision of her beauty, in faultless ornamented dán díreach, a metre used by professional bards. In the reply given here, she says that if he had addressed her with inept amateur verse (dán bog) like everyone else, he might have made a better impression, but the poem which he sent was all too clearly the work of a professional poet such as Eochaid Ó hEoghusa (as indeed it most likely was). Her reply is in an amateur's metre, syllabic in organization, so is possibly at least in part her composition—especially since the poem would lose most of its rhetorical point if it had been wholly 'ghosted' by another hand.

But here we reach the crux of her authorship, queried by Cathal G. Ó Háinle, which itself hinges on the fascinating position which Brigid Fitzgerald occupied within the complex society of occupied Ireland in the early seventeenth century. She was the daughter of Henry, the twelfth earl of Kildare; and this exchange presumably dates from early in her marriage to Rudhraighe O'Donnell, Earl of Tyrconnell, *c.*1604, before Maguire, the putative author of the first poem, went into exile in Flanders in *c.*1607. Despite her marriage to a rebel Earl, Brigid's own family were loyal to the English regime, and indeed her mother and grandmother were of English origin. She lived mostly at Maynooth in Co. Kildare, geographically positioned not far from English-dominated Dublin. When, in 1607, she had to defend herself to the Lord Deputy against charges (which she did in a letter written in perfect English) of receiving money from her outlaw husband, through a Franciscan intermediary, she claimed that she barely spoke enough Irish to understand the messenger, and that she had need of an interpreter for that language. This claim is unlikely to have been wholly true, in view of the cultural circumstances of her upbringing and the obvious expediency of claiming ignorance, so her own disclaimer of her knowledge of Irish is to be treated with some suspicion. For the moment, although her precise role in its composition is not wholly clear, the poem in her voice is a fascinating document coming precisely from a point where Irish and English cultures touch without integration.

95   '*A mhacoimh dhealbhas an dán*'

A mhacoimh dhealbhas an dán
    tig aníos ar scáth na sgol;
an dán lér chuiris do chlú,
    maith a dhéanamh, is tú id' thocht

Na roinn-se do-rinne sibh,   5
    adéarthaoi rinn, a fhir ghráidh,
nach tú do dhlighfeadh an duas
    dá dteagmhah a luach 'nar láimh.

An dán do ghabhais fá seach —
    go bhfios damhsa — ní breath cham —   10
is d'fhior a ndéanta más fíor
    do ba tugtha díol na rann.

Beagán dána 'na dhán cheart,
    maith a dhéanamh, a dhearc mhall;
is gan tusa it' adhbhar suadh,   15
    iongna linne cruas na rann.

Ní chuirfinn i n-iongnadh ort
    do dhán go holc gibé fáth;
gidh eadh, is ró-iongna linn
    sibhse do bhreith gill ar dhán.   20

Dar do láimh, a dhuine ghrinn,
is tú féin do mhill bhur modh,
mar nach tángais fear-mar-chách
ar cuairt chugam le dán bog.

Mac Con Midhe, Fearghal Óg.   25
Ó Dálaigh Fionn, róimh na sgol—
leo do cumadh an gréas glic
más fíor dom aithne, a mhic Con.

Ó hEoghusa, oide na suadh—
fear a ndéanta go luath maith—   30
is é do-rinne na roinn;
nó neach éigin do Chloinn Chraith.

Acht gibé acu sin saoi
lé ndearnadh an laoi gan locht,
ní mheasaim nach mór an slad   35
a chlú do bheith ar mhac Con.

Ní ionneosad ainm an fhir
do dhuine ar bith gibé fáth:
is cuma liomsa cia hé,
acht nach deachadh dh'éag dom' ghrádh   40

Mo schloinneadh ní chluinfe cách
uaimsi go dtí an lá iné;
atá mh'ainm, gidh bé lérb áil,
ar mhnaoi do mhnáibh fhlaithis Dé.
A mhachaoimh

(1603–7)

25–6 *Mac Con Midhe, Fearghal Óg, Dálaigh Fionn*: three very distinguished professional bardic poets: Giolla Brighde Mac Con Midhe flourished in the thirteenth century, Gofraidh Fionn Ó Dálaigh was a late medieval poet, while Fearghal Óg Mac an Bhaird was a contemporary   26 *róimh/rome*: capital or head, just as Rome is the capital of Christendom   29 *Ó hEoghusa*: Eochaidh Ó hEoghusa, a well-known professional poet, became poet to Cú Chonnacht Mág Uidhir *c*.1585–6, and remained in the service of his sons, Aodh (lord from 1589–1600) and Cú Chonnacht Óg (1600–8). He is therefore the obvious suspect for a suspiciously professional poem in the name of Cú Chonnacht Óg   43 *mh'ainm/my Christian name*: Bríd, after St Brigit of Kildare, the major female saint of Ireland. Teasing concealment/revelation of a name is a motif in Irish poetry: e.g in the contemporary Piaras Feiritéar's 'Léig dhíot th'airm' ('Lay your weapons down, young woman'), which similarly devotes the last stanza to a name-riddle

95   *'O young man who composes the poem'*

O young man who composes the poem,
stop sheltering behind the poets.
The poem, by means of which you spread your fame,

is well made, while you remained silent.

These quatrains which you made,   5
it would be said to me, dear man,
that it is not you who would deserve the prize (for them)
if I should happen to have the price of them in my hand.

The poem which you have recited in sequence,
it is to the man who made the quatrains   10
that payment for them should be given, it is said—
it is no false judgment as far as I know.

Few poems are faultless, well is [your poem] made,
O [you of the] steady eye,
Seeing that you are not [even] a student-poet,   15
I find the difficulty of your quatrains amazing.

It would be no surprise to me
that your poem should be inferior, for whatever reason;
howver, I find it truly amazing
that you should take the palm for a poem.   20

[I swear] by your hand, my fine fellow,
[that] it is you yourself who has spoiled your performance,
because you did not come like any ordinary man
to visit me bringing me a facile poem.

[Giolla Brighde] Mac Con Midhe, Fearghal Óg [Mac an bhaird],   25
O Dálaigh Fionn, [who was] 'rome' of the schools [of poetry],
it was by them that the ingenious poem was composed,
if I am not mistaken, O son of Cú.

[Eochaidh] Ó hEoghasa, teacher of the poets
—one who makes quatrains quickly and well—   30
it was he who made the quatrains,
or one of the Mác Craighs.

But whichever of these learned men
made the flawless lay,
I do not consider that it is not a great robbery   35
That the son of Cú should have the fame [for having composed] it.

I shall not tell the man's name to anyone
for whatever reason,
I do not care who he is, but I know that
He would not die for love of me.   40

No-one will hear my surname
Until yesterday returns,
My Christian name, whoever may wish to know it,
Is borne by one of the women in God's heaven.

ANONYMOUS (redacted by JENNET DEVICE)
(fl. 1612)

THIS charm comes from the depositions amassed at the 1633/4 trial of the Lancashire Witches. It is here as a representative of a vast, amorphous body of oral lore available to early modern women: it is interesting to note the extremely Catholic content of this verse. Lancashire was a county noted for recusancy, but other versions of this charm survive from elsewhere, suggesting that popular culture was tenacious of some of the distinctive features of the older faith, especially in areas—such as apotropaic prayer/charm/spells—which Protestantism was unwilling to endorse. Jennet Device was 9 years old at the time of the trial: this verse, which she produced, is variously said to have been used by her mother Elisabeth and her older brother James, suggesting perhaps that it is older than either of them. Jennet's grandmother was also a witch, Elisabeth Sowthernes, known as 'old Demdike': the essentially Catholic character of the Lancashire witch-rhymes may be connected with the fact that she must have been born *c*.1530.

96   *Charm*

Upon Good-Friday, I will fast while I may
Untill I heare them knell
Our Lords owne Bell,
Lord in his messe
With his twelve Apostles good,   5
What hath he in his hand
Light in leath wand:
What hath he in his other hand?
Heavens doore key,
Open, open Heaven doore keyes,   10
Steck, steck hell dore.
Let Crizum child
Goe to it Mother mild,
What is it yonder that casts a light so farrandly,
Mine owne deare Sonne that's naild to the Tree.   15
He is naild sore by the heart and hand,
And holy barne Panne,
Well is that man
That Fryday spell can,
His Childe to learne;   20
A Crosse of Blew, and another of Red,
As good Lord was to the Roode.
Gabriel laid him downe to sleepe
Vpon the ground of holy weepe:
Good Lord came walking by,   25

Sleep's thou, wak'st thou *Gabriel*,
No lord I am sted with sticke and stake,
That I can neither sleepe nor wake:
Rise up *Gabriel* and goe with me,
The stick nor the stake shall never feere thee.   30
Sweet Iesus our Lord, Amen.

(1612)

11 *Steck*: stick   12 *Crizum child*: child just confirmed, and anointed with chrism   14
farrandly: bravely   17 *barne Panne*: brain-pan (skull)   19 *spell*: read?   24 *ground of
holy weepe*: perhaps Golgotha, site of the crucifixion   27 *sted*: held down   30 *feere thee*:
make you afraid

ANONYMOUS GENTLEWOMAN
(early 1600s)

NOTHING is known of this witty gentlewoman: the poem is preserved in a
miscellany volume compiled by a University graduate, and seems to record a
riposte sent either to himself or to a friend.

97 *A Gentlewomans answer to one, that sayd
he should dye, if shee refuse his desires*

You say sir that yor-life depends
Upon my love, and with it ends;
In this you commit sacriledge
For it is Joves great Priviledge
To rule the fates, the starres and all   5
That's heavenly or terrestriall
His Pouer you flatly doe deny;
In sayinge if I refuse, you dy
To him thus false if you can be,
I wonder what you'le prove to me?   10
And since that you so lavish art
Of such a precious drop a Hart
Desiringe me to take of you,
Some of that rich and heavenly dew:
I need not any, I can spend   15
A hart upon a private freind.
Hereafter be not so profuse
But keepe them for your proper use;
And yet I care not if I borrow
One heart to wast in publicke sorrow   20

Ffor thy great Foly: that all men may see
How fooles are payd with theyr owne treasurie.

MARY OXLIE
(fl. 1656)

MARY OXLIE'S authorship of commendatory verses prefixed to the *Poems* of William Drummond of Hawthornden (published in 1656) implies that she was a friend of his. The content of her verse suggests a fair amount of education, and a light touch. Nothing else is known of her: Edward Phillips, the editor of the posthumous edition of Drummond in which her work appears, speaks of her as 'Mary Morpeth'. Her poem amplifies the argument of a sonnet which appeared in the 1614 and 1616 editions of Drummond's verse (signed 'Parthenius'), but may have been written considerably later. She may perhaps be the author of two broadsides printed by David Laing in *Various pieces of fugitive Scotish Poetry, chiefly of the seventeenth century* (Edinburgh: W. and D. Laing), a 'hecatombe to John, Earl of Lauderdale' (1670), and 'Welcome to James, Earl of Perth' (1684). As is usually the case with Laing's work, the whereabouts of the source-texts for these poems is unstated, and they are probably now lost. They are clearly by the same hand, and are signed off M.M (perhaps for 'Mary Morpeth'). If this is so, then it is probable that she was relatively young when she wrote the poem we give here, and flourished in the mid- to late seventeenth century.

98   *To William Drummond of Hawthornden*

I Never rested on the Muses bed
Nor dipt my Quill in the Thessalian Fountaine,
My Rustick Muse was rudely fostered,
And flies too low to reach the double mountaine.
Then do not sparkes with your bright Suns compare,   5
Perfection in a Woman's worke is rare;
From an untroubled mind should Verses flow;
My discontents makes mine too muddy show;
And hoarse encumbrances of houshold care
Where these remaine, the Muses ne're repaire.   10

If thou dost extoll her Haire,
Or her Ivory Forehead faire,
Or those Stars whose bright reflection
Thrals my heart in sweet subjection:
Or when to display thou seeks   15
The snow-mixt Roses on her Cheekes,
Or those Rubies soft and sweet,
Over those pretty Rows that meet.
The Chian painter as asham'd,

Hides his Picture so far fam'd;   20
And the Queen he carv'd it by,
With a blush her face doth dye,
Since those Lines do limne a Creature
That so far surpast her Feature.
When thou show'st how fairest Flora   25
Prankt with pride the banks of Ora, .
So thy Verse her streames doth honour,
Strangers grow enamour'd on her,
All the Swans that swim in Po
Would their native brooks forgo,   30
And as loathing Phoebus beames,
Long to bath in cooler streames,
Tree-turn'd Daphne would be seen
In her Groves to flourish green,
And her Boughs would gladly spare.   35
To frame a garland for thy haire,
    That fairest Nymphs with finest fingers
    May thee crown the best of singers.

But when thy Muse dissolv'd in show'rs,
Wailes that peerlesse Prince of ours,   40
Cropt by too untimely Fate,
Her mourning doth exasperate
Senselesse things to see thee moane,
Stones do weep, and Trees do groane,
Birds in aire, Fishes in flood,   45
Beasts in field forsake their food,
The Nymphs forgoing all their Bow'rs
Teare their Chaplets deckt with Flow'rs;
Sol himselfe with misty vapor,
Hides from earth his glorious Tapor,   50
    And as mov'd to heare thee plaine
    Shews his griefe in show'rs of raine.

Mary Oxlie of Morpet.
(1656)

---

2 *Thessalian fountain*: Hippocrene, on Mount Parnassus, home of the Muses   4 *double mountaine*: Parnassus   19 *The Chian painter*: probably intended to signify Zeuxis, creator of an ideal portrait of Helen (though he was from Heraclea in Lucania)   26 *Ora*: the Ore in Fife   33 *Daphne*: a nymph, who metamorphosed into a laurel tree when pursued by Apollo. Poets were therefore crowned with laurel wreaths   40 *Prince*: Henry, son of James VI, who died in 1612, at 18

MRS WINCHCOMBE
(fl. 1614)

AUTHOR of an epitaph on her husband's tomb, otherwise unknown.

99   *'I lovd thee living and lament thee dead'*

I lovd thee living and lament thee dead
But in what measure cannot be exprest,
Yet love and sorrowe both will needes be read
Even in this marble (Deare) they do their best,
And tis for others too I put this stone   5
To me thy tombe shal be my heart alone.
Twise eighteene yeares he viewed Heavens day,
Sixteen he spent in happy wedlocks bonds,
The Graces, Muses and the Fates did lay
Untimely on his webb theire hastening hands,   10
Of heire his house, of all their hopes his friends
Of progenie his wife bereft, he ends.

                                                         (1614)

10 *webb*: the web of his life, woven by the Fates

HONOR STRANGMAN, JENNYFER BENNY
(with JOHN DIER, BENJAMIN STRANGMAN
and others)
(fl. 1616)

OUR only information on this group of people comes from the same Star
Chamber document (PRO, STAC 8 202/30) which contains the text of their
jointly composed 'infamous, obscene and scandalous libell'. The piece was
composed at St Columb in Cornwall in April of the year 1616. The victims of
the piece were Mary Lawry and her husband Hugh, a carpenter. It is obvious
that it is the wife who is the target of the attack. The local sectarian quarrel,
family antagonism, or boundary dispute which may have started the ill-feeling
which explodes into this rough and robust verse is unknown. What is known,
however, is something of the purposes and methods with which the Strangmans
and their associates went about disseminating their composition. They were
accused of 'the stirring up and nourishing of descorde and debate betwixt man
and wief' and that they did 'unlawfully plot, practise and combyne together and
consult how they might blemish the reputation of [the] said subjects' with a libel
'contayning most filthy and reprochfull matter of slander and disgrace... They
have openly and with a lowde voyce read, rehearsed, spoken, uttered, sung,

proclaimed, published and divulged in most scoffing and disgracefull manner
the words, matter and effect of the said libell.'

100   *'Yf there be any man that can tell*
me quicklye'

Yf there be any man that can tell me quicklye,
a Medicyne for to cure a Wench that is greeved sore and sicklye,
Let him come at St Collomb Towne and there he shall have newes
Where lyes this Wench oppressed sore as it will make you muse.

The ground of this here is, as I have heard it spoken   5
Shee always doth bedue her sheats her flood hatch it is broken,
and the streame of it runneth through the brooke as shee lies
   sleeping.
her vilme was broken with a thrust for out her pisse doth flye,

Which greef of hers to help full many hath assaide,
but all their labor was in vayne, they could not cure the Mayd,   10
then shee thought on another trick shee needs would change her lief
shee sold away her Mayden hood and is become a Wief

and then there came a Carpenter who thought sure with a Pyn
to mend her floodgate and thereby to keepe her water in,
he tooke greate Payne and wore his flesh and loked thin and pale,   15
but all his labor was in vayne he could no good at all.

then out she cries most bitterly and still the time doth curse
that shee the chamber pott should hold and ope her neither purse,
Wherein dispaire entred and oft the strapps rented
Which brooke her gate and spilde her state which runneth like a
   vent   20

Yf soon shee be not cured great Pynnes will beare greate price,
a great Pyn for a Chamber pott because shee will not rise,
then she a Mayde perforce must hire the chamber pott to sett
Which still will stand her a greate Pynne els shee bedd must weatt

But I have heard her say of late such vertue is in Myse,   25
they are very good for the disease so they be baked in pies,
first they must stripp away the skyn and afterward them bake,
and for full three dayes after no other meate must take,

and then they must take the skins and heate them good and warme,
uppon a chaffer dishe and coles least cold should doe her harme,   30
and clapp some on her breast and some uppon her nall,
butt let her put most part of them uppon her what I call,

therefore all you good farmers when you doe turne your corne,

save up all the mice you catch for Mistress and bring downe unto
   her house,
it shalbe for your gayne   35
for shee will content you for your cost and payne.

but yf this will not serve alack what shall I saye,
some other physick lett her take her greef for to allay,
yf phisick will not helpe then lett her goe with speede
and take some heare and sue her geare and bite away the threade.   40

6 *sheats*: bedsheets   8 *vilme*: perhaps a by form of 'film', used with the sense of
'membrane', hence 'maidenhood'   13 *Pyn*: by implication, penis   25 *Myse*: traditional
remedy for bed-wetting   31 *nall*: noll (head)   40 *heare*: hair; *sue*: sew; *geare*: sexual
organs

FIONNGHUALA, ÌNGHEAN UÍ DOMHNAILL
BHRIAIN (O'BRIEN)
(*c.* 1617)

THE following accentual lament by a wife for her husband is one of the earliest
examples of its genre in the post-Classical period of Irish literature. Its author,
Fionnghuala Ní Bhriain was the daughter of Domhnall Ó Briain, a politically
significant figure who contested the leadership of the Ó Briain patrimony in
Thomond with his nephew, Conchubhar Ó Briain, the third Earl, in a protracted campaign from the middle years of the sixteenth century. Eventually he
was reconciled with the reformed political organization of the Lordship of
Thomond, in which the Crown, through the offices of the third Earl, exercised
an ever increasing degree of influence, and he was appointed in 1576 to the office
of Sheriff of Clare. Fionnghuala, then, was the daughter of a man who was
important locally, and one who had occupied the minds of not a few senior
officials in London and elsewhere during the third quarter of the sixteenth
century. She was married to Thomas FitzMaurice, Lord of Lixnaw in County
Kerry, but he put her away in December 1579 in order to marry the widow of
James FitzMaurice, his former political rival: adding insult to injury, this
woman was Fionnghuala's stepsister. Since her father Domhnall Ó Briain had
died in October of the same year, Fionnghuala found herself in an unenviable
position as the year drew to its close, rejected by her husband and lacking the
protective authority of her father.
    Fortunately for her, despite her father's dispute with the Earls of Thomond,
her first cousin, Conchubhar, or Conor, Ó Briain, the third Earl, and his son the
fourth Earl, Donnchadh, who was ruling when she composed her lament in
1617, were concerned to defend her interests. The third Earl seems to have
rescued her from her predicament of 1579 (as the poem indicates, when it refers
to the Earl as her 'protector' in times of 'hardship') by arranging a second
marriage for her with Uaithne Mór Ó Lochlainn, the last leader of his sept, who
ruled over the area of North Clare known as the Burren, a marriage which took
place in 1580. The third Earl died the following year and the six lines in

question mark Fionnghuala's affection and fond memory of that nobleman and her indebtedness to him. Her closeness in blood and, quite likely, in friendship with the Earls of Thomond furnishes a cogent explanation for a strange feature of the lament, the only composition of hers which seems to have survived: her earnest reference to the death of an Earl of Thomond (27–33) even as she laments the death, in conventional terms, of her second husband.

Ó Lochlainn's death in 1617 left Fionnghuala Ní Bhriain in a vulnerable position yet again. No heir or heiress had issued from their marriage. Consequently or, perhaps, incidentally, Ó Lochlainn had nominated two first cousins of his own, women of the Burke family, as co-heiresses, Fionnghuala receiving, I assume, only the value of her marriage dowry in accordance with the law and custom that obtained in the sixteenth century. In a sequence of nine lines (34–43) she refers to this state of affairs as her 'loss of precedence', articulating indirectly the dissatisfaction she undoubtedly felt with Ó Lochlainn's will, but placing it in a wider context of political and social turmoil. She specifically alludes to the collapse of Ó Néill's hegemony in Ulster and argues astutely that now only the Ó Briain have any claim to a position of pre-eminence amongst the noble families of Ireland. Dr Liam Ó Murchú perceives in this latter assertion a coded appeal for help to the contemporary Ó Briain ruler, Donnchadh, the fourth Earl of Thomond. The latter had already fought for and had won significant advantages or *freedoms* for the Ó Lochlainn nobility and for Fionnghuala's brother, Toirdhealbhach Ó Briain, Lord of Corcomroe, in North Clare, in the 1585 Composition of Connacht. Unfortunately, due to lack of evidence, it is not possible to say how successful this appeal was, but it appears to be certain that Fionnghuala had to vacate the Ó Lochlainn castle at Muicinis soon after her husband's death.

Thus, though short, this elegy is a complicated literary document. Finnghuala Ní Bhriain's references to genealogical lore (9–21) would point to her having had some contact with the literary culture of her time and it is not far fetched to assume that she was familiar with at least some of the work of the Ó Bruaideadha poets and historians who were attached officially to the Ó Briain nobility. The accentual metre in which she composed her elegy is that which another woman poet of County Clare known as Caitilín Dubh used over the following twenty years (post 1620) to memorialize members of the Ó Briain nobility (Caitilín Dubh's work is not now available, but will shortly be published by Liam Ó Murchú under the imprint of the Irish Texts Society). A dearth of evidence again prevents us from stating whether this female literary activity was a County Clare phenomenon or was replicated in other parts of Ireland at the beginning of the seventeenth century.

101   *Fionnghuala Inghean Domhnaill*
        Uí Bhriain cecenit.

A nainm an Spioraid Naoimh h'imrighe, 'Uaithne,
is triall ó thigh bhig go tigh mhuar sibh;
béara an tAirdrígh dá lánbhrígh suas tu
don ádhbhadh ann nách fuighir gábhadh ná guasacht.

Biaidh Mórmhac na hÓighe gan ghruaim riot   5
do bhrígh tú bheith sgaoilteach fá a bhfuarais
'snach raibh stór cófra ná guais ort,
eaglais is aos ealadhan gan ghruaim riot.

D'inneosainn beagán beagán dot dhualgus:
cúig rígh fhichiot do bhí uaitse   10
ar Éirinn nár bhféidir a ruagadh,
deich rígh is fiche rígh gan truailleadh

do ríogh cóigeadh, gér mhór a ttuairisg,
do churadhaibh lé ccurthaoi gach cruaidhthreas.
Muna leor so dot eolas uaimse   15
do gheabhthar sgeol ort a leabhar na suadha

'sgur libh an céadlaoi dá nduantaibh.
Nár agra an tAirdrígh atá thuas ort
gur sibh féin do réigh so uatha
gur fhortabhair an tromdháimh trí huaire   20
is fir Éireann dá léirsgrios uatha.

Is mun bheith mur tharrla mé i ngruaim riot
do bheadh mac do mháthar dom buaireadh,
ó do síneadh gaois go luaith leat
is réidhteach ar sgéaltaibh ba muarcheisd,   25

do dhaonnacht gan aonbhuille cruais ann.
Sgéal fábhaill atá dom buaireadh:
atáim cráidhte ó bhás Iarla Tuadhmhan,
mo chré chúil, do bhrúigh go muar me,

árdfhlaith aga mbíodh cás im chruadhtan   30
ó bhfuighinn fáilte ghrádhmhar shuaimhneach
is fuighle badh binn liom am chluasaibh
is cáta tar a lán do mhnáibh uaisle.

Ní oile is iongnadh go muar liom:
cé a nÉirinn éinneach do luaidhfiodh   35
tús na slíghe do bhreith uaimse
ó chuaidh tréine Uí Néill ar buairiodh,

Síol Eoghain dár chóir bheith uasal,
'sgur eadruibh féin do bhí an mhuardhacht.
San sgéal so ní faighthior bréaga uaimse   40
gur bhé dlíghe na tttréinfhear gan truailleadh,

gidh bé díobh budh sinnsior an uair sin
an dís oile do stríocadh anuas dho.
a Éire atá taomannach buaidhiortha
ní buan do ré d'éinneach dár dhual tu;   45

's a mhéirdreach ó thréigise h'uaisle
is cuma liom féin cia an té fá mbuailfir.
Is é do bhás tar chách do bhuaidhir me
'sa nainm an Spioraid Naoimh h'imrighe, 'Uaithne.

37 *Uí Néill/Ó Néill:* one of Ireland's most important ruling families, particularly in the North   38 *Síol Eoghain/race of Eoghan:* the Eoganacht, also called the O Briens, were the ruling family of Munster, the most important power in the South   46 *mhéirdreach/ harlot:* the ancient personification of Ireland as a woman acquired new negative connotations when the English seized control of most of the country: 'she' was perceived as faithless to her old rulers

101   *Fionnghuala daughter of Domnall*
       UÓ Briain composed (sang) this

May your journey, Uaithne, be in the name of the Holy Spirit,
you move from a small to a big house;
the Supreme King in his omnipotence will bring you
to the abode where you will encounter neither peril nor anxiety.

The great Son of the Virgin will meet you in no surly fashion   5
since you were lavish with what you got,
and since the hoarding of coffered wealth cannot possibly be imputed to you.
(as) the church and men of art (were) not disappointed with you.

I would briefly relate a little of your heredity:
before you were twenty-five kings   10
over Ireland that could not be displaced,
thirty uncorrupted kings

who ruled a province, though their fame was great,
warriors by whom each tough conflict was fought.
If this knowledge I give of you is insufficient   15
your story can be found in the book of the poets,
considering that to you belongs the first poem of their compositions.

May the Supreme King on high not bring against you
that you obtained this from them,
that you thrice succoured the oppressive company of poets   20
when the men of Ireland were ridding themselves of them.

And were it not that I have been mourning for you,
I would (still) be troubled by you being your mother's son,
since wisdom was associated with you early on,
as was the solving of grave affairs,   25

your kindliness held not the slightest harshness.
Another affair troubles me much:
I am grieved since the death of my protector the Earl of Thomond,
which (death) oppressed me greatly,

a great lord who concerned himself with my hardship,   30
from whom I got loving, soothing salutation,

and speech which was sweet to my ears,
and honour above many noble ladies.

Another matter that I find quite surprising:
where in Ireland is anyone   35
who would cite my lack of precedence
considering that the might of Ó Néill has dissipated,

the race of Eoghan to whom it would have been proper to behave nobly;
and greatness was shared by each of you.
In this matter I do not lie, (I say)   40
that it was the unbroken rule of the mighty ones,

to whichever one of you was superior then,
the other two would bow down.
Ireland, restless and tormented,
no lasting reign has he who has proper claims to you;   45

and, harlot, since you deserted your nobles
I don't care to whom you attach yourself.
Your death, beyond everyone, has oppressed me,
and may your journey be in the name of the Holy Spirit, Uaithne.

BAPTINA CROMWELL (née PALAVICINO)
(1595/8–1618)

SIR HORATIO PALAVICINO, descendant of a Genoese family of diplomats and businessmen, married Anna Hooftman at Frankfurt in 1591, the daughter of a banker and businessman of Antwerp. The couple lived at Babraham in Cambridgeshire, and had three children, Henry, Toby, and Baptina (named after Horatio's mother, Battina Spinola). They were a Protestant family: he had apostasized in 1582. In his will, Sir Horatio left his daughter an annuity of £150, with directions that her marriage-portion was to be £5,000: a level of generosity which left her as well dowered as the daughter of an English peer. Unfortunately his intentions towards his children were overturned by his much younger wife. After his death in 1600, Anna Palavicino remarried as soon as she decently could: the ceremony took place a year and a day after her first husband's death. Her chosen partner was Sir Oliver Cromwell of Hinchinbrook (great-uncle of the Lord Protector), hospitable, prodigal, and several thousand pounds in debt. Though his father, Sir Henry Cromwell, was one of the wealthiest men in late Elizabethan England, the old man was inconveniently long-lived: he died in 1604, leaving his son with an income of £5,000 a year. Again, as soon as it was legally possible, Sir Oliver and Lady Cromwell married the three Palavicino children to Sir Oliver's children by a previous marriage, as follows: Henry Palavicino (14) married Catherine Cromwell (12), and Toby Palavicino (12) married Jane Cromwell in 1606. It was not possible to marry off Baptina simultaneously, since she can have been no more than 10: her marriage to Sir Oliver's heir, Henry, followed c.1608/10. This threw the entire Palavicino fortune, including Baptina's dowry, into Sir Oliver's dubious control:

the texture of their life may be indicated by the diary of John Manningham, who noted in 1602, 'there lives a housefull at Hinchinbrooke, like a kennell'.

Sir Oliver, like many noblemen of his time, contrived to spend both the Cromwell and Palavicino fortunes on the entertainment of King James, who was inclined to favour Hinchinbrook as a convenient hunting-lodge. He lived to the age of 93, overwhelmed by debt. Baptina's husband, Sir Henry, inherited the family propensity. By 1649, his debts were £11,000, with a mortgage for £2,000, while his landed income was reduced to £65 a year. Father and son had run through two fortunes (with a sizeable chunk of a third, since Sir Cornelius Hooftman, Baptina's wealthy uncle, left property to be divided between the children of his sister). Perhaps fortunately for herself Baptina died young, in April 1618, followed two months later by her 2-year-old daughter. Her epitaph in BL Harley 2311, fos. 23-4, emphasizes her extreme piety; and it certainly seems as if hers was a life in need of the comforts of religion.

Baptina Cromwell's verse is preserved in a family book belonging to Anna Cromwell, later Williams, who described it as 'A booke of severall devotions collected from good men by the worst of sinners'. The volume includes other family poetry by Elizabeth Cromwell to her sister Mary, Mrs Price (below)

102   *Verces made by Mistress Battina Cromwell, wife to Henry Cromwell esq. Sir Oliver Cromwell's sone*

Eternal power from whose allseeing eye
nothing though masqued can remaine unknowne
thou that regardest sinners when they cry
be pleased to looke on mee as on thine owne
vouchsafe t'accept this exercise of mine   5
not for my sake but for that sonne of thine
I feere I confess I am and have beene such
that hadst thou not still lovd mee more then much
I now with little hope my state might rue.
But thy abounding mercy more than sinne   10
Hath freed mee from the slavery I was in.
Deare god what love is this thou hast shewed mee
In giveing life when death my soule did chase
and wanting power, nay will to come to thee
thou gavest both of thee I might not loose   15
and with such sweetness hast me happie made
that where thou mightst compell thou didst perswaid

My righteousness could be no gaine to thee
my wickedness could purchase thee no Losse
Mine only is the gaine godly to bee   20
If wicked I am mine only is the crosse,
In this thy mercy then did most appeare
that only for my good thou heldst me deare

ffor all thy goodnes now what may I render
that may be gratious in thy acceptation   25
even of thine owne I heere make tender
which will be pleasing in thy estimation
that thankfullness which thou hast given to mee
I heere unfeinedly returne to thee.
And now I crave what only thou canst grante   30
the grace I have received encrease it still
In each respect so as I never want
sufficient power, to execute thy will.
this I ambitiously aspire unto
O bless my ambition that aspireth so.   35

ELIZABETH STUART, later QUEEN OF BOHEMIA
(1596–1660)

DAUGHTER of James VI and sister of Charles I, Elizabeth's life was not a happy
one. She was separated from her mother in babyhood, the result of a trial of
strength between Anne and James. When James succeeded to the English throne
in 1603, she was sent to be brought up by Lord Harington of Exton at Coombe
Abbey, near Coventry (father of Lucy Harington, Countess of Bedford). She
was taught French, Italian, music, and dancing. She proved to be an expensive
charge, and in typical Stuart fashion, the honour brought the Harington household deep into debt. She also wrote verse and loved hunting. In 1612 she was
betrothed to one of the leading Protestant monarchs of Europe, Frederick V,
Elector Palatine. They married on St Valentine's Day 1613 in London, then
went on progress to Heidelberg, where they were to live. In 1619 the Elector was
elected King of Bohemia, as Protestant champion, and Elizabeth was crowned
Queen. This action precipitated the Thirty Years War, and two years later, the
Battle of the White Mountain put a definitive end to his control of both Bohemia
and the Palatinate. The couple took refuge in Holland, and for the rest of her
life, she was dependent on handouts from her brother and the Stadhouder of the
Netherlands. She bore thirteen children, who included both a Protestant and a
Catholic abbess, the future mother of George I (making her the conduit through
which the present house of Windsor traces its 'legitimacy') and two artists,
Louise Hollandine, and Rupert of the Rhine, inventor of the mezzotint as well as
one of Charles I's most distinguished soldiers. Her homes in exile were a house
in the Hague, the Wassenaer Hof, and a summer house at Rhenen, not very far
below Arnheim, described by Evelyn as 'a neate, & well built Palace or Country
house, built after the Italian manner as I remember'. Her children lived at the
Prinsenhof in Leiden, and summered with her in Rhenen. Elizabeth was
widowed in 1632. Her son, Charles Louis, was restored to the Palatinate in
1648, but she remained in Holland. After the restoration of her nephew, she
returned to England, and resided at the house of William, Lord Craven, but the
suggestion that they were secretly married is almost certainly false. She died at

his house, shortly after the Restoration. The verses here, the only poem she is known to have written, were given by her to Lord Harington, and probably pleased him greatly, since their sentiments are irreprochable. The psalm translations in Heidelberg sometimes attributed to her are in German, and are the work of her daughter-in-law.

103   *Verses by the Princess Elizabeth, given to Lord Harington, of Exton, her preceptor.*

I
This is joye, this is true pleasure
If we best things make our treasure,
And enjoy them at full leasure,
Evermore in richest measure.

II
God is only excellent,   5
Let up to him our love be sent,
Whose desires are set or bent
On ought else, shall much repent.

III
Theirs is a most wretched case,
Who themselves so far disgrace,   10
That they their affections place
Upon things nam'd vile and base.

IV
Let us love of heaven receave,
There are joyes our harts will heave
Higher than we can conceave,   15
And shall us not fayle or leave.

V
Earthly things do fade, decay,
Constant to us not one day;
Suddenly they pass away,
And we can not make them stay.   20

VI
All the vast world doth conteyne,
To content mans heart, are vayne,
That still justly will complayne,
And unsatisfyde remaine.

VII
God, most holy, high, and greate,   25
Our delight doth make compleate;
When in us he takes his seate,
Only then we are repleat.

VIII

Why should vain joyes us transport,
Earthly pleasures are but shorte,   30
And are mingled in such sorte,
Greifs are greater then the sporte.

IX

And regard of this yet have,
Nothing can from death us save,
Then we must unto our grave,   35
When we most are pleasure's slave.

X

By long use our soules will cleave
To the earth: then it we leave;
Then will cruell death bereave,
All the joyes that we receive.   40

XI

Thence they goe to hellish flame,
Ever tortur'd in the same,
With perpetuall blott of name,
Flowt, reproach, and endless shame.

XII

Torment not to be exprest,   45
But, O then! how greatly blest,
Whose desires are whole addrest
To the heavenly thinges and best.

XIII

Thy affections shall increase,
Growing forward without cease,   50
Even untill thou dyest in peace,
And injoyest eternall ease.

XIV

When thy hart is fullest fraught
With heavens love, it shall be caught
To the place it loved and sought,   55
Which Christs precious bloud hath bought.

XV

Joyes of those which there shall dwell,
No hearte thinke, no tounge can tell;
Wonderfully they excell,
Those thy soule will fully swell   60

XVI

Are these things indeed even soe?
Doe I certainly them know,
And am I so much my foe?

To remayne yett dull and slowe?

XVII

Doth not that surpassing joy, 65
Ever freed from all annoy,
Me inflame? and quite destroy
Love of every earthly toy.

XVIII

O how frozen is my heart,
O my soule how dead thou art, 70
Thou, O God, we maye impart,
Vayne is humane strength and art.

XIX

O, my God, for Christ his sake,
Quite from me this dulness take;
Cause me earths love to forsake, 75
And of heaven my realm to make.

XX

If early thanks I render thee,
That thou hast enlightened me,
With such knowledge that I see,
What things most behoofull bee. 80

XXI

That I hereon meditate,
That desire, I find (though late)
To prize heaven at higher rate,
And these pleasures vayne to hate.

XXII

O enlighten more my sight, 85
And dispell my darksome night,
Good Lord, by thy heavenly light,
And thy beams most pure and bright.

XXIII

Since in me such thoughts are scant,
Of thy grace repayre my want, 90
Often meditations grant,
And in me more deeply plant,

XXIV

Worke of wisedome more desire,
Grant I may with holy ire,
Slight the world, and me inspire, 95
With thy love to be on fire.

XXV

What care I for lofty place,
If the Lord grant me his grace,

Shewing me his pleasant face,
And with joy I end my race.   100

XXVI

This is only my desire,
This doth set my heart on fire,
That I may receave my hyre,
With the saints and angels quire.

XXVII

O my soule of heavenly birth,   105
Doe thou scorn this basest earth,
Place not here thy joy and wirth,
Where of bliss is greatest dearth.

XXVIII

From below thy mind remove,
And affect the things above: 110
Sett thy heart and fix thy love
Where thou truest joyes shalt prove.

XXIX

If I do love things on high,
Doubtless them enjoy shall I,
Earthly pleasures if I try,   115
They pursued faster fly.

XXX

O Lord, glorious, yet most kind,
Thou hast these thoughts put in my mind,
Let me grace increasing find,
Me to thee more firmly bind.   120

XXXI

To God glory, thanks, and praise,
I will render all my dayes,
Who hath blest me many wayes,
Shedding on me gratious rayes.

XXXII

To me grace, O Father, send,   125
On thee wholly to depend,
That all may to thy glory tend,
Soe let me live, soe let me end.

XXXIII

Now to the true Eternal King,
Not seen with human eye,   130
The immortall, only wise, true God,
Be praise perpetually!

(?1609)

MOR NIGHEAN UISDEIN
(*c*.1615)

WAULKING songs constitute the largest body of surviving folksong in Scottish Gaelic. Their survival and transmission was ensured till the 1930s by their use as a musical accompaniment to the tedious job of fulling ('waulking') cloth once it had been taken off the loom. The cloth was shrunk and the fibres matted by a three-hour rhythmic pounding, carried out in the Highlands by women. Some of the songs may well have been composed extempore; others appear to have been adapted from existing songs. Individual women took turns in singing the words, while the whole group (consisting of an even number between twelve and sixteen) would sing the chorus of meaningless vocables at the end of every line or couple of lines. The event took on a festive and hypnotic air, the single sex audience allowing for unusual frankness. The songs often concern dramatic events in courtship (rape, abandonment, infidelity), but their formulaic nature suggests they may not all be factual or biographical.

104   *'Hé mandu'*

Hé, mannd' thu!
Gur h-é mis-e,
Hé, mannd' thu!
Rinn an t-socharadh.
Hé, mannd' thu!   5
'N oidhche bha mi,
Hao ri, ho ró.
'N còir an locha!
Hò, mannd' thu, Hao ò
Hò rò i, hao ò!   10

'N oidche bha mi
'N còir an locha;
'N oidche dhiùlt mi
Fear a phoca.

'N oidche dhiùlt mi   15
Fear a phoca.
C'àit am faic mi
Fear a choltais;

C'àit am faic mi
Fear a choltais;   20
Bho nach maireann

Fionn no Osgar,

Bho nach maireann
Fionn no Osgar,
Torcul donn   25
Gu cur cloiche

Torcul donn
Gu cur cloiche
No Driuchd–Uaine
Mac Righ Lochlainn?   30

24 *Fionn no Osgar/ Fionn and Oscar*: Finn, leader of the Fenians, a group of legendary
heroes celebrated in Ireland and Gaelic Scotland, and his grandson   25 *Torcul/Torcail*: a
legendary Swedish king (Thorkell)   30 *Lochlainn/Norway*: as the previous note suggests,
several Norse heroes were remembered in Gaelic song, but this name is completely garbled

104   *'Ay, bashful thou!'*

Hé mandu
It was me
Hé mandu
Who made the blunder
Hé mandu   5
The night I was
Hé mandu
Beside the water.
Hé mandu, Hì ri o ró
Hó ró, Hù ó.   10

The night I was
Beside the water,
The night I refused
The man with the game-bag.

The night I refused   15
The man with the game-bag,
Where can I see
A man of his likeness?

Where can I see
A man of his likeness,   20
Since Finn and Oscar
Are not living.

Since Finn and Oscar
Are not living,
Nor brown-haired Torcail,   25
Masterful at putting,

Nor brown-haired Torcail,
Masterful at putting,
Nor Driùchd-Uaine
Prince of Norway?   30

HESTER PULTER, née LEE
(1596–1678)

LADY HESTER PULTER was the daughter of James Ley, first Earl of Marlborough, by his first wife Mary, daughter of John Pettie of Stoke Talmage,
Oxfordshire, one of eleven children. Though Marlborough rose to be Lord
Treasurer, he is a figure of little political significance, whose reputation never
recovered from the fact that he was Buckingham's appointee. She married
Arthur Pulter, who had a modestly successful public life, culminating in becoming Lord Lieutenant of Hertfordshire. On the outbreak of civil war, he retired
into the country, and spent his time building a house on his estate at Broadfield.
Despite his firmly maintained neutrality, it is clear that his wife was a vehemently committed royalist. Her work is preserved in a single manuscript, which
appears to be a scribal fair copy with her own corrections, containing some 120
poems together with a romance written between 1646 and 1665, entitled
'Hedassa's chaste fancies' (Hedassa being another name for the biblical Esther).
It encompasses a considerable variety of genres: satires, love-poetry, elegies,
emblems, allegories, and also includes a long romance in two parts, the second of
which is incomplete, called *The unfortunate Florinda*. Her own persona in this
work is as Fidelia, an aristocratic Moroccan girl who carries a black lead pencil
in her pocket. At first reluctant to join her brother's Italian and Spanish lesson,
she changes her mind because of the 'many Excellent books' she will be able to
read. She later puts her knowledge to good use while disguised as a boy and
employed as a slave in the country house of a London merchant. Debating with
the misogynist Don Alphonso, she argues that girls are naturally quicker than
boys: 'and so it is where learning hath not made a difference, for all possible
knowledg is infused into Men, And woemen are bred up in as much Ignorance
as is possible' (ff. 26^{r-v}).

   She was the mother of fifteen children, all but one of whom she outlived; and
by her own account, tended to write poetry during her confinements (which,
according to the childbirth practice of the seventeenth century, left her mewed
up in her room for prolonged periods of time). The absence of any mention of
her husband in her poetry, together with their political divergence, may suggest
a lack of sympathy between them. Despite her considerable skill, she appears to
have had no connection with any other known poets, and her writing is not
mentioned by anyone else; a far more unusual state of affairs with women poets
of her time than is generally believed. However, she was apparently reading the
works of other contemporaries, most notably the poet Andrew Marvell, whose
work she appears to have accessed in manuscript before its publication. Of the
poems included here, 'Upon the imprisonment of his Sacred Majestie' picks up
Thomas Carew's often-recycled line, 'Ask me no more', while 'Upon the Death
of my deare and lovely Daughter' draws in more subtle ways on Marvell's
'Nymph Complaining for the Death of her Fawn'.

105   *The complaint of Thames 1647 when the*
       best of Kings was imprisoned by the worst
       of Rebels at Holmbie

Late in an evening as I walk'd alone,
I heard the Thames most sadly make her moane:
As shee came weeping from her western Spring,
Shee thus bewaild the learned Shepherd King.
Amintas sad Amintas sits forelorne   5
And his faire Cloris now's become the Scorne
Of Troynovants ingreate licentious Dames
Noe Merveile thus if poore aflicted Thames
With Salt abortive teares dos wash this Citty
As full of Blood and lies as voyd of pittie   10
Perfidious Town know thou the power of fate
Thy long felicitie shall find a date
And I may live to see another turn
When thy proud fabrick shall unpittied burn
Then Heaven Just Heaven withold thy raine   15
And I will leave my channil once againe
As when my holy Albians blood was spilt
Seeing to wash away thy Horrid guilt
Is more impossible than 'tis to change
The Skins of Negros that in Aphrick range   20
Then when thou tryest in vengfull flames of fire
Thy scorched genious reddy to expire
Thy tong and mouth sable as Salamander
With speaking gainst thy King and Queene such slander
Then not a drop of my coole Cristall Wave   25
To coole thy Sulpherous Tongue or life to save
But when I have of thee seene all my lust
And all thy pride and Glory Turn'd to dust
Then I Triumphant with my watery traine
Will make this Cittie Quagmires once againe   30
But O thy Blood and Perjuries repent
Then Heaven I hope in mercie will relent
Thy King restore call home his Queene and mine
Or all thy prayer and fasting is in vaine
Hast thou forgot (Aye me) soe have not I   35
Those Halcian dayes the Sweete Tranquillity
That we injoyed under his happy Reigne
Which Heaven will once restore to us againe
Unles the dismale line of dissolution
(Which ô forbid) bee drawn upon this Nation.   40
Oft have I born upon my silver Brest
His lovely Cloris like Aurora drest

With youth and beuty with her Princely Spouse
Envied I was by Severn, Humber, Owes
The sacred Dee said shee noe more would boast   45
Her shewing Conquest on the conquering Coast
Though Edgares Glory from her River springs
When hee in Triumph by eight Captive kings
Was Rowed upon her famous Cristall streame
Those former Honours shewed now like a dreame   50
Nay the Danube said she would ner'e rehearse
Her being biggest in the Universe
Even Tigris would not brag of Golden sands
But said shee envied more my happy strands
Soe said the Loyer in envie Poe tooke on   55
Thou shee were Honour'd by a Phaiton
And Ægipts Glory Nillus stately streame
Said her felicities were but a dreame
When on her or'e flowing waves were seene
The Roman Eagles and her black ey'd Queen   60
And silver Gangers said the sacrifice
The Bamans brought with elivated eyes
Though all theire Carcases by fire calcin'd
Were in her Purifieing Waves refin'd
Though all theire wealth and Treasure in they hurl   65
And Shee were Lady of the Easterne world
Yet all that Glory shee did count a toye
Compar'd shee said with happy Thames her Joy
Tiber said of Horatias vallure brave
Shee ner'e would speake but I the praise should have: 70
Cristall Euphrates never did envie
The Glory of noe other floud but I
Though from a Thousand Founts her streame doth springe
Yet did shee never beare soe good a King
Through lofty Babilon her River flowes   75
And earthly Paradice shee doth inclose
Though brave Symerrimus enlarge her fame
Yet doth shee envie still the English Thame
But now alas they envie me noe more
But with theire Tears my heavy loss deplore   80
Oft have I borne my sacred Sovereigns Barge
Being richly guilt, most proud of such a charge
My waves would swell to see his Princely face
Each billow loth to give his fellow place
Sometimes they would rise to kiss his Royall hand   85
And hardly would give back at my command
Billow with billow strive and ruffling Rore
Scorning the blow of either hand or owre
But now insulting on my billowes Ride

The Kingdooms Schourg's and this Citties pride   90
Which make my Trembling Streame lamenting Rore
And her sad loss with troubled brest deplore
Come kind Caribdis com ô com and help's
Sweete lovely Scilla bring thy barking whelps
Then should they need noe Monument nor Tombe   95
But Ocianus dark and Horrid Womb
Should them involve. but wishes are in vaine
I will Rore out my grieve unto the Maine
Now all the bewty that my Waves adorne
Are Surrey swans that sadly swim forlorne   100
Nor doe they in the sun their Feathers Prune
As they were wont, nor yet theire Voyces Tune
But in dispares hanging theire head and wing
This Kingdomes Derges they expireing sing
O that it in my power were to refuse   105
To see this Towne like Cristall Arethuse
Below this curssed Earth would hide my head
And run amongs the Caverns of the Dead
Where my pure wave with Acharon should mix
With Leathe, Phlegethon, Cocitus, Stix: 110
Then would I wafte them to the Stigian shade
Examples unto Reybels to be made
Ô my sad heart these are but foolish dreames
For they Triumph Upon my Conquered Streames
Yet this I'le doe while Sighs breaths up my Spring   115
I'le trickle teares for my aflicted King
And looke how fare one drop of Cristall Thames
Doth run, so fare I'le Memorise theire Fames:
Soe shall my griefe imortalise their Names
I hearing these complaints Though time to sleepe: 120
Satt sadly Down and with her gan to weepe.

3 *western Spring*: the source of the Thames is in Gloucestershire, and the river flows
South-East   5 *Amintas*: typical pastoral name, standing for Charles I   6 *Cloris*: Queen
Henrietta Maria   7 *Troynovants*: London's (the citizens of London supported the parliamentarians); *ingreate*: ungrateful   14 This line may be a clue that the fair-copy, sole
manuscript of Pulter's poems, was revised after 1661   17 *Albian*: St Alban, a British
martyr parted the waters of the Thames and walked dryshod on the river-bed   19–20 cf.
Jeremiah 13: 23, 'Can the Ethiopian change his skin, or the leopard his spots? Then may ye
also do good, that are accustomed to evil'   23 *Salamander*: mythical lizards believed to
live in fire   36 *Halcian days*: days of total calm, thought to be the days when the
kingfishers (halcyons) bred   44 *Owes*: Ouse   45–50 Edgar, an Anglo-Saxon king,
forced this gesture of submission upon eight Welsh rulers   51 *Danube*: the longest
river in Europe   55 *Loyer*: Loire; *Poe*: Po. In Greek myth, when Phaeton, son of Apollo,
lost control of the chariot of the sun, which he was driving, he fell into the river Po   60
Queen: Cleopatra   61 *Gangers*: Ganges   62 *Bamans*: Brahmins   63 The Ganges is
sacred to Hindus: Hindu dead are cremated on its banks and the ashes thrown in the water;
calcin'd: turned to ashes   69 *Horatia*: either Horatio (Livy 1) or she is thinking of Cloelia.
Livy I. 26; *vallure*: valour   77 *Symerrimus*: Queen Semiramis of Babylon   88 *owre*:

oar   90 *Schourg's*: scourges   93–6 *Caribdis…Scilla*: Classical monsters on either side
of the strait of Messina: Charybdis was a whirlpool, Scilla a dogheaded monster. Travellers
fell prey to one or the other   96 *Ocianus*: the ocean   101 *Prune*: preen   106 *Arethuse*:
Arethusa a nymph transformed into a fountain, united with the river Alpheus, to flow
under the sea   109–10 *Acharon…Leathe, Phlegethon, Cocitus, Stix*: rivers of the Classical
underworld

106   *Upon the imprisonment of his*
             Sacred Majesties that unparaleld
             Prince King Charles the First

Why I sit sighing here ask me no more
My Sacred Soveraigns thraldom I deplore
Just Nemesis (whom they pretend to Adore)

Put on thy Sable blood-besprinkled Gown
And thy or'e flowing vengence thunder Doun   5
On these Usurpers of our Caesar's Crown

They have his Sacred Person now in hold
They have their king, and Countrey bought and sould
And hope of Glory, all for Cursed Gold

Then seeing they eternity thus sleight   10
Let Acharons fierce Ishew them afright
Till endles horrour doth their souls benight

Then let our Job like Saint rise from the Ground
For Piety and Patience soe renownd
That for the best of kings hee may be Crownd   15

Then ask noe more why I'm in tears dissolv'd
Whilst our Good King with sorrow is involv'd
To pray and weep for him I am resolv'd.

3 *Nemesis*: goddess of justice who punishes human pride and arrogance   11 *Acharon*:
Acheron, a river of hell or by metonymy, hell itself   13 *Job*: Charles I. Job is an image of
guiltless suffering patiently endured

107   *Upon the Death of my deare and lovely*
             Daughter J.P. Jane Pulter, baptized
             May 1 1625 and died Oct 8 1646 Aet. 20

All you that have indulgent Parents been
And have your Children in perfection seen
Of youth and beuty; lend one Teare to mee
And trust mee I will doe as much for thee
Unlesse my own griefe do exhaust my store   5

Then will I sigh till I suspire noe more
Twice hath the earth Thrown Cloris Mantle by
Imbroidered or'e with Curious Tapestry
And twice hath seem'd to mourn unto our sight
Like Jewes, or Chinesses in snowey white   10
Since shee laid down her milkey limbs on Earth
Which dying gave her virgin Soule new birth
Yet still my heart is overwhelm'd with griefe
And tears (helas) gives Sorrow, noe reliefe
Twice hath sad Philomele left of to sing   15
Her mortifying sonnets to the Spring
Twice at the Silvian choristers desire
Shee hath lent her Musick to compleat theire Quire
Since al devouring Death on her took seasure
And Tellys Wombe involv'd soe rich a Tresure.   20
Yet styl my heart is overwhelm'd with griefe
And time nor teares will give my woes reliefe
Twelve times hath Phoebe horned seemed to fight
As often fil'd them with her Brothers light
Since shee did close her sparkling Diamond eyes   25
Yet my sad Heart for her still pineing Dies
Through the Twelve houses the illustrious Sun
With splendentie his Annuall Jorney Run
Twice hath his firey furious horses Hurld
His blazeing Chariots to the Lower World   30
Shewing his luster to the wondring eyes
Of our (now soe well known) Antipodies
Since the brack of her spotles virgin story
Which now her soule doth end in endles Glory.
Yet my aflicted sad forsaken soule   35
For her in tears and Ashes still doth Rowle
O could a ffevour spot her snowey skin
Whose Virgin soule was scarcely soyld with sin
Aye mee it did, soe have I sometimes seene
Faire Maydens sit incircled on a green   40
White lillies spread when they were making Poses
Upon them scatter leaves of Damask Roses
E'ne soe the spots upon her faire skin shows
Like Lilly leaves sprinkled with Damask Rose
Or as a stately Hert to Death pursued   45
By Ravening Hounds his eyes with tears bedewed
An Arrow sticking in his trembling breast
Her lost condition to the life exprest
Soe trips hee or'e the Lawns on trodden snow
And from his side his guiltles blood doth flow   50
[Soe did the spots upon her faire skin shew
Like drops of blood upon unsullied snow]

But what a heart had I, when I did stand
Holding her forehead with my Trembling hand
My Heart to Heaven with her bright Spirit flyes   55
Whilst shee (ah mee) closed up her lovely eyes
Her soule being seated in her place of birth
I turnd a Niobe as shee turn'd earth.

7 *Cloris Mantle*: Chloris is the Spring; spring flowers   10 White is a colour associated
with mourning by Jews and the Chinese   15 *Philomele*: the nightingale, which does not
sing in winter   20 *Tellys*: Tellus, the earth   33 *brack*: break, or perhaps mistakenly
written for wrack   37 *spot*: Perhaps measles, but more probably smallpox, which was
frequently fatal   41 *Poses*: posies   58 *Niobe*: in Greek myth, she boasted herself superior as a mother to Latona, mother of Apollo and Artemis. These gods, incensed, killed all
her children, and Niobe turned to a weeping stone.

108   *On those two unparalleld friends,*
          S^r: G: Lisle and S^r: C: Lucas, who
          were shott to death at Colechester

Is Lisle and Lucas slaine? Oh say not soe
Who could kill love and valour at a blow?
Just as Minerva's darling clos'd his eyes
Love kissing wept and on his bosome dies
Ah me what horrid Hidra had the hart   5
Them in theire Deaths thus to unite and part
Mars on the Areopagie once was tried
His vallour sav'd him or he else had died
His Judg and Jurie were the best of Gods
These worst of Men, ô me what ods   10
Had Joves three sons of everlasting fame
Borne of a mortall and Celestiall flame
Had they bin here this busines to deside
Then these two Noble Gallants had not died
Or had Astreus (lover of the Moon   15
Of whose bright womb her brighter babe was born)
Had he bin here hee would have tooke delight
To save theire lives that for his child did fight
Then had theire Judges bin the Gods eternall
Or upright Men, nay or the powers infernall   20
This unambiguous busines to deside
Then this unparaleld friendship had not died
But Jewes, Turks, Atheists Independents all
That Cursed Rabble, made these gallants fall
How could they doe it were they not Amazed   25
When as the cruell Parcae sat and Gazed
On theire perfections as Lachis drew the thred

What wont you part a sunder then shee sed
They striving in theire lives to imbrace each other
Shee twirl'd and twisted both of them together   30
Then Clotho at theire constant love did wonder
And in meere pitty pul'd them not asunder
Shee being it seems the Tendrest hearted Lass
Goe Noble Soules shee said and let them pass
But Atropos inrag'd begun to chide   35
Saying these trew loves knots should be untied
But seeing theire Lives she could not stay to untwist
Let those sit Idling here (she said) that list
How can wee give account unto those powers
That us imploy, in trifeling out our houres   40
Then scolding at her sisters for theire sloth
Shee with her fatal Cizers snipt them both
Shee then cryed out, alas but hurring fate
Forced her poore Girle, her pitty came too late.
Licaon Tantall tender to this brood   45
Who fed on Hostagis and Infants blood
Why are they now more cruell then at first
Theyr Drunk with Christian blood yet still they thirst
Doth that ould Vulture and his preying brood
Think to grow young with sucking spritely blood   50
Oh let them next suck Nessus's poys'und gore
Like mad Alcides let them Rave and Rore
And as they have bin three kingdooms sore annoyers
Let them like him at last be selfe destroyers
Had these undaunted loving Heros died   55
In former times they had bin Deified
Then theire Renown and love had spread as far
As those two famous Thunderbolts of War
Effigies, Piramids, Collums, Collosses,
Had bin erect to memorise our losses   60
But wee are now denied, our Just desires
Trew gratefull love in this our age expires
Yet som sad Swan I know there will be found
That for this onely Action will be Cround
That shall beare lovely Lisle, and Lucas name   65
Unto the Temple of Eternall fame.
When that black Armie after theire short Dreame
Shall floating bee on Stix his Sable Streame
They by the Angrey billowes shall be tost
Till in oblivious Horrid womb ther'e lost   70
If he that fired Diana's Phane for fame
Lost both his expectation and his name
If covetous Cambices who presum'd
To rob the Gods till sand his mein consum'd

Or that Fierce Gaule who Delphus ment to plunder   75
Till firey Phebus routed him with Thunder
If these live now in Honour then noe doubt
Fame shall attend this Sacrilegi'us rout
Who have our Truths defenders over powerd
And Temples, Alters, Victims, all devourd,   80
But these victorious soules live now above
And gloriously goe on in endles love
Whilst theire faire frames which here did close their lives
Shall live in fame till they in Glory rise.

1 *Lisle and Lucas*: Sir George Lisle (d. 1648) and Sir Charles Lucas (1613–48), Royalist commanders in the First and Second Civil Wars; both were in arms with the Royalist insurgents that occupied Colchester from 14 June 1648 until the city fell to Fairfax on 27 August. Lucas and Lisle were shot to death on Fairfax's orders for breaking their parole, the occasion of much Royalist recrimination   3 *Minerva's darling*: more probably Sir Charles Lucas.   5 *Hidra*: many-headed ravening monster slain by Hercules   7 *Mars on the Areopagie*: It was on the 'hill of Ares' (Mars) near Athens that the god answered for his adultery with Aphrodite (Venus)   11 *Joves three sones*: perhaps the sons of Zeus and Europa, Rhadamanthus, Minos, and Sarpedon, since two out of three were famous judges; or perhaps Hercules, son of Alcmena, Dionysus, son of Semele, and a third   15 *Astreus*: Astraeus, a Titan, husband of Aurora/Eos (Dawn), and father of the winds   23 *Independents*: sectaries and militant Parliamentarians   26 *Parcae*: the three Fates, Lachesis, Clotho, and Atropos   42 *Cizers*: scissors   43 *hurring*: hurrying   45 *Licaon Tantall*: by comparison with Tantalus, who butchered his own son and made a feast of him for the gods   51 *Nessus's*: the centaur Nessus had venomous blood: a shirt dipped in it was given to Hercules (Alcides) by his wife Iole, who believed it to be a love-charm, and he died in agony   58 *Thunderbolts of War*: Castor and Pollux   64 *Cround*: Crond MS   68 *Stix*: one of the rivers of the underworld   71 *he*: the great temple of Diana at Ephesus, one of the wonders of the ancient world, was destroyed by Herostratus, who hoped this vandalism would make his name immortal   73 *Cambices*: Cambyses of Persia, his story is told by Herodotus   75 *Fierce Gaule*: Brennus, who raided Delphi in 279 BC and was repelled by a miraculous snowstorm sent by Apollo, which was commemorated by the festival of Soteria

ELIZABETH BANCKES AND GEORGE JAMES
(1616)

THIS verse is the subject of a libel case brought before the Star Chamber. The plaintiffs were Henry Bressye of Escott, gent., and Lucy his wife; the defendants, George James of Lutterworth, Leicestershire, plaintiff's servant, and Elizabeth Banckes. The libel was circulated after Mrs Bressye had taken away George James's livery coat with intent to dismiss him. The aggrieved George called in an associate, Elizabeth Banckes, to help him concoct this poem in 1616. This suggests that it was she who had a way with words; while George was more or less responsible for the contents. Quite a number of libels of this kind were made by women, and are of some importance for the history of women's culture, since these actions for libel and slander bear witness to a lively oral working-class culture, both urban and rural, of verse-making for ritual insult. For example, in 1606, Joan Gomme of Thetford, Norfolk, was brought before the Ely Diocesan Court 'for that she hath made and doth exercise the makeing of libellous and lascivious ballads by and [divers] of her neighbours', and Elisabeth Johnson of Stretton upon Dunsmore was presented to the Warwickshire Easter Sessions in 1693 as a common nightwalker, and for making a song or ballad in derision of her uncle and his son, and setting it up with a picture upon her uncle's ground '23 March last in the night time'. Unfortunately, though they were necessarily heard by the court, they were seldom kept as part of the proceedings: this crude, energetic piece, with its ambiguous authorship, stands as an indication of what this kind of working-class women's verse was like. It also has something to tell us about what constituted good repute. Unusually, the verse does not accuse Mrs Bressye of sexual incontinence; but focuses on the allegation that she originated in a lower station in life than she now inhabits, and on her avarice: it is interesting that these were perceived as damaging enough to force the Bressyes into an expensive court-case.

109   *'Roysters give Roome, for here comes a Lass'*

Roysters give Roome, for here comes a Lass:
Thoughe shee never sold Broome, nor had a good face
yet is shee stoute, corrageous, and bolde:
more shameles and impudent, than shee is yeres olde.
For taking of false oathes she does not care   5
For pickinge of pocketts, or Locks she is rare.
For stealing of cloakes, gold Buttons, or Bandes
or cuffes for to weare to grace her false handes.
No oyster-queane putteth her downe for use of Tongue
Nor Kitchin-stuffe Drabb if she doe doe a Wronge.   10
To sell Aqua-vitae sometyme she did use:
No labor nor travayle this Dowde did refuse.
From England to Ireland this Dowde shee is gone:
But back agayne to her shame nowe shee is come home.

                                                    (1616)

1 *Roysters*: roisterers   2 *Broome*: furze twigs, sold for making brooms   9 *oyster-queane*: woman oyster seller (fishwives in general were proverbially foul-mouthed)   10 *Kitchin-stuffe Drabb*: kitchenmaid   11 i.e. she used to sell whisky   12 *Dowde*: shabby slattern

'CONSTANTIA MUNDA'
(fl. 1617)

ALTHOUGH recent writers have doubted whether the polemics against Swetnam signed by Esther Sowernam and Constantia Munda are genuinely by women, Rachel Speght's *Dreame* (printed here, see no. 111), suggests that they were both read as women's work in their own time. *The Worming of a Mad Dogge* has been judged too educated, too Latinate, and aristocratically intolerant to be a woman's work. But if it was thus regarded in its own time, it is at least potentially empowering to other women, by pushing back the boundaries of 'feminine' discourse. Whoever she (or 'she') was, Constantia Munda knew Latin, Italian, and perhaps a little Greek (though her Greek has a somewhat second-hand look about it, and may well consist entirely of tags culled second-hand from Latin authorities). At various points, the text quotes Ovid's *Ibis*, Virgil, Juvenal, Scaliger, Sophocles' *Ajax*, and the *Iliad*. She was capable of constructing (and recognizing as such) a syllogism, and knows a little of the vocabulary of law. She was also notably attached to her mother, who is a 'Lady', and by implication, also a scholar. The combination of skills represented here are not impossible by any means. Among women of the right generation represented in this anthology, we might instance Lady Tanfield, who knew all the relevant languages except Greek, and was expert in law, but was unfortunately not on good terms with her mother. Bathsua Makin is another woman with the right kinds of knowledge but is unlikely to have described her mother as a 'lady', a term which was not used loosely in the early seventeenth century. However, there were certainly other educated gentlewomen born *c.*1590–1600 who could have written such a work, not all of whom are known to us: for example, the earls of Huntingdon, the Audleys, the Herberts, and the Ishams of Lamport in Northamptonshire were all gentry or noble families with a strong commitment to the education of daughters.

110   *To the Right Worshipful Lady her Most*
       Dear Mother, the Lady Prudentia Munda,
       the true pattern of Piety and virtue,
       C.M. wisheth increase of Happiness.

As, first, your pains in bearing me was such
A benefit beyond requital that 'twere much
To think what pangs of sorrow you sustained
In child-birth (when mine infancy obtained
The vital drawing-in of air); so your love,   5
Mingled with care, hath shown itself above
The ordinary course of nature. Seeing you still
Are in perpetual labour with me, even until
The second birth of education perfect me:
You travail still, though churched oft you be.   10
    In recompence whereof what can I give,
But what I take?—even that I live,
Next to the heavens, 'tis yours. Thus I pay
My debt by taking up at interest, and lay
To pawn that which I borrow of you: so   15
The more I give, I take; I pay, I owe.
Yet lest you think I forfeit shall my bond,

I here present you with my writing hand:
Some trifling minutes I vainly did bestow
In penning of these lines that all might know   20
The scandals of our adversary; and
I had gone forward had not *Hester hanged*
Haman before (yet what here I wrote
Might serve to stop the cur's wide throat
Until the halter came). Since which I ceased   25
To prosecute what I intended, lest
I should be censured that I undertook
A work that's done already. So his book
Hath 'scaped my fingers—but in like case
As a malefactor changeth place   30
From Newgate unto Tyburn, whose good hope
Is but to change his shackles for a rope.
  Although this be a toy scarce worth your view,
Yet deign to read it and accept in lieu
Of greater duty: for your gracious look   35
Is a sufficient patron to my book.
This is the worst disgrace that can be had:
A Lady's daughter 'wormed a dog that's mad.'

Your loving daughter
CONSTANTIA MUNDA
(1617)

10 *churched*: the ceremony of churching was held forty days after the birth of a child. 'Constantia' implies that her mother's educational efforts are as toilsome as her original labour in childbirth (and that she frequently attends church)   14–16 I am forced to borrow to discharge my debt, thus making it bigger and bigger   22 *Hester*: a reference to Ester Sowernam, *Ester hath hang'd Haman* (1617), which in turn refers to the Book of Esther 7: 9–10   31 *Newgate . . . Tyburn*: respectively, one of London's most important prisons, and its place of execution   38 *wormed*: cut out the tendon in a dog's tongue that was thought to make it rabid

RACHEL PROCTER (née SPEGHT)
(1597–after 1621)

RACHEL SPEGHT'S date of birth is arrived at by counting back from the year of her marriage in 1621, when she was described as being 24. She was the daughter of a Calvinist minister, James Speght, who was the rector of two London churches, St Mary Magdalen in Milk Street from 1592, and St Clement, Eastcheap, from 1611, holding both appointments till his death in 1637. He had some association with the Goldsmiths company, and enjoyed some patronage from Sir Baptist Hicks. He also published some brief pamphlets, and was clearly an educated man. About her mother, who was clearly of importance to her, we know nothing, except that she died shortly before 1621. Rachel Speght may have been educated at home by her father, or possibly sent away to school: the former, given the very masculine range of knowledge she displays, is perhaps the more likely. A number of conspicuously learned women were educated by their fathers in early modern England: Margaret, daughter of Sir Thomas More, is a very famous example, but nearer in time and social class to Rachel Speght, we may point to women such as Elizabeth Withypoll, née Lucar (1510–37), daughter of a wealthy citizen of London, who learned Latin, Spanish, and Italian, Bathsua Makin, née Rainolds, daughter of a schoolmaster (see nos. 117–18), and Rachel Jevon (see nos. 173–4), daughter of an Anglican clergyman. She dedicates *Mortalities Memorandum* to her godmother, Mary Moundford, so it is possible that the Moundfords may also have supported her decision to publish her work: Thomas Moundford, a well-known London physician, was a partisan of the learned Arbella Stuart. The fact that she apparently perceived no social or other problems with publishing her work suggests that she had the full support of her immediate family and friends, in which she resembles other marginally genteel women such as Isabella Whitney and Aemilia Lanyer. All her publications date from before her marriage, which took place on 2 August 1621, to William Proctor, gent., a cleric, at St Mary Woolchurch Haw. William Proctor also became a minister, and may have held a cure at Upminster in Essex in the years immediately following the marriage. Two children of the marriage were baptized, Rachel in 1627 and William in 1630, both at St Giles, Cripplegate, which suggests that the family was back in London by 1627.

Rachel Speght in writing this dream-vision, in which she is guided by a series of allegorical personifications, is essentially reviving a medieval form, familiar from poems such as the *Romaunt de la Rose* (written by Jean de Meun and translated by Chaucer), and *The Floure and the Leafe*, in a woman's voice, and tentatively attributed to a woman's authorship. The only text of *The Floure and the Leafe* which survives is a printed text, dated 1598, edited by one Thomas Speght, best known for his edition of Chaucer. It is therefore legitimate to wonder if she herself had access to this text, and used it as a model.

111   *The Dreame.*

When splendent *Sol*, which riseth in the East,
Returning thence tooke harbour in the West:
When *Phoebe* layd her head in *Titans* lap,
And Creatures sensitive made hast to rest;
When skie which earst look't like to azure blew,   5
Left colour bright, and put on sable hew.

Then did *Morpheus* close my drowsie eyes,
And stood as Porter at my sences dore,
Diurnall cares excluding from my minde;
Including rest, (the salve for labours sore.)   10
Nights greatest part in quiet sleepe I spent,
But nothing in this world is permanent.

For ere *Aurora* spread her glittering beames,
Or did with roabes of light her selfe invest,
My mentall quiet sleepe did interdict,   15
By entertaining a nocturnall guest.
A *Dreame* which did my mind and sense possesse,
With more then I by Penne can well expresse.

At the appoyntment of supernall power,
By instrumentall meanes me thought I came   20
Into a place most pleasant to the eye,
Which for the beautie some did *Cosmus* name,
Where stranger-like on every thing I gaz'd,
But wanting wisedome was as one amaz'd.

Upon a sodeyne, as I gazing stood,   25
Thought came to me, and ask't me of my state,
Inquiring what I was, and what I would,
And why I seem'd as one disconsolate:
To whose demand, I thus againe replide,
I, as a stranger in this place abide.   30

The Haven of my voyage is remote,
I have not yet attain'd my journeyes end;
Yet know I not, nor can I give a guesse,
How short a time I in this place shall spend.
For that high power, which sent me to this place,   35
Doth onely know the period of my race.

The reason of my sadnesse at this time,
Is, 'cause I feele my selfe not very well,
Unto you I shall much obliged bee,
If for my griefe a remedie you'le tell.   40
Quoth shee, if you your maladie will show,
My best advise I'le willingly bestow.

My griefe, quoth I, is called *Ignorance*,
Which makes me differ little from a brute:
For animals are led by natures lore,   45
Their seeming science is but customes fruit;
When they are hurt they have a sense of paine;
But want the sense to cure themselves againe.

And ever since this griefe did me oppresse,
Instinct of nature is my chiefest guide;   50
I feele disease, yet know not what I ayle,
I finde a sore, but can no salve provide;
I hungry am, yet cannot seeke for foode;
Because I know not what is bad or goode.

And sometimes when I seeke the golden meane,   55

My weaknesse makes me faile of mine intent,
That suddenly I fall into extremes,
Nor can I see a mischiefe to prevent;
But feele the paine when I the perill finde,
Because my maladie doth make me blinde,   60

What is without the compasse of my braine,
My sickenesse makes me say it cannot bee;
What I conceive not, cannot come to passe;
Because for it I can no reason see.
I measure all mens feet by mine owne shooe,   65
And count all well, which I appoint or doe.

The pestilent effects of my disease
Exceed report, their number is so great;
The evils, which through it I doe incur,
Are more than I am able to repeat.   70
Wherefore, good *Thought*, I sue to thee againe,
To tell me how my cure I may obtaine.

Quoth she, I wish I could prescribe your helpe;
Your state I pittie much, and doe bewaile;
But for my part, though I am much imploy'd,   75
Yet in my judgment I doe often faile.
And therefore I'le comment unto your triall
Experience, of whom take no deniall.

For she can best direct you, what is meet
To worke your cure, and satisfie your minde;   80
I thank't her for her love, and tooke my leave,
Demanding where I might *Experience* finde.
She told me if I did abroad enquire,
'Twas likely *Age* could answer my desire.

I sought, I found, She ask't me what I would;   85
Quoth I, your best direction I implore:
For I am troubled with an irkesome griefe,
Which when I nam'd, quoth she declare no more:
For I can tell as much, as you can say,
And for your cure I'le helpe you what I may.   90

The onely medicine for your maladie,
By which, and nothing else your helpe is wrought,
Is *Knowledge*, of the which there is two sorts,
The one is good, the other bad and nought;
The former sort by labour is attain'd,   95
The latter may without much toyle be gain'd.

But 'tis the good, which must effect your cure,
I pray'd her then, that she would further show,

Where I might have it, that I will, quoth shee,
In *Eruditions* garden it doth grow: 100
And in compassion of your wofull case,
Industrie shall conduct you to the place.

Disswasion hearing her assigne my helpe,
(And seeing that consent I did detect)
Did many remoraes to me propose,   105
As dulnesse, and my memories defect;
The difficultie of attaining lore,
My time, and sex, with many others more.

Which when I heard, my minde was much perplext,
As as a horse new come into the field,   110
Who with a Harquebuz at first doth start,
So did this shot make me recoyle and yeeld,
But of my feare when some did notice take,
In my behalfe, they this reply did make.

First quoth Desire, Disswasion, hold thy peace,   115
These oppositions come not from above:
Quoth Truth, they cannot spring from reasons roote,
And therefore now thou shalt no victor prove.
No, quoth Industrie, be assured this,
Her friends shall make theeof thy purpose misse.   120

For with my sickle I will cut away
All obstacles, that in her way can grow,
And by the issue of her owne attempt,
I'le make the *labor omnia vincet* know.
Quoth Truth, and sith her sex thou do'st object,   125
Thy folly I by reason will detect.

Both man and woman of three parts consist,
Which *Paul* doth bodie, soule, and spirit call:
And from the soule three faculties arise,
The mind, the will, the power; then wherefore shall   130
A woman have her intellect in vaine,
Or not endevour *Knowledge* to attaine.

The talent, God doth give, must be imploy'd,
His owne with vantage he must have againe:
All parts and faculties were made for use;   135
The God of *Knowledge* nothing gave in vaine.
'Twas *Maries* choyce our Saviour did approve,
Because that she the better part did love.

Cleobulina, and *Demophila*,
With *Telesilla*, as Historians tell,   140
(Whose fame doth live, though they have long bin dead)

Did all of them in Poetrie excell.
A Roman matron that *Cornelia* hight,
An eloquent and learned style did write.

Hypatia in Astronomie had skill,   145
Aspatia was in Reth'ricke so expert,
As that Duke *Pericles* of her did learne;
Areta did devote her selfe to art:
And by consent (which shewes she was no foole)
She did succeed her father in his schoole.   150

And many others here I could produce,
Who were in Science counted excellent;
But these examples which I have rehearst,
To shew thy error are sufficient.
Thus having sayd, she turn'd her speech to mee,   155
That in my purpose I might constant bee.

My friend, quoth she, regard not vulgar talke;
For dung-hill Cocks at precious stones will spurne,
And swine-like natures prize not cristall streames,
Contemned mire, and mud will serve their turne.   160
Good purpose seldome oppositions want:
But constant mindes *Disswasion* cannot daunt.

Shall every blast disturbe the Saylors peace?
Or boughes and bushes Travellers affright?
True valour doth not start at every noyse;   165
Small combates must instruct for greater fight.
Disdaine to bee with every dart dismayd;
'Tis childish to be suddenly affrayd.

If thou didst know the pleasure of the place,
Where *Knowledge* growes, and where thou mayst it gaine;   170
Or rather knew the vertue of the plant,
Thou would'st not grudge at any cost, or paine,
Thou cast bestow, to purchase for thy cure
This plant, by which of helpe thou shalt be sure.

Let not *Disswasion* alter thy intent;   175
'Tis sinne to nippe good motions in the head;
Take courage, and be constant in thy course,
Though irkesome be the path, which thou must tread.
Sicke folkes drinke bitter medicines to be well,
And to injoy the nut men cracke the shell.   180

When *Truth* had ended what shee meant to say,
Desire did move me to obey her will,
Whereto consenting I did soone proceede,
Her counsell, and my purpose to fulfill:

And by the helpe of *Industrie* my friend,   185
I quickly did attaine my journeyes end.

Where being come, *Instructions* pleasant ayre
Refresht my senses, which were almost dead,
And fragrant flowers of sage and fruitfull plants,
Did send sweete savours up into my head;   190
And taste of science appetite did move,
To augment *Theorie* of things above.

There did the harmonie of those sweete birds,
(Which higher soare with Contemplations wings,
Then barely with a superficiall view,   195
Denote the value of created things.)
Yeeld such delight as made me to implore,
That I might reape this pleasure more and more.

And as I walked wandring with *Desire*,
To gather that, for which I thither came;   200
(Which by the helpe of *Industrie* I found)
I met my old acquaintance, *Truth* by name;
Whom I requested briefely to declare,
The vertue of that plant I found so rare.

Quoth shee, by it Gods image man doth beare,   205
Without it he is but a humane shape,
Worse than the Devill; for he knoweth much;
Without it who can any ill escape?
By vertue of it evils are withstood;
The minde without it is not counted good.   210

Who wanteth *Knowledge* is a Scripture foole,
Against the *Ignorant* the Prophets pray;
And *Hosea* threatens judgement unto those,
Whom want of *Knowledge* made to runne astray.
Without it thou no practique good canst show,   215
More then by hap, as blind men hit a Crow.

True *Knowledge* is the Window of the soule,
Through which her objects she doth speculate;
It is the mother of faith, hop, and love;
Without it who can vertue estimate?   220
By it, in grace thou shalt desire to grow;
'Tis life eternall God and Christ to *Know*.

Great *Alexander* made so great account,
Of *Knowledge*, that he oftentimes would say,
That he to *Aristotle* was more bound   225
For *Knowledge*, upon which *Death* could not pray,
Then to his Father *Phillip* for his life,
Which was uncertaine, irkesome, full of strife.

This true report put edge unto *Desire*,
Who did incite me to increase my store,   230
And told me 'twas a lawfull avarice,
To covet *Knowledge* daily more and more.
This counsell I did willingly obey,
Till some occurrence called me away.

And made me rest content with that I had,   235
Which was but little, as effect doth show;
And quenched hope for gaining any more,
For I my time must other-wayes bestow.
I therefore to that place return'd againe,
From whence I came, and where I must remaine.   240

But by the way I saw a full fed Beast,
Which roared like some monster, or a Devill,
And on *Eves* sex he foamed filthie froth,
As if that he had had the falling evill;
To whom I went to free them from mishaps,   245
And with a *Mouzel* sought to binde his chaps.

But, as it seemes, my moode out-run my might,
Which when a selfe-conceited Creature saw,
Shee past her censure on my weake exployt,
And gave the beast a harder bone to knaw;   250
Haman she hangs, 'tis past he cannot shun it;
For *Ester* in the Pretertense hath done it.

And yet her enterprize had some defect,
The monster surely was not hanged quite:
For as the childe of *Prudence* did conceive,   255
His throat not stop't he still had power to bite.
She therefore gave to *Cerberus* a soppe,
Which is of force his beastly breath to stoppe.

But yet if he doe swallow down that bit,
Shee other-wayes hath bound him to the peace;   260
And like an Artist takes away the cause,
That the effect by consequence may cease.
This franticke dogge, whose rage did women wrong,
Hath Constance worm'd to make him hold his tongue.

Thus leaving them I passed on my way,   265
But ere that I had little further gone,
I saw a fierce insatiable foe,
Depopulating Countries, sparing none;
Without respect of age, or sex, or degree,
It did devoure, and could not daunted be.   270

Some fear'd this foe, some lov'd it as a friend;
For though none could the force of it withstand,

Yet some by it were sent to *Tophets* flames,
But others led to heavenly *Canaan* land.
On some, it seazed with a gentle power,   275
And others furiously it did devoure.

The name of this impartiall foe was *Death*,
Whose rigour whil'st I furiously did view,
Upon a sodeyne, ere I was aware;
With pearcing dart my mother deare it slew;   280
Which when I saw it made me so to weepe,
That teares and sobs did rouze me from my sleepe.

But, when I wak't, I found my dreame was true;
For *Death* had ta'ne my mothers breath away,
Though of her life it could not her bereave,   285
Sith shee in glorie lives with Christ for aye;
Which makes me glad, and thankefull for her blisse,
Though still bewayle her absence, whom I misse.

A sodeine sorrow peirceth to the quicke,
Speedie encounters fortitude doth try;   290
Unarmed men receive the deepest wound,
Expected perils time doth lenifie;
Her sodeine losse hath cut my feeble heart,
So deepe, that daily I indure the smart.

The roote is kil'd, how can the boughs but fade?   295
But sith that *Death* this cruell deed hath done,
I'le blaze the nature of this mortall foe,
And shew how it to tyranize begun.
The sequell then with judgement view aright,
The profit may and will the paines requite   300

Esto Memor Mortis

4 *sensitive*: possessed of senses   7 *Morpheus*: god of sleep   22 *Cosmus*: the cosmos (in Greek, 'arranged', therefore, 'made beautiful'   36 *race*: life   105 *remoraes*: impediments. Remoras were fish which were thought to attach themselves to the bottom of ships and slow them down   110 *into the field*: into battle   111 *Harquebuz*: arquebus, an early form of musket   124 *labor omnia vincet*: work conquers all   126–32 based on 1 Thess. 5: 23   133 *talent*: Luke 19: 3   137 *Maries*: Mary Magdalen 'chose the better part', listening to Jesus rather than helping her sister Martha (Luke 10: 40–2) 139–40 *Cleobulina … Demophila … Telesilla*: Greek women poets. Cleobulina of Rhodes (6th c. BC), famous for solving riddles; Damophyle of Pamphilia (contemporary with Sappho), a lyric poet; Telesilla of Athens, (15 c. BC) lyric poet famous for arming the women of Argos after the men had been defeated by the Spartans   143 *Cornelia*: daughter of Scipio Africanus, mother of the Gracchi. Fragments of her writing, praised by Cicero, may have been preserved   145 *Hypatia*: an Alexandrian mathematician and philosopher, murdered at the instigation of bishop Cyril of Alexandria in AD 415   146 *Aspatia*: Aspasia, mistress of Pericles, ruler of Athens in the fifth century BC. Plato in *Menexenus* declares that she taught Pericles rhetoric   148 *Areta*: the philosopher Arete daughter of Arestippus, who succeeded him as head of the Cyrenian school   205 Colossians 3: 10   211 Proverbs 19: 2   213 *Hosea*: *passim*, but especially ch. 4   223 *Alexander*: Alexander the Great, conqueror of Persia and

son of Philip of Macedon, had the philosopher Aristotle as his tutor   244 *falling evil*: epilepsy   246 *Mouzel*: Speght's *A Mouzell for Melastomus*, printed in 1617   252 a reference to Ester Sowernam, *Ester hath hang'd Haman*, printed in 1617; *Pretertense*: pluperfect   255 *childe of Prudence*: the pseudonyous 'Constantia Munda', who names her mother as 'Prudentia Munda', published *The Worming of a mad Dogge, or A Soppe for Cerberus the Jaylor of Hell*, also in 1617   264 *worm'd*: cut out the tendon in a dog's tongue that was thought to make it rabid   273 *Tophets*: a site south-west of Jerusalem in the Valley of Hinnom where according to Jeremiah worshippers of Baal burned their sons and daughters as offerings (figuratively, hell)   274 *Canaan land*: ancient name for Lebanon and Israel, the Promised Land (figuratively, heaven)   301 'be mindful of death'

MRS BOUGHTON
(*c*.1600–after 1650)

MRS BOUGHTON's husband, the subject of this epitaph, and formerly Rector of Bray in Berkshire, was a graduate of Oxford: he may have been the John Boughton who graduated from St Edmund's Hall in February 1610, and he, in turn, may have been the John Boughton who was vicar of Boughton Aluph in 1629. One of the predecessors of Mr Boughton, the subject of this epitaph, was the famous Vicar Aleyn of Bray, who kept his living from the reign of Henry VIII to Elizabeth I, through the reigns of Mary Tudor and Edward VI: 'Being taxed by one for a turncoat and an unconstant changeling, "not so", said he, "for I always kept my principle, which is this, to live and die the Vicar of Bray"' (T. Fuller, *The Worthies of England*, ed. J. Freeman (London, 1952), 23). There was obviously something special about Bray, since Boughton, who was incumbent during the reign of Charles I, was deposed by Cromwell, and a Presbyterian minister intruded, who proved almost equally flexible, since he survived in post despite the ups and downs of religious politics from Cromwell through Charles II, James, William and Mary, into Anne. It is impossible to date this poem with any precision, as the year of Boughton's death is not known, although it must have been in or after 1650, the year in which he was ousted from his parish.

112   *Epitaph*

When Oxford gave thee two degrees in art
And love possest thee master of my heart
Thy colledge fellowshipp thow lefs't for mine
And nought but deathe could seprate me from thine.
Thirty five yeares we liv'de in wedlocke bands   5
Conjoyned in our hearts as well as handes
But death the bodies of best friendes devides
And in the earths close wombe their relyckes hides
Yet here they are not lost but sowen that they
May rise more glorious at the Iudgment Day.   10

2 a play on Master of Art   3 Holders of Oxford college fellowships could not marry, so Mrs Boughton is using 'fellowship' in two different senses

ELEANORA FINCH, née WYATT
(late 1590s–1623)

ELEANORA WYATT was from the family of Sir Thomas Wyatt. She was the third daughter (after Anne and Catherine) of Sir George Wyatt, the only son of Sir Thomas Wyatt the younger, who rebelled against Queen Mary and was executed in 1554. George, who was an infant at the time of his father's execution, became a minister of the Church of England. Her mother was Jane, daughter of Thomas Finch. The family attainder was lifted in the thirteenth year of the reign of Queen Elizabeth. Eleanora married John Finch, presumably a cousin, in 1619, according to the register preserved in the family papers, which were collected together by Richard Wiat in 1727 (BL Add. 62135). Despite the existing connection of the families, and the presence of courtship poems from John Finch in Richard Wiat's collection, implying a personal relationship between the couple before their union, the marriage got off to a poor start: a long and dignified letter from Eleanor Wyatt to her estranged husband was sent from the home of Sir William Twisden (a friend of her brother's) on 9 November in 1619 (fos 370ʳ–371ʳ). His reply is also preserved. A poem on fo. 334, possibly by Thomas Carew (who also wrote 'An Elegie on E.F.', fos. 352ᵛ–353ᵛ) implies that her death was the result of her first child, which died in the womb. An apparently contemporary poem on her two dead sisters, probably by the local vicar, George Case, is firm in describing Eleanora as 'joined in most chaste marriage' (*coniugio iunctam perhonesto*): perhaps, given the estrangement of the couple, Case is anxious to stress that the child was indeed her husband's.

Richard Wiat's collection includes a booklet of poems apparently compiled and copied by Sir Francis Wyatt, including a poem of his own, to his brother, Haut Wyatt, a number of poems by Thomas Carew, Sir Henry Wotton's famous poem on Elizabeth of Bohemia, and a number of poems in a female voice signed E. It is highly probable that they should be attributed to his sister Eleanora, especially since one of them seems directly answered by a poem signed I.F. (John Finch).

113 *"Tis true I weepe, I sigh, I wring my hands'*

'Tis true I weepe, I sigh, I wring my hands,
But thou, o love, hast yet no cause to laffe:
    For whilst I wring my hands, I thence shake off
What I once held for ornaments thy bands.
    And those deepe sighes to fanne the fire that serv'd,   5
To blow away the stormes are now reserv'd.

E

4 *bands*: bonds, but bands were also decorative collars or cuffs, which might be given as presents

114 *'Lady weare those bayes, you may'*

Lady weare those bayes, you may,
    You from me have wonne the day.

Looke not there, this conquest owe you
   Unto nought your glasse can show you.
None of all your beauties charmes
   Were of this the fatall armes.
In his heart, not in your eies,
   Of this change the first cause lies.
You may worthier soone enough
   Be then I, yet this no proofe.
She from whom I wonne the field,
   Not lesse faire I therfore held.
Nay perhaps sett both together,
   Might be worthier judge'de than either.
To your dressing nor impart
   Half so much of cost or art.
Pouder, crispe not curle your haire,
   Scarse for you he'ele take that care.
Whilst so curiously you spred
   On your cheekes the blushing red:
Time may come, when he to you
   May give cause of blushes true.
Of that white the tincture pure,
   Then his love shall last more sure.
Colours not more false and vaine,
   Then he shall returne againe.
Beauty blowen off with his breath,
   Whilst he closely whispereth.
His so deepe-vow'd love, shall last
   Longer then that idle breath.
Nor so many rules observe,
   So precisely to preserve
Youth and beauty, t'is his use
   Not to stay for that excuse.
Let swift time be faster sett,
   Lett your youth prevent it yett.
Ere your youth, your beauty part,
   Change before your face your heart.
Hee'le be first, his Cupids farre
   Swifter wing'd then others are.
Would you keepe what you have got,
   If it might be, love him not.
If you love, then to retaine
   Measure were but wish't in vaine.
Love but let him then not know,
   Vaild it best becomes, when so
Both our love and beauties worne
   Clouded still does best adorne.
Still give hopes, assurance never,

5

10

15

20

25

30

35

40

45

Sometimes doubts, light quarrels ever.   50
But slight favours reconcil'd,
   Grants as forc't, repulses mild.
Since t'is he that doth pursue
   Variety, still find him new.
Now severe, now careles seeme,   55
   Now in jealousy extreame.
Of a rivall, but be sure
   He from one be ne're secure.
Somewhat on his desires to stay
   Must on them be cast away.   60
But how much soere you store,
   Then you give, reserve much more.
All these rules too well are knowne,
   You have more yet of your owne.
Would they serve, or I not knew   65
   You might me, Ide not teach you.
Best of rules that could be got,
   Were to do what I did not.
Could you but the art discover
   A respectfull silent lover   70
To preserve him, whilst his fire
   But his heart and eies inspire.
But his love, that instant he
   Sweares it is, it leaves to be.
Whilst he blushing fearfull is,   75
   You may feare him then the lesse,
Yet beware him then, in proofe
   You may find him dare enough.
Aske him, for you will I know,
   If he lov'd me, he'le say no: 80
I (alas) may take that oath
   Now for me and may for both.
He will sweare, I lov'd him deare,
   Which how true or false so ere.
In his words how is it true.   85
   Since t'is more than ere he knew.
He will say, I favours gave,
   Such as he from you would have:
For the rest, what he denies,
   Faintly, yet his looke implies.   90
Nor believe, they say he'ele ly,
   Any way that you dare try.
Since the most of mine amisse,
   Onely was in pardoning his.
She that did instruct his youth,   95
   Could she but have taught him truth.

Equall then to her affections
  How she render'd his perfections.
Had she reft him of this one,
  Faults she then had left him none.   100
But how faultles he so ere,
  Yet with some in you he'ele beare.
Way since yet was never knowen
  Him to keepe, preserve your owen.
Since you cannot his desire,   105
  Keepe your vertue yet entire.
Not that that will serve, his spirit
  Is not fixt by art nor merit.
Had that held, then never he
  Had lov'd you, perhaps nor me.   110
Could you keepe what you have wunne,
  Happier never saw the Sunne

                                    E

1 *bayes*: victory wreath

115   *'When I first was brought to light'*

                    1
When I first was brought to light,
Rather into darknesse throwen,
  Midst of such a stormy night,
As i'th dark could not be knowen.
  But unseene have past untold   5
  Not among the rest enrol'd.

                    2
Not a beame of light was seene,
Not a starre peep't through the skies,
  Fled from Heaven the nights pale Queene,
Nor my birth would patronize.   10
  Blew the trembling tapers burn'd,
  All fayre eyes in blacknes mourn'd.

                    3
The first light that greetes mine eyes,
Was the blaze of lightning flashes,
  Which a proud tower rais'd to skies   15
In an instant struck to ashes.
  In such darknes have I seene,
  By such light still blinded beene.

                    4
Me my sad forsaken mother
(Then her love eclipsed remaining)   20
  Bred me not at first from other,

After from her breast sustaining
　　Me, who from her woes did borrow
　　But the pure extract of sorrow.

                    5
I was still brought up in woe,   25
Musicke pleased me not so well,
　　As of those that felt the blow
Weeping for to hear them tell
　　Of that storme, which threat'ning all
　　Onely on our house did fall.   30

                    6
Other stories oft suppli'd
Though our owen might well content
　　Being borne on either side
To much woe by due discent.
　　And I would our races fate   35
　　In my harms might terminate.

                    7
Mourning blacke best pleas'd mine eyes,
And mee thought became mee best,
　　Sad and direfull tragedies
Still I lik'd above the rest   40
　　And those best I ever lov'd
　　Who most spite of fortune prov'd.

                    8
Saddest looks had sweetest grace,
Griev'd with griefe content yet shewing,
　　Nought so well became the face,   45
As the cheekes with teares ore flowing.
　　Wreathed armes, neglected haire
　　Best methought adorn'd the faire.

                    9
From my walking hower of birth
To this present weeping houre,   50
　　Never had I joy on earth,
But what served to make me more
　　Feele my harmes, and brought with it
　　Greater ylls, then that could quitt.

                    10
My desires were nere effected,   55
But where I mine yll desir'd,
　　Else they came so long protracted,
That the tide was back retir'd
　　When they came and let me see
　　Such as these thy wishes be.   60

11

Any gift had fortune lent me,
Not that I can boast of many.
Any grace had nature sent me,
Yet I say I had not any.
Not so little can be thought, 65
As were great the harmes they brought.

12

Yet would mine accursed starre
Had in me his beames confined,
Whose infection spreading farre
Struck at those to me were joyn'd 70
In acquaintance, love and bloud,
More or lesse as neere they stood.

13

Some in their estates were wrack't,
Somme prou'd lucklesse in their love,
Some with false defame were black't, 75
Some their friends unkindnesse prove.
Those the least of ylls have tride,
Who (alas) untimely dyde.

14

Thou most causelesse wert forsaken
For a ruine-bringing love. 80
Death from thee thy love hath taken,
Left alone sad fates to prove.
Thee thy parents fatall doome
Buries in a living tombe.

15

Happy thou hadst thy desire, 85
But your nuptial tapers sett
Both your houses on a fire,
So from Troy the flame was fette;
Thou long-sought thy love did'st find,
Find (alas) but prov'd unkind. 90

16

But thy woes should I awake
Woes with thee in silence sleeping,
All the rest would theirs forsake,
Thine alone thought worth the weeping.
Had not fate cutt off thy story, 95
Thine had rob'd from mine the glory.

17

Yet for many harmes of theirs,
And the greatest of mine owen
Vpon any of the spheares

Would I might the blame have throwen   100
   Whilst they of the ylls they sent
   Made of my selfe the instrument

18
Setting at the races end
As the doubtfull combat still,
   Wheresoere my wishes bend,   105
As still bend to one they will,
   There the losse still lights and brought
   Farther mischiefes with it oft.

19
Helpe to any gave I ever,
Or advise to any lent   110
   Well to any wisht I never,
Where it came to good event.
   But O, where most good of all
   I desir'd, most yll did fall.

20
Thou whose harmes were doubly mine,   115
Where least yll to have redeemed
   Willingly I would resigne
What my greatest good I deemed
   Not alone must wretched be
   But must owe the cause to mee.   120

21
Whilst I gave my selfe for thee
Of that gaine yet may I boast
   And whilst thou to purchase me
All thy world beside hast lost.
   By this match what have we wonne,   125
   Both undoing and undone.

22
Not that I my woes desire,
Vented thus to make them lesse,
   Or ells pitty thus require,
So to sweeten my distresse.   130
   Those which that had best deserved
   Still are in my heart reserved.

23
But I sett my griefes to shew
Where nor light nor eyes are neere.
   And I story out my woe,   135
Where there are no eares to heare.
   But with silent words unfold
   What by me shall nere be told.

E

9 *Queene*: the moon   11 *Blew*: candleflames burn blue when the oxygen level is low: this was thought to signify approaching death   21 *bred*: E. was breast-fed by her mother, not entrusted to a wet-nurse: babies were believed to imbibe the nurser's temperament with her milk   84 This line would most naturally refer to a baby that died in the womb: Eleanora Finch died of such a child, which may suggest (if it is appropriate to read this poem as autobiographic in any literal way) that this poem was written in her last weeks of life (i.e. in 1623), after her baby had stopped moving.

ALICE SUTCLIFFE, née WOODHOWS
(fl. 1620s–1630s)

ALICE was the daughter of Luke Woodhows of Kimberley in Norfolk, and was related to Sir Thomas Woodhouse, an attendant on Prince Henry Stuart, son of James VI and I. She married John Sutcliffe, an 'Esquire of the Body to King James', nephew to Matthew Sutcliffe, one of the royal chaplains, by 1624. She had a daughter, Susan, perhaps named for the Countess of Denbigh. Her husband is also described as an 'ancient servant of Buckingham', the notorious favourite of both James I and Charles I, in a petition for a wreck dated about 1627. John Sutcliffe was something of a projector: another petition from 1634-5 (which describes him as 'his Majesty's servant') details a money-making scheme concerning the powder in the Tower.

Alice Sutcliffe's only published work, *Meditations of Man's Mortalitie* was entered in the Stationers Register on 30 January 1633, and a second edition, enlarged, was printed in 1634. Her work is dedicated to the Duchess of Buckingham, widow of the Duke, and her sister-in-law, Susan Feilding, Countess of Denbigh. Alice Sutcliffe who appears from this dedication to have received some patronage from both: 'you have beene more then a Mother to mee, I having onely from her received life, but next under God from your Grace, & your honourable Sister the being both of mee and mine.' The second edition includes a set of commendatory poems from Ben Jonson, Thomas May, George Withers, and Francis Lenton, all of which emphasize the piety and propriety of her writing. Most of her book is in prose, with the addition of a 528-line poetic summary of Christian belief, from which we excerpt the first sixteen stanzas.

116   From '*Of our losse by ADAM, and our gayne by* CHRIST; *the first* Adam *was made a living soule, the second* Adam *a quickning Spririt; For as in ADAM wee all dye, so in* CHRIST, *shall all be made alive. I* Corinth. *15.*'

GOD by his Wisdome, and all seeing Pow'r
Ordained Man unto Eternitie,

Sathan through malice, turnes that sweet to sowre,
Man eating the forbidden Fruit must Die:
No remedy was left to scape this Curse,   5
The sore still looked on became the worse.

He out of that delightsome place is throwne
To travell in the World with woe distrest,
Through all his life a Pilgrim he is knowne,
With Cares and Sorrowes, and with griefes opprest: 10
The more he lookes into his wretched state,
The more he rues his fact but all too late.

Whereas he was created King of all
The Creatures God on Earth created bad,
His Glory bated is by this his Fall,   15
No creature now on Earth remaines to bad:
The sencelesse Beast the sence of this has found,
And having Man possest with death doth wound.

The Earth disdaines to yeeld to him her strength
But pricking Thornes and Brambles forth doth send,   20
Till with his sweat and labours she at length
Onely for sustenance some food doth lend:
Thus he that was a heavenly Creature form'd,
By disobedience to a wretch is turn'd.

Of all the Trees that in the Garden grew,   25
He onely was forbidden that alone,
His Wife from that obedience soone him drew,
And taste thereof he did although but one:
O wretched man! what hast thou lost hereby
Wicked woman to cause thy husband dye.   30

T'is not saying, the Serpent thee deceiv'd,
That can excuse the fault thou didst commit;
For of all Joyes thou hast thy selfe bereav'd,
And by thy Conscience thou dost stand convict.
Thy husband not alone the falt must rue,   35
A punishment for sinne to thee is due.

For as thou now conceives thy seed in sinne,
So in great sorrow thou must bring it foorth,
The game which thou by that same fruit didst winne,
Thou now dost find to bee of little worth: 40
Obedience to thy Husband yeeld thou must,
And both must Dye and turned be to Dust.

The Truth sometimes is used by the Divell
When as he sayd, Your eyes, should opened bee,
And that you should discerne the good from evill,   45

When you the Fruit had tasted of that tree:
But hee told not your actions, should be sinne
And Death should be the good which you should winne.

For now your strength to weakenesse turned is,
You know the Good but have no powre to chuse't,   50
Your eyes is ope, to see your owne amisse,
And to behold the blisse you have refus'd:
You see your nakednesse made vilde by Sinne,
And now seekes for a place to hide you in.

But O alas! your deeds discover'd are,   55
You naked lye to those all-seeing eyes,
He viewes your actions and doth see you bare,
Bare of all Goodnesse, vilde deformities:
And in your selves you have no power to mend,
For all your strength is sinne Sathan doth lend.   60

Now seizes on your sicknesse Griefes and Feares,
Which night and day with trouble will torment;
Your sweet Delights, are turned all to teares,
And now what you have done, with woe repent!
Nothing but Griefes and Feares and sad annoyes,   65
You now possesse, in stead of endlesse Joyes.

You were immortall, but are mortall made;
You were created pure, but now are vilde;
Your splendant Glories turned all to shade,
Your Innocence the Devill hath beguilde: 70
You were created Children of the Lord,
But now are loathsome Dung, to be abhorr'd.

Which way, can you recouer this your losse?
What friend have you, that will this great debt pay?
Can you gaine, pure gold from filthy drosse?   75
Or have you power to call againe that Day;
No, you are in a laborinth of woe,
And endlesse is the maze in which you goe.

Yet courage Woman, whose weake spirit's dead,
GOD in his love a helpe for thee hath found,   80
Bee sure thy Seed shall bruise the Serpents head,
CHRIST by his Death shall Sathan deadly wound:
This Lyon of *Iudea* resist who can,
In him is blest the whole Off-spring of man.

This Promise in due time fulfill'd hath GOD,   85
Vnto the comfort of each mortall weight;
CHRIST payes our Debt hee's beaten with that rod
That doth belong unto our Soules of right:

His Fathers wrath was powred upon him,
Which doth belong as due to us for Sinne.   90

Hee dy'd vpon the Crosse and conquered Death.
That though wee dye yet live againe wee must,
He buried was and risen is from Earth,
And raignes with God in Heaven amongst the Just:
With him, our Soules and Bodies rais'd hath hee,   95
And from death's thraldome now, hath set us free.

BATHSUA MAKIN (née RAINOLDS)
(1600–after 1673)

BATHSUA was the granddaughter of Henry Rainold, who lived in Ipswich until the 1680s or 1690s, and is known to have translated two books of Latin sermons by the German humanist Christopher Hegendorff (STC 13021–2). His son, her father (also Henry), moved to Stepney by 1600, the year of her birth, and became a schoolmaster. He also wrote a broadside of Latin poems praising James I, Charles I, and Henrietta Maria, printed in 1625 (STC 20840): she is thus the product of a highly educated family, and her own *Musa Virginea* can reasonably be seen as having been written under her father's direction. This book of poetry in five languages (Latin, Greek, French, Hebrew, and Italian) was published by her at the age of 16. It is addressed to James I, and also includes poems to his queen, Anne of Denmark, his son Charles (later Charles I), and the Elector Palatine, his son-in-law. It is probable that, like her contemporaries Elizabeth Weston and Aemilia Lanyer, she was attempting to use poetry as a stepping-stone to social or financial advancement. A well-known anecdote from the commonplace-book of John Colet shows James dismissing a learned maid with contemptuous indifference: the young woman thus dismissed is almost certainly Bathsua Rainolds.

   This teenage authoress returned to the public eye much later in her life, under the name Bathsua Makin, and as such, has been hailed as the first significant feminist writer in England. As far as her personal life goes, she married Richard Makin in 1621, and became the mother of a son. Makin was a minor court servant in the 1620s and 1630s, but then lost his place, which may explain why Bathsua herself was seeking court preferment in the 1640s, and became tutor to the Princess Elizabeth, a coup which may have resulted from a combination of Makin's court connections, and her own *Musa Virginea*. She appears to have had a special relationship with the Huntingdon family: in her *Essay* of 1673, she declares 'I am forbidden to mention the *Countess* Dowager of *Huntington* (instructed sometimes by Mrs Makin) how well she understands *Latin, Greek, Hebrew, French*, and *Spanish*; or what a proficient she is in arts, subservient to Divinity, in which (if I durst I would tell you), she excels.' This would suggest that she had been private tutor to the Countess as well as to Princess Elizabeth. The Countess's daughter, Lady Elizabeth Langham, and her sister Mary, were educated at the school Bathsua Makin opened at Tottenham High Cross in the 1670s. Elizabeth Drake, mother of Elizabeth Montagu, née

Robinson, the eighteenth-century bluestocking, is reported to have been another pupil at this school.

A copy of her Latin verses on the Parliamentarian Sir Henry Vane survives in Bodl. Rawl. Poet. 116, a MS belonging to the Elyot nephews of her admirer Sir Simonds d'Ewes (who had been one of her father's pupils): though of course her position is a complex one. Many of her sympathies and her friends were parliamentarian, but she herself was directly dependent on royal patronage. It was Simonds d'Ewes who put Bathsua in touch with the prodigiously learned Dutchwoman Anna Maria van Schurman, who lived in a Labadist community (a Protestant sect not unlike the Quakers). She sent Makin two letters in Greek on the education of women, preserved in her printed *Opuscula*, 162–4

Bathsua Makin's literary activity appears strictly pragmatic; it was produced as part of an overworked and underpaid life, for practical ends. *Musa Virginea* was written to attract attention to herself. After decades of silence, the verse she produced later in her life seems intended to make, or enhance, relations with patrons. Her famous *Essay* was written as an advertisement for her school: having outlined the value of an academic education for girls, she ends by stating that such an education can best be found at Tottenham High Cross (it appeared anonymously, thus its many references to the excellencies of Mrs Makin do not appear at first to be self advertisement). Noel Malcolm has suggested that the second half of the *Essay*, an approach to grammar, was written by Mark Lewis, a minor Comenian educationalist. Frances Teague has recently found an autograph letter from Makin to the famous physician Baldwin Hamey (see her *Bathsua Makin, Woman of Learning* (Lewisburg, Pa.: Bucknell University Press, 1998), 103–4).

117   *AD Fridericum V.G.D. comitem*
Palatinum longè maximum et illustrissimum
Rheni, Bavariæ Ducem, Principem
Electorem, et Archidapiferum Sacri Imperii
Romani, et, sede vacante, Vicarium
&c. Encomiasticon Bathsvæ Reginaldæ,
Anno salutis, 1616. Londini.

Italiæ pars una fuit Trinacria, NEREUS
    Fecit ut aufugiens insula sola foret;
Roma tamen sarcire volens dispendia tanta,
    Italiæ junxit sæva per arma suæ.
En pelago toto divisos orbe Britannos,   5
    Germanis junxit pax pia, lætus Hymen!
Papa tremit, quidni? tremat hic, timeatque Leonis
    Rugitum; duplicem qui facit inde metum:
At quot magnanimos spirantes arma Leones
    Fert Atavum clypeis Elizabetha potens!   10
En Tibi quanta (TRICEPS) miniantur bella

Quos clypeo septem Dania lata gerit; (Leones;
Verticibus qui bella tuis septena minantur!
Verticibus septem, Bellua fæda, cave:
Quatuor inde suos Genitor, quintumque Maritus   15
    Iungit, in exitium, perfida Roma, tuum;
Qui Mahometanum possint compescere Turcam,
    Vt primi Turcis quinque fuêre duces.
Roma cave; blanda es meretrix, jam sumere pænas
    Incipit hoc facto fœdere, spretus Hymen;   20
Lætus Hymen nobis quos unit pace cupita,
    Læthifer Italidis, Papicolisque tuis;
Haud secus ac moritur Scarabæus odore rosarum,
    Emoreris nostris, invida Roma, rosis:
Iam Petri claves tempus demergere Tibri,   25
    Et gladium Pauli sumere, and arma manu;
Et sed enim vanum est, Petrum diadema Philippo
    Mittere, vel magnos sollicitare duces;
Pro nobis Deus est, qui vincla jugalia nectit,
    Quæ non Paparum rumpere Bulla potest.   30

(1616)

1 *Trinacria*: a poetical name for Italy; *NEREUS*: a sea god   5 *toto*: Virgil, *Eclogues* 1, 65,
'et pene toto divisos orbe Britannos': 'and Britons, separated from the whole world'   5–6
Elizabeth Stuart, eldest daughter of James I, married Frederick V, the Elector Palatine in
1613   10 Refers to the royal coat of arms, with its lions   12–14 *septem ... septena ...*
septem: seven is a righteous number in Revelations: the slain lamb has seven horns and
seven eyes (Rev. 5: 6)   14 *Bellua fæda*: the papacy identified as the beast of Revelations   19 *meretrix*: Rome as Babylon, 'the great whore' of Revelations   30 *Bulla: ex
cathedra* pronouncements by the Pope are referred to as 'bulls', from the lead seal ('bullæ')
used to authenticate them

117   *To Frederick V, by the grace of God,*
    for a long time the most great and illustrious
        count Palatine, Duke of Bavaria,
        Chief Elector and Steward of the
        Holy Roman Empire, and, when the
    throne is empty, its Vicar: an Encomiastic
        by Bathsua Rainolds, in the year of
            grace 1616, from London

That Trinacria was made one part of Italy,
Nereus arranged, so that fleeing, he might be in that island alone;
Savage Rome, nevertheless, wishing to make good so great an expense,
Linked it to Italy by force of her arms.

Lo, happy Hymen has linked the Britons, divided from the whole world
    by the sea,   5
With the Germans, in a holy peace!
The Pope trembled, and why not? Let him tremble,
And fear the roar of the Lion, at which he makes a double fear:
Moreover, as many great-souled Lions as there are breathing,
Puissant Elizabeth bears as arms in the shields of her Ancestors!   10
Lo, however many wars are threatened against you, Three-crowned one
Broad Denmark bore seven of them on a shield
(Lions which threaten sevenfold war from your heights!)
Stinking Beast, beware the seven on the height:
From them the Father links four, and the Husband five,   15
Treacherous Rome, to your ruin;
Who would be able to to restrain the Mahometan Turk
So that at first, there were five dukes for the Turks.
Rome beware, you are a smooth-talking harlot, already
Disdainful Hymen begins to choose torments, to disgrace you with this
    event;   20
Happy Hymen, who unites us in a desired peace,
Death bringer to the Italians, and to your Pope-worshippers;
Just as the Scarab beetle dies from the smell of roses,
Envious Rome, you will die from these roses of ours.
It is time to drown the keys of Peter in the Tiber,   25
To sieze the sword of Paul, and arms in the hand;
Even though it is in vain, to send Peter the Philippian diadem,
or to incite great war-leaders,
God is for us, who confines in chain and yoke
That the Popes' Bull is not able to break.   30

118   *Upon the much lamented death of*
the Right Honourable the
Lady Elizabeth Langham

     Pass not, but wonder, and amazed stand
     At this sad tomb; for here enclosed lie
     Such rare perfections that no tongue or hand
     Can speak them or portray them to the eye;
     Such was her body, such her soul divine!   5
     Which now ascended, here hath left this shrine.
     To tell her princely birth, her high descent
     And what by noble Huntingdon is meant,
     Transcends the herald's art, beyond the rules
     Of Or, or Argent, Azure, or of Gules;   10
     To that nobility her birth had given
     A second added was, derived from heaven;
     Thence her habitual goodness, solid worth,
     Her piety; her virtues blazon forth;

Her for a pattern to all after ages,   15
To be admired by all, expressed by sages,
Who when they write of her, will sadly sorrow
That she did not survive to see their morrow.
So good in all relations, so sweet
A daughter, such a lovely wife, discreet   20
A mother; though not hers, not partial
She loved, as if they had been natural.
To th'Earl and Ladies she a sister rare,
A friend where she professed, beyond compare.
Her hours were all precisely kept, and spent   25
In her devotions; and her studies meant
To share some for her languages which she
In Latin, French, Italian happily
Advanced in with pleasure; what do I
Recount her parts? her memory speaks more   30
Than what can be, or hath been said before:
It asks a volume, rather than a verse,
Which is confined only to her hearse.
But now blessed soul, she is arriv'd at heaven,
Where with a crown of life to her is given   35
A new transcendent Name, to th'world unknowne,
Not writ in marble, but the saint's white stone:
Inthron'd above the stars, with glory crown'd,
Installed with bliss, and Hallelujahs sound.

                                                   (May 2, 1664)

This poem was sent by Makin to the Countess Dowager of Huntingdon condoling with
her on the death of her daughter. Lady Elizabeth was the daughter of Ferdinando
Hastings, sixth Earl of Huntingdon (b. 1609), and second wife of Sir James Langham, a
scholarly Northamptonshire gentleman and admirer of learned ladies. She married on 18
November 1662, and died on 28 March 1664   10 *Azure...Gules*: blue and red in
heraldry   21 *mother*: she was stepmother to the children of the first marriage   23
Earl and Ladies: Theophilus Hastings (b. 1650), seventh Earl of Huntingdon and his
sisters.

KATHERINE, LADY DYER (née D'OYLEY)
(*c*.1600–1654)

KATHERINE was the daughter and co-heir of Thomas D'Oyley of Merton,
Oxfordshire, and wife of Sir William Dyer of Colmworth, Bedfordshire, from a
cadet branch 'of the Antient Family of the Dyers in Somerset'. Her husband was
the son of Sir Richard Dyer (d. 1607?), a gentleman of the privy chamber to
James I. He died in 1621 at the age of 36. Their eldest son, Lodowick (Lewis), of
Staughton, Co. Huntingdon, was created a baronet in June 1627, at the age of

about 21, and in or before 1637, married Elizabeth, the daughter of Sir Henry Yelverton, and was a colonel in the royal army during the Civil War.

In 1641, Lady Katherine put up a magnificent funeral monument to her husband in the chancel of the Church of St Denis, Colmworth, from which the epitaph included here has been taken (there is a photograph of the tomb between pages 188 and 189 of *The Victoria County History, Bedfordshire*, vol. iii). The monument, which is of black and white marble, has alabaster effigies, at two levels, of Sir William and his wife: both are excellent pieces of workmanship. Lady Katherine is holding a small book in her right hand. Below them on the panelled base, between figures of Faith, Hope, and Charity, are four sons and three daughters (her suggested date of birth is based on the obvious assumption that they were married for the best part of a decade). The sons are Lodowick, Richard, Doyley, and James. Lady Dyer bought estates for Richard and Doyley, but the youngest son, James, is not mentioned in her will. The daughters are Ann, Mary, and Katherine. They each received a dowry of £1,500 and were married 'in good manner'. At Lady Dyer's feet is the small figure of Henry, Lodowick's only son, who died in infancy on 22 September 1637. In her will (P.C.C. 11/251, fo. 460), made on 8 October 1653, she complains that her 'losses have become very great since those late troubles' and she includes a codicil specifying what she would have given had these losses not occurred. She also asks that her funeral sermon be postponed until all her children and grandchildren can be assembled together. The will was proved in 1655.

A number of D'Oyleys were associated with Lord Falkland, and it is therefore possible that the loss of papers in the Falkland fire may have destroyed other work of hers, leaving only these three epitaphs. Verse of this quality and confidence, however, suggests that Lady Dyer was considerably more than an occasional poet.

119   *M.S. Sir Will: Dyer, Kt: Who put*
on Immortality Aprill the
29th Anno Domini 1621

If a large hart: Joyned with a Noble minde
Shewing true worth, unto all good inclin'd,
If faith in freindship, Justice unto all,
Leave such a Memory as we may call
Happy, Thine is: Then pious Marble keepe   5
His Just Fame waking, Though his lov'd dost sleepe.
And though Death can devoure all that hath breath,
And Monuments them selves have had a Death,
Nature shan't suffer this, to ruinate,
Nor time demolish't, nor an envious fate,   10
Rais'd by a Just hand not vaine glorious pride
Who'd be conceal'd, wer't modesty to hide
Such an affection did so long survive
The object of't: yet lov'd It as alive.
And this grate Blessing to his Name doth give   15
To make It by his Tombe, and Issue live.

My dearest dust could not thy hasty day
Afford thy drowzy patience leave to stay
One hower longer; so that we might either
    Sate up, or gone to bedd together?   20
But since thy finisht labor hath possest
    Thy weary limbs with early rest,
Enjoy it sweetly; and thy widdowe bride
Shall soone repose her by thy slumbring side;
Whose business, now is only to prepare   25
    My nightly dress, and call to prayre:
Mine eyes wax heavy and the day growes old
    The dew falls thick, my bloud growes cold;
Draw, draw the closed curtaynes: and make roome;
My deare, my dearest dust; I come, I come.   30

                   (1621)

Title *M.S.*: *memoriae sacrum*: sacred to the memory of   16 *Issue*: children   19–20 It is
possible that the stonecutter has introduced error into these lines. The text here is given
literally from the monument: 'have' needs to be understood as an auxiliary to 'sate
up'   26 *nightly dress*: nightclothes, also shroud   27 *wax*: grow

DAME GERTRUDE (HELEN) MORE
(1604–1633)

DAME GERTRUDE is unusually well documented for a nun, in that her
spiritual director, Dom Augustine Baker, who admired her enormously, wrote
a lengthy biography of her. She was a great-great-granddaughter of Sir Thomas
More (Lord Chancellor of Henry VIII, Catholic martyr, and the father of
famously learned daughters), and was highly conscious of her intellectual and
spiritual heritage. Baker describes her as 'of a very extroverted disposition, with
an active imagination, and much prone to talking and recreations, and to every
kind of interest imaginable . . . she had great aptitude for friendships . . . she was
particularly delighted with historical works, and was more attracted to verse than
prose. Indeed, when but a child of four or five, she used to make rhymes in
conversation with her father, to his great entertainment.'
    At 18, she decided to become a nun. Unable to find anywhere suitable for her,
her father decided to found, and financially to endow, a new Benedictine
convent at Cambrai for her reception. There she was joined by her younger
sister Bridget, and by her two first cousins. Her life as a nun was very nearly a
disaster. She became very depressed, and only the fact that the community were
financially dependent on her kept her in place. The problem was that the
Council of Trent had decreed that convents should be strictly enclosed and
contemplative institutions; and the life did not suit her active, extrovert temperament: she would have been better suited, perhaps to a teaching order, a form
of monastic life for women that Mary Ward was just about to invent. It was Fr.
Baker who introduced her to a form of interior prayer which fitted her temperament and allowed her to make sense of her life, and thereafter, she became a

gifted contemplative. Her poems belong to the last period of her life, after she had achieved this reconciliation. She was still liable to periods of spiritual aridity, and therefore put together private notebooks of thoughts and ideas which had been helpful to her, for recourse during these periods. These notebooks also included her poems. One of the great griefs of her life was that Fr. Baker and his method came under suspicion from the hierarchy, and she was ordered to stop using it—since she had come to regard it as almost literally a lifeline, this caused immense strain. She had the happiness of seeing Baker vindicated shortly before her early death from smallpox.

120   *A dittie to the same subject.*

In sorrow deepe, I wake, I sleepe with griefe my Hart opprest;
My Watry eyes like winter skies bedew my mournefull breast.
For when I see my love for mee, in flames of love to burne,
My Lord, my Love, my *God* above, and why should I not mourne?

With feete, and hands transfixed hee stands uppon a fatall beame;   5
And from his side a wound most wide poures out a bloddie streame.
A peircinge Crowne his head pulls downe, his face quite wanne doth turne
He for my sake these paines did take, and why should I not mourne?

While in this paine, he did remaine, his drink was mixt with Gall.
His Corps lay bare, his Clothes they share, each as by lott did fall.   10
His Foes about did laugh and shout and at his vertues spurne,
Thus was his breath shutt up by death, and why should I not Mourne?

The earth did quake, the rockes did shake, and rented all in sunder.
The Corps from Graves and hollow Caves arose to see this wonder.
The sunne so bright forsooke his light and all most wanne did turne   15
Thus heaven and earth lament his death, and why should I not mourne?

Loe when I see uppon a Tree his breathless Body lye,
I grieve, I groane, I sigh, I moane, I payne, I Faint, I dye.
For thee Alone: my life being gone untill thou backe returne
In endlesse greife without reliefe I'll never cease to mourne.   20

121   *A short oblation of this smal work by the*
writer gatherer thereof to our most sweet
and merciful God

My GOD to *thee* I dedicate
This *simple* work of mine.

And also with it hart and soul
　　To be for ever thine.
No other motive wil I have   5
　　Then by it *thee* to praise
And stir up my poor frozen soul
　　By *love* it-self to raise.
O I desir neither tongue, nor pen
　　But to extol *Gods* praise,   10
In which exces ile melt away
　　Ten thousand thousand ways,
And as one that is sick with *love*
　　Engraves on every Tree
The Name and Praise of him she loves   15
　　So shal it be with me.

JANE HAWKINS
(fl. 1629)

THE surviving verses of Jane Hawkins are included here because of the enormous interest of their context. The kind of prophetic writing which they
represent is normally seen as a feature of the Civil War period and the decades
following: the story of Jane Hawkins opens up the fact that the social rifts
revealed by the Civil War had a long history. Our knowledge of this woman and
her context comes from the Bishop of Lincoln, who on 28 April 1629 wrote a
long letter to the authorities in London, telling them about an incident which
developed in a remote country parish.

The weoman is not yeat (Generallye) of any good; and hath beene of very badd fame. Very
precise, and deere unto the viccar of the towne, soe addicted, whom with much a doe, for
feare of deprivation, I brought to conformite, some two years sithence. She is a wittye and
a craftie Baggage. And the chief in this Imposture. Fayninge herself in a trance, she began
(like the Eleventh Sibill) to preach in verse. But not any thinge (as the report went)
concerninge the state or the Government of the Church, But onely by waye of Aunswere
to private temptations of hire owne, and magifienge the Ministrye of Mr Tokey (the
viccar)... this versifienge continued for 3 dayes and 3 nights, in an Auditorye of very neare
two hundred people, the most beinge of the weaker sex. The viccare, and one Mr Wise, his
wise Curate, and another schollar, sittenge composedlye at the beds feete, and Coppienge
out the verses, which the poore weoman (for she is but a pedlar) did dictate which
(amounting to some thousands) they had transcribed and written out fayre, wth intent to
printe and divulge them, when, comminge thither suddenlye, I seazed upon the Coppye
and the Originalls.

What we have here, then, is a High Church bishop, one of those who will in
future support the Laudian reforms, trying to keep control over a Low Church,
or Puritan, vicar, Mr Tokey. Jane Hawkins is a 'precisian', that is, a Puritan; and
a supporter of Mr Tokey. What is interesting is that he is sufficiently impressed
by her gifts that he forms an alliance with her which cuts across boundaries of
class and gender.

122   *'O lett it be for ever told'*

O lett it be for ever told
  to ages that succeed,
That they may lay it up in store
  for then will be most need.
When that you see those fearfull times   5
  which now in parte you feare,
for they are sure to come to us,
  o they drawe wondrous neare.
And then (good truth) you may believe
  I take it still for grant   10
that punishment will follow sinn
  and ever will it haunte.
And therefore now in shortest speech
  o labour to believe
Least afterwards it be too late,   15
  when you so sore shall grieve.

DIANA PRIMROSE
(fl. 1630)

THE most notable member of the Primrose family was Gilbert, a Scot (b. 1573) head of the reformed church in France, and later chaplain in ordinary to James I. The relationship of Diana Primrose to this man (if any, but the name is uncommon) is unknown. Her long poem in praise of Elizabeth I is apparently intended as an oblique criticism of the personal rule of Charles I. The motto, *Dat Rosa mel apibus, qua sugit Aranea virus* [The Rose, from which the Spider sucks poison, gives honey to the bee] seems to imply a reading strategy: the poem, or the author (Prim-*rose*) is the rose, from which the virtuous reader will extract nectar, and the vicious one poison, a definite suggestion that her work carries double meanings. *Dat Rosa mel apibus* is a Rosicrucian slogan used by Robert Fludd: Rosicrucian texts were always intended to mean one thing to initiates and another to outsiders.

123   *The Eight Pearle*
               SCIENCE

Among the Vertues Intellectual,
The Van is lead by that we *Science* call;
A Pearle more precious than th'Ægyptian Queene,
Quaft off to *Anthony*; of more esteeme
Then *Indian Gold*, or most resplendent Gemmes,   5

Which ravish us with their translucent Beames.
How many Arts and Sciences did decke
This HEROINA? Who still had at becke
The *Muses* and the *Graces*, when that *Shee*
Gave Audience in State and Majestie: 10
Then did the Goddess *Eloquence* inspire
Her Royall Brest: *Apollo* with his *Lyre*.
Ne're made such Musicke, On her Sacred Lips
Angells enthron'd, most heavenly *Manna* sips.
Then might you see her *nectar-flaming* Veine   15
Surround the Hevens; in which sugred Streame,
SHEE able was to drowne a World of men,
And drown'd, with sweetnes to revive agen.
Alasco, the Embassador *Polonian*,
Who perorated like a meere *Slavonian*,   20
And in rude rambling *Rhetoricke* did roule,
SHEE did with *Atticke Eloquence* controule
Her Speeches to our *Academians*,
Well shew'd *Shee* knew among *Athenians*,
How to deliver such well-tuned Words,   25
As with such Places punctually accords.
But with what *Oratory*-ravishments,
Did *Shee* imparadise her *Parliaments*?
Her last most Princely Speech doth verify,
How highly *Shee* did England dignify.   30
Her Loyall Commons how did *Shee* embrace,
And entertaine with a most Royall Grace?

2 *Van is lead*: (led): a military term of art   3 *Ægytian Queene*: Cleopatra, who dissolved a precious pearl in vinegar as a toast to Anthony: a story from Plutarch, also used by Shakespeare in *Anthony and Cleopatra*   5 *Indian Gold*: gold brought from the recently discovered mines of South America   19 *Alasco*: A Polish ambassador came to London in 1597 and complained in Latin about the confiscation of Polish grain ships bound for Spain. Cecil reported to Essex 'To this, I swear by the Living God that Her Majesty made one of the best answers extempore in Latin that ever I heard.'   20 *Slavonian*: Slav   22 *Atticke*: Classical Greek   23–4 *Academians . . . Athenians*: scholars of Oxford and Cambridge   29 *Princely Speech*: Elizabeth's so-called 'Golden Speech', delivered in 1601, and widely circulated for 200 years.

ANONYMOUS [? 'LADY LOTHIAN']
[*circulating* 1630s]

THIS didactic poem, evidently by a woman on the basis of its last stanza, is attributed to a Lady Lothian of whom nothing is known (the use of the term 'Lady' in early modern Scotland need imply nothing more than gentry status), and circulated in manuscript in Scotland. One of the copies, now in Aberdeen, is in a large, childish hand, suggesting that it was used for the instruction of the young. 'Tak tyme at the tyd' is a Scottish proverb, and the whole text has a strong flavour of proverbial wisdom.

124   *Ane godlie Instructione for old and young* 'The Lady Lothian's Lilt'

On yeir begines ane other endis
Thus Tyme doeth come and goe
All thus to your Instructione tends
Give we culd tak it so
The sommeris heat the winters cold   5
Quhois seasonis lets us see
Quhan youth is gone and we wax old
Lyk flouris we fade and die.

Men for the most pairt dois rejoyce
Quhan sonis to them ar borne   10
Quhois weiping noice bevailles thair vois
and folis chanes to scorne
Thes ar the mesengeris to schow
Our tyme is passing fast
Quhan We deceas still they do grow   15
Till death us pairt at last

Now let us learne to spend our dayes
In vertue as we ought
In doing guid mak no delay
put sleuth out of our thought   20
The sleuthfull nevir yit ateind
To honour wealth nor fame
But many hath by vertue gaind
ane long long lasting name

In spring tyme of our youth we suld   25
The seidis of learning Saw
Weid furth our vyces give we could
our sinfull lustis overthraw
quha in the pryme of youth taks paines
Thair service to bestow   30
In harvest of his age againe
The grapes of grace do grow

Thus all tymes begines and ends
No thing bot fame remaines
hapie is he quha wyslie spends   35
His Tym in Vertues paines

Bot quhan the paine is past away
the pleasor sall abyde
Now hapie thryse ar such I say
That taks tyme at the tyd   40

The tyd of tyme it floweth fast
and quickly ebes away
Bot if our schip lacks saill or mast
Our Voyage mast delay
our bodies ar that brittle barks   45
That sailles that floodes of fame
Bot if throue sleuth we miss [the] marke
we sinke in seas of schame

Occatione haveth hear befoir
Bot scho is beld behind   50
Tint tyme no travell can restoir
as many folles may find
the little ant the hony bee
In sommer layeth up stoir
for to provyd for winters stormes   55
man most and suld do moir

Thus I have done to pleas your Will
Now let me have my hyre
I have bewray'd my want of skill
In doing your desyre   60
The Weakness of a Woman's Witt
Is not to natures fault
Bot lack of educatioune fitt
Makes nature quhylls to halt.

1 *On yeir*: one year   4 *Give*: if   6 *Quhois*: whose   7 *Quhan*: when   8 *flouris*: flowers   11 *bevailles*: bewails   12 *folis chanes*: folly's chains   20 *sleuth*: sloth   26 *seidis*:
seeds; *Saw*: sow   27 *Weid furth*: weed out   29 *quha*: who   39 *thryse*: thrice   40 *taks
tyme at the tyd*: seizes the moment   49 *Occatione*: Occasion. This follows the traditional
iconography: she can be seized by the forelock, but once she has passed, there is no hair to
clutch at on the back of her head; *hear*: hair   50 *beld*: bald   51 *Tint tyme*: lost time   56
most and suld: must and should   64 *halt*: limp

SIBELLA DOVER née COLE
(perhaps in Collaboration with THOMAS COLE)
(fl. 1630)

THIS is a rather elegant and sophisticated piece of writing involving extensive
wordplay. Internal evidence and particularly the closing pun 'Silabii/Sibellae'
would point to Sibella Dover as author. The title-page of *Annales Dubrensia*

however says that the author of the 'Syrinx' is Oxon. which would usually mean 'of the University of Oxford', thus obviously excluding any woman. But in its other sense 'Of Oxfordshire' it would suit Sibella Dover well. Her father had been president of Corpus Christi College Oxford. Her brother Thomas Cole was a fellow of that college. As a girl she had lived at Lower Heyford in Oxfordshire. A family collaboration, in which Sibella supplied the English and her brother supplied the Latin anagrams and apparatus is perfectly possible. It is not, however, impossible that the daughter of a learned family might herself have had all the knowledge necessary to compose an elegant and allusive, though not deeply learned, piece such as this one.

If the poem is read from the top down it makes a certain sense as coming from Sibella or Sibilla Dover, if it is read, following the hint given by the original numbering, from the bottom upwards, it makes rather more sense as a speech by Lady Modesty, showering benefits from heaven on mortals including Dover. The poem is in the shape of a syrinx or pan-pipe: pattern poetry was a learned game from late antiquity, particularly in Alexandria (there is a syrinx-shaped poem in Greek attributed to Theocritus). Pattern poems enjoyed some popularity in England: there is a long discussion of the form in Puttenham's *Art of English Poesie* (1589), 75–80. George Herbert is probably the most notable exponent: his 'Easter Wings' and 'The Altar' are among the best-known English examples of the genre.

125 *TO HER MODEST MIRTH-MAKING*
Friend, Mr Robert Dover, *this pastorall Pipe,*
by the name of a Syrinx, *dedicates her selfe,*
with her annexed Annagrams.

Incerti Authoris opus.
Τῆς ἐκκλησίας ἀγίόν οὐρανόθεν φύλακος
Dos et Robur versu.
Rubor et dos versu.
Robertus Doverus.

Sing, Sing, Sing, Numen, Lumen, Numen, 20
Pretty Lady nimphs, and all yee young-men; 19
*Mirths deitie: for a laught at his birth, and he will smile at his
   ending:* 18
Ballanced rejecteth. But his merry, merry heart doth inherit 17
Lowdly ecchoed praises: nor timorously his just merrit, 16   5
For he little valueth the pompious Turk-*like Sopheys* 15
This subsideriall rundle : him I deck with Trophies, 14
Which whirryeth his Fame in circuit all over 13
Whose nimble motion is like the first mover, 12
Heroick, spritefull, mirth-making Dover, 11   10
Above the rest my best dearest lover, 10
(Richest favours) friendly befriending. 9
Showring downe, lovely sweet kisses, 8

With more then humane blisses, 7
To whom my rayes give light, 6   15
Doe deck, every wight, 5
Above the skie, 4
Modesty, 3   Verus Rubor dotes) *Ana.*
Lady 2   Robertus Doverus)
I 1   20

[printed vertically in the r.h. margin]
Sirinx sine fistula pastoricia Constans,
Ex centum et nonaginta Sillabii.

translation of Latin and Greek: The work of an unknown author; [Gk.]To the beloved,
heaven-tending, of the holy church; Talent and strength in verse; modesty and gifts in
verse (both anagrams of Robertus Doverus). Anagram at end: Endowed with true modesty.
Marginal Latin couplet: a faithful Sirynx (pan-pipe) without a pastoral pipe, out of 190
syllables (pun on Sillabii and Sibyllae: of Sibylla). NB: this poem can also be read from
bottom to top.   1 *Numen, Lumen*: God, light (Latin)   9 *first mover*: the primum mobile,
the first mobile sphere of early modern astronomy   6 *Sopheys*: the Grand Sophy was a
title for the leader of the Ottoman Empire (there may be an unrecoverable sly reference to
a neighbour or friend called Sophie or Sophia). The author corrects Robert Griffin's
comparison of Dover (elsewhere in The *Annales*) to a Persian Sophie. Or this may be a
legal coterie joke: the Lord of Misrule at the Inner Temple was called The Prince of
Sophie   7 *subsideriall rundle:* the world. A rundle is a kind of barrel, so it is envisioned as
a rolling object under the stars

ANNE BRADSTREET (née DUDLEY)
(1612–1672)

ANNE BRADSTREET was born in 1612 in Northampton, daughter of Thomas
Dudley, who was at that time chief steward in the household of the Earl of
Lincoln. It was apparently with his encouragement that she read widely as a girl:
she described him as 'a magazine of history'. As the daughter of so senior and
trusted a servant, she had free run of the extensive library at Sempringham
Castle, and made good use of it: to judge from her own poems, Du Bartas and
Sir Philip Sidney were particular passions of hers, while Edmund Spenser was
particularly influential on her own practice as a poet. At 16, she married Simon
Bradstreet, nine years her senior, a graduate of Emmanuel College, Cambridge,
and also a dependant of the Earl of Lincoln. About this time, Thomas Dudley
was deeply impressed by the Puritan preachers Dodd and Hildersham, and
converted to Presbyterianism, taking his family with him. As William Laud,
Bishop of London from 1629 and Archbishop of Canterbury from 1633, began
enforcing conformity to an Anglicanism which became increasingly imitative of
Catholicism in its forms and ceremonials, and cracked down on Puritans, a
number of leading Puritans decided to retreat to America. Thus, twelve heads of
families, including Thomas Dudley and John Winthrop, came together in 1629
at Cambridge, and agreed to found the Massachusetts Bay Colony. In 1630,
Dudley, his daughter and his son-in-law travelled with the party of John
Winthrop to New England aboard the *Arbella*, a journey of seventy-two days.

In America, the young couple lived briefly in Salem, Boston, Cambridge, and Ipswich, before settling (between 1638 and 1644) on a farm at North Andover, Massachusetts, near the Merrimac River. Her father, Thomas Dudley, came to occupy a prominent position in the public life of the Massachusetts Bay Colony, and Simon Bradstreet also became a distinguished citizen, judge, legislator, royal councillor, and ultimately governor of the colony. She was childless for the first five years of her marriage, a great grief to her at the time, but thereafter, eight children followed in quick succession, despite her rather delicate health. Anne Bradstreet died of consumption at the age of 60. She was luckier than many early modern women in being survived by all but one of her children, and her husband.

The poem 'Upon the burning of our house' records a traumatic event in the life of the family: her son noted that apart from the financial loss, the fire destroyed more than 800 books, a sizeable library for a private household. The long poem which we have included here is interesting for its approach to the English Civil War, which began in 1641. It makes good use of her extensive reading in English history, but she appears to regard it as an almost exclusively religious issue—in fact, she gives the impression that the whole thing was the fault of Archbishop Laud for perverting the cause of true religion. We give the version from the first edition of *The Tenth Muse*, published in her lifetime, and evidently written before the execution of Charles I (perhaps, on internal evidence, *c.*1643–4). There was quite extensive revision for the second edition, all of which tends to tone down her support for Parliament and radical, even millenarian, Presbyterianism: it is possible that Anne Bradstreet herself suffered a revulsion of feeling after the execution of the king, as many did, but it is equally possible that the editorial hand is another's.

126   *Prologue [to the Tenth Muse]*

I

To sing of Wars, of Captaines, and of Kings,
Of Cities founded, Common-wealths begun,
For my mean Pen are too superiour things,
Or how they all, or each, their dates have run:
Let Poets, and Historians set these forth,   5
My obscure Verse, shal not so dim their worth.

2

But when my wondring eyes and envious heart
Great *Bartas* sugar'd lines, do but read o're
Foole, I do grudge, the Muses did not part
'Twixt him and me that over-fluent store;   10
A *Bartas* can, doe what a *Bartas* wil,
But simple I, according to my skill.

3

From School-boyes tongue, no Rethoricke we expect,
Nor yet a sweet Consort, from broken strings,
Nor perfect beauty, where's a maine defect,   15
My foolish, broken, blemish'd Muse so sings;
And this to mend, alas, no Art is able,
'Cause nature, made it so irreparable.

4

Nor can I, like that fluent sweet tongu'd *Greek*
Who lisp'd at first, speake afterwards more plaine   20
By Art, he gladly found what he did seeke,
A full requitall of his striving paine:
Art can doe much, but this maxime's most sure,
A weake or wounded braine admits no cure.

5

I am obnoxious to each carping tongue,   25
Who sayes, my hand a needle better fits,
A Poets Pen, all scorne I should thus wrong;
For such despight they cast on female wits:
If what I doe prove well, it won't advance,
They'l say its stolne, or else, it was by chance.   30

6

But sure the Antic *Greeks* were far more milde,
Else of our Sex, why feigned they those Nine,
And poesy made, *Calliope*'s own childe,
So 'mongst the rest they plac'd the Arts Divine;
But this weake knot, they will full soone untye,   35
The *Greeks* did nought, but play the foole and lye.

7

Let *Greeks* be *Greeks*, and Women what they are,
Men have precedency, and still excell,
It is but vain, unjustly to wage war;
Men can doe best, and Women know it well;   40
Preheminence in each, and all is yours;
Yet grant some small acknowledgement of ours.

8

And oh ye high flown quils that soare the skies,
And ever with your prey, still catch your praise,
If e're you daigne these lowly lines, your eyes   45
Give wholsome Parsley wreath, I ask no bayes,
This mean and unrefined stuffe of mine
Will make your glistering gold but more to shine.

A.B.
(1650)

8 *Bartas*: Guillaume Salluste, Sieur du Bartas (1544–90), Huguenot religious poet   19
Greek: the orator Demosthenes, who conquered a speech impediment by training himself
to speak holding a pebble in his mouth   32 *Nine*: nine Muses of Greek myth   33
Calliope: muse of epic poetry

127   'As loving Hind that
                (Hartless) wants her Deer'

As loving Hind that (Hartless) wants her Deer,
Scuds through the woods and Fern with harkning ear,
Perplext, in every bush and nook doth pry,
Her dearest Deer, might answer ear or eye;
So doth my anxious soul, which now doth miss,   5
A dearer Dear (far dearer Heart) than this,
Still wait with doubts, and hopes, and failing eye,
His voice to hear, or person to discry.
Or as the pensive Dove doth all alone
(On withered bough) most uncouthly bemoan   10
The absence of her Love, and loving Mate,
Whose loss hath made her so unfortunate:
Ev'n thus doe I, with many a deep sad groan
Bewail my turtle true, who now is gone,
His presence and his safe return, still wooes,   15
With thousand dolefull sighs and mournfull Cooes.
Or as the loving Mullet, that true Fish,
Her fellow lost, nor joy nor life do wish,
But lanches on that shore, there for to dye,
Where she her captive husband doth espy.   20
Mine being gone, I lead a joyless life,
I have a loving phere, yet seem no wife:
But worst of all, to him can't steer my course,
I here, he there, alas, both kept by force:
Return my Dear, my joy, my only Love,   25
Unto thy Hinde, thy Mullet and thy Dove,
Who neither joyes in pasture, house nor streams,
The substance gone, O me, these are but dreams.
Together at one Tree, oh let us brouze,
And like two Turtles roost within one house,   30
And like the Mullets in one River glide,
Let's still remain but one, till death divide.
            (*Thy loving Love and Dearest Dear*,
            (*At home, abroad, and every where.*

1 *Hartless*: without a hart (deer), also, without a heart since presumably, he has hers with
him   22 *phere*: fere (companion)

128   *The Author to her book*

Thou ill-form'd offspring of my feeble brain,
Who after birth did'st by my side remain,
Till snatcht from thence by friends, less wise then true
Who thee abroad, expos'd to publick view,
Made thee in raggs, halting to th'press to trudg,   5
Where errors were not lessened (all may judg)
At thy return my blushing was not small,
My rambling brat (in print) should mother call,
I cast thee by as one unfit for light,
Thy visage was so irksome in my sight;   10
Yet being mine own, at length affection would
Thy blemishes amend, if so I could:
I wash'd thy face, but more defects I saw,
And rubbing off a spot, still made a flaw.
I stretcht thy joints to make thee even feet,   15
Yet still thou run'st more hobling than is meet;
In better dress to trim thee was my mind,
But nought save home-spun Cloth i'th'house I find
In this array, 'mongst Vulgars mayst thou roam
In Criticks hands, beware thou dost not come;   20
And take thy way where yet thou art not known,
If for thy Father askt, say, thou hadst none:
And for thy Mother, she alas is poor,
Which caus'd her thus to send thee out of door.

15 *stretcht*: there were traditional techniques for manipulating and massaging the bodies of babies with the intention of straightening them; but with this child/poem 'feet' here refers to metrical feet   17 *trim*: make smart, ornament

129 *A Dialogue between Old England and New; concerning their present Troubles. Anno 1642*

New-England.

Alas dear Mother, fairest Queen, and best,
With honour, wealth, and peace, happy and blest;
What ails thee hang thy head, and crosse thine armes?
And sit i'th'dust, to sigh these sad alarms?
What deluge of new woes thus over-whelme   5
The glories of thy ever famous Realme?
What means this wailing tone, this mourning guise?
Ah, tell thy Daughter, she may sympathize.

Old England.

Art ignorant indeed, of these my woes?

Or must my forced tongue these griefes disclose?   10
And must my selfe dissect my tatter'd state,
Which 'mazed Christendome stands wondering at?
And thou a childe, a Limbe, and dost not feel
My weakned fainting body now to reele?
This Physick-purging-potion I have taken,   15
Will bring Consumption, or an Ague quaking,
Unlesse some Cordial thou fetch from high,
Which present help may ease this malady.
If I decease, dost think thou shalt survive?
Or by my wasting state, dost think to thrive?   20
Then weigh our case, if't be not justly sad,
Let me lament alone, while thou art glad.

New-England.

And thus, alas, your state you much deplore,
In general terms, but will not say wherefore,
What Medicine shall I seek to cure this woe,   25
If th' wound's so dangerous I may not know?
But you perhaps would have me guesse it out;
What, hath some *Hengist*, like that *Saxon* stout,
By fraud, or force, usurp'd thy flowring crown,
And by tempestuous warrs thy fields trod down?   30
Or hath *Canutus*, that brave valiant *Dane*,
The regall, peacefull Scepter from thee tane?
Or is't a *Norman*, whose victorious hand
With English blood bedews thy conquered land?
Or is't intestine wars that thus offend?   35
Doe *Maud*, and *Stephen* for the Crown contend?
Doe Barons rise, and side against their King?
And call in forreign ayde to help the thing?
Must *Edward* be depos'd, or is't the houre
That second *Richard* must be clapt i'th Tower?   40
Or is't the fatal jarre againe begun
That from the red, white pricking Roses sprung?
Must *Richmonds* ayd, the Nobles now implore?
To come and break the tushes of the Boar?
If none of these, dear Mother, what's your woe?   45
Pray, doe not fear *Spains* bragging *Armado*?
Doth your Allye, fair *France*, conspire your wrack?
Or do the *Scots* play false behind your back?
Doth *Holland* quit you ill, for all your love?
Whence is this storme, from Earth, or Heaven above?   50
Is't Drought, is't Famine, or is't Pestilence?
Dost feel the smart, or fear the consequence?
Your humble Childe intreats you, shew your grief,
Though Arms, nor Purse she hath, for your releif:

Such is her poverty, yet shall be found   55
A Supplyant for your help, as she is bound.

Old England.

I must confesse, some of those Sores you name,
My beauteous Body at this present maime;
But forraigne Foe, nor fained friend I feare,
For they have work enough (thou knowst) elsewhere;   60
Nor is it *Alcies* Son, and *Henries* daughter;
Whose proud contention cause this slaughter;
Nor Nobles siding, to make *John* no King
French *Lewis* unjustly to the Crown to bring;
No *Edward*, *Richard*, to lose rule, and life,   65
Nor no *Lancastrians* to renew old strife:
No Crook-backt Tyrant, now usurps the Seat,
Whose tearing tusks did wound, and kill, and threat:
No Duke of *York*, nor Earle of *March*, to soyle
Their hands in kindreds blood, whom they did foyle: 70
No need of *Teder*, Roses to unite,
None knows which is the Red, or which the White:
Spains braving Fleet, a second time is sunke,
France knowes, how of my fury she hath drunk;
By *Edward* third, and *Henry* fifth of fame,   75
Her Lillies in mine Armes avouch the same.
My Sister *Scotland* hurts me now no more,
Though she hath bin injurious heretofore.
What *Holland* is, I am in some suspence
But trust not much unto his Excellence;   80
For wants, sure some I feele, but more I feare,
And for the Pestilence, who knowes how neare?
Famine, and Plague, two sisters of the Sword,
Destruction to a Land doth soone afford;
They're for my punishments ordain'd on high,   85
Unlesse thy teares prevent it speedily.
But yet I answer not what you demand,
To shew the grievance of my troubled Land;
Before I tell the effect, ile shew the cause
Which are my Sins, the breach of sacred Lawes,   90
Idolatry, supplanter of a Nation,
With foolish superstitious adoration;
And lik'd and countenanc'd by men of might,
The Gospel is trod down and hath no right;
Church Offices are sold, and bought, for gaine,   95
That Pope, had hope, to find *Rome* here againe,
For Oaths, and Blasphemies, did ever Eare
From *Beelzebub* himself, such language heare?
What scorning of the Saints of the most high,

What injuries did daily on them lye,   100
What false reports, what nick-names did they take,
Not for their owne, but for their Masters sake;
And thou, poore soule, wert jeer'd among the rest,
Thy flying for the Truth I made a jeast;
For Sabbath-breaking, and for Drunkennesse,   105
Did ever Land prophanesse more expresse?
From crying bloods, yet cleansed am not I,
Martyrs, and others, dying causelessly:
How many Princely heads on blocks laid down,
For naught, but title to a fading Crown?   110
'Mongst all the cruelties which I have done,
Oh, *Edwards* babes, and *Clarence* haplesse Son,
O *Jane*, why didst thou dye in flowring prime,
Because of Royal Stem, that was thy crime:
For Bribery, Adultery, for Thefts, and Lyes,   115
Where is the Nation, I cann't paralize.
With Usury, Extortion and Oppression,
These be the *Hydra's* of my stout transgression.
These be the bitter fountains, heads and roots,
Whence flow'd the source, the sprigs, the boughs and
    fruits;   120
Of more than thou canst heare, or I relate,
That with high hand I did still perpetrate:
For these, were threatned the wofull day,
I mockt the Preachers, put it faire away;
The Sermons yet upon record doe stand,   125
That cry'd, destruction to my wicked Land:
These Prophets mouthes (alls the while) was stopt,
Unworthily, some backs whipt, and eares cropt;
Their reverent cheeks, did beare the glorious markes
Of stinking, stigmatizing, Romish Clerkes;   130
Some lost their livings, some in prison pent,
Some grossely fin'd, from friends to exile went:
Their silent tongues to heaven did vengeance cry,
Who heard their cause, and wrongs judg'd righteously,
And will repay it sevenfold in my lap,   135
This is fore-runner of my after-clap.
Nor took I warning by my neighbours falls,
I saw sad *Germanie's* dismantled walls.
I saw her people famish'd, Nobles slain,
Her fruitfull land, a barren heath remain.   140
I saw (unmov'd) her Armyes foil'd and fled,
Wives forc'd, babes toss'd, her houses calcined.
I saw strong *Rochel* yeelding to her foe,
Thousand of starved Christians there also,

I saw poore *Ireland* bleeding out her last, ⎫   145
Such cruelty as all reports have past;   ⎬
Mine heart obdurate, stood not yet agast. ⎭
Now sip I of that cup, and just't may be
The bottome dregs reserved are for me.

New-England.

To all you've said, sad Mother, I assent   150
Your fearfull sinnes, great cause there's to lament,
My guilty hands (in part) hold up with you,
A sharer in your punishment's my due.
But all you say, amounts to this effect,
Not what you feel, but what you do expect.   155
Pray in plain termes, what is your present grief,
Then let's join heads, and hands for your relief.

Old England.

Well to the matter then, there's grown of late,
'Twixt King and Peers a Question of state,
Which is the chief, the law, or else the King,   160
One saith its he, the other no such thing.
My better part in Court of Parliament
To ease my groaning Land shew their intent,
To crush the proud, and right to each man deal.
To help the Church, and stay the Common-weal,   165
So many obstacles comes in their way,
As puts me to a stand what I should say,
Old customes, new Prerogatives stood on,
Had they not held law fast, all had been gone,
Which by their prudence stood them in such stead,   170
They took high *Strafford* lower by the head,
And to their *Laud* be't spoke, they held i'th Tower
All *Englands* Metropolitane that houre,
This done, an Act they would have passed fain,
No prelate should his Bishoprick retain;   175
Here tugg'd they hard indeed, for all men saw,
This must be done by Gospel, not by law.
Next the *Militia* they urged sore,
This was deny'd, I need not say wherefore.
The King displeas'd, at York himself absents,   180
They humbly beg return, shew their intents;
The writing, printing, posting too and fro,
Shews all was done, I'le therefore let it go.
But now I come to speak of my disaster,
Contention's grown 'twixt Subjects and their Master;   185
They worded it so long, they fell to blows,
That thousands lay on heaps, here bleeds my woes.

I that no warres so many years have known,
Am now destroy'd and slaught'red by mine own,
But could the field alone this cause decide,   190
One battel, two or three I might abide,
But these may be beginnings of more woe
Who knows, the worst, the best may overthrow.
Religion, Gospell, here lies at the stake,
Pray now dear child, for sacred Zions sake,   195
Oh pity me in this sad perturbation,
My plundred Townes, my houses devastation,
My ravisht virgins, and my young men slain;
My wealthy trading faln, my dearth of grain,
The seed time's come, but Ploughman hath no hope   200
Because he knows not, who shall inn his crop:
The poor they want their pay, their children Bread,
Their woful mother's tears unpitied.
If any pity in thy heart remain,
Or any child-like love thou dost retain,   205
For my relief now use thy utmost skill,
And recompence me good, for all my ill.

New-England.

Dear mother cease complaints, and wipe your eyes,
Shake off your dust, chear up, and now arise,
You are my mother, nurse, I once your flesh,   210
Your sunken bowels gladly would refresh;
Your griefs I pity much, but should do wrong,
To weep for that we both have pray'd for long,
To see these latter Dayes of hop'd for good,
That Right may have its right, though't be with blood;   215
After dark Popery the day did clear,
But now the Sun in's brighness shall appear.
Blest be the Nobles of thy Noble Land,
With (ventur'd lives) for Truths defence that stand,
Blest be thy Commons, who for Common good,   220
And thy infringed Lawes have boldly stood.
Blest be thy Counties who do aid thee still
With hearts and states, to testifie their will.
Blest be thy Preachers, who do chear thee on,
O cry: the sword of God, and *Gideon*:   225
And shall I not on those wish *Mero*'s curse,
That help thee not with prayers, arms and purse,
And for my self, let miseries abound,
If mindless of thy state I e're be found.
These are the dayes, the Churches foes to crush,   230
To root out Prelates, head, tail, branch and rush.
Let's bring *Baals* vestments out, to make a fire,

Their Myters, Surplices, and all their tire,
Copes, Rotchets, Crossiers, and such trash,
And let their Names consume, but let the flash   235
Light Christendome, and all the world to see,
We hate *Romes* Whore, with all her trumperie.
Go on brave *Essex*, shew whose son thou art
Nor false to King, nor Countrey in thy heart,
But those that hurt his people and his Crown,   240
By force expell, destroy, and tread them down:
Let Gaoles be fill'd with th'remant of that pack,
And sturdy *Tyburn* loaded till it crack,
And yee brave Nobles, chase away all fear,
And to this blessed Cause closely adhere   245
O mother, can you weep, and have such Peeres.
When they are gone, then drown your self in teares
If now you weep so much, that then no more
The briny Ocean will o're flow your shore,
These, these are they (I trust) with *Charles* our King,   250
Out of all mists, such glorious dayes will bring;
That dazzled eyes beholding much shall wonder
At that thy setled Peace, thy wealth and splendour,
Thy Church and Weal, establish'd in such manner,
That all shall joy that thou display'dst thy banner,   255
And discipline erected, so I trust,
That nursing Kings, shall come and lick thy dust:
Then Justice shall in all thy Courts take place,
Without respect of persons, or of case,
Then Bribes shall cease, and Suits shall not stick long,   260
Patience and purse of Clients for to wrong:
Then high Commissions shall fall to decay,
And Pursevants, and Catchpoles want their pay,
So shall thy happy Nation ever flourish,
When truth and righteousnesse they thus shall nourish;   265
When thus in Peace: thine Armies brave send out,
To sack proud *Rome*, and all her Vassals rout:
There let thy name, thy fame, thy valour shine,
As did thine Ancestours in *Palestine*
And let her spoils, full pay, with int'rest be,   270
Of what unjustly once she poll'd from thee,
Of all the woes thou canst, let her be sped,
Execute to th'full the vengeance threatned;
Bring forth the beast that rul'd the world with's beek,
And tear his flesh, and set your feet on's neck,   275
And make his filthy Den so desolate,
To th' 'stonishment of all that knew his state.
This done, with brandish'd swords, to Turky go,
(For then what is't, but English blades dare do),

And lay her wast, for so's the sacred doom,   280
And do to *Gog* as thou hast done to Rome.
Oh Abraham's seed lift up your heads on high,
For sure the day of your redemption's nigh;
The scales shall fall from your long blinded eyes,
And him you shall adore, who now despise,   285
Then fulnes of the Nations in shall flow,
And Jew and Gentile, to one worship go,
Then follows dayes of happiness and rest,
Whose lot doth fall, to live therein is blest:
No Caananite shall then be found i'th' Land,   290
And holinesse, on horses bells shall stand,
If this make way thereto, then sigh no more,
But if at all, thou didst not see't before;
Farewell dear mother, Parliament, prevail,
And in a while you'l tell another tale.   295

(1642)

28 *Hengist*: Hengist and Horsa were the legendary leaders of the Anglo-Saxon conquest of Britain in the fifth century   31 *Canutus*: Cnut the Great, king of both England and Denmark, succeeded peacefully in 1016 and ruled until 1035   33 *Norman*: the Norman duke William conquered England in 1066   36 *Maud*: daughter of Henry I, and Stephen, grandson of William the Conqueror, fought a civil war for the throne of England   39 *Edward*: Edward II was deposed by his wife Isabella and her lover Mortimer in 1327   40 *Richard*: Richard II, died 1400   42 *Roses*: the 'Wars of the Roses' between the house of York and the house of Lancaster   43 *Richmond*: the Earl of Richmond, the future Henry VII. The Boar is Richard III   46 *Armado*: the Armada, a fleet sent by Philip II of Spain to conquer England, was wrecked in the channel in 1588   61 *Alcies Son*: Stephen, son of Alice (actually Adela) daughter of William the Conqueror, who disputed the throne with his cousin Maud, daughter of Henry I; *Henries daughter*: Maud, already mentioned, daughter of Henry I of England   63 *John*: his nobles conspired against him   67 *Crook-backt Tyrant*: Richard III, disposed of Edward V and his brother Richard   69 *Earl of March*: Roger Mortimer, who conspired with Queen Isabella to depose Edward II   73 a *second time*: the second Armada of 1639   112 *Edwards babes*: Edward V and his brother, sons of Edward IV; *Clarence hapless son*: George, Duke of Clarence (1449–78) was murdered in the Tower in a butt of malmsey   113 *Jane*: Lady Jane Grey, put on the throne by her father-in-law after the death of Edward VI and reluctantly executed by Mary Tudor in 1554   116 *paralize*: stand parallel with   118 *Hydra's*: mythical beast slain by Hercules: if one head was cut off seven grew in its place   128 *cropt*: crept ed.   138 *Germanies*: destruction of Germany in the Thirty Years War   142 *forc'd*: raped 143 *Rochel*: La Rochelle was a Protestant stronghold in sixteenth- and seventeenth-century France: besieged by the French king, it fell in 1626   145 *Ireland*: the uprising of the Ulster Catholics and the 'massacre' of the Protestants in October 1641 171 *Strafford*: Thomas Wentworth, Earl of Strafford, Lord Lieutenant of Ireland. Impeached by the Long Parliament for incensing the King against his subjects, and executed in 1641 172 *Laud*: Archbishop Laud, a high-churchman loathed by the Presbyterian party and many moderates, impeached by the Long Parliament and imprisoned in the Tower in 1641 (beheaded 1645): 'laud' also means 'praise', so this is a cynical pun   225 *Gideon*: judge-deliverer of Israel (Judges 6: 1–8: 21) 226 *Mero's*: Meroz   238 *Essex*: the Earl of Essex, son of Elizabeth I's rebellious favourite, was appointed Lord General of the parliamentarian forces in 1642 (the parliamentarians claimed to be protecting the King from his own evil counsellors)   263 *Catch-poles*: a contemptuous word for a bailiff   271 *poll'd*: a reference to the annual tax for the support of the Catholic church, called 'Peter's Pence'   274 *beek*: beck (nod)   281 *Gog*:

ruler of the land of Magog in Asia Minor (Ezekiel 38–9); here, the Ottoman Empire (the Book
of Revelation refers to a Satanic invasion of Gog and Magog, 20:7–10)   282 *Abraham's seed*:
the Jews: their conversion would precede the Second Coming of Christ   291 *horses bells*:
probably a sarcasm directed at ritualism, such as the ringing of a bell at the moment of the
consecration of the host

130   *Before the Birth of one of her Children*

All things within this fading world hath end,
Adversity doth still our joyes attend;
No tyes so strong, no friends so dear and sweet,
But with deaths parting blow is sure to meet.
The sentence past is most irrevocable,   5
A common thing, yet oh inevitable;
How soon, my Dear, death may my steps attend,
How soon't may be thy Lot to lose thy friend,
We both are ignorant, yet love bids me
These farewell lines to recommend to thee,   10
That when that knot's unty'd that made us one,
I may seem thine, who in effect am none.
And if I see not half my days that's due,
What nature would, God grant to yours and you;
The many faults that well you know I have,   15
Let be interr'd in my oblivious grave;
If any worth or virtue were in me,
Let that live freshly in thy memory
And when thou feel'st no grief, as I no harms,
Yet love thy dead, who long lay in thine arms: 20
And when thy loss shall be repaid with gains
Look to my little babes my dear remains.
And if thou love thy self, or loved'st me
These O protect from step Dames injury.
And if chance to thine eyes shall bring this verse,   25
With some sad sighs honour my absent Herse;
And kiss this paper for thy loves dear sake,
Who with salt tears this last Farewel did take.

                                        (before 1649)

131   *Upon the burning of our house, July*
         10th, 1666, copyed out of a loose paper.

In silent night when rest I took,
For sorrow neer I did not look,
I waken'd was with thundring nois
And pitious shreiks of dreadfull voice.

That fearfull sound of fire and fire,   5
Let no man know is my Desire.
I, starting up, the light did spye,
And to my God my heart did cry
To strengthen me in my Distresse
And not to leave me succourlesse.   10
Then coming out beheld a space,
The flame consume my dwelling place.
And when I could no longer look,
I blest his Name that gave and took,
That layd my goods now in the dust: 15
Yea so it was, and so 'twas just.
It was his own: it was not mine;
Far be it that I should repine,
He might of All justly bereft,
But yet sufficient for us left.   20
When by the Ruines oft I past
My sorrowing eyes aside did cast,
And here and there the places spye
Where oft I sate, and long did lye,
Here stood that Trunk, and there that chest   25
There lay that store I counted best
My pleasant things in ashes lye,
And them behold no more shall I.
Under thy roof no guest shall sitt,
Nor at thy Table eat a bitt.   30
No pleasant tale shall 'ere be told,
Nor things recounted done of old.
No Candle 'ere shall shine in thee,
Nor bridegroom's voice ere heard shall bee.
In silence ever shalt thou lye   35
Adieu, Adieu; All's Vanity.
Then streight I gin my heart to chide,
And did thy wealth on earth abide,
Didst fix thy hope on mouldring dust
The arm of flesh didst make thy trust?   40
Raise up thy thoughts above the skye
That dunghill mists away may flie.
Thou hast an house on high erect
Fram'd by that mighty Architect,
With glory richly furnished,   45
Stands permanent tho' this bee fled.
'Tis purchasèd, and paid for too
By him who hath enough to doe.
A Prise so vast as is unknown,
Yet, by his Gift, is made thine own.   50
Here's wealth enough, I need no more;

Farewell my pelf, farewell my Store.
The world no longer let me Love,
My hope and Treasure lyes Above.

(1666)

11 *a space*: for apace?

LUCY HASTINGS, née DAVIES, COUNTESS OF HUNTINGDON
(b. 1613)

SHE was the daughter of Eleanor Audley (the prophetess) and her first husband, Sir John Davies of Englefield, Berks, and spent her early years in Ireland, where her father was Attorney General. She married Ferdinando, son and heir of Henry Hastings, fifth Earl of Huntingdon, in 1623, at Englefield. Bathsua Makin, in her *Essay*, p. 10, indicates that she acted as the Countess's private tutor: 'I am forbidden to mention the *Countess* Dowager of *Huntington* (instructed sometimes by Mrs Makin) how well she understands *Latin*, *Greek*, *Hebrew*, *French*, and *Spanish*; or what a proficient she is in arts, subservient to Divinity, in which (if I durst I would tell you), she excels.' Lucy Hastings gave proof of the education with which Mrs Makin credits her by translating the Latin poetry of Peter du Moulin, as we know from Huntington, CH HA 9465, a letter from du Moulin to the countess thanking her for her translations. Bathsua Makin sent her a Latin poem on the death of her son, among the Huntingdon papers at the Huntingdon library, which was possibly written for, but not included in, the *tombeau* of verses on his death, *Lachrymae Musarum*, a collection of nearly one hundred other elegies for the young man. Lady Hastings was also the mother of two daughters, who were educated by Mrs Makin. Although Ferdinando was ostensibly neutral in the Civil War, his brother Henry was a notorious Royalist and the families' sympathies were clearly with the King. Ashby Castle, the family's country seat, fell to Fairfax in March 1646, and it was a condition of the terms of surrender that the castle be 'slighted' or demolished, forcing the family to move permanently to Donnington Park. Ferdinando died on 13 February 1656, to be succeeded by Theophilus, their fourth but only surviving son. Lady Hastings died on 14 November 1679 and was buried at Ashby.

132   *autograph written in her copy of the 1650 issue of* Lachrymae Musarum, *now in the Huntington*

The Bowells of the Earth my bowells [h]ide
Whilst these Dear relicks here interrd abide
Thus I die Living, thus alass mine Eyes,
My funerall see, since hee before me Dyes
Whom I brought forth my Dear Son here he Lies.   5

Clear up mine eyes hee Lies not here,
His Soul is he, which when his Dear
Redeemer had refin'd to a height
Of Purity, and Solid Weight,
No Longer would he let it Stay,   10
With in this Crucible of Clay,
But meaning him a richer Case,
To raise his Luster, not imbase,
And knowing the infectious Dust
Might Canker the bright piece with Rust,   15
Hasted him hence, into his Treasure
Of Blessed Spirits, where the Measure
Accomplish'd bee of the Elect,
They rest, and Joyfully expect
The image of our Lords perfection,   20
In the approaching Resurrection.

                          (1649)

8 *refin'd*: the central metaphor in this poem is chemical/alchemical: the refining of pure,
precious metal from various contaminants by heating it in a crucible

DAME CLEMENTIA (ANNE) CARY
(1615–1671)

THE annals of the Benedictine convent of Our Blessed Lady of Good Hope, in
Paris, where she spent the second half of her life, describe her thus: 'The
advantages of witt and Beauty which she abundantly received from nature rendred
her extreamly acceptable in all conversations . . . She became so much in the favor
of Henerettae Mariae Daughter of France and Queene of England, that she
continued in her Majesty's Court for some years, & seemed much pleased with
the gaity & delight of such a life.' She followed her three younger sisters into
religion only at 35, at Cambrai in 1639. She spoke excellent French, and was, like
Dame Gertrude More, devoted to Augustine Baker: 'She was much drawen by the
atracts of divine Love, to which she did faithfully correspond having a great
propention for contemplative interne prayer, as apears by severall bookes of her
owen collections besides her *spirituall sonngs* which she composed for the solace of
the sicke and infirme; the instructions she followed, and the mentall exercises
which she practised were those of venerable Father Augustin Baker of happy
memory.' The last comment shows that she shares the cultural milieu of Dame
Gertrude More (nos. 120–1). She went to Paris for the cure of a disorder in 1651,
and gained the support of Henrietta Maria in establishing a convent of her Order
there. Out of humility, she declined to become its first Abbess, and Dame Bridget
More was therefore given that honour. Her mottoes were, 'in nidulo meo moriar
mundo ut vivam solus Deo' (may I die to the world in my little nest [my cell], that I
may live only for God) and 'Domine quamvis adagendum nequeam, cellulam
tamen meam servandam valeam' (O Lord, whatever I may fail to do, may I always
manage to keep my cell).

133   *'You blessed Soules, who stand before'*

You blessed Soules, who stand before
Th'eternal King, and so long see
The glory that you changed be
Into that Glory you adore,
Prayze that great Founder, and above,   5
Admire His Power, and blesse his Love.

You who when Lucifer did fal,
Kept your first standing, and remain
Commanders of that mighty Train
Of which our Lord is General,   10
Angels, extoll the Almighty King,
And songs of Triumph to Him sing.

Thou, too, who with a borrowed ray,
When all the Lamps of Heaven hang out,
In the Night's silence walkst about,   15
And when the torch restorest the Day,
Fair Moon and Stars, extol God's Name,
And in your dance His Power proclaim.

MÀIRI NIGHEAN ALASDAIR RUAIDH
(MARY MACLEOD)
(*c*.1615–after 1705)

MÀIRI NIGHEAN ALASDAIR RUAIDH ('daughter of Alasdair') may have been
born in Rodel, Harris, *c*.1615, and died *c*.1705: there are many stories about
her, but few of them are substantiable. Tradition states that she spent part of her
childhood in Bracadale in Skye. She was a semi-professional poet of clan
MacLeod, and may have been a nurse in the household of the MacLeod chief-
tain at Dunvegan, or associated with another MacLeod household, at Berneray.
Her work has been described as 'the prime example of the developed panegyric'
in Scots Gaelic; which is to say, professional bardic poetry of a high order. She
was passionately devoted to Sir Norman Macleod of Berneray in Harris, third
son of Sir Roderic Mór. A number of Màiri's poems, of which this is one, speak
of the pangs of exile; there is no surviving tradition of why it was that she was
exiled from MacLeod territory, or what she was doing during this time: some
traditional material suggests that the chief was angered by her preference for his
brother and his family. The consensus of tradition is that she was exiled for a
period, and allowed to return only on condition that she stopped composing.
However, the recovery of Roderic Mór's son from illness drew a song from her,
which incurred the chief's displeasure. To his remonstrance against her making
songs without his permission she replied 'it is not a song it is only a *crònan*' (i.e.
a mere ditty).

She was known as Màiri Seud, Mary the Jewel. She used to wear a tartan *tonnag* and carry a silver headed staff, and she was much given to whisky and snuff. She herself directed that she should be placed face downward in the grave (a Norse mode of burying witches, adopted into Hebridean culture, and used for the burial of at least two early modern women poets, Màiri and Mairearad nighean Lachainn), and her burial place is known: in the south transept of Tùr Cliamain, St Clements church in Rodel.

The first of the songs from her extensive oeuvre which we include is an indication of why the MacLeods were suspicious of her sharp tongue, despite her poetic gift. It is a reflection of the intensely aristocratic and status-conscious character of Highland culture. The subject of the second song, Iain Garbh MacGille Chaluim of Raasay, was drowned on April 1671 on his way home from visiting the Earl of Seaforth, a tragedy which evoked several surviving songs and laments. It was widely rumoured that his foster-mother brought this about by employing a number of famous witches to raise a storm against him— her motives are unknown, though a version of the story recorded in 1861 suggests it was for the sake of money. This is one of many laments composed by Màiri: they were one of the principal forms required of a professional poet.

134   *Mairearad nan Cuireid*

Oran a rinn Màiri nighean Alasdair Ruaidh, is Mair-
earad nan cuireid a' togail oirre gun robh i leatromach

Ach, a Mhairearad nan cuireid,
Cuime a chuir thu orm br breug:
   Hi riri o hiri o hi o.

Gun robh leanabh gun bhaisteadh
Go aisne mo chléibh',   5

Ann an làraich mhic tighearn'
Far nach bithinn 's fhéin.

Cuim' nach innseadh tu an fhìrinn
Cho cinnteach rium fhéin?

Cha b'ionann do m' bhràithrean   10
Is do g'ghàrlaich gun spéis.

Cha b'ionann do ar tighean
An àm laighe do 'n ghréin:

Gum faightre an tigh m'athar-s'
Sitheann 's cnàimhean an fhéidh: 15

Is e gheibte an tigh t'athar-s'
Sùgh is cnàimhean an éisg.

An àm dìreadh o'n bhaile
Is trom 's gur h-annamh mo cheum.

Gur a diombach mi 'n chaile   20
Thog sgannal nam breug;

Dubh iomall na tuatha,
Buinneag shuarach gun spréidh,

Le farmad 's le mìorun
Chuir mìchliu orm fhéin;   25

Thog ormsa an droch alladh,
Is ortsa, a Chaluim nam beus,

Air an d'fhàs an cùl dualach
Tha 'na chuaileanan réidh,

Is e sìos mu d' dhà shlinnean   30
Mar an fhidheall fo theud.

17 *Sùgh* (*bree*, trans. 18): thin broth   23 *spréidh* (*cattle*, trans. 25): symbol of wealth and
status (dowries tended to be reckoned in cattle)

134   *Tricky Margaret*

A Satiric Song to Tricky Margaret, who had spread a
slanderous report of the poetess.

Nay, Margaret, thou trickster,
why hast thou spread a false tale of me? –
    (*refrain*: Hi riri o hiri o hi o)

That a babe unbaptized
lay within my womb,   5

In the dwelling of a noble's son,
where I and thou would not be together;

Or why wouldst thou not speak
the truth as surely as I?

Not alike were my father,   10
you slanderer, and yours,

Not alike were my brothers
and your unlovely louts,

Not alike were
our dwellings at sunset: 15

In my father's house were found
venison and bones of the deer;

In thy father's house bree
and bones of the fish were your fare.

As I climb from the town   20
my step is heavy and lagging,

I am ill-pleased with the hussy
that has hatched this lying story,

The basest refuse of the folk,
a light jade without cattle,   25

That for envy and malice
hath spread ill-fame of me,

Evil gossip of me
and of thee, honest Calum,

Thou whose curling hair   30
floweth down in ringlets smooth,

Like the strings over the fiddle,
over thy two shoulders.

135   *Marbhrann*

*Do Iain Garbh Mac Ghille Chaluim Ratharsaidh a chaidh a
    dhìth le ainneart mara.*

Mo bheud is mo chràdh
Mar a dh'éirich dà
An fhear ghleusta ghràidh
Bha treun 'san spàirn
Is nach facear gu bràth an Rathasaidh.   5

Bu tù am fear curanta mór
Bu mhath cumadh is treoir
O t'uilinn gu d' dhòrn
O d' mhullach gu sd' bhròig:
Mhic Mhuire mo leòn   10
Tho bhith an innis nan ròn is nach faighear thu

Bu tù sealgair a' gheoidh,
Làmh gun dearmad gun leòn
Air am bu shuarach an t-òr
Thoirt a bhuannachd a' cheoil,   15
Is gun d'fhuair thu na's leoir is na chaitheadh tu.

Bu tù sealgair an fhéidh
Leis an deargta na béin;
Bhiogh coin earbsach air éill
Aig an Albannach threun;   20
Càite am faca mi féin
Aon duine fo'n ghréin
A dhèanadh riut euchd flathasach?

Spealp nach dìobradh
an cath no an srì thù,   25
Casan dìreach
Fada fìnealt:
Mo creach dhìobhail
Chaidh thu a dhìth oirnn
Le neart sìne,   30
Làmh nach dìobradh caitheadh oirre.

Och m'eudail uam
Gun sgeul 'sa chuan
Bu ghlé 's ri fuachd,
Is e chlaoidh do shluagh   35
Nach d'fheud thu an uair a ghabhail orra.

Is math thig gunna nach diùlt
Air curaidh no rùin
Ann am mullach a' chùirn
Is air uilinn nan stùc: 40
Gum biodh fuil ann air tùs an spreadhaidh sin.

Is e dh'fhàg silteach mo shùil
Faicinn t'fhearainn gun sùrd,
Is do bhaile gun smùid
Fo charraig nan sùgh,   45
Dheagh mhich Chaluim nan tùr á Ratharsaidh.

Mo bheud is mo bhròn
Mar a dh'éirich dhò,
Muir beucach mór
Ag leum mu d'bhòrd,   50
Thu féin is do sheoid
An uair reub ur seoil
Nach d'fheud sibh treoir a chaidheadh orra.

Is tu b'fhaicillich' ceum
Mu'n taice-sa an dé   55
De na chunnaic mi féin
Air faiche nan ceud
Air each's e'na leum,
Is cha bu slacan gun fheum claideamh ort.

Is math lùbadh tu pic   60
O chùlaigh do chinn
An ám rùsgadh a' ghill
Le ionnsaigh nach till,
Is air mo làimh gum bu chinneach saighead uat.

Is e an sgeul cràiteach   65
Do'n mhnaoi a dh'fhàg thu,

Is do t'aon bhràthair
A shuidh 'nad àite:
Di-luain Càisge
Chaidh tonn-bhàidte ort,   70
Craobh a bh'àirde de'n abhall thu.

(1671)

135   *Dirge*

For Iain Garbh mac Ghille Chaluim of Raasay, who
was drowned in a violent storm.

It is harm to me and anguish,
that which has befallen
the deft well-loved man
that was strong in conflict
and shall be seen in Raasay never more.   5

You were a great hero,
You were well proportioned
from your elbow to your fist,
from your crown to your shoe;
son of Mary! it is my hurt,   10
that you are in the seals' pasture and will not be found.

You were a hunter of the wild goose,
Your hand was unerring and unblemished
It was a light thing to it to bestow gold
for the maintenance of music;   15
for you had plenty, and all that you had, you would spend.

You were a hunter of the deer,
by whom [their] hides were reddened;
trusty hounds would the mighty man of Alba
hold on leash;   20
where have I beheld
beneath the sun
one man who would vie with you in a princely feat?

A gay gallant were you,
that shrank not in strife or battle;   25
thy limbs straight,
long and shapely;
alas, I am sadly reft,
you are lost to us
by strength of tempest, you whose hands would not cease
    to make your vessel speed.   30

alas for my treasure reft from me,
who was very beautiful to see
in sun and in cold,
lost in the ocean without trace;

that is what has bowed down your people, that you could not
   reach them in that hour.   35

A gun that readily answers,
well would it become my dear warrior
in the cairn's summit
or on the elbow of the peaks;
blood would flow in front of its discharge.   40

What has left my eyes tearful
is to see your land cheerless,
now that you have a homestead without smoke
under the wave-lashed rock,
O man from Raasay, excellent son of Calum of the towers.   45

It is hurt and sorrow to me,
that which has befallen him;
a great roaring sea
leaping about thy boat;
yourself and thy stout crew,   50
when your sails ripped,
that you could not bend your might upon them.

At this hour of yesterday
you were the most wary of step
of all that I saw upon the green   55
where hundreds thronged,
upon a horse as it sprang;
and a sword was no useless wand when you wore it.

Well could you bend a bow
from behind your head,   60
in the hour of declaring your pledge of valour,
with an onset unretreating;
and by my hand! your arrow sped surely.

this is a sore tale
for the wife you have left,   65
and for your only brother
that has sat in your seat;
the Monday of Easter
a drowning wave came upon you;
you who were the loftiest tree of the orchard.   70

GERTRUDE THIMELBY, née ASTON
(c.1615–c.1670)

GERTRUDE ASTON was the fourth daughter of Sir Walter Aston of Tixall in
Staffordshire. Despite their firm commitment to the Catholic faith, her family
held a significant position in late Jacobean and Caroline England. Her father Sir
Walter was twice ambassador to Spain, in 1623–4, as part of the negotiating

team for the projected marriage of Prince Charles with the Infanta, and again in
1635–8. He died in 1638. The family acted as patrons to Michael Drayton, and
had significant connections with both Richard Fanshawe and Edmund Waller.
They also composed verse of their own (see 'Poets of the Tixall Circle').
Gertrude was instrumental in collecting poetry: the main evidence for this is
her commonplace book, now in the Huntington Library, California.

She married Henry Thimelby (brother of her own brother's wife, her close
friend Katherine Thimelby) in the late 1630s or early 1640s. Her husband and
their only child both died young, and she subsequently sought the consolation of
religion, and retired to the convent in Louvain where her sister-in-law Winefrid
Thimelby was abbess. She lived there till her death.

Attribution is not always an easy matter with the Tixall poets (the fact that
Tixall verse survives in family collections, or printed from one such collection,
means that there is no help to be got from manuscripts on this point). However,
several poems by Gertrude are identifiable which very much establish a case for
her as a woman poet who wrote under the self-perception of being a poet. She
uses verse to respond to family arguments and debates, to express her affection
for her husband, to celebrate family weddings, and to offer consolation to family
mourners. She is sometimes self-conscious about the limitations of her gift, most
notably in her touching elegy on her father, and her poem 'To the Lady
Southcote on her Wedding-Day'.

136   *Mrs Thimelby, on the*
        Death of Her Only Child

Deare Infant, 'twas thy mother's fault
So soone inclos'd thee in a vault:
And fathers good, that in such hast
Has my sweet child in heaven plac'd.
I'le weepe the first as my offence,   5
Then joy that he made recompence:
Yet must confesse my frailty such
My joy by griefe's exceeded much:
Though I, in reason, know thy blisse
Can not be wish'd more than it is,   10
Yet this selfe love orerules me soe;
I'de have thee here, or with thee goe.
But since that now neyther can be,
A vertue of necessitie
I yet may make, now all my pelf   15
Content for thee, though not myselfe.

137 *To Her Husband, on New Year's Day 1651*

How swiftly time doth passe away
Wher happiness compleates the day.

Weeks, months, and years but moment prove
To those that nobly are in love.
This computations only knowne   5
To them that our pure flame can owne.
Succeeding yeares example take
By those are past; ther numbers wake
Envy, whilst with a will resigned
No will is knowne til th'others mind.   10

138 *Upon a Command to Write On My Father*

Teares I could sonne have brought unto this hearse
And thoughts, and sighs, but you command a verse;
And here it is, I am so much concern'd
If ere I write I am againe unlearn'd.
For griefe does all things els annihilate,   5
As not consistent with his high estate.
If you will [be] obay'd, Ile hold the pen,
But you must guide my hand, instruct me then.
Dead must I say? I doe the authour see
That gave me life, and not that death kill me!   10
If, when alive, he was the cause of breath,
Why, being dead, does he not cause my death?
This is a miracle from you I know,
For I must live whilest you have it so.
Nor can this new giv'n life be better spent   15
Then to contemplate this sad monument:
Th'inclosure of a worth the world nere knew,
But in his time, and it was from him too.
So sweet a winning way he had on all,
None knew but lov'd him, no desert so small   20
But he would grace, and still did something say,
That none could goe unsatisfy'd away.
We may presume in heaven he went to less,
By his so soone conferred happines.
Could we consider this but as we ought,   25
How vane's our sorrow! what is ever sought
By all our prayres but now he does possess,
Tis then most fit that we should acquiesce.

ANNA LEY, née NORMAN
(before 1620–1641)

ANNA LEY was daughter of Thomas Norman of Dorset, a graduate of St Alban Hall, Oxford, where he was registered as 'pleb' rather than 'gent', and his wife Anne. She married a clergyman, Roger Ley, the curate of the church of St Leonard's Shoreditch, where John Squire was Rector. Squire was one of the most controversial figures in the Church: he was accused of asserting that papists were the King's best subjects, of writing himself 'priest' and despising the appellations 'minister' and 'pastor', and of upholding priestly excommunication; he decorated his church with 'Pictures of the *Virgin Mary*, of *Christ*, and his 12 Apostles at his last supper in Glasse'. Squire's parishoners went so far as to raise a petition against him: 'hee hath peremptorily said, that none shall come hear to Preach, but himselfe or his Curate, so long as hee hath anything to doe in the place' (London, British Library, Thomason Tracts E137.2 (21)). Anna's husband must also have been of the Laudian (or High Church) persuasion, and it is clear from the poem included here that she, too, supported the direction in which Archbishop Laud and the King were taking the church. Her own loyalty to Squire is celebrated by an acrostic, which is one of the poems included in her book.

All that is known of her life derives from a book containing her poems, letters, and other reflections, apparently compiled by her husband from her loose papers, and kept in her memory. One interesting fact which it records is that she was Latin-literate, and taught Latin to university standard in her husband's school. One of the poems included here was written for a pupil. It sheds some interesting light on how one of the 'commonplace books' which survive in quantity from the seventeenth century was supposed to be used by its compiler. A number of her letters are in Latin. She was buried in the churchyard of St Leonards, Shoreditch, on 22 October 1641.

139   *Upon the necessity and benefite of learning written in the beginning of a Common place booke belonging to W.B. a young scholler.*

As from each fragrant sweet the honny Bee
Extracts that moysture is of so much use;
Like carefull labour I commend to thee;
Which if performd much profit will produce.
In this great universe what may compare   5
To learnings worth which beautifies the minde
Adornes the body makes it seeme more faire
And with the best doth kind acceptance finde.
All other hopes how soone they may decay
Like faire flowers nipt with suddaine blast   10
Friends are but mortall riches flie away,

Tis onely this proves constant to the last.
Which to obtaine imploy your cheifest skill,
Heere is an hive to treasure up your store,
Which with each usefull sentence you may fill   15
T'will be a meanes that you aloft may soare
To learnings pitch, where that you once may rest
Il'e lend a hand, doe you but doe your best.

Title: Hoole, *The Ushers Duty*, 1659, sig. C3, recommends that young children keep 'a little paper-book, wherein to gather the most familiar phrases'

140   *Upon a booke written at the*
             beginning of the Parliament 1640

Can nothing serve thy turne but summum ius,
And can a man of God be altred thus?
Loe heere the cause whence the effect did spring,
Your amor lucri wrought this wonderous thing.
Before thy lot fell in that tainted place   5
Unspotted inocence shin'd in thy face,
To please the people thou hast struck thy mother,
Envie hath made thee to disgrace thy brother.
Dost thou reward the Church of England so
Out of whose breasts thy nourishment did flow?   10
Wilt thou incite harsh justice to proceede
Nor canst thou rest till those thou hatst doe bleed?
Instead of water to alay the flame,
Now adding fuel to augment the same,
Goe on yet know God can prevent thine aime.   15

Our Ecclesiasticks those grave learned men
Are vilifide and scornd by thy rude pen,
as subtle shallow quite deprivd of wit,
Good for no bussnesse but a hint or fit,
Foule mouthd detraction thus to slander those   20
Because by them thy stile no higher rose,
Is this the way to gaine the vulgars vote,
Now made with prejudice against that coat,
On their desired ruins wilt thou raise
Thy folorne hopes, and looke for better daies,   25
Had but a miter grac'd thy worthlesse head
Theire fame had livd, thy malice had ben dead.
Which heretofore dark riddles did conceile
But now strange impudence doth full reveale.
O tempora when everie one may vent   30
His own vile thoughts not fearing to be shent,

If some have threatned to draw their swords
Against delinquents, kill them not with words.
One deaths enough to expiate great crimes,
Blast not their pretious names for future times.   35
The Court if justice needs no such directions,
Nor will we hope be moved by thy invections,
To goe beyond that which is right and good,
To please the factious who delight in blood
They know theire actions must be scand above   40
By him whose title is the God of Love.
In which deare attribute that they may share
Justice and mercie both that lovely paire
Shall meet in one, theire censures is direct,
To punish vice and virtue to protect,   45
But if to either side they step a wry,
Rather on mercie let the errour lie,
And they which would have mercie quite rejected
When most they seeke it, may be most neglected.

Title: possibly with reference to Stephen Marshall, the 'sm' of 'Smecytmnuus', whose writing was particularly resented by the Laudians   1 *summum ius*: the highest law   4 *amor lucri*: love of money   30 *O tempora*: oh, these times! (by implication, unusually bad), a half-quotation from Cicero   43 *Justice and mercie*: cf. Psalm 85: 10

KATHERINE ASTON, née THIMELBY
(*c*.1620s–1650s)

KATHERINE THIMELBY was the daughter of John Thimelby of Irnham, Lincolnshire, and the sister of Sir John Thimelby of Lincoln. She married Herbert Aston of Tixall in 1638. The marriage was encouraged by Katherine's intimate friend, Herbert's youngest sister, Constance or Constantia Aston. Herbert Aston's account of his wife after her death describe her as both an author and a collector of poetry. There are also touching descriptions in Herbert's devotional writings of her deathbed instructions to her beloved children. The daughter Catherine to whom she addresses her poem later joined her aunts Gertrude Thimelby and Winefrid Thimelby at the convent in Louvain, where she was professed on 19 August 1668. Her son assumed the name of Barret, attended the English College at Rome, went to St Omer's college in 1684, and joined the Society of Jesus. Katherine Thimelby sustained a number of close female friendships during her life, observing in one letter recounting the progress of the serious illness from which she was to die, 'The world I confess I never lovd, but some friends, perhaps, too much.'

141 *To my Daughter Catherine on Ashwednesday
1645, finding her weeping at prayers, because
I would not consent to her fasting*

My dearest, you may pray now it is Lent,
But ought not fast: nor have you to repent,
Since then in all you've thought, or said or done,
No motes appear though sifted by the sun.
Lent made for penance, then to you may be,   5
Since you are innocent, a jubily.
If not for others then, why don't you spare
Those tears which for yourself prophaned are.
Hymns of thanksgiving and of joy befit
Such a triumphant virtue, and for it   10
Not to rejoice, were as preposterous ill,
As in your vices to be merry still.
But if you reply, 'tis fit you sigh and grone,
Since you have made my miseries your owne;
You feel my faults as yours, so them lament,   15
And expiate those sins I should repent.
O cease this sorrow doubly now my due,
First for my self, but more for love of you.
Ile undertake what justice can exact
By any penance, if you will retract   20
Those sorrows you usurp, which doe procure
A payne I only cannot well endure.

(1645)

142   *Upon the LD saying KT could be
sad in her company*

Madem you say I am sad I ansure noe
unlesse it be because you say I am soe
I know some praysed for speaking what is true
But mores your wright whoes truth does wate of you
Before you spoke I found no cause of griefe   5
But in your speach you tooke all wished reliefe
From me your servant, placed me in want
Of meanes to show my poverty and scant
For I had now atayn'd what I desire'd
And consequently happy, now's required   10
Why I am sad, oh worde of most heigh price
To torne me misserable with in the house
For I am greved that my exteriour show
Should contradict the joye I have from you.

For madem doe me wright I doe protest   15
Ther is no joy if not by me possest.
When in your conversation I can find
Ther be all treasures to delight the mind
And I unworthy shuld this possesse
Which might rewarde the worthyes and blesse   20
Those that had ventur'd most for your deare sake
And I receave this from you, and not take
It as a blessing given to me by you
That from this time I should no sorrow know
Were I in this doubt I would bequeth   25
My place to others weare the willow reath
Therefore by these your favors I intreate
You will beleeve my joye in you compleate.

26 *reath*: reach MS: wreath (i.e. to other disconsolate lovers)

LADY DOROTHY SHIRLEY, née DEVEREUX,
later STAFFORD
(1600–1636)

LADY DOROTHY SHIRLEY was a close friend of Constance, or Constantia
Fowler, a member of the Aston family of Tixall, and a central participant in
their family habit of compiling, as well as composing, verse. She was the
younger daughter of Robert Devereux, second Earl of Essex, born the year
before his death. Her first husband was Sir Henry Shirley: he died in 1634, and
she married again, to William Stafford of Blatherwick, Northants, in the same
year. Her brother was a famous Parliamentary General. She had two sons, one of
whom (Robert) survived her.

143   *The LD ansure*

Deare Cosen pardon me, if I mistowke
I thought the face had bin the truest boke
To reade the hart in, but a face that's good
It seames by dull wits is not understood
Since curious lines that drawne by Art and Skill   5
Study they may but ignorant be still
I fear'd you sad because that smileing grace
Which oft hath joy'd me was not in your face.
Joy me it did because it made me see
You pleas'd to tollerate this place and me   10
But in this act your favors doth not end
You not only like but doe comend

Freindship occasions this and you alasse
Doe view me threw a multiplying glasse
But, what I can be unto you I will   15
And with increase in me for your sake still
which by your company I hope that I
Shall gaine soe much I shall you satisfye
But thinke not like a thefe I will conceale
From whome I stole the truth I will reveale   20
And say to you that have inriched mee
For whose sake I did wish to steale from thee
But this beleeve you canot favoure shew
To one more yours and will be ever so.

MARY FAGE
(fl. 1637)

THE author identifies herself as 'wife of Robert Fage the younger, Gentleman', and posterity knows no more of her than this. Her one work, *Fames Roule*, is a poem of unmistakably professional intentions. It consists of a series of more than four hundred separate acrostics on secular and religious aristocrats, organized in hierarchical sequence, and is evidently an attempt to gain the patronage of as many of its subjects as possible. Each subject is anagrammatized, and an acrostic written on the anagram of the name, as in the example below. Though anagrams were a popular game of the time, the fact that no more is heard of her suggests that she was unsuccessful in attracting the attention she sought.

144   *to their most excellent majesty of*
           Great Brittaines *Monarchy*

CAROLUS-MARIA-STUARTE

anagramma

AU! VESTA, TRAC SOL, MARRY

Cheerly firme Vesta, clad in verdant Green,
Au! is an emblem of our glorious Queen;
Rendring a stable, fast, well knitted heart,
On our great SOL plac't, thence not to depart:
Likely a higher Goddesse cannot be,   5
Vesta like, ruling in her chastity,
Shining in vertues gracious increase.

Much glory hath this *Vesta*, but no peace
Au! doth to her true soul at all remain,
Returning till she doth her SOL retain;   10

In whom she doth delight, whom in her pace
Admiring she doth follow in true trace.

So *Vesta traceth* SOL, and did not tarry,
Till their united Graces they did MARRY,
Vertues conjoyned thus, SOL in his heat,   15
And *Vesta* in her chast, and plenteous great
Rare right increase, doth truly multiply,
Thrusting so forth a great posterity,
Ever to last unto eternity.

6 *Vesta*: goddess of the hearth   12 *trace*: track

POETS OF THE TIXALL CIRCLE
(fl. 1630s–1650s)

TIXALL in Staffordshire, situated near the confluence of Sow and Trent, was the seat of the Aston family and something of a provincial literary centre. Drayton enjoyed the patronage of Walter, first Lord Aston, who had been twice ambassador to Spain: in 1619, and in 1635–8. The Astons and their children had some acquaintance with Sir Richard Fanshawe and Edmund Waller, and at the least access to unpublished texts by Richard Crashaw, Edwin Sandys, and John Davenant. Arthur Clifford, descendant of the Astons through the female line, published a generous selection of Aston poetry from the seventeenth century under the title of *Tixall Poetry* in 1813: the manuscripts have since been lost. The attributions of certain poems to specific members of the family are contestable in some instances, and he seems to underrate the work of Gertrude Thimelby (see above) in particular.

The people who wrote and collected the poems contained in *Tixall Poetry* consisted of five distinct families and their friends: Fowler of St Thomas, Aston of Tixall, Aston of Bellamore, Persall of Canwell (all in Staffordshire), and Thimelby of Irnham (in Lincolnshire). The principal authors appear to have been children of the first Lord Aston: Herbert Aston of Bellamore, his sister Gertrude Aston, wife of Henry Thimelby, and his sister Constantia, later Fowler. To these Aston poets we may add Sir Walter Aston himself, and Edward Aston. Other members of their circle who wrote occasional verse include Lady Dorothy Shirley and Sir William Persall.

Another important poetic manuscript associable with the Tixall circle is Constance Aston's collection of poems by herself, her family, and their friends, now in the Huntington Library in San Marino, California, a section of which is in the same hand as a Roman Catholic collection of verse compiled in the 1650s (Bodleian Library, Add. MS 36452). There are also substantial collections of letters, which are invaluable for contextualizing the poems. The Tixall circle in some ways resembles the social circle in which Anne Finch grew up: a milieu of cultivated, literary gentlefolk content to live remotely in the country. It differs, however, in that the Astons and their friends were Catholic.

It is notable in the Tixall poetry that the family and their friends seem to exchange series of poems on related themes, and even to carry on debates in verse, which seems to have had a central function in their social interactions. Poetry had a pivotal function in their social interactions of the Tixall circle: they exchanged sequences of poems on related themes and even carried on debates in verse. The prime examples are the debate on the vexed question of which sex is the more inconstant between Dorothy Shirley and an unidentified man, and the exchange between Lady Shirley and Katherine Thimelby given above.

145   *TO A GENTLEMAN* THAT
             COURTED SEVERAL LADYS

Since, Coridon, you have a hart can pay
So many sacrifices in a day,
And that you can one for her wit adore,
And then another for her beauty more,
I have no inclination to confine   5
Your general offering to a single shrine.
No, Coridon, I'le quit you of your vow,
You here or there may court, when, where, or how,
Your artful love your fancy shall perswade,
And when you've done, and many conquests made,   10
Back on your honor looke, and there you'le see,
A ruine greater than your victory.
It easy is our weak sex to betray,
But falshood still doth stain on honor lay.
A general pitty is a vertue taught,   15
But general love a crime was ever thought.
Nature to man does but one hart allow,
But they do multiply it to hundreds now;
And to each object, which your covetous sense
Makes you desire, you can a hart dispence.   20
Like those appearing spirits, form'd of air,
Which come to touch, we find no substance there.
Thus you turn cheats in love, and juglers play,
And seem to give, yet nothing give away.
Your bounty never makes your wealth grow less,   25
The harts you're born with, dying you possess;
Only you brought them without perjur'd stain,
But with a thousand carry them back again.
'Tis those false vows and oaths which you express
Give your love credit, and your hopes success.   30
Thus to your pride you injur'd trophys raise,
But they at last will wither all your bays.
Seeking to ruine, you may ruine finde;
Fortune is sometimes just as well as blind.
They'r less than child, will lend their money out,   35
When they both principal and interest doubt.

And men contract such debts in love, that they
Compounding, can't one of a hundred pay;
Yet from our trust they do imperious grow,
And think it glorious they so much can owe.   40
They boast that none shall rule their harts alone,
They'l have a commonwealth, and not a throne.
Indeed, you doe all traiterous subjects prove,
But you are excellent levellers in love:
For least that jealousy grow from mistake,   45
You now in common all your courtships make.
No, Coridon, had all the world been sought,
And all perfections from all persons brought;
Had Solomon his wondrous wisdom lent,
And Alexander all his courage sent;   50
Had Nature rifled her exhaustless store,
And all those noble heroes we adore,
To place in you what each did but enjoy,
Your fickle humour would my love destroy:
I should, as others did, your worth admire,   55
But never flame would take at such a fire.

146 *FROM A SICK POETESSE TO*
MRS ST GEORGE ON HER
FEEDING THE SWANS

Two freezing winters, and one summer's heat,
To the poore sufferers both seeming great,
A lovely payre of swans in pond had past,
Which pleasant walkes and shady willows grac't.
In all which time, in all within their view,   5
Of heaven or earth, they nothing saw or knew
Like to themselves, soe delicately white,
In brightest day, nor clearest moonshine night.
Who then can blame that pride should enter there,
Where we possesse all that wee know is faire?   10
Such shew'd this payre to each observing eye,
By bridled necks, and wings erected high;
By stately motion girding through the waves,
A posture that commands a look, not craves.
Their feet the oares, by which they steered aright,   15
But plac'd by Nature kindly out of sight.
With these in state they oft to shore did row,
Where creatures kind did food on them bestow.
But nere more proud than when the vizard maske,
And long wel-spread black scarfe performed that taske. 20

For contraries with greatest lustre shine,
When by position close they nearest joyne.
But oh! sad hap to this long happy payre!
A hand, employ'd in this kind practis'd care,
A hand, by chance, or purpose, now unveil'd,   25
Shew'd farr more white than all their stock could yield.
Which seene, down fell the snowey sailes, their wings;
Each huffing feather now more closely clings.
Noe food would downe, but sick, and quite undone,
What they could not excell they wisely shunn.   30
Away they fly, and in close covert hide,
Their shame, to be outdone in all their pride.

147   *A Confession*

Since you will needs my hart possesse,
Tis just to you it should confesse
The faults to which tis given;
It is to change much more inclin'd
Then women, or the sea, or wind,   5
Or ought that's under heaven.
Nor will I hide from you this truth,
It hath been from its very youth
A most egregious ranger;
And since from me it often fled,   10
With whom it was both born and bred,
Twill scarce stay with a stranger.
Therefore, the gay, the blacke, the sad,
Which makes me often thinke twere mad,
With one kind looke could win it;   15
Soe naturally it loves to range,
That it hath left successe for change;
And what was glory in it.
Nay, I to it became a sport,
When I did soundly chide it fort,   20
It would in smiles be saying,
Your debts of love you must dispaire
To pay to all thats kind or faire,
If long with one you're staying.
And now, if you are not affraid,   25
After these truths which I have said,
To take this arrant rover;
Be not displeasd if I protest,
I doubt the hart within your breast
Will prove just such another.   30

SEÒNAID CHAIMBEUL
(JANET CAMPBELL)
(c.1645)

THERE is nothing known about the author of this song, and this is the only work attributed to her. Her lover however was MacNaughton of Dundarave, who owned land between Loch Awe and Loch Long in Argyll, and supported Alasdair mac Colla in the Montrose Wars. The song incorporates elements of courtly love (the dream of the loved one), of panegyric (his hunting prowess), of lament (the incremental repetition of the second verse), and of the ancient beliefs in the supernatural power of poetry (the curse on the poet's sister).

148   *' 'S tha 'n oidhche nochd fuar'*

'S tha 'n oidhche nochd fuar
Och mo thruaighe gur fad i;
Ged tha càch 'nan sìor shuain
Gur beag mo luaidh-s' air a' chadal.

Chan e giorrad mo rùim;   5
Chan e cuingead mo leapa;
Ach fear òg a' chùil duinn
Chuir an truim' so air m'aigne.

Gun a bhruadair mi 'n raoir
Thusa luaidh a bhith agam   10
'N a mo leabaidh chaol mhìn,
'S tu bhith sìnte 'nam ghlacaibh.

Ach nuair thionndaidh mi null
Bha do rùm-sa fuar falamh,
Gun do shil air mo shùil   15
Gum b' fhada rùin tho o m' shealladh.

A dheagh Mhic Neachdainn an dùin,
'S tu o thùr nan àrd bhaideal
'S a fhad' a dh' aithnichinn do chùl
A' dìreadh stùc, agus chreagan.   20

Le d' ghunna, 's le d' chù,
Le d'cheum lùthmhor mar ghaisgeach,
'S le d'chuilbheir chaol ùr,
'S i nach diùltadh an t-sradan

Leam bu mhìlse do phòg   25
Na mil shòghail nam beachan,
Na ùbhlan nan craobh,
Gum bu chaoine leam d'anail.

'S math thig bonaid ghorm ùr
Air do chùl bhòidheach dathte;   30
'S math thig dag dhut is sgian,
'S claidheamh giar, guineach, sgaiteach.

An té thug bhuam-sa m' fhear fhéin,
'S a chuir na creuchdan fo m'aisnean.
Nar a faicear ort bréid   35
Là féille no clachàin.

Nar a faicear do chlann
Dol a theampull a'bhaistidh,
Ach 'gan càradh san uaigh,
'S tu bhith buan dheth gun mhac leinn.   40

Gum bi leac shleamhainn ri d' bhonn;
Talamh tolltach fo d' chasan,
'S boinne snighe fliuch, fuar,
Bhith mu bhruachan do leapa.

Mur a b' e do dhroch bheus   45
Bu mhór leam fhéin sin a thachairt,
'S ged is cruaidh e ri ràdh
'S i 'n aona mhàthair a bh'againn.

Tha 'n oidhche mochd fuar
Och mo thruaighe gur fad i;   50
Ged tha càch 'nan sìor shuain
Gur beag mo luaidh-s' air chadal.

148   *'This night tonight is cold'*

This night tonight is cold,
And, alas, it is long,
Though others are sound asleep,
Little mention do I make of slumber.

It isn't the shortness of my room   5
Or the narrowness of my bed,
But the young man of the brown hair
Who cast this weight on my spirit.

Last night I dreamed
That you, love, were with me,   10
In my narrow soft bed,
With you stretched in my arms.

But when I turned round
Your space was cold and empty,
And my eyes shed tears   15
That you, love, were far from sight.

O fine MacNaughton of the fort
From the tower of the high battlements,
I could recognise you at a distance
Climbing peaks and crags.   20

With your gun and with your dog,
Your vigorous stride like a hero,
With your slender new musket
That would never fail to fire.

Sweeter was your kiss to me   25
Than the fragrant honey of bees,
And softer was your breath to me
Than the apples of the trees.

Well does a fresh blue bonnet
Suit your fine, richly-coloured hair,   30
Well does a dirk and pistol suit you
And a sharp, wounding, lopping sword.

The woman who took my man from me
And who set the wounds under my ribs,
May you never be seen as a wife   35
Amongst the crowd at fair or church.

May your children not be seen
Going to the temple to be baptised,
But being laid out in the grave,
And you forever without a son.   40

May a slimy flag be at your door,
Pitted earth under your feet,
And dripping cold damp ooze
Be dropping onto the top of your bed.

If it wasn't for your wicked deeds,   45
I would gladly see that happen,
Though it is hard to say it,
As we had the same mother.

This night tonight is cold,
And, alas, it is long,   50
Though others are sound asleep,
Little mention do I make of slumber.

ELIZABETH CROMWELL
(?fl.1636/40)

THIS poem is recorded in the manuscript miscellany of Anna (Cromwell)
Williams, who explains that it was written by her aunt Elizabeth and addressed
to her mother Mary Price, previously Cromwell. The names Elizabeth and Mary
in this verse, though presumably adventitious (both names were very common),

inevitably evoke the visit of the Virgin Mary to Elizabeth when they were pregnant with, respectively, Jesus and John the Baptist. It is interesting in these occasional verses of undoubtedly Protestant origin to find that Mary Price is deliberately compared with the Virgin (as well, of course, with the 'Mary who chose the better part', Mary Magdalen): this may suggest that, while Mary was, and is, a very marginal figure in Protestant theology, her image perhaps retained some potency in the private world of women interacting with one another. It may, however, be relevant that although the Cromwells were Protestant, after the death of Anna (Cromwell) Williams' father in 1626, her mother (Mary) chose to marry a Catholic, Robert Apreece (Price) of Washingley, who was murdered by Parliamentary soldiers in Lincoln in 1644 for admitting his Catholicism, and is calendared as one of the English Martyrs. The widow then made a third marriage to Humphrey Orme, before 1647. Apart from Anna, she had a surviving son, Robert, by her first husband: the poem before us suggests that there were other siblings. Since the addressee Mary is glossed by Anna (Cromwell) Williams as Mrs Price, the poem was written after 1626 and before 1647, i.e. during her second marriage.

New Year was the normal season for the exchange of gifts in early modern England: poems were quite often given at this time (see also no. 4). Mrs Cromwell's poem includes a piece of bestiary lore, an interesting survival from the Middle Ages: pigeons were believed not to have a gall-bladder (and were hence without bitterness/sin). The verses are interesting as an expression of women's intimate concerns; rejoicing unselfconsciously in handsome, healthy children—though their focus on the childrens' potential godliness would be alien to many modern mothers.

149 *The Sisters newyearsgift from Elizabeth to Mary a happie mother of good children*

Happie newyear god grant may ever stande
in which with gifts ffriends kis each others hande
They out of superfluety distribute parte of store
I have but this ♥ and I can give no more

(O) gratious meeke blest mary, a mother milde I may thee call   5
religious, charitable, humble, a dove that hath no gall,
from these perfections maiest thou never starte
the worlds incumbrances taketh not thy heart
And those distractions banishest from thee
hindrances to religion, or thy pyetie,   10
wisely foreseeing what might cause thy smarte
a blessed Mary to chuse the better parte
which part (from god) thou maiest a blessing call,
with all his other giftes Angellicall,
now in the middle a senter thou maiest stand   15
behinde, before, and in each hand
gaurded about with branches of thine owne
true olive branches, and they fully blowne

with such perfections as God sees most meete
in there young yeares, so beautifull, so sweete,   20
yet tis not th'outward feature
though curiously adorned hath nature
with all rich jems which shee may call her owne
seldom on one steme are such rare flowers knowne
these young born babes, attired thus they bee   25
with modest comely gravitie
a way to religion, which in the bud appeares
wee gess a springe tyme in the riper yeares
a springe of vertue may there ever bee
this is the beauty only praised by mee,   30
perfections glory in her gifts are free
now happie mother I returne to thee,
a life of grace a heavenly light to bee
god grante unto thy selfe and thy posteritie
a joyfull progress maiest thou ever see,   35
with life large crowned betweene thy babes and thee
a period to thy dayes (when this)
maiest thou be taken to everlasting bliss
Now happie Mary, invessed
in those white robes which best thee sute   40
Emblems of purity a choyce fruite
This is thy newyearsgifte or Elizabeths sallute.

DIORBHAIL NIC A BHRIUTHAINN
(DOROTHY BROWN)
(*c*.1620s–late seventeenth century)

DIORBHAIL NIC A BHRIUTHAINN belonged to Luing, an island in Argyle-
shire. It is uncertain when she was born, but she was contemporary with the
famous MacDonald bard Iain Lom, and was, like him, a Jacobite and bitterly
opposed to the Campbells. Her song to Alasdair mac Colla (the Marquis of
Montrose's MacDonald co-warrior in his campaign on behalf of Charles I) was
composed on seeing his birlinn (ship) pass through the sound of Luing on an
expedition against the Campbells, in revenge for the death of his father Colkitto,
whom they had killed some time before. The poem seems to have been composed during Alasdair's recruiting journey through the islands. It is an example
of the trope *tearc enghmais*, a woman falling in love with a warrior through
accounts of his exploits alone, without necessarily ever meeting him (a motif
which is also found in medieval troubadour poetry, most famously in the case of
Gaufré Rudel's love for the Countess of Tripoli). She composed many songs of
which only two survive: this, and another song: a lament for the duchess of Coll.
Long after her death, one Colin Campbell, a native of Luing, who was at a
funeral in the same burying ground where she was laid, trampled on her grave
imprecating curses on her memory. But she still had her supporters: Duncan

Maclachlan of Kilbride in Lorn pulled him off the grave, sent for a gallon of whisky, and had it drunk to her memory on the spot.

150   *Oran do dh' Alasdair mac Colla*

Alasdair a laoigh mo chéille,
Co chunnaic no dh' fhag thu'n Eirinn,
Dh' fhag thu na miltean 's na ceudan
'S cha d' fhag thu t-aon leithid féin ann,
Calpa cruinn an t-siubhail eutruim,   5
Cas chruinneachadh 'n t-sluaigh ri chéile,
Cha deanar cogadh as t-éugais,
'S cha deanar sìth gun do reite,
'S ged nach bi na Duimhnich reidh riut,
Gu 'n robh an rìgh mur tha mi féil dut.   10

        E-hò, hi u hò, rò hô eile,
        E-ho, hi u ho, 's ri ri ù,
        Hò hi ù ro, o hò ô eile,
        Mo dhiobhail dìth nan ceann-fheadhna.

Mo chruit, mo chlàrsach, a's m' fhiodhall,   15
Mo theud chiùil 's gach àit am bithinn,
'Nuair a bha mi òg 's mi 'm nighinn,
'S e thogadh m'intinn thu thighinn,
Gheibheadh tu mo phòg gun bhruithinn,
'S mar tha mi 'n diugh 's math do dhligh oirr'.   20

        E-hò, hi u hò, rò hô eile, *etc.*

Mhoire 's ma run am fìrionn,
Cha bhuachaille bhò 'sa 'n innis,
Ceann-feadhna greadhnach gun ghiorraig,
Marcaich nan seud 's leoir a mhire,
Bhuidhneadh na cruintean d'a ghillean,   25
'S nach seachnadh an toir iomairt,
Ghaolaich na 'n deanadh tu pilleadh,
Gheibheadh tu na bhiogh to sìreadh.
Ged a chaillinn ris mo chinneach—
Pòg o ghruagach dhuinn an fhirich.   30

        E-hò, hi u hò, rò hô eile, *etc.*

'S truagh nach eil mi mar a b' âit leam,
Ceann Mhic-Calein ann am achlais,
Cailein liath 'n deigh a chasgairt,
'S a 'n crunair an deigh a ghlacadh,
Bu shunndach a ghelbhinn cadal,   35
Ged a b' i chreag chruaidh mo leabaidh.

E-hò, hi u hò, rò hô eile, *etc.*

M'eudail thu dh' fheara' na dìlinn,
'S math's eol dhomh do shloinneadh innse,
'S cha b'ann an cagar fo 's 'n iosal,
Tha do dhreach mar dh' òrdaich rìgh e,   40
Falt am boineid tha sinteach,
Sàr mhusg ort go cuilibhear,
Dh'eighte geard an cuirt an rìgh leat,
Ceist na 'm ban o 'n Chaisteal Ileach,
Dorn geal mu 'n dean an t-òr sniamhan.   45

      E-hò, hi u hò, rò hô eile, *etc.*

Domhnullach gasdu mo ghaoil thu,
'S cha b'e Mac Dhonnchai Ghlinne-Faochain.
Na duine bha beò dheth dhaoine,
Mhic an fhir o thùr no faoileachd,
Far an tig an long fo h-aodach,   50
Far an òlte fion gu greadhnach.

      E-hò, hi u hò, rò hô eile, *etc.*

Mhoire 's e mo rùn an t-òigear,
Fiughantach aigeanntach spòrsail,
Ceannard da ceathairne moire,
'S mise nach diultadh do chòmhradh,   55
Mar ri cuideach no am onar,
Mhic an fhir o 'n innis cheolar,
O 'n tìr m faighte na geoidh-ghlas,
'S far am faigheadh fir fhalam stóras.

      E-hò, hi u hò, rò hô eile, *etc.*

Bhuailte creach a's speach mhor leat,   60
'S cha bhiodh chridhe tigh 'n a t-fheoraich,
Aig a liuthad Iarla a's mòrair,
Thigheadh a thoirt mach do chòradh,
Thig Mac-Shimidh, thig Mac-Leod ann,
Thig Mac-Dhomuill duibh o Lochaidh,   65
Bidh Sir Seumus ann le mhor fhir,
Bidh na b' annsa Aonghas òg ann,
'S t-fhuil ghreadhnach fein bhi ga dortadh,
'S deas tarruinn nan geur lann gleoiste.

      E-hò, hi u hò, rò hô eile, *etc.*

'S na 'n saoileadh cinneadh t-athar,   70
Gu 'n deanadh Granntaich do ghleidheadh,
'S ioma fear gunna agus claidhcamh,
Chotaichean uain' 's bhreacan dhathan,
Dh' eireadh leat da thaogh na h-amhunn,

Cho lionmhor ri ibht an draighinn,   75
  E-hò, hi u hò, rò hô eile, *etc.*

Mhoire 's iad no run an comunn,
Luchd na 'n cul buidhe a's donna,
Dheanadh an t-iubhar chromadh,
Dh' oladh fion dearg na thonnadh,
  Thigeadh steach air mointich Thollaidh,   80
'S a thogadh creach o mhuinntir Thomaidh.

  E-hò, hi u hò, rò hô eile, *etc.*

150   *A Song to Alasdair Mac Colla*

Alasdair, O calf of my senses,
Who did you see or leave in Ireland?
You left hundreds and thousands,
And left no-one who was your equal;
Rounded calf of light movement,   5
Leg that mustered hosts together,
War cannot be waged without you,
Nor peace be made without your settlement;
Though the Campbells are not your allies,
May the King deal with you as I would.   10

  E-hò, hi u hò, rò ho eile,
  E-hò, hi u ho, 's ri ri ù,
  Hò hi ù ro, o hò ro eile,
  The lack of leaders is my downfall.

You are my lute, my harp, my fiddle,   15
Wherever I go, my string of music,
When I was young and a little girl
My spirits would be raised by your arrival,
You would get my kiss without pressing,
Safe your right to it today, the way I am feeling. 20

  E-hò, hi u hò, rò ho eile, etc.

Oh Mary, I love that hero,
No cowherd, he, in the meadow,
Magnificent leader of troops, unflinching,
Riders of steeds, plenty carousing,
His lads would win crowns at gambling   25
And not avoid further playing;
Beloved one, if you'd return
You would get what you were seeking:
Though with it I would lose my kindred—
A kiss from the brown-haired girl of the mountain. 30

  E-hò, hi u hò, rò ho eile, etc.

It is a shame I am not as I'd like to be,
With MacCailein's head in my armpit,

Grey Colin having been slaughtered,
The Crowner having been captured;
Cheerfully then would I slumber   35
Even were the hard rock my mattress.

    E-hò, hi u hò, rò ho eile, etc.

Of all men on Earth, you are my treasure,
Well do I know how to recite your ancestry,
Not under my breath in a whisper;
Your appearance is as a king would wish it,   40
Hair under a tasseled bonnet,
A fine muzzle to your musket,
You would summon the guard to the king's court,
Darling of the women in Islay Castle,
A white hand with gold encircled.   45

    E-hò, hi u hò, rò ho eile, etc.

You are my beloved fine MacDonald,
Not Robertson of Glen Faochain,
Or anyone else of his people;
Son of the Laird from the tower of welcome,
Where the ship comes in under sail,   50
Where wine would be quaffed gladly.

    E-hò, hi u hò, rò ho eile, etc.

Mary, the young man is my sweetheart,
Powerful spirited, fun-loving,
Leader of a great fighting-band,
I would not refuse your converse,   55
Either alone or with others,
Son of the Laird from the sheltered tuneful valley,
From the land where were found the grey-legs,
Where men were found who'd spend their riches.

    E-hò, hi u hò, rò ho eile, etc.

When you would plunder cattle and riches,   60
Neither earl nor lord would have the courage
To come and ask you ought about them.
These would come to defend your honour:
The Chief of the Frasers and MacLeod too,
Black MacDonald would come from Lochy,   65
Sir James would be there with a great army,
Angus Og would be there, the best-loved darling,
With the ready drawing of blades sharp-burnished,
If your own noble blood were spilling.

    E-hò, hi u hò, rò ho eile, etc.

And if ever your father's people wondered   70
If Grant could succeed in holding you,
There's many a man with sword and musket,
Green coat and plaid of tartan,
Would rise with you either side of the river,

As numerous as a wren has feathers.   75

E-hò, hi u hò, rò ho eile, etc.

Mary, beloved to me that company,
The people of the brown and yellow ringlets,
Who would make the yew bow buckle,
Drink of the red wine in billows,
Who would come in on the moor of Tollie   80
And raise plunder among the Frasers.

E-hò, hi u hò, rò ho eile, etc.

LUCY HUTCHINSON, née APSLEY
(1620–after 1662)

LUCY HUTCHINSON was born in the Tower of London (as was the early eighteenth-century poet Elizabeth Tollet), the daughter of the Lieutenant of the Tower, Sir Allan Apsley, and his third wife Lucy, daughter of Sir John St John of Lidiard Tregoze in Wiltshire, where a prodigious collection of early modern monuments still survive. She was a precocious child: according to her own account of her life, she could read by the age of 4, and by the time she was 7, she had eight tutors in languages, music, dancing, writing, and needlework. She also learned Latin, at the express wish of her father. Her mother's intellectual interests are suggested by the fact that she helped to finance some of Sir Walter Raleigh's experiments with chemistry while he was in the Tower, and she may also have contributed to her daughter's education.

Her husband, Colonel John Hutchinson, was the scion of an ancient Nottinghamshire family, a skilled fencer, viol-player, and marksman and a graduate of Peterhouse, Cambridge, a college noted for 'popish superstitious practices', and a late convert to Calvinism. Her introduction to Colonel John Hutchinson was a romantic one: he came across a sonnet of hers, admired it, and sought her out. Though she was unlucky enough to catch smallpox before her marriage, which took place in 1638, Hutchinson's love for her was undaunted by the damage to her looks. They had four sons (including twin boys in 1639) and four daughters, the last born in 1662. In the idealizing portrait drawn by his wife, John Hutchinson was a senatorial virtuoso, the embodiment of Classical virtue and Renaissance connoiseurship. He was Parliamentarian governor of the Castle and Tower of Nottingham during the Civil War and he was elected to the Long Parliament in 1646. At London, he purchased paintings, sculptures, engravings and other curiosities from the confiscated collections of Royalists and also 'a very neate Cabinett' to house them. Both husband and wife were sympathetic to the political programme of the Levellers. Hutchinson was a regicide, one of the signatories in January 1649 of the death warrant of that 'man of blood', Charles Stuart, and a member of the English Republic's Council of State. After Cromwell's dissolution of the Long Parliament in 1653, he retired to his country seat at Owthorpe, where he harboured an implacable hostility towards Cromwell, whom they both regarded as having been corrupted by power. After the Restoration, Hutchinson escaped execution for regicide, but died in September 1664 at Sandown Castle, on the coast of Kent, of a fever caused by the damp conditions. After her husband's death Lucy lived partly on the equity in property which she still owned, partly on the assistance of relatives and patrons.

By her own account, she began writing poetry in her teens. She also notes, 'I thought it no sin to learn or hear witty songs and amorous sonnets or poems, and twenty things of that kind, wherein I was so apt that I became the confidant in all the loves that were managed among my mother's young women.' In the later 1660s she wrote an account of her husband and their life together, *Memoirs of the Life of Colonel Hutchinson*: transcribed (in part) out of a diary and intended only for her children, this is the most brilliant of all the Civil War memoirs. It remained unpublished until 1806, and was, until very recently, all that she was remembered by. However, in this decade, a number of her poems have been discovered at Nottingham (three of which are printed here), which have been edited by David Norbrook. Although Nottingham was a little remote from the court and London, she was by no means isolated from the wider literary world. She also wrote a scornful reply to Edmund Waller's panegyric on Cromwell: there is a copy endorsed by the Earl of Clarendon in the British Library (Add. MS 17018, fos. 214–17ᵛ). Sir John Denham's translation of Virgil's *Aeneid* II–VI, his earliest known poetic composition (*c.*1636), survives only in a verse miscellany compiled by Lucy (Nottinghamshire Records Office, HU/3, pp. 5–135, which also contains part of Sidney Godolphin's translation of the same text). Her translation of Lucretius' *De Rerum Natura* survives (now edited by Hugh de Quehen, Ann Arbor: University of Michigan Press, 1997), while another Classical translation, of part of Virgil's *Aeneid*, which was in the possession of the vicar of Tisbury in Wiltshire in the late nineteenth century, seems to have been lost. Professor Norbrook has also discovered that a long and ambitious religious epic on *Genesis* (previously attributed to her Royalist brother, Sir Allen Apsley), called *Order and Disorder; or the world made and undone*, 1679, is her work, making her one of the most important poets, man or woman, of the mid-century.

151   *The Argument of the third booke*

Praysing that Greeke who did these mysteries find
He treats the mortall nature of the mind
Confuting such who dread of Hell derive
From a beliefe that soules their flesh survive
Affirms that Minds are a distinct part of Man,   5
Not Harmony, as the sage Greeks maintaine.
But a comanding power, thrond in the brest
Ruling th'inferior soule, through all the rest
Of the fraile limbs disperst, Both which are found
Of subtile slender attomes, smooth and round   10
That they spring from mixt seeds of breath and heate
And ayre and that seed which doth sence begett
And as any of these predominates
It angrie, mild, bold, cowardly soules creates.
That soules and bodies one conception have   15
One birth, one growth, one wast, one death, one grave
That phisick workes on both, wine and disease

Both Change admitt, substraction and encrease.
That soules departing passe not forth entire
And no power bodies can with them inspire   20
Because oblivion thence doth things deface
And dispositions are in every race
Peculiar and successive; thence doth presse
That passions mortall nature must confesse
And since death, souls and bodies, both doth kill   25
Wee therefore ought not to dread any ill
In death, which doth our woes in Lethe steepe
And when our day expires gives us sweete sleepe
That none can the trackt paths of death decline
But to their next successors must resigne   30
That life they from the former race received;
Nor living have they reason to be grievd
With thoughts of what shall after death befall;
The plagues which poets feignd in hell, being all
Allusions only to the payne men find   35
When guilt or passion workes upon the mind.
The Poet hence perswades us to embrace
Gladly our death, since even the longest race,
The most illustrious, and the best all tend
Unto Mankinds inevitable end.   40

1 *Greeke*: Epicurus   6 *Greeks*: principally Aristoxenus, a pupil of Aristotle   32–7 she
slants this to treat Lucretius's argument as a defective one: if there was no life after death,
this would be logical, but as a convinced Christian, she knows he is wrong.

152   *Another on the Sun Shine*

Heavens glorious Eie, which all the world surveyes,
This morning through my window shot his rayes
Where with his hatefull and unwellcome beames
He guilt the Surface of aflictions Streames;
In anger at their bold intrusion I   5
Did yet into a darker Covert fly:
But They like impudent Suters brisk and rude
Me even to my thickest Shade persude,
Whome when I saw that I could no where shun
I thus began to chide th'immodest Sun.   10
'How, Gawdy Masker, darst thou looke on me
Whose Sable Coverings thy reproaches be?
Thou to our murtherers thy taper bearst,
Th'oppressive race of men thou warmst and Chearst,
The blood which thou hast Seene pollutes thy light   15
And renders it more hatefull than the Night.

All good men loath thee growne a common bawd
The Brave that Leadst Impieties abroad,
Who Smiling doest on lust and rapine shine
Nor Shrinkst thy head in at disgorgd wine,   20
Which Sinners durst not let the see before.
Now thy conniving lookes they dred no more,
Becas thou makst their pleasant gardins growe
And Chearishest the fruitefull seeds they sowe
In feilds, which unto them descended not,   25
By Violence briberry and oppression gott.
Thou sawst the league of God himselfe dissolvd
Which a whole Nation in one curse Involvd,
Thou Sawst a thankelesse people slaughtring those
Whose noble blood redeemd them from their foes,   30
Thy staind beames into the Prison came
But lost their boasts, outshind with vertues flame.
Thou sawst the Innocent to exile Led,
And for all this veildest not thy radiant head,
But comst as a gay courtier to deride   35
Reuines we would in Silent shadows hide.
Since then thou wilt thurst into this darke roome,
By thyne owne light read thy most certeine doom,
Darkenesse shall shortly quench thy impure light
And thou Shalt Sett in Everlasting Night.   40
Those whome thou flattriest shall se thee expire,
And have no light but their one funerall fire;
Theire shall they in a dreadfull wild amaze
At once see all their glorious Idolls blaze.
Thy Sister, the pale Empris of the Night,   45
Shall never more reflect thy borrowd light,
Into black blood shall her darke body turne
While that polluted spheres about yow burne,
And the Elementall heaven like melting lead
Drops downe Upon the impious rebells head.   50
Then Shall our King his Shining host display
At whose approach our mists shall fly away
And wee Illuminated by his Sight
No more shall neede Thy everquenched Light.'

(after 1664)

7 *Suters*: probably intended to evoke the legendarily chaste Penelope besieged by her suitors
in the Odyssey   11 *Masker*: performer in a masque. Although several godly households
themselves staged masques, the primary association of the genre was with the increasingly
extravagant and distant court of Charles and Henrietta Maria   21 *the*: thee   23: *Becas*:
because   36 *Reuines*: Ruines   37 *thurst*: thrust   40 ff. cf. Thomas Campion (1567–
1620) imitation of Catullus, *Carmina* v. 5–6, 'My sweetest Lesbia': 'But, soone as once set
is our little light | Then must we sleepe one ever-during night'   42 *one*: own   49 *melting
lead*: molten lead was a useful *ad hoc* weapon of defence in sieges

153   *To the Gardin att O: [Owthorpe] 7:*th

Poore desolate Gardin, smile no more on me
To whome glad lookes rude entertainments be;
While thou and I for thy deare Master mourne
Thats best becoming that doth least adorne,
Shall wee for any meaner Eies be drest   5
Whoe had the Glorie once to please the best,
Or shall wee prostitute those Joys againe
Which once his noble soul did entertaine,
Forbid it honour and Just Gratitude,
Tis now our best grace to be wild and rude.   10
He that empaled the from the common Ground
Whoe all Thy walls with shining frutetrees Crownd,
Me alsoe above vulgar Girles did rayse
And planted in me all that yelded prayse—
He that with various beauties dect thy face   15
Gave my youth lustre and becoming grace,
But he is gone, and these gone with him too.
Let now thy flowers rise Chargd with weeping dew
And missing him shrink back into their beds,
Soe my poore Virgins hang their drooping heads   20
And missing the deare object of their sight
Close upe their Eies in sorrows Gloomy Night.
Let Thy young trees which sade and fading stand
Dried upe Since They lost his refreshing hand
Tell me too sadely how your noblest Plant   25
Degenerates if it usuall Culture want,
There spreading weeds which, while his watchfull eies
Checkt Their pernitious growth, durst never rise
Let them orerun all the sweete fragrant bankes
And hide what growes in better orderd rankes: 30
Too much alas this Paraliell I find
In the disordred passions of my mind,
But thy late lovelinesse is only his [. . .]
Mine like the shadow with its substance fled.
An nother Gardiner and another Spring   35
May into thee new grace and lustre bring
While beauties seedes doe yet remaine alive,
But ah my Glories never can revive,
No more than new leaves or new smiling fruite
Can reinvest that tree thats dead at roote.   40
When to his worthy memory thou then
Hast offerd one yeares fruit, thou mayst agen
In gawdy dresses to thy next lord shine
And shew weake semblance of his grace in thine:

How all thats generous healthfull sweete and faire 45
Inperfect emblimes of his vertue are.
But could I call back hasty flying time
The vanisht glories that once dect my prime,
To one that resurrection would be vaine
And like ungathred flowers would die againe, 50
In vaine would doting time, which can no more
Give Such a lover, Lovelinesse restore.

(after 1664)

154 *On my Visitt to WS which I dreamt of
That Night xi:th*

Fancy, that Sleeping makes us reenjoy
Those objects which our wakeing sence employ,
My Thoughts with Cheating dreames did excercise
While the dull Charme prevaild upon my Eies
And me backe to an empty mansion Led— 5
Which I the day before had Visited—
And where I once with Sweete content did dwell
Where various Accedents my youth befell.
Me thoughte that having a vast circle run
Hither I came and where I first begun 10
To respire, love resolved to sigh away my Breath
Till all my sorrow found releife in death.
'What Power' Saide I 'hath led me to This place
To See an emblime of my one disgrace:
These naked walls stript of all ornament 15
Did once a Thousand pleasant Things present
Here ware the Gardins, the well painted groves
Where Nimps and Sheapheards treated gentile love
The arras Storries did our fancies rayse—
To what The Poeits faind of Golden days, 20
When Innocence chast love and Constant truth
Shind in the converse of untanted Youth—
He thought to aemulate the Virtues of that age
But Soone those Actors left an empty stage.
The Nobler living guests that filld these roomes 25
Are now withdrawne and shut upe in their Tombs.
Even I whoe here did once in Splendor burne
Doe now a dimme expiring snuffe returne.
There twas' (I syghd) 'ah me twas even their
Philocles breath perfumd and warmd the ayre 30
That circled me; which whilst he did respire
Carried into my soule Life light and fire,

But Since Pale death those dores of motion seald
My Joys Stand Still like streame with Ice Congeald
No day Those amorous whispers can restore   35
No wounded ayre can heale me any more—
Here kind instructions did I oft attend,
Here a true merror Stood a faithfull freind
That taught me how to pollish the rude masse
And dresse my Soule in that nere flattring glasse,   40
But Sorrow, age, death, rewin hath destroyd
Whatere I here or any where Enjoyd.
No tapstrey now decks This naked roome
But what comes from the Spiders dusty loome,
On the defield flowers no Carpitt [Lies]—   45
No other pleasant object greets our Eies.
The place no more affords glad sight or sound;
Nothing but dessolation now is found
In Sollitude and silence reigning here
Where soule and sence so often feasted were.   50
But new Inhabitants may restore
The grace and beauty This Place had before:
I a Polluted Pallace must remaine
No ornaments can decke me vp againe.

Title: WS: probably Welbeck Abbey in Sherwood Forest   17 *ware*: were   18 *Nimps*:
nymphs   19 *arras*: tapestries   22 *untanted*: untainted   30 *Philocles*: name for John
Hutchinson, from the Greek, *philos*, 'loving', and *kleos*, 'fame'   45 *defield flowers*: defiled
floors   53 Isaiah 14

AN ANONYMOUS WOMAN OF THE CLAN CAMPBELL
(fl. 1645)

THE Battle of Inverlochy was fought on 2 February 1645 near the present town
of Fort William, between the Royalist forces led by Alasdair mac Colla (see no.
150) and the Marquis of Montrose, and the Covenanting army led by Campbell
of Auchinbreck for the Earl of Argyll, one of the few Highland chiefs to be a
Protestant and a significant figure in both Highland and Lowland politics.
Alasdair mac Colla was a MacDonald of Antrim in Northern Ireland rather
than a Scot (there were Mac Donalds on both side of the sea), and brought a
substantial body of Irish troops over to fight on behalf of Charles I, to the horror
and dismay of the Scots. Montrose and mac Colla came over Ben Nevis in
winter, taking the Campbells completely by surprise, since this had been
considered impossible, and devastated the Campbells, leaving 1,500 of them
dead. The Earl of Argyll, who had spent that night aboard his galley in the loch,
took advantage of his mobility and fled, deserting his clanspeople. The sparse
emotional tone of the song is characteristic of the vernacular tradition of Gaelic
poetry, which was largely the work of women; it records the events of the battle

from the perspective of someone who suffered from it but was unable to
influence the course of events.

155   *Oran air blàr Inbhir Lòchaidh*

O, gur mi a th'air mo leònadh,
Na hì ri ri ri hó hò;
O, gur mise th'air mo leònadh,
Na hì ri ri 's o ho ró.

Bho latha Blàr Inbhir Lòchaidh,   5
Na hì ri ri ri hó hò;
Bho latha Blàr Inbhir Lòchaidh,
Na hì ri ri 's ri o ho ró.

Bho ruaig nan eireannach dhoithte
Tháinig a dh'Albainn gun stòras,   10
Le bha dh'earras air an cleòcaibh,
Thug iad spionnadh do Chlann Dòmhnaill,
Mharbh iad m'athair is m'fhear pòsda,
'S mo cheathrar bhràithrean 'gan stròiceadh,
'S mo cheathrar mhacanan òga,   15
'S mo naoinear chodhaltan bòidheach;
Mharbh iad mo chrodh mór gu feòlach,
'S mo chaoirich gheala 'gan ròsladh,
Loisg iad mo chuid coirc' is eòrna.

O, gur mi a th'air mo chlaoidheadh   20
Mu mhac Dhunnchaidh Gleanna Faochan,
Tha gach fear a's tìr 'gad chaoineadh
Thall 's a bhos mu Inbhir Aora,
Mhathan 's a bhasraich 's am falt sgaoilte.

O, gur mi a th'air mo mhilleadh   25
Mu mharcaich' nan strian 's nam pillein,
Thuit 'sa chaonnaig le chuid ghillean;
Thug Mac Cailein Mór an linn'air,
'S leag e 'n sgrìob ud air a chinne!

                        (1645)

5 *Inbhir Lòchaidh/Inverlochy*: Montrose, Charles I's general in Scotland, surprised the
pro-Parliament Campbells at their base at Inverlochy after a near-impossible traverse of
mountain passes in winter   9 *eireannach/Irish* Alasdair mac Colla had raised troops in
Ireland for the Royalists   22–3 The Earl of Argyll had taken to sea before the battle.

155   *The battle of Inverlochy*

                O, I have been wounded
                Na hì ri ri ri hó hò;

O, I have been wounded
Na hì ri ri ri hó hò;

by the day of Inverlochy,   5
Na hì ri ri ri hó hò;
Bho latha Blàr Inbhir Lòchaidh,
Na hì ri ri 's ri o ho ró.

from the charge of the grim Irish
who came to Scotland without anything   10
but what they had on their cloaks;
they added strength to Clan Donald.
They killed my father and my husband,
they struck down my four brothers,
they killed my four young sons   15
and my nine handsome foster-children;
they slaughtered my great cattle,
and my white sheep they roasted,
they burnt my oats and my barley.

O, I have been anguished by the death   20
of Duncan of Glen Faochan,
whom all in the land are lamenting
round about Inverary,
women beating their hands, dishevelled.

O, I have been devastated,   25
for the horsemen of reins and bridles
who fell with his men in the battle;
the Earl of Argyll took to the water
and let that blow fall on his kin!

FRANCES (DOROTHY) FEILDING, née LANE,
later JAMES
(?1650–1709)

FRANCES FEILDING, whose given name was Dorothy, was the daughter of
Francis Lane of Glendon by Rothwell, Northamptonshire and fourth and last
wife of Basil Feilding, second Earl of Denbigh, the Civil War hero. At the time of
her marriage, she was considerably younger than her husband. After his death in
1675 she married Sir John James. Though not the only person of her name to be
listed in late seventeenth- and early eighteenth-century Feilding genealogies, she is
probably the signatory of a versified compliment to Christabella Rogers, which
survives in the Berkshire Record Office (Barrett & Belson papers, D/EBT Z34).
She was most probably the compiler of a MS now at Yale (Beinecke Library,
Osborn MS B 226), a collection of original poems, copied poems, prayers, recipes,
and remedies, written by a female member of the Feilding family in the late
seventeenth century, and containing several powerful confessional poems reacting
to the author's widowhood. This MS is of particular interest, since most of the
'private' verse which women allowed to survive casts the writers in a more or less
edifying light, this, by contrast, contains a variety of verse reflecting a range of
emotions including depression, self-pity, and rage. Frances Feilding's friend and

correspondent Christobella Rogers was the author of substantial quantities of verse: one of her poems survives in the British Library's Losely microfilms (M 437, no. 125), 'A songe made by Mrs Christabell Rogers', beginning 'Cupid away for I defy', addressed to 'my much honourd Cosen Al. ffennell'.

156 *one the morening the king was taken ill my dreame of him*

in a deep sleep
a sene of darknes did my soule a fryght:
I saw mee thout a man home I beefore had seene
throune cross a chair pale and coold as if hee dead had beene
one of his arms held up a surgion by   5
to Lett him bloud in this Extreamity
in great distraction I crying said,
hoe is itt hould him up a Lass I am a fraid
that he can never Bleed, for sure that arm is dead
with my still asking hoe hee was mee thought the Roome did ring   10
in this confution I heard one say, oh god itt is the king.

2 *a fryght*: affright   3 *home*: whom   4 *throune*: thrown   6 Draining a pint or two of blood from the arm was considered restorative   8 *hoe*: how; *a Lass*: alas   10 *hoe*: how

THE NURSE OF DONALD GORM
(*c*.1650)

THIS is a lullaby, composed for Dhomhnaill, or Donald, Gorm of Sleat in Skye by his nurse. Curiously, it is the only lullaby included in this collection: while it is certain that early modern women sang to their babies, such compositions are remarkably hard to find in written form. The nurse looks forward to a future in which the infant Dhomhnaill will display all the virtues of a Gaelic hero, the inheritor of an ancient, warrior culture. By the time Dhomhnaill was born, Irish and Scottish Gaelic singers had celebrated Cú Chulainn, Finn, Osein (Ossian), and Oscar for a thousand years. But while the contents of the nurse's song is based on the tropes of professional, bardic praise poetry, she does not use the complex, classical bardic metres, but a simple folksong metre, in whch lines are linked by assonance in the penultimate syllable. The refrain is meaningless as it stands, but may be a corruption of an originally meaningful invocation of Nàile, a Scottish saint, one of the disciples of St Columba (Columcille) of Iona.

157 *Tàladh Dhòmhnaill Ghuirm, le a mhuime*

Nàile bho hì nàile bho h-àrd
Nàile bho hì nàile bho h-àrd
Ar leam gur h-ì   a' ghrian 's i ag éirigh

Nàile bho h-àrd   's i a' cur smàl
Nàile bho h-ù air na reultaibh   5

Nàile nàile nàile ri triall hò
Gu cùirt Dhòmhnaill   nan sgiath ball bhreac
Nan lann ceanngheal   nan saighead siùbhlach
Nan long seòlach   nam fear meanmnach.

Nàile nàile hò nàile   gu triall   10
Moch a màireach.   Gun d' fhaighnich a' bhean
De' n mhnaoi eile: Na, có i an long ud,
Siar an eirthir   'sa' chuan Chanach?
Don-bìdh ort   C' uim' an ceilinn?
Có ach long Dhòmhnaill   long mo leinibh   15
Long mo rìgh-sa   long nan Eilean.
Is mór leam an trom   atà 'san eathar.
Tha stùir òir oirr'   trì chroinn sheilich.
Gu bheil tobar fiona   shìos 'na deireadh
Is tobar fioruisg   'sa' cheann eile.   20

Hó nàile nàile nàile ri triall
Moch a màireach.   Nàil chuirinn geall
Is mo shean-gheall: Am faod sibh àicheadh?
An uair théid mac mo   rìgh-sa dh' Alba
Ge bè caladh   tàimh no àite   25
Gum bi mire   chluiche is gàire
Bualadh bhròg   is leòis air deàrnaibh
Bidh sud is iomairt hò   air an tàileasg
Air na cairtean   breaca bàna
Is air na dìsnean   geala chàmha.   30

Hó nàile nàile nàile le chéile
Ge bè àite   an tàmh thu an Alba
Bidh sud mar ghnàths ann   ceòl is seanchas
Pìob is clàrsach   àbhachd's dannsa
Bidh cairt uisge   suas air phlanga,   35
Ol fiona is   beòir ad champa
Is gur lìonmhaor triubhas   saoithreach sean ann.

Nàile nàile   n àile hó nàile
An uair théid mac hó   mor rìgh-sa deiseil
Chan ann air chóignear   chan ann air sheisear   40
Chann ann air naoinear   chan ann air dheichnear:
Ceud 'nan suidhe leat   cheud 'nan seasamh leat.

Ceud eile, hó, bhith cur   a' chupa deiseal dhut
Dà cheud deugh bhith   d'anamh chleasa leat
Dà cheud deugh bhith   cur a' bhuill-choise leat   45
Dà cheud deugh bhith   'n òrdugh ghleaca leat.

Nàile nàile hó nàile so hugaibh i
An uair thìd mac mo   rìgh fo uigheam

Chan i a' Mhórthir   a cheann-uidhe
Ile is Cinn-tìre   an Ròimh 's a' Mhumhan   50
Dùthaich MhicShuibhne   is d'uthaich MhicAoidh cuide riutha.

Cha liutha dris   air an droigheann
No sguab choirce air   achadh foghair
No sop seann-todhair   air taobh taighe
Na an cùirt Dhòmhnaill   sgiath is claidheamh   55
Cloghaide gormdheas   is bald-shaighead
Bogha iubhrach   is tuagh chatha.
Gur lìonmhor bonaid   ghorm air staing ann
Is coinnle chéire   laiste an lanndair.

Nàile nàile hó nàile le chéile   60
An uair théid mac mo   righ-s' na éideadh
Gu robh gach dùil mar   tha mi fhéin da.
Ciod e ma bhios? Cha   tachair beud da.
Gu bheil mi dhut mar   tha do phiuthar:
Mur 'eil mi bàrr   tha mi uibhir.   65

Neart na gile   neart na gréine
Bith eadar Dòmhnall   Gorm 's a léine.
Neart a fhochainn   anns a' Chéitean
Bith eadar Dòmhnall   Gorm 's a léine.
Neart nan tonna   troma treubhach   70
Bith eadar Dòmhnall   Gorm 's a léine.
Neart a' bhradain as   braise leumas
Bith eadar Dòmhnall   Gorm 's a léine.
Neart Chon Chulainn   fa làn éideadh
Bith eadar Dòmhnall   Gorm 's a léine.   75
Neart sheachd cathan   feachd na Féine
Bith eadar Dòmhnall   Gorm 's a léine.
Neart Oisein bhinn neart   Osgair euchdaich
Bith eadar Dòmhnall   Gorm 's a léine.
Neart na stoirm' 's na   toirmghaoith reubaich   80
Bith eadar Dòmhnall   Gorm 's a léine.
Neart an torrain is na   beithreach éitigh
Bith eadar Dòmhnall   Gorm 's a léine.
Neart na miala   móire a' séideadh
Bith eadar Dòmhnall   Gorm 's a léine.   85
Neart nan dùl is   chlanna-speura
Bith eadar Dòmhnall   Gorm 's a léine.
Gach aon diubh sud   is neart Mhic Dhé
Bith eadar Dòmhnall   Gorm 's a léine.
Ciod e ma bhios? Cha   tachair beud dut.   90

Ar leam gur h-ì a' chrian 's i ag éirigh
Nàile bho hì nàile bho hò h-àrd.

1 *Nàile*: perhaps St Naile of Iona; *hì/Iona*: island off Mull, off the SW coast of Scotland   7 *Dhòmhnaill/Donald*: Donald Gorm of Sleat, on Skye   16 *Eilean/Islands*: the

Hebrides   24 *mac mo rìgh-sa/my King's son*: Charles Stuart, the future Charles
II   27 *Bualadh bhròg/beatings with slippers*: tradional forfeit for the loser in a card-
game was six strokes of a slipper on the palm of the hand   51 *Dùthaich MhicShuibhne
. . . MhicAoidh/the land of Mac Sween and MacKay*: NW Scotland and Gigha   74 *Chon
Chulainn/Cu Chulainn*: aristocratic legendary hero of Ulster   76 *Féine*/Fenians: Irish
heroes, the focus of popular legend   78 *Oisein/Ossian*: son of Finn, leader of the Fenians,
poet and singer; *Osgair/Oscar*: grandson of Finn, leader of the Fenians

157   *Lullaby of Donald Gorm, by his nurse*

Nàile from Iona, Nàile from above,
Nàile from Iona, Nàile from above,
I think that is   the sun as it rises
Nàile from above   that is casting a haze
Nàile from Iona   over the stars.   5

Nàile Nàile Nàile travelling hó
to the court of Donald   of the studded targes
of the swords bright-pointed,   of the flying arrows,
of the many-sailed birlins,   of the spirited clansmen.

Nàile Nàile hó Nàile travelling   10
early tomorrow.   The woman questioned
the other woman,   'Well, what is that vessel
west of the coastline   in the Sea of Canna?'
Starvation take you!   why should I hide it?
Whose ship but Donald's,   the ship of my baby,   15
ship of my own King,   ship of the Islands?
Heavy the cargo   she carries within her.
She had a golden rudder,   three masts of willow,
there's a well of wine   down at her sternage,
and a well of spring-water   up at her bowsprit.   20
Hó Nàile Nàile Nàile travelling
early tomorrow.   Nàile I'd wager
with my old bet,   can you refuse it?
When my King's son   reaches Scotland
whatever the port of   call or lodging,   25
there will be merriment,   sport and laughter,
beatings with slippers   and palms with blisters,
that, and playing   hó at back-gammon,
gambling at cards   patterned and gleamming,
and throwing of dice of   white ivory.   30

Hó Nàile Nàile Nàile together,
whatever the place you   stay in Scotland
this will be usual: music and talking,
piping and harping,   mirth and dancing,
quarts of whisky   up on the table,   35
drinking of wine and   beer in encampment,
and many pairs of breeches   tight and well-fashioned.

Nàile Nàile   Nàile hó Nàile
when the son of   my King travels southwards
it isn't with five men,   it isn't with six men,   40

it isn't with nine men,   it isn't with ten men,
but one hundred with you sitting,   one hundred standing.

A hundred sending   sunwise the cup to you,
twelve hundred others   to frisk and sport with you,
twelve hundred driving   the football across to you   45
twelve hundred standing   in battle array with you.
Nàile Nàile hó Nàile to you with this,
when the son of my   King goes on board ship
not the mainland   his destination,
but Kintyre and Islay,   Rome and Munster,   50
the land of MacSween   and MacKay as well.

Not more the prickles   on the blackthorn
or stooks of corn sheaves   on a field in autumn,
or wisps of old straw   at the side of a bothy,
than the swords and targes   in the court of Donald,   55
the bows of yew-wood   and battle-axes;
many the blue bonnet   hanging on the stand there
and waxen candles   blazing in lanterns.

Nàile Nàile hó Nàile together
when the son of   my King is in armour   60
may every being   be as I am to him.
What if it is? No   harm will befall him.
I am to you   like your sister,
if not as much   then I am more so.

Might of the brighness,   might of the sun's rays   65
be between Donald   Gorm and his shirting,
might of the green corn   in May time
be between Donald   Gorm and his shirting,
might of the breakers,   heavy and hurtling,
be between Donald   Gorm and his shirting,   70
might of the salmon,   boldly leaping,
be between Donald   Gorm and his shirting,
might of Cu Chulainn,   dressed for battle,
be between Donald   Gorm and his shirting,
might of the seven   bands of the Fenians   75
be between Donald   Gorm and his shirting,
might of sweet Ossian   and valiant Oscar
be between Donald   Gorm and his shirting,
might of the storm and   ripping tempest
be between Donald   Gorm and his shirting,   80
might of the thunder   and lurid lightning
be between Donald   Gorm and his shirting,
might of the monstrous   whale blowing
be between Donald   Gorm and his shirting,
might of the elements   and hosts of Heaven   85
be between Donald   Gorm and his shirting,
every one of those and   the might of God's Son
be between Donald   Gorm and his shirting,
What if it is? No   harm can befall you.

I think it is   the sun as it rises   90
Nàile from Iona, Nàile from above.

JANE CHEYNE (née LADY JANE CAVENDISH)
(1621–1669)

LADY JANE was the daughter of William Cavendish, Duke of Newcastle, poetaster, equestrian, Cavalier hero, and husband of the famous Duchess, whose influence over her father Jane viewed with suspicion. Her mother was the Duke's first wife, Elizabeth Bassett, who was daughter and heir of William Bassett of Blore, Stafford. Her poetry is mostly concerned with her family: many of them speak of the devoted affection between herself and her sister Elizabeth, and also of her adulation of her father. She wrote copiously from her early years. Much of her youth was spent at Welbeck. The sisters also wrote a play together, *The Concealed Fanseys*, at some time in the mid-1640s, when they were living together at Bolsover in Derbyshire, another of the family's castles, at the height of the Civil War. This survives in two presentation manuscript copies (Yale University, Beinecke Library, Osborne MS b. 233; Bodleian Library, Rawl. MS poet 16) and has been edited by Nathan Starr. Their father was then in exile in the Low Countries, and the play is full of reference to the sadness of being parted from loved ones. The sisters were guarding the house on their father's behalf, and remained there until they were taken prisoner.

One of the poems included here reminds us that her paternal great-grandmother was 'Bess of Hardwick', one of the Elizabethan era's most redoubtable dowagers. This poem is interesting for what it says of family politics and women's power. It is one of a cycle of twelve elegies for members of her family, carefully selected: note that in the poem included here (and in the others which are not), the Countess has completely suppressed the existence of her great-aunt Elizabeth, Bess's daughter, and of her cousin, Arbella Stuart; 'Bess of Hardwick''s attempt to put Cavendish blood on the throne of England which must have seemed best forgotten by the 1650s.

Lady Jane was deeply pious and filled several volumes with religious meditations, which have been lost, and she adhered rigidly to a thrice-daily routine of prayer. She married Sir Charles Cheyne, Viscount Newhaven, in 1654, who bought the manor and estate of Chelsea, and was responsible for its development: Cheyne Walk is named after him. In 1668 she became epileptic and her death soon followed. There is a monument to her by Bernini in black and white marble on the wall of the north aisle of St Luke's Church in Chelsea. An elegy by Thomas Lawrence, a Chelsea neighbour, was printed anonymously at the end of her funeral sermon by Adam Littleton, and also survives in a manuscript version (Nottingham University, Portland MS Pw V. 19). Lawrence commended her for confining her poetry to a small circle of family and neighbours: 'Wandring abroad small *Poets* does become | Great *Wits* (like *Princes*) best are seen at home.'

158   *On the 30th of June to God*

This day I will my thankes sure now declare
By Sermons, Bounties of each harty prayer
To thee great God, who gave thy bounty large
Saveing my Father from the Enemyes charge

Not onely soe, but made him victour lead   5
Chargeing his Enemyes with linckes of lead
To let them now thy workes plaine see
Sayeing my litle Flock shall Conquerors bee
And it was true Fairfax was then more great
But yet Newcastle made him sure retreat   10
Therefore I'le keepe this thy victoryes day
If not in publique by some private way
In spite of Rebells who thy lawes deface
And blot the footsteps of thy sonns blood trace
Thus will my soules devotion to thee send   15
And all my life in thankes an votery spend

Title *30th of June*: 30 June 1643, date of the Battle of Adwalton Moor, a comprehensive
defeat inflicted on the Yorkshire Parliamentarians of Ferdinando, Lord Fairfax, by the
Royalist forces of the Earl of Newcastle, near Bradford in the West Riding of Yorkshire   6 *linckes*: chain-shot

159   *On my honorable Grandmother,*
       Elizabeth Countess of Shrewsbury

Madam
You were the very Magazine of rich
With spirit such and wisdome which did reach
All that opprest you, for your wealth did teach
Our Englands law, soe Lawyers durst not preach   5
Soe was your golden actions, this is true
As ever will you live in perfect veiw
Your beauty great and you the very life
And onely Pattern of a wise, good wife
But this your wisdome was too short to see   10
Of your three sonns to tell who great should bee
Your eldest sonn your riches had for life
'Caus Henry wenches lov'd more than his wife
Your second children had, soe you did thinke
Soe William you did make, before your Charles to goe   15
Yet Charles his actions have beene soe
Before your Williams sonn doth goe before
This your great house is now become the lower
And I der hope the world shall ever see
The howse of Charles, before your Williams bee.   20
For Charles his William hath it thus so chang'd
As William Conqueror hee may well be nam'd
And it is true, his sword hath made him great
Thus his wise acts will ever him full speak.

Title *Grandmother*: great-grandmother: the celebrated and much-married 'Bess of Hard-wick' who died as Countess of Shrewsbury, colossally rich. The Duke of Newcastle himself wrote an epitaph for her tomb in Derby Cathedral, so Jane Cheyne's interest in this remote ancestress may have been suggested by his   9 *Pattern*: this is a strictly Cavendish perspective: she sacrificed the fortunes of her last two husbands, William Saint Loe and George Talbot, Earl of Shrewsbury, and her Talbot stepchildren to secure the interest of her own Cavendish offspring   13 *Henry*: her first son, born 1550, was disinherited by the dynasty-minded Bess *c.*1580 because he had no legitimate offspring. But he had many bastards, and was remembered a hundred years later as 'the common bull of Derbyshire and Staffordshire'   15 *William*: her second son, born 1551; *Charles*: her third son, born 1553. She bought lands for William, her designated heir, at a cost of £15,900, and only £8,800-worth for Charles   20 *William*: her own father William Cavendish, b. 1592, was the son of Charles Cavendish

160   *An answeare to my Lady Alice Edgertons*
Songe of I prithy send mee back my Hart

> I cannot send you back my hart
> for I have lost my owne
> And that as Centry stands apart
> Soe Watchman is alone.
>
> Now I doe leave you for to spy   5
> where I my Lampe will place
> And if your Scouts, do bring alye
> May bee your selfe will face.
>
> Then if you challenge mee the feild
> And would me battle sett   10
> I then as Maister of the feild
> Perhaps may prove your nett.

The metaphoric structure of this poem is entirely based on the rules of professional warfare in the seventeenth century   12 *prove*: test

ANNE DUTTON, née KING, later HOWE
(1621–after 1671)

ANNE was the last child of John King, Bishop of London, and Joan Freeman, and the sister of Henry King, poet, and Bishop of Chichester. Three other brothers—John, William, and Philip—were also poets. In 1648 she became the second wife of John Dutton of Sherborne, Gloucestershire, a graduate of Exeter College and the Inner Temple, and Doctor of Civil Law. He was twenty-five years her senior and one of the richest men in England. Known as 'Crump Dutton' because of his hunch-back, he is said to have been a strict disciplinarian in his own household, but affable and unassuming in the company of his friends, who included the poet Endymion Porter. A moderate member of the Long Parliament, he later defected to its rival version at Oxford, but afterwards reconciled himself to the Protectorate and even proposed a marriage alliance between his family and Cromwell's. He died early in 1657. She was very much part of her brother's social circle, and known within it as a poet. She was also a competent artist: Izaak Walton records her making a memorial drawing of John Hales, which she accompanied by an apologetic poem (see also London, British Library Add. 22,603, fos. 27ʳ–29ʳ, verses on Anne King's book of pictures). Walton also presented Anne with copies of the third edition of *The Compleat Angler* (1661) and *The Life of Dr Sanderson, late Bishop of London* (1678). By 1671, she had married again, to Sir Richard Grobham Howe of Great Wishford, near Salisbury, a great landowner in Wiltshire. Her son, another Sir Richard, succeeded his father and died in 1730

161   *An essay upon Good-Friday,* *3° April, 1640, by A.K.*

Stay, and behold; and see the greatest wonder,
Nayl'd to this Crosse! It is the God of Thunder
Amaz'd, confused, my hayres they stand upright,
To see such contumely; such dispight
Done to the Sonne of God; nay, God himselve   5
O thou inhumane Salvage! Romane Elfe
Pylate! how couldst thou doe this fact? Thy joynted
Lymes should tremble, when the great Lord's annoynted
Suffers by thy crueltie? Yet do'est free
Barabbas, a Robber? This should not bee;   10
An Innocent to dye; a Thiefe to Live?
This, savyng thyne, and Herods', all, elfe, grieve.
   But stay! I am a Xrian; Pylate, none.
And yet this act of thyne should make thee one;
When lesser wonders, thousands did convert;   15
And this (the greatest) never wrought thy heart
To consternacion, for this foul'st offence
That ever Deputy committed, since
Judas his tyme; or, Since the world began;
To crucifie (at once) both God, and man?   20
"Thou dy'st, heart-broake, despis'd, exyled from Rome
"To France thou com'st, and Lyons is thy tombe.
But oh sad day, that ever man beheld!
Thy very darknesse, blacknesse, sholde have quell'd
The haughty'st romane spirit; when that cloud   25
(Which made the Grecian Dennys cry aloud;
That God did suffer, or the world was done)
Obscur'd the bright sunne, from the brightest sonne
That ever Mortall saw; that glorious starre
That rose agayne; by which, we mounted are   30
And 'Rolled in the Booke of Life, above:

Where none ascends by Meritt, but through Love,
Which Love's the cause, that this day (more than others)
   We pray for Jewes, and Infidells, as Brothers.
And yet this day (though then esteem'd a sad day)   35
By that dyre fact is made for us, a glad day
For so the Church doth celebrate the same;
And now, Good-friday calls it; That's the Name.

6 *Elfe*: elf, deeply pejorative   13 Xrian: Christian   22 *Lyons*: based on the chapter on
'The Passion of our Lord' in the *Golden Legend* of Jacobus de Voragine: one of the most
popular books of the Middle Ages, this work was translated into English in 1483 by
William Caxton   26 *Dennys*: Dionysius the Areopagite: the most widely distributed
version of this story is also found in the *Golden Legend* (under SS. Dionysius, Rusticus,
and Eleutherius)

HANNAH WOLLEY, later CHALLINOR
(*c*.1621–74)

HANNAH WOLLEY is one of the few women writers of her generation who can
be indentified as anything like a middle-class professional. According to her own
comments in *The Queen-Like Closet*, both her mother and her sister were well
skilled in 'Physick and Chirurgery'. She herself went into the household of an
unnamed noble lady from 17 to 24, where she learned to cook, and even esoteric
skills such as preserving, sugar-work, wax-model-making (she is able to offer
'directions for the more curious working and adorning of the Images of the
poetical Gods and Goddesses'), and the care of exotic fabrics. The noble lady
was of a charitable disposition, so she was also able to experiment with remedies
on the various poor people who came to the house for help. At the age of 24 she
married the Master of Newport Grammar school, Benjamin Wolley, a Newport
scholar, who came to the school as an usher in 1635. Their marriage produced
four sons. The school was large and flourishing: they 'often had at one time
above three score in number' and at least three scholars were admitted to St
John's College, Cambridge. For seven years they resided at Newport Pond in
Essex, near Saffron Waldon, before moving to Hackney. In 1661 (i.e. shortly
after the Restoration) she began to write manuals of housewifery: which is to say,
she was able to capitalize on the experience of being a servant in an aristocratic
household by revealing the secrets of how to prepare and present food in an
upper-class manner to the socially aspirant. Her address to the reader in *The
Queen-Like Closet* makes it clear that she envisages an audience of relatively
underemployed middle-class women anxious to imitate aristocratic manners, and
possessed of the time and the resources to prepare elaborate food. Her combination of snob-appeal and technical clarity was, then as now, a recipe for commercial success as a food writer. The *Closet* went into eleven editions, and was
also translated into German. Benjamin Wolley died before 1666, the year in
which Hannah married Francis Challinor of St Margaret's Westminster. She
was, however, widowed again, and by 1674 she was living in the Old Bailey at
the house of Richard Wolley, MA, Reader at St Martin's, Ludgate, probably her
son.

162   From *The Queen-Like Closet*

Ladies, I do here present you
That which sure will well content you,
A Queen like Closet rich and brave;
(Such) not many Ladies have,
Or Cabinet in which doth set   5
Gems richer than in Karkanet;
(They) only Eyes and Fancies please,
These keep your Bodies in good ease,
They please the Taste, also the Eye;
Would I might be a stander by,   10
Yet rather would I wish to eat,
Since ' bout them I my Brains do beat;
And 'tis but reason you may say,
If that I came within your way;
I sit here sad while you are merry,   15
Eating Dainties, drinking Perry;
But I'me content you should so feed,
So I may have to serve my need.

6 *Karkanet*: carcanet   16 *Perry*: a cider-like drink made from pears rather than apples

ANNA TRAPNEL
(*c*.1622–after 1660)

BY her own account, Anna Trapnel was the daughter of William Trapnel, shipwright, who lived in Poplar, in the parish of Stepney. She says also that she was literate: 'I was trained up to my book and writing.' Following her mother's death in 1642, she became subject to religious raptures and began to utter prophecies. In 1645, after her father's death, she donated her possessions to the Parliament's war effort and became a house companion to a Mrs Harlow in the Minneries, Aldgate. It was probably in the summer of 1646 that she experienced what she regarded as her first true visions while suffering from a high fever and following a bout with Satan. In 1647 she left Mrs Harlow and moved in with a relative, Mrs Wythe, on Fenchurch Street. In 1650 she joined the congregation of the Baptist preacher John Simpson at St Botolph's Church in Aldgate. After briefly dabbling with Familism (1652) she aligned herself with the Fifth Monarchists, a group of religious extremists who expected the imminent return of Christ to rule the world in glory (the 'Fifth Monarchy'). Their ideas had infiltrated Simpson's Baptist congregation. By 1654 Trapnel was a figure of public notoriety. On 7 November, while accompanying the Welsh Fifth Monarchist Vavasor Powell to an examination at Whitehall, she fell into a twelve-day trance. She lay in bed with 'her eyes shut, her hands fixed' and delivered a series of visions in extempore verse on the second coming of Christ, together with a denunciation of Cromwell's betrayal of the revolution. Her utterances were taken down verbatim and published as *The Cry of a Stone*. One witness of Trapnel's visions, a certain 'B.T.', was distinctly puzzled: 'it is (to be playne) to me a very strange dispensation, yet I am perswaded she hath communion with God in it, but under what sens to ranke it, I am at some stand.' He also notes that, '(she saith) she cannot make a verse when she is in her selfe'. Later in 1654, Simpson's congregation sent her on a propaganda tour of Cornwall, which got her into trouble with the authorities. She was held prisoner at Plymouth before being transported back to London, where she was briefly imprisoned in Bridewell. These picaresque episodes were the subject of two tracts in that summer: *A legacy for saints: being several experiences of the dealings of God with Anne Trapnel* and *Anna Trapnel's report and plea, Or a narrative of her journey from London into Cornwall*. She returned to Cornwall in 1655, but the mission was unsuccessful, and she may have contemplated emigrating to America. She had driven her body and spirit to breaking-point: for some ten months, from October 1657 to August 1658, confined to her bed and sustained only by a 'little small beer' and an occasional piece of toast, she poured forth a torrent of prophecies in a series of fifty-odd sessions that are recorded in two works, *A voice for the king of saints* (1658) and a thousand-page folio manuscript in the Bodleian Library, Bod. S. 42.I.Th.

A number of prose pamphlets were printed by her or on her behalf. In addition to those already mentioned, there is *Strange and wonderful newes from Whitehall: or, the mighty vision proceeding from Mistris A. Trapnel...concerning the Government of the Commonwealth...and her revelations touching...the Lord Protector, and the army* (1654). Nothing is heard of her after 1660, and this silence is probably best explained by her death. She may have been the sister of Ursula Adman, another Fifth Monarchist of some notoriety.

163   *Having prayed for, and made much mention of the Merchants, she Sings the following Hymn to them.*

> O merchants! oh turn to the Lord!
> What he to you reports,
> Look into the written word so sure,
> And see what he brings forth.
> Oh do not grieve at losses great,   5
> Though all your ships do split,
> Oh look to that bottom wherein
> Cannot come any leak.
> O take up now your time for that
> Which is precious and most sweet,   10
> And shall be given forth to you,
> That will receive meat.
> Oh Merchants! I fain would that you
> Might have true gold indeed:
> O I desire sweet preserves, which   15
> Christ unto you doth leave.

The sweet preserves come from the seas
And from those forraign parts,
Which are made up by those Indians
That are so full of Arts.   20
You have your Canded Ginger, and
Your Preserved Nutmegs too:
That so you may delight therein,
And your mouths overflow.
But oh, there's canded things indeed,   25
Which is covered with Gold,
There is not such preserves as they
Which shall be turned to mould.
But these preserves continue shall,
No mouldy skins shall be   30
At all of them; But the longer
You keep them, you shall see
They are as fresh and lovely as
They were when first he brought,
They do not lose their taste at all,   35
Oh that you would have sought.
These things indeed as pleasant, all
That you would feed upon
Them which will strengthen you always
And lead you to mount Sion.   40
Oh Merchants cloath your selves with robes,
Which will never be wore
Not that which will to rags be turn'd,
Nor that which can be tore.
But here is cloathing substantial;   45
Oh it is costly too!
Oh it is white! Oh it is that
Which Christs blood bought to you!
That you might be cloathed herewith,
And herein still may go,   50
No nail or splinter can these tear,
Nor can remove the show.
Tis glorious and substantial too,
And it abides for ever,
No enemy can rent it from,   55
Oh none can it you sever.
Oh merchants then lift up your heads,
Though losses you may have;
Oh the more of Christ you do now beg,
Which will make you most brave.   60
O you that are proud, and with stout necks
And mincingly goe you,
With your black spots and powdred locks

Thinking to make a show.
And so you go unto those which   65
Are carnal hearts with you,
But oh the spirituals do see,
They do hate it, and spue.
They cannot endure your company,
Oh cover then your skins,   70
Remember when that *Adam* fell,
He covered was leaves in.
His nakednesse with leavy skins
At length must be his cloaths;
Oh therefore all you naked ones,   75
Oh do not Scripture oppose.
Oh you that sport it forth with that
Which is jesting most vile,
The Lord himself does to you say,
That he will you rob and spoil.   80
O you that think to do that which
Is injury to Saints:
O the Lord he draws them more unto
His lovely open gates.
Where he takes them into himself,   85
When others are shut out,
Then *Mordicai* must be call'd in,
Haman must hang without.
Oh thou dear Lord, they chains would do
Thine injury therein   90
They cannot, for the Lord their God
He is their onely King.
Oh sing! oh soul! that I am fain,
And do lift up my heart,
Unto thy beloved so high,   95
Which is exceeding great.
Hallelujah unto *Jehovah*,
I will without fear sing,
Unto him which creatures al brings forth,
Oh! thou art the great King.   100
That store and plenty to thine,
Rivers and streams are there,
Oh thou dost so much love unfold,
That does the heart so chear.
While it sings songs to others, and   105
At the mentioning
Of the perfumes and costly things,
Which are esteemed dear.
They must esteem, and count them dear
That receive from a Christ   110

For it cost his most precious blood,
To bring forth interest.
Into these Royalties it was,
A Saviour led therein,
Thy going to the grave, oh Lord,   115
And rising up a King.
Oh he was willing for to be
Crown'd with a thorny one,
That crowns unto his children might
Be brighter then the Sun.   120
O he was willing to drink gall
And vinegar so sharp,
That so his Saints might drink sweet wine
For to revive their heart.
He willing was, that they should with   125
Their spears that then were sharp,
Run into his own sides, that so
His children might not feel smart.
But that water and blood might come,
For to cleanse, and throw out   130
All their defilements that came when
Man he was driven out.
Of that old Paradise, before
A Christ a new one brings,
Which shall abide for evermore,   135
Where thine shall in it sing.
O how greatly then are those Saints
Established by thee,
That hast a rest brought forth to them,
Where they shall always be.   140
O it is much more better, sure
Then *Adams* state before;
O here is one that is so strng,
None can it rend or tore.
O Saints, love Christ, love him dearly   145
That hath for you thus shown
Great dignity, and his power,
Which set you on his thron.
O Saints rejoyce! O take your harps
Down from your willows now: 150
And play your tunes unto the Lord,
For none shall make you bow.
Great *Babylon*, it shall not mock,
Nor injure your sweet songs,
In the enjoyment of a King,   155
That cast out hath those throngs.
O you Saints that Christ tarry on,

When he hath taught you play,
His melody shall you sound forth,
In the sun-shiny day.   160
Therefore desire, and wrestle too
By faith and prayer, while
The Lord hath brought you forth from all
That endeavour you to spoile.
O fear not! do not tremble, but   165
Go on couragiously.
Let Prayer, let Faith, let Zeal go out,
And through your tongues let fly.
O Prophets all, do you speak out,
With bold courage for him,   170
For unto you he shall draw near,
And appear even when
That the rotten wals are thrown down,
And the great Chaos fals,
A fabrick true that you shall have,   175
That by faith on him calls.
Oh he wil not be slack, though men
They shift and put you off,
Yet he will suddenly relieve,
And let his Canons off,   180
That shall all forts and bulkwards here,
All foes that do upstand,
Shall be laid flat upon the ground
And thine shall enter the land.
Oh they are fruit that are most sweet,   185
They are not rot within,
They have no blemish in them all,
He will fill you to the brim.
You are my *Joshuahs* and are
My *Calebs* that I love,   190
And you also do shew to me
That you climb up above,
Oh unto you I now do speak,
They shall go on apace,
And enter into *Canaans* Land,   195
And dwell in those sweet rayes.
Therefore take heed oh Israelites,
How you do speak and pray
Unto the feeblest of the flock,
To keep them from the way,   200
Wherein they shall green things behold
And milk and hony eat,
Oh therefore awaken them not
Do not the sickly beat.

But like true *Calebs* do go forth,   205
With courage bold and stout,
And speak well of Gods *Canaan*,
Which others seek to rout.
Oh do go tell the goodnesse of
The place and might therein;   210
The Fortifications thereof
Which are made by our King.
Oh speak well of your *Canaan*,
And of its Bulkwards there,
Oh tell of its most glistering walls,   215
And tell what can compare.
What rooms, what wals, what hangings can
Set forth of what is there?
What meat and drink, can be to that
Which is so sweet and clear?   220
I tell you God will take it well,
When well you do report,
Concerning his sweet *Canaan*,
And his salvation cups.

73 *leavy*: perhaps for heavy   87–8 *Mordicai... Haman*: in *The Book of Esther* Haman plots to kill Mordecai and all the Jews in the Persian empire (3: 1–4: 17) but this threat is averted by the courage and shrewdness of Esther and Mordicai, with the aid of a series of fortuitous circumstances (5: 1–8: 14). Haman is hanged on the gallows he had built for Mordecai (7: 9–10)   189 *Joshuahs*: following the death of Moses, Joshua led the people of Israel in occupying the Promised Land, allocated it to the Twelve Tribes and led them in the renewal of their covenant with Yahweh (*The Book of Joshua*)   190 *Calebs*: see Numbers 14: 24

MARGARET CAVENDISH (née LUCAS), DUCHESS OF NEWCASTLE (1624–1674)

KNOWN to many contemporaries by such names as 'Mad Madge' and publicly mocked and ridiculed for her literary efforts, Margaret Cavendish, Duchess of Newcastle, launched on a literary career with the express purpose of achieving both knowledge and fame. Born Margaret Lucas, she was the eighth and last child of Thomas Lucas of Colchester and Elizabeth, née Leighton, a London girl who had born him a son out of wedlock before they eventually legitimized their relationship. Her father died when Margaret was 2: he was described as a 'gentleman... of good quality being a man of £4000 [per annum] in lands'. His wife took over the management of the family estates: she made herself deeply unpopular with her tenants and neighbours by her enclosing activities and rackrenting. Her daughter was later to apply the same methods, with the same results, to the management of the Cavendish estates. Margaret was allowed, as a child, to daydream and indulge her own tastes. Her education (at home) was half-hearted: she blamed the incompetence of her teacher, an 'ancient decay'd gentlewoman', for the fact that she could neither write grammatically nor spell, and she never developed a properly formed script. At the outbreak of Civil War in 1642, the Lucas family moved to the Royalist headquarters at Oxford, where Margaret, despite her bashful, dreamy character, volunteered to serve as Maid of Honour to Henrietta Maria. In 1644 she accompanied her royal mistress into exile in Paris. There she met her future husband William Cavendish, the Marquis of Newcastle, who was her senior by at least thirty years and the father of daughters slightly older than herself (both of whom are represented in this collection). At the same time, he was handsome, gallant, a notable horseman, and interested in literature. They married in 1645 and for the next fifteen years, they lived on credit on the Continent, mostly in Antwerp, in a splendid mansion belonging to the painter Pieter Paul Rubens. In 1651, the Duchess went to England with her brother-in-law to try and raise money and retrieve what they could from the Cavendish estates, which had been confiscated by the revolutionary government. This unsuccessful enterprise took eighteen months, during which the Duchess began writing poetry to console herself. In 1653 she published *Poems and Fancies* and *Philosophicall Fancies* (in prose and verse). The latter was revised as part of *Philosophical and Physical Opinions* (1655 and 1663) and as *Grounds of Natural Philosophy*. On a copy of the second edition of *Philosophical and Physical Opinions* owned by the poet Edmund Waller, the first flyleaf bears this couplet in ink: 'New Castles on the air this Lady builds | While nonsence with Philosophy she guilds' (Huntington, RB 120156). *Nature's Pictures* (1656) contained an autobiographical account of herself, 'A True Relation of my Birth, Breeding and Life'. She was the first Englishwoman to write such a work. She also wrote some closet dramas at Antwerp, but their publication was postponed until 1662 after the manuscript was lost at sea.

At the Restoration they returned to England, and when the Duke was excluded from Charles II's government, they settled on their estates and spent the rest of their lives writing and publishing. In addition to her new works, which included books of orations, fictional letters, and utopian fiction, the Duchess supervised a number of reissues and revised editions. Her major project was a biography of her husband, which took five years to complete, *The Life of the Thrice Noble, High and Puissant Prince William Cavendish, Duke, Marquess and Earl of Newcastle* (1667). The Newcastle's marriage was childless but singularly happy. They idolized each other, and admired one another's writings to an extent which sometimes looked from the outside like *folie à deux*. The Duchess wrote for publication, with supreme self-confidence: 'I confess my ambition is restless and not ordinary.' Her works were published not (as were those of most contemporary women writers), in octavo and other small formats, but in large, expansive folios, like classical texts, which she presented, insistently, to University libraries: the Dutch poet Constantijn Huygens, who was an acquaintance of hers from her Low Countries days, records dealing with one of these embarrassing gifts. She was widely dismissed as an eccentric, both because of her writing, and because of her fantastic apparel and idiosyncratic behaviour, which included a relish for bawdy language. The Duke and Duchess paid a lengthy visit to London in the spring of 1667. She created a sensation: on May Day Pepys went to the park with the rest of London to see her. He spent the entire day trying to get a close view of her— unsuccessfully, although he did see enough to be shocked by her extreme décolletage. She was invited to visit the new Royal Society and shown a series of scientific demonstrations by Hooke and Boyle, which forced her to abandon her position that microscopic images were mental delusions. Her 'scientific' work is aristocratic and amateur, like that of her contemporary Sir Kenelm Digby, but, as several of these poems show, she was an extremely acute observer of natural phenomena, with a keen and sensitive awareness of the animal world. She died suddenly at Welbeck in December 1673 at the age of 50. Her body was embalmed, transported to London, and interred at Westminster Abbey. The Duke, who outlived her by three years, designed a monument for them both in the North Transept of the Abbey. Lady Margaret is represented holding a book, and she has also been supplied with a marble ink-stand and a pencase.

164 *Of* Cold Winds.

As *water Rarified* doth make *Winds* blow,
So *winds* when *Rarified* do *Colder* grow;
For if they much be *Rarified*, then they
Do further *Blow*, and spread out every way;
So *Cold* they are as they like *Needles* prick;   5
Through *thinness* they do break, and cannot stick,
But into *Atomes* fall, whose *Figures* be
Sharp, and peirce *porous Bodies*, as we see.
Yet some will think, if *Air* were parted so,
The *winds* could not have such strong force to blow: 10
True, *Atomes* could not peirce, if they were found
To be all *Dull, Flat, Heavy, Blunt* or *Round*;
But by *Dividing* they so *Sharp* do grow,
That through all *porous Bodies* they do go;
But when the *Winds* are soft, they intermix   15
As *Water* doth, and in one *Body* fix;
They rather wave than blow, as *Fans* are spread,
Which *Ladies* use to cool their *Cheeks* when red:
Or like as *Water drops*, that disunite,
Feel harder, than when mixt they on us light,   20
Unless such *Streams* upon our heads do run,
As we a *shelter* seek, the *Wet* to shun;
But when a *Drop* congealed is with *Cold*,
As *Hail-stones* are, then it more strength doth hold;
For *Flakes* of *Snow* may have more *quantity*   25
Than *Hail-stones*, yet they've no such force thereby;
They fall so *Soft* that they scarce strike our *touch*,
Hail-stones we feel and know their *weight* too much.
But *Figures* that are *Flat* are *dull* and *slow*,
Make weak *Impressions* wheresoe're they go;   30
For let ten times the quantity of *Steel*
Be beaten small, no hurt by that you'l feel;
But if that one will take a *Needle* small,
Whose *point* is *sharp*, and prick the *Flesh* withall,
Strait it shall hurt, and put the *Flesh* to pain,   35
Which greater strength doth not of what is *plain*;

For though you press it hard against the *Skin*,
'T may heavy feel, but cannot enter in:
And so the *Wind* that's thin and rarifi'd
May *press* us down, but never *peirce* the side.   40
Or take a *Blade* that's *Flat*, though strong and great,
And with great strength upon ones *Head* it beat,
You'l break the *Skul*, but not knock out his Brains;
Which *Arrows sharp* soon do, and with less pains.
This what is small, is subt'ler and more quick;   45
For all small *Points* in *porous* Bodies stick.
Winds broken small to *Atomes*, when they blow,
Are *Colder* much than when they streaming flow:
For all that's joyned and united close,
Is stronger much, and gives the harder *Blows*.   50
This shews what's closest in it self to be,
Although an *Atome* in its small degree;
Take *Quantity* for *Quantity* alike,
And *Union* more than *Mixture* hard shall strike.

165   *The* Hunting *of a* Stag.

There was a Stag, did in the Forest lye,
Whose Neck was long, whose Horns were Branch'd up high,
His Haunch was broad, Sides large, and Back was long,
His Legs were Nervous, and his Joynts were Strong;
His Hair lay Sleek and Smooth, he was so Fair,   5
None in the Forest might with him Compare.
In Summer's Heat he in Cool Brakes him lay,
Which being High did keep the Sun away;
In Evenings Cool and Dewy Morning he
Would early Rise and all the Forest see;   10
Then was he Walking to some Crystal brook,
Not for to Drink, but on his Horns to Look,
Taking such pleasure in his stately Crown,
His Pride forgot that Dogs might pull him down;
From thence he to a Shady Wood did go,   15
Where streightest Pines and talest Cedars grow;
Olives upright, imbrac'd by th'Loving Vines,
Birches which Bow their Heads to^a Golden Mines;
Small *Aspen* stalk, which shakes like Agues cold,
That from perpetual Motion never hold;   20
The sturdy *Oak*, which on the Seas doth Ride;
Firr which tall Masts doth make, where Sails are tied;
The weeping *Maple*, and the *Popler* green,
Whose cooling Buds in Salves have Healing been;

The fatting *Chestnut*, and the *Hasle* small,   25
The smooth-rind *Beech*, which groweth Large and Tall;
The loving *Mirtle* fit for Amorous kind,
The yielding *Willow* for Inconstant Mind;
The *Cypress* Sad, which makes the Funeral Hearse,
And *Sicomors*, where Lovers write their Verse;   30
And *Juniper*, which gives a pleasant Smell,
With many more, which were too Long to tell,
Which from their Sappy Roots sprout Branches small,
Some call it Under-wood, that's never Tall;
There walking through the *Stag* was hinder'd much,   35
The bending Twigs his Horns did often Touch;
While he on tender Leaves and Buds did brouse,
His Eyes were troubled with the broken Boughs;
Then strait he sought this Labyrinth t'unwind,
Though hard it was his first way out to find;   40
Unto this Wood a Rising Hill was near,
The sweet wild Thyme and Marjoran grew there,
And Winter-Sav'ry which was never Set,
Of which the Stag took great delight to Eat;
But looking down into the Vallies low,   45
He saw, there Grass and Cowslips thick did grow,
And Springs, which Digg'd themselves a passage out,
Much as like Serpents, wind each Field about;
Rising in Winter high, they'ld over-flow
The flow'ry Banks, but make the Soil to grow;   50
And as he went thinking therein to Feed,
He 'spied a Field, which Sow'd was with Wheat-feed,
The Blades were grown a handfull high and more,
Which Sight to Taste did soon Invite him o're;
In haste he went, Fed full, then down did lye;   55
The Owner coming there, did him Espy,
Strait call'd his Dogs to Hunt him from that place;
At last it prov'd to be a Forest chase;
The Chase grew hot, the Stag apace did run,
The Dogs pursu'd, more Men for Sport came on;   60
At last a Troop of Men, Horse, Dogs did meet,
Which made the Hart to try his Nimble feet;
Full swift he was, his Horns he bore up high,
The Men did Shout, the Dogs ran Yelping by,
And Bugle Horns with several Notes did blow,   65
Huntsmen, to cross the *Stag*, did Side-ways go;
The Horses beat their Hoofs against dry Ground,
Raising such Clouds of Dust, their ways scarce found,
Their Sides ran down with Sweat, as if they were
New come from Watering, so dropt every Hair;   70
The Dogs their Tongues out of their Mouths hung long,

Their Sides did like a Feaverish Pulse beat strong,
Their short Ribs heav'd up high, and then fell low,
As Bellows draw in Wind that they may Blow;
Men Tawny grew, the Sun their Skins did turn,   75
Their Mouths were Dry, their Bowels felt to Burn;
The Stag so Hot as glowing Coals may be,
Yet swiftly Ran when he the Dogs did see.
Coming at length unto a Rivers side,
Whose Current flow'd as with a falling Tide,   80
There he Leap'd in, thinking some while to stay
To wash his Sides, his burning Heat t'allay,
In hope the Dogs could not in Water swim,
But was deceiv'd, for they did follow him
Like Fishes, which to Swim in Waters deep;   85
He Duck'd, but Out, alas! his Horns did Peep;
The Dogs were cover'd over Head and Ear,
Nothing did of them but their Nose appear;
The *Stag* and River like a Race did show,
He striving still the River to Out-go,   90
Whilst Men and Horses down the Banks did run,
Encouraging the Dogs to follow on,
Where in the Water, like a Looking-glass,
He by Reflexion saw their Shadows pass;
Fear did his Breath cut short, his Limbs did shrink,   95
Like those which the Cramp makes to th' Bottom sink:
Thus out of Breath no longer could he stay,
But leap'd on Land, and swiftly Run away;
For Change brings Ease, ease Strength, in Strength Hope lives,
Hope Joys the Heart, and Joy light Heels still gives.   100
His Feet did like a Feathered Arrow fly,
Or like a winged Bird that mounts the Sky;
The Dogs like Ships, that Sail with Wind and Tide,
Do Cut the Air, and Waters deep Divide;
Or like as Greedy Merchants, which for gain   105
Venture their Life, and Traffick on the Main;
The Hunters like to Boys, which without fear,
To see a Sight, will hazard Life, that's Dear:
For they are Sad when Mischief takes no place,
And out of Countenance as with Disgrace,   110
But when they see a Ruine and a Fall,
They come with Joy, as if they'd Conquer'd all:
And thus did their three several Passions meet;
First the *desire to Catch* the Dogs made Fleet,
Then *Fear* the *Stag* made Run, his Life to save,   115
Whilst Men for *love of Mischief* digg'd his Grave.
The angry Dust flew in each Face about,
As if 't would with Revenge their Eyes put out,

Yet they all fast went on, with a huge Cry;
The Stag no hope had left, nor help did 'spy,   120
His Heart so heavy grew with Grief and Care,
That his small Feet his Body scarce could bear;
Yet loath to Dye, or yield to Foes was he,
And to the last would strive for Victory;
'Twas not for want of Courage he did Run,   125
But that an Army was 'gainst him alone;
Had he the Valour had of *Cæsar* stout,
Yet Yield he must to them, or Dye, no doubt;
Turning his Head, as if he Dar'd their spight,
Prepar'd himself against them all to Fight;   130
Single he was, his Horns were all his helps,
To Guard him from a Multitude of Whelps;
Besides, a Company of Men were there,
If Dogs should fail, to strike him every where;
But to the last his Fortune he'ld try out,   135
Then Men and Dogs did Circle him about,
Some Bit, some Bark'd, all Ply'd him at the Bay,
Where with his Horns he Tossed some away:
But Fate his Thread had Spun, he down did fall,
Shedding some Tears at his own Funeral.   140

[a] *Golden* Mines *are found out by the* Birches *bowing.*

16–31 This catalogue of trees with their qualities and associations is a mixture of English woodland, such as she would have known around Bolsover, and Mediterranean trees with strong emblematic associations, which are too tender to grow here, producing a sort of arboreal never-never land   17 *Olives . . . Vines*: Roman farmers used to grow their vines up olives: the practice is recorded by agricultural writers such as Columella. Vines can be grown in southern England, but not olives   18 *Birches*: NB the Duchess's own note   19 *Aspen*: descriptive: the light leaves are always moving   21 *Oak*: used to make the bodies of ships   22 *Firr*: the usual wood for ships' masts   23 *Popler*: poplar   25 *Chestnut*: sweet chestnut: the nuts are starchy and nourishing; *Hasle*: hazel, more a large bush than a tree   27 *Mirtle*: myrtle, too tender to grow outdoors in England, is a Mediterranean shrub sacred to the goddess Venus   28 *Willow*: associated with disappointed love   29 *Cypress*: used for funeral wreaths, associated with death   30 *Sicomors*: Sycamores   42–3: *Thyme . . . Marjoran . . . Winter-Sav'ry*: three native English aromatic herbs used for cooking   43 *Set*: not planted, but growing wild   127 *Cæsar*: Julius Caesar, the great Roman general

166   *The* Ruine *of this* Island

This Island Liv'd in Peace full many a Day,
So long as she unto the Gods did Pray;
But she grew Proud with Plenty and with Ease,
Ador'd her Self, and did the Gods displease,
She flung their Altars down, and in their Stead   5

Set up her Own, and would be Worshipped:
The Gods grew angry, and commanded Fate
To Alter and to Ruine quite the State,
For they had Chang'd their Mind of late, they said,
And did Repent, unthankfull Man th'had made;   10
Fates wondred much to hear what said the Gods,
That they and mortal Men were at great Odds,
And found them apt to Change, thought it did show,
As if the Gods did not poor Men fore-know;
For why, said they, if Men do Evil grow,   15
The Gods, fore-seeing all, Men's hearts did know
Long, long before they did Man first Create;
If so, what need they change or alter Fate?
'Twas in their Power to make them Good or Ill,
Wherefore Men cannot do just what they will;   20
Then why do Gods complain against them so,
Since Men are made by them such ways to go?
If Evil power hath Gods to oppose,
Two equal Deities it plainly shows;
The one Pow'r cannot keep Obedience long,   25
If Disobedient power be as Strong;
And being Ignorant how men will prove,
Know not how Strong or Long will last their Love:
But may't not be the Course of God's Decree,
To love Obedience, wheresoe're it be?   30
They from the first a Changing power Create,
And for that Work make Destiny and Fate;
It is the Mind of Man that's apt to Range,
The Minds of Gods are not subject to Change.
Then did the Fates unto the Planets go,   35
And told them they Malignity must throw
Into this Island, for the Gods would take
Revenge on them, who did their Laws forsake;
With that the Planets drew like with a Screw
Bad Vapours from the Earth, and then did View   40
What place to Squeeze that Poyson on, which all
The Venom had, got from the World's great Ball;
Then through Mens Veins like Molten Lead it came,
And did like Oyl their Spirits all Inflame,
Where Malice boyl'd with Rancor, Spleen and Spight,   45
In Warr and Fraud, Injustice took delight,
Thinking in what way their Lusts they might fulfill,
Committed Thefts, Rapes, Murthers at their will;
Parents and Children did Unnat'ral grow,
And every Friend was turn'd a Cruel Foe;   50
Nay, Innocency no Protection had,
Religious Men were thought to be stark Mad;

In Witches, Wizzards, they did put their trust,
Extortions, Bribes were thought to be most Just;
Like Titan's Race all did in Tumults rise,   55
And 'gainst the Heavens utter Blasphemies;
The Gods in Rage unbound the Winds, to blow
In a strange Nation, formerly their Foe,
Where they themselves did Plant, the Natives all
Were by them Kill'd, for th' Gods had Sworn their fall;   60
Compassion wept, and Virtue wrung her hands,
To see that Right was Banish'd from their Lands:
Thus Winds, and Seas, the Planets, Fates and all
Conspir'd to work her Ruine and her Fall;
But those that keep the Laws of God on high,   65
Shall Live in Peace, i'th'Grave rest Quietly;
And ever after like the Gods shall be,
Injoy all Pleasure, know no Misery.

Title: companion poem to 'A Description *of an* Island': both clearly, though indirectly, describe England before and during the Civil War   36 *Malignity*: a term with strong Civil War resonance: a Parliamentarian term for Royalists   55 *Titan's*: in Greek myth, the Titans conspired against Zeus and the Olympian gods, were defeated only with difficulty and confined beneath mount Etna

MARY CAREY, née JACKSON, later PAYLER
(fl. 1643–80)

MARY CAREY (the name she apparently used throughout her life) was the daughter of Sir John Jackson of Berwick. Her first husband was Pelham Carey, son of Henry, fourth Lord Hunsdon, created Viscount Rochford in 1621 and Earl of Dover in 1628. In later life, she remembered her life with him as frivolous and pleasure-seeking, devoted to 'Carding, Dice, Dancing, Masquing, Dressing, vaine Companye, going to Plays, following Fashions, & yᵉ like'. He was a Royalist, and the colonel of a regiment of Oxford scholars from 1644 to 1666. Her second husband, George Payler, whom she married early in the 1640s, in the early stages of the Civil War, was a Parliamentarian officer, paymaster of the Parliamentarian forces in the Berwick garrison. Her husband's military life took them all over the country, from garrison to garrison: looking back at the age of 45, she notes that she had lived in 'Barwick, London, Kent, Hunsden, Edenbroughe, Thistleworth, Hackney, Tottridge, Grenwicke, Bed-nell-grene, Claphame, York, Mountaine, James's, Newington, Coven-garden and deare Katherine's.' ('Mountain' is Nun-Monkton in Yorkshire, the Paylers' family home). Her life, since it was spent almost entirely in garrisons, was a relatively secure one for the times. The great tragedy of her life was her disastrous record of motherhood. She bore child after child, only to see them die: as she heart-rendingly says, 'all my Children were only Children (each child when it died was all I had alive)'. At the time of her memoir, two children, Nathaniel and Bethia, had survived infancy, and appeared to be healthy. Most of the verse in her memoir is agonized meditation on her obstetric history. She is also the author of a memorial poem on Lady Fairfax, preserved by her husband, 'The Lady Caryes Elegy on my deare wife d. 16 Oct. 1665, in Oxford, Bodleian Library MS Fairfax 38, p. 267, and Fairfax 40, pp. 596–7.

167   *Written by me at the death of my*
        4th son, and 5th Child, Peregrine Payler

1   I thought my All was given before
    But Mercy order'd me one more.
2   A Peregrine, my God me sent
    Him back againe I doe present.
3   As a Love-Token, 'mongst my others   5
    One Daughter, and her four deare Brothers;
4   To my Lord Christ, my only bliss
    Is, he is mine, and I am his:
5   My dearest Lord, hast thou fulfill'd thy will,
    Thy Hand-Maid's pleas'd, compleately happy still   10

    Grove-Street, May 12th, 1652   Mary Carey

3 *Peregrine*: Latin, *peregrinus*, pilgrim

ANNE DOCWRA, née WALDEGRAVE
(1624–1710)

ANNE DOCWRA was a Quaker controversialist, who employed her pen both on the Quaker case for religious toleration, and on personal controversy: Phyllis Mack, *Visionary Women* (Berkeley and Los Angeles: University of California Press, 1992), 320, describes her as 'The Quaker church's chief female gadfly and curmudgeon'. She was born in Bures in Suffolk, the daughter of William Waldegrave, a Justice of the Peace, and notes in her tract, *An Apostate-Conscience Exposed*, that her father encouraged her to read his law-books (pp. 24–5). She was a gentlewoman (like Anne Whitehead, but unlike the majority of early Quakers), and lived near Cambridge.

From 1699, she engaged in a pamphlet war with the apostate Quaker Francis Brigg (her nephew), an activity approved by her Quaker meeting. She argues for women's active participation in the Church, in *An Epistle of Love and Good Advice to my Old Friends and Fellow-Sufferers in the Late Times, the Old Royalists and their Posterity, and all others that have any sincere desire towards God* (n.d.). But she was not always a friend to other Quaker women. Anne Whitehead wrote a letter of rebuke to her in 1683, advising her to 'attend upon the teachings of the Lord in silent subjection as becomes us'. Docwra, who clearly did not number tact among her gifts, had accused the Quaker Women's Meetings (in which Whitehead was instrumental) of being of little purpose 'but to shelter great bellies' (illicit pregnancies: an accusation which seems completely malicious and unfounded). An unknown reader of her tract noted on the copy preserved with the A. R. Barclay MSS (vol. 324, no. 237), 'thou hadst better have studied to be quiet and have kept down that unruly, willfull, ravenous spirit and have power over that before thou had set up thyself in print and usurped authority.'

168   *'The Mystery of Profession great'*

The Mystery of Profession great,
And Lifeless Forms I here repeat,
That all may see, that want of Light
Makes men like Bats and Birds of Night.

Profession was a lovely Tree   5
And very green appeared to bee,
With Blossoms fair as Eye can see;
And when the times with it did suit,
It seem'd as it would bear some fruit.

Great Storms of Persecution blew,   10
That nipt the bud, and chang'd the hew,
And so, away the Blossoms flew.
What fruit can then expected be,
From a seared and blasted Tree?

The Husband-man did his good Will,   15
No fault is found, nor want of Skill:
What's done in love can think no Ill.
And when that he expected Fruits,
It brought forth nothing but Disputes.

This Tree stands still upon the Ground,   20
Small hopes of Life, it being Unsound.
Who knows how Mercy may abound?
None can pluck up, but only he
That plants and plucks to Eternitie.

Profession thus grows out of Date,   25
Through change of times and change of State,
In steps the Monster of Debate.
I'l show her in her Colours true,
And set her forth to public view.

Make-bate Opinion, she appears   30
With swarms of jealousies and fears,
Sets men together by the Ears;
And courts the times whatsoe'er they be,
And make that pass for Loyaltie.

The Sun hath shin'd so long upon her   35
Her brood grows great, and comes to Honour,
And strives to be as big as BONNER.
These Vipers in the Sun do play,
Makes all the year a Holy day.

But storms will come to make them Creep   40
Into their Holes, in hopes of Sleep;
Instead of Rest, with Sorrow weep.
This is the Portion that will be
Due to so great Hypocrisie.

37 BONNER: Bishop Bonner: Sir John Harington, *A briefe view of the state of the Church of England, as it stood in Q. Elizabeths and King James his reigne, to the yeere 1608* (1653), 15–16: 'he was so hated, that every ill-favoured fat fellow that went in the street, they would say, that was *Bonner*.'

MAIRI CHAMARAN, NIGHEAN FREAM CHALLAIRD (MARY CAMERON)
(b. *c*.1625?)

MARY CAMERON was the daughter of Cameron of Callart. A plague carried off her father, her mother, and all her brothers and sisters, leaving only Mary alive. Patrick Campbell, son and heir of Campbell of Inverawe, was in love with Mary and went to see her. At his request she walked to the sea, stripped off her clothes, and washed herself thoroughly. She then wrapped her lover's plaid around her and went off with him. He took her to Inverawe and married her. He built a house in the woods for her, and kept her there three months. He then took her home to live with him. He was severely wounded at the battle of Inverlochy in 1645, and died shortly afterwards. His father forced the young widow to marry the Prior of Ardchattan. The husband of her choice and love was buried near her new home; her second marriage was loveless and unhappy.

169   *Oran Broin*

A Mhic-Dhonnachaidh Inbhir-atha,
Is coimheach a ghabhas tu 'n rathad;
Ged tha Mairi Chamaran romhad,
'S òg a chail mi riut mo ghnothach.

Rìgh, gur mis' a th' air mo sgaradh,   5
Bhi dol le fear eil' a laighe,
Is m' fhear féin air cùl an taighe,
Sealgair nan damh donn 's nan aighean.

Eudail a dh-fhearaibh na Dàlach,
Thug thu mach a taigh na plàigh mi,   10
Far an robh m'athair 's mo mhàthair,
Mo phiuthar ghaoil 's mo choignear bhràithrean.

Eudail a dh-fhearaibh na gréine,
Thog thu taigh dhomh 'n coill nan geugan,
'S bu shunndach ann mo laighe 's m' éirigh;   15
Cha b' ionghnadh sud, oir b' ùr mo chéile

169   *A Song of Sorrow*

O Robertson of Inverawe,
You take the road as a stranger;
Though Mary Cameron lies in front,
Young did I lose any interest in you.

God, it is I who am undone,   5
Going to lie with another man,
With my own man behind the house,
Hunter of the brown stags and hinds.

Darling of the men of the Dale,
You took me out of the house of plague,   10
Where my father and mother lay,
My dear sister and five brothers.

Darling of all men under the sun,
You built me a house in the spreading woods,
Joyful there my lying down and rising,   15
No wonder that—for I was new-wed.

KATHERINE AUSTEN (née WILSON)
(1628–1683)

KATHERINE AUSTEN's commonplace book, dated 1664, tells us much of her interest in dreams, angels, mysticism, and religion, less of the quotidian details of her life: interestingly, it includes an account (fo. 34^r) of the twelfth-century mystic, St Hildegard of Bingen. We do learn that her parents were Robert Wilson and Katherine Rudd, and that she had three children, Thomas the heir, Robert, and Anne. It also looks beyond her life to public events, such as the 'Eng. and Dutch quarel', 1665. Another interesting memorandum records the Great Plague in the same year: 'On goeing to Essex the 28th Aug. the day before I went there there was dead that week before I went 7400.' She was widowed in 1658, when she was only 29 (her husband's will was proved on 15 December that year, P.C.C. 11/285, fo. 338), and one of her principal practical concerns during the time in which she was composing this book was the need to fight a court case to retain an estate at Highbury: 'what a merciful allay and mitigation, that God did not lay the triall and hazard of our estate at my first widdowhood, but hath forbore six years.' A series of entries through 1665, in ever-deteriorating handwriting, record the fluctuations of Mrs Austen's reactions to this legal battle, which she appears to have won. The book records two potentially conflicting strains in Mrs Austen's concerns, her struggle as a widow to maintain and enhance her family's status and material welfare (particularly in securing the Highbury estate for her son), and her attempt to live a life directed by God. An indication of the uneasy relationship between these preoccupations is a prayer that the Austens will get Highbury, written, then scratched out. Her poem 'On the Situation of Highbury' (fo.104^r) falls into the category of 'country house poem' (of which Aemilia Lanyer's 'Description of Cooke-Ham' is also an example), but is unusual in being a description of her *own* estate, passionately fought for; the pleasure expressed in this poem is the pleasure of possession. The provisions for her children in her husband's will, which survives, made it financially prohibitive for her to marry in the first seven years of her widowhood. This period was nearing an end when she wrote this book; she had a suitor, and considered remarriage, but decided against: 'for my part I doe noe Injury to none by not Loveing. But if I doe I may doe real Injuries where I am already engadged. To my Deceased friends posterity.' As a widow, she was free to spend her energy on rebuilding her childrens' fortunes.

She did not get on with her sister-in-law—there is a prose meditation 'upon Sist^r Austens unkindnes to me upon all occasions'. A prose memorandum dated 12 Feb. 1665 refers to 'Sister Austens renewing again her pretention for the Red Lion'—presumably a public house, and another item of family property. The book was intended to be read by her children after her death: there are memoranda to each of them. That to her daughter suggests that Mrs Austen's own rather depressive temperament is a family trait: 'may you be defended from the passion of [your grandmother's] mallancholy...her too great love occasioned much unhappiness to her by it'. The book, as it developed, gradually turned into a private example of the 'Mother's Advice' genre from its original character as an expression of personal interests and concerns, perhaps under the impetus of the Great Plague, which made human life a frighteningly uncertain matter even by seventeenth-century standards, and perhaps left her wanting to give her children some solid advice to cling to in case of her sudden death. She died in 1683 after twenty-five years of widowhood: her will, made on 19 September 1683 and proved in 1684, bequeaths her property to her two sons, Thomas and Robert (P.C.C. 11/375, fo. 1).

170   *Dec. 5th 1644 Upon Robin Austins recovery of the smal pox and General Popams son John diing of them—a youth of a very forward growth and their ages the same. popham 3 yeares for growth more.*

> How does thy mercies stil renew
> How does thy benefites pursue.

My childe lay sicke, while darts of death
Was ready to exhale his breath.
A dangerous infectious Dart   5
Might have seized upon his heart
Expeld his vital powers in haste
And early in his noneage waste
His slender life. Then could not pay
His offerings by a longer stay.   10
His life was in the twilight sky,
Nor knew he not thy praise most high.
O let him live and praise thee who
Doest ade more daies and life renew.
Why was mine spar'd and one so strong   15
Whose lively health, judg'd to live long
A verdant youth, in's growing Spring
The Prince of all the Schollars. Him
A jewell in his parents eye
And this so lov'd a youth, did dye.   20
He strong by nature, and mine frail
Was spar'd, the other did exhail.
Was it his sin, or our desert,
Made mine to live, and him to part?
O noe my Lord. My handes (I doe) uphold   25
It was thy will, nor dare be bold
To search thy secrets, or ask why
My weak son liv'd, a strong did dye.
Thy glory, and thy mercy too
As well in death as life insue.   30

                                  (1644)

14 *ade*: add

171   *On the Situation of Highbury*

So fairely mounted in a fertile Soile
Affords the dweller plesure, without Toile
Th'adjacent prospects gives so sweet a sight
That Nature did resolve to frame delight
On this faire Hill, and with a bountious load   5
Produce rich Burthens, makeing the aboad
As full of Joy, as where fat vallies smile
And greater far, here sickenes doth exhile
Tis an unhappy fate to paint that place
By my unpollishet Lines, with so bad grace   10
Amidst its beauty, if a streame did rise

To clear my mudy braine, and misty Eyes
And find a Hellicon t'enlarge my muse
Then I, no better place then this wud choose
In such a Laber and on this bright Hill   15
I wish Parnassus to adorne my quill.

1665

3 *sweet*: 'rare' is given as alternative   13 *Hellicon*: the hill in Greece where the Muses
lived

ELIZABETH EGERTON, née CAVENDISH, LADY ELIZABETH BRACKLEY, later COUNTESS OF BRIDGEWATER (1626–1663)

DAUGHTER of William Cavendish, first Duke of Newcastle by his first wife, Elizabeth Bassett, who was daughter and heir of William Bassett of Blore, Stafford. At the age of 15, she married John Egerton, Viscount Brackley (1622–1686), who became the second Earl of Bridgewater in 1649 (as a child, he had been the Elder Brother in the first performance of Milton's *Comus*). She left a fair amount of prose writing, and a very few verses, and collaborated with her sister on *The Concealed Fanseys*. Her husband was an opponent of the Restoration government, and when she died in childbirth in her thirty-seventh year, it was at Black Rod's house in Westminster, where she had gone to visit her husband who was in custody there at the time. She is buried in the church of St Peter and St Paul at Little Gaddesden, in a chapel reserved for the Earls of Bridgewater. The papers of the Egerton family, many of them of a literary nature, are in the Huntington Library, San Marino.

172   *On my Boy Henry.*

Here lyes a Boy the finest Child from me
Which makes my Heart and Soule sigh for to see
Nor can I think of any thought, but greeve,
For joy or pleasure could me not releeve,
It lived dayes as many as my years,   5
No more, which caused my greeved teares;
Twenty and Nine was the number;
And death hath parted us asunder,
But thou art happy, Sweet'st on High,
I mourne not for thy Birth, nor Cry.   10

(1655)

RACHEL JEVON
(1627–after 1662)

RACHEL JEVON emerges out of provincial obscurity in 1660 as the author of two parallel Restoration Odes, one in English and one in Latin. She was the daughter of a Worcestershire Clergyman, Daniel Jevon of Sedgeley Hall, Staffordshire (b. *c*.1590), a scholar at Trinity College, Cambridge in 1608, and his wife Elizabeth. She was christened in 1627 in Broom, Worcestershire. In 1662 she petitioned Charles II 'for the place of one of the meanest servants about the Queen. Her father, a loyal clergyman of the diocese of Worcester, though threatened and imprisoned, contrived to preserve his flock, so that not one took arms against His Majesty, but could only give his children education, without maintenance'. She followed this up with another petition described simply as 'For the place of Rocker to the Queen'. It seems possible that her father educated her with the intention of allowing her to attract attention and capitalize on the interest thus gained by finding a patron, as the fathers of sixteenth-century women Latinists such as the Italian Olimpia Morata and the Spanish Luisa Sigea had done.

173   *CARMEN* ΘPIAMBEYTIKON
REGIÆ MAIESTATI Caroli II,
PRINCIPUM ET CHRISTIANORUM
OPTIMI IN EXOPTATISSIMUM
EIUS RESTAURATIONEM

REGUM PIISSIMO, SERENISSIMOQUE, Carolo II,
Hoc Carmen Gratulatorium humillimè offert
Ancillarum indignissima

Alme PATER Patriae, Celeberrime CAROLE REGUM!
Clarior è tenebris, æternum vive, MONARCHA:
Ante Pedes sacros incondita Carmina pono,
Te mihi suppliciter poscens ignoscere Musam,
Primitiasque, meas vultu lustrare benigno: 5
Nam licet ipsa negem, facit EXULTATIO Carmen

CAROLE VIVE DIU, POPULIS CHARISSIMUS ESTO:
VIVE, DIUQUE TIBI POPULUS CHARISSIMUS ESTO

Exoptatus ades, Regum mitissime, CÆSAR,
E superis ortus, dignissima stirpe Propago,   10
Prælucens *Phoebo* Sydus quoque, splendor Avorum,
Martyris occisi vivens regalis imago,
IRIDE nata ROSA ex *Bellâ* pulcherrima Florum.
Ferte pii calami famam venientibus ævis.
Nobis *Parnassi* veniam concedite Musæ,   15

PRINCIPIS ejecti duros recitare labores
Pro patria subitos; CAROLI post aspera fata.
Primi (cujus honos æternus ad æthera tendit,
Quamvis Elysiis spatiatur splendidis agris)
Fallax ejectum revocabat *Scotia* REGEM,   20
Et super HÆREDEM sistunt Diadema Parentum.
Traditus hinc Anglis, illumque furore sequuntur
Per mare, per terras (*heu*!) *sic potuere rebelles.*
Absit præteritos tristes renovare Dolores;
At memorare iuvet, cladem vitâsse VIGORNÆ,   25
Hostibus è mediis, ubi tot cecidere *Britanni*
Stragibus indignis, *quæque ipsa miserrima vidi*
Non quorum pars magna fui, mœstissima solum
Heu! quoties tristis ploravi fata Nefanda?
Heu! quoties Lachrymas sacris libavimus aris,   30
Ut Sobolem placeat Superis umbrare periclis?
Numine ductus eras, cum tot discrimina passus
Terris, et subitò tandem jactatus in alto:
En pelagi Numen magis est tibi mite Tyrannis;
Æolus immites Ventos conjurat in Antrum,   35
Neptunus sævi compescit Murmura ponti,
Advehit unda Ratem placata ad littora spontè;
Tum requiem quærens per inhospita Regna vagatus,
EXTORRI, totus, terrarum clauditur orbis.
At pius ÆNEAS noster vult ferre Penates,   40
Deferet cultus nec sævi tempore fati
Antiquos Patrum, jus ut repararet Avorum
Pectoribus populi PRINCEPS regnavit ubique
Devictis pietate suâ, quæ fortior armis.
Gallia fusa comis civili Marte cruenta   45
Lætatur, NUMEN tantum rediisse quietis;
NUMINIS ob causam, dilectâ pace reversâ
Barbara REGALEM QUERCUM *Ampelona* rejecit
Hostis in obsequium naturæ vincula solvens;
Ast immota fide *Gallorum Lilia* fugit.   50
Cessit ad *Austriacos*, ubi proditione nefandâ
Horrendum Monstrum tentabat tollere Vitam.
Post JOVIS ARBOR agros *Batavum* repetebat aquosos,
Italia effugium venienti ingrata negavit.
At nimbis Quassam, generosa recepit OLIVA.   55
Mox sequitur secura quies, atque, Arma reponunt.
Spectantes *Aliæ* deposcunt fœdere jungi
Tandem Fata jubent, *Sylvæque Druina* Reduxit
Natali supplex, Dominum regnare potentem.
Pectoribus populi subductis, pace Triumphans,   60
Languida nativum revocabat Patria REGEM.
Classibus ecce tuis quam gaudent æquora scindi,

Te PACIS NUMEN Regnis affere superbæ.
Carbasa decertant auris implere secundis
Afflantes Venti, Parcísque, faventibus adsis.   65
Advena Pax rediit quoque tecum NUMINE *Pacis,*
Et tibi subjectis Terris Astrea revertit
Aurea ferratis redierunt tempora Regnis
Multus honor genti, Te Defensore reverso
Antiquæ Fidei, Templis Cultusque redibunt,   70
Cultus enim Templi, REGI *Turresque Coronæ*:
Aspice quàm Thamesis gaudet portando Carinam
Auratam Domini, quàm stratis accipit undis!
Metropolisque senex nuper Lacerata Tyrannis
Induit ornatam Te nunc redeunte juventam.   75
In TE lætantes Populi quàm Lumina figunt!
Quàm glomerant Cives densis spectare catervis!
Quàm simul exultant quia REX dignetur ab illis,
Hospitio recepi! quam Compita plena Triumphis!

O DEUS in terris, PROLES *Coelestis*, adoro   80
TE CHRISTUM DOMINI nobis mortalibus Alti
A CHRISTO DOMINO demissum culmine Cœli
Nos ut vivificet miseros Præsentia sacra,
MARTYRIS occisos, regalis morte cruentâ:
Non fuimus tanquam projecta cadavera terris,   85
Spiritus at nobis animasti corpora vita:
En tetigisse Pedes portantes munera Pacis,
Florum deliciis Tellus vestita superbit
Irradians veluti Phœbus cùm Lampade terras
Lustrat post hyemen, teneras refrigerat herbas   90
Lumine sic claro radiâsti Regna per Orbem
Divinæ ut fructus edant virtutes amœnos.
Aut velut *Aprilis* flores produxerit Imber,
Nativo siccæ detentes carcere terræ.
Sic fusis Lachrymis, *tua Fata* aspersa piorum,   95
BASILICIS immersa Tuis, ad Sydera tendunt;
Numine placato, multâque; tulere Coronas,
Quæ Caput exornare Vestrum, CELEBERRIME REGUM,
Prima coruscabit Superis æterna Corona.
Altera flagravit claris Virtutibus, *intra*   100
Cor Regale Tuum, penitus Virtute repletum.
Tertia plaudentis Populi resplendet Amore,
Lætitiâ mentes connexæ suaviter omnes.
Quartáque completa est vestrâ Pietate supernâ
Quæ vicit duros hostes, ignovit iniquis.   105
Quinta refulgebit Gemmis Auróque decora,
In Caput exsuperans Reges, PRÆCLARE MONARCHA
Omnipotensque Deus faxit florescere Lætè,

Donec in æternum coelestis STELLA corusces.
Quis non miratur quod Turtur doceret albus, 110
Vestibus indutam fœdatis sanguine Sponsam:
CAROLUS en, purus noster sine felle COLUMBUS,
Adveniens *Arcæ* folio frondentis *Olivæ*,
Angliam in uxorem duxit, quæ fœda cruore,
Regināeque, dedit formam complexibus almis. 115
Plaudite nobiscum Gentes, celebrate per Orbem,
Sponsales thalamos REGIS, clamate perenne,
VIVAT IN ÆTERNUM DILECTUS CAROLUS ÆVUM:
Exsultate simul Saltus venantibus apti,
Nobilis adveniet vobis *Venator* in agros. 120
En (LEO) REX vester, jubilate animalia Campi;
Et saliant Sylvæ, præsenti *Robore sacro*,
Nymphæ dum resonant, *O terque quaterque beati*
Queîs licet illustris QUERCUS *recubare sub umbrâ*
Expansâ, Sanctis atros depellere nimbos, 125
Quæ Templo Domini quadrata secando COLUMNA;
Nos ubi vivamus, Laudes cantare sonoras,
Cordibus et citharis, plectris, et vocibus altis,
Ipsi qui DAVID, nostri non vota rejecit;
Regii, at angores Eius complevit amaros, 130
Seminis, et fecit Carolum *Grandemque Bonumque*
Atque, super Solium REGEM Patris extulit altè
Luceat ut toto terrarum splendida STELLA
Orbe, die Medio, rursum contendere Phoebo,
Omnes sub Pedibus dires calcare Tyrannos. 135
Puribus exactis tendem Florentibus annis,
CAROLE NATE DEI, Cœlos ascende Triumphans
VICTOR, in Æternum felici Pace fruendos.

Μόνῳ Θεῷ Δόξα
140

174 *Exultationis Carmen*
TO THE KINGS MOST
EXCELLENT MAJESTY UPON
HIS MOST *Desired Return*

By Rachel Jevon, Presented with her own Hand, Aug. 16th

TO THE *MOST PIOUS* and *MOST SERENE* OF KINGS, The
Unworthiest of His MAJESTIES HAND-MAIDS With all
Humility Offers this Congratulatory Poem.

Dread Soveraign *CHARLES!* O King of Most Renown!
Your Countries Father; and your Kingdoms Crown;

More Splendid made by dark Afflictions Night;
Live ever Monarch in Coelestial Light:
Before Your Sacred Feet these Lines I lay, 5
Humbly imploring, That, with Gracious Ray,
You'l daign these first unworthy Fruits to view,
Of my dead Muse, which from her Urn You drew.
Though for my Sexes sake I should deny,
Yet EXULTATION makes the verse, not I; 10
And shouting cryes, *Live Ever* CHARLES, and *Be*
Most Dear unto Thy People, They to Thee.

Welcome Milde *Cæsar*, born of Heav'nly Race,
A Branch most Worthy of your Stock and Place,
The Splendour of Your Ancestors, whose Star 15
Long since out-shin'd the golden *Phœbus* far;
The living Image of our Martyr'd King,
For us His People freely suffering;
Sprung from the *Rose* and *Flower-de-luce* most fair,
The Spacious World ne're boasted such an Heir. 20
Ye Pious Pens, pluckt from a Seraphs Wing,
Of His high Fame, teach future Times to sing.
Ye lofty Muses of *Parnassus* Hill,
Auspicious be to my unlearned Quill,
Vouchsafing leave the Travels to recite 25
Of this Great Prince, long Banish'd from His Right;
Which Valiant He, did stoutly undertake
For his Religion, and His Countries sake.
After the murther of our CHARLEMAIN,
(Whose lasting Honour ne're shall know a Wane, 30
But to the Skies Tryumphantly ascend,
As His bright Soul did to *Elizium* tend,)
The Scots our CHARLES th'undoubted Heir recall,
And with His Grandsires Glory Him Install;
But after this *(O cruel Fates !)* betray'd 35
He was to th'English, who with a rage assay'd
Him to accost, throughout this British Isle;
   Could ever Rebels act a part so vile?
Hence, hence sad sorrows, and all past annoys,
Let nought approach You but tryumphant Joys; 40
And let us now remember with delight
Your strange escape from *Worc'sters* bloody fight,
Through Thundring Troops of armed foes, whose strife
Was to bereave You of Your sacred life.
Where many thousand *Brittains* spilt their blood, 45
Weltring in gore, for King and Countries good:
How oft have I Your cruel fates bewail'd ?
How oft to Heaven have our Devotions sail'd,

Through tides of briny tears, and blown with gales
Of mournful sighes, which daily fil'd the Sails?   50
That Heaven it's sacred Off-spring would defend,
And to their sorrows put a joyful end.
Propitious were the Heavens to our just Prayer:
You on their Wings the blessed Angels bare
Through thousand dangers, which by Land You past,   55
Till suddenly into the Sea being cast,
The Deities of *Pontus* flowing Stream,
Did unto You than men far milder seem.
Great *Æolus* himself hasts You to meet
Prostrates the winds before Your Sacred Feet;   60
Then with his power commands the fiercer Gales,
Into their Den, lest they disturb Your Sails:
Neptune straight calms the raging of the Sea,
Before Your Stern the pleasant *Dolphins* play;
The surly Waves appeas'd, most gladly bore,   65
The happy Vessel to the happier Shore.
Then wandring through inhospitable Lands,
Still seeking rest, the world amazed stands
To see Him banished from every part
Of its great Orb, Yet from His Faith not start;   70
Nor to regain His Fathers Rights would He,
From th'ancient Worship of His Fathers flee,
For every Kingdom He subdu'd by Charms
Of Love and Piety, more strong than Armes.
France with her hair dishevel'd, torn and sad,   75
With bloody Robes of civil War beclad,
With joy receives this Deity of peace
Who having caus'd those civil Wars to cease,
The barbarous Vine the *Royal Oak* refus'd,
To please the Tyrants, natures bands she loos'd;   80
But He unmov'd in faith their *Lillies* fled,
And to th'unstable Willows wandered.
Who most ungratefully did Him reject,
That them the rebel brambles might protect.
The *Royal Oak* by storms of leaves bereav'd,   85
The generous *Olive* to its soil receiv'd;
Streight follows peace, its Deity being come,
Aside they lay their Arms, Sword, Pike and Drum;
The other Trees all shivering as a Reed,
To make a League with th'*Royal Oak* agreed;   90
At length *Druina* ravished with love,
Humbly recalls Him to His native *Grove*,
In peace to tryumph, and to Reign a Lord
O're hearts subdu'd by Love, not by the Sword.
His Native Country faint and languishing,   95

Humbly implores the presence of her King:
Loe how the late revolted Sea obeys,
How gladly it the Billows prostrate lays
Before Your Royal Navy, proud to bring
Three widdow'd Kingdoms their espous'd King!   100
How do the winds contend, the spreading Sails
Of Your blest Ships, to fill with prosperous Gales;
The Fates are kind; Conduct You to the Shoar,
To welcome You the Thundring Canons roar;
Your ravisht Subjects over-joy'd do stand,   105
To see the stranger, *(PEACE)* with You to land,
With You to earth *Astræa* fair is come,
And Golden times in Iron ages room:
Much Honour hath both Church and State adorn'd,
Since You, our Faiths Defender, are return'd;   110
For of the Church the Honour and Renown,
Are unto Kings the strongest Towre and Crown:
    Behold how *Thames* doth smooth her silver Waves!
    How gladly she, Your gilded Bark receives;
    Mark how the courteous Stream her Arms doth spread,   115
    Proud to receive You to her watry Bed.
    The old *Metropolis* by Tyrants torn,
    Your presence doth with beauteous youth adorn.
    On You how doe the ravish't people gaze ?
    How do the thronging Troops all in a maze   120
    Shout loud for joy, their King to entertain,
    How do their Streets with Triumphs ring again.
Great CHARLS, Terrestrial God, Off-Spring of Heaven,
You we adore, to us poor mortals given,
That You *(Our Life)* may quicken us again,   125
Who by our Royal MARTYRS death were slain:
For we on earth as Corps inanimate lay,
Till You *(Our Breath)* repaired our decay:
Loe how old *Tellus* courts Your Sacred Feet,
Array'd with flowery Carpets peace to greet;   130
As *Phœbus* when with glorious Lamp he views,
Earth after Winter, tender grass renews;
So through the world Your radiant Vertues Shine,
Enlightening all to bring forth Fruits Divine:
Or as the drops distil'd by *April* showrs,   135
Produce from dryest earth imprison'd flowers;
So Your sad Fates sprinkled with holy eyes,
Plung'd in Your Kingly tears, have reacht the skies,
And from the appeased Deity brought down;
T'adorn Your Sacred Temples many a Crown.   140
The first of glory which shall ever last,
In Heaven of Heavens, when all the rest are past;

The Second shines with Virtues richly wrought
Upon Your Soul, with Graces wholy fraught.
The Third resplendent with your peoples Loves,   145
Their Hearts by joy being knit like Turtle-Doves.
The Fourth's compleat by Your high Charity,
Which hath subdu'd and pardon'd th'enemy.
The Fifth shall shine with Gold and Jewels bright,
Upon Your Head, *O Monarch* ! our Delight;   150
Where the Almighty grant it flourish may,
Until in Heaven You shine with Glorious Ray.
Who doth not stand amazed thus to see
The spotless Turtle Dove Espous'd to be
Unto a Bride whose Robes with blood are foul;   155
Loe Lovely CHARLES with Dove-like Galless Soul,
(Coming to th'Ark of His blood delug'd Land,
With peaceful Olive in His Sacred Hand)
Espoused is to *Albion* dy'd in gore;
And to her Princely Beauty doth restore;   160
Then celebrate the Espousals of our King,
With us let far and near all Nations Sing;
Let all the World shout loud perpetually,
    LET CHARLES LIVE LOV'D UNTO ETERNITY.
Rejoyce ye Forrests, your choice pleasures yeild,   165
The Royal Hunter Crowns the verdant field:
And Leap for joy ye Beasts of every Plain,
Behold Your King (the Lion) comes to Reign.
Let shady Woods and Groves together dance
To see the *Royal Oak* to them advance,   170
Whilst Nymphs resound, O thrice, thrice happy they!
Who have the Honour, their faint Limbs to lay
Under the shadow of th'Illustrious *Oak*
Expanded, to depell from Saints the Stroak
Of Tyrants tempests, and a Pillar (squar'd   175
By Crosses) for the Church of God prepar'd;
Where we may live to sing aloud His Praise,
With heart and voice, and Organs sweetest Lays,
Who hath our DAVIDS Prayer not withstood,
But made his Off-spring, CHARLES the *Great*, and *Good*;   180
And banishing all sorrow from His Seed,
Highly Enthron'd Him in His Fathers stead;
That He may shine a Splendid Star to damp
Throughout the world at noon bright *Phœbus* Lamp;
And trample down those Tyrants with His Might,   185
Who dare contemn His Universal Right;
At length Your rip'ned Years being Crown'd with Glory,
Justice and Peace, unparallel'd by story:
Cœlestial CHARLES Triumphantly Ascend

T'enjoy the Heavens in Bliss without all End.   190

GLORY TO GOD ALONE
THRICE BLESSED THREE IN ONE

NB: these poems are parallel, but the line numbers do not correspond: the first number
refers to the Latin text, the second to the English. Where a note refers to only one of the
two versions, * is used in place of the other number.   13/18 *Iride...Rosa/ Rose...*
Flower-de-luce: floral symbols of England and France. Charles II's mother was Henrietta
Maria, daughter of Henri IV   * 29–31 *CHARLEMAIN*: This title for Charles the Great
of France (742–814) was revived for Charles I by a number of Royalist poets. The
constellation Ursa Major had long been known in England as 'Charles's Wain' (i.e.
wagon): the same group of poets associated it with Charles I   25/42 *VIGORNÆ/
Worc'sters*: The Battle of Worcester, 3 September 1651, a decisive defeat for Charles and
his supporters as they attempted to put him back on the throne   35/59 *Æolus*: Greek
god of the winds 40/72 *pius ÆNEAS*: hero of Virgil's *Aeneid*. Aeneas rescued his paternal
gods from burning Troy: Charles II, Jevon suggests, refused to become Catholic as the
price of help from his mother's French relatives   50/75–6 *France...civil War*: the
Fronde (1658–52), two revolts against royal absolutism during the minority of Louis
XIV: the first began as a protest against war taxation by the *Parlement* of Paris; the second
began in 1651 with Mazarin's arrest of the arrogant and overbearing Condé   53/79
Ampelona/Vine: The allegorical scheme of this section derives from the popular satirical
romance by James Howell, *Dendrologia. Dodona's grove, or, the vocall forest*, first published
1640. In Howell's work, 'Vine' is the French king, 'Oke' signifies the King of England
REGALEM QUERCUM/ Royal Oak: Charles II was associated with oak-trees after he was
forced to hide in one after fleeing the battle of Worcester   52* *Horrendum Monstrum*:
recalling Virgil, *Aeneid* III.658   53/83 *Willows*: the Dutch (*agros Batavum aquosos*, the
soggy fields of the Batavians in the Latin text)   */84 *brambles*: the Parliamentarians.
This differs from Howell, who signified 'the great Turke' by 'bramble', but the meaning is
clear.   53/85 *JOVIS ARBOR*: the oak 55 *OLIVA/Olive*: 'King of Spaine, from the
abundance of Oyle and Olives which the Country yieldeth' (Howell) 58/91: *Druina*: the
nymph of the oak-tree: Charles, in keeping with his sexual reputation, seems to have
seduced her   112/151 *sine felle*: doves and pigeons have no gall-bladder   129/179
DAVID: Charles II succeeds Charles I just as David was succeeded by the more glorious
Solomon

KATHERINE PHILIPS (née FOWLER)
(1632–1664)

BORN on New Year's Day 1632, she was the daughter of John Fowler, a
prosperous London cloth merchant, and Katherine, the daughter of Dr Daniel
Oxenbridge and Katherine Harby, described by John Aubrey as an acquaintance
of 'Mr Francis Quarles, being much inclined to poetrie herselfe'. She was
related to the St John family of Wiltshire, and thus to at least two other
women poets, Lucy Hutchinson and Anne Wharton. In the last year of his
life, Dryden claimed a relationship with her: comparing the poetry of Elizabeth
Thomas with that of Orinda, he speaks of her as one 'to whom I had the Honour
to be related, and also to be known' (*Miscellanea*, i. 149). Her early education
was at home: she was taught to read by a cousin named Blackett, who claimed
that Philips had read the entire Bible by the time that she was 4. Her background and upbringing were solidly Presbyterian and the young Katherine used

to pray aloud for the destruction of the bishops. She was often taken to sermons, 'had an excellent memory and could have brought away a sermon in her memory'. At the age of 8, she was sent to Mrs Salmon's school in Hackney and there met Mary Aubrey, the 'Rosania' of her poems.

John Fowler died in 1642 and on his widow's remarriage in 1646 to Sir Richard Phillips of Picton Castle in Pembrokeshire, Katherine was taken to Wales. At 16 she was married to Colonel James Philips, a kinsman of her stepfather. Thirty-eight years her senior, Philips was an ambitious local politician, who strongly identified himself with the Cromwellian regime. Katherine succumbed to the cult of the royal martyr propagated by *Eikon Basilike*, Charles I's ghosted apologia, and the couple seem quietly to have agreed to differ in their politics. Throughout the Interregnum, Katherine lived quietly at her husband's house, the Priory in Cardigan, reading, writing, and bearing two children—a son, Hector, who died before he was a month old, and a daughter called Katherine—in April 1655 and April 1656. She seems to have begun circulating poetry by 1651, since Henry Vaughan took notice of her writing in that year. James Philips's public position perhaps gave Katherine some opportunities to visit and make friends in London. She also formed an intense platonic friendship with one of her neighbours, Anne Owen (Lucasia), who received her first poem from Katherine in July 1651. Her celebrated 'Society' was neither a *côterie* nor a salon: they were simply her friends—drawn from her neighbours in West Wales and the Cavalier literati at London—and the recipients, through the post, of her poems and unsolicited advice. She was a translator (of Horace and Corneille) as well as a lyric poet in her own right.

At the Restoration James Philips lost much property, his seat in Parliament and narrowly escaped prosecution as a regicide, but Katherine's loyal writings and contacts at court protected their fortunes. She acquired an influential friend at court in the person of Sir Charles Cotterell ('Poliarchus'), Master of Ceremonies to the King. Anne Owen married the distinguished Anglo-Irish Royalist, Marcus Trevor, of County Down, and in June 1662 Katherine accompanied her friend on the nuptial journey to her husband's house at Rostrevor. Katherine's reputation as a poet preceded her and she was enthusiastically received by Dublin society. The Earl of Orrery, having seen her translation of a single scene, 'earnestly importuned' her to execute a complete translation of Corneille's *La Mort de Pompée*. This was ready by November and produced at the Theatre Royal, Smock Alley, Dublin, in February 1663. She remained in Dublin, supervising the publication of *Pompey*, before taking ship for Milford Haven in mid-July and returning to her husband at Cardigan. In January 1664 a pirated edition of her poems went on sale at London: the publisher, Richard Marriot, was leant on by Katherine's friends and he claimed (probably disingenuously) to have withdrawn all copies from sale. She died of smallpox in June 1664 at the age of 32. She had finished nearly four acts of a translation of Corneille's *Horace*, which was completed by Sir John Denham and performed in London in 1668-9.

Her original poems and translations were edited by Charles Cotterell and published together three years after her death. During her lifetime, she was careful and fastidious about the circulation of her work, and did not seek publication, though she was happy to make her verse available to admirers such as Dryden and Cowley. Her 'virtue' (both her life, and her subject matter) caused contemporaries to consider her exemplary as a woman poet, and she was repeatedly compared to Behn to the latter's disadvantage. The real contrast, however, was a social rather than a moral one: both Philips's writing and her

attitude to it are profoundly influenced by her sense of her status as a gentlewoman, which was wholly different from Behn's position. She was interested in
popular verse and wrote out verses in inns, and mottoes in windows, in her
personal miscellany, which, unfortunately, does not survive. Also lost are 'the
excellent discourses she writ on several subjects' mentioned by Cotterell in his
1667 edition of her poems. The women poets who paid tribute to Philips's verse
include Aphra Behn, Ephelia, Anne Killigrew, and Anne Finch (all of whom are
represented in this anthology).

175   *Friendship in Emblem, or the*
           Seale, to my dearest Lucasia

I

The hearts thus intermixed speak
A Love that no bold shock can break
For Joyn'd and growing, both in one
Neither can be disturbd alone.

2

That meanes a mutuall knowledge too,   5
For what is't either a heart can doe,
Which by its panting centinell
It does not to the other tell?

3

That friendship hearts so much refines,
It nothing but it self design's   10
The hearts are free from lower ends,
For each point to the other tends,

4

They flame, 'tis true, and severall ways
But still those flames doe so much raise
That while to either they incline   15
They yet are noble, and divine.

5

From smoak or hurt those flames are free
From grosseness or mortallity
The hearts (like Moses bush presum'd):
Warm'd and enlighten'd not consum'd.   20

6

The compasses that stand above
Express this great imortall Love
For friends like them can prove this true,
They are, and yet they are not two.

7

And in their posture is express'd   25
Friendships exalted interest
Each follows where the other Lean's,
And what each doe's, the other meane's.

8

And as when one foot doe's stand fast,
And t'other circles seeks to cast,   30
The steady part doe's regulate
And make the wanderer's motion streight

9

So friends are onely *Two* in this,
T'reclaime each other when they misse
For whose're will grossely fall,   35
Can never be a friend at all.

10

And as that usefull instrument
For even lines was ever meant
So friendship from good–angells spring's
To teach the world heroique things.   40

11

As these are found out in design
To rule and measure every line
So friendship govern's actions best,
Prescribing Law to all the rest.

12

And as in nature nothing's set   45
So Just, as lines, and numbers mett
So compasses for these being made
Doe friendship's harmony perswade.

13

And like to them, so friends may own
Extension, not division.   50
Their points like bodys separate;
But head like soules know's no such fate.

14

And as each part so well is knitt
That their embraces ever fitt,
So friends are such by destiny,   55
And no Third can the place supply.

15

There needs no motto to the Seale
But that we may the Mine reveale
To the dull ey, it was thought fit
That friendship, onely should be writt.   60

16

But as there is degrees of bliss
So there's no friendship meant by this,
But such as will transmit to fame
Lucasia's and *Orinda's* name.

19 *Moses bush*: Exodus 3: 2   21–32 Compare John Donne, 'A Valediction, forbidding mourning'

176   *On the Welch Language*

If honour to an ancient name be due,
Or Riches challenge it, for one that's new,
The Brittish Language claim's in either Sence,
Both for its Age, and for its Opulence.
But all great things must be from us remov'd,   5
To be with higher Reverence belov'd.
So Lantskips, which in prospects distant ly,
With greater wonder, draw the pleased Ey.
Is not great Troy to one dark ruine hurl'd?
Once the fam'd Scene of all the fighting World.   10
Where's *Athens* now, to whom *Rome* learning ow's,
And the safe Lawrell's that Adorn'd her brow's?
A strange reverse of Fate, she did endure,
Never once greater, then she's now obscure.
Ev'n Rome her self, can but some footstepps shew   15
Of Scipio's times, or those of Cicero.
And as the Roman, and the Grecian State,
The Brittish fell, the spoyle of Time and Fate.
But though the Language hath her beauty Lost,
Yet she has still some great remains to boast;   20
For 'twas in that, the sacred Bards of Old,
In deathless numbers did their thoughts unfold.
In groves, by Rivers and on fertil plaines,
They civilised, and taught the Listening Swain's:
Whilst with high Raptures, and as great success,   25
Virtue they cloath'd in musicks charming dress.
This Merlin spoke, who in his gloomy Cave,
Ev'n Destiny herself seem'd to enslave.
For to his Sight, the future time was known,

Much better then to other is their own.   30
And with such state, Predictions from him fell,
As if he did Decree, and not foretell.
This spoke King *Arthur*; who, if fame be true,
Could have compell'd mankind to speak it too.
In this, once, *Boadicia* valour taught,   35
And spoke more nobly, then her soldiers fought.
Tell me what Hero could do more then she,
Who fell at once for Fame, and Liberty?
Nor could a greater sacrifice belong,
Or to her children's, or her Countrey's wrong.   40
This spoke *Caraticus*, who was so brave,
That to the Roman fortune, check he gave;
And when their yoak he could decline no more,
He it so decently and nobly wore,
That *Rome* her self with blushes did beleive   45
A Brittan would the Law of Honour give.
And hastily, his chains away she threw,
Least her own Captive else, should her subdue.

9 *Troy*: the destruction of Troy is the story of Homer's *Iliad*   11 *Athens*: its independence was destroyed by Alexander the Great in the fourth century BC, and it steadily
declined thereafter   16 *Scipio . . . Cicero*: Scipio Africanus and the orator Cicero, famous
names of the Roman republic   21 *Bards*: generic name for Celtic poets   27 *Merlin*: the
magician of Arthurian legend: in Welsh-language sources, there was a strong tradition of
his prophetic gifts   34 *compell'd*: according to Geoffrey of Monmouth's (fictional) *History of the Kings of Britain* (*c*.1140), King Arthur conquered most of Europe   35–6
Boadicia: Queen of the Iceni: her 'words' are those given her by Tacitus. Her forces
conducted terrible reprisals against the Roman civilian population   40 *children's*: her
daughters were raped by Roman soldiers to humiliate her   41 *Caraticus*: again, his words
are put in his mouth by Tacitus   48 *Captive*: with reference to the tag, 'captured Greece
makes her captors captive' (Horace, *Epistolae* II.i. 156)

177   *Lucasia, Rosania, and Orinda*
             parting at a Fountain, July 1663

                            1

        Here here are our enjoyments done,
           And since the Love and grief we weare,
           Forbids us either word, or teare,
        And Art wants here expression,
        See Nature furnish us with one.   5

                            2

        The kind and mournfull Nimph which here
           Inhabits, in her humble Cells,
           No longer her own Sorrow tells.

Nor for it now concern'd appears,
But for our parting, sheds these tears.   10

3

Unless she may afflicted be,
  Least we should doubt her Innocence;
  Since she hath lost her best pretence
Unto a matchless purity,
Our Love being clearer far then she.   15

4

Cold as the streams which from her flow,
  Or if her privater recess,
  A greater coldness can express,
Then cold as those dark beds of snow,
Our hearts are at this parting blow.   20

5

But Time, that has both wings and feet,
  Our suffering Minutes being Spent,
  Will visit us with new content.
And sure, if kindness be so sweet,
  'Tis harder to forget, then meet.   25

6

Then though the sad Adieu we say,
  Yet as the wine we hither bring,
  Revives, and then exalts the Spring,
So let our hopes to meet, allay,
The fears and Sorrows of this day.   30

6 The poem draws on the Classical trope that any water-source will have its own minor
deity ('nymph' or 'genius')

178   *On the 3 September 1651*

As when the Glorious Magazine of Light
Approaches to his Cannopy of night
He with new splendour cloth's his dying rays
And double brightness to his beams conveys.
As if to brave and check his ending fate   5
Put's on his highest looks in's lowest State,
Drest in such Terrour as to make us all
Be Anti-persians, and adore his fall.
Then quits the world, depriving it of day,
While every herb and Plant does droop away   10
So when our Gasping English Royalty

Perceiv'd her period now was drawing nigh,
She summons her whole strength to give one blow,
To raise her self, or pull down others too.
Big with revenge and hope, she now spake more   15
Of Terrour than in many mon'ths before
And muster's her attendants or to save
Her from, or wait upon her to the Grave.
Yet but enjoy'd the miserable fate
Of setting Majesty, to dy in State.   20
    Unhappy Kings! Who cannot keep a throne
Nor be so fortunate to fall alone!
Their weight sink's others; Pompey could not fly
But half the world must beare him company
Thus Captive Sampson could not life conclude   25
Unless attended with a multitude.
Who'd trust to Greatness now, whose food is ayre,
Whose ruine sudden, and whose end despaire?
Who would presume upon his Glorious Birth?
Or quarrell for a spacious share of earth   30
That sees such diadems become thus cheap,
And Heroes tumble in the common heap?
    O! Give me vertue then, which summ's up all,
And firmely stands when Crowns and Scepters fall.

Title *3 September 1651*: date of the Battle of Worcester   1 *Magazine*: the sun, concep-
tualized as an arsenal   8 *Anti-persians*: the (Zoroastrian) Persians adored the rising
sun   23 *Pompey*: Pompey the Great, a Roman general, began the Civil War with Julius
Caesar in 49 BC, and was decisively defeated at Pharsalus in 48 BC   25 *Sampson*: pulled
down the pillars of the temple of Gaza on himself and everyone else inside it: Judges 16: 30

179   *To Antenor*
    On a Paper of mine; which an unworthy
    Adversarey of his threatned to publish,
    to pregiudice him, in Cromwels time.

Must then my folly's, be thy scandall too?
Why sure the Devill hath not much to doe.
My Love, and life, I must confess, are thine,
But not my erroures, they are only mine.
And if my faults should be for thine allow'd,   5

It will be hard to dissipate the cloud.
But Eves rebellion did not Adam blast,
Untill himself forbidden fruit did tast.
But if those lines, a punishment could call
Lasting, and great, as this dark-Lantherns gall,   10

Alone, I'de court the torments, with content,

To testify, that thou art Innocent.
So if my Ink, through malice prov'd a stain,
My bloud should justly wash it off again.
But, since that Mint of Slander, could invent   15
To make that triviall Rime his instrument,

Verse should reveng the quarrell, but he's worse
Then wishes, and below a Poet's curse.
And more then this, wit know's not how to give,
Let him be still himself, and let him live.   20

8 *tast*: Genesis 3: 17

'A LADY' (KATHERINE PHILIPS?)

THIS long poem is something of a curiosity. It appears to be a reworking of a
piece of Katherine Philips's juvenilia, since it is based on one of a pair of poems
'Humbly Dedicated to Mrs Anne Barlow C Fowler' which must predate
Katherine Philips's marriage in 1648, and which were therefore presumably
written when she was 15 or 16. The poem was written to Anne Barlow of
Slebech, eldest daughter of John Barlow, and there is no evidence that it had any
circulation beyond its original recipient: the most likely candidate for this piece
of literary recycling is therefore Katherine Philips herself. It is also possible that
Katherine Fowler, as she then was, copied a piece of commonplace poetry for
her friend, but this seems less likely. Only three lines of the sixteen-line pre-
1648 version are not reused in the longer text. The theme of women's capacity
for self-deception is found only in the long version, which also ponders on the
qualities which make a good husband.

180   *Advice to Virgins*

Madam,
            I cannot but congratulate
The happy Omen of your last Nights fate;
For those that wou'd live undisturb'd and free
Must never put on Hymens Livery.
Perhaps the Outside seems to promise fair   5
but the Liveing only Greive and anxious Care.
But once you let that Gordion Knot be ty'd
That turns the name of Virgin into Bride,
Your life's best Scene, in that fond Act forego
And run into a Labyrinth of Wo: 10
Whose Strange Meanders you may search about,

But never find the Clue to lead you out.
The Married Life affords but little ease,
The best of Husbands are so hard to please.
This in Wive's careful Faces you may Spell,   15
Tho they dissemble their Misfortunes well,
If ought can make the Ills of Marriage less,
Certainly 'tis a husbands Worthiness.
For he must needs prove a tormenting Prize,
Who is not truly virtuous, kind and wise.   20
Obedience do's a grating Duty prove,
If Husband's cannot teach as well as Love.
A Womans humor hardly can submit
To be a Slave to one she do's Outwit.
In Fine, no Plague so great as an ill Head,   25
Yet 'tis a Fate, that few young Ladyes dread.
For Loves insinuating Fire they fan
With the Idea of a God like Man:
And tho one love a Fiend, yet Love is blind
She thinks him like the Image in her Mind;   30
But Marriage do's these cheating thoughts remove,
And let's us see the falsity of love.
Chloris and Phillis gloryed in their Swains,
And sung their Praises to the Neighb'ring Plains
O! they were brave accomplished Saintlike Men!   35
Nay Gods 'till Marry'd, but proved Divels then.
Yet there are some brave Worthy men 'tis true
But they are hard to find, they are so few,
And shaded so in the Dissembling Croud,
That they are like Aeneas in a Cloud.   40
Sure, some resistless power attends on Love,
Else more would Venus and Diana's prove.
A Maiden Life affords the best Content,
'Tis always happy as 'tis innocent.
Clear as Olympias bright and full of ease,   45
And calm as Neptune in the Halcyon days
There are no sleeps broke with domestic cares,
No crying Children to distract our Pray'rs
No pangs of Child birth to extort our Tears,
No blust'ring Husbands create new Fears,   50
No rude upbraiding, that Defect or this,
No great Concern, whoever keeps a Miss.
No sighing, nor Affrightment at the Glass,
When it presents us with a Ruin'd Face;
But such an Object makes a Wife to Start,   55
And almost tempts her to adulterate Art.
Knowing a Husbands Love doth of't decay
As Youth and Beauty Fades and wares away.

And therefore Madam, be advis'd by me,
Turn, turn apostate to Loves Deity   60
Suppress wild Nature, if she dares Rebel,
There's no such Thing, as leading Apes in Hell.

4 *Hymens Livery*: wedding clothes   7 *Gordion Knot*: Gordius, father of Midas, had a
wagon in which the yoke for the oxen was fastened to the pole with a knot so complex that
the story arose that whoever could untie it would gain the empire of Asia. Alexander the
Great visited it in its temple before setting off on his Asian campaign, and cut the knot in
half with his sword   9 *fond*: foolish   40 *Aeneas in a Cloud*: *Aeneid* 1.412–13 '[Venus
enveloped] them by a divine power with a mantle of dense cloud, so that no one might
notice or touch them'   45 *Olympias*: Mt Olympus, tranquil home of the gods 46 *calm*:
the 'Halcyon days', when the kingfishers were believed to breed, were days of dead calm at
sea   52 *Miss*: mistress, kept woman   56 *adulterate Art*: make-up   58 *wares*:
wears   60 *turn apostate*: reject (a god)   62 *leading Apes*: there was a legend that lifelong
spinsters were thus punished

'ELIZA'
(fl. 1652)

THE author of the spiritual biography titled *Eliza's Babes: or The Virgins-
Offering* describes herself on her title page as 'a Lady'. The book does not
contain enough personal information to allow one to break through her anonymity, though her claims to be a lady are supported: some of her female friends
are wealthy enough to be fashionable, she has a friend at court. One of her most
intriguing poems is 'To the Queen of Bohemiah', whom, she says, she always
wanted to see, and finally did so, though this came about through 'thraldome'
and 'trouble'. Elizabeth Stuart left England in 1613, and did not return until
1661: so if 'Eliza' saw her, she must have visited The Hague. The Hague was a
great centre for Royalist exiles, and 'Eliza''s poem 'To Generall Cromwell'
implies that she suffered at the hands of the Parliament, but also that her
sympathies were on the whole Parliamentarian.

Eliza's Babes is dedicated to 'my Sisters', and individual poems are addressed to
sisters 'S.G.' and 'S.S.': these do not have to be sisters in the flesh, of course, but
may be people with whom she is religiously affiliated. Her poems also tell us that
she once also had a brother, who became ill and died, and that 'Mr. C.' was her
spiritual adviser. Though she takes a dim view of earthly marriage in a number of
poems, she appears, on the evidence of several poems included here, to have been
married herself. A sequence of poems chart her changing feelings: her decision to
marry, her lack of enthusiasm for bearing children and preference for writing
poetry, her ambivalent feelings about balancing her love for God with her love of
her husband, and finally, her deep and committed love for this unnamed man.

181   *To my Husband.*

When from the world, I shall be tane,
And from earths necessary paine.

Then let no blacks be worne for me,
Not in a Ring my dear by thee.
But this bright Diamond, let it be   5
Worn in rememberance of me.
And when it sparkles in your eye,
Think 'tis my shadow passeth by.
For why, more bright you shall me see,
Than that or any Gem can bee.   10
Dress not the house with sable weed,
As if there were some dismall deed
Acted to be when I am gone,
There is no cause for me to mourn.
And let no badge of Herald be   15
The signe of my Antiquity.
It was my glory I did spring
From heavens eternall powerfull King:
To his bright Palace heir am I.
It is his promise, hee'l not lye.   20
By my dear Brother pray lay me,
It was a promise made by thee.
And now I must bid thee adieu,
For I'me a parting now from you.

3 *blacks*: immediate relatives of a dead person dressed in black for at least a year   4 *Ring*: 'mourning rings' were a contemporary fashion: usually black enamel and gold, sometimes with the deceased's hair, or with a miniature portrait   11 *Dress*: upper-class mourning rituals involved hanging the house with black cloth   15 *badge of Herald*: armorial bearings: displaying the armorials of the deceased was also mourning practice

182   *To Generall Cromwell.*

The Sword of God doth ever well
I'th hand of vertue! O Cromwel,
But why doe I, complain of thee?
'Cause thou'rt the rod that scourgeth mee?
But if a good child I will bee,   5
I'le kiss the Rod, and honour thee;
And if thou'rt vertuous as 'tis sed,
Thou'lt have the glory when thou'rt dead.

Sith Kings and Princes scourged be,
Whip thou the Lawyer from his fee   10
That is so great, when nought they doe,
And we are put off from our due.
But they for their excuse do say,
'Tis from the Law is our delay.

By Tyrants heads those laws were made,   15
As by the learned it is said.
If then from Tyrants you'l us free,
Free us from their Laws Tyranny.
If not! wee'l say the head is pale,
But still the sting lives in the tail.   20

(after 1649)

19 *head*: probably a reference to the execution of Charles I in 1649

AN COLLINS
(fl. 1653)

A SINGLE copy of An Collins's *Divine Songs and Meditacions* survives, now in
the Huntington Library, and is our sole source for the life of its author. The fact
that much of her poetry is religious meditation means that we know much more
of her state of mind than of the facts of her life. She was a Puritan of some kind,
and certainly no Anglican (this is clear from her long poem 'The Discourse'),
but it is not otherwise obvious to what sect or church she belonged. Her poetry
occupies the middle ground of Puritanism and she does not engage in theological
controversy or polemic. The poem printed here might at first sight be thought to
suggest that she was a Laudian Anglican and a Royalist, but the sentiments here
expressed are not peculiar to Anglicans. Parliamentary government's attempt to
enforce obedience with oaths (l. 43) was also resented and resisted by radical
sectarians such as Quakers, while 'Confiscacion' (l. 46), though associated
particularly with Parliamentarian sequestration of Royalist estates, may also
refer to the compulsory payment of tithes to the established church, which
radicals strongly objected to. The use of the term 'Freinds' in this poem may,
when taken together with the strong objection here expressed to oaths, suggest
that she was actually a Quaker.

   She was unmarried, probably of 'the middling sort' and a chronic invalid from
her childhood. The prefatory poem to her collection speaks of 'being through
weakness to the house confin'd;' her address to the reader, that 'I have been
restrained from bodily employments, suting with my disposicion, which
enforced me to a retired Course of life.' It also sketches her melancholy,
religious, and intellectual temperament: 'Wherein it pleased God to give me
such inlargednesse of mind, and activity of spirit, that this seeming desolate
condicion, proved to me most delightfull: To be breif, I became affected to
Poetry, insomuch that I proceeded to practise the same.' In 'The Discourse' she
states that her family was (at least by her own standards in later life) worldly and
frivolous, so that in her youth, she had access to fiction, which she greatly
enjoyed. At some point, she experienced a personal religious conversion, and
rejected these 'prophane Histories' in favour of prayer and meditation. It is clear
that she was a diligent reader of the Bible, and probably of contemporary
Christian writings.

183 *A Song composed in time of the Civill Warr, when the wicked did much insult over the godly*

With *Sibells* I cannot Devine
  Of future things to treat,
Nor with *Parnassus* Virgins Nine
  Compose in Poëms neat
Such mentall mocions which are free   5
  Concepcions of the mind,
Which notwithstanding will not be
  To thoughts alone confind.

With *Deborah* twere joy to sing
  When that the Land hath Rest,   10
And when that Truth shall freshly spring,
  Which seemeth now deceast,
But some may waiting for the same
  Go on in expectacion
Till quick conceipt be out of frame,   15
  Or till Lifes expiracion.

Therefore who can, and will not speak
  Betimes in Truths defence,
Seeing her Foes their malice wreak,
  And some with smooth pretence   20
And colours which although they glose
  Yet being not ingraind,
In time they shall their luster lose
  As cloth most foully staind.

See how the Foes of Truth devise   25
  Her followers to defame.
First by Aspersions false and Lies
  To kill them in good Name;
Yet here they will in no wise cease
  But Sathans course they take   30
To spoyl their Goods and Wealths increase
  And so at Life they make.

Such with the Devill further go
  The Soule to circumvent
In that they seeds of Error sow   35
  And to false Worships tempt,
And Scriptures falsly they apply
  Their Errors to maintain,
Opposing Truth implicitly
  The greater side to gain.   40

And to bind Soul and Body both
   To Sathans service sure
Therto they many ty by Oath
   Or cause them to endure
The Losse of lightsom Liberty   45
   And suffer Confiscacion,
A multitude they force therby
   To hazard their Salvacion.

Another sort of Enimies
   To Lady Verity,   50
Are such who no Religion prise,
   But Carnall Liberty
Is that for which they do contest
   And venture Life and State,
Spurning at all good meanes exprest,   55
   The force of Vice to bate.

Yet these are they, as some conceit,
   Who must again reduce,
And all things set in order strait
   Disjoyted by abuse,   60
And wakeing witts may think no lesse
   If Fiends and Furies fell,
May be suppos'd to have successe
   Disorders to expell.

How-ever Truth to fade appeare,   65
   Yet can shee never fall,
Her Freinds have no abiding here,
   And may seem wasted all;
Yet shall a holy Seed remain
   The Truth to vindicate,   70
Who will the wrongeds Right regain
   And Order elevate.

What time Promocion, Wealth, and Peace,
   The Owners shall enjoy,
Whose Light shall as the Sun encrease   75
   Unto the perfect Day
Then shall the Earth with blessings flow,
   And Knowledg shall abound.
The *Cause* that's now derided so
   Shall then most just be found.   80

Prophanesse must be fully grown,
   And such as it defend
Must be ruind or over thrown,
   And to their place desend,

The Sonns of strife their force must cease, 85
Having fulfild their crime,
And then the Son of wished peace
Our Horizon will clime.

That there are such auspicious dayes
To come, we may not doubt, 90
Because the Gospels splendant rayes
Must shine the World throughout:
By Jewes the Faith shall be embrac't
The Man of Sin must fall,
New Babell shall be quite defac't 95
With her devices all.

Then Truth will spread and high appeare,
As grain when weeds are gon,
Which may the Saints afflicted cheare
Oft thinking hereupon; 100
Sith they have union with that sort
To whom all good is ty'd
They can in no wise want support
Though most severely try'd.

1 *Sibells*: the Sibyls, pagan prophetesses, were thought to have a true gift of foretelling, and to have prophesied the birth of Christ   3 *Virgins nine*: the Muses   9 *Deborah*: Judges 5   22 *ingraind*: dyed before weaving   50 *Lady Verity*: Truth   91 *splendant*: resplendent   91–6 All these events are part of the expected programme of the Last Days: see the end of Anne Bradstreet, 'A Dialogue between Old England and New' (no. 129)

FRANCELLINA STAPLETON
(fl. 1655)

FRANCELLINA STAPLETON is known from some verses in the poetic miscellany of John Newdigate (compiled 1653/5), a member of a notably intellectual Warwickshire family. She would appear to have been, as her verses imply, a witty friend: Newdigate married young, in 1621. The Stapletons were a neighbouring family, and a number of male Stapletons are mentioned in Newdigate correspondence. Her poem draws on the iconography of friendship in Cesare Ripa's *Iconologia* (first published 1593). Amicita is a young woman: among other attributes, she bears on her heart a motto stating 'longe et prope' (far and near), to which she points, with 'mors et vita' (life and death) written on the hem of her skirt. 'Heat and cold' are not a feature of Ripa's image, however, so she seems to have, or to have created, a variant.

184   *Upon a joynted Ring*

The *Romans* once indeavoured all they could
Of *Freindship* to erect one perfect mould
At last in youthfull shape they fram'd it young
Cause *Freindship* should be permanent, live long:
Whose every Motto orderly I'le cite,   5
On whose pure brest they *Heat* and *Cold* did write
And being expansed with it's finger pointed
Unto the *Hart* where *Farr* and neare were joynted
And on the skirts in spight of *Circe*'s charms
Both Life and death. And these are *Freindships Arms*.   10
Even so am I: for nether *Fortunes* froun
Nor smile can reap the *Freindship* I have sown
Nor can *Oblivion* seize, though farr asunder
Nor nigh at hand though *Jove* should threat and thunder
Nor hope of *Life*, nor feare of *Death* dismay me   15
My freindship shall stand firme though fate betray me
For as this pure white spotles paper (ere
Besmer'd with inck) so, is my love most cleare
But yet suspition may arise from love
Whoe seeming jealous causeless feare may move   20
Yet will I chuse to die with *Dion* rather
Then from my freinds the least distrust to gather
And bind my selfe in *Scipios* freindly band
Philonida: shake freindship by the hand
Apollo call'd that amitye divine   25
Which cannot be seduced: even so is mine
Not *Pylades* for his *Orestes* sake
Endur'd more parries then for my freind I'le take
Then from a *Freind* accept this Emblem Ring
Resembling me more true than any thing   30
For when it seemes to break it is the surest
So where you thinke I faile there am I purest.

1–10 Based (with slight variations) on Cesare Ripa, *Iconologia* (1593 and subsequent
editions), s.v. 'amicitia'   21 *Dion*: Dion, ruler of Syracuse; he was murdered in a room
with many of his friends but they left him to his fate to save their own skins (Plutarch, *Life
of Dion*, ch. 57)   23 *Scipio*: Scipio Africanus (*c*.185–129 BC), destroyer of Carthage and
Numantia; Cicero's *De amicitia* dwells on the friendship of Scipio and Gaius Laelius   27
Pylades . . . Orestes: famously loyal friends of Greek legend

ELIZABETH WITH
(fl. 1659)

THIS extraordinary pamphlet, surviving only in the Thomason collection of
ephemeral literature, appears to represent Mrs Elizabeth With's explanation of
the break-up of her marriage, presumably in answer to critics. While many
women of her generation pamphleteered in support of religious or political
positions, this is a unique survival of a woman's personal polemic (though
probably not the only one to be written). Small-scale, unbound pamphlet
printing of texts of only a few pages was inexpensive, and could be entered on
by very modestly situated people, as we can see from the evident poverty of
some nonconformist pamphleteers. It is just a possibility that she was the
relative that Anna Trapnel went to live with in 1647, the Mrs Wythe who
dwelt on Fenchurch Street.

185   *How* Elizabeth Foole *and her husband*
       parted by means of her Sister in Law

I lived with my old man full nigh ten year,
    But at last (upon condition) I parted from my dear.
He and his sister (yearly) were content
    To allow me forty shillings to pay my rent
I had but six pence in my purse   5
    Which was to buy me bread:
And then I went to be a nurse
    My body for to feed.
Unto a poor woman nurse was I,
    As you may understand: 10
And always at her work was nigh
    And ready at command.
Then did I go to house-keeping
    Which is the best of all:
Three weeks I lay upon a mat   15
    Turn'd up against a wall.
His Sister lent me her flock bed,
    My patience for to prove
But I return'd it her again,
    To choak her with her love.   20
Sometimes I did get sowing work,
    And sometimes I got none:
Had not my son Thomas supply'd my wants
    Full hungry had I gone.

Now when a whole year was almost spent   25
I askt my money to pay my rent:
But he said one penny he would not give

For to maintain me whil'st I do live.
Yet here is a bone for the old man to knaw.
If he will it not me give, ile have it by Law.   30

All you that be disposed
    To abuse me with your tongue,
I pray first consider
    Whether I have done the wrong;
And look home to your own hearts,   35
    And there perhaps you may see
Your minds incline to wandring thoughts
    As much as others be.

---

17 *flock bed*: comfortable futon-type mattress made of woollen wadding   18 *prove*: test   20 *To*: Nor, printed text   21 *sowing*: sewing   30 *Law*: even an estranged wife was entitled to maintenance: Elizabeth Cary, Lady Falkland was granted an order of maintenance of five hundred pounds a year by the Privy Council, despite her open defiance of her husband

ELIZABETH, VISCOUNTESS
MORDAUNT (née CARY)
(d. 1678)

ELIZABETH was the daughter of Thomas Cary, second son of Robert Earl of Monmouth, and she married Henry Mordaunt, later the second Earl of Peterborough. He was a central figure in the futile Royalist intrigues and uprisings of 1658–9, and Clarendon describes his wife as 'a young, beautiful lady of a very loyal spirit and notable vivacity of wit and humour, who concurred with him in all honourable dedication of himself'. Lady Mordaunt kept her diary, which contains occasional verses, from 1656 to 1678, the year of her death. A poem giving thanks for the birth of her son Louis in staunchly Royalist Oxford in 1665, suggests her political affiliations. Louis was one of seven sons and four daughters born to her. After the Restoration, the Mordaunts had a house at Parsons Green, in the London borough of Fulham, which, as she records in this poem, survived the Great Fire of London. Her husband was to die there in June 1675. She was an intimate friend of Margaret Godolphin, and Mary, wife of John Evelyn: quite a few letters to her from Mrs Evelyn survive in the latter's letter-books, preserved as part of the Evelyn collection in the British Library. A famous beauty, her portrait was painted in 1665 by Louise, Princess Palatine, the second daughter of Elizabeth of Bohemia.

186   *Sepr. ye 6th 1666 Thursday A thanks*
       geving for the stoping of the Fire in London

It is to thee, my Derest Lord, that I
For help, and safety, in distress dowe crye,
To thee this fitt, I should all prays retorne,

That when the Sety greate in flames did borne,
My husband, childerne, selfe, and all that's mine   5
Was safely guarded by thy powre devine,
Thy powre I saw, in that devouring fire,
Admired thy Justis, and yet dared desire
That thou wouds't thy destroying Angel bede
To stop, and heare unworthy Mortals plede   10
For mercy, which so often had I felte,
The thoughts of it my soule in teares did melt,
And gave me corag constantely to pray
Tell at the last, thou herd'st, and bede'st him stay,
Saing it is enuff, I will nowe trye   15
Once more whether they'l chuse to live or dye;
O lete us never such a blesing louse,
Refusing mercy, and distroction chuse,
Let the remembrance of thy powr and Love
Rays all our thoughts and prasis high above,   20
That by the strictness of our Lives, we may
Shoe our resentment of the Love, and say
'Tis from thy hands we did this mercy tacke,
O Let us never thy Just Laws forsack;
That ending our Life heare, we may be blest,   25
In Abraham's bosom, with eternall rest.

4 *Sety*: city   9 *destroying Angel*: cf. Exodus 12: 23   17 *louse*: lose

MARTHA, LADY GIFFARD (née TEMPLE)
(1638–1722)

MARTHA, LADY GIFFARD was the daughter of Sir John Temple, Master of
the Rolls, and Mary Hammond, the brother of Henry Hammond, the High
Church rector of Penshurst. She belonged to a circle of educated and cultivated
country nobility and gentry. She lived with her brother from the time she was 12
(when he returned from France). He was Sir William Temple, and they were
extremely fond of one another, fortunately, since her married life consisted of a
tragically brief few days, after which she returned to her brother's house, and
spent the rest of her life with him and his wife Dorothy Osborne, author of a
famous series of letters. Her husband was Sir Thomas Giffard of Castle Jordan,
Co. Meath: they married at Dublin on 21 April 1661, and thirteen days later he
died of some sudden and mysterious disease: this tragedy was romanticized into
the legend that she was 'maid, wife, and widow in one day'. The Temples' life
was peripatetic, moving between households at Sheen, The Hague, and Moor
Park (once the home of Lucy, Countess of Bedford), and their circle was literary:
Katherine Philips, for example, was a friend of Lady Dorothy Temple's, and
wrote to her about the rival translation of Corneille's *Pompey*.

'Of Sleep' is preserved in Lady Giffard's own hand: the repeated punning on
'Temple' (her maiden name) helps support the view that she actually wrote it.

The translation from Horace is, according to Moore Smith, also in her hand. The manuscript from which he took it appears to have been lost: he describes it simply as taken from 'a Yelverton manuscript', but though quite a number of Yelverton manuscripts have found a safe haven in the British Library, a number attested in earlier documents have vanished without trace, including this one. Her other writings included a verse translation of Montemayor's Spanish romance, *Diana*. She died on New Year's Eve 1722 and was buried at Westminster Abbey five days later. In her will (P.C.C. 11/589, sig. 7) she asks to be buried at night: nocturnal funerals were a fashion of the social élite at this time; Katherine Dyer makes the same request in her will. The material possessions mentioned by Lady Martha's will illustrate the kind of exotic luxury goods that were becoming available to the upper classes at the end of the century. They include agate cups and saucers, cups for drinking hot chocolate, an Indian teapot covered with gold, an ebony cabinet, a gold tooth-pick, and '2 Spanish heads' (portraits). She also owned a large number of French and Spanish books.

187   *To Mother Luddwels cave and spring*

13th Ode of ye 3^d Book of Horace

Oh limpid spring! that dost surpass
The clearness of the purest glass
For thee to morrow I will twine
A chaplet with a Boule of wine
To thee a kid Ile sacrifice   5
Whose budding Horns begin to rise

And arm'd for youths adventrous feats
On love and war he Meditates
In vain: for to your Honnour slain
This frisking offspring soon shall stain   10
The streams with his lascivious blood
And turne them to a common flood

The Dogstar in the sultry days
Can't pierce thee with his Noxious rays
From whose malignant scorching heat   15
The wandring flocks to thee retreat.
And oxen panting from the Plough
For thy refreshing coolness low.

If I can give this fountain fame
It shall not want a Noble name   20
Nor will I fail the rock to sing
From whence thy murmuring waters spring
And the tall oaks that bending grow
And overshade its mossy Brow.

4 *Boule*: bowl

188　　*Of Sleep*

Come sleep, thou ease of sickness, want, and care,
Thou only comforter of black despair,
Where even Religion fails, thou great support,
Whom swains enjoy, while princes vainly court.
Come God of slumbers, whither art thou fled　　　　　　5
Tis late, and I have often smooth'd my Bed,
And beat my Doune, and turned and turn'd again
And stretch'd my armes to find thee, but in vain.
Thy soft embraces shall I ne'ere enjoy
Has Meleimda taught thee to be coy?　　　　　　　　10
　　Come Bath my Temple's with thy Heavenly Balme,
My Feaver slacken, and my thoughtes becalme,
Oh how I long to loos the wretched Day
In sweet repose, and dream this World away,
This fruitless World, whose very gain is loss,　　　　　15
Where even success, can our vain wishes cross:
Oh empty Scene, what man has cause to Boast,
When his fruition disapoints us most.
　　Daughter of Innocence, All healing rest,
How shall I tempt thee to this troubled Breast,　　　　20
Oh come and bring theese aching Temples ease
And this disquiet of my soul apease.

7 *Doune*: down pillow　　10 *Meleimda*: reference obscure　　21 *Temples*: with reference to
her headache, but also to her maiden name

ANNE GREENWELL (née DOWNER, later WHITEHEAD)
(1630s–1680)

ANNE WHITEHEAD, celebrated by a group of Quaker men and women in *Piety
Promoted...*, was born Anne Downer, the daughter of a clergyman of the
Church of England, brought up at Charlbury in Oxfordshire, an unusually
middle-class background for an early Quaker. Her education included shorthand
and arithmetic, and after her mother's death, she brought up and educated her
younger sister. Her life was changed by a visit to London in her twenties, when
she became a convinced Quaker, perhaps the first woman in London to join the
movement. She returned to Charlbury, and held services in the town, which
resulted in complete alienation from her family: she then returned to London.
She is known to have interrupted a 'priest' in a church in Stepney during his
service, which resulted in her being committed to the House of Correction, and
detained for ten weeks. Because she refused to work, she was beaten with a
rope's end. In 1654, she entered on a public career, and became the first woman
preacher in London. In 1656, she walked more than a hundred miles to visit

George Fox in prison, where she acted as his secretary and prepared his meals, and prophesied in the neighbourhood.

She was a central member of the London Quaker women's committee from the 1650s. Before 1669, she carried the responsibility for administering the considerable amount of money disbursed for various charitable ends. She kept no regular accounts, and was responsible only to a small circle of personal friends who transacted their church business in their own houses by turns. She jotted down some notes of large transactions in her memorandum book, between 1669 and 1677 (Now Ledger No. 1, in the library of Friends' House, London). The London Women's Meeting was an important institution, which sent letters of advice to women's meetings throughout the country. On one occasion, Anne signed one such communication on behalf of 150 London women. In 1662, she married Benjamin Greenwell but was soon widowed, and in 1670 she married George Whitehead, who was thirteen years her junior. He has a prominent place in Quaker history. From a poor farming background, he was convinced by the preaching of George Fox and at the age of 17 became an itinerant Quaker preacher. After his marriage to Anne he settled in London, and by 1680 he was trading as a grocer in Houndsditch. He was the 'leader of the Quaker lobby at court and Parliament' and after the death of William Penn in 1661 'the acknowledged leader of the Quakers' (J. F. McGregor). *Piety Promoted*... is an indication of the warm regard in which Anne was held by other Quakers, of both sexes. Her own published writings include a collaboration with Mary Elson, *An Epistle for True Love, Unity and Order in the Church of Christ* (1680), which was an appeal for unity, and a collaboration with more than thirty other women, *For the King and Both Houses* (1670).

189   *Some Account of Anne Whitehead's*
        Early Experience, as written by
        her near thirty years ago

> In living Streams that Spring,
> With Tears of Joy now can I Sing,
> Of the Love and Peace that greets
> When the upright hearted meets
> In perfect Truth of living Power   5
> Which lasteth ever down to shower,
> The blessing of the lasting Hill,
> Into the pure Heart to fill,
> With the fulness of his Grace
> Which beholds with open Face   10
> The glory of the holy Spirit
> Which changeth man that life to inherit
> Now being come unto the Life
> The Tree into the Waters of Strife
> That fell to sweeten them   15
> From their bitter sower Leven
> By its own Fruit is known,

True Joy and Peace from Heaven flown,
Here he may take and freely eat
For whom God doth prepare his Meat, 20
Even his own Seed of Israel's Flock
Whose Off-spring is the faithful Flock
Which to his voice alone gives ear, ⎫
Whereby the heart is kept so clear, ⎬
A place only for the pure fear; ⎭ 25
The awe and dread of perfect sight
Which shineth in eternal Light
There the Lamb's kingdom is known
Where Christ the Lord hath only Throne,
Ruling in Life and Spirit meek, 30
Subjecting all under his Feet,
The Earth and Air, and all dark Power
Which may arise to to tempt an houer,
And try if in the upright heart
It can find out any part, 35
There to get in
By Death or Sin
The *Lamb* to Wound and Slay
On whom the Beast would make his Prey
But wasting have the Patience tried 40
The Faith that saves is soon espied,
Which safely keeps the little Flock
That drinketh of the Heavenly Rock,
From which the Water freely springs,
That giveth Life to all good things; 45
And here indeed
There is no need,
Because of right,
All that abide i'th' Light,
May take and eat 50
There daily Meat
And praises gives
To him that Lives
For evermore to Reign
Where there's no Death or Pain 55
Glory, Glory to the Highest
Who brings to peace and perfect Rest.

(1658)

These Verses of dear Ann's own writing, she gave me at her return from the Isle of Wight where she had been travelling in the service of Truth above twenty eight years since, when she had been absent for some space of time.
Mary Stout

14 *Waters of Strife*: Moses sweetened the waters of Marah by dipping his staff in them
(Exodus 15: 23)   19 *freely eat*: cf. Genesis 2: 16   51 *There*: their

JANE VAUGHAN, née PRICE
(fl. mid-seventeenth century)

JANE VAUGHAN was the daughter of Edward Price of Tref Prysg, Llamuwchl-
lyn, a village at the southern tip of Bala Lake in Merionethshire. She married
Rowland Vaughan of Caergai in the same county (*c*.1590–1667). He was a
Royalist poet and translator, whose most influential publication was a translation
of Lewis Bayly's *The Practice of Pity*, *Yr Ymarfer o Dduwioldeb*. Huw Cadwaladr
composed an elegy on his death, suggesting a connection with the family, so he
is probably Jane Vaughan's interlocutor in this dialogue poem.

190   *Ymddiddanion rhwng:*
        Mrs Jane Vaughan o Gaer gae
           a Chadwaladr y prydydd

1 [J.V.]
pob merch yn rhwydd Gwrandewch yn rhodd
I fuw yn y byd fy mryd a'm rodd
A'm llaw yn rhydd mewn llawen fodd
mi fydda o'm gwirfodd gwelwch
gofalon gwir tra fo ynwy ffun   5
mi ddaw i'm calyn coeiliwch
yn fy nydd rhag llygru nwy
dau gwell, a mwy howddgarwch

2 [Cad.]
Ai gwir y glywes baunes byd
ai buw yn ferch Ifangc sy yn ych bryd   10
nid oes yr un o fewn y byd
all roi ddiowryd gwira
nid wyr un gangen glaerwen glud
mo'i thynged hyd yr eithaf
meddwl merch dihareb oedd   15
am droi fel gwyntoedd cyntaf

3 [J.V.]
Y lyfna ei graen: ar dena ei grydd
mewn difir swydd ferch Ifangc sydd

fy fi ai praw mi fydda i prudd
rhag troi llawenydd hebio 20
mi dreia fi ar allo neb
fyw yn rymmus heb ymrwymo
ni chyll un ferch o gwneiff hi yn dda
mo'i chellwer hwya y gallo

4 [Cad.]

Trwy burdeb ferch priodas sydd 25
yn fwy o barch na bod yn rhydd
nid eill un dau mo oedi' r dydd
appwyntio yr Arglwydd Iddyn
os merch naturiol a fydd hi
fo dery i'w ffarti ffortyn 30
ac onide gwell Iddo fo
ymrwymo yn nwylo ei Elyn

5 [J.V.]

Mae llawer mab yn medru ymddwyn
er ynnill clod o fod yn fwyn
yn deg ei raen fel un o'r wyn 35
fo draetha ei gwyn yn dirion
pan ddarfo ymrwymo ag efo yn gaeth
fo dru at waeth 'madroddion
yn bloeddio ai lais fel blaidd o'i le
dan dawli geirie geirwon. 40

6 [Cad.]

Trwy wraig y syrthiwyd Adda i lawr
trwy wraig y sommwyd Samson gawr
O achos merch oedd deg ei gwawr
yr aeth Troia fawr yn wreichion
Ai ddwy ferch a feddwodd Lot 45
O ddiffyg canfod dynion
O nid uch chwi ferch ddifai
gogenwch lai ar feibion

7 [J.V.]

Mae llawer gwedi rhwyno yr llaw
y boreu yn braf heb ronyn braw 50
cyn hanner dydd diammau y daw
ryw wael Esgussion Esgus
ceir gweld dwr yn gwlychu ei bron
ai llygad llon yn llegus

na roed neb rhagdwyn hir nych 55
mo'i Ifiengctyd gwych yn ddibrus

8 [Cad.]

Paham y rhaid mor wylo yr dwr
os meidr merch drwy serch yn siwr
fuw fel Sara gyda ei gwr
diofala cyflwr allan 60
ag onide mae yn rheittiach yw
i hwnnw fuw ei hunan
rhodio yn rhydd a wela i yn haws
na'u wengu anhynaws feingan

9 [J.V.]

Trwy wyllys da mi roes fy mryd 65
rhag gwrando mabiaeth meibion byd
matter gwael eill fynd yn ddryd
nis gwn pa fyd a ddigwydd
rhag meddu'r un o honyn hwy
mi ymgroes fe yn Enw yr Arglwydd 70
mi fydda buw fel Phenith gynt
mi gymra helynt hylwydd

10 [Cad.]

Y Merched glana o fewn y plwy
o ddigerth caffel forwyn ei nwy
o nid un o honyn hwy 75
na fagan glwy neu nychod
ni ddaw byth ar fab mo hyn
mae yn hawdd i bob dyn wybod
a pha un sy yn hawsa i gadw yn ffri
drwy fwynder ei forwyndod 180

11 [J.V.]

ni welai' i ddim bywioliaeth Iawn
ymrwymo a gwr yn siwr pes gawn
gyda'r glana a mwya ei ddawn
'rwy yn ofni cawn anhunedd
mae llawer gwr sy' brafio wr bro 85
yn medru crugo ei gwragedd
pan Elir i gribinnio ar byd
mi cheir un munyd mwynedd

12 [Cad.]

Beth pan ddelo dau ynghyd
a methu buw a llithro'r byd   90
Ai chael hitheu teg ei ffryd
i'w hoel heb wneuthur hyswi
Roi fo yn y gael drwy boenus wedd
yn dristwedd i fuw drosti
Am hyn mod yn rheittia i fab roi nag   95
drwy Prydain rhag priodi

13 [J.V.]

ni cheir ond chwith mor mwynder chwa
yn glwmmi gwr na difir daith
ond gofalon mowrion maith
sydd bob yn saith yn syrthio   100
mi dawa i myn dail y ddol
I Ifiengctyd ffol mom twyllo
llawer lodes gymnes gu
sudd sad am hynny heno

14 [Cad.]

ffortyn sydd yn ledio i'r daith   105
rhwng mab a merch a mwynder maith
na rowch chwithau teg ei hiaith
ddiowryd faith naturiol
Rhag i draserch trwm ych troi
ryw bryd ach rhoi yn Gariadol   110
nid oes matter mawr gan neb
er sorri o'ch wyneb siriol

15 [J.V.]

fo yrrod mabiaith meibion glan
a'i gwen deg a'i gweniaith gwan
lawer lloer i lawr y llan   115
drwy ospri tan dwys prud
na ffeindwch arna i ormod bai
ryw yn gweled rhai yn ddigwilydd
mi garaf bob gwr Ifangc ffel
heb geli fel i gilydd   120

16 [Cad.]

Y Merched oll ar gwragedd da
os llonydd glan ar gan y gaf
Eu goganu nhw mi wnaf
y llestri gwannaf ydyn
Er bod rhai ai llaw yn drom   125

a chafod ffrom yscymmyn
mi wn nad oes na gwr na gwas
heb gariad Addas Iddyn.

Mrs Jane Vaughan a Chadwalader ai [cant]

115 *lawr y llan/parish floor*: perhaps to the grave, or alternatively, undergoing public
penance for fornication.

190   *Debate between Jane Vaughan of Caergai
        and Cadwaladr the poet*

1 [J.V.]

Every girl, without delay, listen intently.
To live in the world my heart is set,
With my hand free in a cheerful manner
I will be, of my own accord, you'll see.
The cares of a husband, while I have breath in me,   5
Will not follow me, believe it,
In my day, lest my vivacity be spoilt,
It would be better and more amiable

2 [Cad.]

Did I hear correctly pea-hen of the world?
Is it your desire to live a young lass?   10
There is not one in the world
that can renounce a husband.
No warm clear-white branch [i.e. girl]
knows her destiny to the end.
A girl's mind was proverbial   15
for turning like the first winds

3 [J.V.]

Smoothest of lustre, and finest of cheek
in all seriousness, is a young girl.
I shall prove it, I'll be wise,
lest I turn happiness away.   20
I shall try if anyone can
to live with strength, without tying the knot.
No girl will lose, if she does well,
her sense of humour, for as long as she may.

4 [Cad.]

Through a girl's purity the love of marriage is   25
more respected than being free.
No two can delay the day
appointed to them by the Lord.
If she be a conventional girl
a fortune will come to her part   30

and is it not better for him
to become entangled in the hands of his enemy

5 [J.V.]

Many lads can behave
in order to win praise for being gentle.
Fair of face, as a lamb,   35
he speaks his grievance mildly.
When you happen to tie the knot tightly with him,
he will resort to worse utterances:
booming his voice, like a wolf that is angry, from his lair
by throwing out harsh words.   40

6 [Cad.]

Adam was felled down by woman;
Samson the giant was disappointed by woman;
because of a girl who was fair of hue,
Great Troy went up in flames.
And his two daughters inebriated Lot   45
because they failed to find men.
O, you are not a blameless girl,
restrain your satire of men.

7 [J.V.]

Many have tied the knot
in the fair morning, without a grain of fright.   50
Before mid-day, doubtless will appear
some poor, false, excuses.
Water will be seen soaking her breast
and her laughing eyes dim.
Let no-one be unmindful of their splendid youth,   55
lest they bring upon themselves long languishing.

8 [Cad.]

Why is it necessary to weep water?
if a girl can live thoroughly by love,
like Sara with her husband
the most carefree situation out,   60
and is it not better for
him to live alone?
Roaming freely seems easier to me
than the dear and fair, white, ungenial girl.

9 [J.V.]

By good faith I put my mind   65
lest I should hear the flattery of men of the world.
A bad matter could be grievous,
I know not what possibility will occur.
Lest I should own one of my them,
I shall cross myself, in the name of the Lord.   70
I will live like Phenith of old,
I'll take considerable trouble.

10 [Cad.]

The fairest girls in the parish
-except when having to quench their passion-
scarcely one of them,   75
does not nurture a disease or weakness.
This will never befall a man
it is easy for all men to know
which one,
is best at keeping her chastity free.   80

11 [J.V.]

I do not see a decent vocation
in being bound with a man, surely, if I did,
With the fairest and most charming
I'm afraid I would suffer from insomnia.
There are many men, that are the pleasantest in the land,   85
who are able to vex their wives.
When it comes to scraping together in the world,
not one pleasant moment is had

12 [Cad.]

What if two were to come together
and failed to live [together] and their world fell apart?   90
And finding one that is fair of face
and mood does not make a housewife.
He through a painful disposition, had
get over her in sadness
It is thus more fitting for a man to say no   95
throughout Britain than to marry.

13 [J.V.]

A sweet taste is not to be had,
In a man's company, nor an agreeable journey.
But large, vast worries
that will fall in sevens.   100
I shall not allow (the meadow leaves insist)
a foolish youth to fool me;
many a warm and dear lass
is prudent tonight because of that.

14 [Cad.]

Fortune leads the way   105
between a girl and a boy and much pleasure
Do not give in your fair terms
a vast natural vow
Lest heavy lust turn you
sometime and render you married.   110
No-one minds much
though your cheerful face will have sulked

15 [J.V.]

The vain talk of pure lads
and their gentle smiles and feeble flattery has driven
many a moon [i.e. girl] to the parish floor   115

by wickedness, under heavy soil
Do not find me too much in error
if I find some impudent
I love every dear young lad
equally, conceal it not.   120

                    16 [Cad.]
All the girls and good wives,
if I find them still and pure in my song
I shall deride them:
they are the weaker vessels.
Though some are heavy-handed   125
with an angry, accursed tongue,
I know that there is not a man or lad
without a suitable lover/sweetheart.

191   *'O f'arglwydd Dduw trugarog' tydi*
             su'n un a thri'

O f'arglwydd Dduw trugarog tydi su'n un a thri
Clyw ochain trwm tosturus a chwynfan merch ai chri
su'n Dersyf cael dygymod er cariad ar un Crist
Dy help ath feddeginiaeth I 'mddiffin fenaid trist

Rwi'n gofyn dy drugaredd am ddwys bechodau maith   5
O'm bedydd hyd y rowan a wneis i'n amla gwaith
pan elwi ger bron Istus rwn gwubod hyn fy hun
nad oes mor Lle sgysodi na chwaith i wadi 'r un

Er hyn mae nghyflawn obaith i'th grasol weithfawr waed
A roisd di ddiodde troswyf o'th goryn hyd dy draed   10
pei golchid ti ag un defnyn fy holl bechodau'n lan
su gochion fel y porphor wae'n union fel y gwlan

Maddeuaist i Fair fagdlen a'r wraig o Ganau wlad
Di a roist y dall i weled ar Cloffion ar eu traed
Di roist y mud ymddieblau a mab y weddw 'n fyw   15
Dod nawdd i mine am bechod o Dduw trugarog Clyw

Rhoist ffrwyth ar goed meusydd ir brig fynd o'r gwraidd
Di a borthaist bobol filoedd ar pump torth bara haidd
Di a fuest Dduw trugarog Do gynt i lawer rhai
nid yw dy wrthie di Etto mi a'i gwn gronyn llai   20

Di iachieist y Claf o'r parlas wraig Diferlif gwaed
Di a ystyriaist wrth Sant peter pan oedd ef wael ai stad
Ynghanol galilea di a drois y Dwr yn win
Duw dod i mine ollyngdod o gaethder pechod blin

Duw cymorth fy nghrediniaith a chadarnha fy ffydd   25
A gollwng fi o gadwynau fy holl bechodau n rhydd
Cariad gras a gobaith oh f'arglwydd imi moes
fy rhaid am Cyflawn iechyd tra rhoddech imi oes

pan roddech imi derfyn o'r bywyd marwol bach
Duw diffodd fy mhechodau gwna mriwie am cleisie 'n iach   30
A Dwg fi i'th fwyn drugaredd i'r nefoedd dan dy law
A chadw fi'n gadwedig y diwrnod mawr a ddaw

finis
Jane Vaughan o gaer gai ai cant

13 *Maddeuaist i Fair...Ganau wlad/Mary Magdalen...woman from Caanan*: Luke 7: 47
and Matthew 15: 22   14 *dall...traed/blind...lame*: Matthew 2: 29 and 9: 33   15 *mab
y weddw/widow's son*: Luke 7: 12   18 *pump/five thousand*: John 6   21 *invalid...woman*:
Matthew 9: 2 and 9: 20   22 *Sant peter/St Peter* John 13: 38 and 21: 15: Peter, having
denied Christ, was nevertheless made prince of the apostles   23 *Dwr/water*: John 2

191   *'O my merciful Lord God, you,*
       who are one in three'

O my merciful Lord God, you, who are one in three
Hear the heavy, pitiful sigh and complaint and cry of a girl
that pleads for your atonement, for the love of one Christ,
your help and salve to protect my sorrowful soul.

I ask for your mercy for many serious sins   5
From my baptism until this hour, I have made much work of sin
When I go before the Justice, I know this myself,
that there is no place to shelter, nor to disown even one sin.

Despite this, my perfect hope is for your gracious, worthy blood,
that you gave from your head and your feet, suffering for my sake.   10
Were you to wash all my sins clean with one drop
that which is red like purple would become as white as wool

You forgave Mary Magdalen and the woman from the land of Canaan.
You caused the blind to see, and put the lame on their feet;
you gave the dumb conversation and you gave life to the widow's son. 15
Give me refuge from sin; Oh merciful Lord, hear me.

You put fruit on the trees of the field, to the summit from the root
You fed five thousand people on five loaves of barley bread
You were a merciful God, yes, long ago to many,
Your miracles are not yet, I know it, a fraction less   20

You healed the invalid from his paralysis and the woman's bloody flux,
you were considerate to Saint Peter when his condition was in a bad
    way.
In Galilee, you turned the water into wine;
God, give me relief, from the confinement of my grievous sin

God help my belief and consolidate my faith   25
and set me free from the shackles of all my sins
Love, grace and hope,
my needs and full health, (oh! give to me, my Lord), while you give me life

When you bring to an end my short, mortal life,
Lord, erase my sins, make clean my wounds and bruises   30
and convey me to your sweet mercy, to Heaven, under your wing,
and keep me in thy keeping until the great day that is to come.

ANONYMOUS BENEDICTINE
NUN OF CAMBRAI

THE English Benedictine convent of Cambrai was founded and financially
endowed in 1623, by Cresacre More, the father of Dame Gertrude More (see
nos. 120–1) because he had been unable to find anywhere suitable for her—the
community still survives, though they have returned to England, and are now at
Stanbrook Abbey. Dame Gertrude was joined at Cambrai by her younger sister
Bridget, and by her two first cousins, though the first Superior was Dame
Catherine Gascoigne. It was a small house: according to the Calendar of State
Papers (Domestic, Charles I 13, p. 28) there were only fifteen of them. Their
constitution is preserved (Lille, Archives départmentales du Nord, 20 H 1), as is a
number of other relevant documents, including a necrology of nuns who died
there from 1631 to 1645 (Lille, 20 H 7). There is also a catalogue of the sisters'
books (Cambrai, bibliothèque publique 1004 (901)), which included a variety of
devotional works in English, French, and Latin. The lives of the sisters of Cambrai
were ascetic and contemplative. They were completely enclosed, unable to leave
the convent, and their lives were mostly spent in the performance of the Divine
Office, private prayer, and contemplation in their separate cells, and reading. The
life at which they aimed is described by Dom Augustine Baker, spiritual adviser to
Gertrude More and other sisters at Cambrai: 'following the Divine Light and
impulses . . . humbling and subjecting the soul to God and to all creatures according to His Will, . . . loving God above all things . . . pursuing prayer, and perform-
ing it according to Divine guidance—all qualities proceeding from the Divine
operation, a state into which none but the Holy Spirit could bring the soul.' This
poem was inserted as a loose leaf into a manuscript volume belonging to one of the
Cambrai sisters, entitled 'For the Use of Sister Anne Benedict of St Joseph',
containing a variety of theological works, particularly those of St Augustine, and
evidently intended to aid Anne Benedict in her private prayer.

192   *'Alone retired in my native cell'*

Alone retired in my native cell,
At home within myself, all noyse shut out,
In silent mourning I resolve to dwell,
With thoughts of death Ile hang my walls about;

All windows close, Faith shall my Taper be,   5
At whose dim flame Ile Hell and Judgment see.

Reflected from these mirrours will appear
The ugly face of Sin without his paint,
And features borrowed only to endear
The world to hearts impatient of restraint;   10
All windows close, Faith shall my Taper be,
At whose dim flame Ile fight for victory.

To hunger after Justice shall be food,
Unto my soul wean'd from the Egiption gust.
My drink shall be thirst after Thee my God,   15
My cloathing to be stript and rent from Dust;
All windows close, Faith shall my Taper be,
On Hope Ile rest, and sleep in Charity.

14 *Egiption gust*: cf. Exodus 16. 3—the Israelites hankered after the luxuries of Egypt

ANNE KEMP
(fl. 1650s)

ANNE KEMP was a gentlewoman, well educated and, on the internal evidence
of her one surviving poem, she lived in Gloucestershire. Nothing else is known
about her. Her poem is a description of a country landscape, in the tradition of
Aemilia Lanyer's poem on Cookham, and Ben Jonson's 'To Penshurst'.

193   *A Contemplation on Bassets down-Hill*[*]
by the most Sacred adorer of the
Muses Mrs. A. K.

If that exact Appelles now did live,
And would a picture of Elizium give;
He might portrai'ct the prospect which this Hill
Doth show; and make the eie command at will.
Heer's many a shire whose pleasauntries for sight   5
Doth yield to the Spectators great delight.
Ther's a large Feild guilded with Ceres gold;
Here a green mead doth many Heifers hold:
Ther's pasture growne with virdant grass, whose store,
Of Argent-sheep shews th'owner is not poore.   10
Here springs doe intricate Meanders make
Excelling farr oblivion's Lethe Lake.

There woods and coppises harbour as many
And sweet melodious Choristers, as any
Elizium yields; whose Philomel'an laies   15
Merit the highest of the Lyrick's praise
Heer's Flora deckt with robes of Or, and Azur,
Fragrantly smelling yeild's two senses pleasure.

Hence Zephirus doth breath his gentle gales
Coole on the Hills, and sweet throughout the vales   20
  How happy are they that in this climate dwell?
  Alas! they can't their owne sweet welfare tell;
  Scarce I myselfe whil'st I am here doe know it
  Till I see its Antithesis to shew it.
Here are no smoaking streets, nor howling cryes,   25
Deafning the eares, nor blinding of the eyes,
No noys orre smells t'infect, and choake the aire,
Breeding diseases envious to the faire.
Deceipt is here exil'd from Flesh, and Bloud:
(Strife only reigns, for all strive to be good.)   30
  With Will his verse, I here will make an end
  And as the crab doth alwaies backward bend
  So, thogh from this sweet place I goe away
  My loyal heart will in this Climate stay.
Thus heartless doth my worthless body rest   35
Whilest my hart liveth with the ever blest.

* neare Meysay Hampton or Down-Ampney in Glocestershire

1 *Appelles*: painter of antiquity famous for his lifelikeness   2 *Elizium*: the Elysian fields
were the abode of the blessed in the afterlife   7 *Ceres gold*: ripe wheat   12 *Lethe Lake*:
Lethe, the river of the Classical underworld whose waters brought forgetfulness   17 *Or,
and Azur*: gold and blue   31 *Will*: Reference is obscure: perhaps the previous lines are
quoted from a fellow poet of that name?

ELIZABETH NEWELL
(fl. 1655–1668)

THE poems of Elizabeth Newell survive in an unbound booklet now in the
Beinecke library at Yale, now 36 pages long, written in a neat but not professional hand, which may be autograph, though two spaces left in the transcription
perhaps hint that it is a copy by another scribe. On two pages, the name
'Elizabeth Newell' is written repeatedly; apparently the name of the author.
Several sheets are apparently missing from the front, since the manuscript as we
have it begins halfway through number 5 of a sequence of sixteen numbered
Christmas Day poems, with dates ranging from Christmas 1655 to 1668 (logic
would suggest that the earliest of the lost poems dated to 1651). Other poems
in the manuscript include 'a Paraphrase on Simeon's Song', 'Changes and

Troubles', 'A Paraphrase on Seneca's Thyestes', and a verse 'wherein the
usefullness excellency and several perfections of Holy scripture are briefly hinted
by J.C.': this is the only verse attributed to anyone other than Elizabeth Newell
herself. The paraphrase on Seneca suggests that Elizabeth Newell was a woman
of some learning, though not necessarily that she read Latin.

194   *A Dialogue*

            Christ   Justice   Sinner

Chr. Bring forth the prisoner. *Just.* thy commands,
        Are done just judge, see here the prisoner stands.
Chr. What hath the prisoner done, say what's the cause
        Of his commitment. *Just.* he hath broken the laws
        Of his so gracious God: conspired the death   5
        Of that great Majesty that gave him breath
        And heap'd transgression Lord upon transgressions
Chr. How know it thou thus: *Just.* Even by his own confession
        His sins were crying and they cried aloud
        They cryed to Heaven; they cryed to Heaven for blood   10
Chr. What sayest thou sinner; hast thou ought to plead
        That sentence should not pass, hold up thy head
        And shew thy brazen, thy rebellious face
Sin. Ah me: I dare not, I am too vile, and base
        To tread upon the earth, much more to lift   15
        Mine eyes to heaven I need no other shift
        Then mine own conscience, Lord I must confess
        I am no more but dust, and no whit less
        Then my Inditment styles me. Ah: if thou
        Search too severe with too severe a brow   20
        What flesh can stand. I have transgress'd thy laws
        My merits pleads thy vengeance, not my cause
Just. Lord shall I strik the blow, *Chr.* Hold Justice stay
        Sinner speake on, what hast thou more to say
Sin. Vile as I am, and of my self abhorred,   25
        I am thy handy work, thy creature Lord
        Stampt with thy glorious Image, and at first
        Most like to thee though now a poore accurst
        Convicted cattiff and degenerous creature
        Here trembling at the bar. *Just.* thy faults the greater   30
        Lord shall I strike the blow. *Chr.* Hold Justice stay
        Speak Sinner has thou nothing more to say?
Sin. Nothing but mercy, mercy, Lord my state,
        Is miserably poor, and disperate,
        I quit renounce my self, the world, and flee   35
        from Lord, to Jesus: from my self to thee,

Just. Cease thy vain hopes, my angry God hath vow'd:
         Abused mercy must have blood for blood:
         Shall I yet strike the blow. *Chr.* Stay Justice hold
         My bowells yern, my fainting blood grows cold   40
         To view the trembling wretch. Mithink, I spy
         My fathers Image, in the prisoners eye
Just. I cannot hold. *Chr.* Then turn, turn thy thirsty blad
         Into my sides let there the wound be made
         Chear up dear soul, Ile redeeme thy life with mine   45
         My soul shall smart, my heart shall bleed for thine.
Sin.   O boundless deeps, oh love beyond degree,
         The offended dyes, to set the offender free,
         Mercy of mercyes, he that was my drudge
         Is now my advocate, is now my Judge   50
         He suffer'd pleads and sentenceth alone
         Three I adore, and yet adore but one.

ELIANOUR HAVEY
(fl. 1658)

NOTHING is known of this Scottish supporter of Cromwell, whose work is datable only by its content. The manuscript which preserves her work contains mostly Royalist poetry.

195   *An Acrostick Eligie on the death of the*
       no less prudent than victorious
       prince Oliver lord Protector

Anagram
Rule well or I come

Our England's victor dead: who can express
Laments sufficient for such worthyness
Immortall fame must bee the trump which may
Unto Eternity thy deeds display
Each tyrant of thy name did trembling stand   5
Reading in it, the ffredome which thy hand
Conquer'd those nations (for but were the sence
Rule well or I come) sent by providence
Oh how his death would us of bless bereft
Middst our success had wee bin wholly left   10
Without a branch of that rich stock whose hight
Envy nor time can blast with all her spite

Live then and prosper, may thy scepter bee
Like his, above the reach of treacherie.

(1658)

9 *bless*: bliss   11 *branch*: Richard Cromwell (1626–1712), in September 1658 he succeeded his father as Lord Protector but was forced to abdicate in May 1659

ANN WILLIAMS (previously CROMWELL)
(fl. 1660s)

A FLYLEAF note by an unknown hand in Mrs Williams's commonplace book
states: 'Ann Cromwell was wife of Henry Cromwell esq. of Ramsy, who was the
son of Coll Henry Cromwell the son of Sir Oliver Cromwell who were all thre
Royalist, and in the year 60 Henry Cromwell of Ramsy changed his name to
Williams being a courtier and from thence she wrate her name Anne Williams,
they died without issue and the estate of Ramsy was sold to Colonell Titus.' She
was the daughter of Richard Cromwell of Upwood, Hunts, and married her
cousin, as the note states. Henry Cromwell was the MP for Huntingdonshire for
most of the years between 1654 and 1673, and the son of Baptina Cromwell. The
death of the child reported here is doubly poignant, since his death meant the
end of the family line. According to the *Victoria County History (Huntingdonshire)*, she was known as 'the Poetess Cromwell'.

196   *Greifes farwell, to an Inherritor of joy*

ffarwell sweet infant; blissfull babe adieu.
thy short, sick Life, hath taught us all to know,
that this short Life of ours is full of rue,
and that there's no contentment here below.
How well art thou, how surely safe, how blest;   5
whose god hath pluckt deaths sting; Laied thee to rest.
who ere thou bee that lov'd him cease to weepe;
ffeare to Lament him as a thing that's lost.
how can that perrish that the Lord doth keepe
that soule miscarry, that so deere him cost,   10
heaven as thou see, hath freed him from annoy
and can your sorowes choose but turn to joy
did thou but know from what a world of ill
from what false joyes, sad cares, afflictive feares,
the hande of mercy hath him taken, you'd fill   15
your mouth with Laughter, not your eyes with teares,
and in a raised Contemplation say
god grante our soules may meete an other day.

and may my soule (o God) so happie bee
as whome I saw in paine in bliss to see.   20

A. Cr.

6 *death's sting*: 1 Corinthians 15: 55

APHRA BEHN (née JOHNSON)
(?1640–1689)

ALMOST everything about the life of Aphra Behn is controversial. However, some probabilities have recently begun to emerge, mostly thanks to the work of Maureen Duffy, who first uncovered the parish registers, and more recently, Janet Todd. She was probably from Kent, the daughter of Bartholomew Johnson, described at his marriage on 25 August 1638 as a yeoman of Bishopsbourne, and Elizabeth Denham, of Smeeth, near Wye. Their first daughter Frances was baptized at Wye a mere five months later–it was customary for a couple to return to the bride's home parish for the baptism of the first child–and on 14 December 1640, at Harbledown just outside Canterbury, they baptized another daughter, 'Eaffry'. This squares with Sir Thomas Colepeper's statement in his *Adversaria* that 'Mrs Been...had also a fayer sister...their names were Franck and Aphra.' Aphra is a name quite common in early modern Kent, but there is a certain irony in the fact that Aphra Behn was put under her patronage, since the original St Afra of Augsburg is probably the only brothel-keeper to have been raised to the altars of the Church (her life is in the *Acta Sanctorum*, under 5 August). Bartholomew Johnson was a barber, and a freeman of Canterbury, who in 1654, became Overseer of the Poor for St Margaret's, an inner-city Canterbury parish. Elizabeth Johnson was employed as nurse to Sir Thomas Colepeper, and the children seem to have spent time with her in the Colepeper household, since he records Aphra's precocious talent: 'from infancy she wrote the prettiest softest engaging verses in the world.' Her origins were lowly but offered her a number of opportunities: she may have learned French from the Hugenot refugees who thronged Canterbury, and Dutch from the exiled colony in nearby Sandwich, and due to her mother's ties with the household, she had the patronage of the Colepepers. She was associated with members of this family throughout her life

In the early 1660s, she seems to have visited Surinam, where 'Astraea' (Behn's codename and *nom de plume*) was mentioned by the deputy governor, William Byam, in his reports in 1663 and 1664. On her return, she married a Mr Behn (usually described as Dutch, though the name is German) about whom nothing whatever is known, although it is hypothesized that he died in the plague of 1665. In 1666, she was sent on a spying mission to Antwerp by Thomas Killigrew to contact William Scot (an old flame from Surinam), the eldest son of the regicide Thomas Scot, who had volunteered to betray his fellow republicans. Her coded intelligence reports, preserved in the Public Records Office, are her earliest extant writings. The enterprise was financially disastrous: by 1668, to keep out of debtor's prison, she was petitioning the king and sending begging letters to Killigrew. From 1667 to 1670 there is very little record of her activities, and then she suddenly appears as the author of *The Forc'd Marriage*, staged in 1670 by the Duke's Company, one of the two theatre companies in London. At about this time she may have been living with a lawyer by the name of John Hoyle. Bulstrode Whitelocke summed him up as 'an Atheist, a Sodomite professed, a corrupter of youth, & a Blasphemer of Christ'. She made a reasonable living as a dramatist until 1682, when the two companies amalgamated into the United Company, halving the demand for new plays. Thereafter she augmented her income with translations from French and Latin (the latter from intermediate English versions), as well as poetry. She also received a royal subsidy for producing 'Tory doggerell': satires, squibs, and songs, which were circulated anonymously in manuscript and are no longer identifiable as her work. Her interest in this type of verse is shown by her personal miscellany, 'Astrea's Book for Songs and Satyrs–1686', now in the Bodleian Library (Firth MS c. 16). She was continually ill from 1686 until her death in 1689, but continued to write at prolific speed as an economic necessity.

She died on 16 April 1689, five days after the coronation of William and Mary, which, as a loyal supporter of the Stuarts, and possibly a secret Catholic, she had had difficulty in accepting. She was buried in Westminster Abbey, where her name appears in the register as 'Astrea Behn'. Behn's literary reputation seemed assured at the time of her death. Defoe ranked her with Milton and Rochester as among the 'great wits' of that era, an interesting triumvirate. Already, however, her *risqué* poems and novels, and reputedly loose morals, had provoked a censorious reaction (e.g. 'The Female Laureat, 1687, in London, National Art Library Dyce MS 25 f 37, fos. 607ʳ–609ʳ), and she was held up as a negative example for aspiring women poets (e.g. poem to Anne Wharton in Edward Young's *The Idea of Christian Love* (1688), pp. vii–viii). However, as many of the subsequent poems in this selection will show, her importance as inspiration and example to women writers of the next generation is incalculable.

The poems selected here are intended to give an impression of the range of her writing. She was a notable translator from French ('The Disappointment' is a version of a French original), and, though she probably did not read Latin, she engaged with Latin literature via English and French translations, so we include her 'Oenone to Paris'. The 'Pindaric'—a loosely structured, rhymed poem with variable line-length—was a fashionable metre of the time, only tangentially related to the poems of Pindar. 'Silvio's Complaint' is interesting for a variety of reasons. It is a political poem on the fall of James Scott, Duke of Monmouth, illegitimate son of Charles II, in eclogue form: a vehicle for discreet political comment since Virgil. It is also interesting linguistically, as an internally consistent, but obviously artificial representation of Lowland Scots: signalled by forms such as 'au' for 'all', and by actual Scotticisms such as 'weys me' (i.e. 'wae's me'), and 'muckle'. The poem to Anne Wharton is a testimony to Behn's increasingly desperate search for patronage; as a response from an established poet to a young admirer, it is extraordinary, but as a reflection of Behn's economic realities, it is revealing. In a somewhat similar fashion, the poem on Queen Mary seeks to reconcile her political loyalties with her need to establish a strategy for survival: she does so by ignoring William, and focusing on Mary as the daughter of James II.

197   *The Disappointment*

I.

One day the Amorous *Lysander*,
By an impatient Passion sway'd,
Supriz'd fair *Cloris*, that lov'd Maid,

Who could defend her self no longer.
All things did with his Love conspire;   5
That gilded Planet of the Day,
In his gay Chariot drawn by Fire,
Was now descending to the Sea,
And left no Light to guide the World,
But what from Cloris Brighter Eyes was hurld.   10

II.

In a lone Thicket made for Love,
Silent as yielding Maids Consent,
She with a Charming Languishment,
Permits his Force, yet gently strove;
Her Hands his Bosom softly meet,   15
But not to put him back design'd,
Rather to draw 'em on inclin'd:
Whilst he lay trembling at her Feet,
Resistance 'tis in vain to show;
She wants the pow'r to say—*Ah! What d'ye do?*   20

III.

Her Bright Eyes sweet, and yet severe,
Where Love and Shame confus'dly strive,
Fresh Vigor to *Lysander* give;
And breathing faintly in his Ear,
She cry'd—*Cease, Cease—your vain Desire,*   25
Or I'll call out——What would you do?
My Dearer Honour ev'n to You
I cannot, must not give——Retire,
Or take this Life, whose chiefest part
I gave you with the Conquest of my Heart.   30

IV.

But he as much unus'd to Fear,
As he was capable of Love,
The blessed minutes to improve,
Kisses her Mouth, her Neck, her Hair;
Each Touch her new Desire Alarms,   35
His burning trembling Hand he prest
Upon her swelling Snowy Brest,
While she lay panting in his Arms.
All her Unguarded Beauties lie
The Spoils and Trophies of the Enemy.   40

V.

And now without Respect or Fear,
He seeks the Object of his Vows,
(His Love no Modesty allows)

By swift degrees advancing—where
His daring Hand that Altar seiz'd,   45
Where Gods of Love do sacrifice:
That Awful Throne, that Paradice
Where Rage is calm'd, and Anger pleas'd;
That Fountain where Delight still flows,
And gives the Universal World Repose.   50

VI.

Her Balmy Lips incountring his,
Their Bodies, as their Souls, are joyn'd;
Where both in Transports Unconfin'd
Extend themselves upon the Moss.
Cloris half dead and breathless lay;   55
Her soft Eyes cast a Humid Light,
Such as divides the Day and Night;
Or falling Stars, whose Fires decay:
And now no signs of Life she shows,
But what in short-breath'd Sighs returns and goes.   60

VII.

He saw how at her Length she lay;
He saw her rising Bosom bare;
Her loose thin *Robes*, through which appear
A Shape design'd for Love and Play;
Abandon'd by her Pride and Shame.   65
She does her softest Joys dispence,
Off'ring her Virgin-Innocence
A Victim to Loves Sacred Flame;
While the o'er-Ravish'd Shepherd lies
Unable to perform the Sacrifice.   70

VIII.

Ready to taste a thousand Joys,
The too transported hapless Swain
Found the vast Pleasure turn'd to Pain;
Pleasure which too much Love destroys:
The willing Garments by he laid,   75
And Heaven all open'd to his view,
Mad to possess, himself he threw
On the Defenceless Lovely Maid.
But Oh what envying God conspires
To snatch his Power, yet leave him the Desire!   80

IX.

Nature's Support, (without whose Aid
She can no Humane Being give)
Its self now wants the Art to live;

Faintness its slack'ned Nerves invade:
In vain th'inraged Youth essay'd   85
To call its fleeting Vigor back,
No motion 'twill from Motion take;
Excess of Love his Love betray'd:
In vain he Toils, in vain Commands;
The Insensible fell weeping in his Hand.   90

X.

In this so Amorous Cruel Strife,
Where Love and Fate were too severe,
The poor *Lysander* in despair
Renounc'd his Reason with his Life:
Now all the brisk and active Fire   95
That should the Nobler Part inflame,
Serv'd to increase his Rage and Shame,
And left no Spark for New Desire:
Not all her Naked Charms cou'd move
Or calm that Rage that had debauch'd his Love.   100

XI.

Cloris returning from the Trance
Which Love and soft Desire had bred,
Her timerous Hand she gently laid
(Or guided by Design or Chance)
Upon that Fabulous *Priapas*,   105
That Potent God, as Poets feign;
But never did young *Shepherdess*,
Gath'ring of Fern upon the Plain,
More nimbly draw her Fingers back,
Finding beneath the verdant Leaves a snake: 110

XII.

Than *Cloris* her fair Hand withdrew,
Finding that God of her Desires
Disarm'd of all his Awful Fires,
And Cold as Flow'rs bath'd in the Morning-Dew.
Who can the *Nymph*'s Confusion guess?   115
The Blood forsook the hinder Place,
And strew'd with Blushes all her Face,
Which both Disdain and Shame exprest:
And from *Lysander*'s Arms she fled,
Leaving him fainting on the Gloomy Bed.   120

XIII.

Like Lightning through the Grove she hies,
Or *Daphne* from the *Delphick God*,

No Print upon the grassey Road
She leaves, t'instruct Pursuing Eyes.
The Wind that wanton'd in her Hair,   125
And with her Ruffled Garments plaid,
Discover'd in the Flying Maid
All that the Gods e'er made, of Fair.
So *Venus*, when her *Love* was slain,
With Fear and Haste flew o'er the Fatal Plain.   130

XIV.

The *Nymph*'s Resentments none but I
Can well Imagine or Condole:
But none can guess *Lysander*'s Soul,
But those who sway'd his Destiny.
His silent Griefs swell up to Storms,   135
And not one God his Fury spares;
He curs'd his Birth, his Fate, his Stars;
But more the *Shepherdess*'s Charms,
Whose soft bewitching Influence
Had Damn'd him to the *Hell* of Impotence.   140

6 *Planet*: the sun   45–50 *Altar*: her genitals   105 *Priapas*: Roman god with an enormous penis, by metonymy, the penis   122 *Delphick God*: Apollo   129 Venus fell in
love with the beautiful but mortal Adonis, who was killed while hunting

198 *A Congratulatory POEM TO HER Sacred Majesty QUEEN MARY, UPON HER ARRIVAL in ENGLAND*

While my sad Muse the darkest Covert Sought,
To give a loose to Melancholy Thought;
Opprest, and sighing with the Heavy Weight
Of an Unhappy dear Lov'd *Monarch's* Fate;
A lone retreat, on *Thames*'s Brink she found,   5
With Murmering Osiers fring'd, and bending Willows Crown'd,
Thro' the thick Shade cou'd dart no Chearful Ray,
Nature dwelt here as in disdain of Day:
Content, and Pleas'd with Nobler Solitude,
No *Wood-Gods*, *Fawns*, nor *Loves* did here Intrude, 10
Nor Nests for wanton Birds, the Glade allows;
Scarce the soft Winds were heard amongst the Boughs.

While thus She lay resolv'd to tune no more
Her fruitless Songs on *Brittains* Faithless Shore,
All on a suddain thro' the Woods there Rung,   15
Loud Sounds of Joy that *Io Peans* Sung.

Maria! Blest *Maria*! was the Theam,
Great Brittains happy Genius, and her Queen.

   The River Nimphs their Crystal Courts forsake,
Curl their Blew Locks, and Shelly Trumpets take.   20
And the surprising News along the Shore,
In raptur'd Songs the wondring Virgins bore;
Whilst Mourning Eccho now forgot her Sighs,
And sung the new taught Anthem to the Skyes.

   All things in Nature, a New Face put on,   25
Thames with Harmonious Purlings glides along,
And tells her Ravisht Banks, she lately bore
A Prize more great than all her hidden Store,
Or all the Sun it self e're saw before.
The brooding Spring, her Fragrant Bloom sent out,   30
Scattering her early Perfumes round about;
No longer waits the Lasie teeming Hours,
But e're her time produc'd her Oderous Flowers;
Maria's Eyes Anticipate the May,
And Life inspir'd beyond the God of Day.   35

   The Muses all upon this Theam Divine,
Tun'd their best Lays, the Muses all, but mine;
Sullen with Stubborn Loyalty she lay,
And saw the World its eager Homage pay,
While Heav'n and Earth on the new Scene lookt gay.   40
But Oh! What Human Fortitude can be
Sufficient to Resist a Deity?
Even our Allegiance here, too feebly pleads,
The Change in so Divine a Form perswades;
Maria with the Sun has equal Force,   45
No Opposition stops her Glorious Course,
Her pointed Beams thro' all a passage find,
And fix their Rays Triumphant in the Mind.

   And now I wish'd among the Crouds to Adore,
And constant wishing did increase my Power;   50
From every thought a New-born Reason came
Which fortifyed by bright *Maria's* Fame,
Inspir'd My Genious with new Life and Flame,

J.R.   And thou, Great Lord, of all my Vows, permit
My Muse who never fail'd Obedience yet,   55
To pay her Tribute at Maria's Feet,
Maria so Divine a part of You,
Let me be Just—but Just with Honour too.
   Resolv'd, She join'd her Chorus with the Throng,
And to the listning Groves Maria's Vertues Sung;   60
Maria all Inchanting, Gay, and Young.

All Hail Illustrious Daughter of a King,
Shining without, and Glorious all within,
Whose Eyes beyond your scantier Power give Laws,
Command the World, and justifie the Cause;   65
Nor to secure your Empire needs more Arms
Than your resistless, and all Conquering Charms;
Minerva Thus Alone, Old *Troy* Sustain'd,
Whilst her Blest Image with three Gods remain'd;
But Oh! your Form and Manner to relate,   ⎫   70
The Envying Fair as soon may Imitate,   ⎬
'Tis all Engaging Sweet, 'tis all Surprising Great; ⎭
A thousand Beauties Triumph in your Air,   ⎫
Like those of soft Young Loves your Smiles appear, ⎬
And to th'Unguarded Hearts, as dangerous are.   ⎭   75

All Natures Charms are open'd in your Face,
You Look, you Talk, with more than Human Grace;
All that is Wit, all that is Eloquence:
The Births of finest Thought and Noblest Sense,
Easie and Natural from your Language break,   80
And 'tis Eternal Musick when you speak;
Thro' all no Formal Nicety is seen,
But Free and Generous your Majestick Meen,   ⎫
In every Motion, every Part a Queen;   ⎬
All that is Great and Lovely in the Sex,   ⎭   85
Heav'n did in this One Glorious Wonder fix,
Appelis thus to dress the Queen of Love
Rob'd the whole Race, a Goddess to improve.

Yet if with Sighs we View that Lovely Face,
And all the Lines of your great Father's Trace,   90
Your Vertues should forgive, while we adore
   That Face that Awes, and Charms our Hearts the more;
But if the *Monarch* in your Looks we find,
Behold him yet more glorious in your Mind;
'Tis there His God-like Attributes we see.   ⎫
A Gratious Sweetness, Affability,   ⎬   95
A Tender Mercy and True Piety;   ⎭
And Vertues even sufficient to Attone
For all the ills the Ungrateful World has done,
Where several Factions, several Int'rests sway,
And that is still i'th'Right who gains the Day;   100
How e're they differ, this they all must grant, ⎫
Your Form and Mind, no One Perfection want,   ⎬
Without all Angel, and within all Saint.   ⎭

The Murmering World till now divided lay,   105
Vainly debating whom they shou'd Obey,
Till You Great Cesar's Off-spring blest our Isle,
The differing Multitudes to Reconcile;
Thus Stiff-neckt Israel in defiance stood,
Till they beheld the Prophet of their God;   110
Who from the Mount with dazling brightness came,
And Eyes all shining with Celestial Flame;
Whose Awful Looks, dispel'd each Rebel Thought,
    And to a Just Compliance, the wilde Nations brought.

                                (1673)

4 *Monarch*: James II   54 *J.R.*: Jacobus Rex   62 *Daughter*: emphasizing that Mary's title is by virtue of being a daughter of James II   63 cf. Psalm 45: 13   69 *Image*: the Palladium, a sacred statue   87 *Appelis*: the Greek painter Appelles, who took features for his portrait of Aphrodite from all the most beautiful women of his time   109–14 Exodus 34: 30

199 *To the Fair* Clarinda, *who made Love to me, imagin'd more than Woman.*

Fair lovely Maid, or if that Title be
Too weak, too Feminine for Nobler thee,
Permit a Name that more Approaches Truth:
And let me call thee, Lovely Charming Youth.
This last will justifie my soft complaint,   5
While that may serve to lessen my constraint;
And without Blushes I the Youth persue,
When so much beauteous Woman is in view,
Against thy Charms we struggle but in vain
With thy deluding Form thou giv'st us pain,   10
While the bright Nymph betrays us to the Swain.
In pity to our Sex sure thou wer't sent,
That we might Love, and yet be Innocent:
For sure no Crime with thee we can commit;
Or if we shou'd——thy Form excuses it.   15
For who, that gathers fairest Flowers believes
A Snake lies hid beneath the Fragrant Leaves.

    Thou beauteous Wonder of a different kind,
Soft *Cloris* with the dear *Alexis* join'd;
When e'r the Manly part of thee, wou'd plead   20
Thou tempts us with the Image of the Maid,
While we the noblest Passions do extend
The Love to *Hermes*, *Aphrodite* the Friend.

200 *On the Death of the late Earl of* Rochester.

Mourn, Mourn, ye Muses, all your loss deplore,
The Young, the Noble *Strephon* is no more.
Yes, Yes, he fled quick as departing Light,
And ne're shall rise from Deaths eternal Night,
So rich a Prize the *Stygian* Gods ne're bore,   5
Such Wit, such Beauty, never grac'd their Shore.
He was but lent this duller World t'improve
In all the charms of Poetry, and Love;
Both were his gift, which feely he bestow'd,
And like a God, dealt to the wond'ring Crowd.   10
Scorning the little Vanity of Fame,
Spight of himself attain'd a Glorious name.
But oh! in vain was all his peevish Pride,
The Sun as soon might his vast Lustre hide,
As piercing, pointed, and more lasting bright,   15
As suffering no viscissitudes of Night.
  Mourn, Mourn, ye Muses, all your loss deplore,
  The Young, the Noble *Strephon* is no more.

Now uninspir'd upon your Banks we lye,
Unless when we wou'd mourn his Elegie;   20
His name's a Genius that wou'd Wit dispense,
And give the Theme a Soul, the Words a Sense.
But all fine thought that Ravisht when it spoke,
With the soft Youth eternal leave has took;
Uncommon Wit that did the soul o'recome,   25
Is buried all in Strephon's Worship'd Tomb;
Satyr has lost its Art, its Sting is gone,
The Fop and Cully now may be undone;
That dear instructing Rage is now allay'd,
And no sharp Pen dares tell 'em how they've stray'd;   30
Bold as a God was ev'ry lash he took,
But kind and gentle the chastising stroke.
  Mourn, Mourn, ye Youths, whom Fortune has betray'd,
  The last Reproacher of your Vice is dead.

Mourn, all ye Beauties, put your *Cyprus* on,   35
The truest Swain that e're Ador'd you's gone;
Think how he lov'd, and writ, and sigh'd, and spoke,
Recall his Meen, his Fashion, and his Look.
By what dear Arts the Soul he did surprize,
Soft as his Voice, and charming as his Eyes.   40
Bring Garlands all of never-dying Flow'rs,
Bedew'd with everlasting falling Show'rs;
Fix your fair eyes upon your victim'd Slave,

Sent Gay and Young to his untimely Grave.
See where the Noble Swain Extended lies,   45
Too sad a Triumph of your Victories;
Adorn'd with all the Graces Heav'n e're lent, ⎫
All that was Great, Soft, Lovely, Excellent   ⎬
You've laid into his early Monument.   ⎭
    Mourn, Mourn, ye Beauties, your sad loss deplore,   50
    The Young, the Charming *Strephon* is no more.

Mourn, all ye little Gods of Love, whose Darts
Have lost their wonted power of piercing hearts;
Lay by the gilded Quiver and the Bow,
The useless Toys can do no Mischief now,   55
Those Eyes that all your Arrows points inspir'd,
Those Lights that gave ye fire are now retir'd,
Cold as his Tomb, pale as your Mothers Doves;
Bewail him them oh all ye little Loves,
For you the humblest Votary have lost   60
That ever your Divinities could boast;
Upon your hands your weeping Heads decline,
And let your wings encompass round his Shrine;
In stead of Flow'rs your broken Arrows strow,
And at his feet lay the neglected Bow.   65
    Mourn, all ye little Gods, your loss deplore,
    The soft, the Charming *Strephon* is no more.

Large was his Fame, but short his Glorious Race,
Like young *Lucretius* liv'd and dy'd apace.
So early Roses face, so over all   70
They cast their fragrant scents, then softly fall,
While all the scatter'd perfum'd leaves declare,
How lovely 'twas when whole, how sweet, how fair.
Had he been to the *Roman* Empire known,
When great *Augustus* fill'd the peaceful Throne;   75
Had he the noble wond'rous Poet seen,
And known his Genius, and survey'd his Meen,
(When Wits, and Heroes grac'd Divine abodes,)
He had increas'd the number of their Gods;
The Royal Judge had Temples rear'd to's name,   80
And made him as Immortal as his Fame;
In Love and Verse his *Ovid* he'ad out-done,
And all his Laurels, and his *Julia* won.
    Mourn, Mourn, unhappy World, his loss deplore,
    The great, the charming *Strephon* is no more.   85

1680

5 *Stygian*: the gods of the underworld   35 *Cyprus*: the cypress was a plant associated
classically with mourning, but 'cypress', or 'cypress lawn' was a light, transparent fabric

used for mourning garments. Behn intends both senses   58 *Doves*: Venus, mother of
Cupid, and of cupids in general, was accompanied by doves   69 *Lucretius*: took his own
life at the age of 44   80 *Royal Judge*: Augustus   82 *Ovid*: Ovid's poetry, like Rochester's, was cynical and sexually explicit. He was thought to have fallen in love with
Augustus's daughter Julia, and to have been exiled for that reason

201   *On Desire A Pindarick. By Mrs.* A.B.

    What Art thou, oh! thou new-found pain?
    From what infection dost thou spring?
Tell me——oh! tell me, thou inchanting thing,
      Thy nature and thy name;
      Inform me by what subtil Art,   5
      What powerful Influence,
You got such vast Dominion in a part
Of my unheeded, and unguarded, heart
That fame and Honour cannot drive yee thence.
Oh! mischievous usurper of my Peace;   10
Oh! soft Intruder on my solitude,
      Charming disturber of my ease,
      That hast my nobler fate persu'd,
And all the Glorys of my life subdu'd.

    Thou haunt'st my inconvenient hours;   15
The business of the Day, nor silence of the night,
      That shou'd to cares and sleep invite,
    Can bid defyance to thy conquering powers.
Where hast thou been this live-long Age
      That from my Birth till now,   20
    Thou never coud'st one thought engage,
Or charm my soul with the uneasy rage
That made it all its humble feebles know?

    Where wert thou, oh, malicious spright,
    When shining Honour did invite?   25
    When interest call'd, then thou wert shy,
Nor to my aid one kind propension brought,
    Nor wou'd'st inspire one tender thought,
    When Princes at my feet did lye.
When thou coud'st mix ambition with my joy,   30
Then peevish *Phantôm* thou wer't nice and coy,
    Not Beauty cou'd invite thee then,
    Nor all the Arts of lavish Men!
Not all the powerful Rhetorick of the Tongue
    Not sacred Wit cou'd charm thee on;   35
    Not the soft play that lovers make,
Nor sigh cou'd fan thee to a fire,

Not pleading tears, nor vows cou'd thee awake,
Or warm the unform'd something————to desire.

Oft I've conjur'd thee to appear   40
By youth, by love, by all their powrs,
Have searcht and sought thee every where,
In silent Groves, in lonely bowrs:
On Flowry beds where lovers wishing lye,
In sheltering Woods where sighing maids   45
To their assigning Shepherds hye,
And hide their blushes in the gloom of shades:
Yet there, even there, thô youth assail'd,
Where Beauty prostrate lay and fortune woo'd,
My heart insensible to neither bow'd   50
Thy lucky aid was wanting to prevail.

In courts I sought thee then, thy proper sphear
But thou in crowds we'rt stifl'd there,
Int'rest did all the loving business do,
Invites the youths and wins the Virgins too.   55
Or if by chance some heart thy empire own
(Ah power ingrate!) the slave must be undone.

Tell me, thou nimble fire, that dost dilate
Thy mighty force thrô every part,
What God, or Human power did thee create   60
In my, till now, unfacil heart?
Art thou some welcome plague sent from above
In this dear form, this kind disguise?
Or the false offspring of mistaken love,
Begot by some soft thought that faintly strove,   65
With the bright peircing Beautys of *Lysanders* Eyes?
Yes, yes, tormenter, I have found thee now;
And found to whom thou dost thy being owe,
'Tis thou the blushes dost impart,
For thee this languishment I wear,   70
'Tis thou that tremblest in my heart
When the dear Shepherd do's appear,
I faint, I dye with pleasing pain,
My words intruding sighing break
When e're I touch the charming swain   75
When e're I gaze, when e're I speak.
Thy conscious fire is mingl'd with my love,
As in the sanctify'd abodes
Misguided worshippers approve
The mixing Idol with their Gods.   80
In vain, alas in vain I strive
With errors, which my soul do please and vex,

For superstition will survive,
Purer Religion to perplex.
Oh! tell me you, Philosophers, in love,   85
That can its burning feaverish fits controul,
   By what strange Arts you cure the soul,
   And the fierce Calenture remove?

Tell me, yee fair ones, that exchange desire,
   How tis you hid the kindling fire.   90
Oh! wou'd you but confess the truth,
It is not real virtue makes you nice:
But when you do resist the pressing youth,
'Tis want of dear desire, to thaw the Virgin Ice.
   And while your young adorers lye   95
All languishing and hopeless at your feet,
   Raising new Trophies to your chastity,
   Oh tell me, how you do remain discreet?
   How you suppress the rising sighs,
And the soft yeilding soul that wishes in your Eyes?   100
   While to th'admiring crow'd you nice are found;
   Some dear, some secret, youth that gives the wound
Informs you, all your virtu's but a cheat
   And Honour but a false disguise,
Your modesty a necessary bait   105
To gain the dull repute of being wise.
Deceive the foolish World——deceive it on,
   And veil your passions in your pride;
But now I've found your feebles by my own,
From me the needful fraud you cannot hide.   110
   Thô tis a mighty power must move
   The soul to this degree of love,
And thô with virtue I the World perplex,
Lysander finds the weekness of my sex,
So *Helen* when from *Theseus* arms she fled,   115
To charming *Paris* yeilds her heart and Bed.

88 *Calenture*: a burning fever   109 *feebles*: foibles   115 *Helen*: Helen was abducted
as a child by Theseus, but as an adult, eloped with Paris

202   SONG. *On her Loving Two Equally.*
          Set by Captain Pack.

I.

How strongly does my Passion flow,
Divided equally 'twixt two?

Damon had ne'er subdu'd my Heart,
Had not *Alexis* took his part;
Nor cou'd *Alexis* pow'rful prove,   5
Without my *Damons* Aid, to gain my Love.

II.

When my *Alexis* present is,
Then I for *Damon* sigh and mourn;
But when *Alexis* I do miss,
Damon gains nothing but my Scorn.   10
But if it chance that both are by,
For both alike I languish, sigh, and die.

III.

Cure then, thou mighty winged God,
This restless Feaver in my Blood;
One Golden-Pointed Dart take back: 15
But which, O *Cupid*, wilt thou take?
If *Damons*, all my Hopes are crost;
Or that of my *Alexis*, I am lost.

Title: Simon Pack, 1654–1701, was a soldier and amateur musician who was well known as
a composer of songs for plays. He contributed a tune to Behn's *The Rover*.

203   *To Mrs. W. On her Excellent Verses*
        (Writ in Praise of some I had made on the
        Earl of Rochester*) Written in a Fit of Sickness.*

Enough kind Heaven! to purpose I have liv'd
And all my Sighs and Languishments surviv'd.
My Stars in vain their sullen influence have shed,
    Round my till now Unlucky Head:
    I pardon all the Silent Hours I've griev'd,   5
My Weary Nights, and Melancholy Days;
    When no Kind Power my Pain Reliev'd,
I lose you all, you sad Remembrancers,
    I lose you all in New-born Joys,
Joys that will dissipate my Falling Tears.   10
The Mighty Soul of *Rochester*'s reviv'd,
Enough Kind Heaven to purpose I have liv'd.
I saw the Lovely *Phantom*, no Disguise,
    Veil'd the blest Vision from my Eyes,
'Twas all o're *Rochester* that pleas'd and did surprize.   15
Sad as the Grave I sat by Glimmering Light,
Such as attends Departing Souls by Night.

Pensive as absent Lovers left alone,
Or my poor Dove, when his Fond Mate was gone.
Silent as Groves when only Whispering Gales,   20
    Sigh through the Rushing Leaves,
As softly as a Bashful Shepherd Breaths,
    To his Lov'd Nymph his Amorous Tales.
So dull I was, scarce Thought a Subject found,
Dull as the Light that gloom'd around;   25
  When lo the Mighty Spirit appear'd,
  All Gay, all Charming to my sight;
  My Drooping Soul it Rais'd and Cheer'd,
    And cast about a Dazling Light.
    In every part there did appear,   30
    The Great, the God-like *Rochester*,
His Softness all, his Sweetness everywhere.

It did advance, and with a Generous Look,
To me Addrest, to worthless me it spoke,
With the same wonted Grace my Muse it prais'd,   35
With the same Goodness did my Faults Correct:
And Careful of the Fame himself first rais'd,
Obligingly it School'd my loose Neglect.
The soft, the moving Accents soon I knew
The gentle Voice made up of Harmony;   40
Through the Known Paths of my glad Soul it flew;
I knew it straight, it could no others be,
'Twas not Alied but very very he.
    So the All-Ravisht Swain that hears
    The wondrous Musick of the Sphears,   45
For ever does the grateful Sound retain,
  Whilst all his Oaten Pipes and Reeds,
The Rural Musick of the Groves and Meads,
Strive to divert him from the Heavenly Song in vain.
  He hates their harsh and Untun'd Lays,   50
Which now no more his Soul and Fancy raise.
  But if one Note of the remembred Air
    He chance again to hear,
  He starts, and in a transport cries,—'*Tis there*!
He knows it all by that one little taste,   55
And by that grateful Hint remembers all the rest.
Great, Good, and Excellent, by what new way
  Shall I my humble Tribute pay,
  For this vast Glory you my Muse have done,
  For this great Condescention shown!   60
  So Gods of old sometimes laid by
  Their Awful Trains of Majesty,
  And chang'd ev'n Heav'n a while for Groves and Plains,

And to their Fellow-Gods preferr'd the lowly Swains.
   And beds of Flow'rs would oft compare   65
To those of Downey Clouds, or yielding Air;
At Purling Streams would drink in homely Shells;
Put off the God, to Revel it in Woods and Shepherds Cells;
   Would listen to their Rustick Songs, and show
   Such Divine Goodness in Commending too,   70
   Whilst the transported Swain the Honour pays
   With humble Adoration, humble Praise.

(after 1680)

204   *A PARAPHRASE ON OENONE to PARIS*

The ARGUMENT

Hecuba *being with Child of* Paris, *dreamt she was delivered of a Firebrand,* Priam *consulting the Prophets, was answer'd the Child shou'd be the Cause of the Destruction of* Troy, *wherefore* Priam *commanded it should be deliver'd to wild Beasts as soon as born; but* Hecuba *conveys it secretly to Mount* Ida, *there to be foster'd by the Shepherds, where he falls in love with the Nymph* Oenone, *but at length being known and own'd, he sayls into* Greece, *and carries* Helen *to* Troy, *which* Oenone *hearing, writes him this Epistle.*

To thee, dear *Paris*, Lord of my Desires,
Once tender Partner of my softest Fires;
To thee I write, mine, whilst a Shepherds Swain,
But now a Prince, that Title you disdain.
Oh fatal Pomp, that cou'd so soon divide   5
What Love, and all our Vows to firmly ty'd!
What God our Loves industrious to prevent,
Curst thee with power, and ruin'd my Content?
Greatness which does at best but ill agree
With Love, such Distance sets 'twixt Thee and Me.   10
Whilst thou a Prince, and I a Shepherdess,
My raging Passion can have no redress.
Wou'd God, when I first saw thee, thou hadst been
This Great, this Cruel, Celebrated Thing.
That without hope I might have gaz'd and bow'd,   15
And mixt my Adoration with the Crowd;
Unwounded then I had escap'd those Eyes,
Those lovely Authors of my Miseries.
Not that less Charms their fatal pow'r had drest,
But Fear and Awe my Love had then supprest;   20
My unambitious Heart no Flame had known,
But what Devotion pays to Gods alone.
I might have wonder'd, and have wisht that He,

Whom Heaven shou'd make me love, might look like Thee.
More in a silly Nymph had been a sin,   25
This had the height of my Presumption been.
But thou a Flock didst feed on *Ida*'s Plain,
And hadst no Title, but *The lovely Swain*.
A Title! which more Virgin Hearts has won,
Then that of being own'd King *Priam*'s Son.   30
Whilst me a harmless Neighbouring Cottager
You saw, and did above the rest prefer.
You saw! and at first sight you lov'd me too,
Nor cou'd I hide the wounds receiv'd from you.
Me all the Village Herdsmen strove to gain,   35
For me the Shepherds sigh'd and su'd in vain,
Thou hadst my heart, and they my cold disdain.
Nor all their Offerings Garlands, and first born
Of their lov'd Ewes, cou'd bribe my Native scorn.
My Love, like hidden Treasure long conceal'd,   40
Cou'd only where 'twas destin'd, be reveal'd.
And yet how long my Maiden blushes strove
Not to betray the easie new born Love.
But at thy sight the kindling Fire wou'd rise,
And I, unskil'd, declare it at my Eyes.   45
But oh the Joy! the mighty Extasy
Possest thy Soul at this Discovery.
Speechless, and panting at my feet you lay,
And short-breath'd Sighs told what you cou'd not say.
A thousand times my hand with Kisses prest,   50
And look'd such Darts, as none cou'd e're resist.
Silent we gaz'd, and as my Eyes met thine,
New Joy fill'd theirs, new Love and shame fill'd mine!
You saw the Fears my kind disorder shows,
And broke your Silence with a thousand Vows!   55
Heavens, how you swore! by ev'ry Pow'r Divine
You wou'd be ever true! be ever mine:
Each God, a sacred witness you invoke,
And wish'd their Curse when e're these Vows you broke.
Quick to my Heart the perjur'd Accents ran,   60
Which I took in, believ'd, and was undone.
'Vows are Loves poyson'd Arrows, and the heart
So wounded, rarely finds a Cure in Art.
At least this heart which Fate has destin'd yours,
This heart unpractic'd in Loves mystick pow'rs,   65
For I am soft, and young as *April* Flowers.
  Now uncontroul'd we meet, uncheck't improve
Each happier Minute in new Joys of Love!
  Soft were our hours! and lavishly the Day
  We gave intirely up to Love, and Play.   70

Oft to the cooling Groves, our Flocks we led,
And seated on some shaded, flowry Bed;
Watch'd the united Wantons as they fed.
And all the Day my list'ning Soul I hung,
Upon the charming Musick of thy Tongue.   75
And never thought the blessed hours too long.
No swain, no God like thee cou'd ever move,
Or had so soft an Art in whispering Love,
No wonder that thou wert Ally'd to *Jove*.
And when you pip'd, or sung, or danc'd, or spoke,   80
The God appear'd in every Grace and Look.
Pride of the Swains, and Glory of the Shades,
The Grief, and Joy of all the Love-Sick Maids.
Thus while all hearts you rul'd without Controul,
I reign'd the absolute Monarch of your Soul.   85
    Each *Beach* my Name yet bears, car'vd out by thee,
Paris, and his *Oenone* fill each Tree;
And as they grow, the Letters larger spread,
Grow still! a witness of my Wrongs when dead!
    Close by a silent silver Brook there grows   90
A Poplar, under whose dear gloomy Boughs
A thousand times we have exchang'd our Vows!
Oh may'st thou grow! to an endless date of Years!
Who on thy Bark this fatal Record bears;
When Paris *to* Oenone *proves untrue,*   95
Back Xanthus *Streams shall to their Fountains flow.*
Turn! turn! your Tide, back to your Fountains run!
The perjur'd Swain from all his Faith is gone!
    Curst be that day, may Fate point out the hour,
As Ominous in his black Kalender;   100
When *Venus*, *Pallas*, and the Wife of *Jove*
Descended to thee in the Mirtle Grove,
In shining Chariots drawn by winged Clouds:
Naked they came, no Veil their Beauty shrouds;
But every Charm, and Grace expos'd to view,   105
Left Heav'n to be survey'd, and judg'd by you.
To bribe thy voice, Juno wou'd Crowns bestow,
Pallas more gratefully wou'd dress thy Brow
With Wreaths of Wit! Venus propos'd the choice
Of all the fairest Greeks! and had thy Voice.   110
Crowns, and more glorious Wreaths thou didst despise,
And promis'd Beauty more than Empire prize!
This when you told, Gods! what a killing fear
Did over all my shivering limbs appear?
And I presag'd some ominous Change was near!   115
    The Blushes left my Cheeks, from every part
    The Blood ran swift to guard my fainting heart.

You in my Eys the glimmering Light perceiv'd ⎫
Of parting life, and on my pale Lips breath'd ⎬
Such Vows, as all my Terrors undeceiv'd.   ⎭   120
But soon the envying Gods disturb'd our Joys,
Declare thee Great! and all my Bliss destroys!
   And now the Fleet is Anchor'd in the Bay
That must to Troy the glorious Youth convey.
Heavens! how you look'd! and what a Godlike Grace   125
At their first Homage beautify'd your Face!
Yet this no Wonder or Amazement brought,
You still a Monarch were in Soul, and thought!
Nor cou'd I tell which most the Sigh augments,
Your Joys of Pow'r, or parting Discontents.   130
You kist the Tears which down my Cheeks did glide,
And mingled yours with the soft falling Tide,
And 'twixt your Sighs a thousand times you said
Cease my Oenone! *Cease my charming Maid*!
If Paris *lives his Native* Troy *to see*,   135
My lovely Nymph, thou shalt a Princess be!
But my Prophetick Fear no Faith allows,
My breaking Heart resisted all thy Vows.
Ah must we part, I cryd! *those killing words*
No further Language to my Grief affords.   140
Trembling, I fell upon thy panting Breast   ⎫
Which was with equal Love, and Grief opprest,   ⎬
Whilst sighs and looks, all dying spoke the rest, ⎭
About thy Neck my feeble Arms I cast,
Not *Vines*, nor *Ivy* circle *Elms* so fast.   145
To stay, what dear Excuses didst thou frame,
And fanciedst Tempests when the Seas were calm?
How oft the Winds contrary feign'd to be,
When they alas were only so to me!
How oft new Vows of lasting Faith you swore,   150
And 'twixt your Kisses all the old run o're?
   But now the wisely Grave, who Love despise,
(Themselves past hope) do busily advise,
Whisper Renown, and Glory in thy Ear,
Language which Lovers fright, and Swains ne're hear.   155
For *Troy* they cry! these Shepherds Weeds lay down,
Change Crooks for Scepters! Garlands for a Crown!
But sure that Crown does far less easie fit,
Than wreaths of Flow'rs, less innocent and sweet.
Nor can thy Beds of State so grateful be,   160
As those of Moss, and new fall'n Leaves with me!
   Now tow'rds the *Beach* we go, and all the way
The Groves, the Fern, dark Woods, and Springs survey;
That were so often conscious to the Rites

Of sacred Love, in our dear stol'n Delights.   165
With Eyes all langishing, each place you view,
And sighing cry, *Adieu, dear Shades, Adieu!*
Then 'twas thy Soul e'en doubted which to do,
Refuse a Crown, or those dear Shades forgoe!
Glory and Love! the great dispute persu'd,   170
But the false Idol soon the God subdu'd.
     And now on Board you go, and all the Sails
Are loosned, to receive the flying Gales.
Whilst I half dead on the forsaken Strand, ⎫
Beheld thee sighing on the Deck to stand,   ⎬   175
Wasting a thousand Kisses from thy Hand.   ⎭
And whilst I cou'd the lessening Vessel see,
I gaz'd, and sent a thousand Sighs to thee!
And all the Sea-born *Neriads* implore,
Quick to return thee to our Rustick shore.   180
     Now like a Ghost I glide through ev'ry Grove, ⎫
Silent, and sad as Death, about I rove,   ⎬
And visit all our Treasuries of Love!   ⎭
This Shade th'account of thousand Joys does hide,
As many more this murmuring Rivers side.   185
Where the dear Grass, as sacred, does retain
The print, where thee and I so oft have lain.
Upon this Oak thy Pipe, and Garland's plac'd,
That *Sycamore* is with thy Sheephook grac't.
Here feed thy Flocks, once lov'd though now thy scorn;   190
Like me forsaken, and like me forlorn!
     A Rock there is, from whence I cou'd survey
From far the blewish Shore, and distant Sea,
Whose hanging top with toyl I climb each day,
With greedy View the prospect I run o're,   195
To see what wish't for Ships approach our shore,
One day all hopeless on its point I stood,
And saw a Vessel bounding o're the Flood,
And as it nearer drew, I cou'd discern
Rich Purple Sayls, Silk Cords, and Golden Stern;   200
Upon the Deck a Canopy was spread   ⎫
Of Antique work in Gold and Silver made.   ⎬
Which mixt with Sun-beams dazling Light display'd. ⎭
But oh! beneath this glorious Scene of State
(Curst be the sight) a fatal Beauty sate.   205
Whilst with your perjur'd Lips her Fingers plaid;
Wantonly curl'd and dally'd with that hair,
Of which, as sacred Charms, I Bracelets wear.
     Oh! hadst thou seen me then in that mad state
So ruin'd, so design'd for Death and Fate,   210
Fix't on a Rock, whose horrid Precipice

In hollow Murmurs wars with Angry Seas;
Whilst the bleak Winds aloft my Garment bear, ⎫
Ruffling my careless and dishevel'd hair,   ⎬
I look't like the sad Statue of Despair.   ⎭   215
With out-stretcht voice I cry'd, and all around
The Rocks and Hills my dire complaints resound.
I rend my Garments, tear my flattering Face,
Whose false deluding Charms my Ruin was.
Mad as the Seas in Storms, I breath Despair,   220
Or Winds let loose in unresisting Air.
Raging and Frantick through the Woods I fly,
And *Paris*! lovely, faithless, *Paris*, cry.
But when the Ecchos found thy Name again.
I change to new Variety of Pain.   225
For that dear Name such tenderness inspires,
As turns all Passion to Loves softer Fires:
With tears I fall to kind Complaints again,
So Tempests are allay'd by Show'rs of Rain.
     Say, lovely Youth, why wou'dst thou thus betray   230
My easie Faith, and lead my heart astray?
It might some humble Shepherds Choice have been,
Had I that Tongue ne're heard, those Eyes ne're seen.
And in some homely Cott, in low Repose,
Liv'd undisturb'd with broken Vows and Oaths: 235
All day by shaded Springs my Flocks have kept,
And in some honest Arms at Night have slept.
Then unupbraided with my wrongd thou'dst been
Safe in the Joys of the fair Grecian Queen.
What Stars do rule the Great? no sooner you   240
Became a Prince, but you were Perjur'd too.
Are Crowns and Falshoods then consistant things?
And must they all be faithless who are Kings?
The Gods be prais'd that I was humbly born,
Even tho' it renders me my Paris scorn.   245
And I had rather this way wretched prove,
Than be a Queen and faithless in my Love.
Not my fair Rival wou'd I wish to be,
To come prophan'd by others Joys to thee.
A spotless Maid into thy Arms I brought,   250
Untouch't in Fame, ev'n Innocent in thought.
Whilst she with Love has treated many a Guest,
And brings thee but the leavings of a Feast:
With Theseus from her Country made Escape,
Whilst she miscall'd the willing Flight, a Rape.   255
So now from Atreus Son, with thee is fled,
And still the Rape hides the Adult'rous Deed.
And is it thus Great Ladies keep intire

That Vertue they so boast, and you admire?
Is this a Trick of Courts, can Ravishment   260
Serve for a poor Evasion of Consent?
Hard shift to save that Honour priz'd so high,
Whilst the mean Fraud's the greater Infamy.
How much more happy are we Rural Maids,
Who know no other Palaces than Shades?   265
Who want no Titles to enslave the Croud,
Least they shou'd babble all our Crimes aloud.
No Arts our good to show, our Ills to hide,
Nor know to cover faults of Love with Pride.
I lov'd, and all Loves Dictates did persue,   270
And never thought it cou'd be Sin with you.
To God, and Men, I did my Love proclaim
For one soft hour with thee, my charming Swain,
Wou'd Recompence an Age to come of Shame,
Cou'd it as well but satisfie my Fame.   275
But oh! those tender hours are fled and lost,
And I no more of Fame, or Thee can boast!
'Twas thou wert Honour, Glory, all to me: ⎫
Till Swains had learn'd the Vice of Perjury,   ⎬
No yielding Maids were charg'd with Infamy.   ⎭   280
'Tis false and broken Vows make Love a Sin,
Hadst thou been true, We innocent had been.
But thou less faith than Autumn leaves do'st show,
Which ev'ry Blast bears from their native Bough.
Less Weight, less Constancy, in thee is born   285
Than in the slender mildew'd Ears of Corn.
    Oft when you garland wove to deck my hair,
Where mystick Pinks, and Dazies mingled were,
You swore 'twas fitter Diadems to bear:
And when with eager Kisses prest my hand,   290
Have said, How well a Scepter 'twould command!
And if I danc't upon the Flow'ry Green,   ⎫
With charming, wishing Eyes survey my Miene,   ⎬
And cry! the Gods design'd thee for a Queen!   ⎭
Why then for Helen dost thou me forsake?   295
Can a poor empty Name such difference make?
Besides, if Love can be a Sin thine's one,
Since Helen does to Menelaus belong.
Be Just, restore her back, She's none of thine,
And, charming Paris, thou art only mine.   300
'Tis no Ambitious Flame that makes me sue
To be again belov'd, and blest with you;
No vain desire of being Ally'd t'a King,   ⎫
Love is the only Dowry I can bring,   ⎬
And tender Love is all I ask again.   ⎭   305

Whilst on her dang'rous Smiles fierce War must wait
With Fire and Vengeance at your Palace gate,
Rouze your soft Slumbers with their rough Alarms,
And rudely snatch you from her faithless Arms:
Turn then fair Fugitive, e're tis too late,   310
E're a wrong'd Husband does thy Death design,
And pierce that dear, that faithless Heart of thine.

79 *Jove*: ruler of the gods, but a notorious seducer of mortal maidens   101 *Venus*: the three
goddesses Aphrodite (Venus), Athena (Pallas), and Hera (the wife of Jove) came naked to
Paris to ask him to judge which was the loveliest. All three took the precaution of attempting
to bribe him, as the poem recounts   179 *Neriads*: Nereids, sea-nymphs   205 *Beauty*:
Helen, wife of Menelaus with whom Paris had eloped   254 *Theseus*: Helen was abducted by
Theseus in her youth   256 *Atreus Son*: her husband Menelaus

205 *To* Damon. *To inquire of him if he cou'd tell me by the style, who writ me a Copy of Verses that came to me in an unknown Hand, by Mrs. A.B.*

Oh, *Damon*, if thou ever werst'
    That certain friend thou hast profest,
Relieve the Pantings of my heart,
    Restore me to my wonted rest.

        Late in the *Silvian* Grove I sat,   5
        Free as the Air, and calm as that;
        For as no winds the boughs opprest,
        No storms of Love were in my breast.
    A long Adieu I'd bid to that
    Ere since *Amintas* prov'd ingrate.   10
    And with indifference, or disdain,
    I lookt around upon the Plain.
And worth my favor found no sighing Swain:
        But oh, my Damon, all in vain
            I triumph'd in security,   15
    In vain absented from the Plain.
        The wanton God his Power to try
    In lone recesses makes us yeild,
    As well as in the open feild;
    For where no human thing was found   20
    My heedless heart receiv'd a wound.
        Assist me, Shepherd, or I dye,
        Help to unfold this Mystery.

No Swain was by, no flattering Nymph was neer,
Soft tales of Love to whisper to my Ear.   25
    In sleep, no Dream my fancy fir'd
With Images, my waking wish desir'd.

Nor to the faithless sex one thought inclin'd;
  I sigh'd for no deceiving youth,
  Who forfeited his vows and truth;   30
  I waited no Assigning Swain
  Whose disappointment gave me pain.
  My fancy did no prospect take
  Of Conquest's I design'd to make.
  No snares for Lovers I had laid,   35
  Nor was of any snare afraid.
  But calm and innocent I sate,
  Content with my indifferent fate.
  (A Medium, I confess, I hate.)
  For when the mind so cool is grown ⎫   40
  As neither Love nor Hate to own,   ⎬
  The Life but dully lingers on.   ⎭

Thus in the mid'st of careless thought,
A paper to my hand was brought.
  What hidden charms were lodg'd within,   45
  To my unwary Eyes unseen,
  Alas! no Human thought can guess;
  But oh! it robb'd me of my peace.
  A Philter 'twas, that darted pain
  Thrô every pleas'd and trembling vein.   50
  A stratagem, to send a Dart
  By a new way into the heart,
  Th' Ignoble Policie of Love
  By a clandestin means to move.
  Which possibly the Instrument ⎫   55
  Did ne're design to that intent, ⎬
  But only form, and complement. ⎭
  While Love did the occasion take
  And hid beneath his flowres a snake
  O're every line did Poyson fling   60
  In every word he lurk'd a sting.
  So Matrons are, by *Demons* charms,
  Thô harmless, capable of harms.

The verse was smooth, the thought was fine,
  The fancy new, the wit divine.   65
But fill'd with praises of my face and Eyes,
My verse, and all those usual flatteries
  To me as common as the Air;
Nor cou'd my vanity procure my care.
  All which as things of course are writ   70
  And less to shew esteem than wit.
  But here was some strange something more
  Than ever flatter'd me before;

My heart was by my Eyes misled:
I blusht and trembl'd as I read.   75
And every guilty look confest
I was with new surprise opprest,
From every view I felt a pain
And by the Soul, I drew the Swain.
Charming as fancy cou'd create   80
Fine as his Poem, and soft as that.
I drew him all the heart cou'd move
I drew him all that women Love.
And such a dear Idea made
As has my whole repose betray'd.   85
Pigmalion thus his Image form'd
And for the charms he made, he sigh'd and burn'd.

O thou that know'st each Shepherds Strains ⎫
That Pipes and Sings upon the Plains;   ⎬
Inform me where the youth remains.   ⎭   90
The spightful Paper bare no name.
Nor can I guess from whom it came,
Or if at least a guess I found,
'Twas not t'instruct but to confound.

206   *Silvio's Complaint: A SONG, to a Fine*
Scotch Tune.

I.

In the Blooming Time o'th'year,
In the Royal Month of May:
Au the Heavens were glad and clear,
Au the Earth was Fresh and Gay.
A Noble Youth but all Forlorn,   5
Lig'd Sighing by a Spring:
'Twere better I's was nere Born,
Ere wisht to be a King.

II.

Then from his Starry Eyne,
Muckle Showers of Christal Fell: 10
To bedew the Roses Fine,
That on his Cheeks did dwell.
And ever 'twixt his Sighs did cry,
How Bonny a Lad I'd been,
Had I, weys me, nere Aim'd high,   15
Or wisht to be a King.

III.

With Dying Clowdy Looks,
Au the Fields and Groves he kens:
Ay the Gleeding Murmuring Brooks,
(Noo his Unambitious Friends)   20
Tol which he eance with Mickle Cheer
His Bleating Flocks woud bring:
And crys, woud God I'd dy'd here,
Ere wisht to be a King.

IV.

How oft in Yonder Mead,   25
Cover'd ore with Painted Flowers:
Au the Dancing Youth I've led,
Where we past our Blether Hours.
In Yonder Shade, in Yonder Grove,
How blest the *Nymphs* have been: 30
Ere I for Pow'r Debaucht Love,
    Or wisht to be a King.

V.

Not au the *Arcadian Swains*,
In their Pride and Glory Clad:
Not au the Spacious Plains,   35
Ere coud Boast a Bleether Lad.
When ere I Pip'd or Danc'd, or Ran,
Or leapt, or whirl'd the Sling:
The Flowry Wreaths I still won,
    And wisht to be a King,   40

VI.

But Curst be yon Tall Oak,
And Old Thirsis be accurst:
There I first my peace forsook,
There I learnt Ambition first.
Such Glorious Songs of *Hero's* Crown'd,   45
The Restless Swain woud Sing:
My Soul unknown desires found,
    And Languisht to be King.

VII.

Ye Garlands wither now,
Fickle Glories vanish all: 50
Ye Wreaths that deckt my Brow,
To the ground neglected fall.
No more my sweet Repose molest,
Nor to my Fancies bring

The Golden Dreams of being Blest   55
With Titles of a King.

VIII.

Ye Noble Youths beware,
Shun Ambitious powerful Tales:
Distructive, False, and Fair,
Like the Oceans Flattering Gales   60
See how my Youth and Glories lye,
Like Blasted Flowers i'th'Spring:
My Fame Renown and all dye,
   For wishing to be King.

(c. 1683)

3 *Au*: aa (all)—Scotticism   5 *Youth*: Charles II's illegitimate son, the Duke of Monmouth (1649–85), claimant to the throne; he was enmeshed by Shaftesbury in the Rye
House Plot (1683), on the discovery of which he fled to the Low Countries. His personal
name was James Scott, hence the transparent fiction of a 'Scotch song'   6 *Lig'd*: lay—
Scotticism   10 *Muckle*: many—Scotticism 15 *weys me*: waes me (woe is me)—Scotticism   18 *kens*: knows—Scotticism   19 *Gleeding*: gliding   20 *Noo*: now—Scotticism
21 *eance*: aince (once)—Scotticism   28 *Blether*: blither   42 *Thirsis*: 'arcadian' name,
standing for the Earl of Shaftesbury, Achitophel in Dryden's *Absalom and Achitophel*
(1681)

JANE SOWLE
(fl. 1680)

JANE was a Quaker, the wife of Andrew Sowle, a one-man Quaker publishing
industry. Sowle suffered frequent harassment by the authorities, and on one
occasion 'about a thousand reams of printed books' were seized. He was
imprisoned several times and Sir Richard Brown, the Lord Mayor, even threatened to have him executed. He died in 1695 at his house in Holywell Lane, aged
67. Jane was described as a printer and bookseller. She was the mother of two
daughters, Tace Sowle and Elizabeth, later Bradford (who also wrote verse, see
no. 255), both of whom were trained as printers. Tace was made free of the
Stationer's Company shortly after her father's death and, assisted by her mother,
and later her husband and a foreman, managed the Sowle press for fifty-four
years. From 1695, Tace printed works in her own name (including the poems of
Mary Mollineux: see nos. 223–5), but though she was practically speaking in
charge, she ensured that her mother Jane always had 'the chief command of the
house'. Few elderly widows of the seventeenth century can ever have been so
honoured and cherished. When Tace married in 1706, the printing-house
imprint became 'J. Sowle', though Jane was by then 75, and can have taken
little part in the hard labour of printing. After Jane's death in 1711, the imprint
became 'assigns of J. Sowle'. In defiance of normal expectations, Tace's husband, marrying into a thriving business run by women, left no mark upon it: his
jobs were the ancillary ones of keeping track of warehousing, accounting, and
distribution. Tace continued to print until she was 83.

207   *A short Testimony for Anne Whitehead*

Dear Ann is gone unto her Rest
Of women sure, one of the Best
True Wisdom had she from above
Filled with Vertue and true Love;
So that to us our loss was such,   5
Caus'd Tears and Sorrow very much:
But since it doth to us befall,
And God did to himself her call;
Let us beg of him that he will
Our Women with his Spirit fill,   10
And make them able to withstand
Truth's Opposers at ev'ry hand,
Till they Gods Work have finished
And all in Peace laid down the head,
And Crown'd with Glory into Heaven   15
So let it be, O Lord, *Amen*

                                        Jane Soule

ELIZABETH WILMOT (née MALET),
COUNTESS OF ROCHESTER
(*c*.1640–1681)

THE wife of the notorious John Wilmot, Earl of Rochester was 'the great beauty
and fortune of the North', according to Pepys, worth £2,500 a year. She was
the only child and heiress of John Malet of Enmore in Somerset, and granddaughter of Lord Hawley. In 1665, when he himself was 17, Rochester
attempted to abduct her, and was punished by a brief confinement in the
Tower. After a somewhat scandal-prone couple of years at court flirting with
her many suitors, she decided to marry him after all, and did so in January
1666/7. Both she and Rochester were still minors. This was a cause for
considerable celebration: her formidable mother-in-law, Lady Wilmot, was in
hopes that the Somerset fortune could be diverted to cover her own enormous
debts. There is no evidence that she succeeded in doing so. The young Countess
had a position at court, as Groom of the Stole to the Duchess of York. Early in
her marriage, she converted to Roman Catholicism, and remained a Catholic
until a few weeks before her husband's death in 1680. Rochester appears to have
been an intermittently more companionable husband than his sexual reputation
and his insistence that his wife live quietly in the country would suggest. He
encouraged his wife to participate in dittying and composing verse exchanges:
four 'Songs' and a pastoral dialogue survive. The couple had four children. Two
of her daughters, Anne Baynton, later Greville, and Elizabeth Montagu, had a
reputation as poets.

208 *Song.*

Nothing ades to Loves fond fire
More than Scorn and cold disdain
To cherish your desire
I kindness used but twas in vain
You insulted on your Slave 5
To be mine you soon refused
I hope not then the power to have
Which ingloriously you used.

Thinke not Thersis I will ere
By my love my Empire loose 10
You growe constant through dispare
Kindness you would soon abuse
Though you still possess my hart
Scorn and rigor I must fain
there remaines noe other art 15
Your love fond fugitive to gain

ANN LEE
(fl. 1660s)

THIS Ann Lee, two poems by whom survive in a commonplace book of the
Paulet family, may be connected with the Lees of Ditchley, since a number of
women of, and connected with, that family are known to have written poetry.
Many of them, alas, were called Ann. This Ann Lee cannot be Ann Wharton,
née Lee: though the *Dictionary of National Biography* puts the latter's birth at
1632, she was actually born in 1659.

209 *On the returne of King Charles 2nd*

If witt may be the Childe of chance and rise
 From love and the inspiration of fair eyes,
If an enthusiastick cup can fire
 Cold blood, and raise low brains to storyes higher,
Create a fancy, pollish every part 5
 Joine Venus beauty to Minerva's art,
And write what all the sober nine cann't doe?
 Why may not Joy dub me a poet too?
Tis not impossible, all our good newes
 Are wonders, and those wonder will infuse 10
Becomming Raptures, who is he can't sing?
 Without a Muse whose Subject is a king?

Come unincumbred thoughts from those soft beds
    Where silence dwells and the fat olive spreads
His peace-emblematizing-branches, where   15
    No eye e're spoke the language of a teare
Noe hand hath learn't to write in blood, noe tongue
    To argue for a profitable wrong:
Come and inspire my pen that I may write
    Wonders, a victory with out a fight: 20
A flood restrain'd by an invisible power
    And what was sea made dry-land the next hour.

    .   .   .   .
    With noble straines or teach me to be dumbe
My lynes goe not a fishing for great friends
    For end they'le have, but they will have no ends   25
This is a royall taske deserves your oyle
    And here the greatest labour is noe toyle
Tis duty guides my pen, nor doe I run
    With flattring lines to court the riseing Sun:
For when my prince labour'd against the streame   30
    He was my prayers that is now my theame
But how I shall present him thats the doubt
    Sunbeames with Sunbeames must be coppyed out.
Colours shew onely shaddows to our sight
    But art ne're found a counterfeit for light   35
Soe majesty that shines in its high ranck
    Cannot be figur'd but with a great blanck.
Words must grow dumbe to speake, it to aspire
    As high as thoughts can reach it is t'admire
I am not eagle-sighted, he that pryes   40
    Into too glorious light hazards his eyes
My quill soars noe such heights, my walke shall be
    To blaze on th'outward skirts of Majesty
Sing of his royall person his great blood
    And valour when he fought against the flood   45
His vertue, his religion and what hopes
    We have of plenty of more things than Ropes
His wisedome his experience bought soe dear
    His justice void, both of revenge and fear:
His mercy to forgive whats done amiss   50
    All the prognosticks of our future bliss:
The peoples love, their joy, at his returne
    As if from hell to heaven they'd adjourne
This is the course I steer, envy stand bare
    My lines are streight and will not interfere   55
Truth needs noe factor, doe but right, and then
    To all I write, thy-selfe shall say Amen
As after a black tempest hath disturb'd

The quiet of the element and curb'd
With cloudy-mufflers the allseeing light   60
(For mischiefe if it want, will make a night)
Unkennel'd all the windes from their strong Caves
And curl'd the peacefull sea with boistrous waves
Dissolu'd the ayer into a stormy rain
And frozen't to bulletts of haile again   65
Fir'd the great Guns of heauen with such a noise
That the eccho dare not to repeat the voice:
Amaze both men, and beasts that nothing hear
But a good conscience can be void of fear.
Yet when the world's bright eye appeares, his rayes   70
Open the clouds, and his kinde heat allayes
The now digested windes, the heavens will weep
Noe more, all thunder too will fall asleep.
Natur's recover'd and is (let art not flout her)
Fayre, tho' shee hath not one black patch about her.   75

Composed by
Ann Lee

7 *nine*: Muses   14 *olive*: fat, because oil-producing, the emblem of peace   22 *dry-land*:
Exodus 14:21 'Moses...made the sea dry land'   25 *ends*: ulterior motives   26 *oyle*:
lamp-oil, i.e. toiling night and day   72 *digested*: alchemical usage: successfully transformed   75 *patch*: elegant ladies wore little black patches as beauty-spots

SARAH GOODHUE, née WHIPPLE
(1641–1681)

A LIFELONG resident in Ipswich, Massachussets, Sarah's families of birth and
marriage were both prosperous. She was the youngest daughter of John and
Susannah Whipple: Ann Bradstreet was probably a visitor to her father's home.
She married Joseph Goodhue on 13 July 1661, and her first child followed
promptly in 1662. She left a few verses in her prose *Copy of a Valedictory and
Monitory Writing* (1681) published in Cambridge, Massachussets, 1681, and
reprinted in 1770, 1773, 1805, and 1850. This is an example of the 'Mother's
Legacy' genre, popular in the sixteenth century, but somewhat archaic in the
late seventeenth. According to the title-page of her *Copy*, she died on 23 July
1681, 'three Days after she had been delivered of two hopeful Children, leaving
ten in all surviving'.

210   *'My first, as thy name is Joseph,
labour so in knowledge to increase'*

My first, as thy name is Joseph, labour so in knowledge to increase,
As to be freed from the guilt of thy sins, and enjoy eternal peace.

Mary, labour so as to be arrayed with the hidden man of the heart,
That with Mary, thou mayst find thou has chosen the better part.
William, thou hast that name for thy grandfather's sake,   5
Labour so as to tread in his steps, as over sin conquest mayest thou
    make.
Sarah, Sarah's daughter shalt thou be, if thou continuest in doing well,
Labour so in holiness among the daughters to walk, as that thou
    may excel.
So my children all, if I must be gone, I with tears bid you all
    farewell.
The Lord bless you all.   10
Now, dear husband, I can do no less than turn unto thee
And if I could, I would naturally mourn with thee:
O dear heart, if I must leave thee and thine here behind
Of my natural affection here is my heart and hand.

                                                            (1681)

BARBARA SYMS AND CAPTAIN COOKE
(fl. 1663)

THERE is a number of song-texts which appear to have been written by women
(we might equally well have included 'Prudence Draper her songe, 1648, in
London, British Library, Harley 2127, fo. 31ʳ, and we do include a song by Lady
Rochester, no. 208 as well as one by Aphra Behn, no. 202): in some circles,
particularly those in contact with the court, women's dittying was perceived as
an elegant accomplishment. There are two other songs attributed to Barbara Syms
in Oxford, Bodleian Library MS Rawl. Poet. 84, Mrs Ba.Syms Song, fo. 39, and
'Goe let alone my swaine and me', fo. 123ᵛ. f[or] Captaine Cooke, *Mrs Barbara
Syms.* is written at the bottom, and it is dated 1663. The book, a miscellany
collection, was first owned by Giles Frampton, who seems to have begun it in
1659. Whoever Barbara Syms may have been, she is strongly associated with the
colourful figure of Captain Henry Cooke. Having begun as a chorister of the
Chapel Royal, he fought for the King in the Civil War, and obtained a captain's
commission for his bravery. At the Restoration, he became Master of the Children
of the Chapel Royal, and held the position until his death in 1672. Samuel Pepys
makes it clear that he was a composer: in 1660, he heard 'a brave anthem of Captain
Cooke's which he himself sung'. Elsewhere, Pepys commments, 'a vain coxcomb
he is, though he sings so well'. The implications of the layout of Barbara Syms's
verses is that Cooke set them to music. The song given here was presumably
written and performed in alternate voices.

211   *Song*

        [CC]   Goe turne away those Cruell Eyes
                For they have quite undone me

　　　　　They usd me for to tyranize
　　　　　When just their glances woon me
[BS]　　But 'tis the custome of you men　　　　　5
　　　　　False men, thus to deceive us
　　　　　They love but till we love againe
　　　　　and then they quickly leave us.

[CC]　　Goe let alone my heart and me
　　　　　that thou hast thus affrighted　　　　　10
　　　　　I had not thought I should have beene
　　　　　by thee thus ill requited
[BS]　　But now I find tis I must prove
　　　　　that men have not compassion
　　　　　when we are won; nor ever love　　　　　15
　　　　　poore weomen but for Fashion

　　　　　　I, Captain Cooke/Mrs Barbara Syms

7 *but till*: only until

DOROTHY WHITE
(1630–1685)

DOROTHY WHITE wrote more Quaker treatises than any other woman except George Fox's wife, Margaret Fell (1614–1702). Her first, *A Diligent Search*, dates to 1659, and she continued to write throughout her life. Although she was a prolific and notable author of religious exhortation, nothing is known of her beyond the basic facts that she was born at Weymouth, in Dorset, and died at London.

212　　*An Epistle of Love and of*
　　　　Consolation unto Israel

　　　And before him you may all rejoyce,
　　　And like Trumpets, lift up your glorious Voice:
　　　And Beloved, our Life is come,
　　　And we shall be cloathed with the Beauty of the Sun:
　　　Who is come to reign in his Majesty,　　　　　5
　　　Who is breaking forth, in this his glorious Day;
　　　Who shall reign, and over the Nations spread,
　　　And under his feet, his Enemies shall tread:
　　　So our Beloved is become our Life,
　　　We are his Virgins, and his Married Wife;　　　　10
　　　Who are to him bound all in one Band,
　　　Who are rejoycing in the Holy Land:

We are come unto the glorious Day,
Therefore all hasten, and to it come away,
That you may all be gathered in,   15
Into the Pallace of the glorious King;
That you all his Beauty may behold,
That in his Love you may be wrapt and fold.
Christ our Life, is now become our Head,
And by his Power, hath rais'd us from the Dead;   20
And unto us he is become our All,
Who in his Mercy hath sav'd us from the Fall.
This is the Day, wherein glad tidings is come,
Therefore with echoes sweet, sing to the holy one.
All you Babes, born of the Royal Birth,   25
All ye that are of the Noble Seed, who are set free from Death.
Lift up your Voice, and like a Trumpet sing.
Sound forth, sound forth, the glory of Zions king;
With ecchoes sweet, give forth the glorious Sound,
Throughout the world, with Glory, Honour, and heavenly renown;   30
That many may come and drink of *Jacobs* Well,
Whose waters sweet, in vertue doth excel;
And in chrystal streams, from his Throne doth flow,
As doth rain descend, and into the Sea doth go.
The *Rest* is come, the Sabbath is known,   35
Glory be given to him, that sitteth on the Throne

31 *Jacobs Well*: John 4: 14

redacted by ISOBEL GILBERT, née GOWDIE
(fl. 1662)

THE confession of Isobel Gowdie (Scotswomen did not take their husband's name) appears to be that considerable rarity, a witch-trial that actually caught a witch. The Scottish legal process of the time required the depositions of defendants to be taken down precisely in their own words: this provides a fascinating linguistic calendar of early modern Scotland: it also means that Mistress Gowdie's account of her experiences is likely to be *verbatim* at least in part. But in this case, the trial documents are of uncertain status, apparently the findings of an ad-hoc local ecclesiastical commission of enquiry. No original documents survive, and the early nineteenth-century antiquarian whose text is the only surviving witness to Isobel Gowdie's confession, gives no indication of their source. According to the inquisition document, she came forward voluntarily, 'appeiring penetent'. However, she also says, 'bot now I haw no power at all': it is not clear whether the loss of her 'power' propelled her into the arms of orthodoxy, or whether her arrest caused the loss of her 'power'. In either case, she seems to have been a practising *malefica* with a system of beliefs which are in

many respects independent of inquisitorial agendas. In particular, she shared
with all levels of Scottish society at the time the belief that prehistoric flint
arrowheads were 'elfbolts', and that she and her fellows could destroy their
enemies by 'spanging' such elfbolts (given them by the Devil) off their thumb-
nails. She was also a visionary, who believed that she had visited the Fairy
Queen at home: 'I was in the Downie-hillis, and got meat ther from the Qwein
of Fearrie, mor than I could eat. The Qwein of Fearrie is brawlie clothed in
whyt linens, and in whyt and browne cloathes, &c.; and the King of Fearrie is a
braw man, weill favoured, and broad faced.' She explains a number of her
practices, besides the shooting of elf-bolts, several of which involve magical
rhymes. Nothing is known of Isobel Gowdie beyond her four documents of
confession: these make it clear that she was married, and suggest that she was a
woman of some standing in the community—certainly not the despised
marginal figure of witchcraft cliché. Her husband was apparently not a witch,
though four members of her coven were husband and wife couples. Mistress
Gowdie's name is therefore standing for a whole substrate of Scottish rural
fantasy, roleplaying, shamanism, and residual pagan belief, which has left few
direct traces in the historical record, but which undoubtedly absorbed the
interest, and cost the lives, of an unknown number of early modern women.

213   *[Charm to destroy the male
            child of the Laird of Parkis]*

We put this water among this meall
For long dwyning and ill heall;
We put it in intill the fyr
To burn them up both stik and stour,
That be brunt with our will,   5
As any stikill on an kill!

1 *meall*: oatmeal   2 *dwyning*: declining;   *heall*: health   3 *intill*: in   4 *stour*:
stake   6 *stikill on an kill*: brushwood in a kiln

214   *[For cadging fish]*

The fisheris ar gon to the sea,
And they vill bring hom fishe to me;
They will bring them hom intill the boat,
Bot they sall get of thaim bot the smaller sort!

3 *intill*: in

215   *[Shapeshifting]*

I sall goe intill ane haire
With sorrow, and sych, and meikle caire;

And I sall goe in the Divellis nam
Ay whill I com hom againe.

Haire, haire, God send thé cair!   5
I am in an hairis liknes now,
Bot I sal be a voman ewin now.
Hair, hair, God send thé cair!

1 *intill*: into; *haire*: hare   2 *sych*: sighs; *meikle*: great   4 *Ay whill*: until   5   *thé*:
thee   7 *voman*: woman; *ewin*: even (i.e. any moment)

ANNA ALCOX
(*c*.1645—?)

ALMOST nothing is known of Anna Alcox. She was the child of a Catholic
family, living in the 1650s at Alveston, near Bristol. She was born in about 1645,
and composed her two surviving poems when still a child of 6, or so the
manuscript states. The age of 7 was legally significant: beneath that age, an
individual could not be held responsible for his or her actions. This may account
for the fact that these are the only poems in this long manuscript miscellany
assembled by recusants which are not anonymous.

216   *'All you that are to mirth Inclin'd'*

All you that are to mirth Inclin'd
consider well and bare in mind
What our Good God hath for us don
in sending his beloved sonne
    for to redeeme our sowles from thrall   5
    who is the saviour of us all.

Let all your songs and praises bee
Unto his heavenly majestie
And evermore amongst your mirth
remember christ our saviours birth   10

The twenty fift Day of December
Good cause have we for to remember
In bethlem upon that morne
there was our blest messias borne

That night before the happie tyde   15
the spotlesse virgin and her guide
Went long time seeking up and downe
to find their lodging in the towne

But marke how all things came to passe
the Inns and lodgings so fild was   20
that they could have no roome at all
but in a sillie oxes stall

That night the virgin mary milde
Was safe delivered of a childe
According unto heavens Decree   25
mans sweete salvation for to bee

Neere bethlem then did sheepheards keepe
Their heards and flocks of feeding sheepe
to them Gods angells did appeare
which put the sheepheards in great feare   30

Prepare and goe the Angells sayd
to bethlehem bee not affraid
theire shall you find this bleassed morne
the princly babe sweete Jesus borne

With thankfull harts and Joyfull minds   35
the sheepheards went this babe to find
And as the heavenly angells told
they did our saviour Christ behold

all in a manger was he layd
the virgin mary by him stay'd   40
attending on the lord of life
being both mother, maide, and wife

Three easterne wisemen from a farre
Directed by a gloryous starre
came bodily and made no stay   45
untill they came where Jesus lay

And being come into that place
Where as our blest messias was
they humbly layd before his feete
their gifts of gold and odoures sweet   50

No costly robes nor rich attire
did Jesus christ our Lord Desire
no musicke nor sweete harmony
till glorious angells from on high
    did in a melodious maner sing   55
    praises unto our heavenly king

All honour glory might and power
be unto christ for evermore
he raised lazarus from his grave
and to the sicke thir health he gave   60

he gave the blind their perfect sight
and made the lame to goe upright
he cur'd the leperous of their evills
And by his power cast out divills
    And to redeeme our soules from thrall   65
    became a saviour to us all.

(1651)

'PHILO-PHILIPPA'
(fl. 1667)

AN Irish admirer of Katherine Philips, her only known work is this poem, perhaps the earliest surviving example of an important strand in late-seventeenth-century feminist thinking, which focused strongly on the disparity between men's and women's educational opportunities. The zeal with which she expressed her feminist opinions led Philips to suspect that the verses might be nothing more than an elaborate hoax (*Letters to Poliarchus*, XXVI) but her suspicions were probably unfounded. Mary Astell, Mary Chudleigh, and others were to make cognate summaries of woman's position in the three decades that follow this poem's appearance in Philips' *Works*.

217   *To the Excellent* Orinda

Let the male Poets their male *Phoebus* chuse,
Thee I invoke, *Orinda*, for my Muse;
He could but force a Branch, *Daphne* her Tree
Most freely offers to her Sex and thee,
And says to Verse, to unconstrain'd as yours,   5
Her Laurel freely comes, your fame secures:
And men no longer shall with ravish'd Bays
Crown their forc'd Poems by as forc'd a praise.
    Thou glory of our Sex, envy of men,
Who are both pleas'd and vex'd with thy bright Pen: 10
Its lustre doth intice their eyes to gaze,
But mens sore eyes cannot endure its rays;
It dazles and suprises so with light,
To find a noon where they expected night:
A Woman Translate *Pompey*! which the fam'd   15
Corneille with such art and labour fram'd!
To whose close version the Wits club their sence,
And a new Lay poetick SMEC springs thence!
Yes, that bold work a Woman dares Translate,
Not to provoke, not yet to fear mens hate.   20
Nature doth find that she hath err'd too long,

And now resolves to recompence that wrong:
Phoebus to *Cynthia* must his beams resigne,
The rule of Day, and Wit's now Feminine.
    That Sex, which heretofore was not allow'd   25
To understand more than a beast, or crowd;
Of which Problems were made, whether or no
Women had Souls; but to be damn'd, if so;
Whose highest Contemplation could not pass,
In men's esteem, no higher than the Glass;   30
And all the painful labours of their Brain,
Was only how to Dress and Entertain:
Or, if they ventur'd to speak sense, the wise
Made that, and speaking Oxe, like Prodigies,
From these thy more than masculine Pen hath rear'd   35
Our Sex; first to be prais'd, next to be feard.
And by that same Pen forc'd, men now confess,
To keep their greatness, was to make us less.
    Men know of how refin'd and rich a mould
Our Sex is fram'd, what Sun is in our Gold: 40
They now in Lead no Diamonds are set,
And Jewels only fill the Cabinet.
Our Spirits purer far than theirs, they see;
By which even Men from Men distinguish'd be:
By which the Soul is judg'd, and does appear   45
Fit or unfit for action, as they are.
    When in an Organ various sounds do stroak,
Or grate the ear, as Birds sing, or Toads croak;
The Breath, that voyces every Pipe, 's the same,
But the bad mettal doth the sound defame.   50
So, if our Souls by sweeter Organs speak,
And theirs with harsh false notes the air do break;
The Soul's the same, alike in both doth dwell,
'Tis from her instruments that we excel.
Ask me not then, why jealous men debar   55
Our Sex from Books in Peace, from Arms in War;
It is because our Parts will soon demand
Tribunals for our Persons, and Command.
    Shall it be our reproach, that we are weak,
And cannot fight, nor as the School-men speak?   60
Even men themselves are neither strong nor wise,
If Limbs and Parts they do not exercise,
    Train'd up to arms, we *Amazons* have been,
And *Spartan* Virgins strong as *Spartan* Men:
Breed Women but as Men, and they are these;   65
Whilst *Sybarit* Men are Women by their ease.
Why should not brave *Semiramis* break a Lance,
And why should not soft *Ninyas* curle and dance?

Ovid in vain Bodies with change did vex,
Changing her form of life, *Iphis* chang'd Sex.   70
Nature to Females freely doth impart
That, which the Males usurp, a stout, bold heart.
Thus Hunters female Beasts fear to assail:
And female Hawks more mettal'd than the male:
Men ought not then Courage and Wit ingross,   75
Whilst the Fox lives, the Lyon, or the Horse.
Much less ought men both to themselves confine,
Whilst Women, such as you, *Orinda*, shine.
   That noble friendship brought thee to our Coast,
We thank Lucasia, and thy courage boast.   80
Death in each Wave could not Orinda fright,
Fearless she acts that friendship she did write:
Which manly Vertue to their Sex confin'd,
Thou rescuest to confirm our softer mind;
For there's requir'd (to do that Virtue right)   85
Courage, as much in Friendship as in Fight.
The dangers we despise, doth this truth prove,
Though boldly we not fight, we boldly love.
   Ingage us unto Books, *Sappho* comes forth,
Though not of *Hesiod*'s age, of *Hesiod*'s worth.   90
If Souls no Sexes have, as 'tis confest,
'Tis not the he or she makes Poems best:
Nor can men call these Verses Feminine,
Be the sense Vigorous and Masculine.
'Tis true, *Apollo* sits as Judge of Wit,   95
But the nine Female learned Troop are it:
Those Laws for which *Numa* did wise appear,
Wiser *Ægeria* whisper'd in his ear,
The *Gracchi*'s Mother taught them Eloquence,
From her Breasts courage flow'd, from her Brain sence;   100
And the grave Beards, who heard her speak in Rome,
Blush'd not to be instructed, but o'recome.
Your speech, as hers, commands respect from all,
Your very Looks, as hers, Rhetorical:
Something of grandeur in your Verse men see,   105
That they rise up to it as Majesty.
The wise and noble *Orrery*'s regard,
Was much observ'd, when he your Poem heard:
All said, a fitter match was never seen,
Had *Pompey*'s widow been *Arsamnes* Queen.   110
   Pompey, who greater than himself's become,
Now in your Poem, than before in *Rome*;
And much more lasting in the Poets Pen,
Great Princes live, than the proud Towers of Men.
He thanks false *Egypt* for its Treachery,   115

Since that his Ruine is so sung by thee;
And so again would perish, if withall,
Orinda would but celebrate his Fall.
Thus pleasingly the Bee delights to die,
Foreseeing he in Amber Tomb shall lie.   120
If that all *Ægypt*, for to purge its crime,
Were built into one Pyramid o're him,
Pompey would lie less stately in that Herse,
Than he doth now, *Orinda*, in thy Verse:
This makes *Cornelia* for her *Pompey* vow,   125
Her hand shall plant his Laurel on thy brow:
So equal in their merits were both found,
That the same Wreath Poets and Princes Crown'd:
And what on that great Captains Brow was dead,
She Joies to see re-flourish'd on thy head.   130
    In the French Rock *Cornelia* first did shine,
But shin'd not like herself, till she was thine:
Poems, like Gems, translated from the place
Where they first grew, receive another grace.
Drest by thy hand, and polish'd by thy Pen,   135
She glitters now a Star, but a Jewel then:
No flaw remains, no cloud, all now is light,
Transparent as the day, bright parts more bright.
Corneille, now made English, so doth thrive,
As Trees transplanted do much lustier live.   140
Thus Oar digg'd forth, and by such hands as thine
Refin'd and stamp'd, is richer than the Mine.
Liquors from Vessel into Vessel pour'd,
Must lose some Spirits, which are scarce restor'd:
But the French wines, in their own Vessel rare,   145
Pour'd into ours, by thy hand, Spirits are;
So high in taste, and so delicious,
Before his own *Corneille* thine would chuse.
He finds himself inlightned here, where shade
Of dark expression his own words had made: 150
There what he would have said, he sees so writ,
As generously to just decorum fit.
When in more words than his you please to flow,
Like a spread Floud, inriching all below,
To the advantage of his well meant sence,   155
He gains by you another excellence.
To render word for word, at the old rate,
Is only but to Construe, not Translate:
In your own fancy free, to his sense true,
We read *Corneille*, and *Orinda* too: 160
And yet ye both are so the very same,
As when two Tapers join'd make one bright flame.

And sure the Copiers honour is not small,
When Artists doubt which is Original.
    But if your fetter'd Muse thus praised be,   165
What great things do you write when it is free?
When it is free to choose both sence and words,
Or any subject the vast World affords?
A gliding Sea of Chrystal doth best show
How smooth, clear, full and rich your Verse doth flow: 170
Your words are chosen, cull'd, not by chance writ,
To make the sence as Anagrams do hit.
Your rich becoming words on the sence wait
As Maids of Honour on a Queen of State.
'Tis not White Satin makes a verse more white,   175
Or soft; Iron is both, write you on it.
Your Poems come forth cast, no File you need,
At one brave Heat both shap'd and polished.
    But why all these Encomiums of you,
Who either doubts, or will not take as due?   180
Renown how little you regard, or need,
  Who like the Bee, on your own sweets doth feed?
      There are, who like weak Fowl with shouts fall down,
Doz'd with an Army's Acclamation:
Not able to indure applause, they fall,   185
Giddy with praise, their praises Funeral.
But you, Orinda, are so unconcern'd,
As if when you, another we commend.
Thus, as the Sun, you in your Course shine on,
Unmov'd with all our admiration: 190
    Flying above the praise you shun, we see
    Wit is still higher by humility.

---

1 *Phoebus*: Apollo, god of the sun and of poetry   3 *Daphne*: pursued by Apollo, she became a laurel (bay) tree   15–16 *Pompey... Corneille*: Pierre Corneille wrote *La Mort de Pompée*, based on part of Lucan's *Pharsalia*, in the winter of 1642–3   18 *SMEC*: Smectymnuus: a group of five Presbyterian ministers who wrote a joint pamphlet attacking episcopacy in 1641 which began a vigorous controversy. The name is formed from their initials   23 *Cynthia*: the moon   63 *Amazons*: a race of woman warriors in Greek myth   64 *Spartan Virgins*: the Spartans, unlike other Greek peoples, expected women to exercise   66 *Sybarit*: the people of Sybaris were notorious for idleness and luxury   67 *Semiramis*: mythical queen of Assyria, who fought at the siege of Bactra   68 *Ninyas*: her effeminate son   69 *Ovid*: his *Metamorphoses* deal with various bodily transformations   70 *Iphis*: her/his story is told in *Metamorphoses*   79–80 *coast...Lucasia*: Philips arrived at Dublin in 1662   80 *Lucasia*: Anne Owen accompanied Philips to Dublin   89 *Sappho*: ancient Greek poetess, born *c*.618 BC on the island of Lesbos, where she spent all her life apart from a short period of exile in Sicily. Known in antiquity as the 'Tenth Muse', two almost complete poems survive, and a number of fragments   90 *Hesiod's age*: Hesiod, Greek didactic poet in the oral epic idiom, lived *c*.700 BC   96 *nine*: the Muses   97 *Numa*: Numa Pompilius, second king of pre-republican Rome, and lawgiver   98 *Ægeria*: a goddess who became counsellor and wife of Numa: in order to commend his laws to the Romans, he declared they had been sanctified and

approved by her   99 *Gracchi's Mother*: Cornelia, daughter of Scipio Africanus, remembered for her prose style as well as her family   107 *Orrery*: Roger Boyle, first Earl of
Orrery (1621–79), author of *Parthenissa*, a romance, and a number of rhymed tragedies   110 *Pompey's widow*: Cornelia, the daughter of Scipio, married Pompey in 52
BC, accompanied him to Egypt after he lost the battle of Pharsalia, and after his murder,
returned to Italy. This will be an allusion to Philips's translation of *Pompey*; *Arsamnes*:
probably for Artamenes, the hero of Madeleine de Scudéry's *Artamenes, or, The Grand
Cyrus*   120–1 *Amber*: this conceit is based on Martial, *Epigrams* IV. 32 and 59   183
weak Fowl: the Roman army practised divination by the behaviour of chickens

FRANCES BOOTHBY ?née MILWARD
(fl. 1669–70)

FRANCES BOOTHBY put on a single play, *Marcelia: or the treacherous friend*, at
Drury Lane in June/July 1669 (thus preceding Aphra Behn as perhaps the first
woman to have a play performed on the professional stage), to little acclaim, and
published nothing else. She may be the Frances, daughter of John Milward, who
married Sir William Boothby, from the Oxfordshire branch of the Derbyshire
Boothbys. Although her immediate background is obscure, Frances Boothby's
connections are made clear by internal evidence. Her play is dedicated to her
Recusant kinswoman, Lady Mary Yate of Harvington Hall in Worcester, whose
granddaughter and heir, Mary, married Sir Robert Throckmorton, one of the
Catholic non-jurors. Elizabeth Cottington, a connection of the equally staunchly
Catholic Aston family of Tixall in Staffordshire, wrote to her uncle Herbert
Aston early in 1669, 'ther is a bowld woman hath offered [a play]: my cosen
Aston can give you a better account of her then I can. Some verses I have seen
that ar not ill: that is commentation enouf: she will think so too, I believe, when
it comes upon the stage. I shall tremble for the poor wooman exposed among the
critticks. She stands need to be strongly fortified agenst them.' This almost
certainly refers to Frances Boothby's play, since the presence of this poem in the
Tixall collection suggests that she was kin to the Astons as well as the Yates. A
Tixall connection would also explain why Elizabeth Cottington and at least one
Aston saw the play in manuscript.

218   *To my most honord Cosen,
MRS SOMERSET on the unjust censure
past upon my poore Marcelia*

    Sigh not, Parthenia, that I'me doom'd to dye,
    Since a false scandal's made the reason why.
    Fortune I ever found my rigid foe,
    And did not hope she now would milder grow.
    A small weake barke by a rough tempest tost,   5
    Can raise noe wonder when we heare 'tis lost;
    When powerfull enemys resolve to kill,
    They heed not justice, strength can do their will;

Ruled by self interest their foes confine,
And word their judgments to their owne designe.   10
This byas made that injuring blow be given,
That thy Arcasia had prophan'd gainst heaven.
But why this furious hurricane did rise
Where by detracting zeale I'm made a sacrifice,
I cannot reach; for sure a woman's pen   15
Is not (like comets,) ominous to men:
Nor could my clouded braine, (wrapt up in night,)
Destroy in all my sex their sunshine light:
The basalisk's poison lys not in my head,
To strike the wits of other women dead,   20
If my dull ignorance could blast them all,
Then should I justly as their victim fall.

(1669/70)

1 *Parthenia*: the virtuous lover and wife of Argalus in Sidney's *Arcadia*, or a name for a chaste maiden (Greek *parthenos*)   11 *byas*: bias   16 *comets*: the appearance of a comet in the sky was thought to presage disaster   19 *basalisk*: the basilisk, a serpent, was so venomous that its stare alone could kill

ELIZABETH POLWHELE
(before 1648–after 1672)

THERE are two principal possibilities for the antecedents of Elizabeth Polwhele. She may have been the daughter of Theophilus Polwhele, vicar of Tiverton, a prominent Nonconformist minister: if so, she was born *c*.1651, the daughter of his first wife, married the Revd Stephen Lobb before 1678, bore five children, and died *c*.1691. But most Nonconformist sectaries were hostile to the stage in the mid- seventeenth century, and so the daughter and wife of a minister is an unlikely playwright. Another possibility is that she was the daughter of John Polwhele (1586–1648), born at St Erme in Cornwall in 1586, educated at Exeter College, Oxford, and a fellow there from 1608 until 1622. He then became vicar of Whitchurch in Devon from 1622 until his death in 1648: since college fellows were not permitted to marry, if he is the father of Elizabeth Polwhele, then his marriage and her birth took place some time after 1622. He left a miscellany manuscript of poetry, now in the Bodleian Library (MS Eng. Poet F 16), which contains poems addressed to Ben Jonson and George Herbert, suggesting that he had some contact with mainstream literary culture, and potentially (through Jonson) with writing for the professional theatre. If this second possibility is pursued, it is likely Elizabeth was born in the 1620s or 30s; and therefore that her public début as a playwright was not made in extreme youth, but in later life, following the example of Aphra Behn and perhaps Frances Boothby.

She is known to to have written three plays in completely different genres, two of which survive. *The Frolicks, or the Lawyer cheated*, is a low-life realistic comedy, though there is no record of its being staged. It is dedicated to Prince Rupert, and she refers in this dedication to an earlier, missing work called

Elysium, perhaps a religious masque. She also wrote a rhymed tragedy in the Jacobean style, *The Faithful Virgins*. (Oxford, Bodleian Library MS Rawlinson Poet. 195, fos. 49–78), composed *c.*1670, and probably performed by the Duke's Company. It is also possible that she is the author of the broadside ballad by 'Mrs E.P' tentatively attributed to her here, written in 1672: in the manuscript of 'The Faithful Virgins', her pen-trials are signed E.P. (fo. 78ᵛ). The royalism of this ballad would be compatible with her dedication of *The Frolicks* to Prince Rupert, and also renders an Anglican background more probable than a Nonconformist one. No other writing is known.

219   *Song*

> If I were tortur'd with greensickness,
> Dost think I would be cur'd by thee?
> I then too soon might swell in thickness—
> A pox upon your remedy!
> The cure may prove worse than the anguish,   5
> And I of a fresh disease might languish.
> But I'll keep myself from such distemper
> In spite of all that you dare do;
> Although you are so free to venter,
> I'll be hanged if I did not baffle you   10

                        (1671)

1 *greensickness*: a disease of virgins, to be cured by sexual intercourse   3 *swell*: become pregnant   9 *venter*: venture

220   *On his ROYAL HIGHNESS*
              His Expedition against the
              DUTCH. By Mrs. E.P

> Proud Hogen Mogen's, we will make you bow,
> Have at you, greasy Butter Boxes now,
> Brave *York* once more against you does advance,
> And in him more then all the Power of *France*;
> 'T'oppose him is in vain, all you can do,   5
> Is nothing, his name's enough to Conquer you.
> But when in Person he vouchsafes to appear
> Prepare to think your day of Doom is near.
> That glorious Hero, never Arms put on
> But he made Victory her self his own;   10
> Who still has wav'd her white Plume o're his head,
> And now to vanquish you, by her is lead.
> Though 'tis a shame, (that worthy) should persue,
> Honour unto such Savage Bores as you.

But you (this never dying fame) shall know,   15
What in his Countreys quarrel he dare do.
Presumptuous Villains, could you find out none,
But *England's* King, to use your jests upon?
Slaves, you e'ere long shall know, none was less fit,
To be a Subject for your scurvy wit.   20
(But *York* in whose Illustrious name are charms,
That Cowards hearts ev'n with pure courage warms,
And does infuse new Soul in ev'ry man,
With much more vigour than dull Brandy can.)
Will punish each affront that you have done   25
To your inevitable destruction.
Hee'l make you curse the time, you Pictures drew,
And draw some of ye, nay and hang you too.
Full of your Fate, he's with our Fleet set forth,
With such a noble train of English youth   30
That when those matchless numbers, you shall veiw,
You'l think the world is come to Conquer you.
Methinks I hear the injur'd Spirits call
(For Vengeance) that did at *Amboyna* fall.
Victims, to your unheard of Cruelty,   35
(To those) that for them will revenged bee.
Their Souls do hover o're our Ships, and seem
To promise Conquest both to us and them.
Our Fleet like to a moving Realm, I see
In Tryumph on the bosome of the Sea.   40
Which bears it proudly, being a Jem of more
(Worth) then sh'has worn upon her brest before.
The Sea-gods wait upon it all along
And thousand water-Nymphs about it throng.
The waves their Royal burden gently court,   45
And all the wind's, with the calm Ocean sport.
Tithon gives *Thetis* leave, to entertain
In all her charmes, our Gallants on the Mayn
And's pleased in spight of age and jealousie,
They shall on his young Mistress Bosome lye.   50
Each Power to us, does kind presages give
That as our cause is just, so we shall thrive.
Wit is too like a common friend, indeed,
Who still forsakes us when we have most need
Or somewhat more should be by me exprest,   55
But let our Canons speak to you the rest.
And tell you to your ruines you must dye
T'apease the wrath of Angered Majesty.

FINIS

(Printed in the Year, 1672)

1 *Hogen Mogen's*: 'The high and mighty', short for the high and mighty States General, the ruling council of Holland, used in England as a name for the Dutch in general   2 *Butter Boxes*: the Dutch diet leaned heavily on dairy products   3 *York*: James, Duke of York, brother of Charles II, as Lord Admiral, led the English forces in a series of Anglo–Dutch naval wars: in 1672 (the third campaign), the English and the French simultaneously declared war on the Dutch. Heavily outnumbered, the Dutch under Admiral de Ruyter nonetheless managed to damage enough ships to prevent the English from capitalizing on their vulnerability   18 Probably a comment on the conclusion of the previous Dutch war: de Ruyter's daring raid on the naval dockyard at Chatham in 1667, where he bombarded the sitting targets, destroyed three large warships, and towed away the king's flagship, the *Royal Charles*. The English failed to see the funny side of this, then or subsequently   27 *Pictures*: Part of the English complaint against the Dutch was that they allowed verbal and visual libels against Charles II to be printed in the Netherlands   34 *Amboyna:* an island in the Moluccas, claimed by the Dutch East India company in 1605. A group of English merchants taken captive there in 1623 were tortured to discourage further competition. It was a key episode in rallying anti-Dutch feeling: Dryden staged *Amboyna: A Tragedy* in 1673   47 *Tithon*: Tithonus was the lover of Aurora, goddess of the dawn, not Thetis. She begged eternal life for him, but forgot to ask for eternal youth. There may be a confusion with Triton, either a generic sea-god, or specifically, son of Neptune and Amphitrite; *Thetis*: a principal sea-nymph, one of the Nereids, often conflated with Tethys, the personified sea herself

ELIZABETH HINCKS
(fl. 1671)

ELIZABETH HINCKS was a Quaker, who describes herself as 'a Woman of the South' on her title-page (with reference to the Queen of Sheba, who came from the South to visit King Solomon). She refers to a friend called T.S. in the first poem in her collection, as her printer (quite probably Tace Sowle, sister of Elizabeth Bradford, and daughter of Jane Sowle), and is otherwise modestly silent about herself and her background. She appears to have been a widow at the time of writing. The rhetorical structure of her work is dialectical: she sets up an objection which could be raised to Quaker religious practice, such as silent prayer, or the absence of hierarchy, and answers it, often at considerable length. Her work is notable for its use of metaphors drawn from women's life and experience.

221   *Something about* SILENCE

Object.

But some do say, *We marvel much, that you can sit* Silent,
We do conceive it no profit, nor are with it content;
For if that we should sit a while, silent from hearing breath,
Our mind a wandring then would be up and down in the Earth:
And so contriving in our hearts, whats to be done, we plot   5
Till there be something we know not that on our heart doth smote:
And if this earthly spirit act, for which we feel this smart,

Some former evil we have done, lyes gnawing of our heart.
So to this outward Ear we must have Objects that do sound,
That the inward Intelect *may, thereby be wholly drown'd:*   10
For that which doth us thus reprove, and on our hearts doth smite,
Doth silence *make our burthen, 'cause it brings that to our sight;*
For this is that to us doth shew, the evils we have done,
In silence *we are made to know, therefore we* silence *shun.*
And so among the trees do run, our selves there for to hide,   15
For this same small still Voice, *at all, by no means we abide.*

16 *Voice*: 1 Kings 19: 20

222   *Some more SCRUPLES clear'd*

Now for the opening of the *Truth*, which is our *strength and stay*.
In *answering* of *Objections* to this same some may say.

Object.
   Oh! here's a Table richly deckt, Oh here are dishes store,
Oh! is all this but one Small Mite, *and from a* Widow *poor:*
Though there are many good Dishes, they have not the right place,
Nor in good Order Usherd in, oh this doth spoile the Grace;
For there are sometimes Dishes come, the which should last be brought,   5
And this Course will not it admit, of this some will find fault,
Though we confess the meat be good, and on the Table store,
But Sauce here is not sutable, to sight it is but poor.

Answ.
   My *Answer* this no *Banquet* is, for them full *Stomacks* have,
But *bitter* things for *hungry Soules*, which newly come from grave,   10
But yet in it ought sweetness find, O this is all my aime,
To praise the goodness of our God, for his *Love* in the same.
And seeing meat is on the Board, if it be'nt rightly set,
Let others take the pains that can the Dishes places fit.
Now for my part when I did taste any dish that was good,   15
I presently brought him to board, to others, for their food.
If in Feasts they first *best Wine bring*, and after that that's worst,
Yet Christ when he *makes Water Wine*, the last's as good as first.
So these *Traditions* we do not, in our minds much admire,
So hungry Souls with *Righteousness* be fed, is our desire.   20

2 *Mite*: see Mark 12: 42, Luke 21:2   17–18 Refers to the miracle at Cana (John 2), esp. 2:
10: 'every man at the beginning doth set forth good wine, but thou hast kept good wine till
now'

MARY MOLLINEUX (née SOUTHWORTH)
(1651–95)

HER cousin Frances Owen, who provides a brief biography in her book *Fruits of Retirement*, notes that Mary was an only child, and her weak eyesight decided her father to educate her in Latin, Greek, arithmetic, 'Physick and Chyrurgy' rather than conventional feminine skills. She preferred to communicate with her husband in Latin, even on her deathbed: one of her last utterances, which he records in his memoir of her, was 'ne nimis solicitus esto' (don't worry about me so much). Her father may have been a Catholic who became a Quaker: the poem on pp. 102–6 (written in 1682) hints as much. Her family came from Warrington. She began writing poetry at the age of 12, in the form of pious exhortations to members of her family. In 1684, Mary Southworth was imprisoned in Lancaster Castle for taking part in a Quaker assembly. In the following year, she married one of her fellow prisoners, Henry Mollineux, at Penketh, near Warrington. She wrote little in English after her marriage, though she continued to write a little Latin verse. In 1690, Henry Mollineux was imprisoned for non-payment of tithes. Mary Mollineux constituted herself his defence, and pleaded his case before Bishop Stratford so well in June 1691 that she managed to effect his release, though he was almost immediately rearrested. There were children of the marriage, though only one can be named, Othniel Mollineux (1686–1732), who became a minister of Lidiat in Lancashire. Mary Mollineux objected to the publication of her work, but her husband and other Quakers were so impressed by the edifying nature of her life that they went against her wishes in this respect. *Fruits of Retirement or Miscellaneous Poems Moral and Divine*, made her famous: there were six editions in England and at least four in Philadelphia before 1783. Her book was printed by the Quaker woman printer Tace Sowle, the sister of Elizabeth Bradford (see no. 207).

223 *'Esuriens agnis quantum concedet in agris'*

Esuriens agnis quantum concedet in agris
    Ipse Lupus, vobis jam dabit iste miser;
Crudelisque rapax, cupidus, sine jure, Sacerdos
    Nummos, non Animas, curat, egetque cupit.

Even what the hungry Wolf in Field would do
    To feeding Lambs, so will the Wretch to you:
The cruel Priest, fierce, covetous, unjust
    For money, not for souls, doth cark and lust.

The translation is by her husband, Henry Mollineux   2 *dabit*: dabid ed.

224   *In a Letter dated the 9th of the Twelfth Month, 1691, she sent to me in Prison these lines, viz.*

I

Qui nocent Sanctis, Dominus locutus,
Hi fui tangunt Oculi Pupillam,
Sentient iram, quoque reddet istis
Praemia dira.

II

Si Deo credis, filioque Christo   5
Quisquis es Vir desipiensque rudis!
Cautus es ne tu Domino repugnas
Cordeque pugnis.

III

Stultus at dixit sibi Corde, nullus
Est Deus: spernens igitur doceri   10
Saepe protervus ruit in ruinam
Absque timore.

M.M.

She signified her Haste in the writing of these, because the Bearer staid for the Letter, and that she had not made any of such Quantities for above twenty years.

I

The Lord, of them that hurt his Saints, doth say
They touch the Apple of his Eye, and they
Shall feel his Anger; he will them requite
With dreadful Plagues, in Death's eternal Night.

II

If then thou believest God, and Christ his son,   5
Whoe'er thou art, thou rude and foolish Man,
Beware, lest then the Lord of Heaven resist
And Fight against him both with Heart and Fist.

III

But in his heart the foolish Man hath said
There is no God; and therefore not dismay'd,   10
To slight his Teachings: he, in Froward Wrath
Runs fearless on in Ruin's dreadful path.

Englished by H.M.

225   *Meditations on Persecution*

Cold hungry Seamen, tho' they oft endure
Day-darkning Storms and Tempests, to procure
The winged Treasures of this fading World
Although they run the Hazard to be hurl'd
On wrecking Rocks, or quick devouring Sounds,   5
Or cast as Captives on some foreign Lands
To spend their wretched Days in Misery,
Instead of what they sought for to enjoy,
Abounding Wealth, if to their wished Shore,
They safe arrive; venture again, yet more   10
Undaunted than at first, in hopes to be
With more Success, kept from those Dangers free
Then why should such Faint-heartedness appear,
In Israel's Camp, that ought of right to fear
None but the Lord? Can any doubt, that have   15
The Word of an almighty King, to save
Them to the uttermost? What! though he see
To tarry long, his own appointed time
Is always best; in greatest Streights, we do
Wholly depend on, and acknowledge too,   20
Salvation only from above; for then
We find, 'tis vain to hope for Help from Men.
Ah, was not Israel thus beset? Could they
Encounter furious Pharaoh's Host, or th'Sea?
Yet was Deliverance near; the Sea must be   25
A Path to them, a Grave to th'Enemy;
Pharaoh might follow, to his own Destruction;
While Israel is prov'd, to gain Instruction:
That these may learn whom they should chiefly fear,
And whom to trust, when Tribulation's near.   30
Ah, then is this our Gospel-Dispensation,
Why should the children of this Generation
Seem so far wiser, or more valiant, then
The sacred Off-spring of Jerusalem?
Those hazard Life for transitory Toys;   35
And shall not these, for everlasting Joys;
Resign up Visibles, yea, Life and all,
To him that gave it, if he please to call
To such a Trial? Can we baulk the Way
Wherein he leads, except we run astray?   40
We must through Exercises overcome,
And bear the Cross, if we would wear the Crown,
And fully follow him: The Recompence
Will far exceed when we are parted hence,

But who art thou, that art so loath to give 45
Up on Estate? A Thief may soon deprive
Thee of a greater Store, than he requires;
Some suffer more by Carelessness and Fires;
Which justly Heaven permits, to let them see
How vain these poor, these trifling Treasures be. 50
Or dost thou fear Confinement? Heav'n may send
Grievous Diseases, which Physician's Hand
Cannot remove, and to th'uneasy Bed
Make thee a Pris'ner when thy Health is fled
But if thou be confin'd for Jesus sake 55
He will a Prison much more pleasant make
Than any spacious Palace: For he'll be
Fullness of Joy, and saving health to thee.
Now, tho' some shun the Cross, as worldly wise
As from the Path of Truth apostasize, 60
And yet the Judgments do not soon ensue,
(Altho' they be in dreadful Vengeance due)
So that the Wicked did of old aver,
Surely the Lord his Coming doth defer:
Yet shall they not have Peace, but feel the Rod 65
Of a displeased, of a jealous GOD;
Whose Word can never fail, although he try
Some with Long-suffering, and great Clemency
Ah, kiss the Son, lest that his Anger be
Incens'd! For he alone can comfort thee: 70
And let not any taint or start aside
Heaven will support his faithful Ones when try'd.

(1684)

24 cf. Exodus 14

JULEA PALMER
(fl. 1671–3)

JULEA PALMER is the otherwise obscure author of an extensive collection of devotional poems now in the William Andrews Clark Memorial Library. The first of them is preceded with 'Julea Pallmer September 28/1671'. There are two hundred poems, numbered and grouped into two centuries. The dates included in many poems' titles indicate that they were composed or compiled consecutively between 1671 and 1673.

226   *78 The fruit of sin, or a
        lamentation for england*

What cause have we, asham'd to stand
when we doe seriously
Veiw, what sin has, brought on our land
within our memory.

Wee were a terrour far, and neer   5
unto the nations round
Thou maydest us, to them a fear
when they did hear our sound

But now we ar, become a scorne
And byword, round about   10
With dirt, thou hast defil'd our horn
and seemst to cast us out

Thousands in one yeer swept a way
By, the plauge att thy command
Thy dreadfull wrath, thou didst display   15
by emptiing our land

Thy Iudgments, they have been abroad
when on the sea, we fought
Within we are, full of discord
which makes our foes to shout   20

A dreadfull, conflagration
has laid our houses wast
Our statly metripolitan
By fire, was quite defac'd

Yet have we, not return'd to thee   25
but still we are the same
Prodigiously wicked, are wee
dishonoring of thy name

The glory of england is thin
her beauty, waxen leane   30
And yet we act, as if by sin
t'undoe our selfs, wee meane

Great Judgments, o're our heads impend
to think this, we have ground
The quarell is not att an end   35
whilst sin, doth thus abound

We dayly dare, omnipotence
and stand it out with god

As if we meant by violence
to pull on us, his rod   40

Thou standest now on the threshold
as if thou wouldst be gone
And yet how stupid, and how cold
are we, like to a stone

Remember Lord thy covenant   45
thy glory, and thy name.
And let it not be made, the taunt
Of, the wicked, and profane

Take not away thy gospell Lord
though thou aflict us sore   50
Give us thy presence, with thy word
till time shall be no more

A gospell, in its purity
when we cease, to live here
We beg that thou, wilt not deny   55
unto our Children dear.

NB. Since the text is autograph, the capricious punctuation of the original has been
preserved   5–6 Cromwell's admiral, Robert Blake, defeated the Dutch under Tromp
(1652–3) and the Spanish at Cadiz, Santa Cruz, and Jamaica (1656–8); English troops
successfully intervened in Flanders and occupied Dunkirk (1657–8)   11 *horn*: Job 16: 15,
'I have defiled my horn in the dust'   14 *plauge*: the Great Plague of 1665   18 *on sea*:
England's repeated defeats in the Anglo-Dutch naval wars   24 *fire*: the Great Fire of
London, 1666   46–7 deleted line between these two

MARY ENGLISH
(1652?–1694)

MARY ENGLISH was an American, and an indirect victim of the famous Salem
witch trials. She was the daughter of William and Elinor Hollingsworth, and
married a well-to-do Salem merchant, Philip English, in 1675. He was an
Episcopalian. She joined the Congregational church in 1681. Both were accused
of witchcraft in 1692, and escaped to New York, but she died there, affected by
the strain of imprisonment.

227   *'May I with Mary choose the better part'*

May I with Mary choose the better part,
And serve the Lord with all my heart
Receive his word most joyfully
Y live to him eternally.

Everliving God I pray   5
Never leave me for to stray;
Give me grace thee to obey.
Lord grant that I may happy be
In Jesus Christ eternally
Save me dear Lord by thy rich grace   10
Heaven then shall be my dwelling place.

1 *Mary*: Mary Magdalene, Luke 10: 42

MAREY WALLER, later MORE
(fl. 1674)

OUR principal source of information about Marey More is Horace Walpole:

[Marey More was] a lady, who I believe painted for her amusement, [and] was the grandmother of Mr Pitfield; in the family are her and her husband's portraits by herself. In the Bodleian Library in Oxford is a picture by her that she gave to it, which by a strange mistake is called Sir Thomas More, though it is evidently a copy of Cromwell, Earl of Essex. Nay, Robert Whitehall, a poetaster, wrote verses to her in 1674 on her sending this supposed picture of Sir Thomas More.

Her essay, 'The Womans Right' defending the equality of the sexes, is addressed to 'my little daughter Elizabeth Waller' (printed by Margaret Ezell, *The Patriarch's Wife: Literary Evidence and the History of the Family*, (Chapel Hill and London: University of North Carolina Press, 1987) 191–203). The daughter was probably born in 1663 (she married Alexander Pitfield in April 1680 at St Leonard's, Shoreditch, giving her age as 17); and she also had a son, Richard Waller. We may therefore assume that Marey More was married to one Waller in the early 1660s, and subsequently became Mrs More. Elizabeth Waller's marriage license shows that in 1680, her mother was living in the parish of St Andrew's Undershaft, Bishopsgate, but none of her affairs are recorded in that parish. Late in the seventeenth century, on the evidence of the surviving correspondence of Richard Waller, Marey More lived in Crosby Square, and seems to have been a friend of the scientist and inventor, Robert Hooke, who was certainly a friend of Richard Waller's: his diary records paying visits, accompanied by Waller, to a 'Mrs More' who lived nearby, and discussing her dreams with her. She seems to have been well-to-do: both her son and her brother-in-law are described as 'very ingenious and rich' by John Aubrey, and one of the Waller letters indicates that she had servants (plural). In 1713 one of Waller's correspondents enquired anxiously after her health and she was seriously ill when she made her will on 25 December 1714 (P.C.C. 11/554, sig. 180). The will was not proved, however, until September 1716. She names her two granddaughters, Anna and Winifred Pitfield, as her heirs.

    Her son Richard Waller was outstandingly learned: John Evelyn describes him as an 'extraordinary young Gent: & of great accomplishments', noting particularly his skill in painting, that he writes in Latin, and is a poet: 'his house is an Academy of itselfe'. Marey More herself could read Greek and Latin, on the evidence of her essay (she discusses the nuances of New Testament Greek), and, as Walpole suggests, she was known as a painter. As her poem suggests, she made nine copies of a portrait by Holbein then believed to be of Sir Thomas More, though ironically, it is actually of Sir Thomas Cromwell. Two survived into the twentieth century, the one she gave to the Bodleian, and another which was sold by Christie's in 1929 and has since disappeared. There are two other possible surviving portraits from her hand, an unsigned pencil sketch of her son Richard, the frontispiece of his manuscript translation of the *Aeneid*, and a portrait of the historian John Stow, in her parish church, St Andrew's Undershaft, where he is buried.

Her relationship to Robert Whitehall of Merton, whose poem she answers, is complex. His own poem was taken by her as insulting (it begins, 'Madam: Your Benefaction has been such | That few can think it is a Woman's touch'), and also, interestingly, provoked a defence of her and her painting from an anonymous defender, beginning 'Deare Friend! Thy Poetry is such | That all will swear it is thy touch'. Thus, both More herself, and another contemporary, take his poem as essentially belittling of women artists in general, and More in particular. However, it was Whitehall himself who delivered the painting to the library. It is possible, therefore, that the poem was merely a supremely tactless and unsuccessful attempt at light humour: according to Hearne, it was Whitehall in whose company the notorious Earl of Rochester first 'grew debauched', and he may not have realized how unfunny his poem would seem to a woman reader.

228 *An answer: by Marey More: to the Ingenious Mr Robert Whitehall, Fellow of Merton college in Oxon vpon a Coppy of verses sent her by him on Sending a Pickture of her owne Drawing*

To; OXON

Jeare your Benefactress, that's but Just
And I can Bear't, But why noe woman must
An Artist be in Painting, cause you see
I'me none, make the whole Sex Suffer for me,
It made me Doget Martialls Bitch to Read   5
Besids I Find his Baudy steps you Tread
Fellow, and Batchelor; it must be soe
Hide your Six't line, sure't speakes more than you know
The Holbin Coppier yields, lett's pencills fall
Scearce knows her Poet from's originall   10
Three for our selves, and six for friends Beside
Nine ways att once, what sir your muse squint Eyd
Ile close them upp then, For the view I feare
May prove Catching, I wish you'd doe soe there
Just what I thought, Oxford I knew before   15
How ere take Jeare for Jeare from
Marey More

Xbris 16th 1674 on his verse

5 *Martiall bitch*: Martial, *Epigrams* 1. 110   8 *Six't line*: 'Yet every Lady knows to draw man in': she evidently suspects sexual innuendo   9 Marey More had copied the Holbein portrait of her ancestor, St Thomas More.

EPHELIA
(before 1678–after 1681)

EPHELIA stands as the name on the title-page of an important collection, *Female Poems on Several Occasions* (first published in 1679), and also appears as the signature of a number of minor works; two broadsheets on political themes, a manuscript poem now in the University of Nottingham's Portland collection, and a play, *The Pair-Royal of Coxcombs*, of which only the prologue, epilogue, and songs survive, printed in *Female Poems*. The collection appears largely to be the work of a single author, though not entirely: it was not uncommon for prologue and epilogue of plays to be written by another hand and this Epilogue, which ends 'But if you'l Clap the Play, and Praise the Rime, | She'l do as much for you another time' is unlikely to be by Ephelia herself. It is directly comparable with the experience of another young woman who ventured a play in 1695 ('Ariadne''s *She Ventures and she Wins)*. This has an epitaph by Mr Motteaux, which similarly treats the play as standing for the writer, and the relationship of writer and audience as sexual: 'Our Poetess is troubled in her Mind, | Like some young Thing, not so discreet as kind, | Who, without Tears, has her dear Toy resigned... | ...for, pray, take notice, 'tis her Maidenhead, | (that of her Brain I mean) and you that wed | Feel seldom easie Joys, till that is fled'. The inclusion of this epilogue and some obvious juvenilia suggest that Ephelia was a little pressed for material. However, most of the poems in the collection tell a continuous story: Ephelia falls in love with a man she calls Strephon, or J.G., becomes jealous of Mopsa, and is courted by Cloris. Strephon goes to North Africa on some kind of business, and marries an African lady in Tangier, while Cloris meanwhile falls in love with Marina. Another fact which is clear from the collection is that she received some patronage from Mary, Duchess of Richmond and Lennox, fulsomely praised in the prefatory poem, and possibly also addressed in three poems in the collection addressed to 'Eugenia' ('the well-born lady'). The last of these is an abject apology: Ephelia apparently spoke of her patroness in some unduly public context, which the lady resented. The fact that Ephelia disappears without trace after 1681, and that Robert Gould, writing some time in the 1680s, apostrophizes her as 'Ephelia! Poor Ephelia! ragged Jilt' suggests that Ephelia was unable to keep what patronage she had attracted, and that she was unable to make her way either as writer or as kept-woman without assistance. The contents of the second, 1682 edition are even more miscellaneous than those of the first.

The identity of Ephelia is uncertain, and her nom-de-plume itself is a puzzle. It is pastoral in appearance, though in fact is is neither Classical nor a Renaissance coinage. The Greek ἔφηλις, a fairly rare word, means 'pimpled', or at best, 'freckled' and is therefore an unlikely choice of soubriquet: though it could conceivably have been suggested by an educated lover as an unkind joke, and naively adopted. If 'Ephelia to Bajazet' is indeed by this writer rather than by Sir George Etheredge, then her first lover was John Sheffield, third Earl of Mulgrave, who was certainly educated enough, and nasty enough, to have suggested it to her. Another possibility is that it was adopted as a slight variation on Shakespeare's Ophelia, so wounded by Hamlet's rejection that she goes mad and dies for love: a suitable reference-point for a woman whose affairs, as she presents them, were consistently unhappy. It is possible that her original name was Joan Phillips: Aphra Behn, who certainly knew Ephelia, speaks playfully in the prologue to *Sir Patient Fancy* (1678) of a new woman poet called Joan: the date is congruent with Ephelia's poetic début, since her earliest published poem came out in that year, and some of the future contents of *Female Poems* were presumably also circulating in manuscript. Thomas Newcomb, *Bibliotheca*, (1712), refers to a female poet called Phillips 'who in Verse her Passion told': this is unlikely as a reference to Katherine Philips, who could hardly be said to tell her passions in her poetry. There is no poet Joan, or Mrs Philips, writing under those names in the second half of the seventeenth century.

229 *To Madam* Bhen

Madam! permit a Muse, that has been long
Silent with wonder, now to find a Tongue:
Forgive that Zeal I can no longer hide,
And pardon a necessitated Pride.
When first your strenuous polite Lines I read, 5
At once it Wonder and Amazement bred,
To see such things flow from a Womans Pen,
As might be Envy'd by the wittiest Men:
You write so sweetly, that at once you move,
The Ladies Jealousies, and Gallant's Love; 10
Passions so gentle, and so well exprest,
As needs must be the same fill your own Breast;
Then Rough again, as your Inchanting Quill
Commanded Love, or Anger at your Will:
As in your Self, so in your Verses meet, 15
A rare connexion of Strong and Sweet:
This I admir'd at, and my Pride to show,
Have took the Vanity to tell you so
In humble Verse, that has the Luck to please
Some Rustick Swains, or silly Shepherdess: 20
But far unfit to reach your Sacred Ears,
Or stand your Judgment: Oh! my conscious Fears
Check my Presumption, yet I must go on,
And finish the rash Task I have begun.
Condemn it Madam, if you please, to th'Fire, 25
It gladly will your Sacrifice expire,
As sent by one, that rather chose to shew
Her want of Skill, than want of Zeal to you.

230 *SONG*

I.

You wrong me Strephon, when you say,
I'me Jealous or Severe,

Did I not see you Kiss and Play
With all you came a neer?
Say, did I ever Chide for this,   5
Or cast one Jealous Eye
On the bold Nymphs, that snatch'd my Bliss
While I stood wishing by?

2.

Yet though I never disapprov'd
This modish Liberty;   10
I thought in them you only lov'd,
Change and Variety:
I vainly thought my Charms so strong,
And you so much my Slave,
No Nymph had Pow'r to do me Wrong,   15
Or break the Chains I gave.

3.

But when you seriously Address,
With all your winning Charms,
Unto a Servile Shepherdess,
I'le throw you from my Arms: 20
I'de rather chuse you shou'd make Love
To every Face you see,
Then Mopsa's dull Admirer prove,
And let Her Rival me.

231   *To one that asked me why I lov'd J.G.*

Why do I Love? go, ask the Glorious Sun
Why every day it round the world doth Run:
Ask *Thames* and *Tyber*, why they Ebb and Flow:
Ask Damask Roses, why in *June* they blow:
Ask Ice and Hail, the reason, why they're Cold: 5
Decaying Beauties, why they will grow Old:
They'l tell thee, Fate, that every thing doth move,
Inforces them to this, and me to Love.
There is no Reason for our Love or Hate,
'Tis irresistable, as Death or Fate;   10
'Tis not his Face; I've sence enough to see,
That is not good, though doated on by me:
Not is't his Tongue, that has this Conquest won;
For that at least is equall'd by my own:
His Carriage can to none obliging be,   15
'Tis Rude, Affected, full of Vanity:
Strangely Ill-natur'd, Peevish, and Unkind,

Unconstant, False, to Jealousie inclin'd;
His Temper cou'd not have so great a Pow'r,
'Tis mutable, and changes every hour: 20
Those vigorous Years that Women so Adore,
Are past in him: he's twice my Age and more;
And yet I love this false, this worthless Man,
With all the Passion that a Woman can;
Doat on his Imperfections, though I spy   25
Nothing to Love; I Love, and know not why.
Sure 'tis Decreed in the dark Book of Fate,
That I shou'd Love, and he shou'd be ingrate.

232   *Advice to his GRACE.*

Awake, vain Man; 'tis time th'Abuse to see; ⎫
Awake, and guard thy heedless Loyalty   ⎬
From all the Snares ere laid for It and thee. ⎭
No longer let that busie Juggling Crew
(Who to their own mis-deeds entitle You,)   5
Abuse Your ear: Consider, Sir, the State
Of our unhappy Isle, disturb'd of late
With *causeless* Jealousies, *ungrounded* Fear,
Obstinate Faction, and *Seditious Care*;
Gone quite distracted for Religion's sake;   10
And nothing their hot Brains can cooler make,
(So great's the deprivation of their sence,)
But the excluding of their lawful Prince:
A Prince, in whose each Act is clearly shown
That Heaven design'd Him to adorn a Throne;   15
Which (*tho' He scorns by Treason to pursue,*)
He ne'r will quit, if it become His due.
Then lay betimes your mad *Ambition* down;
Nor let the dazling Lustre of a Crown
Bewitch Your Thoughts; but think what *mighty care*   20
Attends the Crowns that lawful Princes wear;
But *when ill Title's added to the weight*
How insupportable's the Load of State!
Believe those working Brains Your Name Abuse;
You only for their Property doe use.   25
And when they're strong enough to stand alone;
You, as *an useless Thing*, away'l be thrown.
Think too, how dear you have already paid,
For the fine *Projects* Your false Friends had laid.
When by the Rabbles *fruitless Zeal* You lost   ⎫   30
Your Royal Fathers Love, Your growing Fortune cross'd ⎬
Say, was Your Bargain, think ye, worth the Cost? ⎭

Remember what Relation, Sir, you bear
To Royal *Charles*, Subject and Son You are;
Two Names that *strict Obedience* does require;   35
What Frenzy then does Your rash Thoughts inspire,
Thus by *Disloyal Deeds* to add more Cares
To them of the bright Burden that he wears?
Why with such eager speed hunt You a Crown
You're so unfit to wear, were it Your own?   40
With Bows, and Legs, and little Arts, You try
A rude, unthinking *Tumults* love to buy:
And he who stoops to do so mean a Thing,
Shows he, *by Heaven*, was ne're designed for *King*.
Would you be Great? do Things are *Great* and *Brave*;   45
And scorn to be the *Mobile's* dull Slave;
Tell *the base Great Ones*, and the *Shouting Throng*,
You scorn a *Crown* worn in *anothers wrong*.
Prove your high Birth by Deeds Noble and Good,
But strive not to Legitimate Your Blood.   50

Ephelia

(1681)

13 *excluding*: Exclusion Crisis, the attempt to exclude the Catholic James, Duke of York,
from the succession. After the discovery of the 'Popish Plot' the Whigs tried in three
successive parliamentary sessions to force through a bill to change the succession but all
three attempts (1679, 1680, 1681) failed   31 *Royal Father*: the Duke of Monmouth was
son of Charles II and Lucy Waters   41 *Legs*: a formal deep bow, with one leg extended
forward, the toe pointed (a token of deep respect)   46 *Mobile*: *mobile vulgus*, the fickle
crowd, a phrase from Ovid, *Tristiae* I. 9. 11

JANE BARKER
(1652–1732)

JANE BARKER was a Jacobite gentlewoman. She was baptized on 17 May 1652
in Blatherwycke, Northamptonshire. Her father, Thomas Barker, bore a coat of
arms. He attended the court of Charles I, possibly as a servant to the Lord
Chancellor, Keeper of the Great Seal. Her mother was a Cornishwoman, Anne
Connock. Her father fought on the King's side in the Civil War, an uncle fought
for James II against William, and another uncle fought against Monmouth at
Sedgemoor, where he was killed. She herself was as ardent a supporter of the
Stuarts as any of her male relatives, and a convinced Jacobite. By 1662 the family
had moved from Northamptonshire to Wilsthorp, Lincolnshire, where Thomas
Barker managed a sizeable farm belonging to John Cecil, Earl of Exeter. Jane
Barker herself had been sent to school in Putney, and returned about this time to
her family. In her early teens, she learned how to manage a farm, and at 15 or so,
was sent to an aunt in London, probably to acquire citified manners.

One of her greatest interests was medicine, and she became a practising herbalist. She was related to Richard Lower, a London physician, and co-founder of the Royal Society. Her brother Edward matriculated at St John's College Cambridge, in 1668, and completed his MA at Christ Church Oxford, in 1674–5. He taught her Latin, the use of herbs, and anatomy, and his early death in 1675 grieved her greatly. She was extremely serious about her own medical practice: in a poem in *Poetical Recreations*, she renounces poetry in favour of reading Galen and Hippocrates (in Latin: she does not claim to read Greek); in another, she expresses her delight in finding that an apothecary had filed her bills with the doctors'. She was not the only woman in her generation to practise medicine semi-officially: a contemporary, Mary Trye, learned medicine from her father, and kept his practice going after his death, as she explains in *Medicatrix, or the woman-physician* (1675).

Jane Barker lived contentedly in Lincolnshire for a decade, exchanging verses with friends and family, and working on her fiction, but in 1685, she and her mother left the farm, besieged by bad luck and debt, and went to London, where she joined the court of Mary of Modena (like Anne Finch and Anne Killigrew) and converted to Catholicism, whilst continuing to practise as a herbalist. Religion is another major theme of her writing. When James II was driven into exile in 1688, she was one of the almost 40,000 supporters who followed him. She settled in St Germain-en-Laye with a number of Connock relatives, notably her cousin, Colonel William Connock. She made contact with the English Benedictine convent of Pontoise, and witnessed the profession there of Arabella FitzJames, illegitimate daughter of James II. Her manuscript collection of Poems Refering to the Times (1700: London, BL Add. MS 21,621) was, according to its dedication, compiled as a gift for James II. Another early collection of poems was published in 1688, *Poetical Recreations*, a collection of her own work together with poems by Cambridge friends, and some by the publisher, Benjamin Crayle. She lived in France for a time after the exile of James II, though towards the end of her life, she was living in London. From the 1680s onwards, she became interested in fiction, and the first of several novels was published in 1715 (*Exilius*). By 1696, she was nearly blind with cataracts, which were couched—whether this improved her sight, is not clear. She returned to England in 1704, and took over the farm at Wilsthorp. In the early 1730s, she was one of those who argued for the canonization of James II: she claimed that the touch of a cloth dipped in the dying king's blood cured a 'death's head', an apparently cancerous growth, about the size of a 'grain of oatmeal', on her breast. She returned to France towards the end of her long life, because she died and was buried at St Germain-en-Laye, on 29 March 1732.

The subject of the third poem included here is more presumably a member of the English Augustinian house of canonesses at Paris than of the other English Augustinian convent at Louvain. This kind of fancy-work was very much part of nun's culture: for example, a recruit to the English Benedictine house at Ghent in 1623 is described as 'the mistress of making and teaching ye silke flowers in both ye monasterys and she who first found out ye art of printing leaves', and a pair of recruits to the 'Blue Nuns' of Paris in 1690 who were skilled, respectively, in making watches and studded watch-cases, 'declared they would not be admitted on the score of being obliged to work more than their Religious duties would with eas permit, and as the rest of the Community'. All this reflects a continual financial problem in English convents: the abbess of Ghent comments with obvious relief, that they had 'by severall marchaunts very good vent for theyr silk flowers'.

233   *On the DEATH of my Dear Friend*
         and Play-Fellow Mrs. E.D. having
         Dream'd the night before I heard thereof
         that I had lost a Pearl

I dream'd I lost a pearl, and so it prov'd;
I lost a Friend much above Pearls belov'd:
A Pearl perhaps adorns some outward part,
But Friendship decks each corner of the heart;
Friendship's a *Gem*, whose Lustre do's out-shine   5
All that's below the heav'nly Crystaline.
Friendship is that mysterious thing alone,
Which can unite, and make two Hearts but one;
It purifies our Love, and makes it flow
I'th' clearest stream that's found in Love below;   10
It *sublimates* the Soul, and makes it move
Towards Perfection and *Celestial* Love.
We had no by-designs, nor hop'd to get
Each by the other place among the great;
Nor *Riches* hop'd, nor Poverty we fear'd,   15
'Twas Innocence in both, which both rever'd
Witness this truth the *Wilsthorp-Fields*, where we
So oft enjoy'd a harmless *Luxurie*;
Where we indulg'd our easie Appetites,
With Pocket-Apples, Plumbs, and such delights,   20
Then we contriv'd to spend the rest o'th'day,
In making Chaplets, or at Check-stone play;
When weary, we our selves supinely laid
On beds of *Vi'lets* under some cool shade,
Where the Sun in vain strove to dart through his *Rays*   25
Whilst Birds around us chanted forth their *Lays*;
Ev'n whose we had bereaved of their yong
Would greet us with a *Querimonious* Song.
Stay here, my Muse, and of these let us learn,
The loss of our deceased Friend to mourn: 30
Learn did I say? alas, that cannot be,
We can teach Clouds to weep, and Winds to sigh at Sea,
Teach *Brooks* to murmer, *Rivers* to ore-flow
We can add Solitude to Shades of *Yeaugh*.
Were *Turtles* to be witness of our moan,   35
They'd in compassion quite forget their own:
Nor shall hereafter Heraclitus be
Fam'd for his Tears, but to my *Muse* and me;
Fate shall give all that *Fame* can comprehend,
Ah poor repair for th'loss of such a *Friend*.   40

17 *Wilsthorp-Fields*: Wilsthorpe, near Market Deeping, in Lincolnshire   20 *Pocket-Apples*: apples in their pockets   22 *Check-stone*: chequers   27 *bereaved*: birds-nesting, or collecting birds' eggs, was a children's pastime—rather a tomboyish one for two little girls   28 *Querimonious*: Jane Barker read Latin, so this may be a pun, conflating 'cere-monious' with Latin 'querelae', laments, complaints   34 *Yeaugh*: yew   35 *Turtles*: turtle-doves   37 *Heraclitus*: concerned with the fleeting nature of the world, and hence known as 'the weeping philosopher'

234   *Necessity of Fate*

I

In vain, in vain it is, I find
   To strive against our *Fate*,
   We may as well command the Wind
Or th' *Seas* rude Waves to gentle manners bind,
   Or to *Eternity* prescribe a date,   5
As frustrate ought that *Fortune* has design'd.
For when we think we're Politicians grown,
   And live by methods of our own;
   We then *obsequiously* obey
Her Dictates, and a blindfull Homage pay.   10

II

For were't not so, surely I cou'd not be
Still slave to Rhime, and lazy Poetry
   I who so oft have strove,
   My freedom to regain;
And sometimes too, for my assistance took   15
Business, and sometimes too a Book,
Company, and sometimes Love:
   All which proves vain,
For I can only shake but not cast off my Chain.

III

Ah cruel Fate! all this thou did'st foreshow   20
   Ev'n when I was a Child;
   When in my *Picture*'s hand
   My Mother did command,
There shou'd be drawn a Lawrel-Bough:
Lo then my *Muse* sat by and smil'd,   25
To hear how some the Sentence did oppose,
   Saying an *Apple*, *Bird*, or *Rose*
Were objects which did more befit
My childish years, and no less childish wit.

IV

But my smiling Muse well knew that constant Fate   30
   Her promise wou'd compleat;

For Fate at my *initiation*,
    In the *Muses* Congregation,
As my Responsor promis'd then for me,
    I shou'd forsake those *three*,   35
Soaring honours, and vain sweets of pleasure,
And vainer fruits of *worldly treasure*,
All for the *Muses* Melancholy Tree,
E're I knew ought of its great *Mystery*
    Ah gentle Fate, since thou wilt have it so   40
    Let thy kind hand exalt it to my brow.

24 *Lawrel-Bough*: proper to a poet   38 *Tree*: the laurel

235   *To Dame——Augustin nun*
           on her curious gum-work

Oft have I strove t'asscend that lofty ground,
Where th'immortal raritys are found,
But all in vain, Parnassus is too high,
And I to weak either to climb or fly.
Then pardon madam that I bring to you,   5
Such flowers as I cou'd scramble up below,
Which so insippid are, compar'd to yours,
As dayses, amongst finest gilliflowers,
But whosoe'er pretends to immitate,
Your works, and not live in your holy state }   10
Deserves to suffer proud Arachnas fate.
For those who will pretend to work like you,
Must do the work of saints and Angells too
For every Alaluja you repeat,
And every hym, or antiphon you set,   15
Makes either Rose, pink, lilly, violet.
Which holy Angells fresh in water keep
(That water which for others sins you weep)
To dress heav'ns altars up, on propper days
When Augustin saints sing Alalujas.   20
And when in Rapture you are carryed there,
Thence in your minds the beautious figgures bear,
And like an other wonderous Moses you,
Transcribe heavens works, and natures far outdo,
Or like those painters who best pictures make   25
Who for a pattern their own children take.
    We need not to Italion villas go
Nor yet versails, the Toileries st Cloud,
T'admire the works of nature or of art,

Since you excell em all in every part,   30
Thus the great world, byth' little world's outdone,
Not' only so, but by the heart alone,
For the vast universe can never show,
So fine a structure, such a motion too,
Now though this member's small, and cloyster'd lives,   35
Yet to the whole, it animation gives,
So you bless'd Dames, insensibly dispence,
On all your sex, your vertuous influence,
Whilst you your selves, gain what this world can't give
A perfect life, heav'ns representative.   40

Title *gum-work*: a fashionable craft, along with waxcraft and beadwork: a technique for producing small three-dimensional or high-relief pictures   8 *dayses*: daisies; *gilliflowers*: pinks or carnations   11 *Arachna*: Greek myth. Arachne, a champion spinner, matched her skill against the goddess Minerva and was turned into a spider   19 *propper*: days consecrated to particular saints   20 *Augustin*: saint associated with the Augustinian order   23 *Moses*: thought to be author of the first five books of the Old Testament   28 *versails*: Versailles, originally a royal hunting-lodge but greatly expanded by Louis XIV into the principal royal palace; the decoration of the interior was carried out by Charles Le Brun; *Toileries*: Tuileries, a royal palace adjoining the Louvre; *st Cloud*: St Cloud   31 [author's note: 'man, the little world']

MARY ADAMS
(fl. 1676)

MARY ADAMS was a working-class prophetess, who published a two-page pamphlet in 1676, which attracted enough interest to be reprinted in 1678. She may have been connected with a Baptist minister called Richard Adams, from Leicester, who was at Shad Thames, in Bermondsey, South London, in 1689, but the impersonal nature of her text does not allow us to place her in any way.

236   *'Oh LONDON*
             I once more to thee do speak'

Oh LONDON I once more to thee do speak
    Because thy Pride has made my Heart to ake
To See thy Pride and eke Abomination
    Which causeth the Lord to send such Visitations,
As Plague and Pestilence, Fire and Sword,   5
    Because thou will not hearken to his Word,
Which cut off Thousands in a little time,
    Methinks it should not so soon be out of mind;
Also the great Fire which raged up and down,
    Throughout the City, till 'twas almost consum'd   10

That Thousands were left without habitations;
  Oh! do not forget the Lord in such great visitations.
I must confess the Judgments were very great,
  But to what End I to you must relate,
That you should see by those his Visitations   15
  Your horrid Sins and great Abominations
What Pride and Pleasures are found in this great City,
  With Oaths and other great Abominations, which makes me pity
To see the Sad and Deplorable State thou art in
  Which will cause the Lord more Plagues on thee to send.   20
What Sins were found in Sodom and Gomorrah,
  Also the Great Cruelty of Pharaoh
That is not found in this Wicked Generation?
  Therefore repent with speed, lest it prove your Damnation.

(1676)

8 refers to the outbreak of bubonic plague in London, 1665   9 The Great Fire of
London, which broke out in 1666

KATHERINE COLYEAR (COUNTESS OF
DORCHESTER), née SEDLEY
(1657–1717)

KATHERINE SEDLEY was the daughter of a minor literary figure, Sir Charles
Sedley, poet and playwright, and his wife Katherine, née Savage. Circa 1672, he
sent his wife to a nunnery at Ghent, and went through a form of marriage with a
gentlewoman called Ann Ayscough. When Katherine was only 15, she was
already describable (by John Evelyn) as 'none of the most virtuous but a witt'.
Despite her lack of obvious charms and her determined Protestantism, James,
Duke of York fell in love with her. She commented, 'It cannot be my beauty, for
he must see I have none; and it cannot be my wit, for he has not enough to know
that I have any.' She became a Maid of Honour to the long-suffering Mary of
Modena (though obviously, of the opposite party at court to the virtuous and
devoted Anne Finch and Anne Killigrew). She was well educated: a book of
songs with her bookplate and the date 1678 contains both drinking-songs, and
religious pieces in Latin (London, BL Add. MS 30382). For what it is worth, in
Curll's edition of Rochester of 1709, the long heroic epistle 'Ephelia to Bajazet'
is headed 'An Letter from the lady K. S.—to the ... Earl of Rochester', suggesting that she had a literary reputation. She bore James a daughter, called Lady
Catharine Darnley, in March 1679, and a son, James Darnley, who died on the
day of his father's coronation. In 1686, James created her Baroness of Darlington
and Countess of Dorchester, with a pension of £5,000 a year. When he became
king, he resolved to stop seeing her, a resolution he broke within the year. She
survived the revolution of 1688: in May 1691 William and Mary granted her a
pension of £1,500 a year, and in 1703, her former pension of £5,000 was
renewed by a grant in the Irish parliament.

She married David Colyear, first Earl of Portmore, in 1696, and had two sons by him. She is said to have advised them, when they went to school, 'if any body calls either of you the son of a whore, you must bear it, for you are so: but if they call you bastards, fight till you die; for you are an honest man's sons.' A contemporary key to Delarivier Manley's *New Atalantis* (1707) identifies her as the Lesbian lover of Catherine Cockburn, née Trotter; though Greer *et al.* suggest that Manley's 'Zara' is more probably Lady Sarah Piers—'Daphne' is almost certainly Catherine Trotter.

Catherine Frazier, the subject of this lampoon, was another of the more raffish Maids of Honour, daughter of Sir Alexander Fraser, the King's physician, and mistress of Sir Carr Scrope, a friend of Rochester's. Katherine Sedley and Carr Scrope were notoriously at feud: according to a letter from Lady Chaworth to her brother on 30 January, 1676, 'Mis Sidley and Sir Carr Scroope [had] too loud quarells twice in the Q[ueens] drawing roome, upon some lampoone made of her that she judged him the author, which says she is as mad as her mother and as vicious as her father.' She retaliated in kind, with these verses. Carr Scroope was in love with Catherine Frazier, but was alarmed by her extravagance: Lady Chaworth also notes, 'mighty bravery in clothes preparing for the Queen's birthday, especially Mis Phraser whose gowne is ermine upon velvet imbroidered with gold and lined with cloth of gold, 'twill come to 300l., and frights sir Carr Scroope, who is much in love with her, from marrying her, saying his estate will scarce maintaine her in clothes.'

237   *'As Frazier one night at her*
           Post in the Drawing Room stood'

As Frazier one night at her Post in the Drawing Room stood
Dunbarton came by, and she cryd O My Lord, woud—you
   woud!—
What is your will, Madam, for I am in haste and cant tarry,
The thing is soon done, I will swear—it is nothing but—marry.
Why Madam says he, do you think the Devil is i'me   5
To marry with you when I can have as good for a Guinea;
Pray look not so high, nor toss up your dangling locks:
Go marry Car Scrope, and your Father will cure his pox.

(1676)

1 *Frazier*: Fazier MS. Caroline Frazier, lady-in-waiting to the Duchess of York   2 *Dunbarton*: Sir George Douglas, Earl of Dumbarton   4 *marry*: her sudden and urgent need for a husband may be intended to imply that she is pregnant   8 *Car Scrope*: Sir Carr Scroop, versifier and man of fashion; *Father*: Her father Sir Alexander Fraser was the King's physician-in-ordinary from June 1660. He also had a reputation as an abortionist.

MARGARET, LADY GODOLPHIN, née BLAGGE

(1652–1678)

MARGARET BLAGGE was the daughter of Colonel Thomas Blagge (b. 1613), Groom of the Bedchamber, and his wife Mary, daughter of Sir Roger North, of Mildenhall, Suffolk. Sir Henry North, Margaret's uncle, was a poet and romance writer; his wife, Dame Sara, was a collector of verse and epitaphs (British Library, Add. MS 18220; Add. MS 36755). Thomas Blagge was a hard-line Royalist. He followed Charles II into exile on the Continent and became a Lieutenant Colonel of the King's Lifeguards. He died soon after the Restoration: his widow was granted a £500 annuity in March 1661. In 1666, Margaret, at 14, became a Maid of Honour to Anne Hyde, the Duchess of York, and at court she met and fell in love with Sidney Godolphin, a 21-year-old Cornishman and up-and-coming courtier. He proposed to her and they were betrothed, but the marriage did not take place for nine years, as Godolphin lacked the means to establish a suitable household. In 1672, under the influence of her tyrannical spiritual mentor, John Evelyn, she pledged to withdraw from the court and dedicate the remainder of her life to God. Evelyn devised for her a punishing regime of prayer, repentance, and fasting, in the form of a series of 'offices', which seem designed to sublimate her sexuality. When Godolphin returned from the Continent in the autumn of 1672, he found that she was prepared to end their engagement. The unflappable Godolphin began to scheme to win her back. He persuaded her to leave the court for Berkeley House, in what is now Mayfair: Lady Berkeley was related to Godolphin through his mother and could be relied upon as an ally, while Goring House, where Godolphin was in residence, was nearby. Throughout the remainder of 1673 and into 1674 Godolphin patiently subverted Evelyn's influence over Margaret, and rebuilt their own relationship. In late 1674 Margaret was ordered to return to court to act the part of Diana in John Crowne's masque, *Calisto*, and Godolphin seized the opportunity to press his suit. On 16 May 1675 they married in a secret wedding at the Temple Church in London, and kept Evelyn, and the rest of the world, in the dark about their marriage for nearly twelve months. It may have been Margaret's pregnancy that forced them to divulge the truth. On 3 September 1676 she gave birth to a boy, christened Francis. The celebrations were short-lived as her condition rapidly deteriorated. She became delirious, pimples and running blisters erupted across her skin, and she died after imbibing a potion of *Aurum potabile* (potable gold), a medicine of last resort sent to her by Elizabeth Mordaunt (see no. 186). Godolphin's grief was acute: he never married again. Evelyn wrote a 'Life of Mrs Godolphin', a hagiographic work which he left in manuscript. The brief satirical verses given here are an indication that for all her piety, she had cast an amused and observant eye on the affectations of her fellow maids of honour. Her other writings, which are extensive, are religious meditations, with one hymn, which she herself describes as incompetent but sincere (London, British Library Evelyn Bound F. 38, fo. 19ʳ). The selections from her 'Devotions', copied out by Evelyn (London, British Library Evelyn MS, Bound F. 38) suggest that she read Latin with ease.

238   *Song:*

On a Lady newly come out of France, &c.
To the Tune of——

I

As F—at her Toilet sat
  Her beauty to renew
Ah fy, Sayd she, I'm grown so fat
  I know not what to do:

2

She sigh'd and cry'd, I must be leane   5
  Or I shall *perdre taille*
The finest shape that 'ere was seene,
  Said her Mother † *Missrael*

3

But Miss'raell, what shall I do
  An *Earle* for to obtaine?   10
None else *ta chere Maistresse* shuld woo
  None else her Coeur shall gaine:

4

But if I shoud this Conquest make
  Then I must bid *adieu*
Too all those hearts that lie as sleeke   15
  And follow now *ma queue*:

5

La bouche si belle, les yeux si doulx
  Le tour de mon visage,
Enough to send a Soul to Hell
  Et faire un sot d'un sage: 20

6

No more your Mistris you shall see
  Attentive un douceure
But I an English Wife must be
  Subjet a les douleurs:

7

But when of Evils there are two,   25
  'Tis great to choose the least
For this Appartement with you
  Missrael I love best

8

My Glasse, my Thoilet and my Bed,
    Si propre a la francaise   30
That I had rather much be dead
    Than *Vivre* al'Anglois.

† the mayd

---

1 *F—*: perhaps Caroline Frazier again?   6 *perdre taille*: lose my shape   11 *ta chere*: her
darling   16 *ma queue*: my tail/the tail of my dress   17–18 The mouth so beautiful, the
eyes so soft, the shape of my face   20 and to make a fool out of a wise man   22 waiting
for a present   24 subject to their griefs   30 So neat, in the French taste

AMY HAMMOND (née BROWNE)
(?–1693)

AMY BROWNE came from Gloucestershire. Her father may have been James
Browne (1615–*c*.1685), of Mangotsfield in that county, who matriculated at
Oriel College, Oxford in 1634 and took his BA in 1638. He was a chaplain in
the Parliamentarian army in Scotland, and as a General Baptist (Bunyan's sect)
he sought debates with Presbyterian preachers who viewed him with horror as a
heretic. Anthony à Wood claims that he conformed at the Restoration but his
Scripture Redemption Freed from Men's Restrictions (1673) suggests otherwise,
since it is clearly the work of a committed Baptist. Amy married Anthony
Hammond (1641–80) of Somersham Place, Huntingdonshire, an ancient, moat-
ed house belonging to the Bishops of Ely, which had fallen into a state of ruin,
though it still had one habitable wing. Their son, Anthony Hammond (1668–
1738) was a poet and pamphleteer. According to one story, while at Cambridge
he shared rooms with Susanna Centlivre (b. 1666–7), the playwright, who was
attending the university dressed as a man.

239   *Verses by my mother in her own hand*

To my affections what a slave am I?
That I cannot prevaile more easily
To resigne my Relations unto thee

When I consider my dayly prayers bee
Thy will be done, with words soe readyly   5
I must conclud tis all hypocricy.

Excessive love is due to God alone
Who is all Goodnesse and Perfection
And doth returne a hundred fold for one.

To hold what is most deare, with a loose hand   10
Freely to let it goe at his command
O that my hard heart were thus meekly fram'd.

Grant me Lord to attaine this victory
Over my stubborne flesh, before I dy
And soe retire to the grave peaceably.   15

To have noe wil but thine what liberty
Should I injoy? How highly should I fly?
At thy summons, to Blest Eternity.

ANONYMOUS IRISHWOMAN

THIS Irish poem dates from the seventeenth century, and it is in a popular, rather than a bardic metre, so is apparently one of the relatively few sets of amateur verses to survive from so early. Ireland had maintained a class of professional poets and guardians of culture, the *filid*, since before the birth of Christ, who passed knowledge from one generation to the next via a highly efficient system of oral teaching. Since poetry was thus a profession, akin to, and of equal status with, law, involving a long, complicated, and gruelling apprenticeship, it is hardly surprising to find that it excluded women. The honoured ranks of poets (*filid*), were literate, learned professionals, while ordinary people entertained themselves with verse which was completely distinct from the activities of the professionals, but did not write it down. In professional Irish poetry of the thirteenth and fourteenth centuries, there are derogatory references to women fortune-tellers and women balladeers, who compose popular *abhrán* verse. Such verses reluctantly admit a 'great demand' for this low-status, popular composition, but also indicate indirectly why none of this verse survives: the only literate professionals capable of recording it not only held it in contempt, but regarded it on some levels as dangerous competition. According to the professional poets, women's proper relation to bardic activity is as patrons, and they are frequently mentioned in this capacity.

The contents of this poem suggest that it is one of the satirical songs composed by women against men which were seen (by Irish men) as a particularly heinous variety of female misconduct: many later examples survive, particularly from Gaelic Scotland (which also produces a considerably earlier one, too early, alas, for this volume: a satirical poem on her chaplain's penis by Isabella, fifteenth-century Countess of Argyll). This example, with its playful hyperbole, seems well calculated to deflate the masculine ego.

240   *'Ní binn do thorann lem thaoibh'*

Ní binn do thorann lem thaoibh,
  a mhacaoimh shaoir na bhfonn ngharbh;
gé decair dhúinn gan a chleith
  dob fhearr liom tú do bheith marbh.

Do dhúischechadh mairbh a huaigh 5
 leis gach fuaim dá dtig ód shróin;
a chaomhthaigh luigheas im ghar,
 is doiligh dhamh bheith dod chóir.

Dá mbeith cheachtar dhíobh im chionn,
 doba lugha liom de ghuais 10
gáir chaoilcheann ag tolladh chrann
 ná do shrann ag dol im chluais.

Binne liom grafainn na muc
 ná gach guth lingeas ód shróin;
binne fós—ní bhiam dá cheilt— 15
 gaineamh agá meilt i mbróin.

Binne bodharghuth lag laoigh,
 díoscadh drochmhuilinn mhaoil bhrais,
nó géis gairbh-easa chaor mbán
 le lingeadh de lár tar ais. 20

Binne bloiscbhéime na n-all
 ná gach srann dá dtig ót ucht,
's is binne donál na bhfaol
 ná gach claon chuireas tú id ghuth.

Binne guth lachan ar linn 25
 ná glothar do chinn id schuan,
agus is binne fá seacht
 fuaim garbhthonn ag teacht i gcuan.

Is binne búirthe na dtarbh,
 gáir chlogán, gé garbh an dórd; 30
gol leinibh, go siabhradh cinn,
 is binne linn ná do ghlór.

Mná in iodhnaibh go ngoimh ag gul
 gan árach ar scur dá mbrón,
Caoi chadhan in oidhche fhuair, 35
 is binne ná fuaim do shrón.

Sceamhgal scine le scrios práis
 ní mheasaim gur páis dom cheann,
ná géim cairte le cloich chruaidh,
 ón dord tig uait ar mo pheall. 40

Ceannghail tonn le creataibh long,
 uaill fhearchon, gé lonn a sian,
is míle finne céad uair
 ná gach fuaim lingeas ód chliabh.

Árach ní fhaghaim ar shuan, 45
 do tógbhadh leat gruag mo chinn;

gach bolgfhadach tig ód cheann,
dar Brighid, dar leam, ní binn.

240   *'Ugly your uproar at my side'*

Ugly your uproar at my side,
    my fine young man of the harsh hymns!
I confess (though it goes hard)
    I would rather you were dead.

The dead would wake in their graves   5
    with each noise that leaves your nose.
Partner, lying close,
    it is bad to be beside you.

Of the two, if I had to choose,
    I would pick as the lesser pain   10
a woodpecker drilling a tree
    than your snoring in my ear.

Pigs' grunts are sweeter, I find,
    than the noise that starts from your nose.
Sweeter still, I won't deny   15
    is sand crunched in a quern,

or the hollow weak moan of a calf,
    the creak of a wrecked, great rackety mill
or the rough falls' roar in a white mass
    rebounding out of its bed.   20

Loud blows on cliffs are sweeter
    than the snores that leave your breast,
and sweeter the howling of wolves
    than the twists you give your voice.

Ducks on a pond are sweeter   25
    than the sleep-rattle in your head,
and sweeter seven times
    rough waves as they enter harbour.

Sweeter the bellowings of bulls
    or a bell calling with hard clang.   30
A child crying till it racks your brain
    is pleasanter than your noise.

Women's feverish cries in their pangs
    with no hope of their troubles' end
or geese grieving in the cold night   35
    are nicer than your nose-noise.

Screech of knife scraped across brass
    would torture my head no more
(or a cart grinding on hard stone)
    than your tune upon my pillow.   40

Waves pounding ships' ribs,
   the howl of wild dogs whining mad,
are sweeter a hundred thousand times
   than the sound that starts from your chest.

I have lost all hope of sleep.   45
   You have swept the hair from my head.
Each gust out of your skull,
   by Bridget, ugly it is!

MARY, LADY CHUDLEIGH (née LEE)
(1656–1710)

THE future Lady Chudleigh was the daughter of Richard Lee of Winslade in
Devon. In February 1674, at the age of 17, she married George Chudleigh,
thirteen years her senior, the eldest son of Sir George Chudleigh of Ashton,
Devon, to whose baronetcy he succeeded in 1691. Their marriage is said to have
been an unhappy one, though she was the mother of two sons and a daughter,
Eliza Maria, whose early death she commemorated in one of her poems. She
corresponded with a number of literary friends, including Mary Astell, Elizabeth Thomas, and John Norris of Bemberton, and led what she called a 'rough
and unpolished life' in the country, where she spent much of her time alone with
her books and her thoughts.
   The early poem from Lady Chudleigh which is included here is a testament
to the excited response generated to Mary Astell's *A Serious Proposal to the
Ladies*, published in 1694 (Elizabeth Thomas's 'To Almystrea' is another). After
A Serious Proposal, the extensive literature of the defence of women received a
considerable augmentation by women themselves, which is not so evident in
earlier stages of this controversy. Lady Chudleigh herself also published a long
poem, *The Ladies Defence*, in 1701, a verse debate defending women's right to
education and self-expression, written in reply to *The Bride-Womans Counsellor*
(1699), a wedding sermon by the Nonconformist preacher John Sprint which
articulated the doctrine of wifely obedience in its most extreme form. She
published her *Poems on Several Occasions* in 1703, which went into another
four editions in her lifetime, and also *Essays upon Several Subjects in Verse and
Prose*. In later life, she was immobilized by rheumatism. She died at Ashton and
was buried there. Manuscripts of unpublished plays and translations, and of her
poems, are in the Houghton Library, Harvard, and the Huntington Library in
San Marino.

241   *To Almystrea*

I.

Permit *Marissa* in an artless Lay
To speak her Wonder, and her Thanks repay:

Her creeping Muse can ne'er like yours ascend;
She has not Strength for such a towring Flight.
Your Wit, her humble Fancy do's transcend;   5
She can but gaze at your exalted Height:
Yet she believed it better to expose
    Her Failures, than ungrateful prove;
        And rather chose
To shew a want of Sense, than want of Love: 10
But taught by you, she may at length improve,
And imitate those Virtues she admires.
Your bright Example leaves a Tract Divine,
She sees a beamy Brightness in each Line,
And with ambitious Warmth aspires,   15
Attracted by the Glory of your Name,
To follow you in all the lofty Roads of Fame.

2.

Merit like yours, can no Resistance find,
But like a Deluge overwhelms the Mind;
    Gives full Possession of each Part,   20
Subdues the Soul, and captivates the Heart.
Let those whom Wealth, or Interest unite,
    Whom Avarice, or Kindred sway
    Who in the Dregs of Life delight;
And ev'ry Dictate of their Sense obey,   25
Learn here to love at a sublimer Rate,
To wish for nothing but exchange of Thoughts,
        For intellectual Joys,
        And Pleasures more refin'd
Than Earth can give, or Fancy can create.   30
Let our vain Sex be fond of glitt'ring Toys,
Of pompous Titles, and affected Noise,
Let envious Men by barb'rous Custom led
        Descant on Faults,
        And in Detraction find   35
Delights unknown to a brave gen'rous Mind,
While we resolve a nobler Path to tread,
    And from Tyrannick Custom free,
View the dark Mansions of the mighty Dead,
    And all their close Recesses see;   40
    Then from those awful Shades retire,
        And take a Tour above,
    And there, the shining Scenes admire,
        Th' Opera of eternal Love;
View the Machines, on the bright Actors gaze,   45
Then in a holy Transport, blest Amaze,

To the great Author our Devotion raise,
And let our Wonder terminate in Praise.

(after 1694)

39 *Mansions*: i.e. read Classical literature. In her 'Epistle Dedicatory' to *The Ladies Defence* (London: John Deere, 1701), Lady Chudleigh exhorts women to read Classical writers in translation   42 *Tour above*: study religious literature

ANNE WENTWORTH
(fl. 1676–1679)

MRS WENTWORTH, who apparently lived with her husband in White-Cross Street in London, is known only by two pamphlets, *A Vindication of Anne Wentworth* (1677) and *The Revelation of Jesus Christ* (1679). Her sketch of her background in these works aligns her with other prophets in many eras: the long illness, suddenly cured and the sense of mission which follows on from it are classic in accounts of the formation of prophets. According to her own account, people spoke against her because she lived apart from her husband, but as she explains, he 'will not suffer me to live with him, unless I deny the Lord, and his Message, and avow to be deluded by a lying spirit'. Thus, she warns, the vessels of wrath are to be emptied on the heads of 'Hanserd Knollys with his Church, and Nehemiah Cocks, my Husbands Pastor, Thomas Hicks, William Dicks, Philip Boarder [who had refused to take her as a tenant], my Relations, and hundreds more, that have a hand in setting my Husband against me, so that he will not own me, and then they go on to blame and defame me, and say, that I am run away from him.' Here we have a picture of a woman completely estranged from her community, religious, social, and familial: Knollys is presumably her own pastor. She is, however, not without resources. Even though she failed to convince anyone from her original environment to accept her message, she found believers elsewhere. One was sufficiently impressed to print this little pamphlet of her prophecies; another, or others, after her husband had turned her out and taken away all her furniture, reinstated her in some comfort. The author of the pamphlet claims not to know the identity of this benefactor, attributing the situation, rather, to the hand of the Lord. Anne Wentworth's career is an interesting illustration of the costs and benefits of religious enthusiasm: in pursuit of her vocation as a prophetess, she estranged herself from every possible avenue of support, but succeeded in building an alternative structure round herself and ended up, apparently, better off than she had started. It is interesting that, while her prophecies show very little sense of the world beyond her immediate environment, one of the few things which does impinge is Titus Oates's Popish Plot, which alarms her considerably. Her writings illustrate the way that the spirit of prophecy cut across social hierarchy, including gender: in *A Vindication . . .*, she asks: 'what authority this unbeleeving husband hath over the conscience of his beleeving wife; it is true he hath authority over her in bodilly and civill respects, but not to be a Lord over her conscience; and the like may be said of fathers and masters.' As Anne Wentworth's own story indicates, when imperatives were ranked thus, 'bodily and civill' authority often got short shrift; one reason why prophets were generally greeted with alarm and suspicion by the authorities.

242   *Revelation V, October 8*

When I had writ this, then the Lord said further concerning the
King

> Woe to *England*, when the Kings Life is gone!
> All may pray that no hurt to him be done.
> Now the Plot is found out, all yet is not past,
> For it's well, if that his life do escape at last,
> He now warning hath, if he will notice of it take,   5
> We may pray hard for his Life, for *Englands* sake!

                                    (1678)

1 With reference to the so-called 'Popish Plot', fabricated by the unbalanced Titus Oates in 1678

243   *Revelation VIII, March 31*

> Full *eighteen years* in sorrow I did lye,
> Then the Lord *Jesus* came to hear my cry;
> In one nights time he did me heal,
> From head to foot he made me well.
> With Ointments sweet he did me anoint,   5
> And this work he then did me appoint,
> A hand in Babylons *Ashes* I must have,
> For that end the Lord took me from the Grave,
> And said, a new Body I the Lord will give thee,
> To convince thy Enemies, if they could but see;   10
> For they are both deaf, and also very blind,
> That I the Lord may serve them in their kind:
> They do know how I the Lord did make thee whole,
> But they see not the Spirit of God in thee burn like a Coal:
> For with a Coal from my Altar I the Lord touched thee,   15
> Which none but the pure Spiritual Eye can see.
> I the Lord will openly and surely avenge thy cause,
> Upon all thy Enemies, for their unjust Laws;
> For all thy cries and groans entered into my Ear,
> And I the Lord will make them stand in awe and fear.   20
> For my Childrens wrongs I the Lord will not forget,
> But strike a blow and all of them will I then hit.
> From Heaven will I the Lord come to appear,

For to make them all my own voice to hear:
And all those, that long to see this thing done,   25
Must patiently wait till I the Lord do come.

(1676)

7 cf. Jeremiah 51   15 *Coal*: 'Then flew one of the seraphims unto me, having a live coal in his hand . . . And he laid it upon my mouth, and said, Lo, this has touched thy lips; and thine iniquity is taken away' Isaiah 6: 6–7

ANNE WHARTON
(1659–1685)

ANNE WHARTON was the second daughter of Henry Lee of Ditchley, by Anne, daughter of Sir John Danvers of Cornbury, who was the heir-at-law to the estate of her uncle, Henry Danvers, Earl of Danby. Anne Lee was a double orphan. Her father died of smallpox before she was born, and her mother eleven days after the birth. The two motherless babies, Anne and Ellinora, became the wards of their grandmother, Anne Wilmot (née St John: she was the sister of Lucy Hutchinson's mother, Lucy Apsley, née St John), whose children included John Wilmot, the future poet and Earl of Rochester (from a second marriage). Anne Wharton was thus Rochester's niece, but in terms of her experience of family life, something more like his sister: he was only twelve years her senior. When Lady Wilmot was widowed for the second time in 1658 she was left solely responsible for six children, two of whom were joint heiresses to the fortune of Henry Danvers, Earl of Danby, theoretically worth £12,000 a year. With the assistance of a number of trustees, Lady Wilmot battled for the fortunes of her brood of fatherless children, and acquired enormous debts. In 1662, it was conceded, against various other claims and counter-claims, that Ellinora and Anne were indeed the heirs at law of the Danby fortune. Lady Wilmot's difficult financial position was doubtless complicated by her career as a courtier (always an expensive business): she became Groom of the Stole to Anne Hyde, Duchess of York in 1664. It is probable that her granddaughters went to court with her, and became the playmates of the princesses Mary and Anne. Both Ellinora and Anne were said to be pretty, though it must be said that any girls that wealthy would tend to be perceived in a golden light. The Duchess's court was as cynical and sexually libertarian as that of the Duke's brother, Charles II: the Duke had many mistresses, and the Duchess had a notorious affair with Henry Sidney, so the tone of court life may either account for, or give credence to, a later accusation that Anne 'was at first debaucht for mony by my Lord Peterborough when mighty young'. Since Lady Peterborough was the Duchess's Lady of the Bedchamber, he could certainly have known her in the simpler sense of the word. Apart from whatever she may or may not have learned at court, Anne Lee leaned French and Italian, and according to her later elegy on Rochester, learned versifying from her uncle, to whom she was evidently devoted.

The Lee girls' fortunes, in their minority, were naturally managed by a group of trustees, though there is evidence that they were taking an interest in their financial affairs (and lending money to their uncle Rochester) from their early teens. Both girls caught smallpox in 1669, but made good recoveries. Eleanor married James Bertie, Lord Norreys of Rycote, in 1672, when she was only 14. Anne was mysteriously ill again that year, and was sent to Bath for at least three months to recover. The Berties were by this time pressing for the payment of Ellinora's £8,000 dowry, a sum which could not be raised from income (since the Lee girls were still minors, they could not touch the capital): it was perhaps due to her battles with the Berties that Lady Wilmot decided suddenly that it would safeguard her other granddaughter's interests to be married without delay. Meanwhile Philip, fourth baron Wharton, a friend of Sir Ralph Verney, who was one of the Lees' trustees, was the father of four daughters for whom he had to find dowries, and urgently looking for an heiress to marry his son Thomas. Negotiations went forward in secret, and the pair were married on 16 September 1673 without any publicity. Once again, there was trouble over the dowry.

The couple moved to Wharton's house at Winchendon, near Wooburn, where he continued to pursue his main interest, which was breeding and racing horses, and to visit his mistress, Jane Dering. He was a dashing and glamorous figure, to be seen at all race-meetings of any significance. Like Rochester, he required his wife to live in retirement in the country, and seldom visited her there. One consolation was provided by Rochester himself: during the autumn and winter of 1675, he was in disgrace, and living at Adderbury, twenty miles or so from Winchendon, amusing himself by exchanging playful verses with various members of his family. Further strain was put upon the relationship by Wharton's need for money: horses, and his other hobby of politics, were both expensive, and so he brought an action against Lady Wilmot in 1679. Meanwhile, Anne Wharton was working on a verse tragedy in five acts (now BL Add. MS 28693) called *Love's Martyr*, celebrating the love of Ovid for the emperor Augustus's daughter Julia (this was entered in the Stationer's Register in February 1686, but never printed or staged). When Anne reached her majority and the trust was finally wound down, Anne's half of the estate which had seemed so enormous amounted to only £2,281.6s.10d. In addition to whatever trouble or embarassment resulted from these financial problems, Anne Wharton suffered from a series of 'convulsion fitts' which alarmed her friends. In 1680, when Rochester died, Anne was too weak herself to go to his bedside. The elegy on his death which she circulated was admired by, among others, Jack Howe and Edmund Waller. From that time on, she worked seriously at poetry, and corresponded with a number of literary figures, including Aphra Behn. She had many admirers. Robert Wolseley professed to find her poetry far superior to that of Katherine Philips ('While soaring high above Orinda's flights', in the library of the University of Nottingham, Portland MS Pw V 516).

It seems clear that no sympathy was ever established between Anne Wharton and her husband. She flirted with her husband's brother, Goodwin Wharton: according to his own account, after her death, she attempted to seduce him, but he refused her. To put this in context, according to her grandmother, Wharton had refused to sleep with her for the three years before her death: Goodwin Wharton, remembering her approach to him, recalled that, 'she freely once said she would be content to be dam'd rather than not to have her desires which expression was lick the desperate greatnesse of her spirit'. It was Goodwin Wharton who recorded the story about the Earl of Peterborough, and also that she had had an affair with her uncle Rochester, and a brief fling with Jack Howe.

Anne Wharton's health was never good. Apart from 'convulsion fitts', she had problems with her throat from as early as 1672. In 1680, she went to Paris in search of a cure. Two charming autograph letters written to her husband from Paris are in the British Library (Add MS 4162, fos. 232–5). On her return, she was still far from well. At this time, she made friends with Bishop Burnet, who had been instrumental in her uncle's spectacular deathbed conversion, and exchanged poems and correspondence with him. He criticized her for failing to revise her first drafts, and also for her reluctance to make her poetry public. Her last illness was long and painful. She left her entire estate to her husband (breaking the entail, and cutting out her own family, including her grandmother), with the major exception of a provision for a £3,000 portion for Rochester's daughter by the actress Elizabeth Barry. Germaine Greer has suggested that she suffered from syphilis contracted before her marriage, and that her apparent generosity to a husband from whom she was certainly estranged was the price of avoiding a divorce or a posthumous court-case implicating her entire family. Certainly, any sexual contact with courtiers carried the risk of syphilis; and both sore throats and blinding headaches (which Anne is recorded to have suffered) were possible symptoms.

244   *A Song.*

How hardly I conceal'd my Tears?
    How oft did I complain?
When many tedious Days my Fears
    Told me I Lov'd in vain.

But now my Joys as wild are grown,   5
    And hard to be conceal'd:
Sorrow may make a silent Moan,
    But Joy will be reveal'd.

I tell it to the Bleating Flocks,
    To every Stream and Tree,   10
And Bless the Hollow Murmuring Rocks,
    For Echoing back to me.

Thus you may see with how much Joy
    We Want, we Wish, Believe;
'Tis hard such Passion to Destroy,   15
    But easie to Deceive.

245   *My Fate.*

Raising my drooping Head, o'er charg'd with Thought,
Having each Scene of Life before me brought;

I chid myself because I durst repine
At Nature's Laws, or those that were Divine.
Throughout the whole Creation 'tis the same,   5
The Fuel is devoured by the Flame;
Each peaceful, harmless, unoffending thing
Is to the Offender made an Offering:
Even God himself. Hold, my aspiring Thought;
Descend, my Muse, thy flight too high is wrought;   10
Tell not, how He, all peaceful and all kind,   ⎫
Was offer'd for the vilest of Mankind;   ⎬
A Victim for the vilest was design'd.   ⎭
Descend, I say, my Muse; low things afford
Theams high enough for thee: Touch not the Word,   15
Till he hath touch'd thy Wings with Grace Divine,
Then, only his, thou shalt the World decline.
The harmless Dove the Falcon doth betray;
The Lamb is to the Wolf become a Prey;
And Men to whom free will Heaven doth impart,   20
To follow still the Counsels of his Heart,
If wrack'd with doubt; if harmless, he designs
Peace to his Heart, and still his Wish confines
Justice to Peace, and Love to Quiet joyns.
Why then the Dove-like Fate will sure be his;   25
Short is his Life, unsettled is his Bliss:
Hard Fate; that choice we eagerly pursue,
Is, or to be undone, or to undo.

DAMARIS, LADY MASHAM (née CUDWORTH)
(1659–1708)

LADY MASHAM was born in Cambridge, where her father, the Platonist and philosopher Ralph Cudworth, taught for forty-three years, and was brought up in the Master's Lodge of Christ's College. Her considerable intellectual gifts were recognized from an early stage, and she was encouraged to think for herself. She married Sir Francis Masham (1646?–1723), third baronet of Otes, Essex, in June 1685, thus acquiring nine stepchildren. She had one child of her own, Francis Cudworth Masham, who was born in 1686. She reared her son according to Locke's theories, expressed in his *Thoughts Concerning Education*, and taught him Latin, learning the language herself as they went along. She published *A Discourse Concerning the Love of God* in 1696, anonymously, but not secretly: it was widely known to be hers. Another book, *Occasional Thoughts in Reference to a Vertuous or Christian Life* (1700) advocates women's education, and generally, defends rationality against social prejudice. A letter to Locke suggests that in 1685, she toyed with publishing her verse: 'How ever perhaps you may see me in Print in a little While, and then need not be Beholden to me, it being

growne much the Fasion of late for our sex, Though I confess it has not much of
my Approbation because (Principally) the Mode is for one to Dye First; and at
this time if I might Have my owne Choice I Have no Great Inclination That
Way'—another, of the same year, points in a rather different direction: ''Tis in
Vain that you bid me Preserve my Poetry; Household Affairs are the Opium of
the Soul.' The Masham's country mansion was a large and well-known house. In
1691, when his health began to fail, Locke went to live there as a paying guest,
and remained there until his death. While he lived there, Otes was 'one of the
most important addresses in the world of European letters'. He assembled a
library of nearly 4,000 volumes and in his will he bequeathed to Lady Masham
any four folios, eight quartos, and twenty-four smaller books of her own choice.
Lady Masham's mother also joined the household after the death of her husband: she was buried at High Laver Church and her epitaph was written by
Locke. Lady Masham died before her fiftieth birthday and was buried in Bath
Abbey.

246   *The Irreconcilable*

I

I little thought (*my Damon*) once, that *you*
Could prove, and what is more, to *me*, *untrue*.
Can I *forget* such *Treachery*, and *Live*?
Mercy it self would not this Crime forgive.
Heaven's Gates refuse to let *Apostates* in,   5
No that's the *Great unpardonable Sin*.

II

Did you not vow by all the Powers above,
That you could none but *dear Orinda* love?
Did you not swear by all that is Divine,
That you would *only* be and *ever* mine?   10
You did, and yet you live *securely* too,
And think that *Heaven's false* as well as *you*.

III

Believe me, *Love's* a thing *much* too *divine*
Thus to be *Ape'd*, and made a mere *design*.
'Tis no less Crime than *Treason here* to *feign*,   15
'Tis Counterfeiting of a *Royal Coin*.
But Ah! *Hypocrisy*'s no where so common grown
As in *Most Sacred* things, *Love* and *Religion*.

IV

Go seek *new Conquests*, go, you have my leave,
You shall not *Grieve* her whom you could *decieve*.   20
I don't *lament*, but *pitty* what you do,

Nor take that Love as *lost*, which ne'r was *true*.
The way that's left you to *befriend* my Fate,
Is now to prove *more constant* in your *Hate*.

247   *On Damons Loveing of Clora.*

Say wherefore is't that Damon flys,
From the Weake charms of Cloras Eyes?
Weake Charms they surely needs must bee,
Which till this Houre he could not see,
Nor is she now more Faire, than when   5
Theire first acquaintance, they began,
When the Gay Shepherd Laugh'd at love,
Swore it no Gen'rous Heart could move,
Disease of Fools, Fond Lunacie,
To Cloras Face oft would he cry,   10
For mee your Friendship but bestow,
(Friendship, the onely Good below)
Faire shepherdess, Ile ask no more,
Since more to give, exceeds your Pow'r,
Damon the Mightie Gift then gain'd,   15
With Witt exalted now maintain'd
No Happy Lovers greatest Bliss
More then a shadow was to his,
Which all Refin'd, found no alloy,
And like to Fate, nought could destroy.   20
Long did the Happy Youth thus live,
Hee could not ask, nor could shee give,
Till wandering the other Day
To, on the Ground the Shepherd lay,
Pensive, as unseene Clora thought,   25
Whom, heedless steps had thither brought
To heare bewail his Miserie,
Complain of loss of Libertie,
Curse his owne stubborn Pride, and then
With Teares, and sighs, begin againe,   30
Ask Pardon of Philosophy
For Passions rude Apostacie,
Resolve he would no Captive bee,
But set Himself by Reason free,
Hee Paus'd on this awhile, but strait   35
Ah Damon cry'd, it is too late,
Thou yesterday the Will didst lose,
To Day the Power to refuse,
Condemn'd a Sacrifice to bee,

Oppose not then thy Destinie,   40
Appease loves God, let Clora know
How much to thee her charms do owe,
Her Pitty she cannot Deny
Though all her Powers thou didst Defy,
More difficult the Conquest is   45
The Nobler sure esteem'd it is.
Mistaken, Damon, she Reply'd,
Did herself no longer hide,
Conquests so hardly gain'd do show
Wee nothing to the Conquer'd owe.   50
Nor can I challenge any part
In captivating thy rough Heart,
Since I am still the same as, when
My Powers, and loves, you did disdaine,
Just Destinie, thy love does cause,   55
Submiting thee to Humane Laws,
Who proudly woud'st exempted be
Through Ignorance, or Vanitie.
The Friendship once I gave retaine
But think from me no more to gaine,   60
To whom thy Passion comes too late,
That scorne a Conquest giv'n by Fate.
With this, she left the trembling swaine
Half Dead with Greife at her disdaine,
Who for his love no lure can find   65
But Breaths his Plaints unto the Wind
Not Dareing Cloras Eyes to see
Since her injust Severitie,
Who still insensible remaines,   ⎫
His Constant Passion still disdains,   ⎬   70
And laughs at all his Greife, and Pains.   ⎭

                        (1682)

SÌLEAS NA CEAPHAICH
(SILEAS MACDONALD)
(c.1660–c.1729)

SÌLEAS NIGHEAN MHIC RAGHNAILL, or na Ceapaich ('of Keppoch'), was
born c.1660, allegedly at Bohuntin, two miles or so up Glen Roy from Keppoch
in Inverness-shire. Her father, Mac Mhic Raghnaill, was the fifteenth chief of
the MacDonalds of Keppoch, and himself a poet. Her descent was thus a
markedly aristocratic one, with a family tradition of verse. Her mother may
have been a Cameron, Mary, daughter of Duncan MacMartin, sixth chief of the

Camerons of Letterfinlay, though this is not certain. She had at least four brothers and three sisters. She was married to Alexander Gordon of Camdell, a farm a mile North of Tomintoul, in Banffshire, hereditary factor, or chamberlain, to the family of the Duke of Gordon: the contract was drawn up on 1 August 1685. She was the mother of a number of children: five sons are mentioned in various sources (George, James, Gilleasbuig, Iain, and Alasdair), and at least three daughters (Màiri, Katerine, and Anna). Her husband died in 1720.

Sìleas was a much-admired poet, many of whose works were preserved within the oral tradition. Nine of the poems attributed to her, including the early 'Conversation with Death', are written in the old syllabic metres, while the rest are in the stressed metres which began to become popular in the seventeenth century, including five apparently based on the metres and tunes of popular songs.

248 *Còmhradh Ris a' Bhàs*

Ochòin, a nocht mar a thà,
   'S am Bàs air teachd orm gun fhios;
Labhair e gu calma cruaidh:
   'S éiginn uair a dhènamh ris.

Fhreagair mise gu bochd truagh: 5
   'Gu dé ghruaim a chuir mi ort,
'Nuair thàinig thu cho coimheach garg,
   'S nach do ghormaich snàithn' dhe m' fholt?

Bàs: 'Cha b' e sin a b' fhasan domh fhéin,
   Feitheamh ris gach té bhith liath;   10
Gabhaidh mi an sean 's an t-òg—
   'S math mo chòir air luchd nan srian.'

Ise: 'Chan eil mo chuideachd ach maoth;
   S còir bhith caomhail ris a' chloinn
Gus an àraichear an t-òg,   15
   'S a' chuid as mò dhiùbh chur an greim.'

Bàs: 'Gu dé 'n t-iomradh th' agad dhiùbh,
   'S nach dèan aon neach dhiùbh do riar?
B' fheàrr dhuit an leigeil air chùl,
   'S an aire thoirt gu dlùth air Dia.'   20

Ise: 'Nan saoilinn gum biodh tu rìreadh,
   Dhèannainn gu cinnteach riut comunn,
Gun tugadh tu mi gu m' Shlànair,
   'S comas a bhith 'ghnàth 'na shealladh'

Bàs: 'Nì mise mo chid de 'n bheart sin,   25
   Nì mi do leagail o 'n àrdan;

Fàgaidh mi do chasan caol is
Nì na daolagan dìot fàrdach.'

Ise: 'Ochòin, ma tha thu dha rìreach,
      'S nach faigh mi sìneadh no dàil bhuat,   30
    Feuch an toir thu orm ìsleadh,
      Gus an dèan mi sìth ri m' Àrd-righ.'

Bas: ''S iomadh latha fhuair thu roimhe,
      'S bu bheagh t' omhail air a' chàs sin;
    O nach do sheall thu na b' fheàrr romhad,   35
      Nì mise 'n gnothach and dràsda.'

Bhuail e buille mhór 'sa' taobh orm;
    Cha d' fhogainn a h-aon na dhà leis,
Gus an tug e orm bhith glaodhaich,
    'S bu bheart fhaoin domh buntainn dhà-san.   40

'Nuair a thuig mi e bhith rìreadh,
    Thug mi sgrìob fo sgéith mo Shlànair;
Rinn E rium ro-mhóran caoimhneis
    'S thug E air an Aog bhith sàmhach.

Bàs: 'Cha toir Mise tuille péine   45
      Do 'n chreutar bhochd tha mì-thaingeil,
    Feuch an tig i orm na's ùmhlaidh',
      'S an cuir cùl ris an àrdan.'

                        (*c*.1690–1710)

248   *A Conversation with Death*

Alas! the state of things tonight:
Death having come upon me unawares;
strong and harsh he spoke;
an appointment must be made with him.

I answered weakly and piteously,   5
'What sorrow have I caused you
that you come here, so fierce and cruel,
though not a hair of my head has turned grey?'

Death: 'It has not been my own custom
      to wait for everyone to go grey: 10
      I take young and old,
      and I have a good claim on those streaked with grey'.

Me: 'My family are still young:
      the children ought to be treated kindly
      until the young ones are reared   15
      and most of them have been put in charge of affairs.'

Death:	'What consideration do you give them,	
	since not one of them will attend you?	
	You would be better to turn your back on them	
	and give close attention to God.'	20

Me: 'If I thought you were in earnest
        I would certainly make an agreement with you,
        that you would take me to my Saviour,
        allowing me to be forever in His sight.'

Death: 'I shall do my part of the bargain,   25
        I shall humble your pride;
        I shall leave your legs scrawny
        and the worms will make you their home.'

Me: 'Alas! if you are in earnest
        and I am to get no reprieve or respite from you,   30
        try to make me humble,
        so that I may make peace with my High King.'

Death: 'You have had many days before now,
        and you paid little attention to that matter;
        because you did not look better to the future,   35
        you must make do with me now.'

        He gave me a heavy blow in the side,
        and one or two were not enough for him,
        till finally he made me scream,
        and it was a vain task for me to strike him.   40

        When I understood he was in earnest
        I went under my Saviour's protection;
        He was extremely kind to me
        and bade Death be at peace.

Death: 'I will give no more pain   45
        to this poor ungrateful creature,
        to see if she becomes more humble for me,
        and if she turns away from pride.'

ANNE KILLIGREW
(1660–1685)

ANNE KILLIGREW was born shortly before the Restoration, the daughter of Dr Henry (1613–1700) and Judith Killigrew. The connection between the poet Anne Killigrew and the Elizabethan scholar-poet Katherine Killigrew is a very remote one: she is the great-granddaughter of Sir Henry Killigrew's brother William. More immediately, her father and two of his brothers, Thomas and William, were dramatists, as was her cousin Thomas, and she was thus the child of a notably literary family. At the Restoration, her father was appointed master of the Savoy Hospital—a reward for his loyalty during the Interregnum—while two of her brothers, Henry and James, went on to distinguish themselves as naval officers.

Anne Killigrew was a self-consciously ambitious poet. Her first poem was an *Alexandreis*: an abortive attempt to begin an epic account of the deeds of Alexander the Great Her ambivalence about this effort is indicated by her remark, with respect to Alexander,

Nor will it from his Conquests derogate
A Female Pen his acts did celebrate.

Her verse is self-consciously classicizing, indicating her familiarity with at least the content of the Classical curriculum (though she probably acquired this knowledge through translations). She was placed in the household of Mary of Modena, Duchess of York, as a maid of honour. Her work reflects court life, particularly the somewhat pathetic personality of the Queen to whom she was devoted (as were most of her other servants). As Carol Barash has observed, 'Mary of Modena's court was as close as England ever came to the world of the précieuses. She provided a model of women's patronage of women artists, a world where women exchanged various kinds of writing' (*English Women's Poetry 1649–1714: Politics, Community, and Linguistic Authority*, (Oxford: Clarendon Press, 1996) 150). Her choice of poetic subjects tends to be figures who experienced loss and sorrow. Anne Killigrew's poetry, though not published until after her early death, was circulated by her: one indication of this is the verses to, and by, other poets in the published collection, another is the surviving manuscript poems which either imitate her work, or hail her as a writer (e.g. Oxford, Bodleian Library Montagu e 13, fo., 160^v, and Rawlinson Poet. 94, fos. 149–52). She was also an artist, and painted portraits, biblical and mythological subjects, and landscapes inspired by the Dutch and Flemish masters and Claude Lorraine. Three of her paintings are known to survive: a portrait of James II is at Windsor Castle, and a portrait of Mary of Modena and a 'Venus and Adonis' are in private hands.

In 1680, a Mrs Killigrew was recorded by the English Benedictine nuns of Paris as living 'en pension' with them. Her family was Anglican, but a number of women in the circle of Mary of Modena became sympathetic to Catholicism, and some, including Jane Barker, actually converted. This may, therefore, be our Anne Killigrew, since the convent boasted a variety of connections with court circles. Killigrew died of smallpox six weeks after the coronation of James II and was buried in the chancel of St John the Baptist's Chapel in the Savoy Hospital. As a tribute to her memory, Anne's father collected and published a slim volume of her poems, which appeared with the famous prefatory ode by John Dryden to 'Mrs Anne Killigrew, Excellent in the two Sister-Arts of Poësie, and Painting'.

249   *Upon the saying that my* VERSES *were made by another.*

Next Heaven my Vows to thee (O Sacred *Muse!*)
I offer'd up, nor didst thou them refuse.

O Queen of Verse, said I, if thou'lt inspire,
And warm my Soul with thy Poetique Fire,
No Love of Gold shall share with thee my Heart, 5
Or yet Ambition in my Brest have Part,
More Rich, more Noble I will ever hold
The Muses Laurel, than a Crown of Gold.
An Undivided Sacrifice I'le lay
Upon thine Altar, Soul and Body pay; 10
Thou shalt my Pleasure, my Employment be,
My All I'le make a Holocaust to thee.

The Deity that ever does attend
Prayer so sincere, to mine did condescend.
I writ, and the Judicious prais'd my Pen: 15
Could any doubt Insuing Glory then?
What pleasing Raptures fill'd my Ravisht Sense?
How strong, how Sweet, Fame, was thy Influence?
And thine, False Hope, that to my flatter'd sight
Didst Glories represent so Near, and Bright? 20
By thee deceiv'd, methought, each Verdant Tree,
Apollos transform'd *Daphne* seem'd to be;
And ev'ry fresher Branch, and ev'ry Bow
Appear'd as Garlands to empale my Brow.
The Learn'd in Love say, Thus the Winged Boy 25
Does first approach, drest up in welcome Joy;
At first he to the Cheated Lovers sight
Nought represents, but Rapture and Delight,
Alluring Hopes, Soft Fears, which stronger bind
Their Hearts, than when they more assurance find. 30

Embolden'd thus, to Fame I did commit,
(By some few hands) my most Unlucky Wit.
But, ah, the sad effects that from it came!
What ought t'have brought me Honour, brought me shame!
Like *Esops* Painted Jay I seem'd to all, 35
Adorn'd in Plumes, I not my own could call:
Rifl'd like her, each one my Feathers tore,
And, as they thought, unto the Owner bore.
My Laurels thus an Others Brow adorn'd,
My Numbers they Admir'd, but Me they scorn'd: 40
An others Brow, that had so rich a store
Of Sacred Wreaths, that circled it before;
Where mine quite lost, (like a small stream that ran
Into a Vast and Boundless Ocean)
Was swallow'd up, with what it joyn'd and drown'd, 45
And that Abiss yet no Accession found.

Orinda, (*Albions* and her Sexes Grace)
Ow'd not her Glory to a Beauteous Face,
It was her Radiant Soul that shon With-in,
Which struk a Lustre through her Outward Skin;   50
That did her Lips and Cheeks with Roses dy,
Advanc'd her Height, and Sparkled in her Eye.
Nor did her Sex at all obstruct her Fame,
But higher 'mong the Stars it fixt her Name;
What she did write, not only all allow'd,   55
But ev'ry Laurel, to her Laurel, bow'd!

Th'Envious Age, only to Me alone,
Will not allow, what I do write, my Own,
But let 'em Rage, and 'gainst a Maide Conspire,
So Deathless Numbers from my Tuneful Lyre   60
Do ever flow; so *Phebus* I by thee
Divinely Inspired and possest may be;
I willingly accept *Cassandras* Fate,
To speak the Truth, although believ'd too late.

(1685)

22 *Daphne*: a nymph pursued by Apollo, and transformed into a laurel   24 *empale*:
encircle. A laurel wreath was a classical prize for poetry   35 *Jay*: one of Aesop's fables.
The jay dressed itself up in bright feathers shed by other birds, and briefly dazzled all who
beheld it   47 *Orinda*: Katherine Philips   63 *Cassandra*: daughter of Priam of Troy:
cursed by Apollo with the gift of true prophecy which was, however, never believed in
time.

250   *On the Birth-Day of Queen Katherine*

While yet it was the Empire of the Night,
And Stars still check'r'd Darkness with their Light,
From Temples round the cheerful Bells did ring,
But with the Peales a churlish Storm did sing.
I slumbr'd; and the Heavens like things did show,   5
Like things which I had seen and heard below.
Playing on Harps Angels did singing fly,
But through a cloudy and a troubl'd Sky,
Some fixt a Throne, and Royal Robes display'd,
And then a Massie Cross upon it laid.   10
I wept: and earnestly implor'd to know,
Why Royal Ensigns were disposed so.
An Angel said, The Emblem thou hast seen,
Denotes the Birth-Day of a Saint and Queen.
Ah, Glorious Minister, I then reply'd,   15

Goodness and Bliss together do reside
In Heaven and thee, why then on Earth below
These two combin'd so rarely do we know?
He said, Heaven so decrees: and such a Sable Morne
Was that, in which the *Son of God* was borne.   20
Then Mortal wipe thine Eyes, and cease to rave,
God darkn'd Heaven, when He the World did save.

(1685)

ANNE FINCH (née KINGSMILL),
COUNTESS OF WINCHILSEA
(1661–1720)

ANNE KINGSMILL was born at Sydmonton, Hampshire in April 1661, the month of King Charles II's Coronation. Her parents, Sir William Kingsmill and Anne Haslewood, were both members of old and respected Royalist gentry families. They had married in 1654, and Sir William, unlike many of his contemporaries, was able to keep most of his land intact during the Interregnum. He died, leaving his widow with three children under four, in the year of Anne's birth, and therefore had no personal impact on his daughter's life, though it is interesting to note that he was himself a poet (there is a collection in Lichfield Cathedral Library: Sir William Kingsmill, *Vana non Ludibria. Carmina Ventosa*). The bulk of the family estates was left to his son, also William, but the two daughters, Bridget and Anne, were left two thousand and fifteen hundred pounds respectively, to be paid with accrued interest when each either married or turned 21. His will also stressed that his daughters should be carefully educated. In 1662, Lady Kingsmill married Sir Thomas Ogle. The only child of this marriage, Dorothy Ogle, became an intimate friend of Anne Kingsmill's, and the subject of a number of her poems. Anne's mother died in 1664. The orphans' property, and the responsibility for them, then became the subject of an acrimonious lawsuit between their stepfather and their maternal uncle, Sir William Haslewood, finally settled in the childrens' favour. Between 1664 and 1671, Anne and Bridget were in fact brought up by their maternal grandmother, Bridget, Lady Kingsmill, in London, at 55 Charing Cross, while their brother lived with his uncle: Dorothy Ogle lived with her father until his death in 1671, and then became the ward of Sir Richard Campion. In 1671, the Kingsmill girls went to join their uncle, brother, and three cousins at Maidwell in Northamptonshire, and their grandmother died in the following year. The Maidwell household, while remote and rural, was by no means uncultivated. Anne was brought up among a circle of lively-minded, intellectual country gentlefolk. Sir William's neighbour, Sir Justinian Isham of Lamport Hall, was a member of the Royal Society, who had been a student of Sir Francis Bacon's, and was the father of a family (also of two girls and a boy) of compatible age, and the families regularly dined and visited. The Isham girls were tutored along with their brother in Latin, Greek, mathematics, and algebra: some of their lessons may perhaps have been shared with their neighbours the Kingsmills. Anne, though there is no indication that she learned Latin, was familiar with Classical myth; and she could certainly read French and Italian. She was also very well read in contemporary English literature.

In her twenty-first year, Anne became maid of honour to Mary of Modena when she was brought to England in 1682, and moved from Maidwell to St James's Palace. The relationship between Mary and her attendants seems to have been an affectionate one: Anne Finch certainly remembered it as such, in 'On the Death of the Queen'. Other members of the circle who had poetic connections include Katherine Sedley (no. 237), Anne Killigrew (nos. 249–50), and the Countess of Roscommon, wife of the poet Wentworth Dillon. The court milieu, while stimulating, was not welcoming to authorial aspirations by young women: Anne herself comments, 'itt is still a great satisfaction to me, that I was not so far abandon'd by my prudence, as out of a mistaken vanity, to lett any attempts of mine in Poetry, shew themselves while I liv'd in such a publick place as the Court, where every one wou'd have made their remarks upon a Versifying Maid of Honour; and far the greater number with prejudice, if not contempt.' (Preface, *Miscellany Poems*, 7–8).

It was at St James's Palace, probably in 1683, that Anne Kingsmill met Heneage Finch, second son of the second Earl of Winchilsea: a member of an old and noble family, but occupying a very subordinate place within it. He himself was a courtier, a soldier, and in his private life, a man of antiquarian tastes. He seems to have wooed with determination, while Anne was initially reluctant. Her unresponsiveness may be linked to a private tragedy which may have left her unable to think about her own affairs: her only brother killed his cousin William Haslewood in a duel in 1683, and was tried and found guilty of manslaughter on 29 January 1684. Anne and Heneage married on 15 May 1684: a month later, Charles II granted William Kingsmill a full pardon. Anne resigned her post as maid of honour upon her marriage, though Heneage continued to serve James as gentleman of the bedchamber. They then lived in Westminster Palace. Heneage served a year as a Member of Parliament, and was promoted in 1687 to lieutenant-colonel. The marriage was close, affectionate, but childless.

The government of James II reached crisis in 1688. Heneage Finch was not merely a colonel, but also still one of James's personal attendants. After the successful coup of William and Mary, James was ordered to leave England, and he departed for France in December 1688. The position of the Finches, as of all those who owed personal loyalty to James and his family, was extremely difficult: in their case, it also left them homeless. 1689 was spent in the homes of various friends and relatives. The Finches refused to swear an oath of allegiance to the new monarchs, and thus became part of the group known as Nonjurors. In 1690, Heneage Finch attempted to flee to France to join the exiled Stuart court at St Germain, but was captured, taken prisoner, and tried for treason. He remained in custody for most of a year; a period of personal and political anguish, but a productive one for Anne Finch as a poet. Thereafter the couple lived with Finch's nephew Charles, Earl of Winchilsea at Eastwell in Kent. Their status had changed completely: from what had been a promising career and a responsible role in the life of the court, they became dependent country-dwellers facing a probable future of persecution and financial hardship. The landscape of Kent became a consistent element in her poetry.

It is an expression of the unusually close relationship between Anne Finch and her husband that very shortly after his case had been dismissed in 1690,

Heneage Finch enlivened his leisure by appointing himself his wife's editor. She had begun a collection shortly before his release, employing an amanuensis. After 87 pages of this anonymous scribe's work, Heneage Finch took over the work of compilation. The book had a plan and a structure: it began with 'The Introduction', an apology for women's writing, and then moved into her most recent work on the themes of loss and suffering. Gradually, like many such volumes, the manuscript degenerated from a fair-copy book into a notebook. Heneage Finch began another manuscript, this time in folio, in 1694 or 1695. His support of her writing, evidenced by these secretarial contributions, is evident throughout the thirty-odd years of their life together; a situation which is explained in part by the abundant leisure which their political non-conformity gave them, but also by the unusually companionate quality of their relationship, uninterrupted as it was by either children or career. The interest in local history and antiquarianism which is shown by many of her poems of the 1690s perhaps derives from a parallel and reciprocal impulse in Anne Finch to share her husband's interests.

During the reign of Queen Anne, the Finches emerged to some extent from retirement. Heneage made several unsuccessful attempts to become an MP, and by 1708, they had taken up residence in London; important to his wife's literary development, since it was at this stage in her life that she became friendly with Jonathan Swift, who wrote a long poem to her and seems to have encouraged her to think in terms of publication. 'The Spleen' had appeared anonymously in Charles Gildon's miscellany in 1701, but in 1709, two poems appeared in Delarivier Manley's *New Atalantis* in 1709: anonymously, but accompanied by biographical information sufficient to guess the author's identity, and in the same year, she published three pastorals in Jacob Tonson's *Poetical Miscellanies*. In 1713, she published her own volume of verse, with Swift's own publisher, John Barber (who was, gossip had it, the lover of Delarivier Manley). By that time, she had become the Countess of Winchilsea, on the death of her husband's nephew Charles in 1712, a rise in status which brought them, unfortunately, yet further financial problems. It may, however, have eased her status as an author: while the first edition came out with 'Written by a Lady' on the title-page, subsequent title-pages printed later that year bore the name 'Lady Winchilsea'.

The poems given here include 'The Introduction' (to her first manuscript collection of poems) which shows that Anne Finch was, like the author of 'The Emulation', Mary Astell, Mary Chudleigh, and other contemporaries, coming to the conclusion that education was the key to solving the problem of women's position; one of the several poems expressing her love for her husband, which has been chosen also because it shows something of her lighter and more playful side, an epigram which focuses her sense of betrayal after King James's fall, and lastly, an unexpected and rather ambitious attempt at an heroic epistle focused on a passionate friendship between two men, which demonstrates a close and careful reading of North's translation of Plutarch.

251   *The Introduction*

Did I my lines intend for publick view,
How many Censures, wou'd their Faults pursue,

Some wou'd, because such words they doe affect,
Cry their insipid, empty, uncorrect;
And many have attain'd, dull, and untaught,   5
The name of witt, only by finding fault
True judges, might condemn theire want of witt,
And all might say, they're by a woman writ.
Alas! a woman that attempts the Pen,
Such an intruder on the rights of men,   10
Such a presumptuous Creature, is esteem'd,
The fault, can by no vertue be redeem'd.
They tell us, wee mistake our sex, and way,
Good breeding, fashion, dancing, dressing, play,
Are the Accomplishments wee should desire,   15
To read, or write, or think, or to enquire
Wou'd cloud our beauty, and exhaust our time,
And interrupt the Conquests of our prime.
Whilst, the dull manage of a servile house,
Is held by some, our utmost art, and use.   20
    Sure 'twas not ever thus, nor are we told
Fables of women that excell'd of old;
To whome, by the diffusive hand of Heaven,
Some share of witt, and poetry was given.
On that glad day, on which the Ark return'd,   25
That holy pledge, for which the Land had mourn'd,
The joyfull Tribes, attend it on the way, ⎫
The Levites, doe the sacred Charge convey, ⎬
Whilst various Instruments before it Play; ⎭
Here, holy Virgins in the Consort joyn, ⎫   30
The Louder notes, to soften, and Refine, ⎬
And with alternate verse, Compleat the Hymn Devine. ⎭
Loe! the Young Poet, after Gods own heart,
By him inspir'd, and taught the Muses art,
Return'd from Conquest, a bright Chorus meets,   35
That sing his slayn ten thousand in the streets,
In such Loud numbers they his Acts declare,
Proclaim the wonders of his early warr,
That Saul, upon the vast applause does frown,
And feels its mighty Thunder, shake the Crown;   40
What can the threat'n'd Judgment now Prolong?
Half of the Kingdom is already gone,
The fairest half, whose influence guides the rest,
Have David's Empire, o're their hearts confest.
A woman here, leads fainting Israel on,   45
She fights, she wins, she Triumph's with a Song;
Devout, Majestick, for the Subject Fitt,
And far above her Arms, exalts her witt;
Then, to the peacefull, shady palme withdraws,

And Rules the rescu'd Nation, with her Laws.   50
How are we faln', faln by mistaken Rules?
And Educations, more than Nature's fools;
Debard from all improvements of the minde,
And to be dull, expected and dessigned;
And if some one, wou'd soare above the rest,   55
With warmer fancy, and ambition prest,
So Strong, th' opposing faction still appears,
The hopes to thrive, can ne're outweigh the fears,
Be caution'd then my Muse, and still retir'd,
Nor be despis'd, aiming to be admir'd,   60
Conscious of wants, still with contracted wing,
To some few Freinds, and to thy sorrows sing.
For Groves of Lawrel, thou wert never meant;
Be dark enough thy shades, and be thou there content.

14 *play*: playing cards   25 1 Sam 6: 2–5   33 *Young Poet*: David   36 1 Sam.
18: 7   45 *a woman*: Deborah, Judges 4–5

252   *A Letter to Daphnis*

Sure of successe, to you I boldly write,
Whilst Love, does every tender line endite.
Love, who is justly President of verse,
Which all his servants write, or else rehearse.
Phœbus, how'ere mistaken Poets dream,   5
N'er us'd a Verse, 'till Love became his theam,
To his stray'd Son, still as his passion rose
He rais'd his hasty voyce, in clamerous prose,
But when in *Daphne*, he wou'd Love inspire,
He woo'd in verse, sett to his silver lyre,   10
In moving Verse, that did her heart assail,
And cou'd on all, but Chastity prevail.
The Trojan Prince, did pow'rfull numbers joyn,
To sing of War, but Love was the design,
And sleeping Troy, again in flames was drest,   15
To raise the like, in pittying Dido's breast.
Love, without poetrys refining aid,
Is a dull bargain, and but coursly made;
Nor e're cou'd Poetry, successfull prove
Or toutch the soul, but when the sence was Love.   20
Oh! cou'd they both, in absence now impart
Skill to my hand, but to describe my heart.
Then shou'd you see, impatient of your stay,
Soft hopes contend, with fears of sad delay.

Love, in a thousand pleasing motions, there,   25
And lively images of you appear.
But since the thoughts, of a poetick mind,
Will n'er be half, to sylables confind,
And whilst to fix, what is conceav'd we try,
The purer parts, evaporate and dye.   30
You must perform, what they want force to doe,
And think, what your Ardelia thinks of you.

(Eastwell, Oct. 21, 1690)

Title: *Daphnis*: correction over Mr Finch; 'at London' supplied in smaller letters   5
Phœbus: probably with reference to his rebellious son Phaeton   9 *Daphne*: a nymph
wooed by Apollo who was turned into a laurel   13 *Trojan Prince*: Aeneas, who recounts
the fall of Troy to Dido in the first three books of Virgil's *Aeneid*   32 *Ardelia*: correction
over Areta: a pen-name she used for a time

253   *Cæsar and Brutus*

Though Cæsar falling, shew'd no sign of fear,
Yett Brutus, when thou did'st appear,
When thy false hand, against him came,
He vail'd his face, to hide that shame,
Which did on the mistake attend   5
Of having own'd thee, for his Freind.

1 *Caesar*: Julius Caesar was assassinated in 44 BC by a republican conspiracy headed by
Brutus and Cassius   2 *Brutus*: Marcus Junius Brutus, leading conspirator, and Caesar's
adopted son

254   *An* EPISTLE *from* Alexander *to* Hephæstion *in His Sickness*

With such a Pulse, with such disorder'd Veins,
Such lab'ring Breath, as thy Disease constrains;
With failing Eyes, that scarce the Light endure,
(So long unclos'd, they've watch'd thy doubtful Cure)
To his *Hephæstion Alexander* writes,   5
To soothe thy Days, and wing thy sleepless Nights,
I send thee Love: Oh! that I could impart,
As well my vital Spirits to thy Heart!
That, when the fierce Distemper thine wou'd quell,
They might renew the Fight, and the cold Foe repel.   10
   As on *Arbela*'s Plains we turn'd the Day,
When *Persians* through our Troops had mow'd their way,

When the rough *Scythians* on the Plunder run,
And barb'rous Shouts proclaim'd the Conquest won,
　　'Till o'er my Head (to stop the swift Despair)   15
The *Bird* of *Jove* fans the supporting Air,
Above my Plume does his broad Wings display,
And follows wheresoe'er I force my way:
Whilst *Aristander*, in his Robe of White,
Shews to the wav'ring Host th'auspicious Sight;   20
New Courage it inspires in ev'ry Breast,
And wins at once the Empire of the East.
Cou'd He, but now, some kind Presage afford,
That Health might be again to Thee restor'd;
Thou to my Wishes, to my fond Embrace;   25
Thy Looks the same, the same Majestick Grace,
That round thee shone, when we together went
To chear the Royal Captives in their Tent,
Where *Sysigambis*, prostrate on the Floor,
Did *Alexander* in thy Form adore;   30
Above great *Æsculapius* shou'd he stand,
Or made immortal by *Apelles* Hand.
But no reviving Hope his Art allows,
And such cold Damps invade my anxious Brows,
As, when in *Cydnus* plung'd, I dar'd the Flood   35
T' o'er-match the Boilings of my youthful Blood.
But *Philip* to my Aid repair'd in haste;
And whilst the proffer'd Draught I boldly taste,
As boldly He the dangerous Paper views,
Which of hid Treasons does his Fame accuse.   40
More thy Physician's Life on Thine depends,
And what he gives, his Own preserves, or ends.
If thou expir'st beneath his fruitless Care,　⎫
To *Rhadamanthus* shall the Wretch repair,　⎬
And give strict Answer for his Errors there.　⎭   45

　　Near thy Pavilion list'ning *Princes* wait,
Seeking from thine to learn their *Monarch's* State.
Submitting *Kings*, that post from Day to Day,
To keep those Crowns, which at my Feet they lay,
Forget th'ambitious Subject of their Speed,   50
And here arriv'd, only Thy Dangers heed.
The *Beauties* of the Clime, now Thou'rt away,
Droop, and retire, as if their God of Day
No more upon their early Pray'rs would shine,
Or take their Incense, at his late Decline.   55
Thy *Parisatis* whom I fear to name,
Lest to thy Heat it add redoubl'd Flame;
Thy lovely Wife, thy *Parisatis* weeps,

And in her Grief a solemn Silence keeps.
Stretch'd in her Tent, upon the Floor she lies,   60
So pale her Looks, so motionless her Eyes,
As when they gave thee leave at first to gaze
Upon the Charms of her unguarded Face;
When the two beauteous Sisters lowly knelt,
And su'd to those, who more than Pity felt.   65
To chear her now *Statira* vainly proves,
And at thy Name alone she sighs, and moves.

But why these single Griefs shou'd I expose?
The World no Mirth, no War, no Bus'ness knows,
But, hush'd with Sorrow stands, to favour thy Repose.   70
Ev'n I my boasted Title now resign,
Not *Ammon*'s Son, nor born of Race Divine,
But Mortal all, oppress'd with restless Fears,
Wild with my Cares, and Womanish in Tears.
Tho' Tears, before, I for lost *Clytus* shed,   75
And wept more Drops, than the old Hero bled;
Ev'n now, methinks, I see him on the Ground,
Now my dire Arms the wretched Corpse surround,
Now the fled Soul I wooe, now rave upon the Wound.
Yet He, for whom this mighty Grief did spring,   80
Not *Alexander* valu'd, but the King.
Then think, how much that Passion must transcend,
Which not a Subject raises but a Friend:
An equal Partner in the vanquished Earth,
A Brother, not impos'd upon my Birth,   85
Too weak a Tye unequal Thoughts to bind,
But by the gen'rous Motions of the Mind.
My Love to thee for Empire was the Test,
Since him, who from Mankind cou'd chuse the best,
The Gods thought only fit for Monarch o'er the rest.   90
Live then, my Friend; but if that must not be,
Nor Fate will with my boundless Mind agree,
Affording, at one time, the World and Thee;
To the most Worthy I'll that Sway resign,
And in *Elysium* keep *Hyphæstion* mine.   95

(before 1702)

5 *Hephæstion Alexander*: Hephaestion was the friend and lover of Alexander the Great. The details of his life and death here are from Plutarch. He caught a fever at Ecbatana in Media in the spring of 324 BC, and died after breaking a strict dietary regimen: while his physician Glaucus was at the theatre, he consumed a boiled chicken and a cooler-full of wine (*Life of Alexander*, ch. 72)   10 The great battle between Alexander and Darius in fact took place at Gaugamela (*Life*, ch. 31)   16 *Bird of Jove*: eagle. An eagle hovered for a while over Alexander's head and then flew straight towards the enemy, which impressed the watching troops as a sign of divine favour (*Life*, ch. 33)   29 *Sisygambis*: Alexander

captured the womenfolk of his Persian enemy Darius. When Darius' mother sued for mercy, she mistakenly addressed the taller and more impressive Hephaestion in mistake for Alexander, who responded by saying, 'he is Alexander too'   31 *Æsculepius*: the doctor-god of classical Greece   32 *Apelles*: Greek painter renowned for lifelike effects, who made a portrait of Alexander wielding a thunderbolt   34–40 In the winter of 333, Alexander caught fever after bathing in the icy Cydnus, and the only physician who dared treat him was Philip. Parmenion sent Alexander a letter from the camp warning him to beware of Philip, since Darius had bribed him to murder him. When Philip entered the room with his medicine, Alexander handed him the letter, took the draught, and drank it with a cheerful smile while Philip read the letter in horror and amazement (*Life*, ch. 19) 43–5 Alexander had Glaucus crucified after Hephaestion's death (*Life*, ch. 72)   44 *Rhadamanthus*: the judge of the underworld   56 *Parisatis*: Alexander and Hephaestion married sister princesses, Parasatis, and Barsine, the daughters of Darius and Statira   72 *Ammon's Son*: Ammon was an Egyptian god identified with Zeus: according to one version, Alexander was not the son of Philip, but of Ammon, who came to his mother's bed in the form of a serpent. Alexander visited the shrine of Ammon at Siwa in the Libyan desert, and the priest welcomed him as son of the God: possibly he intended to say '*O paidion*' ('O my son'), but because he was not a native speaker, mistakenly said '*O pai Dios*' ('O son of Zeus') (*Life*, chs 2–3: 27) 75 *Clytus*: ed. has 'old Clytus', with an erratum slip correcting to 'lost'. Alexander killed his comrade Cleitus when drunk   94 *the most Worthy*: Alexander left his empire 'to the most worthy'

ELIZABETH BRADFORD (née SOWLE)
(1663?–1731)

MRS BRADFORD was a Quaker who became one of the first women poets of America. She was born in London, where her father, Andrew Sowle, her mother, Jane, and her sister, Tace, were all printers. She married her father's apprentice William Bradford in 1685 and the couple emigrated to America, where they lived at first in Philadelphia, then moved to New York. William Bradford published *War with the Devil*, a long poem by the Baptist Benjamin Keach, first published in London in 1683: both he and his wife wrote prefatory poems for his New York edition. Though it falls slightly outside the temporal parameters for this anthology, we include this poem for four reasons: because it expresses the suspicion which Quakers felt towards poetry in the seventeenth century (evidenced, for instance, by the response to the verse of Abigail Fisher, an important London Quaker, and by a poem apologizing for the use of verse in Elizabeth Hincks's *The Widow's Mite*, 47), because it is a witness to the Quaker network, because there is so little early women's poetry from America, and because it gives us a glimpse of a family of educated, working-class women: her mother also wrote verse (above, no. 207).

255 *To the Reader, in Vindication of this Book*

> One or two lines to thee I'll here commend,
> This honest poem to defend

From calumny, because at this day
All poetry there's many do gain-say,
And very much condemn, as if the same   5
Did worthily deserve reproach and blame.
If any book in verse they chance to spy,
Away profane, they presently do cry:
But though this kind of writing some dispraise,
Sith men so captious are in these our days   10
Yet I dare say, how e'er the scruple rose,
Verse hath express'd as secret things as prose.
Though some there be who poetry abuse,
Must we therefore, not the same method use?
Yea, sure, for of my conscience 'tis the best,   15
And doth deserve more honor than the rest.
For 'tis no humane knowledge gain'd by art,
But rather 'tis inspir'd into the heart
By divine means; for true divinity
Hath with this science great affinity: 20
Though some through ignorance, do it oppose,
Many do it esteem, far more than prose:
And find also that unto them it brings
Content, and hath been the delight of kings.
David, although a king, yet was a poet,   25
And Solomon also, the Scriptures show it.
Then what if for all this some do abuse it?
I'm apt to think that angels do embrace it,
And though God giv'st here but in part to some
Saints shall have't perfect in the world to come.   30

(1707)

'A YOUNG LADY'
(fl. 1683)

THE author of 'The Emulation. A Pindarick Ode' is evidently a member of the
new generation of women writers such as Lady Chudleigh, Mary Astell, and the
Irishwoman 'Philo-Phillipa' who had begun to formulate a series of radical
criticisms of the position of women in society, particularly of their educational
opportunities: she cannot be identified further than this.

256   *The Emulation. A Pindarick Ode.*

I

Ah! tell me why, deluded Sex, thus we
  Into the secret Beauty must not prye
    Of our great Athenian Deity.
  Why do we Minerva's Blessings slight,
  And all her tuneful gifts despise;   5
Shall none but the insulting Sex be wise?
Shall they be blest with intellectual Light,
Whilst we drudge on in Ignorances Night?
  We've Souls as noble, and as fine a Clay,
And Parts as well compos'd to please as they.   10
  Men think perhaps we best obey,
  And best their servile Business do,
  When nothing else we know
But what concerns a Kitchin or a Field,
  With all the meaner things they yield.   15
  As if a rational unbounded Mind
Were only for the sordid'st task of Life design'd.

II

  They let us learn to work, to dance, or sing,
  Or any such like trivial thing,
Which to their profit may Increase or Pleasure bring.   20
    But they refuse to let us know
    What sacred Sciences doth impart
    Or the mysteriousness of Art.
In Learning's pleasing Paths deny'd to go,
  From Knowledge banish'd, and their Schools;   25
  We seem design'd alone for useful Fools,
And foils for their ill shapen sense, condemn'd to prie
    And think 'em truly wise,
  Being not allowed their Follies to despise.
  Thus we from Ignorance to Wonder run,   30
(For Admiration ceases when the Secret's known)
  Seem witty only in their praise
  And kind congratulating Lays.
Thus to the Repute of Sense they rise,
And thus through the applauder's Ignorance are wise.   35
  For should we understand as much as they,
  They fear their Empire might decay.
  For they know Women heretofore
Gain'd Victories, and envied Lawrels wore:
  And now they fear we'll once again   40

Ambitious be to reign
And to invade the Dominions of the Brain.
And as we did in those renowned days
Rob them of Lawrels, so we now will take their Bayes.

III

But we are peaceful and will not repine,   45
They still may keep their Bays as well as Wine.
We've now no Amazonian Hearts,
They need not therefore guard their Magazine of Arts.
We will not on their treasure siese,
A part of it sufficiently will please: 50
We'll only so much Knowledge have
As may assist us to enslave
Those Passions which we find
Too potent for the Mind.
'Tis o're them only we desire to reign,   55
And we no nobler, braver, Conquest wish to gain.

IV

We only so much will desire
As may instruct us how to live above
Those childish things which most admire,
And may instruct us what is fit to love.   60
We covet Learning for this only end,
That we our time may to the best advantage spend:
Supposing 'tis below us to converse
Always about our Business or our Dress;
As if to serve our Senses were our Happiness.   65
We'll read the Stories of the Ancient Times,
To see, and then with horror hate their Crimes.
But all their Vertues with delight we'll view,
Admir'd by Us, and imitated too.
But for rewarding Sciences and Arts,   70
And all the curious Products which arise
From the contrivance of the Wise,
We'll tune and cultivate our fruitful Hearts.
And should Man's Envy still declare,
Our Business only to be fair;   75
Without their leave we will be wise,
And Beauty, which they value, we'll despise.
Our Minds, and not our Faces, we'll adorn,
For that's the Employ to which we are born.
The *Muses* gladly will their aid bestow,   80
And to their *Sex* their charming Secrets show.
Whilst Man's brisk Notions owe their rise
To an inspiring Bottle, Wench, or Vice,

Must be debauch'd and damn'd to get
The Reputation of a Wit,   85
To Nature only, and our softer Muses, we
Will owe our Charms of Wit, of Parts, and Poetry.

(1683)

3 *Athenian Deity*: Athena/Minerva, goddess of wisdom   18 *work*: sewing   39 Perhaps
with reference to the Greek poetess Corinna, who is said to have beaten Pindar in open
competition

ANONYMOUS SAMPLER VERSE
(late 17th cent.)

VERSE on a sampler, Victoria & Albert Museum, embroidery study collection,
no. 480–1894: late seventeenth-century, in coloured silk on linen, using cross-
stitch, two-sided Italian cross-stitch, satin stitch, double running stitch,
herringbone, Algerian eye, and decorated buttonhole stitches. This is the earliest
appearance of the verse that is known, but it evidently had a continued circulation: a sampler made by Jane Curtis (b. 1815) in 1827, now at Crathes Castle
outside Aberdeen, has a version of it. Whether or not this was written by a
woman, it is of interest for women's culture: the implication of the poem is that
needle skills do not represent entertainment or self-fulfilment, but a potential
path to employment and independence. Since needlework is often thought of as
a device for the suppression of women, it is an interesting insight into an
alternative contemporary perspective.

257   *'When I was young I little Thought'*

When I was young I little Thought
That Wit must be so dearly bought
But Now Experience Tells me how
If I would Thrive then I must Bow
And bend unto another's will   5
That I might learn both art and skill
To Get my Living with My Hands
That so I might be free from Band
And My Own Dame that I may be
And free from all such slavery.   10
Avoid vaine pastime fle youthfull pleasure
Let moderation allways Be My measure
And so prosed unto the heavenly treasure.

8 *Band*: bonds   13 *prosed*: proceed

A LADY OF QUALITY
(before 1685)

This translation of Sappho is notable for its blurring of the gender of the object addressed, and for its use of erotically coded words: though most of the women's writing in the collection it comes from is by Aphra Behn, she would not have referred to herself as 'A Lady of Quality'.

258   *Verses Made by Sappho, done from the Greek by Boyleau, and from the French by a Lady of Quality.*

1.

Happy who near you sigh, for you alone
Who hears you speak, or whom you smile upon:
You well for this might scorn a Starry Throne.

2.

To this compar'd the Heav'nly Bliss they prove,
No Envy raises; for the Powers a Love   5
Ne'er tasted, Joys, compar'd to such above.

3.

When ere I look on you, through every Vein,
Subtil as Lightning flies the nimble Flame,
I'm all o'er Rapture, while all over Pain.

4.

And while my Soul does in these Transports stray,   10
My Voice disdains to teach my Tongue its way;
Each faculty does now its trust betray.

5.

A Cloud of wild Confusion veils my sight,
Sounds vainly strike my Ears, my Eyes the light,
Soft Languishment my Senses disunite.   15

6.

Swift trembling streight o'er all my Body flies,
Life frightned thence, Love dos his place supply,
Disorder'd, Breathless, Pale, and Cold, I die.

Title: *Boyleau*: Nicolas Boileau (1636–1711), French critic, poet and translator   5 *a Love*: *sic*. The syntax is contorted, but the best sense is 'the Powers ne'er tasted a Love, [or] Joys compar'd to such...' Comma supplied after *tasted*   18 *die*: pun on secondary sense of 'have an orgasm'

LADY WYTHENS, née ELIZABETH TAYLOR, later COLEPEPER
(before 1670–1708)

ELIZABETH TAYLOR was the daughter of Sir Thomas Taylor, first Baronet of Park House, Maidstone, Kent, and Elizabeth, daughter and heir of George Hall of Maidstone. The marriage took place in 1657, and Sir Thomas died *c*.1665. She married Sir Francis Wythens in May 1685. That priceless source of literary gossip, Delarivier Manley's *New Atalantis* (1709) describes one 'Olinda', a poetess, romantically linked with a 'young Chevalier': the key identifies the pair with Lady Withers, or Wythens, and Sir Thomas Colepeper (*c*.1657–1723), third and last Baronet of Preston Hall, Aylesford. Elizabeth Taylor's marriage to a man almost as old as her father was not a success, though it lasted long enough to result in more than one child. She left him shortly after the marriage, and presumably became Colepeper's mistress, since she was installed in a house not far from his country villa, and subsequently, she moved in with him, bringing her children by Wythens: Colepeper successfully sued the latter for their support. On Wythens's death, the pair legitimized their relationship by marrying. She was buried at Aylesford in 1708.

An ode in the persona of Olinda, beginning 'Ah poor Olinda never boast', is published in at least two songbooks of the period, *A Collection of Twenty Four Songs* (1684), and *The Theater of Music* (1685). Three poems published in Aphra Behn's 1685 *Miscellany* are attributed to 'Mrs Taylor'. Thus, 'Olinda' and Mrs Taylor are writing similar poetry in the same year, while Olinda is independently identified with Lady Wythens. The case for identifying Olinda with Wythens seems a secure one. She also used the name Lady Wythens: 'A Drinking Song, made Extempore, by the Lady Withins', was collected in a 1720 miscellany by Anthony Hammond (130). She was connected to Edmund Waller's circle and a poem by 'Mrs [Elizabeth] Taylor to Mr Waller' (beginning 'Indeed Anacron I was told') is among the Petty Papers owned by the Earl of Shelburne at Boxwood House (vol. 2, no. 68) and another text appears in a poetic miscellany compiled by the Waller family (Cambridge, Harvard University Houghton Library MS D 6, fo. [47^{r-v}]). The two poems included here are a dramatic instance of how different the same writer's work can look, depending on whether it is preserved in manuscript or print.

259   *Off the Dutchesse made by Mrs Taylor*

    Com all ye Nymphs and evrey Swaine
    To dresse the Grove and strowe the Plaine

Lett nature all her sweets displaye
Bright Gloriana cums to day
Young Pious beautyfull and wise   5
Above all prais doos prais dispise.
Such wonders modestey does ware
As naked truth she can not bare.
For still she doubts wee worshipe more
the stamp of Greatnesse than the Ore   10
Tho she to power dos nothinge ow
Since from her selfe the Glory flow
which all discerne, yet if Commend
for blushing vertue wee offend
which darts out such inforcing Rays   15
As most Divinity betrays.

260   *To MERTILL, who desird her to
           speak to CLORINDA of his Love.*

MERTILL, Though my heart should break,
    In granting thy desire,
To cold *Clorinda* I will speak,
    And warm her, with my fire.

To save thee from approaching harm,   5
    My Death I will obey.
To save thee, sinking in the Storm,
    I'll cast my self away.

May her Charms equal those of thine!
    No words can e're express   10
And let her Love be great as mine
    Which the wou'd only bless.

May you still prove her faithful slave,
    And she so kind and true
She nothing may desire to have   15
    Or fear to Lose,—but you.

BARBARA MACKAY, LADY SCOURIE
(fl. 1660s/70s)

NOTHING is known of this woman, beyond the information which can be
gleaned from her manuscript, Edinburgh, National Library of Scotland,

Wodrow Qu. XXVII, a presentation copy of Lady Scourie's verse paraphrase of the Song of Solomon and the Lamentations of Jeremiah, with the addition of a few original religious and moral poems at the end, inscribed by the author to the Countess of Caithness.

261   *from The Song of Solomon in verse*

Bryd 7 Sonet

As apple tree among the trees of wood
For sight most pleasant and for fruit most good
So my beloved is in every part
Bove all mens sons a treasure to my heart
I sate me doun with pleasure and delyte   5
Under the shaddow off that heavnly sight
O but the fruit that droped from his lipp
Unto my taste how pleasant was and sweet
To full compleate my comfort and my treasure
He did me banquet in his house off pleasure   10
And to enlarge my heart for things above
His only banner over me was Love
Stay me with flaggons, with apples comfort me
I'm sick off love, and I am like to die
But yet to cherish me in this great need   15
His deare left hand it holdeth up my head.
And to make all my feares to take the chase
His glorious right hand dos me still embrace
I heare an aire that makes my heart rejoice
It is the sound of my beloved's voice   20
Upon the mountains leaping for his prey
Upon the hils he skipps to make his way
My deare beloved he's like a pleasant roe
Or faire younge hart that do most statly goe.
Behold behind our walls how he doth stand   25
That wall off Sin the building of our hand
But through the window loe he looketh forth
And through the jallis lets us see his worth
My deare beloved spake and said to me
Rise up my love and make thy journey free   30
My faire one O make no more excuse
But come away and doe not time abuse
For loe the winter of your woe is past
The raine is gone and every stormy blast
The flowers appeare upon the earth, the time   35

Off singing birds is come in its full pryme
And o the turtle is heard in our Land
That pleasant voice that ought us all command
The figtree puteth foorth her pleasant fruit
Her green leaves sheweth that the time is meet   40
The vine most tender with his grapes most fine
And goodly smell do show that all is mine
Therfore my love arise and come away
My fairest one and make no more delay.

Title: the Bride's seventh sonnet   28 *jallis*: shutter

MARY EVELYN
(1665–1685)

THE eldest daughter of John Evelyn the diarist. She died of smallpox at the age of 19 and was buried in the south-east end of the church at Deptford. Evelyn records her gift for comedy in his diary, as well as her excellent education, musical talents, and piety: 'she had a talent of rehersing any Comical part or poeme, as...she might decently be free with, more pleasing than the Theatre...Nothing was therefore so delightfull to her, as the permission I gave her to go into my Study, where she would willingly have spent whole dayes; for as I sayd, she had read aboundance of History, & all the best poets, even to Terence, Plautus, Homer, Vergil, Horace, Ovide, all the best Romances, & modern Poemes, and could compose very happily, & put in her pretty Symbol, as in that of the *Mundus Muliebris*, wherein is an enumeration of the immense variety of the Modes & ornaments belonging to the Sex...' He seems to have decided to publish his much-loved daughter's poem as a memorial to her.

In her short life, Mary Evelyn seems to have had an intellectual life which was quite unknown to her parents, much as they loved her. She read secretly in her room, copying out history and theology into a commonplace book, and planned a correspondence with a clergyman who she asked to be her spiritual mentor, a venture which may have had an eye to the accumulation of a set of publishable letters (British Library, Evelyn MSS). We have included *Mundus Muliebris* in its entirety, because of its interest as a document for social history. The description of a dressing-room became a minor literary genre of the eighteenth century: Swift's far more misogynist *The Lady's Dressing Room* (1732) was answered by Miss W—'s *The Gentleman's Study* (1732): see *Eighteenth-Century Women Poets*, ed. Roger Lucsdale (Oxford, Oxford University Press, 1990) no. 91.

262 *A VOYAGE TO MARRYLAND: OR, THE LADIES DRESSING-ROOM.*

Negotii sibi volet qui vim parare,
Navem, et Mulierem, hæc duo comparato.
Nam nullæ magis Res duæ plus Negotii
Habent, forte si occeperis exornare.
Neque unquam satis hæ duæ Res ornantur,
Neque eis ulla ornandi satis satietas est.

Plaut. Poenelus. Act I Scen.2

Whoever has a mind to abundance of Trouble,
Let him furnish himself with a Ship and a Woman,
For no two things will find you more Employment,
If once you begin to Rig them out with all their Streamers.
Nor are they ever sufficiently adorned,
Or satisfy'd, that you have done enough to set them forth.

He that will needs to *Marry-Land*
Adventure, first must understand
For's Bark, what Tackle to prepare,
'Gainst Wind and Weather, wear and tare:
Of Point *d'Espagne*, a Rich *Cornet*,   5
Two *Night-Rails*, and a *Scarf* beset
With a great Lace, a *Colleret*.
One black Gown of Rich Silk, which odd is
Without one Colour'd, Embroider'd *Bodice*:
For Petticoats for Page to hold up,   10
For short ones nearer to the Crup:
Three *Manteaus*, nor can Madam less
Provision have for due undress;
Nor *demy Sultane*, *Spagnolet*,
Nor Fringe to sweep the Mall forget,   15
Of under Bodice three neat pair
Embroider'd, and of Shoos as fair:
Short under Petticoats pure fine,
Some of *Japan* Stuff, some of *Chine*,
With Knee-high Galoon bottomed,   20
Another quilted White and Red;
With a broad *Flanders* Lace below:
Four pair of *Bas de soy* shot through
With Silver, Diamond Buckles too,
For Garters, and as Rich for Shoo.   25
Twice twelve day Smocks of *Holland* fine,
With *Cambric* Sleeves, rich Point to joyn,
(For she despises *Colbertine*.)

Twelve more for night, all *Flanders* lac'd,
Or else she'll think her self disgrac'd: 30
The same her Night-Gown must adorn,
With two Point Wastcoats for the Morn:
Of Pocket *Mouchoirs* Nose to drain,
A dozen lac'd, a dozen plain:
Three Night-Gowns of rich *Indian* stuff,   35
Four Cushion Cloths are scarce enough,
Of Point, and *Flanders*, not forget
Slippers embroidered on Velvet:
A *Manteau* Girdle, Ruby Buckle,
And *Brilliant* Diamond Rings for Knuckle   40
Fans painted, and perfumed three;
Three Muffs of *Sable*, *Ermine*, *Grey*;
Nor reckon it among the Baubles,
A *Palatine* also of *Sables*.
A Saphire Bodkin for the Hair,   45
Or sparkling Facet Diamond there:
Then *Turquois*, *Ruby*, *Emrauld* Rings
For Fingers, and such petty things;
As Diamond Pendants for the Ears,
Must needs be had, or two Pearl Pears,   50
Pearl Neck-lace, large and Oriental,
And Diamond, and of Amber pale;
For Oranges bears every Bush,
Nor values she cheap things a rush.
Then Bracelets for her Wrists bespeak,   55
(Unless her Heart-strings you will break)
With Diamond *Croche* for Breast and Bum,
Till to hang more on there's no room.
Besides these Jewels you must get
Cuff Buckles, and an handsom Set   60
Of Tags for Palatine, a curious Hasp
The Manteau 'bout her Neck to clasp:
Nor may she want a Ruby Locket,
Nor the fine sweet quilted Pocket;
To play at *Ombre* or *Basset*,   65
She a rich *Pulvil* Purse must get,
With Guineas fill'd, on Cards to lay,
With which she fancies most to play:
Nor is she troubled at ill fortune,
For should the bank be so importune,   70
To rob her of her glittering Store,
The amorous Fop will furnish more.
Pensive and mute, behind her shoulder
He stands, till by her loss grown bolder,
Into her lap *Rouleau* conveys,   75

The softest thing a Lover says:
She grasps it in her greedy hands,
Then best his Passion understands;
When tedious languishing has fail'd,
Rouleau has constantly prevail'd.   80
But too go on where we left off,
Though you may think what's said enough;
This is not half that does belong
To the fantastick Female Throng:
In Pin-up Ruffles now she flaunts,   85
About her Sleeves are *Engageants*:
Of Ribbon, various *Echelles*,
Gloves trimm'd, and lac'd as fine as Nell's.
Twelve dozen *Martial*, whole, and half,
Of *Jonquil*, *Tuberose*, (don't laugh)   90
Frangipan, *Orange*, *Violett*,
Narcissus, *Jassemin*, *Ambrett*:
And some of *Chicken* skin for night,
To keep her Hands, plump, soft, and white,
Mouches for pushes, to be sure,   95
From *Paris* the *tré-fine* procure,
And *Spanish* Paper, Lip, and Cheek,
With Spittle sweetly to belick:
Nor therefore spare in the next place,
The Pocket *Sprunking* Looking-Glass;   100
Calembuc Combs in Pulvil Case,
To set, and trim the Hair and Face:
And that the Cheeks may both agree,
Plumpers to fill the Cavity.
The *Settée*, *Cupée*, place aright,   105
Frelange, *Fontange*, *Favorite*;
Monté la haut, and *Palisade*,
Sorti, *Flandan*, (great helps to Trade)
Burgoine, *Jardiné*, *Cornett*,
Frilal next upper Pinner set,   110
Round which it does our Ladies please
To spread the Hood call'd *Rayonnés*:
Behind the Noddle every Baggage
Wears bundle *Choux* in *English*, Cabbage:
Nor *Cruches* she, nor *Confidents*,   115
Nor *Passagers*, nor *Bergers* wants,
And when this Grace Nature denies,
An Artificial *Tour* supplies;
All which with *Meurtriers* unite,
And *Creve-Cœurs* silly Fops to smite,   120
Or take in Toil at *Park* or *Play*,
Nor Holy *Church* is safe, they say,

Where decent Veil was wont to hide
The Modest Sex Religious Pride:
Lest these yet prove too great a Load,   125
'Tis all comprised in the *Commode*;
Pins tipt with Diamond Point, and head,
By which the Curls are fastned,
In radiant *Firmament* set out,
And over all the Hood *sur-tout*:   130
Thus Face that *E'rst* near head was plac'd
Imagine now about the Wast,
For *Tour* on *Tour*, and *Tire* on *Tire*,
Like Steeple *Bow*, or *Grantham* Spire,
Or *Septizonium* once at *Rome*,   135
(but does not half so well become)
Fair Ladies Head) you here behold
Beauty by Tyrant Mode controll'd.
The graceful *Oval*, and the *Round*,
This *Horse* Tire does quite confound;   140
And Ears like *Satyr*, Large and Raw,
And bony Face, and hollow Jaw;
This monstrous Dress does now reveal
Which well plac'd Curls did once conceal.
Besides all these, 'tis always meant   145
You furnish her Appartment,
With *Moreclack* Tapestry, Damask Bed,
Or Velvet richly embroidered:
Branches, *Brasero*, *Cassolets*,
A *Cofre-fort*, and Cabinets,   150
Vasas of Silver, *Porcelan*, store
To set, and range about the Floor:
The Chimney Furniture of Plate
(For Iron's now quite out of date:)
Tea-Table, *Skreens*, Trunks, and Stand,   155
Large Looking-Glass richly *Japan'd*,
And hanging Shelf, to which belongs
Romances, Plays, and Amorous Songs;
Repeating Clocks, the hour to show
When to the Play 'tis time to go,   160
In Pompous Coach, or else Sedan'd   ⎫
With Equipage along the *Strand*,   ⎬
And with her new *Beau* Fopling mann'd. ⎭
A new Scene to us next presents,
The Dressing-Room, and Implements,   165
Of Toilet Plate Gilt, and Emboss'd,
And several other things of Cost:
The Table *Miroir*, one Glue Pot,
One for *Pomatum*, and what not?

Of *Washes*, *Unguents*, and *Cosmeticks*,   170
A pair of Silver Candlesticks;
Snuffers, and Snuff-Dish, Boxes more,
For Powders, Patches, Waters store,
In silver Flasks, or Bottles, Cups
Cover'd, or open to wash Chaps;   175
Nor may *Hungarian* Queen's be wanting,
Nor store of Spirits against fainting:
Of other waters rich, and sweet,
To sprinkle Handkerchief is meet;
D'Ange, *Orange*, *Mill-Fleur*, *Myrtle*,   180
Whole Quarts the Chambe to bespertle:
Of Essence *rare*, *and le meillure*
From *Rome*, from *Florence*, *Montpellier*,
In *Filgran Casset* to repel,
When Scent of *Gousset* does repel,   185
Though powder'd *Allom* be as good,
Well strew'd on, and well understood.
For Vapours that offend the Lass,
Of *Sal Armoniack* a Glass:
Nor Brush for Gown, nor Oval Salver,   190
Nor Pincushion, nor Box of Silver,
Baskets of *Fil'gran*, long and round,
Or if *Japonian* to be found,
And the whole Town so many yield,
Calembuc Combs by dozens fill'd   195
You must present, and a world more,
She's a poor Miss can count her store.
The Working Apron too from France,
With all its trim Apurtenance;
Loo Masks, and whole, as wind does blow,   200
And Miss abroad's dispos'd to go:
Hoods by whole dozens, White and Black,
And store of Coiffs she must not lack,
Nor Velvet Scarfs about her Back,
To keep her warm; all these at least   205
In *Amber'd* Skins, or quilted Chest
Richly perfum'd, she Lays, and rare
Powders for Garments, some for Hair
Of *Cyprus* and of *Corduba*,
And the Rich *Polvil* of *Goa*,   210
Nor here omit the Bob of Gold
Which a *Pomander* Ball does hold,
This to her side she does attach
With Gold *Crochet*, or *French Pennache*,
More useful far than *Ferula*,   215
For any saucy Coxcombs Jaw:

A graceful Swing to this belongs,
Which he returns in Cringe, and Songs,
And languishing to kiss the hand,
That can Perfumed blows command.   220
All these, and more in order set,
A large rich Cloth of Gold *Toilet*
Does cover, and to put up Rags,
Two high Embroider'd Sweet Bags,
Or a large Perfum'd *Spanish* Skin,   225
To wrap up all these Trinkets in.
But I had almost quite forgot,
A *Tea* and *Chocolate* Pot,
With *Molionet*, and Caudle Cup,
Restoring Breakfast to sup up: 230
Porcelan Saucers, Spoons of Gold,
Dishes that refin'd Sugars hold;
Pastillios de Bocca we
In Box of beaten Gold do see,
Inchas'd with Diamonds, and *Tweeze*   235
As Rich and Costly as all these,
To which a bunch of *Onyxes*,
And many a Golden Seal there dangles,
Mysterious Cyphers, and new fangles.
Gold is her Toothpick, Gold her Watch is,   240
And Gold is everything she touches:
But tir'd with numbers I give o're,
Arithmetick can add no more,
Thus Rigg'd the Vessel, and Equipp'd,
She is for all Adventures Shipp'd,   245
And Portion e're the year goes round,
Does with her Vanity confound.

Whoever...: Translation of *Poenulus*, given above in Latin   5 *Point d'Espagne*: Spanish
point-lace; *Cornet*: lace lappets, hanging down on either side of the face   6 *Night-Rails*:
nightdresses   14 *demy Sultane, Spagnolet*:   15 *the Mall*: London street where the
fashionable walked   20 *Galoon*: A narrow, decorative ribbon, often of gold, used as a
border   23 *Bas de soy*: silk stockings   26 *Holland*: linen   27–8 *Point... Colbertine*:
kinds of lace   33 *Mouchoirs*: handkerchiefs   43 *Grey*: squirrel fur   44 *Palatine*: a
luxurious kind of fur tippet named after Elisabeth Charlotte, Princess Palatine (wife of
the Duc d'Orléans) in 1676   65 *Ombre... Basset*: fashionable card games   66 *Pulvil*:
pillow shaped   75 *Rouleau*: a roll of gold coins   88 *Nell's*: Nell Gwyn, actress and
mistress of Charles II   89–92 *Martial–Ambrett*: gloves were bought impregnated with
perfume   95 *Mouches for pushes*: patches for pimples   97 *Spanish paper*: rouge   101
Calembuc: eagle wood, the fragrant wood of the Indian tree *aquilaria agallocha*   104:
Plumpers: prostheses worn inside the cheek to disguise the hollow effect given by missing
teeth   105–20 Parts of an elaborate formal hairdo   134 *Grantham spire*: famously
tall   135 *Septizonium*: a large structure built as a monument to the emperor
Septimius Severus at Rome   147 *Moreclack*: Mortlake: England's most famous tapestry
workshop   153 *Plate*: silver   176 *Hungarian Queen's*: Hungary Water (eau-de-
cologne)   180 perfumes: 'Angel', 'Orange', 'Thousand Flowers', 'Myrtle' (a scented

shrub)   183–6 *Montpellier...Allom*: deodorants   214 *Pennache*: panache, a tuft of
feathers of something of the same shape, such as a tassel   215 *Ferula*: used by school-
masters to discipline pupils   223 *Rags*: used for sanitary protection   225 *Spanish skin*:
a skin of perfumed Spanish leather   229 *Molionet*: a chocolate, mill   233 *Pastillios de
Bocca*: breath-fresheners   237 *Onyxes*: carved in intaglio, as seals

LADY GRISELL BAILLIE (née HUME)
(1665–1746)

LADY GRISSEL BAILLIE was born on Christmas Day at Redbraes castle in
Berwickshire, daughter of Sir Patrick Hume of Polwarth and Grisell Ker. She
became something of a heroine at an early age. Her father, Sir Patrick Hume,
used her to deliver secret messages to the imprisoned Jacobite Robert Baillie of
Jerviswood. Later, when the family property was confiscated and her father
himself was in hiding, she contrived to smuggle food to him. Her father was
forced to flee Scotland when he was suspected of participation in the Rye House
Plot; and Grisell as the oldest of eighteen children took on the responsibility of
caring for her family. She was the mainstay of the family during their exile in
the Low Countries. In 1688, she and her mother returned to Britain with the
Princess of Orange, who invited her to become a Maid of Honour. She refused,
having fallen in love, and returned to Scotland to marry Robert Baillie's son
George. They had a son and two daughters. Lady Grissel died at Mellerstein,
Berwickshire, on 6 December 1746.

She began to write from an early age and left fragments of poems in a
notebook, 'many of them interrupted, half-writ, some broken off in the middle
of a sentence', as her daughter, Lady Murray, later described them. (She wrote a
memoir of both parents which was eventually published in 1922.) Lady Grissel
also left voluminous memoranda and account books, selections from which were
published in 1911 as *The Household Book of Lady Grizel Baillie*. Some of her
Scottish songs appeared anonymously in Scottish song collections. *Were ne my
Hearts light I wad Dye* is first attributed to her in 1839 in a broadsheet with
music by Charles Kirkpatrick Sharpe, 'the words by Lady Grizell Baillie'. It is a
poem of considerable insight into the processes by which a young man's family
can separate him from a girl deemed unsuitable: it is interesting that the cast of
characters, other than the young man himself, is entirely female: the girl, pitted
against the lover's mother, sister, and fiancée. This type of writing, when
anonymous, is thought of as authorless, created by 'the folk': it is a style of
composition, however, imitable by highly literate individuals such as Robert
Burns.

263   *Were ne my Hearts light I wad Dye*

I

There was an a May and she lo'ed na men,
She Bigged her bonny Bow'r down in yon Glen,

But now she cryes dale and a-well-a-day,
Come down the Green gate and come here away.

2

When bonny young *Johnny* came o'er ye sea,   5
He said he saw nathing so bonny as me,
He baight me baith Rings and mony bra things,
And were ne my Hearts light I wad dye.

3

He had a wee Titty that lo'ed na me,
Because I was twice as bonny as she,   10
She rais'd sick a Pother twixt him and his mother,
That were ne my Hearts light I wad dye.

4

The day it was set and the Bridal to be,
The wife took a Dwalm and lay down to dye,
She main'd and she grain'd out of Dollor and Pain,   15
Till he vow'd that he ne'er wou'd see me again.

5

His Kin was for ane of a higher degree,
Said what had he to do with the likes of me,
Appose I was bonny I was ne for Johnny,
And were [ne] my Hearts light I wad Dye.   20

6

They said I had neither Cow nor Calf,
Nor drops of drink runs thro' the drawf,
Nor Pickles of Meal runs thro' the mill Eye,
And were [ne] my Hearts light I wad Dye.

7

The maiden she was baith wylly and slye,   25
She spyed me as I came o'er the Lee,
And then she ran in and made sick a din,
Beleive your ain Een and ye trow ne me.

8

His bonnet stood ay fu' round on his Brow,
His auld ane lookt ay as well as his new,   30
But now he let's gang ony gate it will hing,
And casts himsell down on the Corn bing.

9

And now he gaes drooping about the Dykes,
And a' he dow do is to hund the Tykes

The live lang night he ne'er bows his Eye,   35
And were [ne] my Hearts light I wad dye.

10

But young for thee as I ha' been,
We shou'd ha' been galloping down in yon Green,
And linking out o'er yon lilly white Lee,
And wow gin I were young for thee.   40

2 *Bigged*: built   7 *bra*: braw (pretty)   8 *And were ne . . . dye*: If I did not have a resilient
nature, I would die   9 *Titty*: sister   14 *wife*: older woman; *Dwalm*: fainting fit   31 he
puts his bonnet on any old how   32 *bing*: bin   34 *hund the Tykes*: persecute the
dogs   40 *wow gin*: Oh, if only

MARY PIX (née GRIFFITH)
(1666–before 1709)

PADDY LYONS and Fidelis Morgan have recently been able to shed some new
light on the 'background of letters and music which formed Mary Pix as a
playwright'. She was born in 1666, the daughter of the Reverend Roger Griffith
and Lucy, née Berriman, in Nettlebed, Oxfordshire. Her mother was described
as a *soundesse*, or musician, on her marriage, 5 October 1665. Her father, a
graduate of both English universities, was rector of the Buckingham parish of
Padbury and Master of the Royal Latin (Free) School in Buckingham. She
probably learnt Latin from her father, or another teacher at the school: in the
satirical play *The Female Wits* (1697) she tries to engage her rivals, Delarivier
Manley and Catherine Trotter, in a 'Latin dispute'. The Reverend Griffith died
early in 1682, but his widow and daughter continued to live at the schoolhouse
for some time afterwards. Mary had a fling with her father's successor, Thomas
Dalby MA, before leaving for London, and on 24 July 1684, in the parish of St
Savior's Benetfink, she married George Pix, a merchant tailor, six years her
senior, and also something of a landed gentleman: from his father he inherited
Pix Hall in Kent, together with a small landed estate. Their first child, also
George, was baptized there in June 1689, but he lived for little more than a year,
and was buried in the local cemetery of Hawkhurst in September 1690. The
following year they went back to London, where their second son William was
baptized at St Andrew's, Holborn, on 12 November 1691. The couple had
dwellings in Southampton Buildings, 'a garden away' from the theatre at
Lincoln's Inn Fields. Her first play, *Ibrahim*, was an Oriental tragedy produced
at Drury Lane in May 1696. In the same year she wrote her only novel, *The
Inhuman Cardinal, or: Innocence Betrayed*, and a successful farce *The Spanish
Wives*. Comedy was her *métier* and among the women playwrights of this period,
only Aphra Behn was more prolific. The performance of Susanna Centlivre's
The Busybody in 1709 was advertised as for the benefit of Mrs Pix's executors.
The implication is that there was something amiss with Mary's will (which has
not been traced) and that the benefit was an attempt to compensate the executor
for the outlays thus incurred.

264   *to Mrs.* Manley, *upon her Tragedy*
       call'd The Royal Mischief

As when some mighty Hero first appears,
And in each act excells his wanting years;
All Eyes are fixt on him, each busy Tongue
Is employ'd in the triumphant Song:
Even pale Envy hangs her dusky Wings,   5
Or joins with brighter Fame, and hoarsly sings;
So you the unequal'd wonder of the Age,
Pride of our Sex, and Glory of the Stage;
Have charm'd our hearts with your immortal lays,
And tun'd us all with Everlasting Praise.   10
You snatch Lawrels with undisputed right,
And conquer when you but begin to fight;
Your infant strokes have such *Herculean* force,
Your self must strive to keep the rapid course;
Like *Sappho* Charming, like *Afra* Eloquent,   15
Like Chast *Orinda*, sweetly Innocent:
But no more, to stop the Reader were a sin,
Whilst trifles keep from the rich store within.
       M.Pix.

                                         (1696)

13 Hercules is said to have strangled snakes even in his cradle   15 *Sappho*: the Greek
poetess; *Afra*: Aphra Behn   16 *Orinda*: Katherine Philips

265   *To Mrs S.F. on her Poems*

Hail to *Clarinda*, dear Euterpe Hail,
Now we shall Conquer, now indeed prevail;
Clarinda will her charming Lines expose,
And in her Strength we vanquish all our Foes.
To these Triumphant Lays, let each repair,   5
A Sacred Sanction to the writing Fair;
Mankind has long upheld the Learned Sway,
And Tyrant Custom forc'd us to obey.
Thought Art and Science did to them belong,   ⎫
And to assert our selves was deem'd a Wrong,   ⎬   10
But we are justify'd by thy immortal Song: ⎭
Come ye bright Nymphs a lasting Garland bring,
In never fading Verse, *Clarinda's* Praises sing;
Read o're her Works, see how Genuine Nature fires,
Observe the sweetness which her Pen inspires.   15
From thence grow Wise, from thence your Thoughts improve,

Here's Judgment piercing Sense and softer Love;
To idle Gayeties true Wit prefer,
Strive all ye Thinking Fair, to Copy her.

(1706)

MARY ASTELL
(1666–1731)

MARRY ASTELL was born on 6 November 1666 in Newcastle upon Tyne, the daughter of Peter Astell, a gentrified coal merchant, and Mary Errington. Her mother was from a family of Catholic recusants, but she allowed her children to be brought up in the Church of England. Mary was the oldest child; one brother, Peter, studied at the Middle Temple and pursued a modestly successful career as a lawyer in his hometown; a second brother died in infancy. According to tradition, Astell was tutored at home by her clerical uncle, Ralph Astell, a Cambridge graduate and published poet. Her father died when she was 12, leaving assets of £500, and dramatically altering the material circumstances of the family. At the age of 20, she moved to London, apparently with the intention of earning her living as either a governess or a writer. She soon settled in Chelsea, the rural location for Sir Thomas More's enlightened household, but recently developed by Sir Charles Cheyne, Lady Jane's husband (nos. 158–60). She was to live there for the rest of her life. Her financial situation rapidly became desperate but it began to improve after an inspired appeal to William Sancroft, the High Church Archbishop of Canterbury, who helped her with pecuniary gifts and contacts. Her poetry was written before she was 22, under the influence of a youthful enthusiasm for Cowley's 'Odes', and survives in a single manuscript booklet in the Rawlinson collection of the Bodleian Library. Her first book, the *Serious Proposal to Ladies*, was issued in 1694 by the leading Tory publisher Rich Wilkin, and projected a scheme for an all-female college or 'Protestant nunnery', which was, in conception, not unlike the secular monasteries of eighteenth-century Denmark. The *Serious Proposal* had a profound impact on many of its women readers, demonstrated here by the poems of Lady Chudleigh and Elizabeth Thomas which we include (nos. 241 and 287). The second part to the *Serious Proposal*, published in 1697, presented rules of rational thinking for women according to Cartesian principles. Her next book, *Some Reflexions on Marriage* (1700), was the last of her feminist texts; in the 1706 preface she asked rhetorically: 'If all men are born free, how is it that women are born slaves.' From 1703 to 1709 she became involved in the party politics of her day and published a series of densely-argued tracts and pamphlets in support of the High Church and Tory positions. In 1709 she opened a school for the daughters of pensioners at the Royal Chelsea Hospital. The school was funded by the philanthropic ladies in Astell's circle: the Countess of Coventry, the Duchess of Ormonde, and Lady Elizabeth Hastings. The generosity of these same patrons provided for Astell's financial security (in spite of an ill-advised investment in the South Sea Bubble), and in 1712 she moved from rented accommodation into her own small house at the bottom of Paradise Row. She died after a mastectomy operation for breast cancer, and was buried in the Chelsea graveyard on 14 May 1731.

266   *In emulation of Mr Cowleys*
           Poem call'd the Motto page I

I

What shall I do? not to be Rich or Great,
    Not to be courted and admir'd,
    With Beauty blest, or Wit inspir'd,
Alas! these merit not my care and sweat,
    These cannot my Ambition please,   5
My high born Soul shall never stoop to these;
But something I would be thats truly great
In 'ts self, and not by vulgar estimate.

II

If this low World were always to remain,
    If th' old Philosophers were in the right,   10
    Who wou'd not then, with all their might
Study and strive to get themselves a name?
    Who wou'd in soft repose lie down,
Or value ease like being ever known?
But since Fames trumpet has so short a breath,   15
Shall we be fond of that which must submit to Death?

III

Nature permits me not the common way,
    By serving Court, or State, to gain
    That so much valu'd trifle, Fame;
Nor do I covet in Wits Realm to sway: 20
    But O ye bright illustrious few,
What shall I do to be like some of you?
Whom this misjudging World dos underprize,
Yet are most dear in Heav'ns all-righteous eyes!

IV

How shall I be a Peter or a Paul?   25
    That to the Turk and Infidel,
    I might the joyfull tydings tell,
And spare no labour to convert them all:
    But ah my Sex denies me this,
And Marys Priviledge I cannot wish;   30
Yet hark I hear my dearest Saviour say,
They are more blessed who his Word obey.

V

Up then my sluggard Soul, Labour and Pray,
    For if with Love enflam'd thou be,

Thy JESUS will be born in thee,   35
And by thy ardent Prayers, thou can'st make way,
 For their Conversion whom thou may'st not teach,
Yet by a good Example always Preach:
And tho I want a Persecuting Fire,
I'le be at lest a Martyr in desire.   40

                                            (Jan. 7 1687/8)

30 *Marys Priviledge*: refers to Luke 2. 27–8

ALICIA D'ANVERS (née CLARKE)
(1668–1725)

ALICIA D'ANVERS, according to Anthony à Wood (manuscript notes in his copy of *Academia*, Bod. Wood 517, Pamphlet 6) was the daughter of Samuel Clarke, a 'sometimes superior Beadle of Law' in Oxfordshire, and also architypographicus to the University. He knew Hebrew, Arabic, and Farsi as well as Latin, and he played a part in the preparation of Brian Walton's polyglot Bible in 1657. A daughter Alice was born to them, and christened in Holy Cross Church at Holywell on 5 January 1668. Her father died when she was 2, but she grew up to marry a sometime scholar of Trinity, Knightley Danvers. The marriage occurred before 3 December 1690, since her first publication was licensed under that name. She was buried, as she had been born, in the parish of Holywell. Her husband became deputy recorder of Northamptonshire.

Alicia D'Anvers is one of the many writers of the seventeenth century who imitated the jingling metre and genial, conversational style of Samuel Butler's *Hudibras* (published in three parts between 1663 and 1678). Another evident model for *The Oxford-Act* is Chaucer's *Canterbury Tales*: after this introduction, Alicia D'Anvers goes on to sketch a series of characters, all on the road to Oxford, before taking us to Oxford itself for the public display of learning which they are all off to witness (including Aldermen, Justices, Woollen-Drapers, Tailors, Prentices, and 'three jolly Landladies'). Her subject, in the introduction to the Oxford-Act, is the less than glorious part played by Oxford (and to some extent Cambridge) in recent history: it is interesting to observe that events of recent history, of passionate interest to some of the women whose work is included in this anthology—Monmouth's rebellion and its aftermath, Judge Jeffrey's 'Bloody Assize', and the 'Glorious Revolution' of 1688 which brought William and Mary to power—all seem very far-away and pointless. The relative frivolity of tone in this and other work of the 1690s may suggest that fifty-odd years of political upheaval (since 1640) had so exhausted the capacity of individuals to respond effectively that political apathy, and a variety of ironic or flippant responses to political engagement was becoming an increasingly attractive option for many.

267   *A True Relation of their Practice*
       at Oxford *Town when there an ACT is.*

Canto I

Half Choakt ith' Dust of our lewd Town,
Tir'd with their Follies and my own;
To breath a Wiser Air, and better,
With many a Token, many a letter,
I tript to t'other *Alma Mater.*   5
Thousands One, Hundreds Six, Tens Ninety
Three Ones the Year exactly point t'ye,
When a remarkable Occasion
Brought there the Learned and Wise oth' Nation;
The *Act* which some believ'd must be   10
Turn'd to a *Jewish Jubilee,*
Whose joyful sound that Nation hears
No more than Once in Fifty Years.
The *Act*, which now they discontinue
So long, some thought, they ne'er had any;   15
But that some forward Scribes in Iniquity
Had feign'd it like their own Antiquity.
Oft wou'd the new created Sophister
Where Boy cry'd, want ye any *Coffee*, Sir?
Start from brown-study, answering rather   20
When comes the *Act*, the *Act*, Dear Father?
The Beardless Father sigh'd, but knew
No more of that than I, or You;
For all his Logick and his History,
This an unfathomable Mystery.   25
Even the grave *Doctors* scarce cou'd tell
Without the help of *Chronicle,*
When last they in their Boots appear'd,
And Bugbear *Terrae-Filius* fear'd.
Now one, and then the other Faction   30
Putting the Dons beyond their Action:
Now Whig, as Nobbs had then bedighted him
With Horns and Tail cried *Bough*, and 'frighted 'em;
Till they stark staring run with one Mouth,
To rail at, and discomfit *Monmouth*:   35
Tho' wiser *Cam* to save his Bacon,
His Picture kept till he was taken,
Then their Lov'd *Chancellor*'s Picture banish,
As *Rome* unfortunate *Sejanus.*
More Loyal *Oxford*, *Windsor* trusted   40
With many a Pondrous Pike and Musket,

Soon form'd in Squadron and Battalions
To swinge the Duke's Tatterdemalions:
But Blessings on that Noble Lord
Who sav'd the Labour of their Sword;   45
Who did the Tall-Young Man betray,
And run most Loyally away.
O happy *Oxford*! happy since
Fate gave thee such a grateful Prince;
True to his Friends beyond comparison,   50
He *Jefferys* sent to pay thy Garrison;
Whose *Musick-Speech* so sore did fright ye
The *Act* that Summer cry'd Good-night t'ye.
Since then, Confusion on Confusion,
All Chaos till the *Revolution*;   55
Till a New World rose from Black Billows,
And *Surges* roll'd as Soft as Pillows.
Yet then Fate had so long been thwarting,
So stunn'd with the old Blows of Fortune,
The Aged Matron did appear,   60
She scarce got Breath in Four long Year;
But now recover'd brisk and Bonny,
As Bridegroom's Self, in Moon-call'd-*Hony*,
An Act as I before have told y'it
She'll have, and all crowd to behold it.   65
Expect not all the Nation over,
From *Cornish Mount* to *Peer* of *Dover*,
I shou'd recite, since did I know it,
'Twould look like *Herald*, not like *Poet*:
Then rest content with what I give ye   70
To further trouble save, believe me.

5 *Alma Mater*: university (Oxford)   17 *Antiquity*: refers to the claim that Oxford was founded by Alfred the Great   28 *Boots*: i.e. as actors   29 *Terrae-Filius*: ordinary people (as spectators)   33 *Bough*: barked like a dog   35 *Monmouth*: the failed rebellion of the Duke of Monmouth (bastard of Charles II) against his uncle James II in 1685   39 *Sejanus*: he rose to great power under the emperor Tiberius, but was destroyed by him   46 *Tall-Young Man*: The Duke of Monmouth   51 *Jeffreys*: Judge George Jeffreys was sent to purge the West Country of traitors, and did so with notorious brutality   52 *Musick-Speech*: Jeffreys had a rasping voice   67 *Cornish Mount...Peer*: St Michael's Mount, in Cornwall, to Dover pier, i.e. from West to East

A LADY
(fl. 1688)

LIKE the poem of 'A Young Lady of Quality' (no. 271) this may possibly be an early work of Delarivier Manley (nos. 275–7). It is interesting for its attestation of the immense importance of Aphra Behn as example and inspiration to other women, and also for its covert declaration of a shared political position—Aphra Behn's response to the Glorious Revolution was to consider the rule of Queen Mary legitimated by her status as daughter of James II, and to ignore William III entirely: the 'Lady' commends her for this delicate balance of exigency and principle.

268   A PINDARICK *to Mrs Behn on her Poem on the Coronation, Written by a Lady*

Hail, thou sole Empress of the Land of Wit,
To whom all conquer'd Authors must submit,
And at thy feet their fading Laurels lay,
The utmost tribute that a Muse can pay,
To thy unlabour'd Song o'th' Coronation day.   5
The subject was Divine we all confess,
Nor was that flame, thy mighty fancy, less.
That cloth'd thy thought in such a pleasing dress,
As did at once a Masculine wit express,
And all the softness of a Female tenderness.   10
No more shall men their fancy'd Empire hold,
Since thou *Astrea* form'd of finer mould,
By nature temper'd more with humid cold,
Doth man excel——
Not in soft strokes alone, but even in the bold.   15
And as thy purer Blood
Thrô more transparent vessels is convey'd
Thy spirits more fine and subtil do thy brain invade.
And nimbler come uncall'd unto thy aide;
So the gay thought——   20
Which thy still flaming fancy doth inspire
New, uncontroul'd, and warm, as young desire,
Have more of kindling heat and fiercer fire;
Not to be reach't, or prays'd, unless by such
As the same happy temperament possess;   25
Since none with equal numbers can reward thy Lays,
May the just Monarch, which you praise,
Daine to acknowledg this.
Not with a short applause of crackling Bays
But a return of that may revive thy days;   30
And thy well-meaning grateful loyal Muse
Cherisht by that bleast theam its zeal did chuse.
Maist thou be blest with such a sweet retreat,
That with contempt thou maist behold the great;
Such as the mighty *Cowlys* well-known feat.   35
Whose lofty Hous I wou'd have all thy own

And in the mid'st a spacious shady Throne,
Rais'd on a Mount that shou'd Parnassus be,
And every Muse included all in thee.
On whose coole top alone thou shoud'st dispense   40
The Laws of Wit, Love, Loyalty, and Sense:
The new Arcadia shou'd the Grove be nam'd
And for the guift our grateful Monarch fam'd.

Amidst the shade, I'd wish a well built House,
Like *Sidneys* Noble Kalendar shou'd stand,   45
Raising its head and all the rest command.
Its out-side gay, its inside clean and neat
With all of lifes conveniences replete,
Where all the Elements at once conspire
To give what mans necessities require,   50
Rich soyle, pure Aire, streams coole, and useful fire.
The fertil spot with pleasure shou'd abound
And with *Elizium*-Spring be ever crown'd.

When thou thy mind unbend'st from thoughtful hours
Then shou'dst thou be refresht with Fruits and Flowrs,   55
    The Gods and Nymphs of Woods and Springs
    Shall Dance in Antique Rural Rings:
While scaly Trytons and grim Satyrs play
Such Tunes, as Birds compose, to welcome day.
Till the glad noyse to distant shores resound,   60
And flying Birds joyn in th' Harmonious sound.
Which listning Echo's catch at the rebound.
Here without toyle, or pining want perplext
Thy Body easy and thy mind at rest,
    With all Lifes valu'd pleasures blest,   65
Thy largest wishes still thou should'st enjoy
Inviron'd with delights that ne're can cloy.

    Accept, thou much lov'd Sappho of our Isle,
    This hearty wish, and grace it with a smile,
    When thou shalt know that thy Harmonious Lire   70
    Did me, the meanest of thy sex, inspire.
    And that thine own unimitable lays
    Are cause alone that I attempt thy praise.
    Which in unequal measure I rehearse
    Because unskill'd in numbers, Grace or Verse;   75
    Great Pindars flights are fit alone for thee,
    The witty Horace's Iambicks be
Like Virgil's lofty strains alas too hard for me.
    And if enough this do not plead excuse,
    Pity the failings of a Virgin Muse,   80
    That never in this kind before essai'd,

Her Muse till now was, like her self—a Maid.
Whose Blooming labours thus she dedicates to you,
　　A Tribute justly to your merits due,
　　At least her part of gratitude to pay   85
For that best Song o'th' Coronation day.
How bad wou'd the Ill-natur'd World requite
　　Thy noble labours if they do not write,
　　Who have, perhaps, been happy in this kind
To own thou'st now out-done all that they e're design'd.   90
　　Sure none with malice e're was so accurst,
　　This to deny but will with envy burst,
Since even thy own more envious sex agree
　　The glorious theam had right alone from thee;
　　The femal Writers thou hast all excell'd,   95
Since the first mother of mankind rebell'd.

ANNE FYCHAN
(fl. 1688)

THIS poem is particularly interesting since it demonstrates a Welsh woman's engagement with events of national significance. In the manuscript, it follows a series of twelve englynion on the Seven Bishops by Edward Morris, the drover poet of Perthi Llwydion. Both Morris and Fychan are reacting to the imprisonment of seven bishops in the Tower of London, charged with treason, after they refused to comply with James II's demand that a second Declaration of Indulgence be read aloud in every parish church. One of the seven was Welsh, William Lloyd, Bishop of St Asaph in North Wales. The reaction of Morris and Fychan is characteristic of Welsh responses to this event.

269　　　　　　　*I'r saith esgob*

Saith ddoeth saith wiwddoeth—saith wyr
　　Saith weithian a weithiodd yn bybyr
　　Saith a gawson ni yn gysur
Saith golofn barch saith galon bur

　　　　　　　　　　Anne Fychan ai cant

269　　　　　　　*On the seven bishops*

Seven wise men, seven fit in their wisdom—seven heroes
　　Seven at least who laboured with vigour
　　Seven who were a comfort to us

Seven pillars of respect, seven pure hearts
Anne Fychan sang it

CLEONE
(fl. 1688)

THE identity of this woman is unknown, but the poem casts an interesting light
on the importance of Aphra Behn to aspirant woman writers.

270   *To Mrs B. from a Lady who had a desire
to see her, and who complains on the
ingratitude of her fugitive Lover.*

Kind are my stars indeed but that so late
And I a stranger to a gentle fate,
If such a one I meet and chance to know,
I have not proper words to call it so,
Wondering at happiness, surpris'd as far   5
As a rough General always train'd to War,
Snatch'd from the midst of cruel fierce alarms,
Into a thousand unexpected charms;
A joy like this, how shall I entertain,
With a heart wounded, and a soul in pain;   10
In my laborious enterprises crost,
My life near *Finis*, and the Day quite lost.
Cleone had a swain, and lov'd the youth
Not for his Beauty but his seeming truth,
Not for a goodly herd or high descent,   15
(Ah that no God my ruin would prevent,)
What thô the Swain had neither Sheep nor land,
I scorned the goods of fortunes partial hand;
So generous was my passion for the slave,
Because I equally suppos'd him brave.   20
Oh! give me leave to sigh one sad adieu,
Then wholly dedicate myself to you
I have no business here but to complain
Of all the treasons of an ingrate Swain,
Since my inhumane perjur'd Shepherd's gone,   25
Night four seven times has put her mantle on,
And three seven times *Aurora* has appear'd,
Since last I from the cruel *Strephon* heard;
Whither he lives, is dead, or on what shore,

(Patience, ye Gods!) alas I know no more,   30
Then why my Stars do my destruction press,
Send me your pity, bounteous Shepherdess;
That I the face of grief no more may know;
If I deserve it that cou'd Love so low;
Consult not that, but charity and give   35
One tender pittying sigh that I may live:
(That I may thus make my complaint to you,)
Kind are my Stars indeed at last 'tis true;
Let not my rude and untam'd griefs destroy,
The early glimmerings of an infant joy: 40
And add not your neglect, for if you doe,
Cleone finds her desolation too!
Know this it yet remains in your fair breast,
To render me the happy or unblest.
You may act miracles if you'l be kind,   45
Make me true joys in real sorrows find;
And bless the hour I hither did pursue
A faithless Swain and found access to you:
Accept the heart I here to you present,
By the ingratitude of *Strephon* rent;   50
Till then gay, noble, full of brave disdain,
And unless yours prevent shall be again;
As once it was, if in your generous brest,
It may be Pensioner at my request
No more to Treasons subject as before   55
To be betray'd by a fair tale no more,
As large as once, as uncontroul'd and free,
But yet at your command shall always be.

A YOUNG LADY OF QUALITY
(fl. 1689)

THE author of this long and ambitious poem on the death of Aphra Behn, which simultaneously claims that the throne of the Tenth Muse is empty, and makes a tacit bid to occupy it, is most probably a youthful Delarivier Manley: since the poem so unmistakably breathes an ambition to occupy a place in the public world of literature, it is probable that its writer is someone who subsequently became more visible. Mrs Manley, daughter of Sir Roger Manley of Denbighshire, could very properly describe herself as a 'young lady of quality', and might already have been looking for a literary career (see biographical entry on Delarivier Manley).

271   *An Elegy Upon the Death of*
Mrs. A. Behn; the Incomparable Astrea.

I

Summon the Earth (the fair *Astrea*'s gone,)
  And let it through every Angle fly,
    Till it has fill'd the mighty Round,
  And thence arise to the expanded Sky,
    In murmurs for the misery done,   5
To see if Heaven, Heaven will our Grief supply,
  With tears enough to mourn her Destiny.
    Assemble all the Crowds below,
    You that Obedience to the Muses owe,
And teach the Sighing Maids to mourn,   10
    With unbound Hair, and flowing Tears,
    In Strains as moving as her Numbers were,
    The mighty Desolation, mighty Woe.
      Teach them in Charming Accents, such as once
She did the list'ning Crowds inform,   15
When high as Heaven her Praise was born,
    And taught the Angels to rejoyce,
    In sweeter, truer Numbers than before,
    In all their bright Seraphick Store.
      Had ever tun'd their Heavenly Voice: 20
And thus prepar'd, let them the Loss deplore,
The charming wise *Astrea* is no more.

II

What have we done? What have our Crimes deserv'd?
    Why this injurious Rape?
      The World is Widdow'd now,   25
    And Desolation every where
    With dismal Groans invades the Air;
      My sullen Muse, that ne're before
      The sacred Title wore,
Untaught, unpractis'd, has preferrd   30
(For none from Mourning can escape)
    In uneven Strains, and much below
      All but my Grief,
    To tell the World their Universal Woe,
      Which ne're can hope Relief: 35
'Tis an implacable Decree,
That Languishments, Diseases, Death,
Must attend all that live on Earth
    Cannot those Hours we here possess,

From Fate, and those attendant Ills, be free,   40
That ravish hence our Happiness,
　　But in Diseases, Murmurs, Strife,
　　Made pass away our hasty Life?
When if it uncontroul'd did bloom,
　　Exempt from Anguishes or Fears,   45
　　Who then would offer up their Tears,
To see their beck'ning Fate were come,
After a Life supinely run?
But now in Pain that ling'ring Span must waste,
Which Sighing terminates in Death at last,   50
And kills with us the sense of Dangers past.

III

Can no distinction here be own'd?
　　Must Death for ever stand thus arm'd,
To snatch a Soul Divinely form'd?
　　Must that then Triumph over all?   55
Give all below a Fatal Wound,
　　Then urge it is but Natural?
　　　Ah! how inglorious is our Fate,
　　　How rigid and how desperate?
We're flatter'd with the pleasing Tale;   60
　　In us the form of Gods are seen;
　　　Fond Ignorance, for they are all Divine,
Exempt from all we fear:
　　Nor can their Beings ever fail,
As those that wander here.   65
Hence then, thou false receiv'd Belief, begone,
And let us see, we're like our selves alone.

IV

Who now, of all the inspired Race,
Shall take *Orinda*'s Place?
　　Or who the Hero's Fame shall raise?   70
　　　Who now shall fill the Vacant Throne?
　　　The bright *Astrea*'s gone,

V

And with her all that heavenly Wit,
And Charming Wonders of her Face,
On which with more we gaz'd,   75
And claim'd a Title to our Praise.
　　The Graces too have made their flight,
　　　All to inglorious Fate submit;
　　To Fate, which draws us to that nearer sight
Of Death, and everlasting Night,   80

Where Silence her chief Empire sways,
And hurls a gloomy Shade around
The hollow unexhausted Ground,
Which all Return denies:
For when the sick'ning Soul decays, 85
Languishes, sighs, and dyes,
She bids an everlasting long Adieu
To all the World, and all she valu'd too.

VI

Let all our Hopes despair and dye,
Our Sex for ever shall neglected lye; 90
Aspiring Man has now regain'd the Sway,
To them we've lost the Dismal Day:
Astrea an equal Ballance held,
(Tho' she deserv'd it all;)
But now the rich Inheritance must fall; 95
To them with Grief we yeild
The Glorious envy'd Field.
Of her own Sex, not one is found
Who dares her Laurel wear,
Withheld by Impotence or Fear; 100
With her it withers on the Ground,
Untouch't, and cold as she,
And Reverenc'd to that degree,
That none will dare to save
The Sacred Relick from the Grave; 105
Intomb'd with her, and never to return,
Fills up the narrow Urn,
Which more Presumption, or more Courage has than we.

VII

In Love she had the softest sense;
And had her Virtue been as great, 110
In Heaven she'd fill'd the foremost Seat.
This failure, or she had Immortal been,
And free as Angels are from Sin;
'Twas pity that she practis'd what she taught;
Her Muse was of the bolder Sex; 115
Such Mysteries of Love she did dispence,
Such moving natural Eloquence,
As made her too much Wit her fault.
Her ever-loyal Muse took no pretext,
To discommend what once it prais'd; 120
And what has most her Glory rais'd,
Her Royal Master she has follow'd home,
Nor would endure the World when he had lost his Throne.

VIII

Hail! the Elizian Shades, and bright *Orinda*, hail!
   They now much happier are than we;   125
   Their Triumphs are but now begun;
   What we have lost, the Shades have won:
      Her Presence makes their Harmony,
      For ever we must disagree.
See then, and do not fail,   130
   To entertain the welcom Guest
   And sing her Praise above the rest,
   For she deserves the Triumph best,
      Meet her, ye Amorous Lovers, and Adore
      Her Shade, before   135
      The Nymphs for whom you Fetters wore.
Her Care was most for you,
For still she gave to Sacred Love its due,
Reveal'd more Mysteries than *Ovid* knew:
Joyn all the Glorious Shades, and sing *Astrea*'s Praise,   140
Whilst her unhappy Monument we raise.

                                  (April 22, 1689)

22 *the charming wise Astrea*: Compare the refrain of Behn's 'On the Death of the late Earl of Rochester', 'The Young, the Noble Strephon is no more'   139 *Ovid*: author of *The Art of Love*

SARAH FIELD (née FYGE, later EGERTON) (1670–1723)

BORN in London, Sarah Fyge Egerton (as she styled herself after her second marriage) was one of the six daughters of Thomas Fyge, a physician and city councillor from an old Buckinghamshire family, and Mary, née Beacham, of Seaton, Rutland. In about 1690 Sarah married Edward Field, an attorney (unwillingly, by her own account). She seems to imply that her publication of the *Female Advocate* (1686, 1687), one of several responses to Robert Gould's anti-feminist satire, *Love Given O're* (1682), led her father to hustle her into matrimony. A few years later Field died, leaving her childless and comfortably off. She then married a second cousin, the Revd. Thomas Egerton of Adstock, Bucks, a wealthy widower and the father of adult children. He was about twenty years her senior. The prospects for this marriage were not good, as Sarah was already in love with Henry Pierce, an attorney's clerk and a friend of her first husband (the 'Alexis' of her poems). In 1704, she sued Egerton for divorce on grounds of cruelty, while at the same time, Egerton sued Sarah Field and her father in Chancery for the estate left her by Field. See Delarivier Manley, the *New Atalantis* (1709), for a representation of their marital discord, which also implies, with witty lack of sympathy, that she was subject to seizures of some kind. Her *Poems on Several Occasions* was published in 1703. Her estranged husband died in 1720. She had no children and died on 13 February 1723, having lived the last years of her life as a wealthy widow (Egerton died in 1720). In her will Sarah asks to be buried near the brass monument of her great-grandfather, Thomas Fyge (d. 1578), which is on the north side of the chancel, in the Church of St Lawrence, Winslow, Bucks, leaving £50 for a marble monument of her own (P.C.C. 11/589, sig. 25). She was known to literary contemporaries as 'Mrs Field', or Clarinda. Dedicatees of her verse include John Norris, the first Earl of Halifax, and Congreve, and she is also associated with Elizabeth Thomas.

272 *The Liberty*

Shall I be one, of those obsequious Fools,
That square there lives, by Customs scanty Rules;
Condemn'd for ever, to the puny Curse,
Of Precepts taught, at Boarding-school, or Nurse,
That all the business of my Life must be,   5
Foolish, dull Trifling, Formality.
Confin'd to a strict Magick complaisance,   ⎫
And round a Circle, of nice visits Dance,   ⎬
Nor for my Life beyond the Chalk advance: ⎭
The Devil Censure, stands to guard the same,   10
One step awry, he tears my ventrous Fame.
So when my Friends, in a facetious Vein,
With Mirth and Wit, a while can entertain;
Tho' ne'er so pleasant, yet I must not stay,
If a commanding Clock, bids me away: 15
But with a sudden start, as in a Fright,
I must be gone indeed, 'tis after Eight.
Sure these restraints, with such regret we bear ⎫
That dreaded Censure, can't be more severe,   ⎬
Which has no Terrors, if we did not fear;   ⎭   20
But let the Bug-bear, timerous Infants fright,
I'll not be scar'd, from Innocent delight:
Whatever is not vicious, I dare do,
I'll never to the Idol Custom bow,
Unless it suits with my own Humour too.   25
Some boast their Fetters, of Formality,
Fancy they ornamental Bracelets be,
I'm sure their Gyves, and Manacles to me.
To their dull fulsome Rules, I'd not be ty'd,
For all the Flattery that exalts their Pride: 30
My Sexs forbids, I should my Silence break,
I lose my Jest, cause Women must not speak.
Mysteries must not be, with my search Prophan'd,
My Closet not with Books, but Sweat-meats cram'd,

A little *China*, to advance the Show,   35
My *Prayer-Book*, and seven *Champions*, or so.
My Pen if ever us'd imploy'd must be,
In lofty Themes of useful Housewifery,
Transcribing old Receipts of Cookery:
And what is necessary 'mongst the rest,   }   40
Good Cures for Agues, and a cancer'd Breast,   }
But I can't here, write my *Probatum est*.   }
My daring Pen, will bolder Sallies make,
And like my self, an uncheck'd freedom take;
Not chain'd to the nice Order of my Sex,   45
And with restraints my wishing Soul perplex:
I'll blush at Sin, and not what some call Shame,
Secure my Virtue, slight precarious Fame.
To keep those Rules, which privately we Curse:
And I'll appeal, to all the formal saints,   50
With what reluctance they indure restraints.

                                                    (*c*.1687)

34 *Closet*: private room or cupboard; *Sweat-meats*: sweets   36 *seven Champions*: The
Famous Historie of the Seven Champions of Christendom, a romance printed *c*.1597: i.e.
ridiculously old-fashioned   42 *Probatum est*: proved by testing

273   *To* Orabella, *Marry'd to an old Man*

TELL me fair Nymph, who justly had design'd,
A charming Youth, to suit your equal mind;
What did seduce you thus to match with one,
Whom if by Nature made she'll scarcely own?
For form'd so many Centuries ago,   5
She has forgot if he's her Work or no;
I think the way to do his Reverence right,
Is to suppose him a Pre-Adamite:
Your blooming Youth in Age beyond decay,   }
Will teach censorious Malice what to say,   }   10
Who spite of Virtue will your Fame betray. }
What strong Persuasions made you thus to wed,
With such a Carcass scandalize your Bed?
Sure 'twas no earthly Gain that charm'd you to't,
Nothing but hopes of heaven should make me do't: 15
But since there's other ways to gain that Bliss }
Dispatching Martyrdom I wou'd not miss,   }
To be secur'd, could I but 'scape from this.   }
The monster Twin whose Brother grew from's Side, }
With all the stench he suffer'd when he dy'd,   }   20
Is a just Emblem of so yok'd a Bride.   }

But Ptisick, Gout and Palsie have their Charms,
And did intice you to his trembling Arms:
Kind amorous Glances from his hollow Eyes,
Did your gay Breast with rapturous Joys surprize   25
Ah! who can blame to see a yielding Maid,
By all these blooming Charms to Love betray'd.
Oh! for a vestal's Coldness to resist
The tempting Softness in such Beauties drest.
The bright Idea soon dissolves in Air,   30
And in it's room the Picture of Despair.
A moving Skeleton he seems to be,
Nature's antientest Anatomy.
Worth observation, hang him up therefore
In *Gresham* College, and I'll ask no more.   35

(probably before 1687)

8 *Pre-Adamite*: Isaac de la Peyrère contended in 1655 that Adam was the father of the Jews only, and the Gentile peoples stemmed from an earlier race   19 *monster Twin*: There are several early modern accounts of semi-twins (two heads/torsos, sharing one lower body): horribly, one twin sometimes predeceases the other. One such is in Montaigne's *Essays*, 'Of a monstrous child', II.30   22 *Ptisick*: tuberculosis   35 *Gresham College*: founded by the financier Sir Thomas Gresham (1519–79) as a college of seven professors in astronomy, geometry, physics, law, divinity, rhetoric, and music

274   *On my Wedding Day*

Abandon'd Day, why dost thou now appear?   ⎫
Thou must no more thy wonted Glories wear;   ⎬
Oh! rend thy self out of the circling Year,   ⎭
With me thou'rt stript of all thy pompous Pride,
Art now no festival Cause, I no Bride: 5
In thee no more must the glad Musick sound,   ⎫
Nor pleasing Healths in chearful Bouts go round, ⎬
But with sad cypress dress'd, not Mirtle crown'd; ⎭
Ne'er grac'd again with joyful Pageantry:
The once glad Youth that did so honour thee   10
Is now no more; with him thy Triumph's lost,
He always own'd thee worthy of his Boast.
Such Adoration he still thought thy due,
I learn'd at last to celebrate thee too;
Tho' it was long e're I could be content,   15
To yield you more than formal Complement;
If my first Offering had been Free-Will,
I then perhaps might have enjoy'd thee still:
But now thou'rt kept like the first mystick Day,
When my reluctant Soul did Fate obey,   20

And trembling Tongue with the sad Rites comply'd, ⎫
With timerous hand th'amazing Knot I ty'd,   ⎬
While Vows and Duty check'd the doubting Bride.   ⎭
At length my reconcil'd and conquer'd Heart,   ⎫
When 'twas almost too late own'd thy Desert,   ⎬ 25
And wishes thou wast still, not that thou never wer't ⎭
Wishes thee till that celebrated Day,
I lately kept with sympathizing Joy.
But Ah! thou now canst be no more to me,
Than the sad Relick of Solemnity;   30
To my griev'd Soul may's thou no more appear,
Be blotted out of Fate's strict Calendar.
May the Sun's Days ne'er be to thee allow'd,
But let him double every thick wrought Cloud,
And wrap himself in a retiring Shroud;   35
Let unmixt Darkness shade the gloomy Air, ⎫
Till all our sable Horizon appear,   ⎬
Dismale as I, black as the Weeds I wear;   ⎭
With me thy abdicated State deplore
And be like me, that's by thy self no more.   40

(after 1687)

8 Cypress belongs to funerals, myrtle to weddings   38 *Weeds*: widows' mourning garments

DELARIVIER MANLEY, née MANLEY
(c.1670/8–1724)

Delarivier Manley was the daughter of Sir Roger Manley, Lieutenant-Governor of the Channel Islands (where she claims to have been born) from 1667 to 1672. His military career was one of modest distinction: he went on to serve as a Captain in the Royal Regiment of Foot Guards, and as governor of Landguard Fort in Suffolk. In addition, he was a writer (in English and Latin) and translator (from Dutch, a language he must have learned as an exile during the Interregnum). Her mother's identity does not seem to be known. Delarivier was one of a number of children, of whom at least two boys and four girls survived to adulthood. The youthful Delarivier, by her own account, fell passionately in love with a young ensign, James Carlisle, serving with her brother-in-law's regiment, which was stationed in Jersey; and was sent to France to recover from this infatuation, where she learned to speak and write good French: it was intended that she should become a maid of honour to the Queen (Mary of Modena). The death of her father, c.1687, and the flight of James II and Mary at the Glorious Revolution of 1688 put an end to this project. John Manley (born c.1654), her cousin, was left as her next of kin, a position he abused by talking her into marrying him in about 1690. Apart from the disparity of age, and his widely-attested hot temper and general charmlessness, he had a living wife of about his own age, a Cornish heiress called Anne Grosse, by whom he had children. He also had a son, John, by Delarivier, born in June 1691. Thus, when the facts of the matter became known, despite her respectable birth and antecedents, the young Delarivier, as an unmarried mother, became *déclassée*. John Manley left her, to return (apparently) to his legitimate wife. Her route out of social oblivion was via one of the least respectable women of the period, the royal mistress Barbara Villiers, Lady Castlemaine, whom she met perhaps by chance—however, she improved the acquaintance until Lady Castlemaine took her as a protégée. It seems also to have struck her, at this time, if not before, that a career as a writer offered her the only possible independence open to her. Her début in print (unless she is 'A Young Lady of Quality') is her poem on Catherine Trotter's *Agnes de Castro* (1695), which suggests a determination on her part to follow Trotter's lead. Her own first plays, *The Lost Lover* and *The Royal Mischief*, followed promptly, in 1596. Subsequently, she abandoned theatrical writing in favour of prose, mostly scandalous semi-fiction about public figures: *The New Atalantis*, which got her arrested for slander, is the best known of these *romans à clef*. In 1700 she edited *The Nine Muses; or, poems written by so many ladies, upon the death of the famous John Dryden*. The four women who contributed to this volume—Sarah Fyge Egerton, Mary Pix, Catherine Trotter, and Susanne Centlivre—are all satirized in the *New Atalantis*, because (in her view) they had proved themselves politically and personally untrustworthy. According to John Richetti, '[Manley] was nothing less than the principal woman of letters of Queen Anne's England' and her reputation as a political satirist was such that in 1711 she succeeded Swift as the chief writer for the Tory periodical, *The Examiner*. For the last years of her life she cohabited with the printer John Barber, a Jacobite womanizer who later became Lord Mayor of London. She died at his printing house in Lambeth Hill and was apparently buried in the middle aisle of St Benet's, Paul's Wharf, although there are different arrangements in her will, which was made in September 1722 (P.C.C. 11/599, sig. 21).

275   *Prologue, Spoken by Mr. Horden*

> The first Adventurer for her fame I stand,
> The Curtain's drawn now by a Lady's Hand ⎫
> The very Name you'l cry boads Impotence, ⎬
> To Fringe and Tea they shou'd confine their Sence, ⎭
> And not outstrip the bounds of Providence.   5
> I hope then Criticks, Since the Cause is so,
> You'l scorn to Arm against a Worthless Foe,
> But curb your spleen and fall, and trial make,
> How our fair Warrior gives her first Attack.
>   Now all ye chattering Insects straight be dumb,   10
> The Men of Wit and Sense are hither come,
> Ask not this Mask to Sup, nor that to show
> Some Face more ugly than a Fifty Beau,
> Who, if your play succeeds, will surely say,

Some private Lover helpt her on her way,   15
As Female Wit were barren like the Moon,
That borrows all her influence from the Sun.
The Sparks and Beaus will surely prove our Friends
For their good Breeding must make them commend
What Billet Deux so e're a Lady sends.   20
She knew old Thread-bare Topicks would not do, ⎫
But Beaus a Species thinks it self still new, ⎬
And therefore she resolved to Coppy You.   ⎭

4 *Fringe*: making fringes, handiwork   13 *Fifty Beau*: a fifty-year-old man of fashion

276   *To the Author of Agnes de Castro*

Orinda, and the Fair *Astrea* gone,
Not one was found to fill the Vacant Throne
Aspiring Man had quite regain'd the Sway,
Again had Taught us humbly to Obey;
Till you (Natures third start, in favour of our Kind)   5
With stronger Arms, their Empire have disjoyn'd,
And snatcht a Lawrel which they thought their Prize,
Thus Conqu'ror, with your Wit, as with your Eyes.
Fired by the bold Example, I would try
To turn our Sexes weaker Destiny.   10
O! How I long in the Poetick Race,
To loose the Reins, and give their Glory Chase;
For thus Encourag'd, and thus led by you,
Methinks we might more Crowns than theirs subdue.

                                          Dela Manley

                                            (1696)

1 *Orinda ... Astrea*: Katherine Philips, Aphra Behn

277   *Song and Musick, set by*
       Mr. Eccles, *and Sung by Mrs. Leveridge*

Unguarded lies the wishing Maid,
Distrusting not to be betraid;
Ready to fall, with all her Charms,
A shining Treasure to your Arms.

Who hears this Story must believe,   5
No Swain can truer Joy receive.
Since to take Love, and give it too
Is all that Love for Hearts can do.

LADY SARAH PIERS (née ROYDON)
(c.1670–before 1720)

SARAH was the daughter of Matthew Roydon, and married Sir George Piers of Stonepit, near Seal in Kent. Little seems to be known of her life. Her husband was an army captain and Clerk of the Privy Seal. We know of her devoted friendship to Catherine Cockburn, née Trotter, from Cockburn's dedications, Lady Sarah's commendatory poems, and the large number of letters exchanged between them from 1697 to 1709, some of which are published in the collected works of Catherine Cockburn. Delarivier Manley hints broadly that their relationship was a sexual one, but the circumstantial evidence would appear to discredit the notion of an adulterous lesbian affair: Lady Sarah was on excellent terms with her husband (they had two sons, one of whom died in 1707), and her relationship with Catherine Cockburn's husband seems also to have been friendly. Her health was not good, and this, combined with her husband's periodic absences on active service, seems to have led her to frequent watering-places. One of her few surviving poems, written in 1708, is on the beauties who were to be found frequenting the spa-town of Tunbridge Wells.

278   *To my much Esteemed Friend*
       on her Play call'd Fatal-Friendship

With what Concern I sat and heard your Play,
None else can Judge, but such a Friend sure may.
The *Indian* Mother cou'd not feel more pain,
Whose Newborn Babe's thrown headlong in the Main,
To prove him lawful: at whose welcome Rise   5
(Her fears disperst) Joy gushes at her Eyes.
Were I but Judge enough I'd do thee Right,
Though yet much more, I want Poetick flight,
And 'twere his folly to repeat a new
Who light a taper the bright Sun to shew,   10
Shou'd I attempt your Praise, but as a Friend,
T'Express my thoughts, is all that I intend.
Your fable's clear, no rule have you transgrest,
Chast all your thoughts, yet Nature still exprest,
Your numbers flow, as if the Muses all   15
Consulted nothing, but their Rise, and fall,
Your Characters are just, and with such art
Your Passions rais'd, they gain th'unwary heart,
And what you feign, effectually Create,
Who was unmov'd, at sad *Felicia*'s Fate?   20
Scarce cou'd the stubbornest deny their Tears,
All felt your Heroes miseries, as theirs,
But as a faithful Friend, he touch'd me most;
By life's most noble, best of blessings, lost;

O Heaven, this my fondest wish Decree!   25
Our mutual Friendship, may ne'er Fatal be.

3 *Indian Mother*: this ancient trope is ultimately traceable to Aristotle's *Politics*

A YOUNG LADY
(fl. 1691)

THE poems 'Henric to Maria' and 'Maria to Henric' is consciously modelled on Ovid's *Heroides*, narrative poems in the person of a series of mythological great lovers. The *Heroides* attracted considerable interest from women poets in the later seventeenth century, following their translation into English: Aphra Behn composed a version of Ovid's *Oenone to Paris* (included in this anthology, no. 204), and Anne Wharton tackled *Penelope to Ulysses*. The idea of writing a heroidic poem on the reigning King and Queen probably also owes somewhat to Drayton's *England's Heroical Epistles*, which is a series of fictitious verse love-letters exchanged between pairs of English, and mostly royal, lovers. Despite the fact that William was notoriously an admirer of his own sex, Queen Mary was devoted to him, a fact which was widely publicized.

279   *MARIA to HENRIC*

Minutes grow tedious, Time too slowly moves,
While *Henric*'s absent, and *Maria* loves.
Each Hour's a Week, and ev'ry Day a Year,
And ev'ry of *Maria*'s Thoughts a Fear:
Not for thy Faith, my Fears are all for Thee,   5
For that dear Heart that nothing holds but me.
    May I demand, of Love e'er taught Thee yet,
To look on lazy Moments with Regret?
If Love has taught Thee his Account of Time?
If *Henric*'s Love be such a Love as mine?   10
If so, my sighs are justify'd by thine;
If so, you cannot frown, and cannot chuse,
But all I sigh, and all I say excuse;
And wish, and speak, and doubt, and act with me,
If Love like mine in a Male Breast can be.   15
Female our Souls, all Masculine our Love,
Strong is your Sense, feebly your Passions move.
Here shrunk my soul, till my kind careless Pen
Run on to *Henric*'s Name—I liv'd agen.
Henric more Noble than the rest of Men!   20
O happy Thought! O blest Maria's Fate!
He loves, does all above the common Rate.

You busy'd yet with all those great Affairs,
Counsels, Debates, and Policy of Wars;
Safety of Kingdoms, all the Mighty Things,   25
Worthy my *Henric*, fit alone for Kings.
This some relief to painful Absence gives,
Diverts the Pangs wherewith Maria strives.

While You the foaming untam'd Gallia chase,
And all Your Snares around the Tigress place;   30
Pleas'd thus to see her all at Your Command,
Whene'er You please to move Your Conquering Hand:
Suffer not fond *Maria* to complain,
That You forget Your own dear am'rous Chain.

On unfledg'd Vict'ries in the Nest You smile,   35
And great Designs Your Love and Hours beguile:
Alone my business, and my all is You,
My self, my Wishes, all I have to do;
Your Name alone perswades me to endure;
That gives the Wound, and that applies the Cure: 40
But there's no Balsom priz'd by me above
The bright Idea of Your Noble Love.

But if Your Love (pardon the dubious Thought)
If You the gen'rous Flame from *Belgia* brought,
Why could it not perswade You to delay?   45
Why could not parting Tears induce Your stay?
How cruel short the pleasing Interview!
Short as 'twas sweet, as short disgustfull too.
Why was I born so Great, or You so Brave?
Were You less so, or were I but a Slave?   50
My servile Consort I in view might have?
Nor think he's now engag'd, a Conqu'rour now,
Dying, perhaps, with Vict'ry on his Brow,
Wounded, or sick, or e'en I know not how.

Lost *Mons*, the worthy Cause, and *British* Isle,   55
Forgive the Queen, that on Your Loss could smile;
Th'unwelcome News no sooner reached my Ear,
But straight I knew my *Henric* was not there:
No Towns are ever lost when he's too near.
You often come indeed too near Your Foes,   60
Your Breast too oft, too daringly expose;
You are too much a Conquerour for me,
I love You better than the Victory:
Yet I love Conquest, and can wish it too;
But why, methinks, must all be done by You?   65
Let others take the Danger; Let them stake
Their Lives, and let them *Henric*'s Glory take——

Ha! What!——What would my fondling Passion do?
Oh, that it might be Great! as Great as now;
And yet incapable to wrong You too!   70

What's State, Respect, or what's a Crown to me?
Poor Joys!——How poor's a Queen depriv'd of Thee?
My very Dreams, the softest Bliss I knew,
My Thoughts, my Dreams, are still employ'd with You,
Pleasing at first, now serve t'afflict me too.   75
My Bed with sad Apprehension shake,
With sudden Shrieks and Cries I start, and wake:
Attendants and officious Guards rush in,
When nothing but her *Henric* wants the Queen;
Shipwrack'd with Doubts and almost sunk by fear,   80
Least swelling *Neptune* so embrace my Dear,
E'en You that took of me so little Care:

You that expos'd in a small Shallop lay,
Defying *Boreas* and a Raging Sea,
By cruel, deadly Sheets of Ice enclos'd;   85
Hunger, and bold obtruding Death oppos'd:
Yet Your Prophetic Valour could inspire
Your glowing Breast with such Heroic Fire;
The Shell, that *Caesar and his Fortunes* bore,
Was destin'd to attain, and reach'd the Shore;   90
Can You suppose with me to perish more?

Cease not to fear (said You) but blush to think,
That *Henric and his Fortunes* here must sink.
Ye Gods!——The Gods were with Thee, and they saw:
These words were follow'd with a sudden Thaw: 95
And kind Heav'n cast Thee on thy Native Shore,
When nothing less was hop'd, You wish'd no more.

If I, of more cow'rdly Sex, had seen
What mighty Perils shut my *Henric* in,
Away had flown my hasty tim'rous Soul;   100
Nor could that Prophecie, so spoke, recall
My fleeting Breath, restoring as it was,
'T had been, to dying me, of little Force.
The fearful Tale, e'en while I knew You safe,
A strange cold shivering to my Senses gave,   105
Methought, and wrapt me in a chilly Wave.

Be kind, my Love, make haste—Be rather slow
And be my kinder Love in being so.
Be kind, and cautious, let me not sustain
Those Dyings, and those Agonies again.   110
While I implore soft Winds, entreat the Sea

To be as gentle as my Sighs for Thee,
And careful as Maria's Thoughts can be;
Safe as Thy Arms, serene as those You give
Your great Protection to, and wish to live.   115
Live you *Maria*'s, she that lives for You.
All Yours—Adieu, my Royal Love, Adieu.

29 *Gallia*: a personified France   55 *Mons*: Louis XIV personally invested Mons in 1691
and accepted its surrender   61 *daringly*: William was noted for his personal courage in
battle. He was shot at the Battle of the Boyne in 1690, and nearly killed on two subsequent
occasions   83 *Shallop*: on 19 October 1688 William set sail from Helvoetsluys, but the
fleet was scattered in mid-Channel by a storm and gradually had to find its way back home.
It put to sea again on 1 November and landed in England, at Brixham, on the fifth

BATHSHEBA BOWERS
(1672?–1718)

BATHSHEBA BOWERS was born in Charlestown, Massachussets, to English
Quakers, Benanuel Bowers and Elizabeth Dunster, niece of Henry Dunster, the
first president of Harvard. Her parents had twelve children in all, some of whom
died in infancy. They sent their four eldest daughters to Philadelphia to escape
religious persecution. Three of them married there, while Bathsheba remained
single. According to her niece, who wrote an account of her in 1739, she was
crossed in love when she was about 18. She 'seemed to have little respect for
riches but her thirst for knowledge being boundless, after she had finished her
house and Garden, and they were as beautiful as her hands cou'd make them, or
heart could wish, she retired herself in them from Society.' This was presumably *c*.1690. Subsequently, she built a small, architecturally eccentric, house by a
spring of water about half a mile from town, subsequently known as Bathsheba's
Bower. She was deeply impressed by the vegetarian Thomas Tryon, and
adopted his principles. She continued to define herself as a Quaker, but her
independent and argumentative character made her in effect a sort of Quaker
Independent. She also wrote the history of her life, printed it, and distributed it
free to anyone who would take it: sadly no copy is known to survive. A voracious
reader, she owned several volumes 'wrote by a female hand filled with dreams
and visions and a thousand Romantic Notions of her seeing Various sorts of
Beasts and Bulls in the Heavens': these may possibly be the works of Anna
Trapnel, Mary Howgill, or others, now lost, of similar tendencies. She wrote a
spiritual autobiography, *An Alarm Sounded to Prepare . . . the world to meet the
Lord*, published in New York in 1709, probably by the Quaker printer William
Bradford. She believed that she could never die, a belief which was tested when
she moved to South Carolina in the last years of her life, and lived through a
native American attack on her settlement with complete equanimity.

280 *Rev. xxii, v 17*

The Spirit saith, come,
And the Bride saith, come,
And let all that hear, come
And take of the water of life freely.

But Lord, if they will not come   5
Without sin, to salvation, do thou come,
And compel them to come,
That we may altogether come,
And forever sing hallelujah to Thee,
In the 1st, 2nd, 3rd, 4th, 5th, 6th and 7th degree.   10

Amen, saith my soul.

(1709)

ANNE MORCOTT
(fl. 1692)

THE extent of women's involvement with the professional writing of ballads is completely unquantifiable. Ballads were normally, though not always, registered without an author's name: though it it highly probable that many ballads were written by women, this is one of only two which seems certain to be so, so is included here to stand for a whole area of women's literary production. Women were involved at every stage of ballad production from printing and publishing to selling. Seven women publishers of broadsides are named by Claude M. Simpson. Among them, Mary Coles and Elizabeth Deacon succeeded their husbands, but Elizabeth Toy printed in partnership with John Wally, and Elizabeth Millet with Alexander Milbourn, suggesting a more deliberately professional type of involvement. Dianne Dugaw (*Warrior Women and Popular Balladry, 1650–1850* (Cambridge: Cambridge University Press) 23) prints a portrait of Mrs Parker, a well known ballad-singer and seller of the 1680s, by M. Laroon which shows her with Roger Teasdell, her apron pocket stuffed with broadsides, and one in her hand. Another well-known woman who hawked ballads on the streets was called 'Parliament Joan'. When it comes to writing, however, the fact that ballads came out (with very rare exceptions) anonymously means that it is seldom possible to identify any particular ballad as a woman's composition. It is gratifying, therefore, that practically the only ballad we can definitely associate with a woman is a conspicuously successful one. Nothing is known of the author of this broadsheet ballad registered at the Stationer's Hall in 1692. It and its tune were immensely popular and influential. In less than a decade, twenty-five or so ballads called for its air. It was, like most others, printed anonymously, but the first three stanzas were printed in a more literary context, Thomas d'Urfey's *Pills to Purge Melancholy*, which is where the authorship of the words is credited to Anne Morcott. The ballad was written shortly before 4 March 1692, when William set out for his second campaign in the Low Countries.

281   *The Loyal English Man's Wish for*
        the Preservation of the King and Queen

1   Let *MARY* Live long,
        She's Vertuous and Witty,
        All Charmingly Pritty,
    Let *MARY* Live long,
        And Reign many Years.   5
    Now the Clouds is gon o're,
    That Troubled us sore:
        Since the Sun-shine apears,
    We shall be Deliver'd,
    We shall be Deliver'd,   10
        From Fury and Fears.

2   God bless the KING at Home,
        With Laurels to Crown him,
        Each Rebel may own him;
    And may he Live long   15
        And Reign many years;
    Now the Conquest is plain,
    And Three Kingdoms Regain'd;
        Let his Enemies fall,
    Whilst *Cæsar* shall Flourish,   20
    Whilst *Cæsar* shall Flourish,
        In spight of 'em all.

3   All Glorious and Gay,
        Let the KING Live for ever;
        May he Languish never never: 25
    Like Flowers in *May*,
        His Actions smell sweet;
    When the Wars are all done,
    And he safe in his Throne,
        Trophies lay at his Feet,   30
    With loud Acclamations,
    With loud Acclamations,
        His MAJESTY Greet.

4   When for *Flanders* he goes,
        May the Enemy fear him,   35
        When e're they come near him;
    May he Conquer his Foes
        As he did at the *Boyn*,
    May his Army march on
    With the Beat of the Drum,   40
        Whilst *Monsieur* doth Fly,

The *English* shall Follow,
The *English* shall Follow,
And Fight till they Die.

Heav'ns Prosper his Arms,   45
  Both at Home and Abroad
  May he always be Lord,
And Guarded from harms
  By the Powers above;
May his Enemies all   50
At his Feet present fall,
  And their Loyalty prove,
Whilst our KING does Enjoy,
Whilst our KING does Enjoy
  Blest MARY in Love.   55

Printed and Sold by *T. Moore*, 1692

12 *KING*: William III, husband of, and joint monarch with, Mary II, daughter of James II who was deposed in their favour on religious grounds   18 *Three Kingdoms*: England, Scotland, and Ireland   34 *Flanders*: After his victory at the Boyne, William spent most of the next six years campaigning in Europe at the head of a Grand Alliance against Louis XIV. For the campaign of 1692, he persuaded his ministers to raise and support a land force of 65,000—vast, by contemporary standards   38 *Boyn*: The Battle of the Boyne (1690). William III and his Protestant army defeated James II, who escaped to France   41 *Monsieur*: probably the French in general, but possibly James II

ELIZABETH TIPPER
(fl. 1693–8)

ALL that we know of Elizabeth Tipper derives from her own work, *The Pilgrim's Viaticum: or, the Destitute, but not Forlorn*. At the time of writing, Elizabeth Tipper was a poor schoolteacher, dependent on the charity of friends, some of whom she names. *The Athenian Spy* (1704) describes her as the 'True Widow' Tipper, suggesting that she would be an 'ingenious wife... for any Dean or Prebend' (letter XLI, *18ᵛ), which suggests that she had been married (this list of marriageable ladies also includes Mary Astell). Her book seems aimed at attracting the patronage of Anne, Countess of Coventry, third daughter of the Duke of Beaufort, and a friend of Lady Elizabeth Hastings, Lady Catherine Jones, and Mary Astell.

She had some association with John Dunton, who claims to have published some of her work in his *Athenian Mercury* (*Life and Errors* (1818) 292): he is a likely associate for this devout Anglican poetess, since he also published Elizabeth Rowe.

282   *Some Experimental Passages of my*
LIFE, with Reflections upon *Jacob's*
Words, *Few and Evil have the days*
of the years of my Life been.

'Tis strange that he Unborn, ere he saw Light,
Destin'd a Victor, and Heaven's Favourite,
Should almost at the Period of his Age,
Give this relation of his Pilgrimage,
Yet 'tis not strange, since *mortal Life* we see   5
No more from *Sorrow* than from *Death* is free.
My *Life* the assertion much has verifi'd,
From Port to Port, by sad Experience try'd,
In all my *Undertakings* still been crost,
And like a *Ball* from hand to hand been tost,   10
Five Years i'th Prime of all my Youth I spent
Recluse as 'twere from the World, in *banishment*:
And Hermit like in all things did I dwell,
An *uncouth Cottage* serving for my *Cell*;
For several Days and Nights sometimes been driven   15
To *Silence*, save the *Words* I spoke to Heaven.
My constant *Visits* Fields and Woods receiv'd,
Who at my oft resorting never griev'd;
But bounteously with Sunshine, Air, and Shade,
Their frequent *Visitant* still happy made;   20
One dear and courteous Tree, above the rest,
Did oft invite me to become her Guest;
Upon her root I hourly *sate*, and *Read*,
Her towering Branches sheltering my Head;
And when I Kneel'd, the kind officious Grass,   25
The verdant Covering of my Cushion was.
The like Good-will have Hedges to me born,
And distant Furrows of the growing Corn:
To this the Evening oft hath met my *Fast*;
And *Tears* the longest day been my Repast: 30
Yet these *Afflictions*, Lord, more *Joy* I own,
Than have the Vicious, who possess a Throne:
Nor can I at a *Flood* of *Tears* repine,
Till I forget that *Bloody Sea* of Thine:
O grant me *Resignation* till I see   35
How 'tis Thy Pleasure to dispose of me.

My Penance now seem'd something to abate,
And glimering Beams of *Sun-shine* dart from Fate:
Two of my greatest *Wants* at once supply'd,
IMPLOYMENT and SOCIETY beside: 40

My *Happiness* this large Addition found,
New Joys with *Honourable Friendship* crown'd.
No more my *Brow contracted* now appears,
Nor Eye-Balls fretted Red with Briny Tears:
Save when in *Penitence* and *Care* I mourn'd,   45
That GOD's withdrawing *Beams* might be return'd.

This *Sun-shine Fortune* did not long remain,
Ere 'twas eclips'd by a dark Cloud again:
My *Comforts* sever'd by that *Unseen Hand*,
Which *Prosperous* and *Adverse Fate* both command.   50

Then, by the Counsel of a real Friend,
I am advis'd my *Precious Time* to spend
No more in a poor Village, but repair
To a City, try the *Smiles* of *Fortune* there.
What this may signify, 'tis GOD best knows;   55
My *Fortune* ever *Ebbs*, but never Flows.
The Wicked, Careless, Foolish; all I see,
Her *Kindness* have, which is deny'd to me:
'Tis so, Great GOD, and to it I submit,
And all thing, else Thy *Wisdom* shall think fit.   60
This only thing I begg, while I have Breath,
Grant me an HONEST LIFE *and* HAPPY DEATH.

                                        (1698)

283 *To a Young Lady that Desired a Verse of*
      My Being Servant One Day,
      and Mistress Another

More than a King's my Word dos rule to day,
His subjects *His*, my betters *Mine* obey;
Quality, Fortune, Beauty, Virtue, Wit,
Do *Govern* others, but to me *Submit*:.
*To Morrow from this *Dignity* I fall,   5
And am a *Servant* at each *Beck* and *Call*:
Next day I'm *free* in *Liberty* and *Power*,
And, as before, a *Mistress* every *Hour*.

Changeable is my *State*, and yet not strange,
When *Day* to *Night*, and *Light* to *Darkness* change: 10
Yet *Fate* I cannot blame, but justly own,
She, in this *Difference, Evenness* hath shown;
For when I'me *Mistress*, none I can *Command*,
When *Servant*, curbed by no *Imperious Hand*:

This is a *Riddle*, yet here wonder why   15
When all the *World*'s a *Riddle*, why not I?

(1698)

* I teach Ladies Writing and Accompts one day, and keep Shop-Books the other
day, in which Business I am a hired Servant.

ELIZABETH ROWE (née SINGER)
(1674–1737)

ELIZABETH ROWE was the eldest daughter of a dissenting Protestant preacher,
who became a clothier, and moved from her birthplace, Ilchester in Somerset, to
Frome, her home for most of her life. She had two sisters, one of whom died in
childhood, the other at 20. According to the biographical notes provided by her
editor Theophilus Rowe in the 1739 edition of her works, she introduced herself
to the Thynne family of Longleat by means of a little book of verses, when she
was nearly twenty: the Thynnes then took an interest in her, and Mr Thynne,
son of Viscount Weymouth, taught her French and Italian from the poems of
Tasso, which she later translated (Nottingham University Library, Portland MS
Pw V376–83). Henry's daughter Frances, at this time a child but later Countess
of Hertford, was to become a life-long friend and correspondent. Another patron
was the High Church bishop and hymnodist Thomas Ken (then in retirement at
Longleat), while her friends included the Countess of Winchilsea, the fifth Earl
of Orrery, Matthew Prior, and Isaac Watts (who became her literary executor),
all of whom were poets. In 1710 she married the young scholar, Thomas Rowe,
son of a dissenting minister and thirteen years her junior. They moved to
London and settled down to a happy but brief married life. Thomas died of
consumption at Hampstead in 1715. She returned to live at her father's house in
Frome and after his death she inherited substantial property at Frome and
Ilchester, half of the income from which she donated to charity. She corresponded with friends but rarely left Frome, except occasionally at the invitation
of the Countess of Hertford.

She began publishing her poetry in 1691, at first anonymously, in a succession
of journals published by the Athenian Society, not revealing her identity to the
editor, John Dunton, until 1695. Her first book came out, edited by Dunton, in
1696, when she was 22: it is therefore this first collection, rather than her mature
work, with which we are here concerned. Some of these poems were written,
according to Theophilus Rowe, 'when she was at a boarding-school in the
country, or soon after leaving it', and they were omitted from later editions of
her collected verse. In it, the young Elizabeth Singer shows a degree of gaiety
and sense of fun which is not a feature of her later work. It also contains political
poetry (unlike her friend the Countess of Winchilsea, she was a staunch Wil-
liamite), and a number of poetic exchanges with the Athenian Society which
show her revelling in playful, witty exchange with fellow poets. There are also
three separate attempts at paraphrase of parts of the Song of Solomon. Later in
her life, Elizabeth Rowe, always profoundly pious, became increasingly austere.
She became uneasy about her early writings: 'not satisfied to have done nothing

that injur'd the sacred cause of virtue, she was displeas'd with her self for
having writ any thing that did not directly promote it.' (1739, vol. i, xvii).
Nevertheless, it is interesting that there is a picture of Sappho among the
paintings mentioned in her will (P.C.C. 11/682, sig. 67). She died in February
1737 and was buried in the same grave as her father in the meeting-house at
Frome.

284   *To a very Young Gentleman
                at a Dancing-School*

I.

So when the Queen of Love rose from the Seas,
Divinely Fair in such a blest amaze,
Th'inamoured watry Deities did gaze.

II.

As we when charming *Flammin* did suprize,
More heavenly bright our whole *Seraglio*'s eyes;   5
And not a Nymph her wonder could disguise.

III.

Whilst with a graceful Pride the lovely boy,
Pass'd all the Ladies (like a *Sultan*) by,
Only he lookt more absolute and coy,

IV.

When with a Haughty air he did advance,   10
To lead out some transported she to dance,
He gave his hand as carelessly as Chance.

V.

Attended with a Universal Sigh
On her each Beauty cast a Jealous Eye,
And quite fell out with guiltless Destiny.   15

                                        (1696)

285   *The Reflection*

Where glide my thoughts, *rash inclinations stay*,
And let me think what 'tis you fool away,
Stay ere it be to late, yet stay and take,
A short review of the great prize at stake.
Oh! stupid folly 'tis eternal Joy,   5
That I'm about to barter for a toy;

It is my *God* oh dreadful hazard where,
Shall I again the boundless loss repair!
It is my *Soul* a Soul that cost the blood,
And painful agonies of an humbled God,   10
Oh blest occasion made me *stay to think*,
Ere I was hurri'd off the dangerous brink,
Should I have took the charming venom in, ⎫
And cop'd with all *these terrors for a sin*,   ⎬
How equal had my condemnation been?   ⎭

ELIZABETH THOMAS
(1675–1731)

ELIZABETH was the daughter of Emmanuel Thomas of the Inner Temple, and Elizabeth Osborne. Her father died when she was 2, and she was brought up by her mother and her mother's mother in straitened circumstances in lodgings in London. Some details of her biography can be gleaned from the 'Life of Corinna' prefixed to her published collection of letters, *Pylades and Corinna* (171–2). This claims that she was taught a little Latin, writing, mathematics, pharmacy, and chemistry (a list of interests which she held in common with a number of early modern literary women, notably Jane Barker). She more certainly read French, since some translations from French are included in her *Miscellany Poems on Several Subjects* (1722). The first symptom of Elizabeth Thomas's literary ambition is that she initiated a correspondence with Dryden in the summer of 1699 by sending him two poems to criticize, of which 'The Dream' is probably one. He responded graciously in November 1699: 'you want neither Vigour in your Thoughts, nor Force in your Expressions, nor Harmony in your Numbers and methinks I find much of Orinda in your Manner (to whom I had the Honour to be related, and also to be known)' (*Miscellanea*, i. 149). It was Dryden who dubbed her 'Corinna', after the most famous Greek woman poet after Sappho. It may be relevant that whereas Sappho was remembered for exquisite short lyrics, Corinna's reputation was for long, complex poems: Byzantine scholars claim that she vanquished Pindar in open competition on one occasion. On the strength of this association with Dryden, she contributed to one of the several elegies in honour of Dryden after his death the following year, *Luctus Britannici* (1700). A further consequence of this was that she attracted Richard Gwinnet ('Pylades'), to whom she was engaged for the next seventeen years; their marriage was postponed while Gwinnet battled with consumption, Elizabeth Thomas nursed her mother through breast cancer, and presumably, the pair tried to get together enough money on which to marry. During this lengthy period, she inadvertently became something of a medical curiosity when she swallowed 'the middle Bone of the Wing of a large Fowl', fell into a 'most violent bloody Flux', and experienced a variety of other bizarrre and unpleasant sequelae. She was treated with mercury, and in 1713, sent to Bath for 'Relief by Pumping'. Gwinnet died in 1717, and bequeathed her £600, but it took an eight-year lawsuit to recover any of this money: all she was able to get, after that, was £213. Meanwhile, her mother died in January 1719, leaving her in debt. In 1727 she was sent to the Fleet prison for debt, and remained there until July 1730. She died destitute in lodgings in Fleet Street in February 1731.

In addition to her friendship with Dryden, Elizabeth Thomas was associated with a variety of distinguished writers. She was friendly with Lady Mary Chudleigh, author of the *Ladies' Defence* (Marissa), Mrs Diana Bridgeman (Musidora), Anne, Lady Dowager De La Warr (Sulpitia), Lady Hester Pakington, and Mary Astell, to whom she wrote a poem as Almystrea (an anagram of her name, also used by Lady Chudleigh) *c.*1700, in response to her defence of women, *A Serious Proposal* (1694). It was Lady De La Warr's daughter-in-law who paid for her burial, which suggests that she may been seen as to some extent a client of Lady De La Warr senior.

286   *The Dream. An Epistle to Mr* Dryden.

When yet a Child, I read great Virgil o'er,
And sigh'd, to see the barb'rous Dress he wore;
The Phrase how awkward, how abstruse the Sense!
And how remote from *Roman* Eloquence!
And mov'd, to see his lofty Epick Rhymes   5
By murd'ring Pens debas'd, to doggerel Chimes;
Ye sacred Maids, cried I, How long? and why
Must *Virgil* under *English* Rubbish lye?
He, who can charm in this Exotick Dress,
What Beauties must his native Tongue express?   10
Ah barren Isle! not One, one gen'rous Quill,
To give Him whole, will none exert their skill,
But who translate incorrigibly ill?

    Then pausing here, I fell into a Dream
If I may call it such? and this the Theam.   15
Methoughts I did the *Delphick Fane* behold,
The Doors, and Roof, were all of burnish'd Gold,
The Floor, and Walls of *Parian* Stone were built,
And these, with ductile Gold, were finely gilt,
Above three Hundred Lamps shone in the Place,   20
And twice six Altars, did the Temple grace;
A golden Tripos, in the Midst arose;
But O! what Pen it's Lustre can disclose?
So nicely grav'd, so lively ev'ry Part,
Nature her self was here out done by Art.   25
The meanest Basis was of costly Wood,
And, on it's Summit, bright *Apollo* stood:
An azure Mantle did his arms invest,
His golden Lyre, he held before his Brest.
A Silver Bow was on his Shoulder bound,   30
And with chaste *Daphne's* Leaves, his Head was crowned.

Ruddy his Cheeks, and flowing was his Hair,
All dazling bright he look'd, and exquisitly Fair.
Around him, sage *Memoria's* Daughters sat;
And all the Graces at his right Hand wait.   35
Then up *Calliope* arose, who sings
Of mighty Poets; and of mighty Kings:
Her lovely Breast, with her fair Hand she stroke,
And after due Obeisance, thus she spoke.

   Thou *Great Director* of our Triple Trine!   40
Thou, who instructed us, and made us thine!
Hast thou forgotten? when my first born Son,
My dearest *Orpheus*, *Pluto's* Favour won;
And how, for too much Kindness to his Wife,
He was by *Bacchannals* depriv'd of Life;   45
Who tore his Limbs, in *Hebrus* cast his Head,
Which sweetly sang his Elogy tho' Dead?
'Twas then, you chear'd me, bid me dry my Eyes,
And said, from me, another Swan should rise:
When *Virgil's* born, he shall thy Joys restore,   50
And, for thy *Orpheus*, thou shalt weep no more.
'Twas said! 'tis done! and Virgil calm'd my Breast,
With *Eagles* Wings, he soar'd above the Rest;
And *Orpheus* Spirit, doubly he possest.
But now twelve Cent'ries past, I've cause to mourn,   55
To see my *Virgil's* Works thus maul'd and torn,
By *French*, *Dutch*, *English*, and each stupid Drone,
Burlesq'd, obscur'd, and in Travesty shown.
Poor mercenary Pens attempt for Gain,
And hungry Wits his sacred Lines profane;   60
'Tis thus they sully, thus disgrace his Name;
And not one gen'rous Bard, is left to clear his Fame.
Hold! he reply'd, there's one has Sense and Truth,
That is my Creature, he shall right the Youth,
New polisht *Maro*; *Maro's* soul express;   65
And cloath him in a more becoming Dress.
And thou bold Girl! (to me) hast done amiss,
To call that barren where my *Dryden* is;
He whom I have ordain'd, by certain Doom,
To honour *Britain*, more, than *Virgil Rome*:   70
And with the self same voice, Eternal Fame,
Dryden and *Virgil's* glory shall proclaim.

   The grateful Muse, profoundly bow'd her Head,
And I still trembling, wak'd, at what was said:
Dryden cried I! ev'n then, I knew your Name;   75
(For who was Ignorant of *Drydens* Fame?)
'Tis he! 'tis only he the Work must do,

Then in some Years I found the Vision true,
And swiftly caught the Blessing as it flew.
The Death of Friends, first gave my Muse a Birth,   80
But you, Sir, rais'd her grov'ling from the Earth:
You taught her Numbers; and you gave her Feet;
And you set Rules, to bound Poetick Heat:
If there is ought in me deserves that Name,
The Spark was light at mighty *Drydens* Flame: 85
But ne'er yet blest with my great Master's Sight.
I fear you'll think it Impudence to write.
Forgive me *Sir*, I long'd to let you know
How much your Pupil to your Works does owe;
Her Muse is yours, and is at your Command,   90
But envies those that in your presence stand.

(1699)

16 *Delphick Fane*: temple of the oracle at Delphi, sacred to Apollo   18 *Parian Stone*: marble   31 *Daphne's Leaves*: laurel   34 *Memoria's Daughters*: the Muses, daughters of memory   36 *Calliope*: Muse of epic   38 *stroke*: struck   40 *Triple Trine*: the nine Muses   43–7 *Orpheus*: famous singer of Greek myth, went to Hades to try and rescue his wife Eurydice. When he failed, he rejected human society, and the female followers of Bacchus, offended by his indifference, tore him to pieces and threw his still-singing head into the river Hebrus   65 *Maro*: Virgil's full name was Publius Vergilius Maro

287   *To Almystrea on her Divine Works*

Hail happy *Virgin*! of celestial Race,
Adorn'd with *Wisdom*! and repleat with *Grace*!
By *Contemplation* you ascend above,
And fill your Breast with true seraphic Love.
And when you from that sacred Mount descend,   5
You give us Rules our Morals to amend:
Those *pious Maxims* you your self apply,
And make the Universe your *Family*.
No more, Oh Spain! thy Saint Teresa boast,
Here's one out-shines her on the British Coast;   10

Directs as well, and regulates her Love,
But in that Sphere, with greater Force doth move.
Whose Soul like hers! view'd its Almighty End!
And to that Center, all its Motions tend:
Like her! the glorious Monuments doth raise,   15
Beyond male Envy! or a female Praise!

Too long! indeed, has been our Sex decryed
And ridicul'd by Men's malignant Pride;
Who fearing of a just Return forbore,
And made it criminal to teach us more.   20

That Women had no Souls, was their Pretence,
And Women's Spelling past for Women's Sense
When you, most generous Heroine! stood forth,
And show'd your Sex's Aptitude and Worth.
Were it no more! yet you bright Maid alone,   25
Might for a World of Vanity Atone!
Redeem the coming Age! and set us free!
From the false Brand of Incapacity.

(after 1694)

9 *Teresa*: St Teresa of Avila (1515–82), famed as writer, mystic, and reformer

ANGHARAD PRITCHARD, née JAMES
(1677–1749)

ANGHARAD JAMES was the ancestor of several of the most eminent Nonconformist preachers of the nineteenth century, and is therefore less obscure than
most Welsh-language women poets. Family traditions recorded in a book on her
great-grandson John Jones Talsarn represent her as a forceful character,
prominent in her neighbourhood, well-educated in classics and the law, a
prolific poet, and a fine harpist (Owen Thomas, *Cofiant John Jones Talsarn*
(Wrexham 1874), 24–5). Several of her poems, including the one given here,
were intended to be sung to well-known tunes. Some of her poems are dated to
the first two decades of the eighteenth century, but it seems reasonable on
grounds of content to ascribe this one to the period before her marriage to
William Pritchard in 1701. Since he was nearly forty years older than she was,
her desire for a mature husband seems to have been fulfilled—it is also possible
that her marriage was already being planned at the time when it was written.
Pritchard died in 1718/19, and her only son Dafydd died in 1729 at the age of
16. A poem expressing her grief at Dafydd's death survives in two manuscripts
now in Cardiff Library.

Angharad James's own library included several books in Latin, a Bible, and a
prayer book heavily annotated in her own hand, as well as a manuscript 'Llyfr
Coch' (Red Book) containing her own and other poets' verses. Ceridwen Lloyd
Morgan has argued that Angharad James must be seen as an educated woman
and an active participant in Welsh literary culture: the reason that her work
remained unpublished is that, like many of her contemporaries, she did not
privilege print media over manuscript and oral forms of dissemination (*Barn* 313
(1989), 14–16). A handful of Angharad James's verses survive, mostly in one or
two versions scattered through National Library of Wales MSS 9B, 436V, and
Cwrt Mawr 436D.

288 *Ymddiddan rhwng Dwy chwaer*
un yn Dewis Gwr oedrannus; ar llall yn
Dewis Ieuaingctydd, iw canu ar fedle fawr

[M.J.]
Byd drwy drafferth heb fawr afiaeth, a'r rhan fwya
Yn rhoddi ei gobeth ar goweth soweth sydd
Rhai yn union o chwant Mamon, am rwi'n coelio
O an-fodd Calon drwy foddion drwg di fudd
Yn wir o'm rhan tra fyddw' i byw   5
Yn era Duw mi gara
Yr hardda ei bryd yn wir heb wad
Yw newis gariad gora
Cael glas-lange mwyn Ifangc mewn aflaeth ydiw 'mryd
Yn ddedwydd a'r gynnydd dda beunydd yn y Byd.   10

[A.J.]
Os wyt Began mor ben chwiban, a mund i garu
Hogiau pur lan anniddan fydd dy fyd
Nid wrth ynadroddion ofer Ddynion, y mae coelio
Eitha ei Calon a'i Moddion hoywon byd
Y Gwr Ifangc tecca ei ddawn   15
Bydd anodd iawn ei ddirnad
Fe dry ei ffydd pan ddel yn ffraeth
Dan Gwlwm Caeth offeiriad
Fe a'n Gostog afrowiog Wr tonnog sirie tynn
Heb Wenn mi chweru and hynny mwy am hynn.   20

[M.J.]
Ow na choeliwch ar hyfrydwch, ma'i Gwyr Ifangc
Au diddanwch yn harddwuch tegwch Tir
Perl Aur Gemau purion Tlysau, dethol ran dawn
Daeth or India howddgarau gorau Gwir
Ni chongcweria dim yn siwr   25
Mo londid Gwr a'i fodde
Y fi mi chara hon ddyn byth
Tra bytho chwyth i'm Gene
Dau mwynach na chleiriach yn swbach afiach yw
Cael Hencyn Ireiddwyn pan felyn teg i fyw   30

[A.J.]
Cymer Gyngor meinir weddol os iw dy fwriad
Yn arferol bu'n raddol i ble yr eir
Na fed yn gynta cyn cynhaya, gwaetha y prifia
Y Dwysen Lasa a Gwag-ca coelia y Ceir
Yr yd addfetta yw'r gore yn siwr   35
Ag fella Gwr mewn oedran

Drwg iw d'amcan am wr da
Yn wir debyga'i Began
Ceir ddewis un Ddilys un moddus gweddus gwar
Di falchedd go sobredd da rinwedd Cyrredd ear   40

[M.J.]
Henaint go brydd aiff yn heubren, rydwi'n tybied
Hyn fy hunan mae gwaetha iw'ch amcan chwi
Gwell Cymdeithas llangc pereiddlas, nid yw'ch Cyngor
Ond rhy ddiles im pwrpas addus i
Yr impin iredd braf o bryd   45
Yw'r goreu ei gyd a gare
Mae fy mwriad i gyd ddwyn
A'i ffedwl mwyn au fodde
Cyn mentro ynrwymo ar un pan grycho'r grudd
Mi brofa mi ymgroesa yn wir mi arhosa yn rhydd   50

[A.J.]
Gwiliwch fynyd gam gmeryd, Mae ich mawrfryd
Yn eich gwynfyd i gael dedwydd fyd da
Pam Brioder chwi a rhyw swagor, yn gwit y derfydd
Yr holl fwynder ar gwychder hoywder ha
Odid un pan bwyso'r Byd   55
Na newidia ei bryd ai fodde
Ni welir Gwen fel yr ydoedd gynt
Yn siccir bun Eglur in welir feinir fael
Y sobre'n mwyneiddia a fuase gore ei gael.

Angharad James ai Canodd a'r Ymddiddan a fu rhyngthi ai chwaer
    Margared James

(*written in the margin alongside the penultimate verse*)
Duw gadwo i mi fel dyma'r gwr
A garu yn hir o Amser
Ag i Farged lysti langc
o swagriwr Ifangc ofer. A.J.

288   *A Conversation between two sisters,*
      one choosing an aged man, and the other
      choosing youth, to be sung to the great medley.

[M.J.]
It is a wicked world of toil without much mirth, and the multitude
Put their hopes on riches, alas.
Some lust entirely for Mammon, I believe,
Reluctant of heart, by wicked and unprofitable means.
Truly, for my part, as I live,   5
In God's name will I love.

The loveliest in appearance, truly, undeniably,
Is my best chosen sweetheart.
To have a fresh and gentle young lad, full of zest, is my desire,
Content and thriving daily in the world   10

[A.J.]

If you, Began, are so dizzy as to go and love
pure and fine lads, you will be malcontent.
It is not by words of insincere men that
the extent of their hearts and their fine worldly means are to be believed.
The most talented of young men   15
will be very diffcut to comprehend.
His faith will flee when he comes swiftly
under the binding knot of the priest;
He will become an ill-natured cur, an inconstant man of mean words
without a smile, he will become embittered but for this more than that.   20

[M.J.]

O! don't become vexed over beauty. Young men
and their amusements are the beauty and fairness of the land.
Pearl, gold, pure gems, jewels, select in talent,
from India adored things, the best indeed.
To be sure, nothing conquers   25
the beauty of a man and his means.
Me, I will never love an old man
while there is breath in my jaws.
Doubly better than having a decrepit man, wizened and unhealthy, is
to have a fresh and pale lad, yellow-haired and fair to live with.   30

[A.J.]

Take my advice comely girl, if your intent
is usual, do not be hasty to reach your goal
Don't reap early before harvest; the worst to grow
is the unripe ear of corn, and, believe it, it will be the emptiest.
For sure enough, the ripest corn is the best,   35
and so too a man of maturity.
Your notion of a good husband is bad,
truly, that's my opinion, Began.
Try to choose correctly, one courteous, proper, genteel,
humble, very sober, of good virtue, an honest friend.   40

[M.J.]

A very weak geriatric will become a hollow tree; I personally believe
that your notion is the worst one.
The company of a sweet youth is better; your advice is
too useless for my genial purpose.
The succulent shoot, with pleasant features   45
is the best of all who love.
It is my intention to bear with
his gentle mind and manners,
before venturing to tie the knot with any man when his cheek wrinkles
I will put it to the test, I will cross myself, I will indeed remain free. 50

[A.J.]

Beware a moment, lest you err. It is your great desire
in your blissful ignorance to find contentedness and goodness.
When you are married to some Lothario, all your bliss
splendour and summer gaiety will quickly cease.
There is a hardly a man who does not change his   55
nature and manners when circumstances are pressing
A smile will not be seen as it was before.
'Tis sure, bright girl, a rich girl does not see the gain that is to be had
from
the gentlest, the soberest that would be the best to have

A.J. composed this and the dialogue occurred between her and her sister
M.J.

May God reserve for me this man
that I would love for a long time;
and for Margaret, a lusty youth,
a young and vain swaggerer.
A.J.

CATHERINE COCKBURN (née TROTTER)
(1679–1749)

CATHERINE TROTTER was the daughter of David Trotter, a naval commander,
and Sarah Ballenden. Her father died of the plague on an expedition to Scanderoon
when she was 4, and thereafter, Catherine, her sister, and her mother lived on a
precarious system of pensions, and subventions from relatives. She was taught
some Latin and logic, and learned French on her own. While still a child, she
surprised her family with some extempore verses on an incident that she observed
in the street. Her first attempt to earn her own living was as a lady companion. She
was politically a Jacobite, and, although she was brought up as a Protestant, she
converted to Catholicism (the religion of her mother's family) as a young woman.
She made her public début at the age of only 14, in 1693, with verses addressed to
the Jacobite poet and historian, Bevil Higgons, on the occasion of his recovery from
smallpox, and an epistolary novel, *Olinda's Adventures, or, the Amours of a Young
Lady*. Her writing was evidently connected with the need to earn money. *Olinda's
Adventures* was successful enough to be translated into French. In 1695, her first
play was produced, the blank verse tragedy *Agnes de Castro*, based on Aphra Behn's
translation of a French short story, and saluted by Delarivier Manley (a favour
which she promptly returned with a gratulatory poem on the latter's *The Royal
Mischief*, published the following year). *Agnes de Castro* was a success, and gained
her some credit as a writer, as well as making money. Her most successful drama,
The Fatal Friendship, was produced at Lincoln's Inn Fields in 1697, and she wrote
three more plays thereafter, but in the early 1700s, she began to be more interested
in philosophy. Her first work in this area was *A Defence of Mr Locke's 'Essay of
Human Understanding'*. Locke was impressed: he sent her a present of books and a
typically gallant letter of thanks. Lady Masham was less generous: she implied, in a
letter to Leibnitz, that Trotter's arguments were not her own. At the age of 22

Trotter left London and settled in Salisbury, Wiltshire, at the house of Dr Inglis, her sister's husband. There she became very friendly with Bishop Burnet and formed a close relationship with his learned wife. Burnet was later to discuss her poetry with Sophia Carlotta, Queen of Prussia, who expressed herself intrigued by the 'Scotch Sappho'.

In 1707, Trotter returned to the Church of England and early in 1708 she married a Scots minister, Patrick Cockburn, curate of St Dunstan's in Fleet Street. At this point, she 'bid adieu to the muses' and concentrated on bringing up her children, although from 1727 (the year in which she and her husband moved to Aberdeen) until her death, she resumed her writing on philosophical topics. Cockburn lost his benefice by his refusal to take the Oath of Abjuration and was reduced to employment as a Latin teacher at a school in Chancery Lane. Cockburn was finally persuaded to take the oath in 1726 and in the following year he was appointed Minister of the Episcopalian Church in Aberdeen. He also accepted the stipend for the parish of Long Horseley, near Morpeth, Northumberland, for over nine years without ever visiting the place. In 1737 the Bishop of Durham took note of his absenteeism, and Cockburn was obliged to abandon Aberdeen and resettle his family at Long Horseley. Catherine was buried in the church there: her tomb bears the inscription 'Let their Works Praise them in the Gates. Prov. xxxi.31'. According to Mrs Manley, whose account of her in the *New Atalantis* (1707) was written after they had become inveterate enemies, she was the lesbian lover of 'Zara', identified in the contemporary key as Catherine Sedley, Countess of Dorchester (*Kissing the Rod: An Anthology of Seventeenth-Century Women's Verse* (London: Virago, 1988) 445) (though Greer *et al.* suggest that Lady Sarah Piers, whose affection for her was publicly acknowledged, is the more likely candidate), and despite her air of virtue, also had a number of male lovers during her youthful career as a professional writer. This is probably slander, but suggests at least that the milieu she moved in as a semi-independent young woman of letters was radically different from that which she inhabited in Aberdeen. Some of her correspondence and literary papers are in the British Library, Add MSS 4264–67, 4371.

289   *Verses sent to Mr Bevil Higgons,*
       On his Sickness and recovery from
       the Small-pox, in the Year 1693

Cruel disease! Can there for beauty be
Against thy malice no security?
Must thou pursue her to this choice retreat?
Enough thy triumphs in her wonted seat,
The softer sex, whose epithet is fair;   5
How coudst thou follow or suspect her here?
But beauty does, like light, itself reveal;
No place can either's glorious beams conceal.

   Thine, as destructive flames, too fatal shin'd,
And left no peace in either sex's mind.   10
The men with envy burn'd, and ev'n the fair,

When with their own, thy matchless charms compare,
Doubt, if they should or love, or envy most,   ⎫
A finer form than they themselves can boast: ⎬
Repine not, lovely youth, if that be lost.   ⎭   15
What hearts it gain'd thee! 'Twas no pride to please, ⎫
To whom that part was lost, which no disease,   ⎬
Nor time, nor age, nor death itself can seize.   ⎭
That part, which thou for ever will retain,
Fewer, but nobler victories will gain   20
And what all felt, when you in danger were,
Shews us how needful to our peace you are.

   When death stood menacing the stroke so near,
That as on certain ills, we left to fear,
Grief seem'd to dart at once a speedier blow,   25
For less of life appear'd in us, than you;
Nor could you doubt our truth, all hearts were known,
Artless and open to you as your own.
Who feign'd to love you, now no longer would,
And who had hid their love, no longer could,   30
What prudence, fear, or modesty conceal'd,
The force of grief like tortures soon reveal'd:
Nor was the highest blam'd for an excess,
All own'd the moving cause deserv'd no less
Whate'er philosophers of old had taught,   35
Here the most sensible was wisest thought.
Silent they wept, nor ceas'd their flowing tears,
Unless to offer more availing prayers,
To which thy life the gracious powers grant,
For fears and prayers make threat'ning heav'n relent.   40

   Go on, brave youth, in all the noblest arts,
And every virtue; exercise thy parts.
The world much will expect, and claim from thee,
But most thy gratitude is due to me,
Who' tho' of numbers, that thy friendship claim,   45
The least recorded in the leaves of fame,
The last in worth, am yet the first to show
What for thy safety we to heav'n owe,
Perhaps the only: less mankind incline
T'acknowledge favors, than at ills repine.   50

   Of ten diseas'd, who heav'nly medicine gain'd, ⎫
Tho' all importunate alike complain'd,   ⎬
And equal all the cure they sought, obtain'd,   ⎭
But one return'd, and he like me unknown,
The blessing giv'n with grateful joy to own.   55

                  (1693)

290   *To Mrs.* Manley. *By the Author*
        of Agnes de Castro.

Th' Attempt was brave, how happy your success,
The Men with shame our Sex with Pride confess;
For us you've vanquisht, though the toyl was yours,
You were our Champion, and the Glory ours.
Well you've maintain'd our equal right in Fame,   5
To which vain Man has quite engrost the claim:
I knew my force too weak, and but assay'd ⎫
The Borders of their Empire to invade,   ⎬
I incite a greater genius to my aid: ⎭
The war begun you generously pursu'd,   10
With double Arms you every way subdu'd,
Our Title clear'd, nor can a doubt remain   ⎫
Unless in which you'll greater Conquest gain, ⎬
The Comick, or the loftier Tragick strain, ⎭
The Men always o'ercome will quit the Field,   15
Where they have lost their hearts, the laurel yield.

                                        (1696)

MARGARET MAULE, COUNTESS OF
PANMURE, née DOUGLAS,
(*c.*1667 – 1731)

THIS poem comes from a packet of 'Verses of my own making' by Margaret
Countess of Panmure, all of them dating from the eighteenth century apart from
the quatrain given here. The archive would undoubtedly repay further study.
Margaret was the youngest daughter of William Douglas (1633–94), who succeeded to the Dukedom of Hamilton by his marriage to Anne (1632–1716), *suo
jure* Duchess of Hamilton. She was a deeply pious woman of Presbyterian
sympathies and attempted to moderate the government's persecution of the
Covenanters before the revolution of 1688. Margaret received a Classical education; that much is clear from the many notes in her own handwriting that appear
on the Latin books in the Panmure library. In 1687 she married James Maule (b.
*c.*1658), Earl of Panmure, a Protestant Jacobite who refused to take the oath of
allegiance to William III. (Margaret's father, conversely, had been one of the
first nobles to desert James II.) Their union was a dynastic alliance, but it was
also a marriage of minds. Margaret, Panmure, and his brother, Harry, were a
notably cultivated family. They were patrons of early neo-classical architecture:
in 1701 the Earl helped to provide a fund to enable his architect Alexander
Edward, to travel through England and Flanders 'for takeing draughts of the
most curious and remarkable houses'. A 'volaire' was added to the exterior of the
new mansion at Panmure and at Brechin Castle they erected park walls with an
outer gate, on the top of which were two great urns. The Panmures also

possessed a substantial collection of musical manuscripts (Edinburgh, National Library of Scotland, MSS 9447–76; for a related collection see MS 9450).

The Panmures adhered with principled stubbornness to one of the family mottoes, *Curo, Pugno, Parco* ('Do, Fight, Forbear'). The Earl 'came out' for James III in the 'Fifteen' and fought at the Battle of Sheriffmuir, where the failure to achieve an outright victory virtually finished the rebellion. In January he entertained James III (the Old Pretender) at Brechin Castle and then, a little later, he followed him into exile. He was indicted for high treason, and his estates were forfeited to the Crown. They were the largest of all the confiscated Jacobite properties. (These estates were eventually recovered for the family by his nephew, William Maule, in 1764.) The Earl died of pleurisy at Paris, in 1723, to be 'succeeded' by Harry, also a Jacobite exile (officially the Panmures had been stripped of all their honours). In their absence, Lady Panmure took over the management of the family's affairs, which she conducted with knowledge and skill. Several of her letters survive. They display a 'great knowledge of human nature and a keen perception of the ludicrous'. She died at Edinburgh in 1731.

291   *'Now let us unto some fair Medow goe'*

> Now let us unto some fair Medow goe
> That wee to other, our love may show
> And there let us in union dwell
> That none may us in good excell.

(1690s?)

'These verses were made when I was 10 years of Age and which my father alwayes wore in his pocket.'

AMEY HAYWARD
(fl. 1699)

'Mrs Amey Hayward, of Limmingtoon' is known only from her book of verses, a collection of religious meditations. There is no indication in them of why she took to print, or which of England's Limingtons or Leamingtons was her home. Her work is addressed to other women, warning them to behave in a godly and upright manner, and devote their thoughts to religious meditation.

292   *A Spiritual Meditation upon a Bee*

> 1. My Soul is like to a little painful Bee
>   To build her *Combs* in Jesus Christ doth flee,
>   And if she willing is to live and thrive,
>   Then she must haste, and get into her *Hive*:

2. Because her *Hive* is in a Garden fair,   5
   Wherein she gather many, and never spare,
   Of blossoms sweet, and Flowers fragrant;
   There is enough to give her full content.

3. My *Bee* with *Honey* there may fill her *Combs*,
   To keep her in the windy Winter-storms: 10
   Because in Winter forth she cannot go,
   By reason of the pinching Frost and Snow:

4. But when the Summer-season is come in,
   My little painful *Bee* is on the Wing;
   Abroad she flys then with a joyful mind,   15
   To work on each sweet Blossom she can find.

5. Over the sweetest Flower she will hover,
   And there she will her painfulness discover;
   And when she's Load, she to her *Hive* will hye,
   To Treasure up her Lading Joyfully,   20

6. To fill her Combs against the time of need,
   That she upon her Honey then may feed;
   But if my Bee a Shower should espy,
   Into her Hive away she then must hye;

7. For if that she doth long the time delay,   25
   The Rain my drive my *Bee* out of her way;
   But while my painful *Bee*, she is at work,
   The *Hornet* and the *Whasp* for her doth lurk,

8. To catch my *Bee*, her *Honey* for to take,
   And then of my poor *Bee* a prey to make: 30
   But if my *Bee* she should become a drone,
   My Bee will quickly then be left alone.

9. Out of the Hive forthwith they will her beat,
   Because their Honey she no more shall Eat;
   And of her Life they soon will her bereave,   35
   Because with them she shall no more receive;

10. For while they laboured to fill each Comb,
   She lost her Sting, and so became a drone:
   Therefore my Soul, do not to sloath incline;
   But labour now, the precious time is thine;   40

11. For if thou should'st be sluggish, and delay,
   Then wo will be to thee another day:
   Labour therefore, to get in Christ, thy Hive;
   There's *Honey* store, which will keep thee alive:

12. And be not thou like to the idle drones,   45
   Which lye and languish in their empty Combs;

Take care in building, 'tis a curious Art,
In building *Combs*, each Bee to have his part;

13. And do not build thy *Combs* confusedly,
     So at the last there is no room for thee;   50
     If thou dost build with Hay, *Wood*, or with Stubble,
     It will bring thee into confused trouble:
     But unto higher things thou must aspire;
     For that is Fuel fit but for the Fire.

The Author's Request

The Stock of Honey now for which I trade,   55
Oh that it may unto me so be made,
Like the increase of the widdow's Oyl,
Which in the Widdow's Vessel ne'er did fail
Until that she in full her debts had paid,
As it is in the Holy-Scripture said.   60

1 *painful*: diligent   58 1 Kings 17: 14

ANONYMOUS ('A LADY OF HONOUR')
(fl. 1699)

THE Scotswoman who wrote *The Golden Island* was seeking to raise support for a Scottish settlement in Panama (the 'Darien Scheme'). This was Scotland's principal attempt to jump on the bandwagon of colonialism, following the model provided by the English East India Company, and was one of the last gestures towards an economically independent Scotland before the Union with England of 1707. The 'Company of Scotland trading to Africa and the Indies' was set up in 1695: its charter gave the Company a monopoly of Scots trade with Asia, Africa, and America for thirty-one years and authorized them to take possession of uninhabited territories. The enterprise began with high hopes. Unfortunately, all that remained to take possession of in the New World after the English, the French, and the Spanish had had their pickings was the isthmus of Panama, directly on the Equator, almost entirely without resources, and rife with yellow fever and other lethal tropical diseases. *The Golden Island* belongs to the second wave of Scots settlement in Panama, which arrived there in November 1699; the first having been almost entirely destroyed by disease.

The poem is a classic example of the literature of heroic colonization; like a miniature of Camoes' *Lusiad*: problems, if any, were with other European countries, while the South is perceived as straightforwardly open to exploitation. The discourse of the poem is also powerfully influenced by the myth of the 'Golden Age', when nature, animal and vegetable, simply offered itself for human consumption. The hedgehog, with its prickles loaded with fruit, also suggests that the Lady's reading had included material derived from medieval bestiaries, such as Topsell's *Historie of Four Footed Beastes*. The poem also records a brief moment in political history when a number of people in both

Scotland and the Netherlands were thinking in terms of a cross-channel alliance against the English (whom the Dutch had recently defeated in the Battle of the Medway).

293 *The Golden Island or the Darian Song.*
In commendation of All Concerned in that
Noble Enterprise Of the Valiant Scots,
by a Lady of Honour.

Some slumbring thoughts possess'd my brain,
   was Prophecied of Old,
That Albanie should Thrissels spread,
   o're all the Indian Gold.
Me thought I heard the Valiant Scots,   5
   beneath the Northern Poll,
Rejoycing of their Prosperous Voyage
   which England did Control.
The Heavens did Favour them so Fair,
   they were into Deaths Jaws,   10
And *Neptune* bowed the loftie Seas,
   and humbled all her Waves,
Untill the Ransomed should pass
   that ventured on the Main,
The English Great, then ventured twice,   15
   and were beat back again.
Sol, Luna, Mars, and *Jupiter*,
   Heavens Canopie did keep,
Be sure some Angel stier'd our Helm,
   when some were faln a sleep: 20
To guide us to that Noble place,
   was promis'd us before,
That will Enrich brave Albanie,
   which Fame does still adore:
It is ordain'd in Holy Write,   25
   Death pay'd our Sacrifice;
The *Thristle* and the *Reed Lyon*
   will Crush our Enemies.
We're Antipods to England now,
   win by a pleasant Toil: 30
We've saild the Gulph against the Tyde,
   come to a Fruitfull Soil.
Who can express what we expect,
   since we are favoured so,
The Lord has thought upon our flight;   35
   some thought to make us low.

All Men that has put in some Stock,
　　to us where we are gone;
They may expect our Saviors words
　　a Hundered reap for One;   40
For to Encourage every One
　　that ventures on the Main,
Come cast thy Bread on Waters great,
　　thou'lt get it back again.
The world durst never *Scotland* Brag,   45
　　for Valour and Renown:
Go pass the Line surrownd the Glob,
　　not such an Ancient Crown.
What One has slighted us before,
　　not want of Honour sure,   50
Brave Noble Spirits in Ancient Land
　　onlie is called Poor.
Our Enemies has the Sun shine
　　so well we know our Foes?
But the *Thrissil* in the *Lyons* hand,   55
　　'gainst *Leopards* and the *Rose*;
The Lord will mend the Broken Reed,
　　and will not *quench the spark*:
Our Enemies shall all fall down
　　as Dagon before the Ark.   60
Fortune put on her Gilded Sails,
　　went to the Antipods:
Heathens receiv'd us with a Grace,
　　as if we had been Gods.
The Gales blew sweet, we Bless the Lord,   65
　　for all our sails were full,
King William did Encourage us
　　against the *English* will.
His words is like a Statly Oak,
　　will neither Bow nor Break;   70
We'll venture Life and Fortune both,
　　for Scotland and his sake.
For he has done such valiant Acts,
　　What Pen can him express?
Lay down your Crowns and Battens all,   75
　　that came by *Adams* Race.
What will be said in future times
　　when Vertue yields her Flowers,
The Babes unborn will then cry out,
　　no Parent's like to Ours.   80
This great Attempt is carried on,
　　by Mortals that has breath,
It seems the Lord does mind to send

Christs Gospel through the Earth:
To writ the parts of these brave Men,   85
   that has sent us away
The Vialactia smiles to see
   Scotlands new Nuptial day.
The Harp play'd us a pleasant spring,
   and Neptune took a dance,   90
Made Monsieur Flower-de-luce to fall,
   into a deadly Trance.
When we were on the Darian Main,
   and viewed the Noble Land,
The Trees joyn'd hands and bowed low,   95
   for honour of *Scotland*.
Young Native Babes that never spake
   Dame Nature bad them cry,
And utter forth some joyfull Notes,
   to welcome Albanie!   100
Refreshing spring and Rivolats
   when we were Landed there,
Came glidding with her jumbling Notes,
   invits us to take share;
The chearming birds, that haunts the Woods,   105
   Meavis, Peacock, and Dow,
Brought Presents in their mouths, and sang
   we pay Tribute to you.
We went in Boats, and come to Land,
   which banisht all our fears.   110
The Seas did mourn for want of us,
   each Oar was droping Tears.
The Woulf, the Lyon, and the Boar,
   the Wyld Tigger and Fox,
did fill their Claws with Golden Dust,   115
   salutes us from the Rocks.
The Tortels in the *Indian Seas*,
   left Eggs upon the Land
And came to see that Noble Fleet,
   was come from *Old Scotland*.   120
The Hurtchon came out of the Woods,
   her prickels Load with fruit,
She mumbled, but she could not speak,
   ye're welcome all come eat.
The Balmie Grass, and blooming Flowers,   125
   were all covered with dew;
Then Phoebus did bid them give a smell,
   and that would pay their due.
The Seas began to roar for joy,
   when we were all past through,   130

And Neptune with's great *Harry Kains*,
   to us was like a Loach,

.   .   .   .   .   .

And still we bless the Lord of Hoasts,   135
   and all our Benefactors,
And drank a health to Albanie,
   for all our Brave Directors.
Nilus Banks did Overflow
   only but *Egypts* land: 140
But your Fame will the World Ov'rspread,
   and Banks of Heathen sand.
We have another Fleet to sail,
   the Lord will Reik them fast;
It will be wonderful to see,   145
   the *Sun rise in the West*!
If I should name each One concerned,
   according to their station,
Ten Quair of paper would not do,
   its known by true Relation: 150
For some are Noble, All are Great,
   Lord bless your Companie,
And let your Fame in Scotlands Name
   O'respread both Land and Sea.

(1699)

3 *Albanie... Thrissels*: Scotland, thistles   6 *Northern Poll*: North Pole   27 *Reed Lyon*: Red Lion, The Scottish King of Arms   47 *Line*: the Equator   55–6 With reference to the coats of arms of Scotland and England   60 *Dagon*: 1 Samuel 5: 4   67 *William*: Stadthouder of the Netherlands   66/68 note rhyme, full/will, an indication of the writer's East-coast origin   87 *Vialactia*: Milky Way   91 *Monsieur*: France   106 *Meavis, Dow*: songthrush, dove   121 *Hurtchon*: hedgehog (porcupine?): its behaviour, spiking fruit on its prickles, is based on medieval bestiaries   131 *Harry Kains*: hurricanes   132 *Loach*: loch (lake)   133–4 The missing couplet here was inadvertently omitted between the bottom of 7 and the top of 8   144 *Reik*: reach, hold   149 *Quair*: quire (5 folio sheets of paper)

ANNE MERRYWEATHER
(d. after 1702)

THIS poem is preserved together with a letter from Lord Rochester—neither the notorious John Wilmot, Lord Rochester, nor his son Charles, who died in 1682, but the first Lord Rochester of the second creation, Lawrence Hyde, son of the Earl of Clarendon, who took the title after Charles Wilmot's death had brought it to extinction (Queen Anne, whose mercy is being sought, was therefore his niece: her mother was Clarendon's daughter Anne Hyde), and a covering note to an unnamed Maid of Honour, as follows:

Madame, this enclosed is a humble petition to her Majesty which I desire may be presented through your Ladyships hands, & I will not trouble you with more words, than that I shall be glad to owe your obligation to your favour, & to be ever sensibly concerned to show it on all the occasions of gratitude and service a man of honour & truth can pay you. I am, with all respect, your ladyships most obedient, humble servant, ROCHESTER.

Mrs Merryweather
This is from a woman of great age that I got out of prison where she had been kept many yeares, & had been brought out several times to be burnt for having despersed treason, but she would never confess who employ'd her.
Cockpit No. 23 1702

The poem, addressed to Queen Anne, which refers to having been 'buryd four thousd Days' suggests that she has been in prison for a good eleven years, (that is) since 1691. The story of her arrest and imprisonment can be pieced together from the state papers in the Public Records Office. She was initially committed to Newgate for 'clipping' coins but on 7 November 1692, she was summoned before the Attorney General to answer charges of high treason in conspiring with their Majesties' enemies. On 16 November a warrant was issued to search her house for seditious and unlicensed papers and pamphlets. Three days later she was examined at Whitehall on the charge of distributing the Declaration of King James. She was allowed to receive visits from her friends and family, among them a Mrs Johanna Merryweather. It was probably hoped that they would be able to persuade her to turn informant. She was sentenced to death for high treason in January 1693. She received several temporary reprieves in February—the threatened burnings mentioned in the note—before receiving a reprieve for an indefinite period later in the month. She was still in prison on 6 July 1702, when the London authorities were instructed to include her in the next general pardon for poor convicts, but without the condition of transportation, and in the meantime she was to be granted bail for her appearance to plead her own pardon. Although apparently a member of the criminal underworld, Merryweather was clearly a woman of some education. Her refusal to turn informant is an indication that she was also a convinced Jacobite like Jane Barker and Anne Finch, although a more directly politically active one. Her poem is interesting for the way it harks back to Queen Elizabeth, and the idea of a glorious tradition of female monarchy as characteristic of England.

294 'The Prince who said an English Senate can'

The Prince who said an English Senate can
Do anything, but make a Woman Man:
That Wonder well performd, might now have seen
Since more than Man they give us in a Queen.
A Queen! whose Conduct will revive again   5
The Happyness of Great Eliza's Reign.
A Queen! (tho' Kings ne're cou'd) will let us see
That Privilege, and Prerogative may agree.
A Queen, whose Power even the Dead can Raise,
The Dead in Law, Buryd four Thousand Days!   10

A Queen, where Good and Powerfull unite
Makes Duty both our int'rest and Delight.
Lett the French Slaves theyr Salique Law admire
Theyr Law, nor theyr Religion we desire.
Unbounded Power may our Dross subvert,   15
But Goodness only wins an English Heart.
An English Parlament will make 'em know
The weaker sex, shall be the stronger now.
French Lillys to the English Rose must Bow!
What can true English wish for, more than this,   20
A Queen whose Heart intirely English is?
What surer Basis for a Throne can prove
Than Loyalty secur'd by English Love?
May these French-envyd Blessings last for ever!
And some small share fall to poor Merryweather.   25

10 *four Thousand Days*: suggests she has been in prison for twelve years   13 *Salique Law*:
French law decreed that the throne had to pass down the male line

SOURCES AND NOTES

ALIA (no. 1) From Oxford, Bodleian Library MS Lat. Misc. c. 66 fo. 93^v, also printed in R. H. Robbins, 'Poems of Humfrey Newton, Esq., 1466–1536', *Publications of the Modern Language Association of America* 65 (1950), 249–81, at 268, and Alexandra Barratt, *Women's Poems in Middle English* (London and New York: Longman, 1992).

ANONYMOUS (no. 2) Cambridge University Library, MS Add. 5943, fo. 178^r, also printed in Barratt, *Women's Writing in Middle English*, 287–8. Light punctuation supplied.

ANONYMOUS (no. 3) Oxford, Bodleian Library, MS Rawlinson c.813, fo. 58^v. See now *The Welles Anthology: MS Rawlinson C 813, A Critical Edition*, ed. Sharon L. Jansen and Kathleen H. Jordan (Binghamton, NY: Medieval and Renaissance Texts and Studies, 1991).

ANONYMOUS (no. 4) Oxford, Bodleian Library MS Rawlinson c.813, fos. 6^b–7^a. See now *The Welles Anthology*, ed. Jansen and Jordan.
27 *turne*: durne MS

ANONYMOUS (no. 5) Oxford, Bodleian Library, MS Rawlinson C 813, fos. 71^r–72^v. See also *The Welles Anthology*, ed. Jansen and Jordan. See further Marion Glastonbury, 'At the mercy of men's dreams', *New Statesman* 102, no. 2042 (6 Nov. 1981), 18.

LADY MARGARET HOWARD, née STEWART, later DOUGLAS, LADY LENNOX (no. 6) London, British Library, Add. MS 17,492 ('The Devonshire MS'), fo. 88^r. Also printed in Kenneth Muir, 'Unpublished Poems in the Devonshire Manuscript', *Proceedings of the Leeds Philosophical Society* 6 (1947), 253–82. See headnote to the poem for the linguistic grounds on which our attributions are made.
14 *whight*: Whight MS

(no. 7) ['the sueden chance ded mak me mues'] fragment, same hand, fo. 67^r, also in Scots.
3 *soe*: sfe MS

CIRCLE OF ANNE BOLEYN (no. 8) London, British Library Add. 17,492 ('The Devonshire MS'), fo. 65^r. Also printed in Muir, 'Unpublished Poems in the Devonshire Manuscript', 253–82.

KATHERINE, LADY BOROUGH, née PARR, later NEVILLE, TUDOR, SEYMOUR (no. 9) Hatfield House, Cecil Papers vol. 314. [Old Library no. G.d.29] fos. 9–59. Extract fo. 14$^{r–v}$. The poem is a verse translation of Katherine Parr's *The Lamentacion of a Synner*, published in 1547 (extract is a translation of sig. A 6^v–7^r). Katherine Parr read French (and Latin), so this may well be a translation exercise of her own, or by another hand from her immediate circle. See further John N. King, 'Patronage and Piety: The Influence of Catherine Parr', in *Silent but for the Word: Tudor Women as Patrons, Translators and Writers of Religious Works*, ed. Margaret P. Hannay, (Kent, Oh.: Kent State University Press, 1985), 43–60.

ALIS FERCH GRUFFVD AB IEUAN AP LLYWELYN FYCHAN (no. 10) Aberystwyth, National Library of Wales, MS Llanstephan 49, p. 132 [fo. 64^v]

(no. 11) Aberystwyth, National Library of Wales, MS Llanstephan 49, p. 132 [fo. 64^v]. Also found in London, British Library Add. 14,892, fo. 64^r, and Add. 14,994, fo. 87^r.

ANNE KYME, née ASKEW (no. 12) Taken from facsimile of *The first examynacyon of Anne Askewe, latelye martyred in Smythfelde, by the Romysh popes upholders* (Marburg, John Bayle, November 1546), 46^{r-v}. Facsimile, ed. Betty Travitsky and Patrick Cullen (Aldershot: Scolar Press, 1996).

(no. 13) *The latter examinacyon of Anne Askewe, latelye martyred in Smythfelde, by the wyced Synagoge of Antichrist* (Marburg, John Bayle, 16 January 1547), 63^r–64^r. Facsimile, as above.

LADY ELIZABETH TYRWHIT (no. 14) Thomas Bentley, *The Monument of Matrones conteining seven severall lamps of virginitie, or distinct treatises . . . compiled for the necessarie use of Both sexes out of the sacred Scriptures, and other approoved authors, by Thomas Bentley of Graies Inne Student* (London, Printed by H. Denham, 1582), 131. The last three lines of the final doxology are found on p. 105: it is clearly intended that they should be supplied here.

(no. 15) Ibid. 129.

MILDRED CECIL, née COOKE, LADY BURLEIGH (no. 16) Cambridge, University Library, MS Ii.5.37 ('the Bartholo Sylva MS'), p. v^r. We are indebted for this translation to Dr Winifred Stevenson, which is based on a slightly emended text. It is probable that a level of error was introduced by the scribe, Petruccio Ubaldini, whose transcription of language he did not, or did not fully, understand (such as English) is, though calligraphically exquisite, very far from accurate.
5 νηρίτου : νηπίτου MS: the fact that the phrase is from Hesiod confirms this emendation.

LADY MARY CHEKE, née HILL, later MACWILLIAM (no. 17) London, British Library, Add. MS 10,309, fos. 108^v–109^r (Margaret Bellasys' commonplace-book, = A) is the chosen copytext. Like many poems which circulated in manuscript, copies vary considerably. Other texts collated: London, British Library Add. MS 15,277, fo. 16 (= C), London National Art Library Dyce MS 44, fo. 72^v (= D), University Library, Nottingham, Portland MS, Pw V 37, 172 (= P). Further texts known to us are in London, British Library Add. MS 12049, fos. 192–3, Cape Town, Gray MS 7, a 29, p. 157, Rosenbach MS 1083/16, pp. 16–17, Cambridge, St Johns College, MS V 26, p. 116, and Yale, Beinecke Library, MS Osborn b 205, pp. 48–48^v.

The attribution to Lady Cheke is found in London, British Library Add. MS 15,227 (The Answer to't by the Lady Cheeke) and Yale, MS Osborn b 205 (An answer by the Lady Check).
significant variants: Title: The Answer to't by the Lady Cheeke London, British Library Add. 15227 (= C) Bible: Scripture A, P   3 *who had*: having C; that had A,P   4 *soe*: his C this A   6 *pappes*: blest the pappes AC   15 *then*: therfore P; *stand much*: stand P Nor marvaile then your preacher stood perplext C   16 *the*: his P

ANNE BACON, née COOKE (no. 18) Cambridge University Library, MS Ii.5.37 viii^r ('the Bartholo Sylva MS').

FRANCES NEVILL (née MANNERS), LADY ABERGAVENNY (no. 19) from 'The Praiers made by the Right Honourable Ladie Frances Aburgauennie, and committed at the houre of her death, to the right worshipfull ladie MARIE Fane (hir onlie daughter) as a Jewell of health for the soule, and a perfect Path to

Paradise'. Thomas Bentley, *The Monument of Matrones conteining seven severall lamps of virginitie, or distinct treatises . . . compiled for the necessarie use of Both sexes out of the sacred Scriptures, and other approoved authors, by Thomas Bentley of Graies Inne Student* (London, Printed by H. Denham, 1582), 131; 139.

EMMA FOXE (no. 20) Monumental brass from Aldeborough, Suffolk, printed in Thomas Ravenshaw, *Ancient Epitaphs* (London: Joseph Masters & Co., 1878), 28.

ELIZABETH I, QUEEN OF ENGLAND (no. 21) From Pierpont Morgan Library copy of Henry Bull, *Christian Prayers and Holy Meditations.* (London: Henry Middleton 1570), owned by Thomas Heneage, Elizabeth's vice-chamberlain. Carl F. Bühler, 'Libri impressi cum notis manuscriptis', *Modern Language Notes* 53 (1938), 245–9.

(no. 22) Henry Harington (ed.), *Nugae Antiquae: being a miscellaneous collection of original papers in prose and verse*, London, W. Frederick (1769), i. 58–60 (The rationale for using this very late text as the copy-text is found in the biographical headnote.) Oxford, Bodleian Library, MS Rawlinson poet. 108, fo. 44^v (= O); London, British Library, Egerton 2642, fo. 237^v (= E); George Puttenham, *The Arte of English Poesie* (London: R. Field, 1589), 247 (= P)
significant variants: 1 *dread*: dowbte OEP; *exile*: exiles: OEP   2 *annoy*: annoys R   3 *fayth*   forth E; *subjects*: subject P 4 *shold*: would EP; *move*: weved OEP   5 *Joyes*: tois P; *cloke*: clothe O   6 *rage*: raigne P; *report*: repent OP; *by chaunged*: to changed O by course of changed mindes P   7 *topps*: topp OP; *suppose*: supposed P; *of Rue*: upward O of ruth P   8 *of*: all P   9 *The*: then P; *with*: which OP; *blynde*: blyndes OP 11 *that . . . sow*: discord aye Joye sows O, that eke discord doth sowe P   12 *former . . . still*: frend rule still; *still . . . know*: hath taught stil peace to grow   14 *Realm*: realm it; *no seditious sexts*: no stranger force   15 *through*: with P 16 *the*: their; *or . . . Joy*: or gapes for further Joy

(no. 23) Paul Melissus, *Mele sive Odae* (Nuremberg, 1580), 72. Also printed in James E. Phillips, 'Elizabeth I as a Latin poet: an epigram on Paul Melissus', *Renaissance News* 16:4 (1963), 289–98.

(no. 24) Greenwich, National Maritime Museum, MS SNG/4, single sheet. Perhaps the most relevant of the many recent works on the Queen to the subject of Elizabeth as an author are Jennifer Summit, 'The Arte of a Ladies Penne: Elizabeth I and the Poetics of Queenship', *ELR* 263 (1996), 388–95, Steven May, *The Elizabethan Courtier Poets: the Poems and their Context* (New York: University of Missouri Press, 1991), 316–21, and Susan Frye, *Elizabeth I: The Competition for Representation* (New York and Oxford: Oxford University Press), 1993.

ANNE LOK, née VAUGHAN, later DERING, PROWSE (no. 25) Cambridge University Library, MS Ii.5.37, p. v^v.

(no. 26) John Taffin, *Of the Markes of the Children of God, and of their Comforts in Afflictions. To the faithfull of the Low Country*, Overseene again, and augmented by the Author, and translated out of French by ANNE PROWSE (London: Thomas Snodham for Thomas Man, 1615), 124^v–126^v. On Anne Lok, see Patrick Collinson, 'The Role of Women in the English Reformation Illustrated by the Life and Friendships of Anne Locke', *Studies in Church History*, ii, ed. G. J. Cuming (London: Nelson, 1965), 258–72, at 265, and Margaret P. Hannay, 'Unlock my lipps: the Miserere mei Deus of Anne Vaughan Lok and Mary Sidney Herbert, Countess of Pembroke', in *Privileging Gender in Early Modern England*, ed. Jean R. Brink, Sixteenth-Century Essays and Studies, 23 (Kirksville, Mo., 1993) 19–36.

CATRIN FERCH GRUFFYDD AB IEUAN AP LLYWELYN FYCHAN OR CATRIN FERCH GRUFFYDD AP HYWEL O LANDDEINIOLEN (no. 27) Aberystwyth, National Library of Wales, MS 6209E, p. 220 (p. 24 original pagination: the third of a group of MSS bound together to make up the volume), written in 1698/9.

ANNE DUDLEY, née SEYMOUR, later UNTON, with MARGARET and JANE SEYMOUR (no. 28) from *Annae, Margaritae, Janae, sororum virginum, heroidum Anglarum, in Mortem Margaritae Valesiae, Navarrorum Reginae, Hecatadistichon*, ed. N. Denisot (Paris: Michel Fezandat & Robert Granlon, 1550), sig A4^{r-v}

Significant variants: 6 luce nec aba jacet 1551 edn. 13 avebar 1551 edn.

LADY JANE DUDLEY, née GREY (no. 29) Thomas Bentley, *The Monument of Matrones conteining seven severall lamps of virginitie, or distinct treatises . . . compiled for the necessarie use of Both sexes out of the sacred Scriptures, and other approoved authors, by Thomas Bentley of Graies Inne Student* London, Printed by H. Denham (1582), 102. These follow on the end of *An Exhortation written by the Ladie Jane the night before she suffered, in the end of the New Testament in Greeke, which she sent to her sister the Ladie Katherine.* See further Carole Levin, 'Lady Jane Grey, Protestant Queen and Martyr', in *Silent but for the Word*, ed. M. P. Hannay (Kent, Oh.: Kent State University Press, 1985), 92–106. The 'Lamentation' of Lady Jane Grey, entered in the Stationers Register (Register A, leaf 89) in 1562–3, is certainly fictional.

ELIZABETH HOBY, née COOKE, later LADY RUSSELL (no. 30) Elias Ashmole, *The Antiquities of Berkshire*, 3 vols. (London: Edmund Curll, 1719), ii. 470–1. The Bisham mortuary chapel, with its fascinating gynocratic ordering of monuments, survives, but the original inscription of this poem on the daughters is completely worn away.

(no. 31) Ibid. 470–1. This poem survives *in situ* at Bisham, but is very hard to read.

ISABELLA WHITNEY (32) *The Copy of a Letter lately written in Meeter, by a yonge Gentilwoman: to her unconstant lover* (London: Richard Jhones, 1567), sig. A2^{r}–5^{v}.

(no. 33) From *A sweet Nosegay, or pleasant Posye, contayning a hundred and ten Phylosophicall Flowers*, (London: no publisher, 1573), sig. E 2^{r}–9^{r}. See further *The Floures of Philosophie (1572) by Hugh Plat and A Sweet Nosgay (1573) and The Copy of a Letter (1567) by Isabella Whitney*, ed. Richard J. Panofsky (New York: Delmar (Scholar's Facsimiles and Reprints), 1982), Betty Travitsky, 'The "Wyll and Testament" of Isabella Whitney', *English Literary Renaissance* 10:1 (1980), 76–93.

KATHERINE DOWE (no. 34) From B.D. [Bartholomew Dowe, her son], *Dairie Booke for Good Huswives* (London: for Thomas Hacket, 1588), sig. C 2^{r}. Facsmile reprint, with Torquato Tasso, *The Housholders Philosophie*, in The English Experience 765 (Amsterdam: Theatrum Orbis Terrarum, 1975).

KATHERINE KILLIGREW (née COOKE) (no. 35) John Harington, *Orlando Furioso in English Heroical Verse* (London: R. Field, 1591), bk. 37. 314. There are also three manuscripts:

Cambridge, University Library, MS Ff.5.14, fo. 107^{r} (the commonplace book of W. Kytton, a puritan preacher, who notes, 'these verses were wrytten by Mrs. Kyllygrewe to my Lady Cycyll') (=C); Dublin, March's Library, 23.5.21, fo. 22^{v} (= M); Oxford, Corpus Christi College, MS 316 (=O).
significant variants: 1 *cures:* curas C   3 *retines, vel:* revires, et H

(no. 36) Taken from an inscription (subsequently lost in the Great Fire of London) by John Stow, *A Survay of London*, enlarged edn. (London: E. Purslow, to be sold by N. Bourne, 1633), 259–60.

MARY STUART, QUEEN OF SCOTS (no. 37) Pierre du Bourdeilles, Seigneur de Brantôme, *Memoires de Messire Pierre du Bourdeille, Seigneur de Brantôme, contenans les Vies des dames Illustres de France de son temps* (Leiden: Jean Sambix, 1665), 121–3.

(no. 38) London, British Library, MS Cotton Caligula B. V., 'Transactions between England and Scotland Temp. Hen. VIII and Eliz.', fos. 323–4, bifolium.

(no. 39) Public Record Office SP 53.12, fo. 58^r (Mary, Queen of Scots XII.31). Rounded humanist display script (possibly holograph) single page presentation sheet: address does not survive. '1582' is on reverse in 19th-c. hand.

ANONYMOUS (no. 40) Edinburgh, National Library of Scotland, Advocates' MS 1.1.6, fo. 228^r ('The Bannatyne Manuscript, written in Tyme of Pest, 1568', compiled by George Bannatyne), ed. W. Tod Ritchie, 5 vols., Scottish Texts Society (STS) (Edinburgh and London: William Blackwood & sons, 1934), iv 293–4. Facsimile edn., Denton Fox and W. A. Ringler (Menston: Scolar Press, 1980).

NIGHEAN DHONNCHADH (THE DAUGHTER OF DUNCAN CAMPBELL OF GLENLYON) (no. 41) *Bardachd Ghaidhlig: Gaelic Poetry 1550–1900*, ed. W. J. Carmichael Watson (Inverness, 1959). It should be reiterated here that with poems in all of the Celtic languages it is perfectly possible that composition and the first written form of the text may be separated by decades, even centuries. See further Katherine Kerrigan (ed.), *An Anthology of Scottish Women Poets* (Edinburgh: Edinburgh University Press, 1991), 56–9.

ELLIN THORNE (no. 42) London, British Library, MS Cotton Vespasian A 25, fos. 152^v–153^r. See also *Tudor Songs and Ballads from MS Cotton Vespasian A 25*, ed. Peter J. Seng (Cambridge, Mass.: Harvard University Press, 1978), 75.

MARIE COLLYN, née HARVEY (no. 43) London, British Library, MS Sloane 93, fo. 80^{r-v}. The book was composed between 1573 and 1580 by Gabriel Harvey, in whose hand it is. It has been edited, as *Gabriel Harvey's Letter-Book*, by E. J. L Scott (London: Camden Society, 1884).

ANNE FIELD, née VAVASOUR, later RICHARDSON (no. 44) Oxford, Bodleian Library, MS Rawlinson Poet. 85, fo. 17, is copytext (= R): this is a text not too far removed from the persons involved, since it is early (1588/90: within eight years or so of the poem's being written), and contains a group of five poems associated with the Earl of Oxford.

Other MSS: Washington, Folger Shakespeare Library V a 89, fo. 6^v (= F), which subscribes to 'vavaser'; Oxford, Bodleian Library, MS Rawlinson Poet. 172, fo. 5^v (= O); London, British Library, MS Harley 6910, fo. 145 (= H), 'finis qd La. B. to N' (it should be noted that Anne Vavasour is referred to by at least one contemporary as 'Baviser': 'N' is of often used to stand for 'some unknown person'). There is also a shortened version in London, British Library, MS Harley 7392, fo. 40 (ll. 17–42 only), subscribed 'Ball', perhaps for 'ballad', or for B. Allott, a name which appears on fo. 77.

Significant variants: 1 *sweet*: my H   2 *acquaint*: annoy FOH   3 *Myne*: my F; *allthoughe*: where O; *saye*: say F;   4 *be*: rest FOH   5 *me*: we FH; I O; *amongest the*

Lynxes: besieged with Argus O among the Linceus H 6 *That pryes innto*: that pries and spies F looks to each privy O pries and spies into each H; *mynde*: mine O...7 *sorrows*: sorrow 8 *my... lookes*: our secret love H 9 *Content... selfe*: thou knowest right well H 10 *shame*: fame O 13–16, 17–20: H reverses order of lines 13 Then think not strange although that I be coy H 14 *conceyts*: conceit O 15 *jestures*: gesture OH 16 *Nor*: and O 18 *live*: lie H dwell L; *envyes*: every H 19 *heartes*: breasts L; *a*: and O; *meaning*: meanings O 20 *reste*: show FOHL; *whiche*: that FOHL; *outwardlye... make*: we by force do make O we are forced to make L 21 So: And H; *lyste*: lust H; *vaunt*: want O 22 *moste*: must FOHL; *desyre... fayne*: live best I always find O desire I seem to move L 24 *I seeme most*: most I seem F 25 *Then:* Thus FOHL; *will*: must O 26 *Thou... oughte*: They shall not find H Thou... hear... judge L 27 *it*: this JL 28 *As*: and OL

CATHERIN LLWYD, née OWEN (no. 45) Aberystwyth, National Library of Wales, MS J. Glyn Davies 1, fos. 192ᵛ–193ʳ.

CHRISTIAN LINDSAY (no. 46) Edinburgh, Edinburgh University Library, De 3 70, fo. 68ᵛ. Edited in *The Poems of Alexander Montgomerie*, ed. James Cranstoun, STS (Edinburgh and London: William Blackwood & Sons, 1887), 103–4.

MARGARET CLIFFORD, COUNTESS OF CUMBERLAND, née RUSSELL (no. 47) Monument formerly in the south aisle of St Mary's Church, Hornsey, Middlesex and moved to the north side of the nave in the course of James Brooks's 1888 rebuilding. Printed in *Notes and Queries*, 7th ser. 4 (July–Dec. 1887), 374.

MARY HERBERT, née SIDNEY, COUNTESS OF PEMBROKE (no. 48) *The Collected Works of Mary Sidney Herbert, Countess of Pembroke*, ed. Margaret P. Hannay, Noel J. Kinnamon, and Michael G. Brennan, 2 vols. (Oxford: Clarendon Press, 1998), ii, 49–51. (The texts of the psalms in this immaculate edition are derived from the manuscript, copied by the writing-master and poet John Davies of Hereford, in the possession of Viscount De L'Isle MBE at Penshurst Place, Kent.)

(no. 49) Ibid. 89–92.

(no. 50) Ibid. 221–2.

(no. 51) *A Poeticall Rhapsody containing, Diverse... Poesies*, London, 1602. *The Collected Works of Mary Sidney Herbert, Countess of Pembroke*, ed. Margaret P. Hannay, Noel J. Kinnamon, and Michael G. Brennan, 2 vols. (Oxford: Clarendon Press, 1998–9), i. 89–91. See further G. F. Waller, *Mary Sidney, Countess of Pembroke: A Critical Study of her Writings and Literary Milieu* (Salzburg: Institut für Anglistik und Amerikanistik, Universität Salzburg, 1979), Margaret P. Hannay, *Philip's Phoenix: Mary Sidney, Countess of Pembroke* (New York and Oxford: Oxford University Press, 1990). 34 *there*: three 1601 text 44 *shine*: thine 1601 text

ANONYMOUS (no. 52) Text re-edited by Dr Meg Bateman from *Sean Dain agus Orain Ghaidhealach... Eoin Gillies...* Clo-bhuailt' am Peairt, 1786/A *Collection of Ancient and Modern Gaelic Poems and Songs*, Perth, printed for John Gillies, Bookseller, 1786, pp. 204–5. See Anne C. Frater, 'The Gaelic Tradition up to 1750', *A History of Scottish Women's Writing*, ed. Douglas Gifford and Dorothy Macmillan (Edinburgh: Edinburgh University Press 1997), 1–14, at 2.

ANNE WRIGGLESWORTH (no. 53) J. W. Ebsworth (ed.) *The Bagford Ballads, Illustrating the last years of the Stuarts* (Hertford, 1878), i, pp. xviii–xix. There is another copy in Oxford, Bodleian Library, Historical Collections for Oxfordshire, MS. XIV (Ecclesiastical Records) fo. 263.

ELIZABETH, LADY TANFIELD née SYMONDES (no. 54) Taken from the monument of Lord Chief Justice Tanfield, North Chapel, Church of St John the Baptist, Burford, Oxfordshire.

ANONYMOUS possibly MARIE LAUDER, née MAITLAND (no. 55) Cambridge, Magdalen College, Pepys Library 2251, fos. 78^v–79^v. See further *The Maitland Quarto Manuscript*, ed W. A. Craigie, STS NS 9 (Edinburgh and London: 1920), 160–2, and Jane Farnsworth, 'Voicing Female Desire in "Poem XLIX"', *Studies in English Literature 1500–1700*, 36.1 (1996), 37–72.

ELIZABETH 'E. D.' [COBURNE, née DOUGLAS] (no. 56) Edinburgh, National Library of Scotland, MS 2065, fo. 4^r.

(no. 57) Ibid. From a manuscript presented to the University by the poet Drummond in 1627: The Triumphs of the most famous Poet, Mr Frances Petrarke, translated out of Italian into Inglish by Mr Wm. Foular, P. of Hawicke, dedicated to Lady Jeane Fleming and Lady Thirlstane, 12 December 1587.

AEMILIA LANYER, née BASSANI (no. 58) From *Salve Deus Rex Judaeorum* (London: Valentine Simmes for Richard Bonian, 1611), sigs. A1^r–H1^v.

(no. 59) Ibid. sigs H2^r–I1^r. See further Barbara Lewalski, 'Of God and Good Women: The Poems of Aemilia Lanyer', in *Silent but For the Word* ed. M. P. Hanuay (Kent, Oh.: Kent State University Press, 1985), 203–23.

ANNE DOWRICHE, née EDGCUMBE (no. 60) From *The French Historie, That is, A Lamentable Discourse of three of the chiefe, and most famous bloodie broiles that have happened in* France *for the Gospel of Jesus Christ* (Exeter: Thomas Orwin for William Russell, 1589), 28^v–29^v.

(no. 61) From Hugh Dowriche, Δεσμοφυλαξ: the Jaylors Conversion, Wherein is lively represented the true Image of a Soule rightlye touched, and converted by the spirit of God (London: John Windet, 1596), sig. A 6^v–7^r.

ANNE DORMER, LADY HUNGERFORD (no. 62) John Bucke, *Instructions for the use of the beades* (Louvain: no printer given, 1589; foldout rear end-paper). While Lady Hungerford's authorship of these verses cannot be finally proved, it is strongly suggested by Bucke's note on p. 6: 'Lastlie I have added some rules to know from whence evell thoughes do proced eand meanes to avoyde them: with a figure or portrature of the beades, conteining your Ladyshippes usuall Meditacion upon them.' (Various features of this text, such as *eand* in the passage cited, suggest that it was typeset by Flemings rather than within the English community.)

JANE SEAGER (no. 63) London, British Library Add. MS 10037, fo. 1^v.

(no. 64) Ibid. fo. 3^v. See further Werner Kramer, 'Zur englischen Kurzschrift im Zeitalter Shakespeares. Das Jane-Seager-Manuskript', *Shakespeare Jahrbuch* 67 (1931), 26–61.

ELIZABETH COLVILLE, née MELVILLE, LADY CULROSS (no. 65) From *Ane Godlie Dreame, compylit in Scottish Meter be M. M. Gentelvvoman in Culros, at the requeist of her freindes* (Edinburgh: Robert Charteris, 1603), sig. B1–B2.

(no. 66) *A Sonnet sent to Blackness* Edinburgh, National Library of Scotland, MS Wod. Qu. XXIX, fo.11^r.

LADY ANNE SOUTHWELL, née HARRIS (no. 67) London, British Library Lansdowne 740, fo. 142^r, autograph.

authorial corrections: 4+ The only touchstone of great natures storye | in whome all artes reside, and hold theyr glorye [struck through in MS] 6+ whose sacred lippes doe never part asunder | but as the Heralds of all grace and wonder [struck through in MS]

(no. 68) Washington, Folger Shakespeare Library MS V b 198, fo. 16ʳ.

(no. 69) Ibid. fo. 19ᵛ.

(no. 70) Ibid. fo. 21ʳ. There is a complete edition by Jean Klene, *The Southwell-Sibthorpe Commonplace Book (Folger MS V.b.198)* (Tempe, Arizona: Medieval and Renaissance Texts and Studies, 1997). See also her 'Recreating the voice of Lady Anne Southwell', in *New Ways of Looking at Old Texts*, ed. W. Speed Hill (Binghampton, NY: Renaissance Texts and Studies, 1993) 239–52.

ESTHER KELLO, née INGLIS/LANGLOIS (no. 71) We are indebted for assistance with this translation to Professor Michael Edwards. Edinburgh National Library of Scotland MS 20498, fo. 23ʳ. Calligraphic MS: Le Livre de l'Ecclesiaste ensemble les lamentations de Jeremie de la main d'Esther Anglois Françoise, A Lislebourg en Ecosse, 1602. See further A. H. Scott-Elliot and Elspeth Yeo, 'Calligraphic Manuscripts of Esther Inglis (1571–1624), a Catalogue', *The Papers of the Bibliographic Society of America* 84 (1990), 11–86.

MARTHA PRYNNE, née DORSETT, later THROUGOOD, MOULSWORTH (no. 72) Yale, Beinecke Library, Osborn MS fb 150. See further Ann Depas-Orange and Robert C. Evans (eds.), *'The Birthday of my Self': Martha Moulsworth, Renaissance Poet* (Princeton: *Critical Matrix*, 1996). Robert C. Evans, *'The Muses Female Are': Martha Moulsworth and other woman writers of the English Renaissance*, Locust Hill Literary Studies 20 (Locust Hill Press, 1996).

LUCY RUSSELL, née HARINGTON, COUNTESS OF BEDFORD (no. 73) Oxford, Bodleian Library MS Rawlinson Poet. 31, fo. 39, is copytext, compared with Oxford, Bodleian Library Ms Eng. Poet. f 9, fos. 122ᵛ–123ᵛ.

Other MSS: London, British Library Harley 4064; San Marino, California, Huntington Library, Bridgewater MS EL 6873; Cambridge, Mass., Harvard College Library, Carnaby MS Eng. 96611; Cambridge University Library, Luttrell MS; ex. the library of Sir Geoffrey Keynes; New Haven, Yale University, Osborn Collection Ms b 148. Also in *Poems by J.D.* [John Donne] *with elegies on the author's death* (London: M.F. for John Mariott, 1635), and subsequent editions, as 'Elegie on Mistris Boulstred'.

significant variants from 1635 and Eng. Poet. f 9 (= E):
2 *flow*: growe E   5–6 *denounce...pronounce*: denounces...pronounces 1635; *joy*: joyes E   8 *The clearer*: This clear   13 *gentle*: greatly   22 *spoyles...weare* Their soules in Triumph to thy conquest beare 1635   24 *hers*: her 1635   30 *the*: those 1635   31 *not*: that   32 *spirit-instructed*: spirit instructed 1635   32 *Which did*: did not   34 *Act*: case E; *saw, heard, felt*: saw and felt 1635   39 *she sayles*: shee's fled E   41 *teach*: preach E; *of her*: which she E; *and*: did E

ELIZABETH JANE LEON, née WESTON ('WESTONIA') (no. 74) Elizabetha Joanna Westonia, *Parthenicon*, ed. G. Martin à Baldhoven (Prague: Paulus Sessius [1608]), bk. ii, sig. C2ᵛ–3ʳ.

(no. 75) Published as a pamphlet, Prague, no printer given, 1606
28 *quum*: MS note corrects to quin.

(no. 76) Elizabetha Joanna Westonia, *Parthenicon*, ed. G. Martin à Baldhoven (Prague: Paulus Sessius [1608]), bk. i, C5ᵛ–6ᵛ.

(no. 77) Ibid., manuscript addition to London, British Library copy (C 61 d 2), second flysheet^{r-v}. There is a facsimile edition of *Parthenicon* in *Neo-Latin Women Writers: Elizabeth Jane Weston and Bathsua Reginald [Makin]*, ed. Donald Cheney, *The Early Modern Englishwoman: The Printed Writings* (Aldershot: Ashgate, 1999), and a critical edition by Brenda Hosington and Donald Cheney. *Collected Writings* (Toronto, Bultalo & London: University of Toronto Press, 2000)

ELIZABETH CARY, née TANFIELD, COUNTESS OF FALKLAND (no. 78) From *The Tragedie of Mariam, the faire Queene of Iewry, Written by that learned, vertuous, and truly noble Ladie*, E. C. (London: printed by Thomas Creede, for Richard Hawkins, 1613), Act III, sc. 3, sig. E3^{v}-4^{r}.

(no. 79) Dedicatory sonnet handwritten in the published prose version of *The Reply of the Most Illustrious Cardinall of Perron* (Douai: Martin Bogart, 1630), Yale, Beinecke Library copy: from Arlene I. Shapiro, 'Elizabeth Cary: Her Life, Letters and Art' (Diss., SUNY Stony Brook, 1984), 81.

LADY MARY WROTH, née SIDNEY (no. 80) From *The Countesse of Mountgomeries Urania. Written by the right honourable the Lady MARY WROATH, Daughter to the right noble Robert Earle of Leicester* (London: Ioh. Marriott and John Grismond, 1621): 'Pamphilia to Amphilianthus' (separately paginated), p. 36 for the beginning and end of the 'crown of sonnets': In this strang labourinth how shall I turne?

(no. 81) Ibid. 22.

(no. 82) Ibid. 25.

(no. 83) Ibid. 44.

(no. 84) Ibid. 18–19.

(no. 85) Ibid. 30.

(no. 86) University of Nottingham Library, Cl LM 85/3. For previous history, see *MSS of Sir Henry Jukes Lloyd Bruce*, HMC Ser. 55 (Reports on MSS in Various Collections), pt. 7 (London, 1914) 124. The cover sheet is endorsed, 'To the Right Ho^{ble} the Lo^r Denny Barron of Waltham in Essex, ffrom Mary Wrothe'. Several copies of the acrimonious exchange of letters, and Denny's original poem, are preserved, but only one copy of Wroth's reply. See further Josephine Roberts, 'An, Unpublished Literary quarrel concerning the suppression of Mary Wroth's *Urania*', *N&Q*, 222 NS 24 (1977), 532–5. See also *Reading Mary Wroth: Representing Alternatives in Early Modern England*, ed. Naomi J. Miller and Gary Waller (Knoxville: University of Tennessee Press, 1991).
20 *Thrid*: Trid MS

ISOBEL BEAUMONT and JOHN COLEMAN, a servant (no. 87) Public Record Office STAC 8/55/26. For context (and it is a Websterian context which more than repays study), see Richard Cust, 'Honour and Politics in Early Stuart England: The Case of Beaumont v. Hastings', *Past and Present*, 149 (1995), 57–94, at 87.

HESTER WYAT (no. 88) Oxford, Bodleian Library Rawlinson d. 360, fo. 63^r, endorsed on verso, 'Mrs Hester Wyat upon women's writing verse'.
18 *lissening*: lisening MS   20 *Pleasures*: plea MS   39 *dye*: dy MS

A MAID OF HONOUR (no. 89) From *The Crown Garland of Golden Roses: Gathered out of England's Royal Garden, Set forth in many pleasant new Songs and Sonets* (London: John Wright, 1631), sig. B 3^{r-v} (first published 1612).

A GENTLEWOMAN (no. 90) London, British Library, MS Add. 22601, fo. 26ʳ. A number of poems in this collection of 'Ancient MS Poems, Ballads, Letters, Plays and Sonnets', are dated 1603.

ANONYMOUS (no. 91) Orally transmitted song, recorded by the antiquarian John Aubrey: London, British Library, MS Lansdowne 231, fos. 101–243, in Aubrey's autograph.
21 [no brader than a thread]: addendum floating above l. 21

ELEN GWDMAN (no. 92) Aberystwyth, National Library of Wales MS 832, 'Llyfr Gwyn Mechell', p. 87. The MS is in the hand of William Bulkeley (1691–1760) diarist and recorder of eighteenth-century Angelsey. 'Y Mesur Rogero' (to the tune Rogero) is added to the title, suggesting that the poem was intended to be sung.

ELEANOR DAVIES, née TOUCHET, later DOUGLAS (LADY ELEANOR AUDLEY) (no. 93) London, Public Record Office SP 16/345/104. See Esther S. Cope (ed.), *Prophetic Writings of Lady Eleanor Davies* (New York and Oxford: Oxford University Press, 1995), 73–5.

(no. 94) THE GATEHOUSE SALUTATION From the Lady *ELEANOR.,* Revelat. cap. 4, Serving for Westminsters Cathedral, their old Service. And Courts of Westminster, those Elders sitting, &c., February, 1646, no publisher given, A2ᵛ–4ʳ. Source text: copy of Lady Eleanor's tracts in the Folger Shakespeare Library. Taken from Cope, *Prophetic Writings of Lady Eleanor Davies,* 218–19. See further Esther S. Cope, *Handmaid of the Holy Spirit: Dame Eleanor Davies, Never soe Mad a Ladie* (Ann Arbor, Mich.: University of Michigan Press, 1992).

BRÍD INÍAN IARLA CHILLE DARA (BRIGID O'DONNELL, née FITZGERALD) (no. 95) From Cathal C. Ó Háinle, 'Flattery rejected: two seventeenth-century Irish poems', *Hermathena* 138 (1985), 5–27, at 17–18, an edition based on the two surviving MSS, Maynooth, University College MS C 59, written in 1645, and Dublin, Trinity College H.4.14, written by Tomás de la Híd in 1694.

ANONYMOUS, redacted by JENNET DEVICE (no. 96) From Thomas Potts, *The WONDERFUL DISCOVERIE OF WITCHES IN THE COUNTIE OF LANCASTER with the Arraignment and Triall of Nineteene notorious WITCHES, At the Assizes and general Gaole deliverie, holden at the Castle of Lancaster, upon Monday, the seventeenth of August last, 1612* (London: W. Stansby for John Barnes, 1613), sig. K1ᵛ–2ʳ.
30 *feere*: deere ed.

ANONYMOUS GENTLEWOMAN (no. 97) London, British Library Add. 22,603, fo. 21ʳ. (This is a Cambridge collection mostly of University poetry from the early seventeenth century: a poem on fo. 19ᵛ is dated 1636).

MARY OXLIE (no. 98) *Poems by That most Famous Wit, William Drummond of Hawthornden*...(London: printed by W.H. and are to be sold in the Company of Stationers, 1656), sig. A7ʳ⁻ᵛ.

MRS WINCHCOMBE (no. 99) Monument, dated 1614, in the Church of S. Peter, Wittenham, Oxfordshire. Printed in *Epitaphs from Oxfordshire,* collected by Patricia Utechin (Oxford: Robert Dugdale, 1980), 1.

HONOR STRANGMAN, JENNYFER BENNY (with JOHN DIER, BENJAMIN STRANGMAN, and others) (no. 100) London, Public Record Office STAC 8 202/30.
38–9 *her take*: take MS; *lett her*: let MS

FIONNGHUALA, ÍNGHEAN UÍ DOMHNAILL BHRIAIN (O'BRIEN) (no. 101), This poem was first edited by Dr Liam O Murchú in *Éigse: A Journal of Irish Studies* 27 (1993), 67–79. A full discussion of its historical and cultural background, along with scholarly apparatus, is to be found there. We are indebted for this edition, translation, and biographical note to Dr Ó Murchú.

BATTINA CROMWELL, née PALAVICINO (no. 102) London, British Library Harley 2311 (A Booke of severall devotions collected from good men by the worst of sinners, Anna Cromwell, 1656), fo. 21^{r-v}.

ELIZABETH STUART, later QUEEN OF BOHEMIA (no. 103) From *Nugae Antiquae: Being a Miscellaneous Collection of Original Papers, in Prose and Verse; Written During the Reigns of Henry VIII, Edward VI, Queen Mary, Elizabeth, and King James: by Sir John Harington, Knt. and by Others who lived in those Times. Selected from Authentic Remains*, 3 vols. (London: John Dodsley, 1779), iii. 296–303: 'This was written by Elizabeth, daughter of King James, 1609, and given to Lord Harington, of Exton, her Tutor.' She would then have been 13. 14 *nam'd*: name ed.   22 *vayne*: mayne ed.   60–1 Harington's text goes from stanza XV to XVII, probably a simple mistake rather than signalling the omission of a stanza

MOR NIGHEAN UISDEIN (no. 104) *One Hundred and Five Songs of Occupation from the Western Isles of Scotland*, collected by Frances Tolmie, reprinted from *The Journal of the Folksong Society* 16, IV.3 (1911), (Felinfach: Llanerch Publishers, 1997), 215–16. Redacted from the singing of Mrs Hector Mackenzie, Dunvegan, Skye, 1864. Translated by Dr Meg Bateman.

HESTER PULTER, née LEE (no. 105) Leeds, Brotherton Library MS LT.q.32, fos. 8^v–10^r (12–15).

(no. 106) Ibid. fo. 33^r, 61.

(no. 107) Ibid. fos. 16^v–17^v, 28–30.

(no. 108) Ibid. fos. 13^v–115^r, 22. There is a forthcoming complete edition of Hester Pulter's collection of poems, by Dr Mark Robson.

ELIZABETH BANCKES and GEORGE JAMES (no. 109) London, Public Record Office STAC 8/59/4. In this Star Chamber case, the plaintiffs are Henry Bressye of Escott, gent., and Lucy his wife, defendants, George James of Lutterworth, Co. Leicester, plaintiff's servant, and Elizabeth Banckes: the said Lucy having taken away the said George's livery coat with intent to dismiss him.

'CONSTANTIA MUNDA' (no. 110) From *The Worming of a Mad Dogge: Or, A Soppe for Cerberus the Jaylor of Hell*, by Constantia Munda — *dux foemina facti* (London: printed for Laurence Hayes, and are to be sold at his shop neere Fleetbridge, over against St Brides Lane, 1617), sig. A1^{r-v}. The names signify 'Chaste Constancy' and 'Chaste Prudence'. 'Dux femina facti' is a tag from Virgil, *Aeneid* I. 364 (a woman is made war-leader: with reference to Queen Dido).

RACHEL PROCTER, née SPEGHT (no. 111) The Dreame: from *Mortalities Memorandum, with a Dream Prefixed, imaginarie in manner; reall in matter* (London: Edward Griffin for Jacob Bloome, 1621), 1–11. See now Barbara K. Lewalski, *The Polemics and Poems of Rachel Speght* (New York and London: Oxford University Press, 1996).

MRS BOUGHTON (no. 112) Epitaph in St Michael's Church, Bray, Berks, still *in situ*.

ELEANOR FINCH, née WYATT (no. 113) London, British Library Add. 62135, fo. 337^r.

(no. 114) Ibid. fos. 337^v–339^r.

(no. 115) Ibid. fos. 334r–336^v.

ALICE SUTCLIFFE, née WOODHOWS (no. 116) *From* 'Of our losse by ADAM, and our gayne by CHRIST; the first *Adam* was made a living soule, the second *Adam* a quickning Spririt; For as in ADAM wee all dye, so in CHRIST, shall all be made alive. I *Corinth*. 15.' In Alice Sutcliffe, *Meditations of Man's Mortalitie. Or, A Way to True Blessednesse* (2nd edn. enlarged, 1634), 141–200 ('Of our losse' occupies pp. 141–200).

BATHSUA MAKIN, née RAINOLDS (no. 117) *Musa virginea graeco-latino-gallica* (London: Edward Griffin for John Hodgets, 1616), sig. B1$^{r–v}$.

(no. 118) Huntington Library MS H.A. 8799. See now *Neo-Latin Women Writers: Elizabeth Jane Weston and Bathsua Reginald [Makin]*, ed. Donald Cheney, *The Early Modern Englishwoman: The Printed Writings* (Aldershot: Ashgate, 1999) and Frances Teague, *Bathsua Makin: Woman of Learning* (Lewisburg: Buchwell University Press, 1998).

KATHERINE, LADY DYER, née D'OYLEY (no. 119) Text from the Dyer monument in St Mary's Church, Colmworth, Bedfordshire.

DAME GERTRUDE (HELEN) MORE (no. 120) *The Holy Practises of a Devine Lover or the Saintly Ideots Devotions* (Paris: Lewis de la Fosse, 1657), p. 289.

(no. 121) *The Spiritual Exercises of the Most Vertuous and Religious D. Gertrude More of the Holy Order of St Bennet and English Congregation of our Ladies of Comfort, Cambray, she called them Amor ordinem nescit And Ideots Devotions. Her only Spiritual Father and Director the Ven. Fa. Baker stiled them Confessiones Amantis a Lovers Confessions* (Paris: Lewis de la Fosse, 1658), 277. NB: there is a manuscript (mostly prose) containing some of the material in *Confessio Amantis*, in Oxford, Bodleian Library, Rawlinson C 581. The thirty-nine-stanza poem on fos. 1^r–7^v shares the same first stanza as 'A short oblation'

JANE HAWKINS (no. 122) London, Public Record Office SP 16/142/19

DIANA PRIMROSE (no. 123) from *A Chaine of Pearle, Or a memoriall of the peerles Graces, and Heroick Vertues of Queene Elizabeth of Glorious Memory. Dat Rosa mel apibus, qua sugit Aranea virus* ['The rose, from which the Spider sucks poison, gives honey to the Bees'] (London: Printed for Thomas Paine, to be sold by Philip Watchouse, 1630), 10–11.

ANONYMOUS [? 'LADY LOTHIAN';] (no. 124) Edinburgh, National Library of Scotland, Advocates MS 5.2.14, fo. 9^r. Other MSS: Aberdeen, Aberdeen University Library, MS 28 fos. 26^r–27^r; Aberdeen, Aberdeen University Library, Special Collections MS 2543, fos. 13^r–15^r (a text in a child's hand); Edinburgh, Edinburgh University Library Laing MS III 488.
15 (and also 37) *Quhan*: qu MS.

SIBELLA DOVER, née COLE (perhaps in collaboration with THOMAS COLE) (no. 125) From *Annalia Dubrensia, upon the yeerely celebration of Mr Robert Dover's Olimpick Games upon the Cotswold-Hills, 1630.*, sig. H 3^r.

ANNE BRADSTREET, née DUDLEY (no. 126) *The Tenth Muse Lately sprung up in America, Or Severall Poems, compiled with great variety of Wit and Learning, full of delight. Wherein especially is contained a compleat discourse and description of The Four Elements, Constitutions, Ages of Man, Seasons of the Year. Together with an Exact Epitome of the Four Monarchies, viz. the Assyrian, Persian, Grecian and Roman. Also a Dialogue between Old England and New, concerning the late troubles.*

With divers other pleasant and serious Poems. By a Gentlewoman in those Parts (London: Stephen Bowtell, 1650), 3–4 (also in revised, posthumous edn. (1678), 3–4). Facsimile reprint, ed. Josephine K. Piercy (Gainsville, Fla.: Scholars Facsimiles and Reprints, 1965).

Significant varia from 1678: 6 *Verse*: Lines 20 *speake...plaine*: in future times speak plain   41 *each...all*: all and each   46 *wholsome*: Thyme or   47 *stuffe*: ure

(no. 127) *Several Poems compiled with great variety of wit and learning, full of delight wherein especially is contained a compleat discourse, and description of the four elements, constitutions, ages of man, seasons of the year, together with an exact epitome of the three first monarchyes, viz. the Assyrian, Persian, Grecian, and beginning of the Romane common-wealth to the end of their last king... with diverse other pleasant and serious poems, by a gentlewoman in New-England* (Boston: John Foster, 1678), 234–5.

(no. 128) Ibid. 256.

(no. 129) *The Tenth Muse Lately sprung up in America, Or Severall Poems, compiled with great variety of Wit and Learning, full of delight. Wherein especially is contained a compleat discourse and description of The Four Elements, Constitutions, Ages of Man, Seasons of the Year. Together with an Exact Epitome of the Four Monarchies, viz. the Assyrian, Persian, Grecian and Roman. Also a Dialogue between Old England and New, concerning the late troubles. With divers other pleasant and serious Poems. By a Gentlewoman in those Parts* (London: Stephen Bowtell, 1650), 180–90.

Significant varia from 1678 (pp. 192–201): 7 *mourning*: mournful   14 *weakned fainting*: fainting weakned   18 *this*: my   30 *And*: Or; *fields*: field   46 *doe not*: do you   50 *this*: the   61 *and*: nor   66–70: No Duke of *York*, nor Earl of *March* to soyle | Their hands in kindreds blood whom they did foil | No crafty Tyrant who usurps the Seat, | Who Nephews slew that so he might be great   74 *of*: oft   86 *thy*: our   93 *And*: Are 94 *is trod*: troden   95 *are*: were   104 *I made a jeast*: was made a jest   111 *which I have*: by great ones   112 *babes*: youths   115 *for Thefts*: omitted   127–30 *These... Clerkes*: I then believ'd not, now I feel and see | The plague of stubborn incredulity   132 *Some...* *went*: Some fin'd, from house and friends to exile went   134 *heard...cause*: saw their wrongs; *wrongs*: hath   143 *yielded*: yeelding   157 *hands*: hearts   162 *My...Parlia-ment*: 'Tis said, my beter part in Parliament   190 *cause*: strife 193–5 *the worst...sake*: but this may be my overthrow   198 *ravisht*: weeping   206–7 *now...ill*: do what there lyes in thee | And recompence the good I've done to thee   212 I once your flesh: and I your flesh   214–17 *Your...blood*: Your griefs I pity, but soon hope to see, | Out of your troubles much good fruit to be; | To see those latter dayes of hop'd for good, | Though now beclouded all with tears and blood: 233 *Prelates*: Popelings   236 *trash*: empty trash   240–1 *shew...heart*: with a Loyal heart, | Not false to King, nor to the better part   243 *By force...down*: As duty binds, expel and tread them down   244–5 *lines omitted*   247 *blessed*: hopeful   270 *thy valour*: and glory   275 *Execute...full*: And on her pour   296 *Parliament*: rightest cause

(no. 130) *Several Poems compiled with great variety of wit and learning, full of delight wherein especially is contained a compleat discourse, and description of the four elements, constitutions, ages of man, seasons of the year, together with an exact epitome of the three first monarchyes, viz. the Assyrian, Persian, Grecian, and beginning of the Romane common-wealth to the end of their last king... with diverse other pleasant and serious poems, by a gentlewoman in New-England* (Boston: John Foster), 1678, 239.

(no. 131) Andover Manuscript Book, a book of meditations dedicated to her second son, Simon, in 1664, fos. 66^v–67^r reproduced in facsimile reprint of 1650 edn., ed. Josephine K. Piercy (Gainsville, Fla.: Scholars Facsimiles and Reprints, 1965).

LUCY HASTINGS, née DAVIES, COUNTESS OF HUNTINGDON (no. 132) flyleaf poem in her own copy of *Lachrymae Musarum*, San Marino, Huntington Library, RB 102354.

DAME CLEMENTIA (ANNE) CARY (no. 133) Lille, Archives Départmentales du Nord, 20H39.

MÀIRI NIGHEAN ALASDAIR RUAIDH (MARY MACLEOD) (no. 134) Mairi Nighean Alasdair Ruaidh, *Orain agus Luinneagan Gaidhlig*, ed. J. Carmichael Watson, Oliver & Boyd for the Scottish Gaelic Texts Society (Edinburgh, 1982), 12–15: prose translation slightly modified.

(no. 135) Ibid. 26–31.

GERTRUDE THIMELBY, née ASTON (no. 136) ?San Marino, Huntington Library, HM 904.

(no. 137) ?San Marino, Huntington Library, HM 904.

(no. 138) ?San Marino, Huntington Library, HM 904. See Jenijoy La Belle, 'The Huntington Aston Manuscript', *The Book Collector* 29 (1980), 542–67.

ANNA LEY, née NORMAN (no. 139) Los Angeles, William Andrews Clarke Memorial Library, MS L6815 M3 C734, fo. 93^{r-v}.

(no. 140) Ibid. fos. 94^r–95^v.

KATHERINE ASTON, néee THIMELBY (no. 141) San Marino, Huntington Library, HM 904.

(no. 142) Ibid. fos. 158^r–158^v.

LADY DOROTHY SHIRLEY, née DEVEREUX, later STAFFORD (no. 143) San Marino, Huntington Library, MS HM. 904 158^v–159^r.

MARY FAGE (no. 144) From *Fames Roule, or the Names of our dread Soveraigne Lord King Charles, his Royall Queen Mary, and his most hopeful posterity ... anagrammatiz'd and expressed by acrostiche lines on their names*, by Mistris Mary Fage, wife of Robert Fage the younger, gentleman (London: Richard Oulton, 1637), p. 5.

POETS OF THE TIXALL CIRCLE (fl. 1630s–1650s) (no. 145) *Tixall Poetry; with Notes and Illustrations*, ed. Arthur Clifford (Edinburgh: James Ballantyne & Co., 1813), 263–5.

(no. 146) Ibid. 287–8.

(no. 147) Ibid. 154–4

SEÒNAID CHAIMBEUL (JANET CAMPBELL) (no. 148) From 'Seann oran Albannach a Ceap Bhreatainn', *Gairm* 9 (1954), 69–70, translated by Dr Meg Bateman. The song was recorded at Cape Breton from the singing of C. I. N. Macleod.

ELIZABETH CROMWELL (no. 149) *A Booke of severall devotions collected from good men by the worst of sinners, Anna Cromwell, 1656*, London, British Library, Harley 2311, fo. 20^{r-v}. Anna Cromwell Williams has endorsed the poem as follows: 'My Aunt Cromwells verces which she meade [o]n my mother and all ous Children, and annotated the original heading: The Sisters newyearsgift from^{Mrs} Elizabeth^{Cromwell} to Mary$^{Mrs\ Price}$ a happie mother of good children.'

DIORBHAIL NIC A BHRIUTHAINN (DOROTHY BROWN) (no. 150) John Mackenzie, *Sàr-obair nam Bard Gaelach* (Glasgow: MacGregor, Polson & Co., 1841), 62–3.

LUCY HUTCHINSON, née APSLEY (no. 151) British Library Add. MS 19,333, fos. 51ᵛ–52ʳ, (antograph).

(no. 152) Nottinghamshire Archives DD/HU2 (not Hutchinson's hand), ix–xi.
19 *rapine*: rampine MS   21 *not*: no MS

(no. 153) Ibid. pp. xxi–xxiv.
8 *his noble soul did*: did his noble Sould MS   9 *Just*: jus MS   30 *orderd*: ordd MS   33–4 There would seem to be 2 lines wanting in the MS at this point   36 *grace and lustre*: grace and new Lustre MS   52 *Such*: Shuch MS

(no. 154) Ibid. pp. xxix–xxxx. See David Norbrook, 'Lucy Hutchinson versus Edmund Waller: An Unpublished Reply to Waller's *A Panegyrick to my Lord Protector*', *The Seventeenth Century* 11 (1996), 61–86, and David Norbrook, 'Lucy Hutchinson's "Elegies" and the Situation of the Republican Woman Writer', *English Literary Renaissance* 27:3 (1997), 468–521. Lucy Hutchinson's translation of Lucretius, *De Rerum Natura*, is ed. with introd. by Hugh de Quehen (Ann Arbor, Mich.: University of Michigan press, 1997).
10 *begun*: begun—MS   14 *an*: a MS   19 *fancies*: fances MS   23 *We*: or He MS   29 *There*: These MS; *syghd*: spghd MS   36 *No*: N MS   42 *any*: any MS

AN ANONYMOUS WOMAN OF THE CLAN CAMPBELL (no. 155) J. L. Campbell, *Songs Remembered in Exile* (Aberdeen, 1900), 245, revised and translated by Dr Meg Bateman.

FRANCES (DOROTHY) FEILDING, née LANE, (later JAMES) (no. 156) New Haven, Yale University, Beinecke Library, Osborn Ms b 226. For information about Frances Feilding and Christobell Rogers, we are indebted to Dr Alison Shell. Punctuation supplied.

THE NURSE OF DONALD GORM (no. 157) From *An Anthology of Scottish Women Poets*, ed. Catherine Kerrigan, with Gaelic Translations by Meg Bateman (Edinburgh: Edinburgh University Press 1991), 18–23.

JANE CHEYNE, née LADY JANE CAVENDISH (no. 158) From her Collected Poems, 1641–9, Oxford, Bodleian Library MS Rawlinson Poet. 16, p. 35. This volume was transcribed by her father's secretary, John Rolleston. There is another copy in Yale University, Beinecke Library Osborn MS b. 233, 38. The poem refers to the Royalist victory of Adwalton Moor, 30 June 1643.

(no. 159) Ibid. 136, also in Yale University, Beinecke Library Osborn MS b. 233, 35.

(no. 160) Ibid. 16.

ANNE DUTTON, née KING, later HOWE (no. 161) Oxford, Bodleian Library, Rawlinson D 398, fo. 235, perhaps autograph: a King family manuscript.

HANNAH WOLLEY, later CHALLINOR (no. 162) from *The Queen-Like Closet, or a Rich Cabinet stored with all Manner of Rare Receipts* (the fifth Edition, London, R. Chiswel, 1684 (licensed 1669)) sig. A 8.

ANNA TRAPNEL (no. 163) From *The Cry of a Stone, or a Relation of Something spoken in Whitehall, by Anna Trapnell being in the Visions of GOD, Relating to The Government, Army, Churches, Ministry, Universities: and The whole NATION, Uttered in Prayers and Spiritual Songs* (London: no publisher given, 1654), 25–8.

MARGARET CAVENDISH, née LUCAS, DUCHESS OF NEWCASTLE (no. 164) *POEMS and PHANCIES, Written By the Thrice Noble, Illustrious, And Excellent PRINCESS the LADY MARCHIONESS of NEWCASTLE* (Second impression, much altered and corrected, London: William Wilson, 1664), 38–9. On Margaret Cavendish's scientific thinking, see Lisa T. Sarasohn, 'A Science turned Upside Down: Feminism and the Natural Philosophy of Margaret Cavendish', *Huntington Library Quarterly* 47 (1984) 288–307.

(no. 165) Ibid. 138–42.

(no. 166) Ibid. 145–7.

MARY CAREY, née JACKSON, later PAYLER (no. 167) Oxford, Bodleian Library, Rawlinson D 1308: 'My Lady Carey's Meditations, & Poetry'. Scribal copy by Charles Hutton made in 1681. The rest of the MS is concerned with Thomas, Lord Fairfax (evidently a close friend, since Mary Carey wrote an epitaph on Fairfax's wife). There is also a surviving autograph MS book, apparently the text from which Hutton copied, since the contents seem to be word for word identical, in the possession of the Meynell family.

ANNE DOCWRA, née WALDEGRAVE (no. 168) From *A Looking-Glass for the RECORDER and Justices of the Peace and Grand Juries for the Town and County of CAMBRIDGE* (no publ. 1682), 9–10.

MAIRI CHAMARAN, NIGHEAN FREAM CHALLAIRD (MARY CAMERON) (no. 169) *Transactions of the Gaelic Society of Inverness* 25 (1904–7), p. 240. Translated by Dr Meg Bateman.

KATHERINE AUSTEN, (née WILSON) (no. 170) London, British Library Add. MS 4454, fo. 44^r–45^r. Dec. 5th 1644 Upon Robin Austin's recovery of the small pox and General Popams son John diing of them.

Title *popham 3 yeares*: pop 3 yeares MS   23 *our*: correction over 'my'   25 *My*: correction over 'with'.

(no. 171) Ibid. fo. 104^r.

ELIZABETH EGERTON, née CAVENDISH, LADY ELIZABETH BRACKLEY, later COUNTESS OF BRIDGEWATER (no. 172) London, British Library Egerton 607, fo. 119^r. See further Betty Travitsky, '*True coppies of Certaine Loose Papers...*', *The MS Journal of Elizabeth Egerton, Countess of Bridgewater* (Binghamton, NY: Centre for Medieval and Early Renaissance Studies, forthcoming).

RACHEL JEVON (no. 173) Rachel Jevon, *Exultationis Carmen* (London: John Macock 1660), Oxford, Bodleian Library, Gough London 2 (6).

(no. 174) Ibid.

KATHERINE PHILIPS, née FOWLER. There are three MS of Katherine Philips's poetry which are of importance here, as well as one single autograph leaf: two MSS and the single sheet are in the National Library of Wales, Aberystwyth, and one MS is in the Harry Ransom Humanities Research Center of the University of Texas at Austin. In the modest schedules of variants (offered for variants between texts circulated in her lifetime) which are here given for her poems, we follow the system of sigla used in Dr Thomas's edition. Aberystwyth, National Library of Wales, MS 775, is a fair copy MS in Katherine Philips's own hand, dating from before 1660 = A. Aberystwyth, National Library of Wales MS 776, a fine fair copy in the hand of a professional scribe, was compiled for Mary Aubrey (the 'Rosania' of Philips's poems) soon after 1664. The dedication, signed by 'Polexander', is a remarkable composition praising the rarified love which the two women had enjoyed. The close resemblance of the sometimes idiosyncratic orthography of this MS to that of MS A would suggest that the poems which it contains were copied from autograph papers = B. The University of Texas at Austin, Harry Ransome Humanities Research Center, Misc. *HRC 151 Philips MS 14,937 (D), a MS in the hand of Orinda's friend Sir Edward Dering, contains seventy-six of her poems, presumably copied by him from her originals when she was in Dublin in the years 1662–3 = D. The posthumous editions are signified by *1664*, *1667* etc., following their dates of publication.

(no. 175) Aberystwyth, National Library of Wales, MS 775, pp. 101–5. Katherine Philips, *Poems*, 1664. *Poems by Katherine Philips*, ed. Patrick Thomas, 106–8.

significant variants: Title: To my dearest Lucasia, friendship in emblem or the seale D   19 *hearts*: Heart B   28 *doe's*: doth D; *the*: each B   29 *doe's*: Doth D   31 *doe's*: doth D   44 *Law* to: unto B   46 *and numbers*: in number B   58 *Mine*: mind B   61 *is*: are D   64 *Lucasia's*: Lucasia B

(no. 176) Aberystwyth, National Library of Wales, MS 776, pp. 340–2. Published in *1667*. B is earliest surviving text. *Poems by Katherine Philips*, ed. Patrick Thomas, pp. 202–3.

(no. 177) National Library of Wales MS 776, pp. 337–8. Published in *1667*. B is earliest surviving text. *Poems by Katherine Philips*, ed. Patrick Thomas, pp. 200–1.

(no. 178) Aberystwyth, National Library of Wales, MS 775, 168–66 [This poem is written in the reversed portion of the MS, fos. 28^r–29^v]. Published in *1664*. A is the earliest surviving text. *Poems by Katherine Philips*, ed. Patrick Thomas, pp. 82–3.

(no. 179) Aberystwyth, National Library of Wales, MS 776, 265–6. Published in *1664*. B is the earliest surviving text. *Poems by Katherine Philips*, ed. Patrick Thomas, 116–17.

Variants from D: Title: To Antenor, on a paper of mine which J. Jones threatens to publish to his prejudice   1 *folly's, be*: crimes become   2+ The weaknesse of the other charge is cleare | When such a trifle must bring up the reare. | But this is mad designe; for who before | Lost his repute upon anothers score?   5 *should be*: must be   8+ 'Tis possible this magazine of hell | (Whose name would turne a verse into a spell, | Whose mischiefe is congeniall to his life) | May yet enjoy an honourable wife. Nor let his ill be reckon'd as her blame, Nor let my follies blast Antenor's name.   16 *that triviall*: so dull

There is a modern edition of *The Poems of Katherine Philips*, by Patrick Thomas, (Essex: Stump Cross Press, 1990); another, by Elizabeth Hageman, is forthcoming from New York, Oxford University Press. The secondary material on Philips is now considerable: most of it either on her techniques of disseminating her work, or on her sexuality. For the first of these topics, see Peter Beal, *In Praise of Scribes* (Oxford: Clarendon, 1998), 147–91, and for the second, Arlene Steibel, 'Subversive Sexuality: Masking the Erotic in Poems by Katherine Philips and Aphra Behn', in *Renaissance Discourses of Desire*, ed. Claude J. Summers and Ted-Larry Pebworth (Columbia and London: University of Missouri Press, 1993), 223–36: both offer further references.

'A LADY' (KATHERINE PHILIPS?) (no. 180) This poem appears to be a reworking of Katherine Philips' early, short poem 'Humbly Dedicated to Mrs Anne Barlow C Fowler' which is found in the single autograph leaf, Aberystwyth, National Library of Wales, Orielton Estate MSS, Parcel 24, envelope 7/ 10/2. This must predate Katherine Philips's marriage in 1648, and was therefore written when she was 15 or 16. The addressee was Anne Barlow of Slebech, eldest daughter of John Barlow. Four copies of the long version survive, suggesting that it was a popular poem in miscellany manuscripts. The chosen copytext is Oxford, Bodleian Library Firth C 15, pp. 335–7 (on which see David M. Vieth, *Attribution in Restoration Poetry: A Study of Rochester's Poems of 1680* (New Haven and London: Yale University Press, 1963), 25–7). Other texts are in Bodleian Library Eng. misc. d.292, fo. 110, Nottingham, University Library, Portland MS PwV 40, fo. 156^{r-v} (from which major variants are given below) and PwV 41, fos. 149–50 (there is also a counter-poem, in Portland PwV 40, fo. 158^{r-v}). The relation of the short and the longer versions is far from clear: the poem brings into focus the problem of appropriation and rewriting in texts preserved in miscellany manuscripts.

significant variants from P:
1: I cannot madam but congratulate   3 *those*: she; *wou'd*: will   6 *Greive:*grief   9 *Your*: You your   25–6: Since there is nothing worse than an ill head | But 'tis a state that few young ladies dread   29 *Fiend*: Friend   31–2 wanting in P   42: Else would more virtuous than Diana prove   45–6 wanting in P   49: No blustring husbands to create our fears   57–8 wanting in P

Short version:

Aberystwyth, National Library of Wales, Orielton Estate MSS, Bundle 24, envelope endorsed 7/ 10/ 2

> A marryd state affords but little Ease
> The best of husbands are so hard to please
> This in wifes Carefull faces you may spell
> Tho they dissemble their misfortunes well
> A Virgin state is crown'd with much content   5
> Its all ways happy as its inocent
> No blustering husbands to creat yr fears
> No pangs of child birth to extort yr tears
> No childrens crys for to offend your ears
> Few worldly crosses to distract yr prayers   10
> Thus are you freed from all the cares that do
> Attend on matrymony & a husband too
> Therefore Madm be advised by me
> Turn turn apostate to love's Levity
> Suppress wild nature if she dare rebell   15
> There's no such thing as leading Apes in hell.

'ELIZA' (no. 181) *Eliza's Babes: or, The Virgins-Offering. Being Divine Poems and Meditations. Written by a Lady, who onely desires to advance the glory of God, and not her own* (London: printed by M.S. for Laurence Blaiklock, 1652), 46–7.

(no. 182) Ibid. 54.

AN COLLINS (no. 183) *Divine Songs and Meditacions Composed by An Collins* (London: printed by R. Bishop, 1653), 63–6. See now An Collins, *Divine Songs and Meditacions*, ed. Sidney Gottlieb, *Medieval and Renaissance Texts and Studies* (Tempe, Ariz., 1996).

FRANCELLINA STAPLETON (no. 184) Oxford, Bodleian Library MS Eng. poet. 112, fo. 81^{v}. The MS is a miscellany composed by John Newdigate (1600–42) which includes a page in a different (italic) hand signed by Francellina Stapleton.

ELIZABETH WITH (no. 185) From *Elizabeth Fools Warning, Being a true and most perfect relation of all that has happened to her since her marriage. Being a Caveat for all young women to marry with old men. Experienta docet.* By Elizabeth With of Woodbridge (London, for Francis Coles in the Old-Bailey, 1659), 6–7.

ELIZABETH, VISCOUNTESS MORDAUNT, née CARY (no. 186) From *The Private Diarie of Elizabeth, Viscountess Mordaunt*, ed. Robert Jocelyn, Earl of Roden Duncairn, 1856), 91–2 (56^r).

MARTHA, LADY GIFFARD, née TEMPLE (no. 187) From *The Early Essays and Romances of Sir William Temple Bt with the Life and Character of Sir William Temple by his sister Lady Giffard*, ed. G. C. Moore Smith (Oxford: Clarendon Press, 1930), 189, and see p. xxviii. Moore Smith claims to have taken it from 'a Yelverton MS' and that it was holograph. It is not with the Yelverton manuscripts now deposited in the British Library (our thanks to Dr Frances Harris of the British Library for investigating this on our behalf).

(no. 188) London, British Library, Egerton 1717, fo. 62^r.

ANN GREEWWELL, née DOWNER, later WHITEHEAD (no. 189) From *Piety Promoted by Faithfulness, Manifested by Several Testimonies concerning that true Servant of God ANN WHITEHEAD* (London: no printer, 1680), 39^{r-v}.

JANE VAUGHAN, née PRICE (no. 190) Aberystwyth, National Library of Wales, Cwrt Mawr MS 204B 'Llyfr Cerddi William Morgan', fos. 53^v–55^r, compiled by William Morgan (d. 1728) for Llammawddwy, Merionethshire. There is a variant text in London, British Library Add. MS 15005.

(no. 191) Aberystwyth, National Library of Wales MSS Brogyntyn Series I, number 3, fo. 625^r.

ANONYMOUS BENEDICTINE NUN OF CAMBRAI (no. 192) Loose sheet in Collection entitled For the Use of Sister Anne Benedict of St Joseph, Lille, Archives Départementales du Nord, 20H25.

ANNE KEMP (no. 193) Oxford, Bodleian Library, Wood 416 (11), single printed leaf.

ELIZABETH NEWELL (no. 194) Yale, Beinecke Rare Book and Manuscript Library, Osborn b 49, fo. 26.

ELIANOUR HAVEY (no. 195) Edinburgh, National Library of Scotland Adv. 19.3.4, fo. 87^r.

ANN WILLIAMS, née CROMWELL (no. 196) London, British Library Harley 2311, fo. 22^r.

APHRA BEHN, née JOHNSON (no. 197) *Poems on Several Occasions: with a Voyage to the Island of Love* (London: R. Tonson and J. Tonson, 1684), 70–7.
emendations: 46 *sacrifice*: sacirfice ed. 63 *appear*: appeat ed.

There is an earlier, variant text in *Poems on Several Occasions, By the Right Honourable, the Earl of Rochester*, 'Antwerp' [i.e. London], 1680, and a later one in *Familiar Letters of Love and Gallantry*, 1718, where it is called 'An Imperfect Enjoyment'. There are also several manuscript texts: 'An Imperfect Enjoyment, by Mris A. Behn', in 'A Collection of Poems', *c*.1690, Cambridge, Mass., Harvard FMS Eng. 6366, pp. 117–24; 'The Imperfect Enjoyment', Stockholm, Royal Library Ms Vu 69, 89–96. See facsimile edition: *The Gyldenstolpe Manuscript Miscellany of Poems by John Wilmot, Earl of Rochester, and other Restoration Authors*, ed. Bror Danielsson and David M. Vieth (Stockholm: Almqvist &

Wiksell, 1967). New Haven, Yale University Library, Osborn Collection b 105, 213, copy of last 10 lines in a quarto miscellany of poems on affairs of state. 118 *of:* f 1684 copy text.

(no. 198) A Congratulatory POEM TO HER Sacred Majesty QUEEN MARY, UPON HER ARRIVAL in ENGLAND (London, R.E. for R. Bentley and W. Canning, 1689). Broadside, signed 'By Mrs A. Behn', printed 1689.

(no. 199) *Lycidus, or the Lover in Fashion, being an Account from Lycidus to Lysander of his Voyage from the Island of Love, Together with a Miscellany of New Poems By several hands* (London: Joseph Knight and Francis Saunders, 1688), 175–6, signed 'By Mrs. B.'.

(no. 200) *Miscellany, being a collection of* POEMS *by several Hands together with* REFLECTIONS *on* MORALITY, *or* SENECA UNMASQUED, ed. Aphra Behn (London: for J. Hindmarsh, 1685), 45–9.

(no. 201) *Lycidus, or the Lover in Fashion, being an Account from Lycidus to Lysander of his Voyage from the Island of Love, Together with a Miscellany of New Poems By several hands* (London: Joseph Knight and Francis Saunders, 1688), 145–51, signed 'By Mrs B.'. There is a manuscript copy of this, University of Nottingham, Portland MS PwV 159.

(no. 202) First published, in a slightly variant form, in *The False Count* (1682), reprinted in *Poems on Several Occasions: with a Voyage to the Island of Love* (London: R. Tonson and J. Tonson, 1684), 89–90.

(no. 203) *Poems on Several Occasions: with a Voyage to the Island of Love* (London: R. Tonson and J. Tonson, 1684), 57–60.

(no. 204) First published by Jacob Tonson, in *Ovid's Epistles, Translated by several Hands* (1680), 77–114, where it is attributed to 'Mrs A. Behn'.

(no. 205) *Lycidus, or the Lover in Fashion, being an Account from Lycidus to Lysander of his Voyage from the Island of Love, Together with a Miscellany of New Poems By several hands, by Mrs. A.B.* (London: Joseph Knight and Francis. Saunders, 1688), 112–17, signed 'By Mrs. A.B.'.

(no. 206) *Poems on Several Occasions: with a Voyage to the Island of Love* (London, R. Tonson and J. Tonson, 1684), 95–8. See further Mary Ann O'Donnell, *Aphra Behn: An Annotated Bibliography of Primary and Secondary Sources* (New York and London: Garland) 1986, Janet Todd, *The Complete Works of Aphra Behn*, 6 vols. (London: William Pickering, 1992–6), Heidi Hunter (ed.), *Rereading Aphra Behn: History, Theory and Criticism* (Charlottesville and London: University Press of Virginia, 1993), Janet Todd, *The Secret Life of Aphra Behn*, (London: André Deutsch, 1996), Janet Todd (ed.), *Aphra Behn Studies.*
3 *Heavens*: Heaves ed.   35 *au*: add ed.

JANE SOWLE (no. 207) From *Piety Promoted by Faithfulness, Manifested by Several Testimonies concerning that true Servant of God ANN WHITEHEAD* (London: no publisher, 1680), 103.

ELIZABETH WILMOT, née MALET, COUNTESS OF ROCHESTER (no. 208) Copytext is draft in her own hand, Nottingham, University Library, Portland MSS PwV 31, fo. 15. The poem circulated very widely, usually ascribed to Rochester.
corrections in draft: 3 *cherish*: *over scored out* highten   4 *I*: supplied   7 *then*: *superscript*
Other MSS and printed texts: New Haven, Yale University, Beinecke Library b. 105, fo. 137; Washington, Folger Shakespeare Library MS b 12, fo. 32[r];

London, National Art Library MS Dyce 43, fo. 106; Leeds, Brotherton Library Lt 54, pp. 120–1 (where it forms stanzas 3–4 of a five-stanza poem). *Poems on Several Occasions, By the Right Honourable, the Earl of Rochester*, ('Antwerp' [i.e. London], 1680), 63 ('The Answer'); 'Ephelia', *Female Poems on Several Occasions, Written by Ephelia*, 2nd edn. (London: James Courtney, 1682), 160; *The Triumph of Wit* (1688) 161; *Poems &c. on Several Occasions... written by the Right Honourable John Late Earl of Rochester* (London: Jacob Tonson, 1691), 56; *A Complete Collection of Old and New English and Scotch Songs* (1735).

ANN LEE (no. 209) Oxford, Bodleian Library, Rawlinson Poet. 84, fo. 10^{r-v}.

SARAH GOODHUE, née WHIPPLE (no. 210) *Copy of a Valedictory and Monitory Writing* (Cambridge, Mass.: James Allen, 1681). Pattie Cowell, *Women Poets in Pre-Revolutionary America, 1650–1775, An Anthology* (Troy, NY: Whitston, 1981), 196.

BARBARA SYMS and CAPTAIN COOKE (no. 211) Oxford, Rawlinson Poet. 84, fo. 231^{v}. There is an ownership signature of Egiguis [Giles] Frampton hunc librum jure tenet, 1659.

DOROTHY WHITE (no. 212) from Dorothy White, *An Epistle of Love and of Consolation unto Israel, from the pouring forth of the Spirit, and holy anointing of the Father* (London: printed for Robert Wilson, 1661), 13.

ISOBEL GILBERT, née GOWDIE (no. 213) From *Confessions of Issobell Gowdie, Spous to John Gilbert, in Lochloy*, printed in Robert Pitcairn, *Ancient Criminal Trials in Scotland, compiled from the Original Records and Manuscripts with Historical Illustrations*, 3 vols. (Edinburgh: Bannatyne Club, 1833), iii 602–16 (MS now lost).

(no. 214) Ibid.

(no. 215) Ibid.

ANNA ALCOX (no. 216) Oxford, Bodleian Library, MS Eng Poet B.5, pp. 50–1.

'PHILO-PHILIPPA' (no. 217) From POEMS by the most deservedly Admired Mrs KATHERINE PHILIPS, The matchless ORINDA (London: J. M. for H. Herringman, 1664), sig. c 2^{r}–d2^{v}.

FRANCES BOOTHBY ?née MILWARD (no. 218) *Tixall Poetry; with Notes and Illustrations*, ed. Arthur Clifford (Edinburgh: James Ballantyne & Co., 1813), 228–9: Frances Boothby put on a single play, *Marcelia: or the treacherous friend*, (1670), at Drury Lane in June/July 1669, to little acclaim, and published nothing else. This poem must therefore date from 1670. No manuscript survives.

ELIZABETH POLWHELE (no. 219) From *The Frolicks, or the Lawyer Cheated* (1671), Act IV, ll. 358–67. Ithaca, Cornell University Library Bd Rare P P77. See *The Frolicks*, ed. Judith Milhous and Robert D. Hume (Ithaca, NY, and London: Cornell University Press, 1977), 119.

(no. 220) Broadsheet, London, Public Record Office SP 29/319/177.

ELIZABETH HINCKS (no. 221) From *The Poor Widow's Mite, Cast into the LORD'S TREASURY, Wherein are contained Some Reasons in the Justification of the Meetings of the People of God called QUAKERS: with an Approbation of several Truths held by them, and the ground of Dark Persecution Discussed*, printed for the use and benefit of such *Bees* as suck their *Hony* from the *Flowers* and

Blossoms that God makes to spring; that they may have to keep *themselves alive* in the *dark stormy Winter* (1671), 20.

(no. 222) Ibid. 44–5.

MARY MOLLINEUX, née SOUTHWORTH (no. 223) From *Fruits of Retirement: Or, Miscellaneous Poems, Moral and Divine. Being Some Contemplations, Letters, &c.* Written on Variety of Subjects and Occasions. By Mary Mollineux, Late of Leverpool, Deceased (London: T. Sowle, 1702), sig. B8ʳ.

(no. 224) Ibid. sig. B8ᵛ.

(no. 225) Ibid. 117–19.

JULEA PALMER (no. 226) Los Angeles, William Andrews Clark Memorial Library P1745M1 P744 1671–3: a volume of devotional poems, apparently the original compositions of Julea Palmer. Her name and the date 1671 appear on the first flyleaf, and the first poem is preceded by Iulea Pallmer September 28 1671. The volume contains 200 poems, numbered and grouped in two centuries. Dates in many titles suggest they were composed or at least compiled consecutively between 1671 and 1673. There is a forthcoming edition of the *Centuries* by Elizabeth Clarke and Vicki Burke.

MARY ENGLISH (no. 227) George F. Chevers, 'A sketch of Philip English . . .', *Historical Collections of the Essex Institute* 1 (1859), 157–81, at 164.

MAREY WALLER, later MORE (no. 228) Oxford, Bodleian Library MS Rawlinson D. 912, fo. 19ʳ. There is another copy in London British Library Harley 3918, fo. 60ʳ.

EPHELIA (no. 229) From *Female Poems on Several Occasions, Written by Ephelia* (London: William Downing, for James Courtney, 1679), 72–3. There is also a second edition, 'with large additions' (London: for James Courtney, 1682).

(no. 230) Ibid. 48–9.

(no. 231) Ibid. 58–9.

(no. 232) Broadside ballad on the Duke of Monmouth (Oxford, Bodleian Library Ashmole G.5 (86)). See now the facsimile edition of the first edition, *Poems by Ephelia (c.1679)*, ed. Maureen E. Mulvihill, Scholars' Facsimiles and Reprints (New York: Delmar, 1992).
41 *Slave*: Slaves ed.

JANE BARKER (no. 233) From *Poetical Recreations: Consisting of Original Poems, Songs, Odes, &c. With Several New Translations. In two Parts. Part I. Occasionally Written by Mrs Jane Barker. Part II. By Several Gentlemen of the Universities and Others* (London: Benjamin Crayle, 1688), 18–19. The Latin motto on the title-page, 'pulcherrima virgo incedit, magna Juvenum stipate caterva' ('a most beautiful virgin goes, accompanied by a great crowd of young men') is an adaptation of Virgil's *Aeneid* 1. 496–7, where it refers to the Carthaginian queen Dido.

(no. 234) Ibid. 38–40.

(no. 235) From Oxford, Magdalen College MS 343, fos. 46ʳ⁻ᵛ. See further *The Galesia Trilogy and Selected Manuscript Poems of Jane Barker*, ed. Carol Shiner Wilson (New York and Oxford: Oxford University Press, 1997).
1.25 painter MS

MARY ADAMS (no. 236) From *A Warning to the Inhabitants of England and London in Particular*, by M.A., (Printed in the Year, 1676), p. 7.

KATHERINE COLYEAR (COUNTESS OF DORCHESTER), née SEDLEY (no. 237) From D. M. Vieth, 'A "Lost" Lampoon by Katherine Sedley?', *Manuscripts* 6 (1954), 160–5. The copytext is Yale, Beinecke, Spence Papers, Box 1319 (on the back of a legal document dated 29 July 1752). There is another text in the Beinecke, Yale, Beinecke, Osborn MSS 4, Box IV, folder 13 (late s.xvii/early s.xviii hand), endorsed 'A song on Mrs Phraziar'.

As Phrazier one Night at her Post in the Drawing Room stood
Dumbarton came by and she crie'd my Lord would you would
What is your will Madam, for I am in hast and cant tarry
The thing is soon done for I swear it is nothing but marry
He laught and cri'd out do you thinke that the Devill is in me
To marry with one that in Time will be mine for a Guinea
Nay look not so coy nor toss your dangling Locks.
but marry Scar croop [Carr Scroop] and your Father may cure his Pox.

Vieth claims that a third copy is extant in London, British Library Add. MS 27408, but we failed to find it.

MARGARET, LADY GODOLPHIN, née BLAGGE (no. 238) London, British Library Evelyn Bound F 38, fo. 19ᵛ. Evelyn, who copied this poem, notes: 'That nothing of her may be lost, & to shew how wittily she reprovd a Young Creature, whose fantastic carriage and affectation became ridiculous, tho' when she had don it (& that barely to reproach the folly) the tendernesse of giving Ready offence, gave her scruples) yett the witt & raillery is so illustrious, so innocent, and so like her, that I shall not scruple to recite it.'

AMY HAMMOND, née BROWNE (no. 239) Oxford, Bodleian Library Rawlinson D 174, fo. 100ʳ. Miscellany of Anthony Hammond Esq., which includes letters and documents dated from between 1642 and 1709.

ANONYMOUS IRISHWOMAN (no. 240) From *An Duanaire, 1600–1900: Poems of the Dispossessed*, Seán ó Tuama & Thomas Kinsella (Mountrath: Dolmen Press, 1981), 35–7.

MARY, LADY CHUDLEIGH, née LEE (no. 241) From *Poems on Several Occasions, Together with the Song of the Three Children, PARAPHRAS'D, by the LADY CHUDLEIGH* (London: W. B. for Bernard Lintot, 1703), 21–2. See now *The Poems and Prose of Mary, Lady Chudleigh*, ed. Margaret Ezell (New York and Oxford: Oxford University Press, 1993).

ANNE WENTWORTH (no. 242) *The Revelation of Jesus Christ, Just as he Spake it in Verses at several times, and sometimes in Prose, unto his Faithful Servant Anne Wentworth, who suffereth for his name* (Published by a Friend. An. Dn. 1679), Revelation V, October 8, pp. 5–6.

(no. 243) Ibid. 9–10.

ANNE WHARTON, née LEE (no. 244) From *A Collection of Poems by Several Hands. Most of them written by persons of eminent Quality* (2nd edn., London: T. Warren for Francis Sanders, 1693), 238–9.

(no. 245) Ibid. 251–2. See further *The Surviving Works of Anne Wharton*, ed. Germaine Greer and Susan Hastings (Stump Cross, Essex: Stump Cross Books, 1997).

DAMARIS, LADY MASHAM, née CUDWORTH (no. 246) From John Norris, A COLLECTION of *Miscellanies* Consisting of POEMS, ESSAYS,

DISCOURSES, *and* LETTERS (Oxford: printed at the Theatre, John Crosley, 1687), 31.

(no. 247) Oxford, Bodleian Library Locke c 32, fo. 19^{r-v}. NB: this is followed by a copy in the hand of Locke's amanuensis, Sylvester Brownover, with a reply ending more happily, probably by Locke (fo. 20^{r-v}).

SILEAS NA CEAPHAICH (SILEAS MACDONALD) (no. 248) Entered from *Bàrdachd Shilis na Ceapaich, c.*1660–*c.*1729, ed. Colm Ó Baoill, Scottish Gaelic Texts Society (Edinburgh: Scottish Academic Press, 1972) 12–15.

ANNE KILLIGREW (no. 249) From *POEMS by Mrs Anne Killigrew*. Immodicis brevis est aetas, & rara Senectus. Mart. I.6.Ep.29. These POEMS are Licensed to be Published, Sept.30.1685. Ro. L'Estrange (London: printed for Samuel Lowndes, over against Exeter Exchange in the Strand. 1686), 44–7 (the motto is from Martial's *Epigrams*: 'the life of the very talented is brief; they rarely achieve old age').

(no. 250) Ibid. 47–8. Facsimile reproduction with introduction by Richard Morton (Gainesville, Fla.: Scholars Facsimiles and Reprints, 1967).

ANNE FINCH, née KINGSMILL, COUNTESS OF WINCHILSEA, (no. 251) Northampton, Northamptonshire Record Office, Finch-Hatton MSS 283 (unfoliated), pp. 1–5. It is also in the folio MS now in the Folger Shakespeare Library, 'Miscellany Poems with Two Plays by Ardelia', which is a copy of the Finch-Hatton MS.

(no. 252) Northampton, Northamptonshire Record Office, Finch-Hatton MSS 283 (unfoliated), pp. 106–8, also in Leeds, Brotherton Library, MS Lt 36, fo. 6^{r-v} and [Anne Finch], *Miscellany POEMS, on SEVERAL OCCASIONS, written by a LADY* (London: for J.B., 1713), 278–9.
significant varia from Leeds MS (=L) and 1713:   4 *or else*: or wou'd L   11–12: *missing* L 1713

(no. 253) Northampton, Northamptonshire Record Office, Finch-Hatton MSS 283 (unfoliated), p. 110. Another copy in the folio MS now in the Folger Shakespeare Library, 'Miscellany Poems with Two Plays by Ardelia'.

(no. 254) [Anne Finch], *Miscellany POEMS, on SEVERAL OCCASIONS, written by a LADY* (London: for J.B., 1713), 97–102. Folger Shakespeare Library, 'Miscellany Poems with Two Plays by Ardelia'. See further Barbara McGovern, *Anne Finch and her Poetry: A Critical Biography* (Athens and London: University of Georgia Press, 1992). Professor Germaine Greer is working on a new edition.

ELIZABETH BRADFORD, née SOWLE (no. 255) Prefatory poem, Benjamin Keach, *War with the Devil. Or the Young Man's Conflict with the powers of darkness* (New York: William Bradford, 1707).

'A YOUNG LADY' (no. 256) From *Triumphs of Female Wit, in Some Pindarick Odes, Or the Emulation. Together with an Answer to an Objector against Female Ingenuity, and Capacity of Learning, by a Young Lady* (London: for T. Malthus and J. Waltho, 1683), 1–5.

ANONYMOUS SAMPLER VERSE (no. 257) Verse on a sampler, Victoria & Albert Museum, embroidery study collection, no. 480–1894.

A LADY OF QUALITY (no. 258) From *Miscellany, being a collection of Poems by several Hands together with Reflection on Morality, or Seneca Unmasqued*, ed. Aphra Behn (London: for J. Hindmarsh, 1685), 212–13.

LADY WYTHENS, née ELIZABETH TAYLOR, later COLEPEPER (no. 259)
Oxford, Bodleian Library MS Rawlinson Poet. 172, fo. 110^r.
1 *evrey*: evey MS

(no. 260) *Miscellany, being a collection of Poems by several Hands together with
Reflection on Morality, or Seneca Unmasqued*, ed. Aphra Behn (London: for J.
Hindmarsh, 1685), 71–2.

BARBARA MACKAY, LADY SCOURIE. (no. 261) From 'The Song of Solomon
in verse', NLS, Edinburgh, MS Wod. Qu. XXVII, fo. 11^{r-v}. This is a presentation manuscript.
24 *statly*: *heavily overwritten over, probably, seafly.*

MARY EVELYN (no. 262) *Mundus Muliebris: or, the Ladies Dressing-Room
Unlock'd and her Toilette spread. In Burlesque. Together with the Fop-Dictionary,
Compiled for the Use of the Fair Sex* (2nd edn., London: printed for R. Bentley,
in Russel-Street in Covent-Garden, 1690), edited in facsimile with an introduction by J. L. Nevinson (London: The Costume Society, 1977).

LADY GRISELL BAILLIE, née HUME (no. 263) From *Orpheus Caledonius or a
Collection of the Best Scotch Songs set to Music by W. Thomson* (London: 2 vols.,
for the author, 1733), i. 88 (first published 1726). Another text in the several
editions of Allan Ramsay, *The Tea-Table Miscellany* (Edinburgh: for J. Dickson,
1775; first published 1723–7): as the variants below indicate, Ramsay's text is
slightly Anglicized. First attributed in 1839 in a broadsheet with music by
Charles Kirkpatrick Sharpe, 'the words by Lady Grizell Baillie'.
Variants from Ramsay 1775:   1 *an*: anes   6 *bonny*: lovely   7 *baight*: heght   18 *likes*:
like   19 *Appose*: Albeit   22 *drops*: dribbles; *drawf*: draff   25 *maiden*: titty   27 *sick a*:
a loud   30 *lookt*: looks; *his*: some's   31 *gang*: wear   32 *casts*: cast   35 *bows*:
steeks   37 *But*: Were I   40 *were*: were but

MARY PIX, née GRIFFITH (no. 264) From *The Royal Mischief. A Tragedy. As
it is Acted by His Majesties Servants. By Mrs Manley* (London: R. Bentley, F.
Saunders, and J. Knapton, 1696), sig. A3^v.

(no. 265) *Poems on Several Occasions, together with a Pastoral*, by Mrs S.F
[Sarah Fyge] (London: printed and to be sold by J. Nutt, [1706]), sig. A 6^{r-v}.

MARY ASTELL (no. 266) Oxford, Bodleian Library MS Rawlinson Poet.154,
fos. 52^r–54^r, from A COLLECTION of POEMS humbly presented and Dedicated To the most Reverend Father in GOD WILLIAM by Divine Providence
Lord ARCHBISHOP of Canterbury, 1689, a complete booklet (fos. 50^r–93^v).
See Ruth Perry, *The Celebrated Mary Astell: An Early English Feminist* (Chicago
and London: University of Chicago Press, 1986).

ALICIA D'ANVERS, née CLARKE (1668–1725) (no. 267) From *The Oxford-Act:
a Poem*. The beginning of the first canto (London: Randal Taylor, near Stationers Hall, 1693), 1–3.

A LADY (no. 268) *Lycidus, or the Lover in Fashion, being an Account from Lycidus
to Lysander of his Voyage from the Island of Love, Together with a Miscellany of
New Poems By several hands* (London: Joseph Knight and Francis Saunders,
1688), 89–94.

ANNE FYCHAN (no. 269) Aberystwyth, National Library of Wales, MS 436B
(also known as Williams MS 638), fo. 60^r, compiled *c*.1710–20. Follows a series
of poems of twelve englynion on the drover poet Edward Morris of Perthi
Llwydion, and is followed by six elegiac englynion attributed to one E.E. on the
death of the Duke of Monmouth.

'CLEONE' (no. 270) *Lycidus, or the Lover in Fashion, being an Account from Lycidus to Lysander of his Voyage from the Island of Love, Together with a Miscellany of New Poems By several hands* (London: Joseph Knight and Francis Saunders, 1688), 172–6.
emendation: 2 l *a*: l ed.   30 closed bracket supplied.

A YOUNG LADY OF QUALITY (no. 271) *An Elegy Upon the Death of Mrs. A. Behn; the Incomparable Astrea. By a Young Lady of Quality* (London: printed by B.J., 1689).

SARAH FIELD, née FYGE, later EGERTON (no. 272) *Poems on Several Occasions, together with a Pastoral*, by Mrs S.F [Sarah Fyge] (London: printed and to be sold by J.Nutt [1706]), 19–21.

(no. 273) Ibid. 36–7.

(no. 274) Ibid. 70–2. See further Jeslyn Medoff, 'New Light on Sarah Fyge (Field, Egerton)', *Tulsa Studies in Women's Literature* 1, 2 (Fall, 1982), 155–75.

DELARIVIER MANLEY (no. 275) From The LOST LOVER; or, The Jealous Husband; a COMEDY, As it is Acted at the *THEATRE ROYAL* by His Majesty's Servants, *written by Mrs.* Manley (London: printed for R. Bentley, in Covent-Garden, 1696), sig. B 1[r].

(no. 276) *Agnes de Castro, a Tragedy, as it is Acted at the Theatre Royal, by his Majesty's Servants, written by a Young Lady* [Catherine Trotter] (London: printed for H. Rhodes, R. Parker, S. Briscoe, 1696), sig. A1[v].

(no. 277) from The Royal Mischief, a TRAGEDY. As it is Acted by his MAJESTIES SERVANTS. By Mrs *Manley* (London: printed for R. Bentley, F. Saunders, and J. Knapton, 1696), 20.

LADY SARAH PIERS, née ROYDON (no. 278) From [Catherine Trotter] *Fatal Friendship: A Tragedy, as it is acted at the New-Theatre in Little-Lincolns-Inn-Fields* (London: Francis Sanders, 1698), sig. A4. Catherine Trotter dedicated two early works to Lady Piers: *The Unhappy Penitent: a Tragedy* (1701), which also includes a poem from Sarah Piers, 'To the Excellent Mrs Catherine Trotter'; and *Love at a Venture*.

A YOUNG LADY (no. 279) from *Maria to Henric And Henric to Maria: Or, The Queen to the King in Holland and His Majesty's Answer, Two Heroical Epistles in Imitation of the Stile and Manner of Ovid. Written by a Young Lady* (London: printed for Joseph Knight at the Pope's Head, in the Lower Walk of the New Exchange, 1691), 1–6.

BATHSHEBA BOWERS (no. 280) From *An Alarm Sounded to Prepare the Inhabitants of the World To meet the Lord in the way of his Judgment* (New York: William Bradford, 1709), from Cowell, *American Women Poets in Pre-Revolutionary America, 1650–1775, an Anthology* (Troy, NY: Whitson, 1981) 211–13. See further William John Potts, 'Bathsheba Bowers', *The Pennsylvania Magazine of History and Biography* 3 (1879), 110–12.

ANNE MORCOTT (no. 281) From *The Pepys Ballads*, ed. Hyder Rollins, 8 vols. (Cambridge: Mass.: Harvard University Press, 1929–32), vi. 161. On women and ballad writing and publishing, see Claude M. Simpson, *The British Broadside Ballad and its Music* (New Brunswick: Rutgers University Press, 1966), which discusses Ann Morcott, pp. 437–8.

ELIZABETH TIPPER (no. 282) *The Pilgrim's Viaticum: Or, the Destitute, but not Forlorn. Being a Divine poem, digested from meditations upon the Holy Scripture* (London: J. Wilkins, 1698), 18–21.

(no. 283) Ibid. 34–5.

ELIZABETH ROWE, née SINGER (no. 284) *Poems on Several Occasions, written by Philomela* (London: printed for John Dunton at the Raven in Jewes-Street, 1696), pt. II, 22–3.

(no. 285) Ibid. 43
Text note: 1 *glide*: gilde ed.

See further *The Poetry of Elizabeth Singer Rowe* (1674–1737), ed. Madeleine Forell Marshall, Studies in Women and Religion 25 (Lewiston and Queenston: Edwin Mellen Press, 1988).

ELIZABETH THOMAS (no. 286) From her *Miscellany Poems on Several Subjects* (London, Thomas Combes, 1722), 18–22 (reprinted as *Poems on Several Occasions, by a Lady*, 1726, 1727).

(no. 287) Ibid. 218 (also in *Poems on Several Occasions*).

ANGHARAD PRITCHARD, née JAMES (no. 288) Aberystwyth, National Library of Wales MS 9B, pp. 390–1 (original pagination pp. 392–3).

CATHERINE COCKBURN, née TROTTER (no. 289) From *The Works of Mrs Catharine Cockburn, Theological, Moral, Dramatic, and Poetical, Several of them now first printed, with an account of the Life of the Author.* Thomas Birch, 2 vols. (London: J. and I. Knapton, 1751), ii. 557–9.

(no. 290) From The Royal Mischief, a TRAGEDY. As it is Acted by his MAJESTIES SERVANTS. By Mrs *Manley* (London: printed for R. Bentley, F. Saunders, and J. Knapton, 1696).

MARGARET MAULE, COUNTESS OF PANMURE, née DOUGLAS (no. 291) Edinburgh, Scottish Record Office, GD 45/26/99 (no. 94) No. 50.

AMEY HAYWARD (no. 292) *A Spiritual Meditation upon a Bee The Females Legacy. containing, divine POEMS, on Several Choice SUBJECTS. Commended to all Godly women* (London: Benamin Harris, in great East-cheap, for the Author, 1699) 87.

ANONYMOUS 'A LADY OF HONOUR' (no. 293) The GOLDEN ISLAND or the *DARIAN SONG*. In commendation of All Concerned in that Noble Enterprise Of the VALIANT SCOTS, by a Lady of Honour (Edinburgh: John Reid, 1699), 3–8.

ANNE MERRYWEATHER (no. 294) London, British Library MS Add. 61474, fo. 63$^{\text{r–v}}$.

INDEX OF TITLES AND FIRST LINES

INDEX OF AUTHORS